ENERGY PRIMER

SOLAR, WATER, WIND, AND BIOFUELS

TABLE OF CONTENTS

FRONT COVER
Photo courtesy of the High Altitude Observatory and NASA. *Sun's hot outer atmosphere, or corona, color-coded to distinguish levels of brightness, reaches outward for millions of miles. A coronagraph, one of Skylab's eight telescopes, masked the sun's disk, creating artificial eclipses. It permitted 8½ months of corona observation, compared to less than 80 hours from all natural eclipses since use of photography began in 1839.*

BACK COVER
Graphic courtesy of Sandicker Studios, Mountain View, California.

Abstract: *The* **Energy Primer** *is a comprehensive, fairly technical book about renewable forms of energy — solar, water, wind, and biofuels. The biofuels section covers biomass energy, agriculture, aquaculture, alcohol, methane, and wood. The focus is on small-scale systems which can be applied to the needs of the individual, small group, or community. More than ¼ of the book is devoted to reviews of books and hardware sources. Hundreds of illustrations and a dozen original articles are used to describe the workings of solar water heaters, space heaters and dryers, waterwheels, windmills, wind generators, wood burning heaters, alcohol stills, and methane digesters. The final section of the book focuses on the need for energy conservation and some of the problems and potentials of integrated energy systems.*

INTRODUCTION

This book was written to fill a void. The groups involved with the *Energy Primer* had been receiving numerous inquiries about methods of supplying energy needs that could be implemented by individuals and small groups. Solar/wind devices and methane digesters seemed to be particularly popular, but there were also the inevitable questions about "organic" gardening and farming, water power, wood and alcohol. There were general questions too: "How can I feed and fuel those around me without relying so much on outside power sources that pollute and that are rising in cost and dwindling in supply?" People wanted to know about food and fuel supplies that came from renewable sources of energy rather than non-renewable oil wells and nuclear reactors.

But it seemed that people were asking much more than just: "*How* can I build a solar collector," or, "*Should* I build a solar collector?" Most questions clearly reflected a growing dissatisfaction with a culture that allowed fewer and fewer options with regard to our control over life's everyday needs. The supermarket and the wall plug are still the major supply sources and there seems no end to it.

So we set out to write a book about renewable energy systems that people could use for themselves; a description of how they work, their limitations and potentials and the hardware and techniques necessary to grow, build and maintain them. But we soon realized that there were limitations. For one thing, the different food and energy systems were in varying states of development and redefinement. New ideas were being offered every day about solar collectors, scaled-down waste systems, wind generators, etc. New companies were starting out all the time in response to the growing demands for devices that harness solar and wind power. Inevitably the book would soon be obsolete. In addition, renewable energy systems were, by their very nature, geared to the local conditions of climate, economy, geography and resources. It made little sense to try and describe endless possibilities and designs that were already described in widely scattered community and regional publications, technical journals, "underground" brochures, survival texts and energy magazines both funky and slick. What we wanted was a sourcebook that brought basic information together, not a cookbook.

And we needed something, too: a perspective to what we were doing.

Energy Scarcity, Conservation and Practical Alternatives:

For generations our culture has been enjoying the benefits of a cheap, easily available energy source . . . fossil fuels. Today, practically all of our luxuries and necessities are totally dependent on coal, natural gas and oil. The fact that reserves of these fossil fuels are limited has become a platform for politicians, a bargaining point for diplomats, a lucrative commodity for the rich and a glaring reality for everyone.

> *Geochemical evidence suggests that every year about 28 million tons of carbon go into the formation of new fossil sediments. Current consumption of fossil fuels is about 6 billion tons of carbon per year. The rate of consumption is therefore over 200 times the rate of deposition. On this basis we can say that fossil fuels are limited and non-renewable.*
>
> —I.T. Rosenqvist
> 1972 Conference on Energy & Humanity

Because we have built our culture and standard of living on easy energy, conventional wisdom pushes harder and harder to find "alternative" energy sources capable of feeding our excessive needs. The most obvious alternative has been the search for more inaccessible deposits of fossil fuels . . . further offshore and deeper in the ground. But very soon the cost of retrieving new reserves will exceed the benefits provided by them. The search for more oil can only be a short term solution with long term implications for the environment.

Further down the line, many see the development of nuclear power as the answer to our energy problems. But we should at least pause for a moment. The development of nuclear power is not only a mistake, but a self-destructive response to a complex problem. In the first place, uranium

itself is a limited resource; reserves can only hope to last for a few generations at best. Moreover, there is the strong possibility that the wide-scale use of nuclear power plants will simply inaugurate an era of world wide nuclear armament and global conditions in which no one can afford to make a mistake . . . political or technical. And finally there are the inevitable nuclear wastes generated and *left behind* by nuclear power plants that threaten the very existence of life as we know it. Of most concern is plutonium, a by-product of breeder reactors and the deadliest, and one of the most persistent elements in the known universe. Plutonium has a half-life of 24,000 years, and to our knowledge there is no way of safely containing anything . . . let alone plutonium . . . for 24,000 years (rockets to the sun and salt mines notwithstanding). For a few generations of more easy energy we give to our future generations the consequences and burdens of plutonium and other nuclear wastes. We view this as insanity.

If we dismiss nuclear fusion as being an undeveloped alternative with its own problems of radioactive waste (albeit far less than those of fission), we are left with one alternative energy source that could supply much of our needs . . . solar power and all of its manifestations in the wind, water and plants.

There are a number of ambitious ideas for harnessing solar energy. For example, some people have suggested that we could cover the southwest deserts with solar reflectors or send satellites into orbit to microwave solar energy back to earth. There are also plans for building bigger hydroelectric dams and massive digesters to recycle manure from oversized feedlots. There are even schemes for covering the mid-west plains and offshore areas with wind generators, and for growing high-yield plants in vast areas of marginal land to fuel power stations. Certainly these alternatives are infinitely more desirable than nuclear energy, and there is little doubt that some of them will be developed to help supply future energy needs. However, in perspective, they must be viewed as nothing more than extensions of the growing tendency to centralize the generation and control of energy and to alienate people further from the natural forces that support them. A central power station, regardless of its source of energy, still requires elaborate transmission grids to disperse the energy. To some degree this may be realistic, but as *the only* way of providing energy in an increasingly unstable social order it leaves few options for people to adopt.

More and more the energy resources of the world are coming under the control of international corporations and energy cartels. Growing scarcities of energy and natural resources will continue to determine major political policies in the future. To balance this trend, we need to diversify and disperse the physical energy base and dilute the growing economic power bases . . . a trend that will help us all. *The most obvious way to do this is to develop and adopt scaled-down renewable energy systems that are utilized where they are needed and designed for local environments and requirements.* The new politics of self-sufficiency . . . relying on ourselves and our own decentralized energy resources . . . will conflict with the present politics of centralized institutions and industry. Hopefully, in time, it will come to supplement this tradition rather than conflict with it. The important thing is that we generate as many options as we can for a future whose course grows more uncertain every day.

> *"It's easier and cheaper to save the energy we get from conventional sources than it is to earn (generate) energy from newer, more expensive sources such as the wind and sun. For example, it's cheaper and easier to insulate a home than to produce energy (from renewable sources) to heat an uninsulated dwelling. . . If we consume all of our fossil fuels in our cars and 'space-hippy' vans, we'll never see the solar-based society to which we must move if we want to survive."*
>
> —Lee Johnson and Ken Smith

We should have no illusions about local energy systems. Our exaggerated needs *cannot* be supplied by solar, wind, water and biofuel energy alone. The prerequisite to using any renewable energy system is CONSERVATION. Without conservation, techniques and devices for using renewable energy will always seem impractical and will always make little economic sense.

It's not very glamorous to deal with energy conservation. Most people would rather concentrate on new pieces of hardware than cultivate living habits that make solar collectors feasible. Unfortunately most strategies for conservation are based on simplifying what we have rather than creating radically new living patterns. Car pools, lowered thermostats, simple appliances and efficient insulation are all important methods of reducing energy consumption. But by themselves they mean little unless they become part of a personal plan to change our standard of living, recycle our materials and wastes, and make do with less. We needn't be austere, only sensible about our habits. Then and only then can the energies from the sun, wind and garden begin to support our needs. *First we must minimize our needs, then we can start changing our hardware.*

There are other realities too. Fossil fuels are an indispensible ingredient for organic chemicals and a valuable fuel for a few high energy processes like ore smelting. At the present time, coal, oil and natural gas are the only practical energy resources that can provide steel for windmills, digester tanks or circulating pumps, and plastic or glass for solar collectors, greenhouses, etc.

Generally speaking, renewable energy devices are still locked into a costly technology that requires high energy resources like fossil fuels to provide construction materials. This is a reality and shouldn't be hidden in the "something for nothing" attitude that renewable energy systems seem to generate. However this needn't always be so. Future energy policies *can* be redirected so that material and construction designs will be oriented for posterity and not planned obsolescence.

The problem is that we just don't know what the trade-offs really are. Perhaps it will take several years for a wind generator to "pay back" the energy costs of making it, and there is some evidence to indicate that this may be so. At what scale are renewable energy systems really practical. . . the household, village, community or city? These and many more questions remain to be asked. As we observe, think and change, we will often be very much on our own. We will be our own "experts" and we will be our own "scientists." In this process we will develop many values and perfect many processes that can and should be shared. A desire to facilitate this exchange of information has been one of the moving forces behind the creation of this book.

—R.M., —C.M., —T.G., —T.W.

SOLAR

SOLAR RADIATION AND ITS USES ON EARTH

John I. Yellott
Professional Mechanical Engineer
and
Visiting Professor in Architecture,
Arizona State University

Astronomers tell us that our sun is only one of untold billions of similar stars, in varying stages of their progression from incomprehensible origins to ultimate extinction. Our particular star is thought to have originated between eight and ten billion years ago and its present rate of energy output, approximately 3.8×10^{23} kilowatts, is caused by the conversion of mass into energy at the rate of some 4.7 million tons per second. It is expected to continue to emit radiant energy at this rate for another four billion years, so, for all practical purposes, it is the only perpetually renewable source of energy which the planet Earth possesses.

It is high time that we get on with the task of learning how to use the massive amounts of energy which the sun gives us each day, and that is what this chapter is all about. Appendix I is a glossary of the words and symbols used in heliotechnology, while Appendix II contains a more in depth mathematical and conceptual approach for the serious student of solar technology. It gives the information needed to make quantitative estimates of how big a solar device must be in order to achieve a desired result. Methods of estimating solar heater performance are in Appendix III, and resources for further work are referred to in Appendix IV.

We will now turn our attention to the uses to which we can put this highly variable but vitally important energy resource, the sun's radiation.

FUNDAMENTAL PRINCIPLES OF SOLAR ENERGY UTILIZATION

There are three primary processes by which the sun's radiation can be put to technical use: (1) Heliochemical, (2) Helioelectrical and (3) Heliothermal. These are derived from the Greek word Helios, meaning "the sun." Other terms often used are: heliostatic, referring to devices which are stationary with respect to the sun or which make the sun appear to stand still; heliotropic, referring to devices which follow or track the sun, and heliochronometry, which means the telling of time by means of the sun. The latter, discussed in a later section, is probably the most ancient of the subjects to be covered in this chapter, since people have been using the shadows cast by various devices to tell time since the days of ancient Eygpt.

Heliochemical

From our point of view, the first of these is by far the most important, since it is the heliochemical process called photosynthesis (App. IV, No. 1) which enables certain wavelengths from the solar spectrum to cause carbon dioxide and water to unite with nutrients from the soil and thus create the plants and oxygen by which we live. All of the coal, oil and natural gas that our planet has ever possessed has come from photosynthesis in ages past, and the food on which we exist today comes from that same process. We are just beginning to understand photosynthesis, but even the greatest laboratory in the world cannot equal a single blade of grass or the leaf of a tree in bringing about this remarkable process.

Man has not yet made much use of heliochemical processes, except perhaps in the field of photography, and so we will turn our attention to the remaining two processes, helioelectrical and heliothermal.

Helioelectrical

Helioelectrical devices are entirely man-made, since nature has not produced anything which converts solar radiation directly into useable electricity. These are also the most recent of the sun-powered devices to make their appearance. Really significant helioelectrical apparatus dates back only two decades to the invention of the silicon solar battery. Silicon solar cells utilize the ability of solar radiation to dislodge electrons from properly treated silicon and thus to cause an electric current to flow.

These were the first sun-powered devices to attain real and unqualified success; the exploration of space and the landing of men on the moon would not have been possible without the arrays of silicon cells which have powered virtually all of our space vehicles. It is to be hoped that the heliothermal apparatus which is about to be discussed will make an equally rapid and significant impact as that made by silicon solar cells.

Heliothermal

Heliothermal devices absorb solar radiation on blackened surfaces and convert it into heat. The black surface will attain a temperature at which equilibrium is established between the rate at which energy is being absorbed and the rate at which the absorbed energy is being lost to the surrounding atmosphere and put to useful service.

The blackened sheet of metal, heavily insulated on the side away from the sun and covered with a sheet of glass to trap the absorbed solar heat, may approach 300°F. The heat absorbed by the metal may be carried away by water circulating through tubes attached to the metal plate, or by air blowing over the sun-heated metal. The glass cover plays a vital part by transmitting as much as 90 per cent of the solar radiation to the plate and by refusing to transmit back to the atmosphere the longwave radiation (heat) which is emitted by the plate. The glass also makes a major reduction in the amount of convective heat loss, i.e., the carrying away of heat by movement of the air at the surface of the plate.

Heliothermal devices have been used with varying degrees of success for more than a century to produce temperatures ranging from below the freezing point of water to nearly 6000°F. We will discuss them in order of the temperature at which they operate, excepting the production of ice. This will be covered in a later section, because even though ice can be produced from solar radiation, it can only be done chemically by using the process of absorption refrigeration which requires a relatively high temperature. Our discussion of heliothermal devices will begin with the solar still, which does its work at temperatures very close to the ambient air temperature.

SOLAR STILLS AND SOLAR DRYERS

Probably the oldest intentional use of the sun's ability to produce heat came when primitive man allowed pools of salt water to evaporate to produce salt essential to the human diet. This process is still in use, as is demonstrated by the great salt works near San Francisco.

Solar Distillation

Controlled evaporation to produce fresh potable water from salt or brackish sources is a much more recent development, but, like most of the heliothermal devices which will be described in this chapter, the basic ideas can be traced back for at least a century. The first large solar still was built at Las Salinas in the Andes Mountains of Chile by J. Harding in 1872, to provide drinking water for the men and animals working in a copper mine. It was nearly an acre in extent, made of wood and glass, and it could deliver some 6000 gallons per day of pure water from a very brackish source.

Its principle of operation is exactly the same as that of the many stills which have been built in the past few years in Australia and on the arid Greek islands in the eastern Mediterranean Ocean. Fig. 1 shows the general idea of these simple devices. A water-tight compartment, made of wood or concrete, is painted black to absorb the solar radiation which enters through the glass roof of the still. Salt or brackish water, or even sewage effluent, is allowed to flow into the channel or box to a depth of four to six inches. The incoming solar radiation heats the water, causing some of it to evaporate and this condenses on the inner surface of the glass roof.

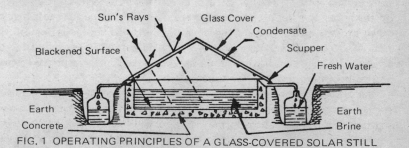

FIG. 1 OPERATING PRINCIPLES OF A GLASS-COVERED SOLAR STILL

Since water will "wet" (App. I) clean glass, the condensation takes place in the form of a very thin film which flows down by gravity into the scupper which leads the condensate off to a suitable container. The water channel is insulated by the earth. After some of the water has been distilled off, the brine which is left is flushed out at intervals. This prevents the concentration of salt from building up to the point when it will cover the the bottom of the still with reflective white crystals.

The product of such a still is distilled water which can be used for drinking, for filling storage batteries or for any other purpose for which pure water is needed. Attempts have been made to use plastic films as still covers, to eliminate the weight and cost of the glass roofs, but the plastic films have not proved to be as reliable as glass. Most films are not "wet" by water and so the condensation takes place in droplets which tend to reflect the sunlight instead of transmitting it into the basin. Also, few films are completely resistant to deterioration from the ultraviolet component of the solar radiation. They are really only useful in stills which are expected to be used for a short period of time.

Fig. 2 shows the desert survival still devised by R. D. Jackson and C. H. Von Bavel of the Water Resources Laboratory in Phoenix. The kit includes only a sheet of transparent plastic and a tin can, since the other needed materials can be found in the desert. Even in the dryest earth there is always some moisture and it can be distilled out by creating a heat trap, as shown in Fig. 2, by using a transparent plastic cover, a rock to weight the cover down in its center and a can to catch the droplets of moisture as they trickle down the inner surface of the plastic. This is the desert version of the ocean rescue still, developed in 1940 by Dr. Maria Telkes, using inflatable plastic bags which, in an emergency, can be used to make drinking water from ocean water.

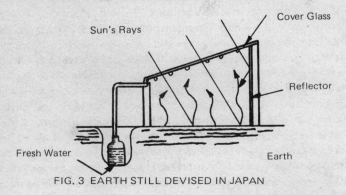

FIG. 2 DESERT SURVIVAL SOLAR STILL

Dr. M. Kobayashi, formerly Managing Director of Nippon Electric Co. of Tokyo, proved that water can be extracted from virtually any kind of soil by the earth-still shown in Fig. 3. He used a typical still construction, complete with cover glass and reflector to increase the amount of solar radiation reaching the earth. He has tested his still at the top of Mt. Fujiyama where the soil is volcanic ash, and in the arid deserts of Pakistan, and he has never failed to produce water that is pure and potable.

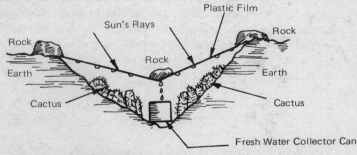

FIG. 3 EARTH STILL DEVISED IN JAPAN

The Brace Research Institute of McGill University has published plans for a simple solar still (App. IV, No. 2) which uses a tray made by folding up the edges of a flat sheet of galvanized steel. The corners are soldered to make the tray water-tight and a drain pipe is soldered to the bottom of the tray. The tray is quite shallow since it is intended to hold less than an inch of water. It is painted black with a flat black waterproof plastic paint after a suitable priming coat has been applied.

The bottom of the still is made of hardboard sheet (Masonite) 1/8 inch thick and the space between the pan and the bottom is filled with wood shavings to act as insulation. In the U.S. glass wool would probably be used as the insulating material, since it is readily available and relatively inex-

pensive. Fig. 4 shows a cross section of the Brace still with enough of the details to convey the essential ideas. The ends of the still are elongated triangles, made of plywood, and the sides are made of single pieces of good quality soft pine, 2 inch by 4 inch, and long enough to suit the dimensions of the tray.

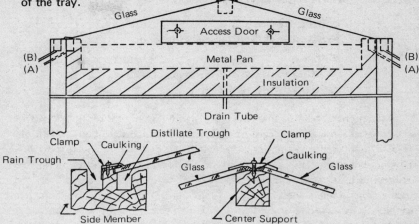

FIG. 4 CONSTRUCTION DETAILS OF A GLASS-COVERED SOLAR STILL, DESIGNED BY BRACE RESEARCH INSTITUTE.

The two troughs serve to carry off the distillate "A" and any rain "B" which may fall on the still (Fig. 4). The cover glasses are supported at an angle of about 15 degrees to the horizontal, with a 1 inch square supporting member which is appropriately beveled. The glass is given a water tight caulking at the upper and lower edges with Dow Corning No. 780 Building Sealant or its equivalent, and a galvanized sheet steel clamp is attached to the supporting member by flat-head screws.

The still is mounted so that the tray is level, with the long dimension running east and west, in a location which is unshaded all day long. The still is filled to a depth of about 1 inch with fresh water each morning. The glass must be thoroughly cleaned before it is installed and the outer surface must be kept clean so that the collected rainwater can also be used.

Where there is adequate sunshine and plenty of non-potable water available, a solar still such as that shown in Fig. 4 is a practical means of turning that water into drinking water at the rate of about one gallon per day for each 10 to 12 square feet of area. Larger stills will produce proportionally greater quantities of distillate, comparable to the 6000 gallons per day produced by the great stills at Las Salinas, Chile, and Coober Pedy, Australia. In summer, temperatures within the tray can be expected to reach 140°F, with considerably lower temperatures attained during the winter months.

There is a very extensive bibliography devoted to solar distillation. App. IV, No. 3 will lead the reader to much of the literature devoted to this subject, including references to the work of the Commonwealth Scientific and Industrial Research Organization (CSIRO). Most of the successful solar stills in use today use long concrete troughs, painted black, covered with tilted glass roofs similar to that shown in Fig. 4. Careful attention to details, particularly to the prevention of leaks, is essential to good performance.

SOLAR CROP DRYERS

Sunshine has been used since time immemorial for the purpose of drying crops. This has traditionally been accomplished by simply exposing the crop to the sun's rays and hoping that no rain would fall until the drying process had been completed. A more sophisticated technology has been evolved during the past two decades to make more effective use of the sun's thermal power and to minimize the usual contamination associated with natural dehydration. The most common sources of contaminants are:

(a) airborne dust and wind-blown debris, such as leaves;
(b) insect infestation and presence of larvae, etc.;
(c) animal and human interference.

To minimize contamination and to maximize the effectiveness of the sun's rays, it is essential that the drying area be covered by a transparent material. Glass is preferred because of its resistance to deterioration, while plastic films such as Mylar have merit because of their low cost and freedom from breakage due to stones, hail, etc. The Brace Research Institute has published (App. IV, No. 4) a very good description of a solar drying unit which can be made by anyone who has access to simple carpentry tools. This dryer is essentially a solar hot box, which can be used to dehydrate fruit, vegetables, fish, or any other product which needs to be dehydrated for preservation. It consists of a solar "hot box," with two layers of transparent covering, which can be either double strength glass or plastic film (Fig. 5).

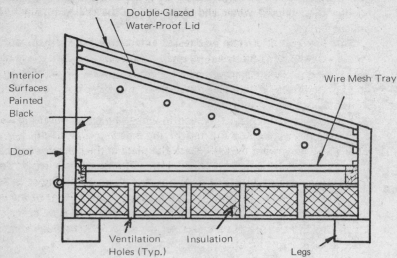

FIG. 5   SECTION THROUGH TRAY-TYPE SOLAR DRYER
(adapted from Brace Research Institute design)

The box itself is generally made of plywood, although larger, permanent dryers may be made of adobe, brick, stone or concrete. The insulation should consist of any materials, such as wood shavings or sawdust, which are locally available and inexpensive, although these are subject to infestation by ants and termites and would have to be treated to prevent this problem. Glass wool is the preferred insulating material since it can survive any temperature which the hot box will attain, and will not support insect life.

The operation of the dryer is quite simple. The ventilation holes at the bottom and the top of the dryer allow air to enter and to carry away the moisture which is removed from the vegetables or other materials by the heat of the sun. The access door in the rear panel enables the materials to be placed on the drying tray, and to be removed when they are dry. The interior of the cabinet should be painted black, while the exteriors of the side and rear panels should be painted with aluminum paint. The number of ventilation holes is determined by the amount of moisture which must be removed from the materials which are being dried.

The angle of slope of the dryer cover should vary with the latitude, but in general an angle of the local latitude minus 10 degrees will be found to be satisfactory. The use of aluminum foil within the cabinet to reflect some of the transmitted rays onto the material may be helpful. The drying trays are made of galvanized wire mesh (i.e., "chicken wire"). Where electricity is available, the use of a small fan to draw air through the dryer would be helpful, but it is not necessary.

The dryer should be glazed, preferably with two layers of glass, fitted in with adequate room for thermal expansion. Ventilation is essential so that the moisture which is "distilled" out of the agricultural material can be removed from the cabinet. This means that screened air holes in the bottom, sides, and the back of the cabinet are essential. One of the most valuable assets of such a dryer is its ability to keep produce dry during rain storms, so the glazed top should be watertight.

Experience with a cabinet dryer of this type indicates that there are upper temperature limits which should not be exceeded for most products. A hot box of this type can readily attain temperatures above 200°F if it is not ventilated, so some degree of care should be taken to prevent overheating of the materials which are to be dried.

SOLAR WATER AND AIR HEATERS

The heating of water and air by solar radiation is one of the oldest and most valuable applications of heliothermal technology. The variety of water heaters and air heaters is almost endless and they all operate on much the same principle.

Solar Water Heaters

Fig. 6 shows a typical flat-plate grid collector for heating water, and Fig. 7 shows the components in an exploded cross-section. The components, progressing inward from the top, are:

(a) The *glazing*, which is usually double strength (1/8 inch) window glass, although 3/16 or even 1/4 inch glass may be used if the size of the pane is so large that the wind loading requires that thickness. Tempered glass is being suggested because of its resistance to breakage, but its extra cost may not be justified in most applications. The glass must be installed with gaskets or caulking which provide enough flexibility to allow the glass to expand when it gets hot and to contract again when it cools off at night. More details on the behavior of glass and other possible glazing materials will be given later in this section.

(b) The *water tubes*, which, in the first generation of heaters built in the 1930's, were generally arranged in a zig-zag pattern. Today's collectors generally use a grid pattern. The metal was formerly copper, but now aluminum and steel are being more widely used for economic reasons. The tubes are usually 1/2 to 3/4 inch inside diameter, with 1 to 1—1/4 inch pipe used for the inlet and outlet headers.

(c) The *flat plate*, which may be any metal—copper, aluminum or steel— that has good thermal conductivity and is reasonable in cost. The term "flat plate" is used to distinguish this type of collector from the concentrator-type which will be discussed later when we deal with high-temperature collectors. The surface of the plate may be corrugated or vee-ed, or fins may be used which are perpendicular to the tubes. The major problem is finding an inexpensive way of fastening the tubes to the plate with a good thermal bond. Thermal cements (App. I) are an efficient way of doing this.

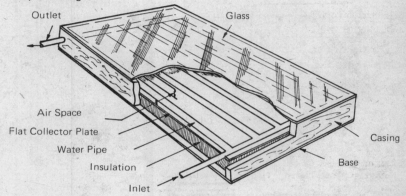

FIG. 6   TYPICAL FLAT-PLATE SOLAR COLLECTOR
(for heating water)

The metal plate must be coated with a radiation-absorbing paint or plating; if painted it should be properly primed before the black coating is applied. There are special coatings available which can absorb most of the sun's rays and re-radiate very little longwave radiation, but these finishes, called "selective surfaces" (App. IV, No. 5) generally require very special equipment and they are really needed only when the collector is intended to operate at quite high temperatures. Flat black paint, properly applied to prevent peeling and cracking, will do a good job for ordinary domestic solar water heaters.

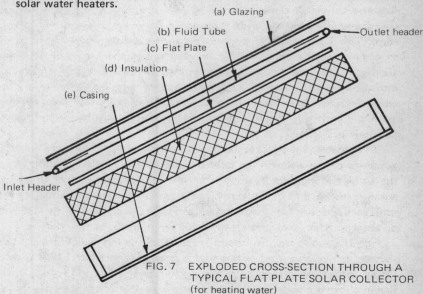

FIG. 7   EXPLODED CROSS-SECTION THROUGH A
TYPICAL FLAT PLATE SOLAR COLLECTOR
(for heating water)

(d) The *insulation*, which may be any low-conductivity material that is available and can withstand temperatures up to 200°F. In India, dried palm leaves have been used, but in the U.S., glass wool is the most widely used insulator because it has a low thermal conductivity (see App. I for definitions and values of this important quantity) and it is available at moderate cost in a wide range of widths and thicknesses. Remember that foil-clad insulation only makes use of the radiation-reducing qualities of the foil when the shiny surface has an air space between it and the adjacent surface. Foamed insulation is being used to some extent in collectors and it can add structural strength. Care must be taken to avoid the high temperatures which will cause the foam to melt when a double-glazed collector is exposed to the sun without any water flowing through it.

(e) The *casing*, which holds the collector together and, in combination with the glazing, makes it water- and dust-proof. A simple wooden box, adequately painted and fitted with a hardboard (Masonite) base, will do. Factory built collectors usually have casings made of sheet metal, rust-proofed and painted to resist deterioration.

The flow of water through flat-plate collectors can occur in many ways, as indicated by Fig. 8.

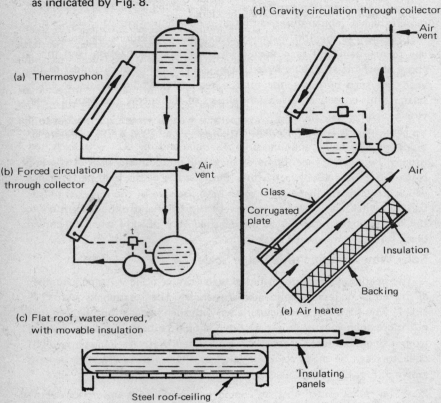

FIG. 8 SOLAR WATER AND AIR HEATERS.

Fig. 8(a) shows the typical thermosyphon system, which will be described in considerable detail in the next section because it is by far the most widely-used heliothermal device. Fig. 8(b) shows a forced-circulation system, with a pump to take water from the lower part of the storage tank and force it upward through the heater to the top of the tank. An extension to the vertical down-comer is shown to represent an air-vent, which will cause the collector to be drained of its water whenever the pump stops. This is necessary to prevent freezing in regions where the outdoor air temperature falls below 32°F for any protracted period of time. An alternative is to use a mixture of water and antifreeze (ethylene glycol is most widely used and readily available), but this requires the use of a heat-exchanger (App. I) between the water circuit and the storage tank. In addition, any antifreeze liquid is certain to be relatively expensive and it may be highly poisonous.

This system would use a thermostat, designated "t" to sense the temperatures of the water in the tank and the surface of the collector. When the sun is shining brightly enough to heat the collector surface to a temperature above that of the water in the tank, the pump is started, and it runs until the sun has moved to a position in the sky where its rays will no longer produce enough heat to enable the collector to operate.

Fig. 8(c) shows the "Skytherm" system invented by Harold Hay of Los Angeles, in which a steel ceiling-roof is covered with water which is contained in shallow plastic bags (e.g., water beds). The insulating panels shown above the water bags can be moved away horizontally by pulling on a cable (not shown) so that the sun's rays can warm the water during sunny winter days. The water will in turn warm the metal ceiling-roof which then becomes a radiant heater for the room below. At night the panels are moved back to cover the water bags and eliminate loss of heat to the cold night air.

During the summer the operation is reversed; the panels remain over the bags during the day and they are rolled back at night so that the water can lose heat to the night sky. During the hottest part of the summer, water can be sprayed on the bags. Some of this exposed water will evaporate, cooling the enclosed water and thus causing the ceiling to function as a radiant cooler.

The "Skytherm" system was tested extensively for eighteen months in Phoenix during 1967-68. It kept a small, one-room structure above 68°F in winter and below 80°F in summer for all except 1% of the 13,140 hours of test conditions. A full-scale "Skytherm" residence is currently in operation at Atascadero, California.

Fig. 8(d) shows a gravity system in which the pump raises the water to a distribution pipe along the top of the collector and gravity makes the water flow downward over the black flat plate in the collector and back to the tank. This is the system which Dr. Harry Thomason uses in his "Solaris" homes. The advantage to this system is that there are no pipes to form a grid in the collector, thus reducing the cost and the weight of the unit. A thermostat performs the same function here that it did for type (b) and the vent at the top of the piping causes the water to drain back to the tank whenever the pump stops.

The Thermosyphon Water Heater

The simplest and most reliable heliothermal device is the thermosyphon solar water heater which is shown in Fig. 8(a), and in more detail in Fig. 9. This combines a flat plate collector with an insulated water storage tank mounted high enough above the collector so that the cold water in the downcomer pipe will displace by convection the sun-heated water in the collector tubes. This causes a slow but continuous circulation of water downward from the bottom of the tank, upward from the collector, and back to the upper part of the tank. The action will continue as long as the sun shines on the collector. In a good sunny location, free from shadows throughout the entire day, a 4 foot x 8 foot collector will give 40 to 50 gallons of hot water per day. The temperature of the water in the upper part of the tank will vary from 165°F on a hot summer day to 115°F on a cold winter day.

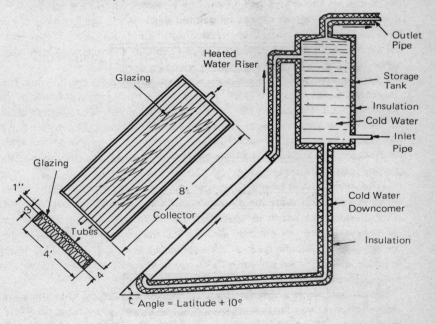

FIG. 9 TYPICAL THERMOSYPHON SOLAR WATER HEATER

A single layer of glass is generally adequate to reduce the heat loss from the surface of most collectors, but in very cold areas double-glazing is desirable. Care must be taken in applying glass, to make sure that it is free to expand or contract, because the inner glass will get very hot by radiation and convection from the collector plate, while the outer glass will remain relatively cool due to the loss of heat to the outdoor air.

The bottom of the storage tank should be at least 1 foot above the top of the collector and the connecting pipe from the downcomer to the bottom header should slope downwards towards the collector.

All piping should be insulated and the tank should be completely surrounded with as much insulation as possible, up to 6 inches in thickness. This should be covered with a thin sheet-metal jacket painted in some dark color to take advantage of the sun's ability to help keep the tank warm during the day.

There are many other ways (Fig. 10) to produce water heater collector plates. The Australians have traditionally used copper tubing soldered to copper sheet as was used in thousands of solar water heaters built a generation ago in the U.S. Now copper is too expensive for large scale use, although its resistance to corrosion and its ease of forming and soldering give it a major advantage over steel and aluminum.

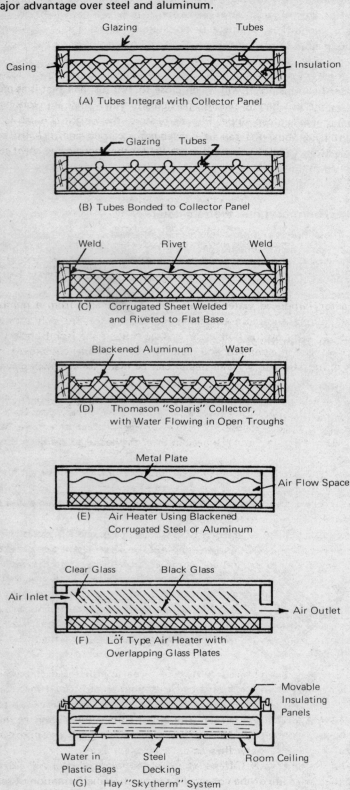

(A) Tubes Integral with Collector Panel

(B) Tubes Bonded to Collector Panel

(C) Corrugated Sheet Welded and Riveted to Flat Base

(D) Thomason "Solaris" Collector, with Water Flowing in Open Troughs

(E) Air Heater Using Blackened Corrugated Steel or Aluminum

(F) Löf Type Air Heater with Overlapping Glass Plates

(G) Hay "Skytherm" System

FIG. 10   FLAT PLATE COLLECTOR TYPES

A factory-made collector plate is shown in Fig. 10(a), representing an integral tube-in-sheet which is made in the U.S. under the Roll-Bond® patents held by the Olin Brass Co. Their process involves the printing (using a very special "ink") of the desired tube pattern on one flat sheet of aluminum. A sandwich is then made by putting a second sheet of aluminum over the first and bonding the two together with heat and pressure over their entire surfaces, except for the printed areas. The tubes are then created by inserting a special needle into an unbonded portion of the edge and inflating the tube pattern with a pressurized fluid. This is the

process by which virtually all refrigerator freezing compartments are made, and patterns of extreme complexity can be produced on panels of relatively large size (up to 3 or 4 feet by 12 feet).

The one major problem encountered with aluminum tube-in-sheet is the corrosion which generally occurs when untreated water comes into contact with bare aluminum. The Showa Aluminum Co. of Japan has a U.S. patent on the use of zinc powder in the special "ink" used in the Roll-Bond® process and this produces the equivalent of a galvanizing action on the water passages which, according to Showa, makes them entirely resistant to corrosion. When these panels become available in the U.S., they will be very valuable components of the large number of collectors which are going to be needed here.

The actual temperature of the water used for domestic purposes in the U.S. ranges from 100°-110°F for bathroom purposes, which is about as high as the human skin can tolerate. Dish washing, to remove grease, may require higher temperatures, although proper detergents can take care of that problem in the 100°F range quite nicely. Institutions are required by law to maintain 180°F in their dishwashers for sterilization, and this is above the limit attainable by a single-glazed collector during most of the year. For such purposes, the solar water heater would be used as a preheater, thus conserving a substantial part of the energy that would otherwise be required.

The Japanese have developed a wide variety of solar water heaters; new types are also being announced in Australia and the U.S. with each new issue of *Popular Science*. Some of these will undoubtedly prove to be successful, but others will lack either the long life or the high performance which a successful installation must have. Beware of the low-cost plastic variety, which are likely to have a very short life and to be susceptible to the high temperatures which are reached very quickly when un-cooled black surfaces are exposed to the sun.

Solar Water Heating on a Large Scale

The heating of large quantities of water can be done by using a number of individual collectors connected in parallel. The Australians (App. IV, No. 7) who have had much experience with such installations, believe that not more than twenty-four riser tubes should be used in parallel coming from a single header. They have demonstrated that very large batteries of collectors can be made to work satisfactorily by using the arrangement shown in Fig. 11.

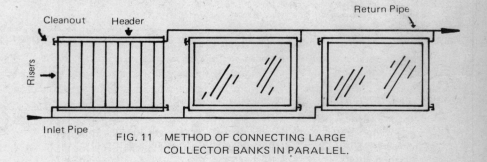

FIG. 11   METHOD OF CONNECTING LARGE COLLECTOR BANKS IN PARALLEL.

They have also shown that relatively high temperatures can be attained for large quantities of water for industrial and commercial purposes by using three types of collector batteries in series. The first, receiving the coldest incoming water, are not covered with glass and hence are relatively inexpensive; the second battery is comprised of single-glazed collectors which are more expensive and also more efficient with warmer water. The third battery, which elevates the water to its final temperature, is double-glazed; these are the most expensive units, but they are also the most efficient at high operating temperatures.

Solar Air Heaters

Fig. 8(e) shows a simple and inexpensive air heater, consisting of a cover glass (plastic film may be used, too), a corrugated plate of sheet steel or aluminum painted black, a space through which the air can flow, a layer of insulation and a Masonite or plywood backing to keep the assembly water-proof. The air can be made to flow by means of a fan or blower, or, if the system is properly designed, it will rise due to convection (the "chimney effect") because the heated air is lighter than the cold air outside.

Air heaters are much less expensive than water heaters because there is no need to worry about freezing, and any leakage which occurs will not cause the kind of damage which water can create. The drawback to air systems is the fact that fans are larger, more expensive and more power-consuming than the small pumps used with some solar water heating systems [Fig. 8(b) and (d)]. Also, the ducts which are used to carry the air are much larger and more costly than the pipes used with water systems. Each type has its advantages and disadvantages, and each prospective installation must be given careful thought to make sure that the best possible choice is made.

The simplest of all solar air heaters, and one which is in increasingly wide use now, employs a heavy southfacing vertical concrete wall (Fig. 12) which is painted a dark color and covered with a sheet of glass. An air space runs between the concrete and the glass, and the chimney effect causes the heated air to rise. Openings at the bottom and top of the wall allow the cold air along the floor to enter the air space and similar openings at the top provide an opportunity for the warm air to re-enter the room behind the wall. The air then circulates through the room, warming the walls and the occupants. Small electric baseboard heaters are used to provide heat during long periods of bad weather.

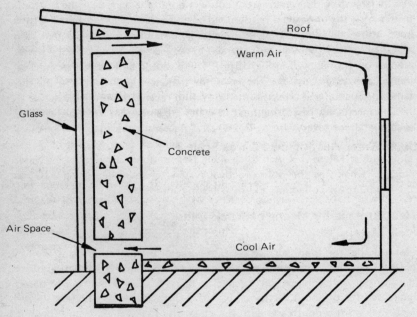

FIG. 12   TROMBE-TYPE SOLAR SOUTH WALL
AIR HEATER USED AT ODEILLO, FRANCE

The overlapping glass plate air heater shown in Fig. 10(f) was invented during World War II by Dr. George Löf, who uses this system in his own home in Denver. The plates are actually divided into two segments, with the upper piece being clear and the lower piece being black. The division was found to be necessary when the first prototype was tested using single sheets of glass with the lower half painted black. These promptly broke from thermal shock as soon as they were exposed to the sun, because the lower part immediately became hot, while the upper part remained cool. Dividing the glass sheets into two parts cured this problem completely, and the Löf house in Denver has been operating satisfactorily since the late 1950's.

Flat metal plates, painted black and covered with glass or plastic glazing, will do a good job of heating air, as Dr. Telkes proved in the solar house which she built at Dover, Massachusetts, in 1939. However, the heat transfer from the metal to the air is improved if the plates are corrugated to increase the amount of surface available for heat transfer. The Australians are making good use of thin copper air heaters, with the copper corrugated into small vees and treated on its outer surface to become selective in its ability to absorb solar radiation and yet not re-radiate much longwave radiation.

Suggestions for Building Solar Water and Air Heaters

There are no hard and fast rules for building satisfactory solar heaters, nor are there any precise dimensions which must be followed. Generally speaking, there should be a single glazing at least, spaced about 1 inch above the collector plate. Glass will generally give much longer life than plastic glazing, but if a shortened life is acceptable, either Mylar or Tedlar (both are duPont films) will do almost as good a job as glass except at very high temperatures.

There are no precise dimensions which must be specified for either air or water heaters. Metal sheets, plywood, Masonite and similar materials are generally available in 4 foot by 8 foot dimensions. Aluminum, galvanized steel, and copper are usually available in 2 to 3 foot widths and almost any specified length. Glass wool insulation is available in thicknesses ranging from 1 to 4 inches. Glass can be purchased in a wide range of dimensions, but individual sheets larger than 4 feet square are difficult for one person to handle.

A 4 foot by 4 foot module, as used in Australia, is a very good choice for a water heater, since it will weigh close to 100 lbs. and that is as much as two people can handle readily, particularly when they are working on a rooftop with a steep slope. For air heaters, the weight is much less and 4 foot by 8 foot units can be conveniently carried and installed by two people. Corrugated aluminum is much lighter than corrugated sheet steel of the same dimensions and it generally costs little if any more per square foot since the thickness of the aluminum can be less than the steel.

Dr. Thomason gives quite detailed instructions for building the aluminum water heater which is the main feature of his "Solaris" house (App. IV, No. 8). The construction details of most of the other solar houses which have been built during the past three decades are to be found in the articles published by their builders and many of them are well described in *Introduction to the Utilization of Solar Energy* by Zarem and Erway (App. IV, No. 3).

Factory-produced water heaters are now available from a number of manufacturers, and more will soon be on the market. The only type which cannot be built by the builder of average skills is the Roll-Bond® variety which is made of aluminum and requires special welding equipment.

A quite satisfactory water heater can be made using 1 inch galvanized steel pipe as the headers and 1/2 inch galvanized tube as the risers. Thin galvanized sheet steel can be used as the collector plate; this is easier to handle if it is used in the form of strips about 6 inches wide. Drill holes large enough to accept the 1/2 inch tubes at 4 inch centers in the headers and solder the tubes into the headers after the headers have been threaded on both ends.

This will produce a grid of pipe and tube which will weigh less than 30 pounds; the addition of the galvanized steel strips will add another 10 to 12 pounds of weight. Let the steel strips overlap lengthwise and solder or cement the tubes to the strips.

Mount the collector in a box with wooden sides and a Masonite bottom. A soft Neoprene gasket and an aluminum cover strip will give the glass the necessary room to expand and contract, while you retain the water-tight feature which is essential. Three inches of glass-wool insulation should be adequate and a few small holes may be drilled along the bottom of the collector box to allow it to "breathe" as its temperature changes. A flat black paint should be applied to the collector plate and the tubes, after they have been primed with the material which is recommended by the paint manufacturer.

The water inlet connection may be made to either end of the bottom header and the other end should be closed with an ordinary 1 inch standard pipe cap. This cap can be removed at appropriate time intervals to remove dirt and scale from the header. The outlet connection should be made at the opposite corner of the upper header, so there will be approximately equal resistance to water flow across the collector grid.

The use of a water softener ahead of the solar collector will greatly extend the useful life of the collector by preventing the formation of scale on the inner surface of the piping in the hot portion of the collector.

Air heaters are much easier to make, since they require only an air-tight box with a glazing material on the top; this may be either glass or a Tedlar or Mylar film. The heat-absorbing panel may be corrugated or rolled sheet metal, preferably aluminum, with a "dead air space" about 1 inch wide between the glazing and the collector. The air-flow space will be along the back of the aluminum, and both sides of the metal should be painted black. The top or upper surface must be black to absorb the solar radiation which will be transmitted through the glazing. The lower surface should also be black so that it can radiate heat to the covering over the glass wool insulation and allow that surface to help in the air heating process.

Unless you are expert at cutting glass, have this job done for you at the hardware store where you buy the glass. A badly-cut piece of glass is likely to have defects along the edges and when temperature differences begin to occur across the glass, as they will when the plate begins to be heated by the sun, thermal stresses may be set up which can break the glass. Four foot by four foot lights (panes) of glass are also much easier to replace if breakage does occur due to hail stones or other objects which may strike the glazing. Breakage of the glass covers due to hail or stones can be lessened by the use of 1/2 inch wire mesh, supported on an angle-iron framework several inches above the glass. The use of this screen reduces effective absorber area by about 15%, so the total absorber area should be increased to compensate for this reduction.

SOLAR SPACE HEATING AND HEAT STORAGE

Solar space heating may be accomplished in many ways and again there are no hard and fast rules. Before undertaking to heat a building by solar energy, a competent estimate must be made of the amount of heat which the structure will need under adverse winter conditions and at night. The solar heater must be able to provide not only the heat which will be needed hour by hour during a sunny day but it must have additional capacity so that heat can be stored during the day for use at night or during cloudy days.

There are three methods of heat storage which are in use today; the first two representing relatively low technology but complete feasibility. The third, although it has been under study for many years, is still in the developmental stage.

Heat Storage in Water Tanks

Large tanks, filled or almost filled with water, represent the best method that is presently available to store large amounts of heat or cold.

Every substance possesses its own "specific heat," which is the amount of heat in Btu's needed to raise the temperature of that substance 1 degree F. On a pound-for-pound basis, one can store more heat in a substance of higher specific heat than in a substance of lower specific heat. Water has a specific heat of 1.0 Btu/lb./°F, an antifreeze such as ethylene glycol has a specific heat of 0.6, but almost all solid materials from rocks to iron and aluminum have a specific heat of 0.2 Btu/lb./°F.

Water weighs 62.4 pounds per cubic foot or 8.34 pounds per gallon. If we heat water 10 degrees F above the temperature at which we need the heat, we can store 624 Btu in a cubic foot or 83.4 Btu in a gallon of water. Assume that it is house heating which we wish to accomplish and that by using a very efficient system of heat distribution we can use water as cool as 90°F. to heat the house.

If we store hot water at 150°F in a cylindrical steel tank, as in Fig. 13(a), we can store 62.4 lb./cu.ft. x (150°F - 90°F) = 3744 Btu in a cubic foot of water or 8.34 lb./gal. x (150°F - 90°F) = 500.4 Btu in a gallon. A 2000 gallon tank of water will thus be able to store about 1,000,000 Btu's at a temperature difference of 60°F.

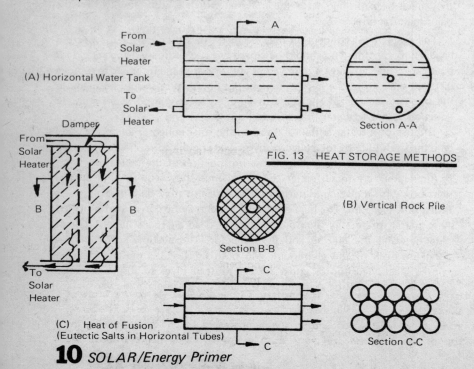

(A) Horizontal Water Tank

Section A-A

FIG. 13   HEAT STORAGE METHODS

(B) Vertical Rock Pile

Section B-B

(C) Heat of Fusion (Eutectic Salts in Horizontal Tubes)

Section C-C

If we insulate the tank with 6 inches of glass wool or, even better, 6 inches of urethane foam, we will lose only about 1000 Btu per hour through the glass wool and half that amount through the urethane (assuming that the tank is 6 feet in diameter and 10 feet long).

The storage of cold is not quite so simple, since we cannot use such a large temperature range without running into the complication of freezing the water. We may well want to do just that, as we will see in the heat-of-fusion section upcoming, but assuming that we want the water to remain in the liquid state and that we want to use it for cooling at 55°F, we have only 23 degrees of temperature at our disposal (water freezes at 32°F). The 2000 gallon tank contains 8.34 lb./gal. x 2000 gal. = 16,680 lbs. of water and can thus store about 16,680 lbs. x 23°F = 383,640 Btu's of "coolth," as compared with nearly three times that much when we are storing "warmth."

Now we see that, if we can allow a 60°F temperature rise and fall, we can store about 1,000,000 Btu in a 2,000 gallon tank but if we restrict ourselves to the 23°F temperature rise and fall for cooling, we will need a tank nearly three times as large, or almost a 6,000 gallon tank. For a 6 feet diameter tank, the length will stretch out to about 30 feet. Obviously, if we want to store very large amounts of "coolth" in a tank of water, the tank is going to have to be very large.

The tank should have an outlet connection at one end, near the bottom, from which the water can be pumped to the solar collector, and a return inlet, above the water level, thus leaving some air space in the tank. An access hole, large enough for someone to get inside the tank, will be a wise precaution (not shown in Fig. 13(a)). There should be two connections on the far end, one above the center of the tank to supply water to the distribution system and one near the bottom to receive the return water.

The mechanics of storing heat in water are simple; in addition, water is available almost everywhere. The disadvantages are the space, weight (8.3 tons for 2,000 gallons, 25 tons for 6,000 gallons), and the cost of a steel tank with a 1/4 to 3/8 inch thick shell. Despite these disadvantages, water storage remains as the only practical system when we are using water as the medium for collecting and distributing the heat.

Heat Storage by Means of Rock Beds

The ability of a solid to *transfer* heat is a function of its surface area per unit volume; the more surface area, the greater the ability to transfer heat per unit volume. The ability of a material to *store* heat is a function of its density per unit volume and its specific heat. A solid cubic foot of basalt has a density of about 184 pounds, but a surface area of only six square feet, making it a poor candidate for a heat transfer system, even though it is a good means of heat storage. If this big cube is broken into many 1/2 inch cubes, we will have 13,824 small cubes and their total surface area will be 144 square feet, giving us a much better heat transfer situation. However, in trying to pack the cubes helter-skelter into the original one cubic foot container, we will find, because of air spaces, the cubic foot will only hold about 89 pounds. This will still give us about 70 square feet of heat transfer surface, compared to the 6 square feet of the original block.

Going back to 23°F as the temperature range over which we were operating with the water tank, 1 cubic foot of basalt pebbles can store 89 lbs. x 0.2 Btu/lb./°F x 23°F = 409 Btu. If we are concentrating on heating and can allow a 60°F temperature difference, we can store almost three times as much heat; 1,068 Btu per cubic foot or 24,000 Btu per ton. To store 1,000,000 Btu with the 60°F temperature range, we would need 41—2/3 tons, which is a formidable pile of rocks.

The practical way to handle a rock pile storage situation is to use the arrangement shown in Fig. 13(b), with the rocks contained in a cylinder, and their weight supported by a steel grill at the bottom of the container. A central pipe with a damper will allow the rocks to be by-passed when the heat is needed directly in the structure.

The air-heated house erected by Dr. George Löf in Denver in 1959 uses two large cylinders, 3 feet in diameter and 18 feet high in the center of the building, to store 12 tons of 1 to 1½ inch rock with a bulk density of 96 pounds per cubic foot. The Thomason houses in Washington, D.C., use 25 to 50 tons of "fist-sized" rocks to provide supplemental heat storage as well as heat transfer surface. Two demonstration houses erected by the writer for the U.S. government in 1958, one in Casablanca and one in Tunis, used the system shown in Fig. 13(b), with a vertical rock pile contained in a Sonotube cylinder.

Rock piles have the advantage that they can neither freeze nor leak, but their capacity is limited. However, they can be safely used under a building since, once they are put in place, very little harm can come to them. The Australians have made particularly effective use of rock beds in the device called the "Rock Bed Regenerator," which will be discussed later.

Heat of Fusion Storage

When a tank of water is cooled by refrigeration, it will give up 1 Btu per pound for each degree that it is cooled until it gets to $32°F$. At that temperature, ice will begin to form and there will be no further change in temperature until another 144 Btu (called the "heat of fusion") have been removed. One hundred forty-four Btu per pound must be added to the ice-water mixture to melt the ice and return it to liquid form again. Its limitation is that $32°F$ is the only temperature at which water will freeze into ice and then melt back again to water.

There are other substances which freeze and melt at more convenient temperatures; the most widely known being Glauber's salt, sodium sulfate decahydrate ($Na_2SO_4 \cdot 10H_2O$). This melts and freezes again at $88°$ to $90°F$, with a heat of fusion of 108 Btu per pound. There are many problems connected with this and similar materials. Their potential value in the storage of warmth and coolth lies in the fact that 1,000,000 Btu's can be stored in only 5 tons of salt as compared with 25 tons of water and 125 tons of rocks (with a $20°F$ temperature swing).

Dr. Telkes of the Institute of Energy Conversion at the University of Delaware has devised ways of adding small amounts of other substances to heat of fusion materials to make them behave properly. The major difficulty appears to be that the heat of fusion materials, unlike water, sink when they freeze and it is not a simple matter to find ways to make them become homogeneous liquids again when they melt. The first attempts to use Glauber's salt in relatively large drums were unsuccessful and now Dr. Telkes has turned to long slim plastic tubes (Fig. 13(c)), similar in shape and size to fluorescent lamps, to provide both storage for the materials and heat transfer surface for the University of Delaware Solar House, "Solar One." Her latest combinations will provide storage of warmth at $120°$ to $126°F$ and coolth at $55°F$.

SOLAR AIR HEATING SYSTEMS

Fig. 14 shows a simple solar air heating system which can be used to provide heat and store excess energy during the day by heating the gravel in the storage tank. One fan and five dampers are needed to enable air to be drawn through the air heater and then to be sent either through the storage cylinder and back to the collector, or diverted directly to the house on cold days. At night, the collector may be by-passed and all of the house air may be circulated through the storage cylinder. For use in most parts of the U.S., an auxiliary electric heater, probably in the form of a grid of resistance wire, would have to be used to guarantee comfort during prolonged periods of bad weather. A fireplace with a Heatalator [see BioFuels—Wood] would do equally well in rural areas where firewood is available.

For heating small, single-story houses, air heaters have a number of advantages, including simplicity and low initial cost. However, the duct-work for the movement of air requires careful planning. Air ducts are many times larger than water pipes in cross-section, and problems can easily develop when one tries to run the ducts in walls and around structural members. Duct-work generally must be purchased from sheet-metal shops, where some pieces probably will have to be custom-made. Fortunately, the temperatures involved in most solar air heaters are such that the air may safely be conveyed in insulated passages between floor or roof joists and through the air spaces which exist in stud walls. Care must be taken to ensure equalized flow through all parts of the air heater. This will generally involve some balancing of the air flow by means of dampers after the system is built.

In summary, an air heating system needs the four elements shown in Fig. 15: (a) is the collector, facing south, steeply tilted and insulated so that the collected heat will go into the air and not be wasted. A fan (b) is needed to circulate the air. A filter on the fan will minimize the dust and pollen problem within the house. The rock bed (c) provides storage of heat in winter and storage of coolth in other seasons when the air at night is cold enough to cool the rocks so that they in turn cool the house during

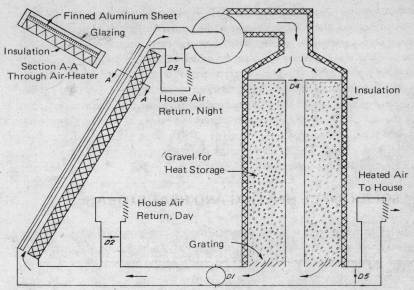

FIG. 14 SOLAR AIR HEATER SYSTEM WITH VERTICAL ROCK BED HEAT STORAGE

the day. An auxiliary heating system in the form of the electric grid (e) can be used to heat the house directly on cloudy, cold winter days or to store heat in the rock bed by properly setting the dampers. Fig. 15 has a maximum of flexibility because its eight dampers permit outdoor air to be brought in, blown through the rockbed and then out again. The rockbed can thus be cooled down at night and the house air can be cooled during the day by blowing it through the cooled rocks.

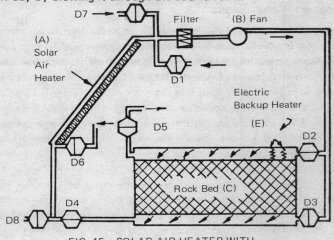

FIG. 15 SOLAR AIR HEATER WITH ROCK BED HEAT STORAGE (8 dampers)

South Wall Air Heaters

A number of houses have been built in southern France using the concept shown in Fig. 12. This is an outgrowth of work done during the past decade by Dr. Felix Trombe of the Solar Energy Laboratory at Odeillo. The major activity at Odeillo is centered around the great solar furnace, but the building which houses the nine-story solar concentrator, and many of the staff homes in the vicinity, use south wall heaters during the winter months, with electric auxiliary heaters for long periods of low insolation.

This idea is just beginning to be used again in the U.S., although the Telkes-Raymond house in Dover, Mass. used vertical south-wall heaters, and "Solar One" at the University of Delaware is employing this system, too.

Solar Water Heating Systems for Space Heating

The basic principles of a solar space heating system using water instead of air as the heat transfer fluid are given in Fig. 16. A collector similar to Fig. 6, or Fig. 10 (a)—(d), is mounted on a south-facing exposure or a flat roof of a structure. Heat storage is provided by an insulated tank which can hold from 2,000 to 20,000 gallons of water depending upon the size of the building and the length of time that heat must be provided from storage.

The house heating system works independently of the solar collecting and storage system (Fig. 16), since the solar-system pump, P1, goes to work whenever the solar thermostat, T1, senses that the temperature of the collector panel is warmer than the water in the storage tank. The pump runs at constant speed and so the temperature of the water leaving the top of the collector will vary from a few to many degrees above the

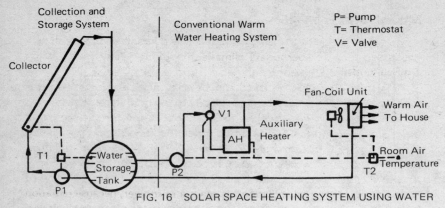

Collection and
Storage System

Collector

Conventional Warm
Water Heating System

P= Pump
T= Thermostat
V= Valve

FIG. 16   SOLAR SPACE HEATING SYSTEM USING WATER

tank temperature.

When the thermostat senses that the collector panel is falling below the tank temperature, the pump will stop and all of the water in the collector panels will drain back into the tank. The system is thus "fail-safe," because it will be protected against freezing since the system will drain itself whenever the pump stops because of power failure or from a signal from the thermostat. There will be enough inertia in the system to prevent it from stopping if a passing cloud happens to cross the sun, but it will stop and remain shut down if prolonged cloudiness sets in.

The actual heating of the building is done by any conventional warm water system (e.g., water circulation pipes and radiators) into which the circulating pump P2 will supply warm water from the storage tank. When the house thermostat T2 calls for heat, it starts P2, and valve V1 directs the warm water into the house heating system, indicated in Fig. 16 as a fan-coil unit. This consists of a fan or blower, driven by an electric motor, and a heater containing finned tubes through which the water flows. In many homes, the fan in such a system runs continuously to give air circulation even when heat is not required. A filter will add to the comfort of the occupants of the house by removing dust and pollen at very little added cost.

Generally, the solar heat collection and storage system will be designed so that enough heat will be available in the storage tank to carry the house through several cold, sunless days. However, it is not feasible to store enough heat for every possible contingency and so an auxiliary heater must be provided. Shown in Fig. 16, this may be a fuel-fired heater or an electric resistance heater. If an auxiliary heater must be used for many hours per year, or if the region is one where summer cooling is needed as urgently as winter heating, then a heat pump (App. I) is the economical answer to this problem.

The heat pump can use cool or even cold water from the storage tank as its heat input and use a small amount of electric power to raise the temperature of the water up to the point where it can do the heating job. This system is discussed in detail in the articles cited in App. IV, No. 9.

The system shown in Fig. 16 has been used in many buildings, including the MIT solar houses which were built in the 1930's. These used large south-facing collectors which constituted the south-facing portion of the roofs, and large water tanks in the basement. Several experimenters have used bare metal roofs with tubes integral with the metal roofing (similar to Fig. 10(a)) as their heat collectors, with water storage tanks and heat pumps to raise the temperature of the circulating water to the point where it can warm the building. Prominent among these experimenters were Mr. Yanagimachi of Tokyo and Mr. and Mrs. Raymond Bliss of Tucson, who designed the University of Arizona Solar Laboratory which was in use for several years until it was torn down to make way for the University's Medical School.

There are two other water heating systems which should be mentioned in this section, the first being the "Solaris" houses built by Dr. Thomason in a suburb of Washington, D.C., in 1959, 1960 and 1963. The Thomason houses all use the open-flow system shown in Fig. 10(d). The collectors are mounted on steeply-pitched south-facing roofs and they receive their water from a perforated pipe which runs along the ridge of the roof. A large (1,600 gallon) water tank in the basement provides the major heat storage and this is surrounded by 50 to 60 tons of river rock. These rocks provide additional heat storage and the heat transfer surface which is needed to warm the air which is circulated through the house by a small blower.

The collectors are covered by a single layer of glass and they drain automatically whenever the pump is shut off by the thermostat which senses

the temperature of the collector surface. Corrugated aluminum roofing, primed and painted black, is used as the collector surface. This is probably the lowest cost collector panel in use today. App. IV, No. 8, gives additional details on the "Solaris" system.

The "Skytherm" solar heated and naturally cooled system (Figs. 8(c) and 10(g)), invented by Mr. Hay, now has its first full-scale application. A building of this design is now in regular use at Atascadero, California. Professors Kenneth Haggard and Philip Niles of California State Polytechnical University did the architectural design and engineering. Technical assistance came from Professor Philip Niles on the instrumentation phase. Funds for building the house were put up by the inventor, Mr. Hay. HUD (the Department of Housing and Urban Development) contracted with Cal Poly to instrument and monitor the operation of the house.

The "Skytherm" system is particularly well adapted to the southwest desert, where the skies are generally clear both winter and summer, and where the summer humidity is low. Daytime temperatures may be very high (110°F and above) but the "Skytherm" system has demonstrated its ability to cope with them.

Another solar-water heated house which should be mentioned is the residence of Mr. and Mrs. Steve Baer, near Albuquerque, New Mexico which uses steel barrels filled with water, behind single glazing, to absorb the winter sun on the southern exposure of the house. An insulating panel, hinged at the bottom, is lowered when the sun begins to strike the south wall, admitting the sun's rays to warm the blackened ends of the barrels. The barrels serve as radiators to warm the building, and an ingenious device allows shutters to open automatically whenever the house needs to be cooled. The exterior insulating panel is raised at night to retain the heat which the barrels have collected during the daylight hours.

SOLAR COOLING

Solar cooling is something of a misnomer, since there is actually no way by which we can use the heat of the sun directly to produce cooling. However, we can use the heat to produce hot water or steam, and with that we can refrigerate, using the process known as absorption refrigeration. There are natural cooling methods which are treated in the next section which might be considered to be sun-related but they do not actually use solar radiation as such.

Heliothermal Cooling Systems

The process by which the sun's radiant heat is used indirectly to produce cooling is known as "absorption refrigeration." This process was discovered almost accidentally by the British scientist, Michael Faraday, in 1824. Faraday was trying to make liquid ammonia, using the apparatus shown in Fig. 17. It consisted of a U-shaped test tube, with silver chloride saturated with ammonia in the left leg, and nothing, at first, in the right leg. A glass of water, or some similar simple cooling means, was provided for the right leg, and a source of heat, shown as a Bunsen burner on the left. As Faraday applied heat gently to the saturated silver chloride, the ammonia gas was driven off, and it condensed as a liquid on the right side.

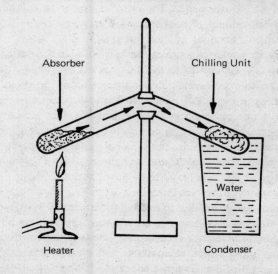

FIG. 17   FARADAY'S 1824 DEMONSTRATION OF ABSORPTION REFRIGERATION.

Faraday then proceeded to cut off the heat, and go on about his business. When he returned, he found, much to his surprise, that the liquid ammonia had disappeared from the right side of the apparatus, but the outer surface of that side was covered with ice. He reasoned, quite correctly, that the ammonia had evaporated, taking heat away, freezing the water as the ammonia went back into absorption in the silver chloride. This was the first absorption refrigeration process, and, about one hundred years later, this principle was used for household refrigerators.

The ammonia-water absorption system was discovered somewhat later. Here the ammonia is the refrigerant and the water, instead of silver chloride, is the absorber. Water can absorb very large quantities of ammonia when it is at a low temperature, but, when the water is heated under high pressure, it will give off the ammonia as a gas. This ammonia can then be condensed back to liquid form and allowed to expand through a valve, where some of the ammonia will evaporate and cool down the rest of it.

This form of absorption refrigeration has been very widely used, with low pressure steam as the heat source. The only mechanical work involved is the power needed to run a small pump to raise the pressure of the ammonia-water. In a high pressure "generator," heat is then applied to drive the ammonia away from the water. Cooling must also be applied at this point to cool the water down again, and to condense the ammonia. So, both heat, and cooling water, such as that obtained from a cooling tower or an evaporative cooler, must be provided.

The ammonia-water system is also under pressure, and building codes require that such apparatus be used in outdoor locations. The chilled fluid which results from this process, generally cold water, can be taken indoors and used to cool air. This system is widely used where there is a large quantity of low pressure steam available which would otherwise be wasted or where very hot water is available.

The absorption process which is being studied in a number of experimental buildings uses lithium bromide as the absorbant and water as the refrigerant. Water has been used as a refrigerant for many years, using centrifugal compressors or steam jets to reduce the pressure on a tank full of water. This causes enough of it to evaporate to chill down the remainder. The compressed water vapor is then condensed by the use of water from a cooling tower or a similar source. It then goes back to the tank to complete the cycle and to be re-used. Attempts have been made to use steam generated in solar boilers to power such a system, but they have not been successful.

The lithium bromide system uses the ability of that substance to absorb large quantities of water when it is relatively cool, and to give up the water vapor when it is heated. The temperature to which the heating must proceed is about 200° to 210°F in conventional commercial units, such as those manufactured by the Arkla-Servel Company. Newer versions of the lithium bromide-water systems use solar-generated hot water at 180° to 200°F to regenerate the strong lithium bromide-water solution, and thus to drive off the water, which must be cooled before it can go back into the chiller tank to complete the cycle and continue the process.

The major difficulty with solar-powered absorption refrigeration at the present time is the temperature at which it has to operate and the relatively low Coefficient of Performance. The latter is simply the ratio of the cooling effect to the amount of heat that must be generated to produce this effect, frequently measured in "tons of refrigeration" (App. I). The Coefficient of Performance of a typical lithium bromide absorption system is no higher than 0.6, as opposed to the 3.0 or better attained by even a small compression refrigeration system driven by an electric motor.

Temperatures in the 200°F range are not easy to obtain with solar collectors, even if two cover plates and a selective surface are used. The efficiency of collection is likely to be no higher than 50% at noon and an hour or two before. After that time, the efficiency falls off rapidly, as the sun moves away from its noon position, and the day-long efficiency of a collector operating at 200°F is likely to be no more than 30%.

There are many other combinations, aside from ammonia-water and lithium bromide-water, which can be used in absorption systems, and these are being carefully reviewed now to see whether a system can be developed which will operate at lower temperatures, with a higher Coefficient of Performance than those which characterize today's absorption systems. Dr. Erich Farber and the Solar Energy Laboratory, University of Florida (App. IV, No. 10) are doing significant work in solar cooling.

Natural Cooling Methods

There are two natural cooling methods which have been used with considerable success in appropriate climatic conditions. These are (1) night sky radiation and (2) evaporation.

Almost everyone has observed the effect of night sky radiation when they have noticed frost on the ground early in the morning, even when the air temperature has not dropped to 32°F. The reason for the cooling of the ground to the freezing point is that, depending largely upon the amount of water vapor in the atmosphere, the sky is a good absorber of radiation. When the sky is very dry, the apparent temperature of the sky, as far as ground heat losses are concerned, may be very low.

The term "nocturnal radiation" is again a misnomer, because radiation from surfaces on the earth to the sky proceeds all day long, but it is generally masked by the incoming solar radiation during the daytime. At night when this source of heat is not present, the cooling effect of radiation to the sky can be very marked indeed. It is most noticeable when the sky is clear and cloudless, and the relative humidity is low. It is least noticeable on an overcast night, because then the clouds tend to radiate back to the earth almost as much heat as they receive from the ground and the grass and buildings which cover it.

Raymond Bliss, when he was planning the solar energy laboratory for the University of Arizona, made a careful study of the water vapor in the atmosphere. He found that the rate of heat loss from a black surface on the ground, at the temperature of the air near the ground, ranged from 20 to 40 Btu (App. I) depending upon the amount of moisture in the air. The dew point of the air at the surface has been found to be a good measure of the total amount of moisture in the atmosphere in any given location, and the Bliss curves (App. IV, No. 11), show that there is very little change in the "nocturnal radiation" rate as the air temperature changes, but there is change from 20 to 40 Btu as the relative humidity of the air changes from 80% to 10%.

Evaporative cooling is the cooling of air by the evaporation of moisture into that air. The process of passing air through pads which are saturated with water, and evaporating some of the moisture picked up by the air, has been used for many years as a means of reducing the temperature of desert air to a tolerable level. The difficulty with this very simple process is that the moisture which reduces the temperature also raises the relative humidity, until the result is cold, clammy air which is almost as uncomfortable as the hot, dry air which entered the evaporative cooler, These devices are frequently called "swamp coolers" in the southwest where they have been widely used for several generations. Today, they are employed most widely to cool cattle sheds, manufacturing operations and large areas where so much heat must be removed that conventional refrigeration would be far too costly.

A modification of the simple evaporative cooler has been developed in Australia, and given the name "Rock Bed Regenerative Air Cooler (RBR)." One such device is shown in Fig. 18, and hundreds of units using this simple principle are in operation in Australia. The system uses two beds of rocks, set side-by-side and separated by an air space in which a damper is located. Water sprays are mounted close to the inner surface of each bed of rocks, and two fans are used. In Fig. 18, the outdoor air is being drawn into the rock bed on the right, which has just been evaporatively cooled, while the rock bed on the left is undergoing evaporative cooling by having the indoor air flow through it on its way outward to the atmosphere.

At the beginning of each cycle, water is sprayed into the rock bed for 10 to 15 seconds, thoroughly saturating the rocks. The air from the house,

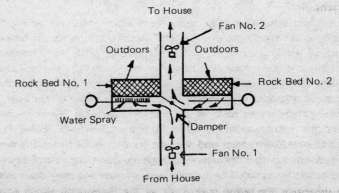

FIG. 18   ROCK BED REGENERATOR

blowing through the rock bed, evaporates the moisture away from the rocks and thereby cools them and the air, increasing the humidity of the air as well. This does no harm, since the air simply goes back to the atmosphere. On the other side of the system, air is being drawn into the house through rocks which have just been cooled. Only a very small amount of moisture is added to the air since it is the rocks which have been cooled, and the only moisture remaining is the small amount which adheres to the surface of the rocks.

The first prototypes in the U.S. are now under construction in Arizona. They will be very useful adjuncts to solar heating systems, since the amount of power that they require is only about 10% of that used by a mechanical refrigeration system, and the amount of water needed is very small. The evaporation of 1.5 gallons of water per hour is equivalent to 1 ton of refrigeration, and the cost of the water is negligible.

The Australians have found that the rock beds can also be used to conserve heat from outgoing ventilation air in the winter. They operate during the winter without the water sprays. The rock bed will be heated almost to the exhaust air temperature in the exhaust portion of the cycle, and the incoming cold outdoor air will then be preheated almost to the indoor temperature by passing through the heated rocks. The RBR system has tremendous promise for both heating and cooling, and it is likely to find wide use in many parts of the United States.

SOLAR COOKING

Cooking by the use of solar heat is a very old art. The first solar cooker was probably that built in Bombay in 1880, and several other ingenious ovens, including that shown in Fig. 19, have originated in India.

Solar Ovens

One of the best solar ovens, little known in this country, was developed by Dr. M. K. Ghosh of Jamshedpur. Shown in Fig. 19, the Ghosh heater consists of a simple wooden box, about 24 inches square and 12 inches deep. It is lined with 2 inches of insulation (glass wool would be very satisfactory here) and it contains a blackened metal liner in which the cooking is done. The interior insulation and the hinged top are lined with shiny aluminum foil, the former to reduce radiation from the oven to the sides and bottom of the box, and the latter to reflect the sun's rays into the oven through the double cover glasses. Since much of India lies near the equator and the sun is nearly overhead at midday, the Ghosh oven does an excellent job of cooking the noon meal.

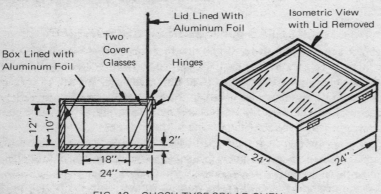

FIG. 19   GHOSH-TYPE SOLAR OVEN
(Top is hinged with two glass panes spaced 3/4" apart, sides and bottom of 3/8" plywood).

Another type of oven, originated by Dr. Telkes, uses a metal box with double glazing over its open end and a hinged, insulated door at the other end. It is contained in a casing which may be made of metal or plywood, and the whole affair is arranged so that it can turn and tilt to follow the sun. Reflecting wings made of shiny aluminum (Alzak® is the best brand) are attached at an angle of 60 degrees to the plane of the cover glasses. These nearly double the amount of solar radiation which can enter the oven. On a bright sunny day, the Telkes ovens can get to 400°F from about 9:00 a.m. to 3:00 p.m.

A simplified version of the Telkes oven is described by Dan Halacy on pp. 51-62 of his excellent do-it-yourself handbook, *Solar Science Projects* (App. IV, No. 6). His oven uses the Telkes principle, but it sets the cover

glasses at an angle of 45 degrees to the oven so that it does not need to be tilted.

The basic principle of operation of a reflector-type solar cooker is shown in Fig. 20, where a simple parabolic reflector, arranged on a sun-following mount, concentrates the sun's rays on a grill which can support a pot or a frying pan. This type of cooker will become hot just as soon as it is adjusted to face the sun and, according to Dr. Farrington Daniels, a 4 foot diameter reflector-type cooker will deliver the equivalent of a 400 watt electric hot plate under bright sunshine. He gives detailed instructions for the construction of a plastic shell of the proper shape which can be lined with aluminized Mylar. App. IV, No. 5, Chapter 5, pp. 89-103 covers the topic of solar cooking; pp. 102-103 gives an excellent bibliography on the subject.

FIG. 20   REFLECTOR COOKER   FIG. 21   SOLAR CONCENTRATORS
(Must be adjustable to follow the sun).

Dan Halacy shows how to make an even simpler reflective cooker out of corrugated cardboard and kitchen-type aluminum foil on pp. 14-27 of *Solar Science Projects* (App. IV, No. 6). He advises the use of sun glasses when you are cooking with his aluminized broiler because the reflectance can be dazzling. The reflecting surface does not get hot, but the grill area does, so be careful when you put on the pots and pans. Also, Brace Research Institute, in *How to Make a Solar Steam Cooker*, Do-It-Yourself Leaflet L-2 ($1.00), describes a steam cooker which uses the simplest of materials for making a broiler. See App. IV, No. 2 for ordering information.

SOLAR FURNACES

While we are dealing with some of the higher temperature solar devices, mention should be made of solar furnaces which can produce small but extremely hot images of the sun. Fig. 21(a) shows the familiar magnifying glass which can be used to start a fire whenever the sun is shining. The diameter of available lenses is not great enough to do much real work with a burning glass. The Fresnel (pronounced Frā-nĕl') lens shown in Fig. 21(b) is available from Edmund Scientific Co. (App. IV, No. 12) in the form of a 12 inch square plastic sheet and you also can buy a booklet entitled *Fun with Fresnel Lenses*. Dan Halacy's book, *Solar Science Projects*, gives explicit details for making a mounting which will convert the Fresnel lens into a miniature solar furnace.

A concentrating curved-mirror solar furnace can reach extremely high temperatures (to 6,000°F, depending on size). Control of the temperature of the target at the focal spot (App. I) may be accomplished by using a diaphragm to "stop down" incoming rays, or by using a cylinder which can be moved to or fro along the axis of the concentrator to regulate the amount of radiation which reaches the target. Military surplus searchlights are the best source of high-precision reflectors at reasonable prices, and Edmund Scientific Co. frequently has some for sale.

The largest solar furnace now in existence is located at Odeillo in the French Pyrenees. There, starting in 1957, Dr. Felix Trombe and the National Center for Scientific Research have constructed a gigantic paraboloid which is nine stories high, uses 63 heliostats, each of which is 24 feet square, to produce an image which is a perfect circle, 12 inches in diameter. The furnace can concentrate 1,000 kilowatts of thermal energy into this small area and temperatures pushing up towards 6,000°F have been reached on sunny days. The first large American solar steam generator will probably be tested in this facility in the summer of 1975.

ELECTRICITY FROM THE SUN

Photovoltaic Devices

About a century ago, when the scientific foundations were being laid for today's heliotechnology, a Frenchman, Becquerel, found that sunlight could produce minute amounts of electricity when it entered a very special kind of "wet cell" battery. Later on, other workers found that sunlight could change the resistance of certain metals and that very small amounts of electricity would be generated when sunlight illuminated discs of selenium or certain types of copper oxide. These devices were very useful as light meters but they could not produce enough power to do anything more strenuous than moving the pointer on a meter or activating a very sensitive relay.

In May, 1954 a one-page report, authored by D. M. Chapin, C. S. Fuller, and G. L. Pearson, appeared in the *Journal of Applied Physics* (Vol. 25, No. 5, p. 676). In brief terms they announced the discovery of a new treatment for ultra-pure silicon, which gave it the property of generating electricity from sunlight with a conversion efficiency of 6%. This was ten times better than any previous efficiency for the direct conversion of sunlight into electricity (the previous record was held by Dr. Telkes with a battery of thermocouples). Drs. Fuller, Chapin and Pearson immediately applied their invention to a small transistorized radio transmitter and receiver.

It was not until the U.S. embarked upon its space program late in 1957 that a unique application was found for the silicon solar battery. There was no other source of power for the satellites which we were planning to launch. NASA was persuaded to put silicon cells on its first permanent satellite, Vanguard One, which was orbited in 1958. They worked so well that all but one of the satellites which have been orbited since that time have been powered by increasingly complex arrays of silicon solar cells. Communication satellites use tens of thousands of silicon cells and Skylab I produces some 20 kilowatts from its array of solar panels.

The details of the theory and construction of silicon cells are beyond the scope of this chapter, so it must suffice to say that, under bright sunlight, each 2 centimeter square cell will produce a short circuit current of 0.10 amperes (100 milliamperes) and an open circuit voltage of 0.60 (600 millivolts). Under optimum load, they produce about 90 milliamps at 400 millivolts, or approximately 36 milliwatts. This is certainly a tiny amount of power when it is compared with today's gigantic steam turbo-generators; but silicon cell technology has advanced so rapidly that tens of thousands of individual cells can be connected together. This can be done rapidly and reliably so that today the communications satellite has become the standard means of intercontinental communication for voice, television and even computer language.

Although the cost is still too high for the installation of great panels of solar cells on every rooftop, great strides have been made and the cost has been reduced from $1000 per watt to $20 per watt, with more reductions on the way. Ways of producing far less expensive silicon cells are now under intensive study. Another approach is to concentrate ten times as much sunshine onto the cells as they would normally receive. The main problem here is to remove the heat which will build up if the cells are not cooled effectively. The more optimistic silicon cell specialists think that, within another decade, the costs will come down to $2 per watt, which will be competitive with conventional methods of power generation.

Although making silicon cells is not a do-it-yourself project, from time to time bargains are available in the way of space-reject cells (Herbach and Rademan of Philadelphia (App. IV, No. 13) is an excellent source), and these are well worth considering for powering radios and other apparatus which require very small amounts of power. Fig. 22 shows a method of mounting solar cells on a sun-tracking device to obtain more power than can be gained from a fixed array. The circuit diagram indicates a series-connected battery of cells which can produce any desired voltage (just use twice as many cells as you need volts, since under load each cells will give just about 1/2 volt). A number of such series-connected groups connected in parallel can produce a respectable amount of power and keep a 12-volt storage battery charged for running a radio or even a small TV set. We are not yet at the point where solar cells will run air conditioners or other large motor loads, but Dr. Boer believes that he can produce another type of cell, using cadmium sulfide rather than silicon, which can be produced at far lower cost than the silicon cells and still retain adequate efficiency to do the job.

Heliothermal Generators

There have been many attempts to produce steam from heliothermal

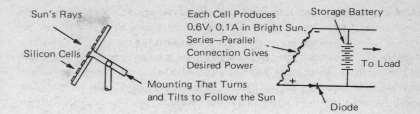

devices, beginning with John Ericsson's work in New York just after the Civil War and reaching its high point early in the 1900's with the building of great solar engines in Arizona and California by A. G. Eneas and in Egypt by F. Shuman and C. V. Boys. None of these attempts succeeded for reasons which are too numerous to be mentioned here.

Flat plate collectors cannot attain temperatures much above 200°F and engines operating at temperatures in that range and discharging their waste heat to air at 80° to 90°F offer little prospect of generating useful amounts of power. Concentrating collectors which do not yet exist, except for laboratory prototypes, are needed to reach temperatures high enough to make engines or turbines operate with competitive efficiencies. When these become available, they will probably use vapors of the Freon family rather than water and they will use the cycle pioneered a century ago by an Englishman, Rankine. For a more detailed account of the various heat-engine cycles, read Chapter 7, *Introduction to the Utilization of Solar Energy* (App. IV, No. 3).

Today's research efforts in the field of heliothermal power generation fall into two categories: (A) small engines using Freon vapor to produce 5 to 10 horsepower to drive pumps, generators or refrigeration compressors and (B) very large installations using vast areas of concentrating collectors to produce enough steam to run a boiler mounted on a tower of moderate height. This is surrounded by a great field of slightly curved mirrors which turn and tilt to reflect the sun's rays into the boiler and thus to produce steam.

The storage of heat to run the solar-power engine at night or on partially cloudy days is a problem which is not even close to solution, so present thinking is that solar steam stations will be tied in with the existing electric power grids. Solar plants will contribute power to the grid when the sun is shining, thus conserving fuel which would otherwise have to be burned or water which would have to run through turbines. The solar plants would be idle at night, when the demand for power in today's air conditioned world is low.

SUNDIALS AND THE TELLING OF TIME

The use of shadows cast by the sun on the earth to designate the passage of time is so ancient that no one really knows who built the first sun dial. They were certainly in use by 1500 B.C. (see App. IV, No. 14 for a comprehensive study of the science of "dialing") and a bewildering variety of sundials is to be found in Europe and Asia. The simplest and most widely-used type is the horizontal dial.

The dial plate is the base upon which the hour lines are inscribed and the "gnomon," attached to the plate and pointing true north (not compass north!), is the element which casts the shadow. The angle between the gnomon and the base must be exactly equal to the local latitude and then, for reasons which an astronomer can readily explain, the gnomon will be aligned exactly with the earth's axis. The hour lines for a properly constructed horizontal dial will always denote the number of hours away from solar noon, and so corrections must be made to account for the Equation of Time and departure of the local longitude from the Local Standard Time Meridian. These corrections are explained in App. II, and the details for calculating hour line angles are given in App. IV, No. 14.

CONCLUSIONS

The purpose of this chapter has been to give the reader the basic principles upon which the rapidly growing field of heliotechnology is based. For those who want to learn more about this fascinating field, the list of resources given in App. IV will prove to be exceedingly helpful. Regular reading of *Solar Energy*, the Journal of the International Solar Energy Society, will help, too.

A Symbol used here to denote the solar azimuth, which is the angle between the south-north line at a given location and the projection of the earth-sun line in the horizontal plane. It is $\angle$HOS in Fig. II.4.

absorptance The ratio of absorbed to incident solar radiation.

ASHRAE Acronym denoting the American Society of Heating Refrigerating and Air Conditioning Engineers, 345 E. 47th St., New York, NY 10017. ASHRAE Handbooks are the source of most of the basic data on heating and air conditioning.

B Symbol used here to denote the solar altitude above the horizontal plane. It is $\angle$HOQ in Fig. II.4.

Btu British thermal unit, which is the amount of heat required to raise the temperature of one pound of water one degree Fahrenheit. (No longer used in England, since they have gone metric!)

Btu Symbol used here to denote "Btu per hour per square foot."

C Designates the Celsius temperature scale where water freezes at 0°C and boils at 100°C. To convert from degrees C to degrees F, multiply the temperature in deg. C by 9/5 (or 1.8) and add 32. Example: convert 18°C to degrees F.; $(18^\circ C \times 1.8) + 32^\circ = 64.4^\circ$F. To convert from degrees F to degrees C, reverse the process and subtract 32 from the Fahrenheit temperature and then multiply by 5/9. Example: convert 112°F to degrees C.; $(112^\circ - 32^\circ) \times 5/9 = 44.4^\circ$C.

coolth A moderate degree of coolness (antonym of warmth).

D Symbol used here to denote the solar declination, which is the angle between the earth-sun line and the earth's equatorial plane, as shown in Fig. II.2. It varies day by day throughout the year from $+23.47^\circ$ on June 21 to -23.47° on Dec. 21.

declination See the definition of symbol D.

deg. Abbreviation used for degrees of arc and also degrees of temperature.

emissivity The property of emitting heat radiation; possessed by all materials to a varying extent. "Emittance" is the numerical value of this property, expressed as a decimal fraction, for a particular material. Normal emittance is the value measured at 90 deg. to the plane of the sample and hemispherical emittance is the total amount emitted in all directions. We are generally interested in hemispherical, rather than normal, emittance. Emittance values range from 0.05 for brightly polished metals to 0.96 for flat black paint. Most non-metals have high values of emittance.

F Designates the Fahrenheit temperature scale, where water freezes at 32°F and boils at 212°F. See the definition of symbol C for the equation to convert degrees F to degrees C.

focal spot The rays of the sun are not precisely parallel, despite its 93,000,000 mile distance, and so they are concentrated not at a point but on a spot, the diameter of which is given by the following formula:

$$\text{Diameter of the focal spot} = \frac{\text{focal length}}{107.3}$$

The number 107.3 is one-half of the reciprocal of the tangent of 16 minutes of arc, which is in turn one-half of the angle which the sun's disk subtends when it is observed from the earth.

G Symbol used here to denote the wall-solar azimuth, the angle in the horizontal plane between the solar azimuth line and the line normal to a specified wall. It is $\angle$HOP in Fig. II.4.

H Symbol used here to denote the sun's hour angle, equal to the number of minutes from local solar noon, divided by 4 to convert to degrees of arc.

heat exchanger A device used to transfer heat from a fluid flowing on one side of a barrier to a fluid flowing on the other side of the barrier. Quite often this is done by running a coil of pipe through a tank.

heat pump A device which transfers thermal energy or heat from a relatively low-temperature reservoir to one at a higher temperature. Heat normally flows from a warmer region to a cooler region; this process is reversed when we supply additional energy to a heat pump.

heliochemical Process which uses the sun's radiation to cause chemical reactions.

heliochronometry Telling of time by means of the sun.

helioelectrical Process which uses the sun's radiation to produce electricity.

heliostatic An adjective referring to devices which make the sun appear to stand still.

heliothermal Process which uses the sun's radiation to produce heat.

heliotropic An adjective referring to devices which track the sun, following its apparent motion across the sky.

hour angle See the definition of symbol H.

I Symbol used to denote solar radiation intensity in Btu.

I_d Symbol used to denote diffuse or sky radiation reaching a specified surface, in Btu.

I_{DN} Symbol used here to denote direct beam solar irradiation on a surface normal to the sun's rays, in Btu.

$I_{D\Theta}$ Symbol used here to denote direct beam solar irradiation on a surface with an incident angle Θ between the sun's rays and the normal to the surface, in Btu.

I_L Symbol used here to denote total insolation on a south-facing surface tilted upward from the horizontal at the angle of the local latitude, in Btu.

I_{sc} Symbol used here to denote the solar constant, the intensity of solar radiation beyond the earth's atmosphere, at the average earth-sun distance, on a surface perpendicular to the sun's rays. The value for the solar constant is 1,353 W/m^2, 1,940 cal/cm^2/min, 429.2 Btu/sq. ft./hr., 125.7 W/sq. ft., or 1.81 horsepower/sq. meter.

$I_{t\Theta}$ Symbol used here to denote total insolation, direct plus diffuse, on a surface with an incident angle Θ between the sun's rays and the normal to the surface, in Btu.

incident angle The angle between the sun's rays and a line perpendicular (normal) to the irradiated surface.

insolation Solar irradiation.

k See the definition of thermal conductivity.

kilowatt One thousand watts. A watt is a unit of power equal to one joule per second. Power is the rate at which work is done. A kilowatt hour is the total energy developed when the power of one kilowatt acts for one hour. This is the common unit of electrical power consumption.

latitude The angular distance north (+) or south (-) of the equator, measured in degrees of arc.

L Symbol used here to denote local latitude in degrees.

Langley The meteorologist's unit of solar radiation intensity, equivalent to 1.0 gram calorie per square centimeter, usually used in terms of Langleys per minute. 1 Langley per minute = 221.2 Btu per hour per sq. ft.

m Symbol used here to denote air mass, the scientist's way of expressing the ratio of the mass of atmosphere in the actual earth-sun path to the mass which would exist if the sun were directly overhead. In space, beyond the earth's atmosphere, m = 0.

micron Unit of solar radiation wavelength, equal to one-millionth of a meter.

normal In geometry, a word which means perpendicular.

photosynthesis The process by which the sun's radiation, in certain specific wavelengths, causes water, carbon dioxide and nutrients to react, thus producing oxygen in plants.

pyranometer A solar radiometer which measures total insolation, including both the direct and the diffuse radiation.

radiometer An instrument which measures the intensity of any kind of radiation. The adjective "solar" is needed to denote instruments, like the pyrheliometer and the pyranometer, which measure insolation.

selective surface A surface which can absorb most of the sun's shortwave radiant energy, 41% of which is visible, but which re-radiates very little longwave (infrared) radiant energy.

solar constant See the definition of symbol I_{sc}.

T Tilt angle, upward from the horizontal.

Tabor surface A black nickel selective surface coating, invented by Dr. Harry Tabor, which absorbs 90% of the incoming solar energy but re-radiates only about 10% as much longwave radiation as would be emitted by a coat of flat black paint.

thermal cement A material which can be used to make metal-to-metal seals which have both high mechanical strength and good thermal conductivity. Generally, the basic composition of such cements is a liquid, such as sodium silicate (water glass), in which a large amount of iron filings is suspended. When exposed to the atmosphere, this mixture hardens and the iron filings give it a thermal conductivity comparable to steel itself. There are many commercial sources for thermal cements, including epoxies, etc.

thermal conductance The amount of heat in Btu which can be conducted through a particular solid material, one foot square, which is 1-inch thick and has a temperature difference of 1°F maintained between its two surfaces. "k" is the symbol used here to designate thermal conductance. Most metals are good conductors and their conductivity varies with their temperature. At 212°F (100°C), silver has the highest conductivity, 2,856 $Btu/(^\circ F/in.)$, while mild steel has a conductivity of 312 <u>Btu</u>/(°F/in.).

thermal resistance	The reciprocal of thermal conductance. The thermal resistance of a material is its thickness, ℓ, in inches divided by its thermal conductivity, k. The resistance of a series of different materials, all in thermal contact with each other, is the sum of the individual resistances.
thermocouple	A thermoelectric device which has a combination of two dissimilar wires with their ends connected together. A millivolt meter is connected in the circuit to measure the voltage which is generated when the two junctions are at different temperatures. If one junction is kept in a bath of ice and water, at 32°F, the voltage generated (measured in millivolts) is a measure of the temperature of the other junction above the 32°F reference point.
thermopile	A large number of thermocouples connected in series with all of the hot junctions located in one region and all of the cold junctions located in another. It is used to measure very small temperature differences with a high degree of accuracy.
thermosyphon	The convective circulation of fluid which occurs in a closed system when less-dense warm fluid rises, displaced by denser, cooler fluid in the same system.
theta	See the definition of symbol Θ.
Θ	Symbol for the Greek letter "theta," used here to designate the angle of incidence between a solar ray and the line "normal" to the surface which is being irradiated.
Θ_L	Symbol used here to denote the incident angle in degrees for solar rays falling on a south-facing surface tilted up from the horizontal at an angle equal to the local latitude, L.
Θ_v Θ_h	Symbols used here to denote the incident angles on vertical and horizontal surfaces, respectively, in degrees.
ton of refrigeration	One ton of refrigeration means the removal of heat at the rate of 12,000 Btu per hour. This unit comes from the fact that melting a ton (2,000 lbs.) of ice requires 2,000 x 144 Btu, which if done over a 24 hour period, requires a heat removal rate of 12,000 Btu per hour.
transmittance	The ratio of radiant energy transmitted to energy incident on a surface. In solar technology it is often affected by the thickness and composition of the glass cover plates on a collector, and to a major extent by the angle of incidence Θ between the sun's rays and a line normal to the surface.
U	Symbol for the heat loss coefficient, in <u>Btu</u>/°F.
wall azimuth	The line in the horizontal plane that is perpendicular to the receiving surface. It is $\angle$SOP in Fig. II.4.
wall-solar azimuth	See the definition of symbol G.
warmth	A moderate degree of heat.
"wet surface"	A surface upon which water will condense in a thin, even sheet, as opposed to forming large, distinct drops. Plastic surfaces can be treated to become "wettable."

APPENDIX II

THE SUN AND ITS RELATION TO THE WHOLE EARTH

The Sun's Radiant Energy

The energy radiated from the sun's outer surface (called the photosphere) travels in spheres of ever-increasing diameter. The intensity of radiation on a unit of area, such as a square foot, or a sq. meter, or a sq. centimeter, varies inversely as the square of the distance from the sun. The intensity of solar radiation at the edge of the Earth's atmosphere, at the average Earth-sun distance, measured on a surface perpendicular to the solar rays, is called the <u>solar constant</u>, I_{sc} (App. IV, No. 15). The average Earth-sun distance, approximately 92,956,000 miles, is called an Astronomical Unit (AU), and at this distance the Solar Constant, I_{sc}, is 429.2 Btu per hour per square foot. ("Btu per hour per square foot" will be used so frequently that we will use the symbol <u>Btu</u> to denote this unit.) Space scientists generally use the International system of units and they say that I_{sc} = 1,353 watts per sq. meter while meterologists use still another system of terminology, in which the solar constant is 1.940 Langleys per minute.

The Earth's orbit is almost exactly circular but the sun is somewhat off-center and so we are further from the sun on July 1 (94,482,000 miles) than we are on January 1 (91,325,000 miles). This variation is great enough to make a detectable change in the intensity of solar radiation at the Earth, but it is more important to space technicians than to others of us on Earth. Here, other and far greater variations exist because of the manner in which the Earth rotates about its own axis.

For nearly two thousand years, between the time of the Greek philosopher Aristarchus of Samos (300 BC) and the Polish astronomer Copernicus (1473-1543), virtually everyone believed that the Earth was the center of the universe and that the

sun and all of the other heavenly bodies revolved about our planet. Thanks to Copernicus, Kepler, Galileo and other courageous men of that era, we now know that the apparent motion of the sun across the sky is actually the result of the Earth's own rotation. We spin at the rate of 360.99 degrees in 24 hours and so the sun appears to move across the sky at the rate of 15.04 degrees per hour.

Time and the Turning of the Earth

Our changing seasons are caused by the fact that, in our annual journey around the sun (it actually takes 365.25 days, which is why we need a "Leap Year" every four years), our rotational axis is tilted at 23.47 degrees with respect to the "plane of the ecliptic" which contains our orbit. Fig. II.1 is the classic method of representing the Earth-sun relationship as it would be viewed by an observer in far outer space. It shows that on December 21 the sun is shining primarily on the southern hemisphere, with the northern half of the globe tilted away. On June 21, the situation is reversed and we receive most of the sunshine, while winter prevails south of the equator.

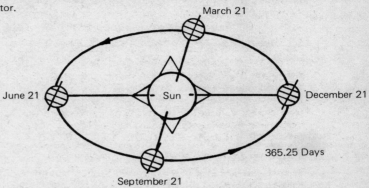

FIG. II.1 ANNUAL MOTION OF THE EARTH AROUND THE SUN.

Fig. II.2 shows the apparent annual motion of the sun with respect to the Earth. The angle made by the Earth-sun line and the equatorial plane is called the sun's "declination" and it varies day by day throughout the year from +23.47 degrees on June 21 to -23.47 degrees on December 21. On March 21 and September 23, the Earth-sun line coincides with the equator and, since the day and the night are each 12 hours long on these two days, they are called the spring and fall equinoxes. We generally think of the Earth as it appears in Fig. II.2, with its axis pointing towards the North Star, Polaris, and a series of circular lines of <u>latitude</u> which are parallel to the equator. Two of these lines, shown on Fig. II.2, are designated as <u>Tropics,</u> with the Tropic of Cancer, at +23.5 degrees North, denoting the most northerly position of the Earth-sun line and the Tropic of Capricorn at -23.5 degrees South, performing the same function in the southern hemisphere.

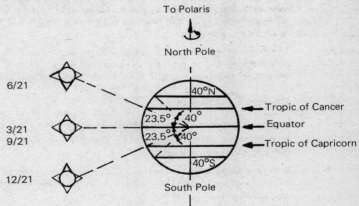

FIG. II.2 APPARENT ANNUAL MOTION OF THE SUN WITH RESPECT TO THE EARTH (caused by the 23.5° tilt of the Earth's axis).

The lines of latitude customarily shown on maps are actually designations of the angle between the equator and a line from the center of the Earth to its surface, as shown by the solid lines on Fig. II.2 which denote 40 degrees North and South latitudes, and the dashed lines which show how the 40 degree angular distance is measured. Latitudes vary from 0 degrees at the equator to 90 degrees at the poles. It is interesting to note that some 75% of the world's population inhabit the land areas between 40 degrees North and 40 degrees South, with 60% living north of the equator.

The declination of the sun for any given date is determined by the year day, starting from January 1, and Table II.1 gives the declinations for the 21st day of each month for the year 1974. For any other year, there will be a very minor difference between the values given in Table II.1 and those given in The Old Farmer's Almanac or some similar reliable sources which obtain their data from the U.S. Naval Observatory in Washington, D.C.

We are primarily interested in the position of the sun with respect to any given location on the Earth at any particular time, but that time must be reckoned by the sun's own peculiar system of chronometry, which differs in some important details from our standard or daylight saving time. First, the velocity of the Earth varies as it pursues its orbital path, because, as Kepler discovered four centuries ago, we speed up as we swing further away from the sun and slow down as we draw nearer. This gives rise to a series of variations, known as "the equation of time," between noon as given by a man-made clock which keeps time uniformly, and solar noon, which is the time when the sun is directly overhead at any given location. Table II.1 gives values of "the equation of time," and its sign is positive (+) when the sun is "ahead" of the clock and negative (-) when the sun is "behind" the clock.

Date	1/21	2/21	3/21	4/21	5/21	6/21
Declination, degrees	-19.9°	-10.6°	0.0°	+11.9°	+20.3°	+23.45°
Eq. of Time, minutes	-11.2	-13.9	-7.5	+1.1	+3.3	-1.4
Date	7/21	8/21	9/21	10/21	11/21	12/21
Declination, degrees	+20.5°	+12.1°	+0.5°	-10.7°	-19.9°	-23.45°
Eq. of Time, minutes	-6.2	-2.4	+7.5	+15.4	+13.8	-1.6

TABLE II.1 DECLINATIONS AND EQUATION OF TIME FOR THE 21st DAY OF EACH MONTH FOR THE YEAR 1974

For purposes of determining time, the imaginary circle which girdles the Earth at the equator has been divided into 24 segments of 15 degrees each and circular lines of longitude extend from the North Pole through each of these division points to the South Pole. Time is reckoned as beginning at the longitude of Greenwich, England and the sun appears to move around the Earth at the rate of 15 degrees per hour or 4.0 minutes per degree.

The world has been divided into 24 Time Zones and those which affect the United States are Eastern, starting at 75 degrees West longitude, Central at 90° West, Mountain at 105° West, Pacific at 120° West, Yukon at 135° West and Alaska-Hawaii at 150° West. At 180° West the International Date Line is reached and the longitude diminishes to reach 0 degrees again at Greenwich.

At any given location, solar time is found by starting with the local standard time (one hour slower than the Daylight Saving Time which, as of 1974, is in force throughout the year in all states except Arizona and Hawaii). Corrections must then be made for the local longitude, since the sun needs 4.0 minutes to traverse each degree between the Standard Time longitude and the local longitude. This correction must be made first and the equation of time must then be added, taking proper account of its algebraic sign.

As an example, we will find the solar time at noon, Pacific Daylight Saving Time, for Palo Alto, California on February 12, when the equation of time is -13.9 min. The longitude of Palo Alto is approximately 122 degrees West, so the time zone correction is 4.0 min./deg. x (122° - 120°) = 8.0 min. The solar time is thus:

Solar time = (12.00 - 1:00) - 8.0 - 13.9
= 11:00 - 21.9
= 10:38.1 a.m.

Solar time may also be expressed in terms of the Hour Angle, H, which is equal to the number of minutes from local solar noon, divided by 4 to convert to degrees. The concept used here involves the imaginary circles shown in Fig. II.3 in which the sun appears to move as our earth turns beneath it. The sun completes its daily journey in 24 hours, so each hour involves a 15 degree progression upward from sunrise in the morning and downward along the circle in the afternoon. The hour angle, H, for the Palo Alto solar noon situation is:

$$H = \frac{11 \text{ hr. } 60 \text{ min. } - 10 \text{ hr. } 38.1 \text{ min.}}{4}$$

$$= \frac{1:21.9}{4} = \frac{81.9}{4} = 20.475 \text{ deg.}$$

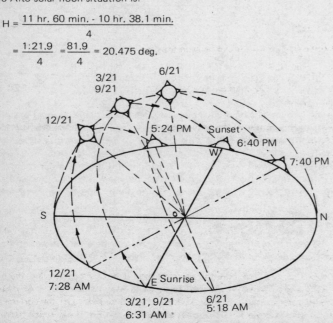

FIG. II.3 APPARENT MOTION OF THE SUN AS SEEN BY AN OBSERVER AT PHOENIX, ARIZONA   (latitude = 33° 30').

Time and the Position of the Sun

The intensity of the sun's radiation at a given time and place and the angle at which its direct rays strike a surface are dependent upon the sun's position in the sky, the season of the year, the degree of cloudiness and the tilt of the surface with respect to the horizontal. The position to the sun is defined by its altitude above the horizon, which in scientific terms is denoted by the Greek letter Beta (β), and by its azimuth.

We will use the letter B to symbolize the solar altitude and the letter A to denote the azimuth, which is the angle between the projection on the horizontal plane of the Earth-sun line and the north-south line in that same plane. A is measured from the south, for our purposes, and so the azimuth line is eastward in the mornings and westward in the afternoons. Fig. II.4 shows the sun in a typical afternoon situation; the surface on which it is shining is a vertical wall, facing south-east.

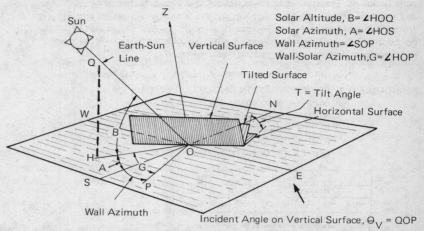

Solar Altitude, B = ∠HOQ
Solar Azimuth, A = ∠HOS
Wall Azimuth = ∠SOP
Wall-Solar Azimuth, G = ∠HOP
T = Tilt Angle
Incident Angle on Vertical Surface, Θ_V = QOP

FIG. II.4 SOLAR POSITION ANGLES FOR AN AFTERNOON CONDITION, WITH THE SUN SHINING ON A VERTICAL SURFACE WHICH FACES SOUTH-EAST.

Using the symbol ∠ to designate an angle, and defining the angles by the letters used in Fig. II.4, the solar altitude B in this case is ∠QOH and the solar azimuth A is ∠HOS. When we know the latitude L and the longitude for the location in which we are interested, and the date and time are specified so that we can determine the declination D and the hour angle H, we can refer to one of the standard texts on this subject (App. IV, No. 16) and find the trigonometrical equations by which the altitude and azimuth may be found.

These are:

Eq. II.1

| Sine of Solar Altitude | = | [Cosine of Local Latitude | x | Cosine of Day's Declination | x | Cosine of Hour Angle] | + | [Sine of Local Latitude | x | Sine of Day's Declination] |

Put into mathematical terms, this is simply:

$$\text{Sin B} = \text{Cos L Cos D Cos H} + \text{Sin L Sin D}$$ Eq. II.1a

After the altitude has been found, the azimuth comes from:

| Sine of Solar Azimuth | = | [Cosine of Day's Declination | x | Sine of Hour Angle] | ÷ | Cosine of Solar Altitude | Eq. II.2

which is:

$$\text{Sin A} = \frac{\text{Cos D Sin H}}{\text{Cos B}}$$ Eq. II.2a

To show that these calculations are not really too complicated in this day of electronic computers, let's find the solar altitude and azimuth for Palo Alto at noon, PDST, on February 21. We have already found that the hour angle H is 20.475 degrees and Table II.1 gives the declination D as -10.6 degrees. The latitude L is found from an atlas to be 37.5 degrees. We can now tabulate the values which we will need, using any convenient set of trigonometrical tables, a slide rule, or a calculator such as the Hewlett-Packard 45 to do the heavy work. For example, we know:

EXAMPLE:

Latitude (L)   = 37.5 deg; Sin L = 0.609; Cos L = 0.793
Declination (D) = -10.6 deg; Sin D = -0.184; Cos D = 0.983
Hour Angle (H) = 20.475 deg; Sin H = 0.350; Cos H = 0.937

Using Eq. II.1a, we find:

Sin B = Cos L Cos D Cos H + Sin L Sin D
= 0.793 x 0.983 x 0.937 + 0.609 x (-0.184)
= 0.730 - 0.112
= 0.618

Then B, equal to the "angle whose sine is 0.618," equals 38.17 degrees.

Cos B = 0.786, so we can then find the azimuth from Eq. II.2a:

$$\text{Sin A} = \frac{\text{Cos D Sin H}}{\text{Cos B}} = \frac{0.983 \times 0.350}{0.786} = 0.438$$

The azimuth, equal to the "angle whose sine is 0.438," equals 25.96 degrees east.

Normally, this kind of mathematical exercise is left for students to do as homework problems. The experienced solar technologist knows that he can find the altitude and azimuth already tabulated for him for the 21st day of each month, at latitudes from 24 to 64 degrees North, in App. IV, No. 16, pp. 388-392. In App. IV, No. 17, pp. 59.5 and 59.6, B and A are given for 40 degrees North. Table II.2 gives in simplified form data similar to those given in App. IV, No. 17.

TABLE II.2 SOLAR POSITION ANGLES, ALTITUDE (B) AND AZIMUTH (A) FOR 32, 40 AND 48 DEG. NORTH LATITUDE; DIRECT NORMAL IRRADIATION IN Btu (I_{DN}); TOTAL INSOLATION (I_L) IN Btu AND ANGLES OF INCIDENCE (θ) FOR SOUTH-FACING SURFACES TILTED UPWARD AT ANGLE L, EQUAL TO THE LOCAL LATITUDE.

Jan 21, Nov 21 Dec.=-19.9	θ_L = Incident Angle at Lat.														
	32° North Lat.					40° North Lat.					48° North Lat.				
Solar Time	Alt.	Azim	I_{DN}	I_L	θ_L	Alt.	Azim	I_{DN}	I_L	θ_L	Alt.	Azim	I_{DN}	I_L	θ_L
6 6	--	--													
7 5	1.5	65.4	2	0	75.9										
8 4	12.7	56.6	196	104	62.0	8.2	55.4	136	72	62.0	3.6	54.7	36	19	62.0
9 3	22.6	46.1	263	190	48.4	17.0	44.1	232	167	48.4	11.2	42.7	179	129	48.4
10 2	30.8	33.2	289	252	35.5	24.0	31.0	268	233	35.5	17.1	29.5	233	202	35.5
11 1	36.2	17.6	301	291	24.8	28.6	16.1	283	273	24.8	20.9	15.1	255	245	24.8
am 12 pm	38.2	0.0	304	304	20.0	30.2	0.0	288	287	20.0	22.2	0.0	261	259	20.0
Day-Long Total, Btu/Ft^2			2406	1980				2128	1778				1668	1448	

Feb 21, Oct 21 Dec.=-10.7	θ_L = Incident Angle at Lat.														
	32° North Lat.					40° North Lat.					48° North Lat.				
Solar Time	Alt.	Azim	I_{DN}	I_L	θ_L	Alt.	Azim	I_{DN}	I_L	θ_L	Alt.	Azim	I_{DN}	I_L	θ_L
6 6															
7 5	6.8	73.1	99	32	75.2	4.5	72.3	48	15	75.2	2.0	71.9	4	1	75.2
8 4	18.7	64.0	229	128	60.5	15.0	61.9	204	113	60.5	11.2	60.2	165	91	60.5
9 3	29.5	53.0	273	208	45.9	24.5	49.8	257	195	45.9	19.3	47.4	233	176	45.9
10 2	38.7	39.1	293	269	31.5	32.4	35.6	280	257	31.5	25.7	33.1	262	239	31.5
11 1	45.1	21.1	302	307	18.0	37.6	18.7	291	295	18.0	30.0	17.1	274	277	18.0
am 12 pm	47.5	0.0	304	320	10.0	39.5	0.0	294	308	10.0	31.5	0.0	278	291	10.0
Day-Long Total, But/Ft^2			2696	2208				2454	2060				2154	1860	

March 21 Sept 21 Dec. = 0.0	θ_L = Incident Angle at Lat.														
	32° North Lat.					40° North Lat.					48° North Lat.				
Solar Time	Alt.	Azim	I_{DN}	I_L	θ_L	Alt.	Azim	I_{DN}	I_L	θ_L	Alt.	Azim	I_{DN}	I_L	θ_L
6 6															
7 5	12.7	8.19	163	56	75.0	11.4	80.2	149	51	75.0	10.0	78.7	131	44	75.0
8 4	25.1	73.0	240	141	60.0	22.5	69.6	230	134	60.0	19.5	66.8	215	124	60.o
9 3	36.8	62.1	272	215	45.0	32.8	57.3	263	208	45.0	28.2	53.4	251	197	45.0
10 2	47.3	47.5	287	273	30.0	41.6	41.9	280	265	30.0	35.4	37.8	269	254	30.0
11 1	55.0	26.8	294	309	15.0	47.7	22.6	287	301	15.0	40.3	19.8	278	289	15.0
am 12 pm	58.0	0.0	296	321	0.0	50.0	0.0	290	313	0.0	4210	0.0	280	302	0.0
Day-Long Total, Btu/Ft^2			2808	2308				2708	2228				2568	2118	

April 21 Aug 21 Dec.=12.1	θ_L = Incident Angle at Lat.														
	32° North Lat.					40° North Lat.					48° North Lat.				
Solar Time	Alt.	Azim	I_{DN}	I_L	θ_L	Alt.	Azim	I_{DN}	I_L	θ_L	Alt.	Azim	I_{DN}	I_L	θ_L
6 6	6.5	100.5	59	7	90.0	7.9	99.5	81	9	90.0	9.1	98.3	99	10	90.0
7 5	19.1	92.8	190	69	75.3	19.3	90.0	191	69	75.3	19.1	87.2	190	67	75.3
8 4	31.8	84.7	240	144	60.7	30.7	79.9	237	141	60.7	29.0	75.4	232	137	60.7
9 3	44.3	75.0	263	212	46.2	41.8	67.9	260	207	46.2	38.4	61.8	254	201	46.2
10 2	56.1	61.3	276	264	32.0	51.7	52.1	272	259	32.0	46.4	45.1	266	252	32.0
11 1	66.0	38.4	282	298	18.9	59.3	29.7	278	292	18.9	52.2	24.3	272	285	18.9
am 12 pm	70.3	0.0	284	309	11.6	62.3	0.0	280	303	11.6	54.3	0.0	274	296	11.6
Day-Long Total, Btu/Ft^2			2902	2296				2916	2258				2898	2200	

May 21 July 21 Dec.=20.5	θ_L = Incident Angle at Lat.														
	32° North Lat.					40° North Lat.					48° North Lat.				
Solar Time	Alt.	Azim	I_{DN}	I_L	θ_L	Alt.	Azim	I_{DN}	I_L	θ_L	Alt.	Azim	I_{DN}	I_L	θ_L
6 6	10.7	107.7	113	14	90.0	13.1	106.1	138	17	90.0	15.2	104.1	156	18	90.0
7 5	23.1	100.6	203	75	75.9	24.3	97.2	208	75	75.9	25.1	93.5	211	75	75.9
8 4	35.7	93.6	241	143	62.0	35.8	87.8	241	142	62.0	35.1	82.1	240	140	62.0
9 3	48.4	85.5	261	205	48.4	47.2	76.7	259	203	48.4	44.8	68.8	256	199	48.4
10 2	60.9	74.3	271	254	35.5	57.9	61.7	269	251	35.5	53.5	51.9	266	246	35.5
11 1	72.4	53.3	277	285	24.8	66.7	37.9	275	281	24.8	60.1	29.0	271	276	24.8
am 12 pm	78.6	0.0	279	296	20.0	70.6	0.0	276	292	20.0	62.6	0.0	272	286	20.0
Day-Long Total, Btu/Ft^2			3012	2250				3062	2230				3158	2200	

June 21 Dec.=23.45	θ_L = Incident Angle at Lat.														
	32° North Lat.					40° North Lat.					48° North Lat.				
Solar Time	Alt.	Azim	I_{DN}	I_L	θ_L	Alt.	Azim	I_{DN}	I_L	θ_L	Alt.	Azim	I_{DN}	I_L	θ_L
6 6	12.2	110.2	131	16	90.0	14.8	108.4	155	18	90.0	17.2	106.2	172	19	90.0
7 5	24.3	103.4	210	76	76.3	26.0	99.7	216	77	76.3	27.0	95.8	220	77	76.3
8 4	36.9	96.8	245	143	62.7	37.4	90.7	246	142	62.7	37.1	84.6	246	140	62.7
9 3	49.6	89.4	264	204	49.6	48.8	80.2	263	202	49.6	46.9	71.6	261	198	49.6
10 2	62.2	79.7	274	251	37.4	59.8	65.8	272	248	37.4	55.8	54.8	269	244	37.4
11 1	74.2	60.9	279	282	27.6	69.2	41.9	277	278	27.6	62.7	31.2	274	273	27.6
am 12 pm	81.5	0.0	280	292	23.4	73.5	0.0	279	289	23.4	65.5	0.0	275	283	23.4
Day-Long Total, Btu/Ft^2			3084	2234				3180	2224				3312	2204	

Dec. 21 Dec.=-23.45	θ_L = Incident Angle at Lat.														
	32° North Lat.					40° North Lat.					48° North Lat.				
Solar Time	Alt.	Azim	I_{DN}	I_L	θ_L	Alt.	Azim	I_{DN}	I_L	θ_L	Alt.	Azim	I_{DN}	I_L	θ_L
6 6	--	--													
7 5	--	--													
8 4	10.3	53.8	176	90	62.7	5.5	53.0	89	45	62.7					
9 3	19.8	43.6	257	180	49.6	14.0	41.9	217	152	49.6	8.0	40.9	140	98	49.6
10 2	27.6	31.2	288	244	37.4	20.7	29.4	261	221	37.4	13.6	28.2	214	180	37.4
11 1	32.7	16.4	301	282	27.6	25.0	15.2	280	262	27.6	17.3	14.4	242	226	27.6
am 12 pm	34.6	0.0	304	295	23.4	26.6	0.0	285	275	23.4	18.6	0.0	250	241	23.4
Day-Long Total, Btu/Ft^2			2348	1888				1978	1634				1444	1250	

Interpolating among the tabulated values is generally quicker and quite sufficiently accurate for most solar purposes, where the other values which are going to be employed later are not precise enough to justify more than slide rule accuracy at most.

There is one more angle which is very important in solar technology and this is the angle between the direct rays of the sun and a line perpendicular (normal) to the surface which is trying to absorb or reflect the sun's rays. This is called the angle of incidence, and it is shown in Fig. II.4 as ∠QOP. It is generally symbolized by the Greek letter theta, θ, and we will use that symbol here because it is both distinctive and easily typed by combining a zero, 0, and a dash, –.

The incident angle can be calculated by using another trigonometrical equation and another angle, G, the wall-solar azimuth, which is the angle in the horizontal plane between the sun's azimuth line, OH in Fig. II.4, and the wall's azimuth, OP, which is the line (in the horizontal plane) that is perpendicular to the wall. The symbol generally used for the wall-solar azimuth is the Greek letter Gamma (γ), but we will use the letter G instead. In Fig. II.4, the wall azimuth is ∠SOP and the wall-solar azimuth G = ∠HOP.

The incident angle can be found from the equation:

$$\text{Cosine of Incident Angle} = \left[\text{Cosine of Solar Altitude} \times \text{Cosine of Wall-Solar Azimuth} \times \text{Sine of Tilt Angle}\right] + \left[\text{Sine of Solar Altitude} \times \text{Cosine of Tilt Angle}\right] \qquad \text{Eq. II.3}$$

In mathematical terms.

$$\text{Cos } \theta = \text{Cos B Cos G Sin T} + \text{Sin B Cos T} \qquad \text{Eq. II.3a}$$

The tilt angle, T, is measured from the horizontal and it can vary from 0 degrees, when the surface is actually horizontal, to 90 degrees, when the surface is vertical. In that case, a look at the basic trigonometrical triangle shows us that Sin T = 1.0 and Cos T = 0.0, so the incident angle for any vertical surface becomes simply:

$$\text{Cosine of Incident Angle for Any Vertical Surface} = \text{Cosine of Solar Altitude} \times \text{Cosine of Wall-Solar Azimuth} \qquad \text{Eq. 11.4}$$

or

$$\text{Cos } \theta_v = \text{Cos B Cos G} \qquad \text{Eq. II.4a}$$

For a horizontal surface, the tilt angle T = 0 degrees, and so Sin T = 0.0 and Cos T = 1.0. Thus for any horizontal surface such as a flat roof, Eq. II.3 tells us that:

$$\text{Cosine of Incident Angle for Any Horizontal Surface} = \text{Sine of Solar Altitude} \qquad \text{Eq. II.5}$$

or

$$\text{Cos } \theta_h = \text{Sin B} \qquad \text{Eq. II.5a}$$

By inspection of Fig. II.4, it can be seen that:

$$\text{Incident Angle for Any Horizontal Surface} = 90 \text{ degrees} - \text{B} \qquad \text{Eq. II.6}$$

If we assign some values to the angles shown in Fig. II.4, we can see how these equations actually work. Given that:

Example:

Local Latitude (L) = 40 degrees
Solar Time = 1:00 p.m.
Date = September 21

From Table II.2, we find that the solar altitude B = 47.7 degrees and the solar azimuth = 22.6 degrees west. If the wall faces south-east, its azimuth is 45 degrees east, so the wall-solar azimuth G = 22.6° + 45° = 67.6 degrees. Let the surface be a vertical wall, so the tilt angle T = 90 degrees and we can use Eq. II.4a, which becomes:

$$\text{Cos } \Theta_v = \text{Cos B Cos G}$$
$$= \text{Cos } 47.7° \text{ Cos } 67.6°$$
$$= 0.673 \times 0.381$$
$$= 0.256$$

and in this particular example, then Θ_v is the "angle whose cosine is 0.256," which turns out to be 75.14 degrees.

There are some useful short-cuts which can simplify the finding of some solar angles. At solar noon, the solar azimuth is always 0.0 degrees and the solar altitude is:

$$B_{noon} = 90 \text{ degrees} - L + D \qquad \text{Eq. 11.7}$$

To return to the Palo Alto example used earlier, at solar noon on February 21, the solar altitude is:

$$B_{noon} = 90 \text{ degrees} - 37.5° + (-10.6°) = 41.9 \text{ degrees}$$

On June 21 in Palo Alto, when the declination is $+23.5°$,

$$B_{noon} = 90 \text{ degrees} - 37.5° + 23.5° = 76 \text{ degrees}$$

Time and the Intensity of Solar Radiation

We have already learned that the intensity of the sun's rays on a surface perpendicular to those rays, located at the average earth-sun distance and outside of the Earth's atmosphere, is 429.2 Btu. April 4 and October 4 are approximately the dates when the average Earth-sun distance is attained (the exact date changes slightly from year to year). The maximum Earth-sun distance occurs on July 4, and then the surface beyond the Earth's atmosphere receives only 415.2 Btu; on January 4, we reach our closest proximity to the sun and the extra-terrestial intensity becomes 443.6 Btu. For those who want to learn more about the sun's radiation in space, App. IV, No. 18, is an excellent and authoritative source of information.

In passing through the atmosphere to reach the surface of the Earth, solar radiation undergoes a number of changes. Ultraviolet radiation which is less than 0.3 microns in wavelength is all absorbed in the upper atmosphere, primarily by the ozone which abounds there. The longwave infrared beyond about 2.6 microns is all absorbed by the water vapor in the lower atmosphere. In between, there are numerous absorption bands caused by other components of the atmosphere, including carbon dioxide.

Some of the incoming radiation is scattered in all directions by the air molecules themselves and this scattered radiation is primarily in the blue portion of the visible spectrum, thus causing the blue color which characterizes a clear sky.

The direct beam radiation is considerably reduced in intensity as it passes through the atmosphere and the amount of the reduction depends upon the length of the atmospheric path which it must traverse. Meteorologists describe this in terms of the air mass, m, which is the ratio of the actual path length OQ to the path length OZ which would exist if the sun were directly overhead. This ratio evidently depends upon the sun's altitude above the horizon, B, and a glance at Fig. 11.5, a much simplified version of the actual situation, will show that:

$$m = \frac{OQ}{OZ} = \frac{1}{\text{Sine of the Solar Altitude}} = \frac{1}{\text{Sin B}} \qquad \text{Eq. 11.8}$$

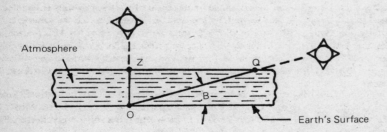

Atmosphere

FIG. 11.5 SIMPLIFIED DRAWING OF THE PATH OF THE SUN'S RAYS THROUGH THE EARTH'S ATMOSPHERE (air mass, m, OQ/OZ = 1/Sin B).

To return to the Palo Alto example, on February 21, the solar altitude at noon is 41.9 degrees and so the air mass is $1.0/\text{Sin } 41.9° = 1.0/0.67 = 1.5$. On June 21, the noon solar altitude is 76 degrees and the air mass at that time and date is $1.0/\text{Sin } 76°$ $1.0/0.97 = 1.03$.

The intensity of the direct beam depends upon the solar altitude, since that determines how much atmosphere the rays have to traverse, and it also depends upon the amount of water vapor, dust particles and man-made pollutants which the atmosphere contains. Water vapor is the primary factor which determines how much direct radiation will reach the earth's surface on a clear day and there is a very marked variation in water vapor content throughout the year.

The probable values of the direct normal radiation intensity on clear days throughout the year and their variation with solar altitude are shown in Fig. 11.6. These values (see App. IV, No. 16, for a more detailed explanation) take into account the annual variation of humidity in the United States. The term "direct normal irradiation" means the intensity of the direct radiation falling on a surface perpendicular or "normal" to the rays, and it is symbolized by I_{DN}.

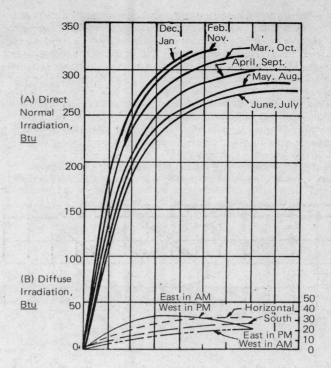

FIG. 11.6 (A) VARIATION OF DIRECT NORMAL IRRADIATION WITH SOLAR ALTITUDE THROUGHOUT THE YEAR; (B) DIFFUSE RADIATION VS. SOLAR ALTITUDE FOR VARIOUS SURFACE ORIENTATIONS.

Most of the surfaces in which we are interested are not normal to the sun's direct rays and so we must return to the angle of incidence, Θ between the incoming rays and a line that is normal to the surface, by using the following equation to find the intensity on any surface for which Θ is known:

| Direct Solar Irradiation on a Surface with an Incident Angle Θ | = | Direct Normal Irradiation | x | Cosine of Incident Angle, Θ | Eq. 11.9 |

or

$$I_{D\Theta} = I_{DN} \text{ Cos } \Theta \qquad \text{Eq. 11.9a}$$

The physical explanation of this very valuable equation (which is the reason for all of the trigonometry in which we have indulged up to this point) is shown in Fig. 11.7. Here we have a beam of direct sunshine which is exactly 1 foot square falling on a horizontal surface with an incident angle Θ which is shown by $\angle$ MOZ. Because the horizontal surface is not normal to the sunbeam, the energy contained in the 1 square foot, represented by the letters MN, is spread over a larger area represented by the letters ON and so the intensity, or the amount of energy per square foot of area is:

$$I_{D\Theta} = I_{DN} \times \frac{MN}{ON} = I_{DN} \text{ Cos } \Theta \qquad \text{Eq. 11.9b}$$

The laws of geometry tell us that $\angle$ MNO is equal to the incident angle $\angle$ MOZ, and the ratio of the two sides of the triangle, MN/ON, is the cosine of $\angle$ MNO, which is also the cosine of the incident angle Θ.

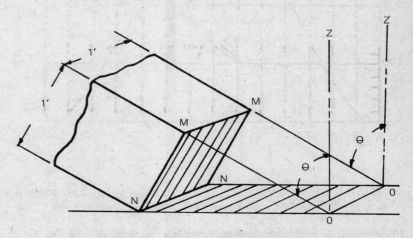

FIG. 11.7 EXPLANATION OF THE COSINE LAW ($I_{D\Theta} = I_{DN} \times \text{Cos } \Theta$).

Most of the surfaces in which we are interested in our study of solar technology will be tilted with respect to the horizontal, but we have learned, thanks to Eq. 11.3, how to find θ for any surface. Because of the sun's apparent daily motion across the sky, shown in Fig. II.3, the incident angle is constantly changing. If we restrict our attention to surfaces which face the south, the incident angle for any particular surface with a fixed tilt will depend only on the time of day and the date, since they determine the sun's altitude and azimuth. Using a surface at 40 degrees north latitude, tilted at 40 degrees upward from the horizontal with July 21 as the date, we find that incident angle varies from approximately 90 degrees at 6:00 a.m. (we will use the 24 hour clock and call that 0600 hours) to a minimum of 20 degrees at noon (1200 hours) and back to 90 degrees again at 1800 hours.

Fig. II.8 shows the hourly variation of θ and it is immediately seen that, for a south-facing surface, the incident angle is symmetrical about solar noon. This means that θ will be the same for a given number of hours away from solar noon in the afternoon as it is for the same hour angle in the morning. The only difference will be that the sun's rays will come from the east in the morning and from the west in the afternoon.

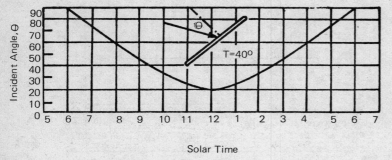

FIG. II.8 HOURLY VARIATION OF INCIDENT ANGLE ON SOUTH-FACING SURFACE (July 21, 40° N latitude, receiving surface tilted upward from horizontal 40°).

Thus far, we have considered only the sun's direct radiation and we appear to have forgotten about the radiation which, in an earlier paragraph, was scattered by the air molecules and the atmospheric dust. Part of this radiation, which is called "diffuse" since it comes from all parts of the sky, reaches the earth's surface and so the total irradiation or "insolation," $I_{t\theta}$, is the sum of this diffuse radiation, which we symbolized by I_d, and the direct radiation, $I_{D\theta}$. In equation form we would say that:

$$\begin{array}{llll}
\text{Total} & \left[\begin{array}{ll} \text{Direct} & \text{Cosine of} \\ \text{Normal Solar} \times & \text{Incident} \\ \text{Irradiation} & \text{Angle, } \theta \end{array} \right. & \begin{array}{l} \text{Diffuse} \\ + \quad \text{Solar} \\ \text{Irradiation} \end{array} & \text{Eq. II.10}
\end{array}$$

Total Solar Irradiation

or

$$I_{t\theta} = I_{DN} \cos\theta + I_d \qquad \text{Eq. II.10a}$$

There is no easy way to estimate the intensity of diffuse radiation, since it too depends upon the amount of dust, moisture and the degree of cloudiness of the sky. On a completely cloudy day, the only radiation that we receive is the diffuse component, while on a clear day it depends upon just how clear the sky really is and how much invisible water vapor it contains. The lower curves in Fig. II.6 give typical values of diffuse radiation for various surfaces in terms of the solar altitude.

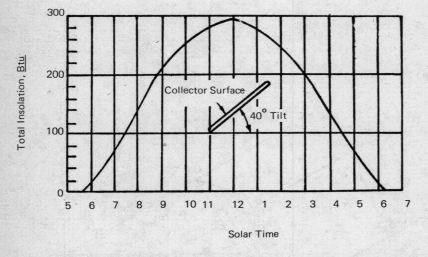

FIG. II.9 HOURLY VARIATION OF TOTAL INSOLATION ON SOUTH-FACING SURFACE (July 21, 40° N latitude; receiving surface tilted upward from horizontal 40°).

The University of Florida has developed a computer program (App. IV, No. 19) by which the total insolation can be computed from ASHRAE data for surfaces with any orientation and any degree of tilt from the horizontal. Table II.2 gives selected values of the solar data which are to be found in App. IV, No. 16 and No. 17. Space does not permit the use of all of the available data and so only a single surface is considered in Table II.2, facing south and tilted at the angle of the local latitude.

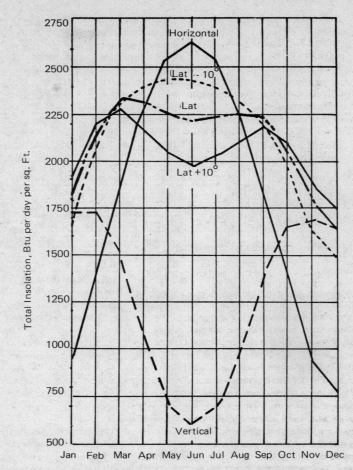

FIG. II.10 VARIATION OF DAY-LONG TOTAL INSOLATION THROUGHOUT THE YEAR FOR SOUTH-FACING SURFACES WITH VARYING TILT ANGLES (on the 21st day of each month).

An extension of the University of Florida program, produced by Miss Ceresse Nada of Alhambra High School, Phoenix, gave insolation data for surfaces facing in directions other than due south. For 40 degrees North latitude, the loss in day-long insolation on January 21 is 1% for a 10 degree deviation, 4% for 20 degrees and 8% for 30 degrees. Thus exact adherence to the general rule about facing due south is not essential for good performance of a solar device. Fig. II.9 shows the hourly variation in total insolation on July 21, for a south-facing surface tilted upward at 40 degrees from the horizontal, at 40 degrees North latitude.

The angle of tilt is very important in the performance of solar collectors, as Fig. II.10 shows. A horizontal surface receives more irradiation in mid-summer and less in mid-winter than any of the other surfaces shown in Fig. II.10. A vertical surface receives a significant amount of irradiation during the winter months when the solar altitude is low, but it receives very little during the summer months when the sun is high in the sky. A surface tilted at the angle of the local latitude (L) will do a good job all year long, but its performance will be exceeded during the summer by a surface tilted at L - 10°, and in winter by one which is tilted at L + 10°. In general, the complexity involved in making a collector adjustable in its tilt angle is not compensated by improved performance. It is preferable to select a suitable angle, based on the function which the collector is intended to serve, and let it remain fixed in place.

Thus far, no reference has been made to radiation which may be reflected from surfaces which are on the south of the collector surface, but this can be significant in the winter when the ground is covered with snow which is a very good reflector. For details on this subject, see App. IV, No. 17, p. 59.9.

Conclusion

The rather tedious mathematical approach contained in the foregoing pages will give to the serious student of solar technology the information which one needs to make quantitative estimates of how big solar devices must be in order to achieve a desired result. The highest intensity attained by the sun's direct rays at sea level does not exceed 304 Btu at 32 degrees North latitude, which means that the atmosphere has filtered out some 30% of the solar radiation even on a clear day. In mid-summer, the highest observed intensity at sea level will be about 280 Btu, indicating that the summer atmosphere absorbs even more of the incoming radiation because of its higher humidity.

We have spoken of clear days and sea-level conditions, and we will find higher intensities at higher elevations and in regions where the humidity is exceptionally low, as it is in the arid southwest. To correct for these situations, App. IV, No. 16, gives a map with "Clearness Numbers," which show that the values given in Table II.2 and Fig. II.10 will be exceeded by as much as 10% in the Rocky Mountain states, while the Gulf Coast and most of Florida will have lower values than the so-called standard, by as much as 10 to 15%.

Clouds present a major problem to the solar technologist, because it is difficult to predict when they will appear and how long they will persist. The local Weather

Bureau (now operated by the National Oceanic and Atmospheric Administration) has long records of the hours of sunshine, or at least the percentage of possible sunshine, on a month by month basis for all major cities. Maps are available in App. IV, No. 20, which show monthly variation of insolation on horizontal surfaces, percent of possible sunshine, number of hours of sunshine per year, and other information which can be used to estimate how much solar radiation can be expected to be available at any given place in an average year.

APPENDIX III

METHODS OF ESTIMATING SOLAR HEATER PERFORMANCE

The technical aspects of collector design and performance estimates are discussed in detail in the publication listed in App. IV, No. 21. The fundamental principles will be treated briefly and simply in the following section.

The first decision which must be made is the angle of tilt of the collector panels. In App. II we have learned that in the northern hemisphere the collectors should face the south while "down under" they should face towards the north. A few degrees deviation from a true south exposure will do very little harm to the collector's performance.

The collector plate can only make use of the heat which actually reaches it, so the ability of the glazing material to transmit the sun's radiation is very important. This property is called transmittance and it depends upon the thickness of the glazing, its composition, and to a major extent upon the angle of incidence θ between the sun's rays and a line normal to the surface (Fig. III.1).

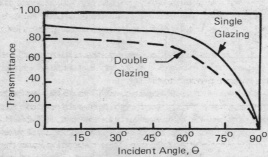

FIG. III.1   TRANSMITTANCE VS. θ FOR CLEAR GLASS.

The equations for finding θ are given in App. II and this angle is very important in determining the intensity of the direct solar radiation falling on a surface tilted away from normal incidence. Table II.2 (App. II) gives data for both the total insolation $I_{t\theta}$, in Btu, and the incident angle θ, for south-facing surfaces tilted upward at the angle of the local latitude, for the 21st day of each month at 40 degrees North latitude. App. IV, No. 17 and No. 19, give similar information for other latitudes. Both $I_{t\theta}$ and θ change minute by minute throughout the day, and so does the collector performance!

The objective of the collector is to heat a fluid and so the following equation is used to see how well the collector is doing its job:

$$\text{Efficiency of Collector, Percent (\%)} = 100 \times \left[\frac{\text{Rate of Fluid Flow} \times \text{Specific Heat of Fluid} \times \text{Fluid Temp. Rise}}{\text{Total Insolation with Incident Angle } \theta, I_{t\theta}} \right] \quad \text{Eq. III.1}$$

The units of measurement are:

$$\% \text{ Efficiency} = 100 \times \left[\frac{\frac{\text{lb.}}{\text{hr.ft.}^2} \times \frac{\text{Btu}}{\text{lb.} ^{\circ}\text{F}} \times {}^{\circ}\text{F}}{\frac{\text{Btu}}{\text{hr.ft.}^2}} \right] \quad \text{Eq. III.1a}$$

The rate of fluid flow is measured in pounds per hour, the specific heat is a quantity of heat in Btu needed to warm a pound of that fluid 1 degree F, and the temperature rise is given in degrees F.

The collector efficiency can also be expressed in terms of what happens to the incoming solar radiation, since we can also say that:

$$\text{Total Incident Solar Radiation} = \text{Heat Carried Away by the Fluid} + \text{Heat Lost from Collector's Surfaces} \quad \text{Eq. III.2}$$

The units of measurement are:

$$\text{Btu} = \text{Btu} + \text{Btu} \quad \text{Eq. III.2a}$$

The collector has six surfaces, but its insulation can easily be made so effective that very little heat is wasted through the back or sides. It is the sun-facing glazed or bare surface which is the hottest and largest in area and so it is responsible for most of the lost heat.

Heat always flows from high temperature to low temperature and the rate of heat flow is equal to the product of the area involved, the difference of temperature between the collector surface and the surrounding (ambient) air, and a factor which the engineer calls the "heat loss coefficient," symbolized by the letter U. The heat loss

coefficient U depends upon (a) the number of cover glasses employed, which may range from zero for a bare collector to three when very high temperatures are needed, (b) the nature of the collector surface and its ability to emit longwave radiation, and (c) the amount of the temperature difference which is causing the heat to flow. App. IV, No. 21, deals with these matters in great detail and Fig. III.2 is adapted from Dr. Austin Whillier's chapter in that reference (p. 32) which gives a great mass of engineering data, most of which is beyond the scope of this chapter. The units for U are $\underline{\text{Btu}}$ (Btu per square foot per hour) per degree F, or $\underline{\text{Btu}}/{}^{\circ}\text{F}$.

The general equation for the collector's performance is:

$$\text{Heat Carried Away by the Fluid} = \left[\text{Radiation Transmitted by Glazing} \times \text{Absorptance of Collector Surface} \right] - \left[\text{Heat Loss Coeff., U} \times (t_s - t_o) \right] \quad \text{Eq. III.3}$$

The units of measurement are:

$$\text{Btu} = \left[\text{Btu} \times \frac{\text{Btu (absorbed)}}{\text{Btu (incident)}} \right] - \left[\frac{\text{Btu}}{{}^{\circ}\text{F}} \times {}^{\circ}\text{F} \right] \quad \text{Eq. III.3a}$$

t_s and t_o are the symbols used here to designate the average temperature of the collector (t_s) and the ambient air temperature (t_o).

Fig. III.2 shows how the heat loss coefficient varies with the number of glass cover plates and with the difference in temperature between the collector plate and the ambient air, starting with an average plate temperature of 100°F and going on up to 240°F, which is just about as hot as a flat plate collector is likely to get. The chart is based on the use of a non-selective black coating on the collector plate, with an emittance (App. I) of 0.95. Page 34 of App. IV, No. 21, gives the remaining assumptions, all of them quite reasonable, upon which Fig. III.2 is based.

The ability of glass or other transparent materials to transmit solar radiation depends upon the thickness and quality of the glass and upon the angle of incidence between the glass and the sun's rays. Table 1 gives values of the transmittance for one, two and three cover glasses for incident angles from zero to 90 degrees. The absorptance for flat black paint is also given for the same incident angles and finally the first two terms of Eq. III.3 are multiplied together to give the decimal fraction of the incoming radiation which reaches and is absorbed by the collector plate.

Incident Angle, θ	0°	10°	20°	30°	40°	50°	60°	70°	80°	90°
n = 1	0.87	0.87	0.87	0.87	0.86	0.84	0.79	0.68	0.42	0.0
n = 2	0.77	0.77	0.77	0.76	0.75	0.73	0.67	0.53	0.25	0.0
n = 3	0.67	0.67	0.67	0.66	0.65	0.61	0.53	0.36	0.11	0.0

TABLE III.1a   VARIATION WITH INCIDENT ANGLE θ OF TRANSMITTANCE FOR SOLAR RADIATION OF n = 1, 2, AND 3 DOUBLE STRENGTH GLASS COVER PLATES

Absorptance	0.96	0.96	0.96	0.95	0.94	0.92	0.88	0.82	0.67	0.0

TABLE III.1b   VARIATION WITH θ OF ABSORPTANCE FOR FLAT BLACK PAINT

n = 1	0.84	0.84	0.84	0.83	0.81	0.77	0.70	0.56	0.28	0.0
n = 2	0.74	0.74	0.74	0.72	0.71	0.67	0.59	0.43	0.17	0.0
n = 3	0.64	0.64	0.64	0.63	0.60	0.55	0.47	0.30	0.07	0.0

TABLE III.1c   PRODUCTS OF TRANSMITTANCE x ABSORPTANCE FOR n = 1, 2 AND 3 DOUBLE STRENGTH GLASS COVER PLATES

We are often interested in knowing what the efficiency of collection is likely to be under a given set of circumstances and Eq. III.1 gave one way to find this. However, we are more likely to know the quantities given in Eq. III.3 and this can be revised to give another way of estimating the efficiency of collection:

$$\text{Efficiency of Collector, Percent (\%)} = 100 \left[\left[\text{Transmittance x Absorptance} \right] - \frac{\text{Heat Loss Coeff., U} \times (t_s - t_o)}{\text{Total Insolation, } I_{t\theta}} \right] \quad \text{Eq. III.4}$$

The units of measurement are:

$$\% \text{ Efficiency} = 100 \left[\left[\frac{\text{Btu (transmitted)}}{\text{Btu (incident)}} \times \frac{\text{Btu (absorbed)}}{\text{Btu (incident)}} \right] - \frac{\frac{\text{Btu}}{{}^{\circ}\text{F}} \times {}^{\circ}\text{F}}{\text{Btu}} \right] \quad \text{Eq. III.4a}$$

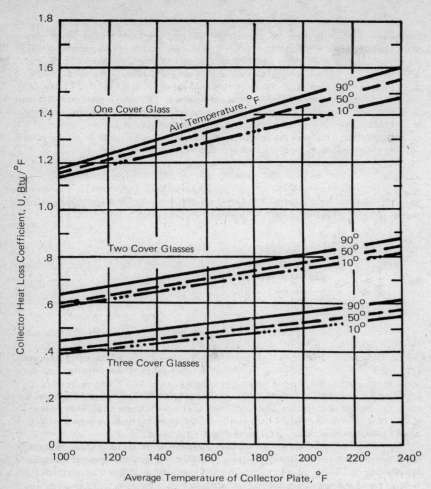

FIG. III.2 VARIATION OF HEAT LOSS COEFFICIENT, U.
WITH COLLECTOR PLATE TEMPERATURE
(non-selective surface).

The general nature of the variation of collection efficiency with temperature rise of the collector plate above the ambient air temperature is shown in Fig. III.3 for a single glazed collector with flat black paint and a collector with a selective surface. At very low temperature differences, the flat black collector will do a slightly better job because its absorptance (0.96) will generally be a few percent higher than the absorptance for the selective surface. As the temperature rises, the heat loss for the collector plate also rises in accordance with Eq. III.3 and the lower longwave emittance of the selective surface soon begins to show its superiority.

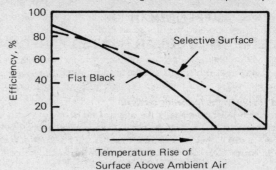

FIG. III.3 TYPICAL SOLAR COLLECTOR PERFORMANCE.

Increasing the number of cover plates from zero to 1 makes a dramatic improvement in collector performance by cutting the heat loss coefficient by a factor of two, and the addition of a second cover glass gives an additional improvement at the higher levels of surface-to-air temperature difference. At the lower temperature differentials, the single glass is better because, as Table III.1c shows, the product of the transmittance times the absorptance falls off sharply as the number of cover glasses increases.

As the time from solar noon increases, there is always a decrease in the insolation of a south-facing collector and an increase in the incident angle which cause the transmittance times absorptance product to fall off.

Generally, the sun must rise to an elevation of 10 to 15 degrees in the sky before its rays are strong enough and the incident angle is favorable enough to permit effective heating. In mid-summer, the sun rises north of east and, as Table II.2 shows, the direct rays of the sun will not reach a south-facing collector until nearly 9:00 a.m. and they will move away again after 3:00 p.m. Thus, depending upon the slope of the collector, there will generally be between 6 and 8 hours of collectable sunshine per day.

EXAMPLE:

To see how this equation works, let us assume that we have a south-facing collector, tilted upward at 90 degrees from the horizontal, at 40 degrees north latitude at 2:00 p.m. solar time, on January 21, at a place where the outdoor temperature is $50°F$. We would like to have the collector run at $110°F$ to provide domestic hot water; Fig. III.2 tells us that the heat loss coefficient, U, will be 1.18 $\underline{Btu}/°F$ for one cover plate, 0.62 for two and 0.41 for three cover plates.

We must next find the total insolation and the incident angle for this condition and Table II.2 tells us that I_{t0} is 237 $\underline{Btu}$ while θ = 35.9 degrees (by calculation, using Eq. II.3a). From Table III.1c, we find the following values for the product of the transmittance and the absorptance at 40 degrees incident angle: 0.81 for n = 1; 0.71 for n = 2; 0.60 for n = 3.

By substituting these values into Eq. III.4 we can easily find the probable value of the efficiency of this collector on a clear winter day, with a 60 degree F temperature difference between the collector plate and the ambient air. For n = 1 (one cover glass) the efficiency is 51%; if we add a second cover glass, the efficiency rises to 55.3% but if we add a third glass, the efficiency drops to 49.6% because the reduction in transmittance more than offsets the reduction in the heat loss coefficient.

For south-facing collectors, tilted at the angle of the local latitude, the collection efficiency is generally highest in the early afternoon, when the incident angle is still below 40 degrees and the outdoor air is at its maximum temperature, thus reducing the heat loss as far as possible with the specified number of cover glasses.

We can easily find the maximum temperature which a particular collector will attain when no heat is being withdrawn from it in the form of hot water or air. In this case the efficiency will be zero and the collector will attain what is called its "equilibrium temperature." For the case just considered, with two cover glasses, the equilibrium temperature is found to be approximately $250°F$.

If we are trying to heat the fluid to an average temperature of $150°F$, the efficiency with two cover glasses will drop to 42%, but if we are content to heat the fluid (let's assume that it is water) to $75°F$, the efficiency would be 69% with one cover glass and 66% with two glasses.

There is one other case which should be considered and that is the minimum rate of insolation which must be attained before the collector can begin to operate. This can also be found from Eq. III.4 by letting the efficiency again become zero and finding the insolation rate. Assuming again that we are dealing with a double-glazed collector, with a relatively low incident angle so that the product of the transmittance times the absorptance remains near 0.71 and the plate-to-air temperature difference is still $50°F$, the minimum insolation which will cause the surface temperature to rise to $110°F$ will be approximately 43 $\underline{Btu}$ which, on a clear January morning, would occur before 8:00 a.m. solar time.

At 8:00 a.m., the air temperature is more likely to be $35°F$ than $50°F$ so the surface-to-air temperature difference would be $75°F$, the heat loss coefficient would be 0.60 and the necessary insolation would be 64 $\underline{Btu}$ which would be reached just before 8:00 a.m.

APPENDIX IV

RESOURCES

No. 1 Virtually every aspect of the subject "Energy" is discussed at great length in the April 19, 1974 issue of Science, published by the American Association for the Advancement of Science, Vol. 184, No. 4134. Photosynthesis is discussed in detail by Dr. Melvin Calvin, University of California, Berkeley, in his article "Solar Energy by Photosynthesis," pp. 375-381 of that publication. Scientific American has had excellent articles on energy in a number of recent issues. In September, 1970, Vol. 223, No. 3, G. M. Woodwell discusses photosynthesis very effectively in "The Energy Cycle of the Biosphere," pp. 64-97. In the September, 1969 issue, Vol. 221, No. 3, John D. Issacs discusses "The Nature of Oceanic Life," pp. 146-165, and he shows that much of the photosynthetic activity on our globe takes place in the oceans. In September, 1971, Vol. 224, No. 3, the entire issue was devoted to a superb survey of the energy situation.

No. 2 Solar still construction can be done in many ways. A good set of directions for making a simple solar still is to be found in Simple Solar Still for the Production of Distilled Water, Technical Report No. T 17, Revised, September, 1967 by T. A. Lawand. This booklet is available for $1.00 plus $0.25 check or mail order handling fee from Brace Research Institute, MacDonald College of McGill University, Ste. Anne de Bellevue, Quebec, Canada H9X 3M1.

No. 3 Distillation of salt or brackish water by stills is discussed in detail by E. D. Howe in Chapter 12, pp. 301-307, of Introduction to the Utilization of Solar Energy, edited by A. M. Zarem and D. D. Erway (McGraw-Hill: 1963) and now available from Xerox University Microfilms. [See Index for page number of this book's review. Ed.] Page 312, references 12-26, covers the subject of solar distillation from the time of Harding and Las Salinas (1872) to the reports issued by the Office of Saline Waters, U.S. Department of the Interior, and the CSIRO, Australia, in the mid-1950's. For later work, the serious student should consult sources such as the Proceedings of the Conference on New Sources of Energy (United Nations: 1964, and recently reissued), held at Rome in 1961, and the publication Solar Energy, issued quarterly by the International Solar Energy Society.

No. 4 Brace Research Institute, Canada, has published How to Make a Solar Cabinet Dryer for Agricultural Produce, Do-It-Yourself Leaflet L-6, Revised, March, 1973 ($1.00), which gives construction details for a simple cabinet-type solar dryer. See Resource No. 2 for ordering information. Much more extensive work on drying, using separate air heaters, has been carried out by the CSIRO in Australia.

No. 5 Selective surfaces possess the property of absorbing a large portion of the shortwave solar radiation which strikes them, while re-radiating only a small fraction of the longwave radiation which a black surface would emit at the temperature attained by the surface. This concept was pioneered by Israeli scientist

Harry Tabor, and his first paper on this subject appeared in the Transactions of the Conference on Scientific Uses of Solar Energy (University of Arizona Press: 1958), held at Tucson in 1955, Vol. 2, Part 1-A, pp. 23-40. In the same publication, J. T. Gier and R. V. Dunkle published their findings on the same subject, pp. 41-56.

Many other papers on the subject have appeared since that time, including specific instructions for preparing selective surfaces on copper sheet, given by Dr. Farrington Daniels in his book Direct Use of the Sun's Energy (Yale University Press: 1964), which was recently reissued by Ballantine Books (No. 23794, $1.95). Since that time, many papers have appeared in Solar Energy Journal, dealing with various aspects of selective surfaces in temperature control for space craft.

No. 6   Thermosyphon water heaters are the most widely used solar devices in the world. They vary in complexity; the very simple zig-zag type is described in detail by D. S. Halacy, Jr., in Chapter 6 of Solar Science Projects (formerly Fun with the Sun) available for $0.75 from Scholastic Book Services, 900 Sylvan Avenue, Englewood Cliffs, NJ 07632.

Brace Research Institute, Canada, has published How to Build a Solar Water Heater, Do-It-Yourself Leaflet No. L-4, Revised, February, 1973 ($1.00), which gives detailed instructions for the building of a corrugated plate absorber and making it into a thermosyphon system. Alternative methods of construction are given, including directions for making a grid-type collector in which a flat metal sheet is wired to the pipes to establish the thermal contact. The use of thermal cement would improve the performance of such a unit. See Resource No. 2 for ordering information.

A detailed study of the performance of thermosyphon heaters with selective surfaces is given in "An Investigation of Solar Water Heater Performance," by J. I. Yellott and Rainer Sobotka. The paper was presented at the Summer Annual Meeting of ASHRAE in 1964, and it is to be found in ASHRAE Transactions, Vol. 70, 1964, p. 425.

No. 7   Flow distribution in solar absorber banks has been studied carefully in Australia, and Paper No. 4/35, presented at the 1970 International Solar Energy Conference by R. V. Dunkle and E. T. Davey of the CSIRO, covers it in considerable detail. Large batteries of solar collectors have not yet been installed in the United States, but experience in this field will soon be gained, and anyone who is planning to make use of more than a few collectors should certainly obtain and study this paper.

No. 8   Dr. Harry Thomason's solar-heated buildings near Washington, D.C. have been described in many papers, including "Three Solar Homes," ASME paper 65 WA/SOL-3, and in Solar Energy Journal, Vol. IV, No. 4, October, 1960. A booklet describing his system, entitled Solar House Plans, is available from Edmund Scientific Co., 701 Edscorp Building, Barrington, NJ 08007 (Catalog No. 9440, $10.00), and a license to build under the Thomason patents (of which there are many) may also be obtained through Edmund (Catalog No. 9441, $20.00).

No. 9   The first office building in the U.S. to be equipped with a solar-assisted heat pump was built in 1956 by Messrs. Bridgers and Paxton, a consulting engineering firm in Albuquerque, NM. Their 4300 square foot building used a large expanse of south-facing wall to support 790 square feet of single-glazed copper-and-aluminum collectors, with a 6,000 gallon storage tank and an electric-powered heat pump. This building is about to be re-activated with new and improved collectors as part of the National Science Foundation's solar energy application program. It is described in detail in Heating, Piping and Air Conditioning for November, 1957, Vol. 27, p. 165 and in the ASHRAE Transactions for 1957, also.

No. 10   The University of Florida, under the leadership of Dr. Erich Farber, has been a leader in solar energy research for the past twenty years. A good reference to their work is "Solar Energy Conversion and Utilization" by E. A. Farber, Building Systems Design, June, 1972, or "Solar Energy, Its Conversion and Utilization," by E. A. Farber, Solar Energy Journal, Vol. 14, No. 3, February, 1973, pp. 243-252. The Solar Energy Laboratory, University of Florida, Gainesville, Florida 32601, can supply reprints of many of their papers, including their outstanding work on solar refrigeration. Write for a list of their publications and current prices.

No. 11   The Bliss curves are described in Solar Energy Journal, Vol. 5, No. 3, 1961, p. 103.

No. 12   Edmund Scientific Co., 701 Edscorp Building, Barrington, NJ 08007, is an excellent source of solar energy devices, and they will gladly send their latest catalog if you simply ask to be put on their mailing list.

No. 13   Silicon solar cells have been used in very large numbers in the space program. Many surplus cells have found their way to the "space surplus" market, and they are available in many forms, from single cells to complete modules. Convenient sources are Herbach and Rademan, Inc. 401 East Erie Avenue, Philadelphia, PA 19134, Edmund Scientific Co. (Resource No. 12), and electronic and radio shops. Silicon cell radiometers called "Sol-A-Meters," calibrated and ready for use, may be obtained from Matrix, Inc., 537 South 31st Street, Mesa, AZ 85204 ($195.00 and up).

No. 14   (a) The best reference on the subject of dials and dialing is Sundials by R. N. and M. L. Mayall (Charles T. Branford, Boston: 1958), now out of print. This 200 page volume tells how to construct dozens of different kinds of sundials, gives values of the solar declination and the Equation of Time for every day in the year, and it is an invaluable aid to anyone who wants to build a sundial. The Encyclopaedia Brittanica also has a good article on this subject.

(b) To calculate the angle between the 12 o'clock line, which always runs exactly true north, and the hour lines, we must make our last excursion into trigonometry and use the following equation:

$$\text{Tangent of Angle X} = \frac{\text{Sine of Local Latitude}}{} \times \frac{\text{Tangent of Hour Angle}}{} \qquad \text{Eq. IV.1}$$

X is the angle between the north-south line and the hour lines; the hour angle is simply the number of hours from solar noon which applied to each of the time lines, divided by 15 degrees per hour (just as we endeavored to explain in App. II). The local latitude (L) must be known exactly and a local surveyor or a good map will give you that information; the sine needs to be found only once.

For the great sundial at Carefree, Arizona, which has a gnomon which is 42 feet long and 4 feet wide (it also carries a solar water heater on its surface), the local latitude is 33 degrees 50 minutes, so the Sine is 0.5567. The angles for the hour lines, measuring southward towards the west for the morning hours and towards the east for the afternoon hours, were calculated as follows:

Time	H, Hour Angle	Tangent of Hour Angle	Tan H x Sin L	X = Angle whose Tangent = Tan H x Sin L
12	0	0.0	0.0	0
11, 1	15	0.2679	0.1492	8.489 = 8 deg. 29 min.
10, 2	30	0.5774	0.3214	17.818 = 17 deg. 49 min.
9, 3	45	1.0000	0.5567	29.105 = 29 deg. 06 min.
8, 4	60	1.7321	0.9642	43.957 = 43 deg. 57 min.
7, 5	75	3.7321	2.0776	64.298 = 64 deg. 18 min.
6, 6	90	Infinite	Infinite	90.000 = 90 deg. 00 min.

No. 15   The most definitive work on this subject is NASA Report SP-8005, Solar Electromagnetic Radiation, May, 1971 Edition, by M. P. Thekaekara. This report is available for $3.00 from National Technical Information Service, U.S. Dept. of Commerce, P.O. Box 2553, Springfield, Virginia 22151. The earlier works of Dr. Charles G. Abbot, published by the Smithsonian Institution, are valuable in relating historical steps towards today's accurate evaluation of the solar constant. Also see Resource No. 18.

No. 16   Solar altitude and azimuth are given in the ASHRAE Handbook of Fundamentals, 1972 Edition, Chapter 22, and in

No. 17   ASHRAE Handbook of Utilization, 1974 Edition, Chapter 59, pp. 59.2 - 59.7. These publications give altitude and azimuth for latitudes from 24 degrees to 64 degrees north, by 8 degree intervals. Values by increments of 1 degree are given in Bulletin No. 214, Volumes 2 and 3, Tables of Computed Altitude and Azimuth, U.S. Government Printing Office, Washington, D.C. 20402. Note that these are intended for navigation purposes, and the azimuth is measured from the north, with noon values being 180°, instead of from the south, with noon values being 0 degrees.

No. 18   Solar radiation in space is well covered by a number of publications written by M. P. Thekaekara. Among these are Solar Electromagnetic Radiation (see Resource No. 15), and Solar Energy Monitor in Space (SEMIS), available free from Dr. M. P. Thekaekara, Code 322, NASA Goddard Space Flight Center, Greenbelt, MD 20771. Similar material by Dr. Thekaekara is to be found in "Solar Energy Outside the Earth's Atmosphere," Solar Energy Journal, Vol. 14, No. 2, January 1973, pp. 109-127. Also see "Evaluating the Light from the Sun," Optical Spectra, March, 1972, pp. 32-35, and "Proposed Standard Values of the Solar Constant and the Solar Spectrum," Journal of Engineering Science, Vol. 4, September-October, 1970, p. 609. For possible variations in the solar constant, see the work of Dr. Abbot and also "Extraterrestrial Solar Energy and Its Variations," by Dr. Thekaekara, in Solar Energy Monitor in Space (SEMIS).

No. 19   Solar irradiation of south-facing surfaces on earth is covered by the work of various ASHRAE committees, for which Resources No. 16 and No. 17 are helpful. The most comprehensive publication is ASHRAE Paper No. 825, "Development and Use of Insolation Data for South-Facing Surfaces in Northern Latitudes," by C.A. Morrison and E.A. Farber of the University of Florida, Gainesville.

No. 20   For actual solar intensities, sunshine hours and percentage of possible sunshine, see Climatic Atlas of the United States, 1968 Edition, U.S. Government Printing Office, Washington, D.C. 20402 ($4.25).

No. 21   Low Temperature Engineering Application of Solar Energy is a 78 page monograph with a somewhat misleading title, since the words "low temperature" were intended to distinguish between the moderate temperatures used in space heating and water heating, and the very high temperatures attained in solar furnaces. Produced by the Technical Committee on Solar Energy Utilization under the editorship of Richard C. Jordan, this volume was published in 1966 by ASHRAE. It was re-issued in 1974, and a new version is now in preparation. This is a highly technical but extremely valuable summary of heliothermal technology as it was in 1966.

Dr. Tabor's chapter on selective surfaces gives specific directions for producing such surfaces on aluminum, galvanized steel, and copper. Dr. Austin Whillier has an extremely valuable chapter on the factors which influence collector performance. Other chapters cover such topics as "Availability of Solar Energy for Flat Plate Collectors," "Measurement of Solar Radiation," "Use of Flat Plate Collectors in Tropical Regions," and "Solar Water Heaters." This booklet is highly recommended to anyone who wants to make a serious study of heliotechnology. It is available from ASHRAE Sales Department, 345 47th Street, New York, NY 10017 for $9.00.

QUANTITATIVE DATA ON SOLAR ENERGY

Matthew P. Thekaekara
Goddard Space Flight Center,
Greenbelt, Maryland 20771

Introduction

Current awareness of the energy crisis has generated a large volume of effort towards the direct conversion of solar energy for practical applications. Quantitative data on available solar irradiance is an essential input parameter for design of collector systems and for computing their efficiency. The spectral distribution of this energy is also important since all collecting devices in general and solar cells in particular are spectrally sensitive, and computation of total solar irradiance at ground level requires integration over all wavelengths of the spectral irradiance curve. Precise measurement of total and spectral irradiance at ground level, at each location all year round, is extremely laborious. This paper will attempt a brief survey of quantitative data on solar energy which is currently available and show how such data can be adapted for use in specific situations.

Extraterrestrial Solar Energy

Two quantities of prime importance in this regard are the solar constant and the extraterrestrial solar spectrum. The solar constant is the amount of energy incident on unit area exposed normally to the sun's rays at the average sun-Earth distance, in the absence of the Earth's atmosphere. The extraterrestrial solar spectrum is the distribution of this energy as a function of wavelength. The currently accepted values of the solar constant and solar spectrum are those published by the American Society of Testing and Materials as the ASTM Standard E 490-73a (Ref. 1). They also form the Design Criteria for NASA space vehicles (Ref. 2).

The value of the solar constant is 1353 W/m² (in the preferred SI units). Expressed in other units which are perhaps more familiar in engineering applications, the value is 1.940 cal/cm²/min, or 429.2 Btu/ft²/hr, or 125.7 W/ft², or 1.81 horsepower/m². The estimated error of this value is ± 1.5 percent. The extraterrestrial solar spectrum can be presented either as a table of values at discrete wavelengths or as a spectral curve as shown in Fig. 1 (identified as Air Mass Zero Solar Spectrum). These values are based on measurements made by different observers, mainly from high altitude jet aircraft. References 3 and 4 should be consulted for detailed information on the derivation of the ASTM standard.

The solar constant is defined for the average sun-Earth distance. As the Earth moves in its annual elliptical orbit around the sun the total solar energy received varies by ± 3.5 percent. There are also small and undetermined variations due to cyclic or sporadic changes in the sun itself. These variations are more significant in certain portions of the spectrum than in others.

Solar Irradiance at Ground Level

Solar energy conversion systems are mostly on the ground. The variability of the energy incident on a ground-based collector is considerably greater than that of the extraterrestrial energy. On days of clear sunshine the energy varies between zero before sunrise and after sunset to a maximum at solar noon. At any moment clouds may intercept the sun and decrease the energy to a low value, that of the diffuse sky radiation. There is also the variation with the seasons of the year; the amount of direct solar energy received on a horizontal surface is least during winter and greatest during summer.

The solar energy received on a surface has two components, that received directly from the sun and that diffused by the sky. A spectral curve of the direct solar radiation is shown in Fig. 1. It is labelled Air Mass One Solar Spectrum. The spectral irradiance values for this curve were computed from those of the extraterrestrial spectrum by taking into account the energy scattered or absorbed by the atmosphere. It is assumed that the sun is at the zenith (air mass is one); the surface is normal to the sun's rays; the atmosphere is one of high clarity; the total amount of ozone is 0.34 cm; and the amount of precipitable water vapor is 2 cm. The total direct solar energy transmitted by the atmosphere in this case is 956.2 W/m² or 70.7 percent of that received above the atmosphere. As solar zenith angle (the angle between the sun's rays and the local vertical) increases, the trans-

mitted energy decreases. Table I gives data on total irradiance at ground level on a surface exposed normally to the sun's rays, for four values of solar zenith angle, and for four levels of atmospheric pollution or turbidity. The effect of pollution is expressed by two parameters α and β of the equation

$$(1) \qquad E_\lambda = E_\lambda{}^\circ e^{-c_\lambda m} \text{ where } c_\lambda = \frac{\beta}{\lambda^\alpha}$$

Here E_λ and $E_\lambda{}^\circ$ are respectively spectral irradiance at wavelength λ after and before transmittance through a turbid atmosphere, and m is the air mass. The values of Table 1 take into account also other factors of atmospheric attenuation, which are ignored in Equation (1), namely Rayleigh and ozone scattering and molecular absorption. The partition of energy between the UV, visible and IR ranges of the spectrum is also shown. It is significant that as air mass increases or turbidity increases, the relative amount of energy in the IR increases and that in the visible and UV decreases.

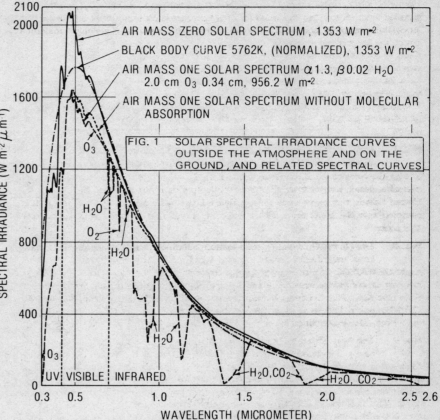

FIG. 1   SOLAR SPECTRAL IRRADIANCE CURVES OUTSIDE THE ATMOSPHERE AND ON THE GROUND, AND RELATED SPECTRAL CURVES

Direct solar irradiance (I_{DN}) discussed above is for a surface normal to the sun's rays. For a horizontal surface or a surface with any other slope, the energy received per unit area is $E_s = E_n \cos\theta$, where θ is the angle between the solar rays and the surface normal. For optimum efficiency of the collector plate, it is advantageous to have low values of θ, especially around solar noon when the air mass is least. For year round operation a surface facing south with a slope equal to the latitude of the place is desirable. For winter heating, but no air conditioning, a greater slope is desirable and for summer heating (of swimming pools, for example) a smaller slope is indicated.

Direct solar irradiance is the major term in the total irradiance on a surface. The next most important term is the diffuse radiation due to the sky. It is available always during day time, even when direct solar radiation is intercepted by clouds. A quantitative treatment of the subject is difficult because of the highly variable parameters of the atmosphere. A representative figure for diffuse sky irradiance on a horizontal surface is between one-fifth and one-sixth of the direct solar irradiance. If the surface is not horizontal but sloping at an angle T to the horizontal, the diffuse sky irradiance is related to that on a horizontal surface by the approximate ratio $\cos^2 (T/2)$.

Another major area where precise quantitative prediction is desirable but almost impossible is the solar energy available at any location over an extended period of time and the relative number of days of sunshine, cloud or rain. "As unpredictable as the weather" is a common expression; statistical data based on previous measurements will have to serve as a guide for the future. An estimate of the energy available at 61 different locations may be made from Fig. 2. It is from Reference 5, Chapter 16, where monthly averages of the daily total insolation are also available for these locations. Station 4, Inyokern, CA, has the maximum value of 569 cal/cm² per day (2381 joules/cm² per day) and Seattle University, Station 24A, has the minimum value of 269 cal/cm². These values of annual means of daily insolation should not be confused with what will be available on any given day and location. Measurements made at Goddard Space Flight Center, Greenbelt, Maryland in suburban Washington, D.C. gave values well outside this range on two consecutive days, 175 cal/cm² on May 13, 1971 and 647 cal/cm² on the next day. Daily total insolation has a wider range of variation from day to day at any one location than the yearly averages of such totals from one location to another. It is also instructive to compare these values with the extraterrestrial solar irradiance.

An area of one cm² exposed normally to the sun's rays outside the atmosphere at the mean sun-Earth distance would receive in 2 hours and 19 minutes the same amount, 269 cal/cm², as the average for Seattle University for a whole day. In most areas of the south-west U.S. the daily insolation is considerably greater than in the north-west. Not all locations in the U.S. are equally cost-effective in solar energy conversion. The increased cost of a collector on a synchronous satellite which has been often discussed in the news media should be weighed against the highly variable and low level solar irradiance at ground locations.

Detailed information on solar energy available on the ground can be obtained from the National Oceanic and Atmospheric Administration (NOAA) which maintains an extensive network of stations. Ninety of these belong to the solar radiation network. There is also a "sunshine switch" network with over 160 stations. Efforts are now being made by NOAA to upgrade and expand the national network for monitoring solar irradiance at ground level. The respository and distribution center for information about solar irradiance data is the National Climatic Center, Federal Building, Ashville, NC 28801.

AIR MASS	SOLAR ZENITH ANGLE (DEGREES)	TURBIDITY FACTORS α	TURBIDITY FACTORS β	TOTAL IRRADIANCE W·m⁻²	RATIO OF TOTAL IRRADIANCE TO SOLAR CONSTANT %	FRACTION OF THE TOTAL ENERGY IN THE UV, λ<0.4μm %	FRACTION OF THE TOTAL ENERGY IN THE VISIBLE 0.4μm<λ<0.72μm %	FRACTION OF THE TOTAL ENERGY IN THE INFRARED λ>0.72μm %
0	0			1353.0	100.0	8.7	40.1	51.1
1	0	1.30	0.02	956.2	70.7	4.8	46.9	48.3
4	75.5	1.30	0.02	595.2	44.0	1.23	44.2	54.5
7	81.8	1.30	0.02	413.6	30.6	0.35	39.4	60.3
10	84.3	1.30	0.02	302.5	22.4	0.102	34.7	65.2
1	0	1.30	0.04	924.9	68.4	4.6	46.4	49.0
4	75.5	1.30	0.04	528.9	39.1	1.04	42.1	56.9
7	81.8	1.30	0.04	342.0	25.3	0.26	35.9	63.8
10	84.3	1.30	0.04	234.5	17.3	0.065	30.3	69.6
1	0	0.66	0.085	889.2	65.7	4.7	46.4	48.9
4	75.5	0.66	0.085	448.7	33.2	1.14	42.4	56.5
7	81.8	0.66	0.085	255.2	18.9	0.30	36.3	63.4
10	84.3	0.66	0.085	153.8	11.4	0.08	30.7	69.2
1	0	0.66	0.17	800.2	59.1	4.5	45.4	50.1
4	75.5	0.66	0.17	303.1	22.4	0.88	38.3	60.8
7	81.8	0.66	0.17	133.3	9.85	0.14	30.0	69.8
10	84.3	0.66	0.17	63.4	4.69	0.039	22.9	77.1

TABLE 1   SOLAR IRRADIANCE ON UNIT AREA EXPOSED NORMALLY TO THE SUN'S RAYS, COMPUTED FOR DIFFERENT AIR MASS VALUES, U. S. STANDARD ATMOSPHERE, 2cm OF H_2O AND 0.34cm OF OZONE.

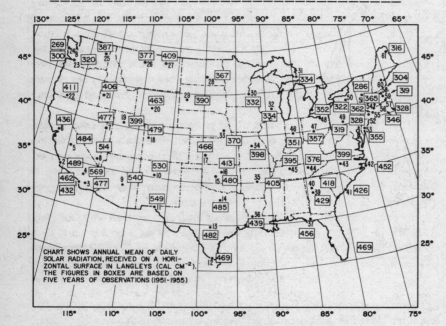

FIG. 2   ANNUAL MEAN OF DAILY INSOLATION RECEIVED ON A HORIZONTAL SURFACE AT 61 LOCATIONS IN CONTINENTAL UNITED STATES

CHART SHOWS ANNUAL MEAN OF DAILY SOLAR RADIATION, RECEIVED ON A HORIZONTAL SURFACE IN LANGLEYS (CAL CM⁻²) THE FIGURES IN BOXES ARE BASED ON FIVE YEARS OF OBSERVATIONS (1951-1955)

Conclusion

The Earth-atmosphere system receives energy from the sun at the prodigious rate of 5.445×10^{24} joules or 1.513×10^{18} KW-hrs per year. The total output of all man-made energy producing systems in the world in 1970 was less than 0.004 percent of this, 2×10^{20} joules. Of this energy 35 percent was produced in the United States, and all but 4 percent from a rapidly dwindling supply of fossil fuels (which after all are stored solar energy). Using today's solar energy for today's needs is a challenge greater than the conquest of space. Knowing how much solar energy is available is part of meeting this challenge.

References

1. Anon: Standard Specification for Solar Constant and Air Mass Zero Solar Spectral Irradiance, ASTM Standard, E-490-73a, 1974 Annual Book of ASTM Standards, Part 41, Philadelphia, PA, 1974.

2. Anon: Solar Electromagnetic Radiation, NASA SP 8005, Washington, D.C., May 1971

3. Thekaekara, M.P., ed., The Solar Constant and Solar Spectrum Measured from a Research Aircraft, NASA TR R-351, Washington, D.C., October 1970.

4. Thekaekara, M.P., Solar Energy Outside the Earth's Atmosphere, Solar Energy, Vol. 14, No. 2, 1973, pp. 109-127.

5. Campen, C.F., et al., ed., Handbook of Geophysics (AFCRL), McMillan Co., New York, pp. 16-15, 1960.

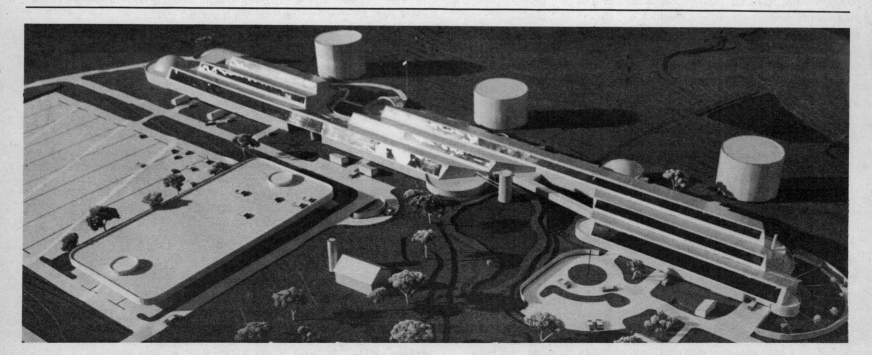

SOLAR COMMENTS
Chuck Missar, Solar Editor

The information presented here on solar energy is just a hint of what is available. For a technology that has had so little practical application, there is ample information available to educate the experimenter and builder. Solar devices for distilling water, heating domestic and swimming pool water, cooking food, and melting materials have been in use for years, the technology is well known and the results are reasonably predictable.

The recent 'energy crisis' resulted in a lot being written on solar energy. *Readers' Digest, Rotarian, Smithsonian Bulletin, Popular Science,* and many other diverse periodicals featured the merits and possibilities of the sun's energy. However, like dozens of articles before them, they were too generalized for us to transfer the technology to practice. Solar energy is well beyond the vague generality stage. The solar chapter attempts to illustrate this by directing you to sources of ideas, plans and hardware from which you can build or buy your own equipment. The beauty of solar energy is that anybody can build a simple system that will decrease demands on our dwindling fossil fuel reserves. A simple cooker or a scrap-fabricated water heater are things you can build tomorrow, if you have sufficient interest.

Let's look at solar energy in historical perspective. Really active research and experimentation on the subject started in the late 19th century. Periodically since then (maybe on 10-15 year cycles), interest in it has risen and then fallen. With oil prices so low for so long and with our "oil will last forever" mentality, we could not justify the expense of solar hardware. Under these conditions of oscillating interest in solar technology, research has been carried out by a small group of dedicated people who believed in the environmental and long term social benefits that could come from the use of solar energy. Maybe that is why this group of pioneering "eccentrics" has so much in common with the burgeoning group of solar advocates today. Together they know that solar energy needs to be developed for the safety and comfort of future generations.

Many large, well established firms are becoming quite involved with solar energy research and hardware. These firms will be the leaders in many solar energy activities, since they have the capital, momentum, and reputation to carry out successful research and development. Most of us interested in doing-it-ourselves will live off the technological fall-out from these firms. By paying close attention to new patents, government information from the National Technical Information Service and the National Aeronautics and Space Administration, trade journals, and our own research, we can learn how to incorporate the latest engineering achievements in our small scale systems without having to support directly large, centralized industries. An appropriate phrase often heard in the hall at Portola Institute is "keep on livin' in the cracks." This applies to solar energy as much as it does to economics or shelter.

Many of us feel uncomfortable with the higher degree of self-sufficiency that "livin' in the cracks" implies. However, as we try to make clear elsewhere in the *Energy Primer,* more self-sufficiency and the understanding of our immediate world that this entails are an absolute necessity in our chaotic world.

THE ABR PARTNERSHIP, ARCHITECTS IN DENVER, AND BRIDGERS AND PAXTON, MECHANICAL ENGINEERS IN ALBUQUERQUE, HAVE DESIGNED A NEW NORTH CAMPUS FOR THE COMMUNITY COLLEGE OF DENVER. 50,000 SQ. FT. OF SOLAR COLLECTORS AND 400,000 GALLONS OF WATER STORAGE WILL BE USED TO HEAT 290,000 SQ. FT. (6+ ACRES) OF FLOOR SPACE IN THE 3-WING BUILDING. SCHEDULED FOR COMPLETION IN LATE 1976, THIS HEAVILY INSULATED, SOLAR HEATED CLASSROOM AND LABORATORY STRUCTURE WILL BE THE LARGEST OF ITS KIND IN THE WORLD. THE SHORTAGE OF NATURAL GAS IN COLORADO PROMPTED THE STATE'S FORESIGHTED GENERAL ASSEMBLY TO FUND THIS INNOVATIVE PROJECT. THE NEW CAMPUS WILL BE LOCATED AT 112TH AVENUE AND LOWELL BOULEVARD, WESTMINSTER, CO.

Self-sufficiency can be expensive. Solar collectors use a lot of metal and glass, they require electronic controls to work efficiently, and maintenance is an ever present reality. We can not expect large segments of the population of the United States, much less the other nations of the world, to use solar energy at the same rate they have been using fossil fuel energy. Besides, the "costs" of solar energy resources and hardware might use up more energy than that gleaned from the sun. Who knows? This whole subject of net energy available from the sun, after recovery costs are calcualted and subtracted from gross energy input, has barely been touched upon. We need immediate and in-depth study of this subject for small and intermediate systems, I think we will confirm what we've suspected all along—the answer to most of our problems is to use less.

Back to what we can do. First, get out there and try to build some solar hardware. Start with a small solar still or dryer, for instance, and work up into something you really feel proud of.

Second, take safety precautions. A collector, left to heat in the sun with water in it but not circulating, can generate enough steam to blow the collector up if there is no means of pressure relief. Many commercial antifreezes are poisonous and should not be used where children or animals might drink the water in which they are mixed. A concentrating collector can blind you almost instantly if you deliberately or accidently look into it, or it can start a fire if it is carelessly aimed. The addition of collector assemblies can alter a structure's deadweight and wind loading characteristics. In short, consider the safety aspects of what you are doing. Dress appropriately for the work to be done and think through each project you undertake. This all sounds obvious, but the techniques of safe driving sound obvious, yet 50,000 people are killed on the road each year in the United States.

Third, keep accurate records of what you are doing and what results you have had. What is your solar hardware cost—in dollars and production energy? How efficiently has it done its job? What problems have you encountered and how did you solve them? Be methodical and accurate. It sounds like school all over again, but it's the only way we're going to generate information that is worthwhile to share.

Fourth, share with others the results of your research and building. There's no better turn-on to solar energy than to see a cooker cook or a heater heat. Many of us grew up with a generation of "tire kickers," let's become a generation of "flat plate thumpers" or some such thing. We must learn to discuss the attributes and shortcomings of solar assemblies just as well as we've been doing with automobiles and the other "necessities" of our age. Information can be shared through publications such as *Alternative Sources of Energy Newsletter, Co-Evolution Quarterly,* regional alternative lifestyle newsletters, or the feature pages of your home town newspaper. Be prepared for lots of visitors and small talk if you build something, since this is one way people become comfortable with the ideas and hardware involved with solar energy.

We haven't done much to stress foreign vendors of solar hardware. Excellent equipment is available from Israel, Australia, Japan and elsewhere. However, with present transportation charges and exchange rates, it hardly makes sense to feature these items. In keeping to what is available in the United States, we have tried to review some of the bad with the good to give you an idea of the range of publications and hardware available.

Prices quoted in the *Energy Primer* are current at the time of publication (Fall 1974). Prices are changing rapidly. Don't be surprised if book and hardware prices are higher on items you order. Also, because solar energy technology is changing so fast, some of the information presented here will soon be obsolete. Read *Alternative Sources of Energy* Newsletter or *Solar Energy Digest* for the newest information.

When you send off for "free" information, *please* send a stamped, self-addresses envelope. Many of the vendors and authors listed here are small operations that can't service an onslaught of "I'm collectingsolarinformation for my___gradephysicsclass" letters. Ask for information judiciously and help pay for it if you need it so badly.

In the following pages of the solar section, reviews and commentary that are not mine are signed by the reviewer. If it is in this typeface, it's a quote from the book or the descriptive literature of the project or hardware being reviewed.

REVIEWS/SOLAR

DIRECT USES OF THE SUN'S ENERGY

This is a book to own; there's so much in it, you'll want it handy. Farrington Daniels wrote much of the book from his own first-hand experience as Director of the Solar Energy Laboratory of the University of Wisconsin. He covers all aspects of solar energy research and application. Without stressing mathematical or engineering details (though including complete references to this material) he describes the full range of work on solar collectors, cooking, heating, agricultural and industrial drying, distillation, storage of heat, solar furnaces and engines, cooling and refrigeration, photochemical conversion, photo- and thermoelectric conversion, and many other uses of solar energy.

Dr. Daniels was concerned with developing low-cost solar applications, principally for the benefit of non-industrialized peoples. He wrote this book to interest others in such possibilities. It's by far the best available introduction to the subject.

—Roger Douglass

Direct Uses of the Sun's Energy
Farrington Daniels
1964

$1.95 paperback

from:
Ballantine Books, Inc.
457 Hahn Road
Westminster, MD 21157

$12.50 hardcover

from:
Yale University Press
92A Yale Station
New Haven, CT 06520

or WHOLE EARTH TRUCK STORE

UNITED NATIONS CONFERENCE ON NEW SOURCES OF ENERGY, ROME, 1961

The three solar energy volumes and the one wind energy volume are back in print! Expensive, to be sure, but nevertheless available. Three thousand sets were printed in 1964; only 2,250 sets have been printed in 1974. If you want some, order soon, as it's doubtful they will be available for very long. The serious researcher will want a personal set; otherwise, ask your library to order them.

Some papers in these volumes are outdated, too technical, too simple or too general. Yet these volumes are probably the most significant collection of reports ever printed on solar energy. They certainly should be studied if you are going into a solar project of any complexity.

The contents are listed below. The numerals in parentheses indicate the number of articles on each subject.

—C.M.

Volume IV: Solar Energy I

II.C.1	Use of solar energy for mechanical power and electricity production
(a)	by means of piston engines and turbines (7)
(b)(i)	by means of thermoelectric converters (7)
(b)(ii)	by means of photo-electric cells (6)
III.A	Solar energy availability and instruments for measurement (21)
III.B	New materials in solar energy utilization (11)

Volume V: Solar Energy II

III.C	Use of solar heating for heating purposes:
.1	water heating (12)
.2	space heating (10)
.3	solar drying (5)
.4	solar cooking (8)
.5	heat storage (3)

Volume VI: Solar Energy III

III.D	Use of solar energy for cooling purposes (10)
III.E	Use of solar energy for production of fresh water (14)
III.F	Use of solar energy for high temperature processing (solar furnaces) (14)

United Nations Conference on New Sources of Energy, Rome 1961
Vol. IV; Solar Energy I
1964; 665 pp

$20.00

Vol. V:
Solar Energy II
1964; 423 pp

$16.00

Vol. VI:
Solar Energy III
1964; 454 pp

$16.00

from:
United Nations
Publications
Room LX-2300
NY NY 10017

or WHOLE EARTH
TRUCK STORE

INTRODUCTION TO THE UTILIZATION OF SOLAR ENERGY

Starting in 1954-55 the UCLA Engineering Extension offered a course by this title, to which many solar energy authorities were invited to lecture. This book contains rewritten and expanded versions of some of these lectures. It was published in 1963 by McGraw Hill "as collateral reading for similar courses that might be given in other institutions and as a volume of general interest for the technical person in any scientific or engineering field." For many technical persons this book will be the most satisfying general introduction to solar energy. It is listed in many technical libraries, but is usually checked out or missing. Now that a Xerox facsimile is available, these libraries may be persuaded to stock duplicate copies. But I think anyone doing technical work in the field will want his own copy.

Following an introduction by Farrington Daniels and a section entitled Energy Sources of the Future which leans heavily on P.C. Putnam's book Energy in the Future (1953), there are chapters on Availability of Solar Energy (total, direct, and diffuse radiation on surfaces on the ground, the sun's hourly position and radiation intensities, thermal atmospheric radiation, measurement, 50 references), Properties of Surfaces and Diathermanous Materials (absorbtion, reflection, emission, transmission curves for glasses and plastics, 26 references), Flat Plate Collectors (by H.C. Hottel and D.C. Erway — calculations of performance curves, 12 references), Concentration of Solar Energy (design equations for mirror and lens systems, 6 references), Conversion of Solar to Mechanical Energy (heat engines, solar pumps, approximately 50 references), Direct Conversion of Solar to Electrical Energy (basic properties and economics of solar photovoltaics, mainly silicon cells, 11 references), and Photochemical Processes for Utilization of Solar Energy (the so-far unproductive search for useful non-biological photochemical reactions to absorb and store solar energy, 49 references).

These excellent chapters on technical aspects of solar energy are followed by a good discussion of the complex Economics of Solar Energy. The author points out that "In an absolute sense, all energy is free . . . the cost is that of extracting, transporting, and converting the energy into useful form" and the cost comparison of solar with other forms of energy is complicated by its widespread, diffuse and periodic nature so that "the various economic peculiarities of solar devices—including the extreme significance of fuel costs, of transmission or transportation costs of competitive energy supplies, of relative financing costs, and of local weather conditions—all emphasize that the competitive economics of solar devices is critically dependent on locale. Any meaningful attempt to compare economic efficiency of a solar device with a conventional device will be valid only for a very limited geographic area." Pollution and other environmental consequences of various energy uses are not considered at all, but the economic aspects of a variety of solar applications are thoughtfully discussed.

The next chapter, by George Löf, is on Heating and Cooling of Buildings with Solar Energy. He discusses a wide variety of possible heating and cooling systems and describes essentially all the solar conditioned houses that had been built to date. The book concludes with a brief chapter on Distillation of Sea Water and other Low-Temperature Applications of Solar Energy (water heating, stoves, greenhouses, 33 references), a chapter on solar furnaces for materials research and processing (10 references), and a chapter on Space Applications of Solar Energy which describes then-current contract research on a wide variety of solar-thermal and photovoltaic electric power plants for satellites and space vehicles.

This book costs $.05 per page, so if you can find the library copy it might be cheaper to do your own duplication of sections of interest to you. Printing, charts and line drawings come through clearly in the Xerox version, the few photographs reproduced poorly. Perhaps if we wait awhile it will be reprinted more cheaply—hope so.

—Roger Douglass

Introduction to the Utilization of Solar Energy
A.M. Zarem and Duane D. Erway
1963; 398 pp

$20.50 hardcopy

$6.85 microfilm

plus tax and shipping

from:
Xerox University Microfilms
300 North Zeeb Road
Ann Arbor, Michigan 48104

SOLAR ENERGY AND BUILDING DESIGN

The copy being reviewed is Bruce Anderson's January, 1973 Masters Thesis in Architecture, which had a limited circulation and is no longer available. Fortunately, there soon should be an updated version published by Arthur D. Little, Inc. A number of people are taking potshots at ADL for their other solar activities, but everyone should agree, I think, that the publication of this book is a good thing. Here's what's in it:

Section One—The Issues: The Global Crisis, the energy crisis, a collection of facts and quotes from *Limits to Growth*, U Thant on the urgency of a global partnership, and Aristotle on the proper size of states. A fact list on the potentials of solar energy, the use of scarce natural resources in solar energy systems and the social implications of the increased cost of housing that they may entail. Solar energy as a political issue, the complications of introducing solar energy into the third world, and philosophy and sociology of a design-with-nature rather than a man-against-nature approach. Also, a questioning of the past attitude of solar engineers that in order to succeed with the public, solar houses should be as much like other houses as possible—that people should hardby be aware that they are using solar energy. Nice

quotes on an ecological code for builders and on awareness of and respect for our proper place in the natural order. Finally, how to calculate the seasonal cost of heating a dwelling—which is an issue since for most situations solar energy will only be used if it is economically advantageous, so long as there are alternatives.

Section Two—Designing with the Sun: Discussions and charts on heat loss and insulation, the effect of wind, wind control and air infiltration on heat loss by a dwelling. Solar heat gain through windows (charts, tables, equations, explanations), heat storage by building material and the effect of different types of construction on daily thermal behavior, and solar control by orientation and building shape. This section won't substitute for the explicit or intuitive knowledge of engineering fundamentals and the use of wisdom and good judgement in their application, but it's a good introduction.

Section Three—Collection and Utilization of Solar Energy: A brief history of existing solar houses. Each house is described in much more detail in Appendix 1, and this is one of the most valuable aspects of the book. Brief surveys of types of solar collectors and heat storage, and systems including auxiliary sources of heat. Several pages of discussion of the architectural and design problems of solar heated dwellings, including the options of collectors separate from the dwelling and of

long-term heat storage. An extended discussion of solar weather with charts and maps, in which Bruce has tried, with admittedly only limited success, to simplify a complex issue.

This is followed by a very extensive bibliography which reflects the author's concern with ecological issues and natural styles of living. The usefulness of the book to designers is enhanced by tables of climatic data, thermal and solar properties of materials, conversion tables for heat and energy units, and a chart from a study by Lof and Tybout showing the effect of collected solar heat.

You won't find Nobel-prize-winning solutions for solar energy collection or storage in this book, or even any original designs for houses or solar systems, but as an introduction to the principles and problems of *Solar Energy and Building Design*, this book is excellent.

—Roger Douglass

Solar Energy and Building Design
Bruce Anderson
1974; approx. 300 pp

Price Not Yet Determined

from:
Arthur D. Little, Inc.
Acorn Park
Cambridge, Massachusetts 02140

or WHOLE EARTH TRUCK STORE

LOW TEMPERATURE ENGINEERING APPLICATION OF SOLAR ENERGY

A basic, excellent book for the solar energy experimenter. A large amount of information packed into 80 pages. Not a how-to-do-it book, but a how-to-calculate-it book. Most useful are the chapters on "Design Factors Influencing Collector Performance" and "Solar Water Heaters." The calculations and formulas presented are comprehensive. The math is a bit involved at times, but many of the basic calculations are very simple. With these calculations, one can evaluate and compare such factors as collector size and placement, materials used in the collector, size of the storage system, heat loss from the collector, etc. There are many charts and graphs which allow comparison or determination of some of the aspects of the design of a solar system without having to go through the calculations.

The article by Liu and Jordan includes an extensive table of value of mean daily insolation (solar energy) on a horizontal surface at weather stations throughout the country for each month of the year. A method is presented for translating this data into predictions of solar output from fixed tilted flat-plate collectors. This article is *the best* source for methods of prediction for cloudy climates.

—Gail Morrison

Low Temperature Engineering Application of Solar Energy
Technical Committee on Solar Energy Utilization, American Society of Heating, Refrigerating and Air-Conditioning Engineers
1967; 78 pp

$9.00

from:
ASHRAE (Sales Dept.)
345 East 47th Street
New York, NY 10017

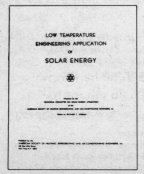

SOLAR ENERGY AS A NATIONAL ENERGY RESOURCE

A panel of 40 scientists and engineers appointed by NASA and NSF prepared this feasibility study of serious government effort to stimulate widespread utilization of solar energy, including conversion of sunlight to thermal and electrical energy, power from wind and from ocean temperature differences, and conversion of organic materials to fuels. One of the panel's conclusions: "A substantial development program can achieve the necessary technical and economic objectives by the year 2020. Then solar energy could economically provide up to (1) 35% of the total building heating and cooling load; (2) 30% of the Nation's gaseous fuel; (3) 10% of the liquid fuel; and (4) 20% of the electric energy requirements." The panel recommends that the federal government take a leading role in this program.

The report is a good general analysis of the basic methods of solar energy conversion, the technical and economic problems inherent in its development, and research and development goals that will lead to the widespread use of solar energy.

—Gail Morrison

Solar Energy as a National Energy Resource NSF/NASA Solar Energy Panel
1972; 85 pp
Stock No. 3800-00164

$1.20

from:
Superintendent of Documents
U.S. Government Printing Office
Wasington, D.C. 20402

SOLAR ENERGY FOR MAN

This basic introduction to solar energy applications covers the same areas as Daniels' *Direct Uses of the Sun's Energy*, but in a very different manner. It's written as an undergraduate science textbook—except that there are no questions or exercises for the student. Each process or application is related, wherever possible, to basic science principles. There are many diagrams, and algebraic equations are derived to provide a simple mathematical description of processes.

As in most science texts, there is little discussion of actual hardware and of how its performance differs from the algebraic idealizations or oversimplified models. So while a non-technical person will find the algebra a barrier to one's understanding, a professional engineer or scientist is likely to find the depth of treatment inadequate. But this book, supplemented by Daniels' book to add some breadth of understanding of what has actually been done, might be a good choice as a text for a technical course on solar energy. Brinkworth uniformly uses MKS units; energy conversion factors are in an appendix of Daniels' book.

—Roger Douglass

Solar Energy for Man
B. J. Brinkworth
1973; 264 pp

$9.95

from:
John Wiley & Sons, Inc.
1 Wiley Drive
Somerset, NJ 08873

or
1530 South Redwood Rd.
Salt Lake City, UT 84104

or WHOLE EARTH TRUCK STORE

SOLAR ENERGY TECHNOLOGY AND APPLICATIONS

According to the preface, this "introduces the various techniques for utilizing solar energy and brings you up to date on work to the present time on the broad spectrum of solar energy systems. Succinctly written for the technical person, it is readily understood by anyone with no background in the field. It is also recommended as a supplementary text for energy related courses."

The book is indeed up to date—a quick look through it reveals that most of the pictures, charts, and diagrams are borrowed directly from recent scientific papers, reports on government contracts, reports of workshops, etc. In fact the book is little more than a very condensed and selective survey of recent solar energy literature. It should serve well the purposes stated in the preface. It is very short, with small pages taken up by half and full-page figures, and should be easy reading for a science or engineering student. There is little if any attempt to provide any overview or evaluation of solar projects or developments, and the book is written in a very impersonal style. Only by looking at the 139 technical references do we learn the names of the persons whose work is being reported.

The book briefly covers the use of solar energy for heating and cooling of buildings, water heating, central station power generation, solar furnaces, crop dryers and stills, fuels from grown and waste organic materials, the ocean thermal gradient power concept, the satellite solar-cell power plant, and wind power. Its extreme brevity is perhaps the book's main drawback. Students of design, architecture or environmental studies should consider Bruce Anderson's or Wilson Clark's book instead. They will get much more for their money.
—Roger Douglass

Solar Energy
Technology &
Applications
J. Richard Williams
1974; 126 pp
$6.95

from:
Ann Arbor Science
P.O. Box 1425
Ann Arbor, MI 48106

or WHOLE EARTH
TRUCK STORE

PROCEEDINGS OF THE WORLD SYMPOSIUM ON APPLIED SOLAR ENERGY

This is the record of the second of two consecutive major solar energy conferences held in Arizona in 1955 by the newly formed Association for Applied Solar Energy (now the Solar Energy Society). The first stressed the Scientific Basis and its 900 pages of transactions were published in 1958 by the University of Arizona. These 300 pages of Proceedings of the World Symposium were first published in 1956 by Stanford Research Institute. This book has found its way into many libraries where it has served over the years to introduce many newcomers to the field of solar energy.

The book gives good general coverage to the principles, problems, and prospects of most fields of solar energy. Except for the development of solar cells as power plants for space vehicles, the state-of-the-art covered in this book has changed little since 1955. Economics was then, and is now, the major barrier to extensive application of solar energy. This is discussed in an introductory article by Farrington Daniels and is the subject of a following article by J. E. Hobson of the Stanford Research Institute. There are articles on solar furnaces, stills, house heating and cooling, heat pumps, solar architecture, and a number of articles on growing algae for food, feed or fuel. A particularly informative article by R. C. Jordan and W. C. Ibele summarizes the history and principles of solar engines, with pictures of some of the notable efforts by pioneers in this field.
—Roger Douglass

Proceedings of the World Symposium on Applied Solar Energy
1956; 304 pp
$15.00

from:
Johnson Reprint Corporation
111 Fifth Avenue
New York, N.Y. 10003

ADVANCED SOLAR ENERGY TECHNOLOGY

A brand new solar newsletter.
$60.00 per year

Advanced Solar Energy Technology Newsletter
1609 West Windrose
Phoenix, Arizona 85029

SOLAR ENERGY

Perhaps the best thing that can be said about this book is that it gives a good account of the history and a few applications of solar energy. The book is an edited and revised version of an earlier translation of the author's *Sonnenenergie* (1958). It's pretty hard to say whose purposes the book might serve, so I'll just describe its contents.

After the usual introductory chapters on the world's limited energy reserves and resources, there's a nice three page chapter on solar mythology. Then, after two easy-to-read chapters on the physics of the sun, the account begins with Archimedes, who reportedly set fire to Roman warships during the seige of Syracuse by means of a "burning mirror" (see page 10, *Harper's*, June 1974). The history of applications covers desalinization of sea water and salt production, heating water, solar heated houses (very sketchy coverage), a solar heat pump system, solar cookers and ovens (lots of detail), solar furnaces (excellent coverage), solar motors and power plants (sketchy), solar-cell powered devices, and experiments on controlled photosynthesis. A chapter is devoted to solar research via, and solar power for, rockets and satellites, with a chronology of launchings! The final chapter was written by Prof. Erich Farber of the University of Florida on the future of solar energy, and that's followed by a table of facts and figures about the sun.

The quality of this book varies from high to the most superficial Sunday supplement level—there are even extended quotes from newspaper articles. It provides little competition for Farrington Daniels' *Direct Use of the Sun's Energy*.
—Roger Douglass

Solar Energy
Hans Rau
1964; 171 pp
$9.95

from:
Macmillan Publishing
Company
Front & Brown Strs.
Riverside, N.J. 08075

or WHOLE EARTH
TRUCK STORE

THE COMING AGE OF SOLAR ENERGY

Whether you are interested in the purity and nobility of solar energy, in the depletion of fossil fuel resources, or in alternatives to a "plutonium economy" which feeds ever increasing amounts of radioactivity and waste heat into the environment, this book is a must. It won't confuse you with useless technicalities or explain how to build a solar water heater (the author's paperback *Solar Science Projects* does that). It will, however, broaden your knowledge and perspective on what has already been done with solar energy (few current developments are really new) and what solar energy might do in the future. The book is short and easy reading, but the author knows his stuff and there's enough substance to the book that you'll be referring back often. Halacy is a good science writer, not of the gee-whiz variety, but one who explains in understandable terms what's really important.

The first half of the book is related to the history and uses of solar energy. The second half of the book details several major current proposals for large-scale solar powerplants, and the last chapter briefly describes others. There's very little space given to solar houses, but the choice of Thomason's and Hay's houses as examples was excellent—they are among the very few solar houses that have been cheap and fully successful.

This book isn't as exhaustive in its coverage as Daniels' *Direct Use of the Sun's Energy*, and it doesn't give references, but it's certainly worth adding to your bookshelf.
—Roger Douglass

Just imagine for a moment that mankind had based his power industry on solar radiation, not fuel, and then the proposal to use different kinds of fuel was put forward. Probably there would have been very many objections. One could imagine that one of the most important arguments in defense of solar energy would be formulated as follows: Solar radiation is a

"noble" form of energy and it was under its influence that life originated and continues to develop on Earth; therefore its use, no matter on what scale, could represent no danger or inconvenience for either the flora or fauna of the world. The use of any other kind of fuel would inevitably be connected with the poisoning of the atmosphere, water and land. Fuel should be used only where there are no other possibilities of obtaining energy, and in the sunny regions of the world the energy of the Sun should be used.
    Professor Valentin Baum
    Tashkent (Russia) Heliotechnical Institute

The Coming Age of Solar Energy
D. S. Halacy, Jr.
1973; 231 pp
$7.95

from:
Harper & Row
Keystone Industrial Park
Scranton, Pennsylvania 18512

or WHOLE EARTH TRUCK STORE

SOLAR HEATING AND COOLING FOR BUILDINGS WORKSHOP

This was an invitational conference staged by the National Science Foundation. About 100 attended, some of whom already had NSF grants and many more of whom wanted them. Many of the 40 papers presented were on work that was underway or being proposed. Many were newcomers to the solar energy field. Sessions are reported dealing with Solar Collectors, Energy Storage, Hot Water Heating, Energy Conservation, Solar Air Conditioning, Foreign Activities, and Solar Heating/Cooling Systems. This book gives summaries of all presentations and in some cases the discussion that followed. Here and there are useful graphs and tables and bits of information but its main value is perhaps as a partial guide to what was being done in the field and by whom. A list of participants and their addresses concludes the book.

—Roger Douglass

Solar Heating and Cooling for Buildings Workshop
Redfield Allen, Editor, 1973; 226 pp; Order No. 223-536
$3.00
from: Nat. Technical Information Service, U.S. Dept. of Commerce, P.O. B. 1553, Springfield, VA 22151

TABLE 2. EXAMPLE ENERGY STORAGE MEDIA

	Temp. Range, F	Melting Temp., F	C_p, Btu/lb	p lb/ft³	K Btu/hr ft F	α ft²/hr	L Btu/lb	Material Cost $/lb	Per Million Btu Vol. Ft³	Weight, lb	Cost $
Water-ice	32	32	0.49	58	1.3	0.046	144	Nil	111	7,000	Nil
Water	90-130	32	1.0	62	0.38	0.0061	--	Nil	400	25,000	Nil
Steel (scrap iron)	" "	--	0.12	489	36.0	0.44	--	0.003	430	210,000	630
Basalt (lava rock)	" "	--	0.20	184	1.14	0.031	--	0.002	680	125,000	250
Limestone	" "	--	0.22	156	0.73	0.021	--	0.002	730	114,000	228
Paraffin wax	" "	100	0.7	55	0.13	0.004	65	0.08	195	10,700	856
Salt Hydrates											
$NaSO_4 \cdot 1OH_2O$	" "	90	0.4	90	--	--	108	0.012	90	8,000	96
$Na_2S_2O_3 \cdot 5H_2O$	" "	120	"	104	--	--	90	0.05	90	9,400	470
$Na_2HPO_4 \cdot 12H_2O$	" "	97	"	94	--	--	120	0.034	78	7,350	250
Water	110-300	--	1.0	62	0.38	0.0061	--	Nil	85	5,300	Nil
Fire brick	110-800	--	0.22	198	0.70	--	--	0.01	33	6,600	66
Ceramic Oxides MgO	" "	--	0.35	224	20.0	0.06	--	0.14	26	4,200	560
Fused Salts $NaNO_3$	" "	510	0.38	140	--	--	80	0.024	21	2,920	70
Lithium	" "	370	$1.0\pm$	33	--	.000435	286	10.00	31	1,020	10,200
Carbon	" "	6,750	0.2	140	2.4	0.103	--	0.20	52	7,200	1,440
Lithium hydride	1,260	1,260	$1.0\pm$	36	4.2	--	1,200	10.00	23	833	8,330
Sodium Chloride	1,480	1,480	0.21	135	3.65	0.13	223	.02	33	4,500	90
Silicon	2,605	2,605	--	146	--	--	607	--	11	1,647	--

Note: By mixing fused salts, any desired melting point between 250 and 1000 F can be attained.

EXPERIMENTS WITH SOLAR ENERGY

SOLAR SCIENCE PROJECTS

These contain diagrams, instructions, parts lists and where to buy the stuff—all an interested kid of any age needs to get started. The second, a paperback version of the author's earlier *Fun With the Sun*, gives instructions for a reflector cooker (parabolic mirror of cardboard and aluminum foil), solar still, solar furnace using a plastic Fresnel lens, solar oven, water heater, motor run by solar cells, and a one transistor radio run by a solar cell.

The first book is usually a bit less explicit about construction techniques, but has more ideas about what has been and can be done, and is more fun to read. There are good instructions for a solar powered airplane using thin-film cadmium sulfide solar cells to run a small motor and propeller. What I liked best was the survival still, made from a piece of any sort of clear plastic sheet and a cup or can. Dig a hole in the ground and cover it with the plastic, weighting the edges with dirt. Water that condenses on the underside of the sheet runs to the center and drips down into the cup in the bottom of the hole. A small rock on top of the sheet helps hold the center down over the cup. Vegetation or waste water can be put in the hole if the soil is too dry. Some soils produce a quart a day. A nicely written book.

—Roger Douglass

Experiments with Solar Energy
D.S. Halacy, Jr.
1969; 147 pp
OUT OF PRINT
published by:
Grosset & Dunlap
New York, NY

Solar Science Projects
D.S. Halacy, Jr.
1974;
$0.75
from:
Scholastic Book Services
900 Sylvan Avenue
Englewood Cliffs, NJ 07632

or WHOLE EARTH TRUCK STORE

WORLD DISTRIBUTION OF SOLAR ENERGY

Probably still the most complete compilation regarding the amount of solar energy available on the earth's surface. The authors gathered all the data they could in 1965, reduced it to a common basis (monthly averages of daily total radiation on a horizontal surface), and presented it in tabular form and as 12 monthly sunshine "contour" maps of the world.

This data forms a basis from which estimates of monthly averages of hourly, daily, total, or direct radiation can be computed for surfaces other than horizontal. References are given for conversion of the data to these forms. A useful table of the US data, along with methods for conversion to tilted surfaces, is given in Liu and Jordan's article in *Low Temperature Application of Solar Energy*. A summary of the Wisconsin compilation was published in the first quarter issue of *Solar Energy*, 1966.

—Roger Douglass

World Distribution of Solar Radiation
G.O.G. Löf, J. A. Duffie and C.O. Smith
1966; 85 pp
Report No. 21
$4.00
from:
Engineering Experiment Station
Research Building
1500 Johnson Drive
Madison WI 53706

TRANSACTIONS OF THE CONFERENCE ON THE USE OF SOLAR ENERGY: THE SCIENTIFIC BASIS

To accommodate investigators who wanted to talk about their own recent work and hear others do the same, the Association for Applied Solar Energy held a two-day conference just before their big 1955 World Symposium in Phoenix. Most of the 80-90 papers were eventually published in these five volumes, which you might find in engineering or science libraries. Some of the material is now rather obsolete, but you might find articles of interest. A virtue of these reports is that they are less condensed, hence easier to read, than most recent technical papers.

SOLAR ENERGY RESEARCH

On September 12-14, 1953, several solar energy researchers met at Madison, Wisconsin. Participants agreed to write brief reports on subjects of their particular interest. The thirty-one contributions which eventually formed this book range from brief abstracts to detailed research reports. Some are quite technical, some are not. Bibliography and references were added. This seems to be the first book on the general status of solar energy utilization. A good deal of it is still interesting today.

Chapter headings are Expected World Energy Demands, Nature and Availability of Solar Energy, Space Heating and Domestic Uses of Solar Energy, Solar Power, Evaporation and Distillation, Atmospheric Phenomena and Conversion of Solar to Electric Energy, Solar Furnaces, Photosynthetic Utilization of Solar Energy, Photochemical Utilization, Miscellaneous Applications and Suggestions. In an appendix, John Duffie chronologically lists 240 United States patents on solar energy dating from one to Ulysses Pratt in 1852 for "Improvement in Process of Bleaching Ivory" up to 1954.

—Roger Douglass

Solar Energy Research
Ed. by F. Daniels and J. A. Duffie
1955; 290 pp
Out of Print
published by:
The University of Wisconsin Press
Madison, Wisconsin

Volumes I to V, respectively, contain papers on solar radiation measurement, collectors and solar furnaces, water and house heating and solar stills and stoves, photochemical processes (photosynthesis in plants and algae), and electrical processes (thermoelectric, photogalvanic, and photovoltaic).

—Roger Douglass

Transactions of the Conference on the Use of Solar Energy: The Scientific Basis
1955;
Out of Print
Published by:
University of Arizona Press

SOLAR ENERGY

This is a really good book on all phases of solar energy, written on a junior high school level. The author is an early writer about science and space, and he has done his homework extremely well. The book starts with a discussion of what energy is and the implications of the earth's limited reserves. This is followed by a short and simple, but accurate, discussion of how the sun works, what sunlight is, and the radiation balance of the earth.

The rest of the book discusses solar collectors, solar heating of buildings, controlled photosynthesis as a source of food and fuel, solar furnaces, coolers, and stills, photovoltaic and thermoelectric generators, and power from the wind and ocean thermal gradients. Although this book is 17 years old, little could be added to it today. This book should be in every school library.

—Roger Douglass

Solar Energy
Franklyn M. Branley
1957; 117 pp

$3.95

from:
Thomas Y. Crowell Co.
666 Fifth Avenue
New York, NY 10019

or WHOLE EARTH
TRUCK STORE

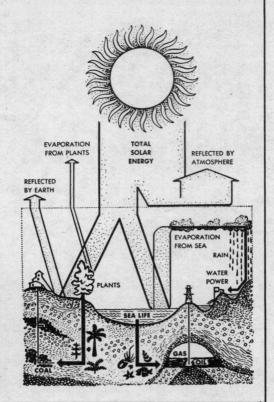

SOLAR ENERGY HANDBOOK

This is an unbound, roughly lithographed, approximately 150 page booklet which the author says is "only a start toward a more comprehensive work." It is intended to offer a practical engineering approach to solar heating and cooling of buildings. There are many tables of data and many lists. Lists of functions to be served, lists of design considerations, lists of desired properties of a material or a system, lists of types of relevant data, lists of components of a system, and even a list of values of trigonometric functions. In between these lists there's often some intelligent discussion of the real world, which usually keeps things from being clear and simple. The discussion seldom penetrates to the point where one has a sufficient basis to evaluate a specific design or intelligently choose among design alternatives.

The author has thought about the problems of engineering a solar house and the book would be of value to someone who has not. But an engineer who wants to design a solar house will be spending much more time with ASHRAE's *Handbook of Fundamentals* and *Low Temperature Engineering Application of Solar Energy* than with this booklet. They would need to in order to evaluate the thermal performance of the house, the available heat from the sun, and the efficiency of the solar collector—matters that just don't receive adequate treatment here. This book is still a long way from being the concise and complete exposition that one associates with the word "handbook."

—Roger Douglass

**Solar Energy
Handbook**
The Landas'
1974; 153 pp

$6.50

from:
The Film Instruction
Company of America
2901 S. Wentworth Ave.
Milwaukee, WI 53207

SOLAR ENERGY

This book is apparently designed for the Junior High School market, although parts of it seem to be even more elementary, such as:

The food that we eat is a product of the sun's energy. The plants we consume every day obtained their energy for growth directly from sunlight by a process known as photosynthesis. And the meats we eat come from animals who also fed upon that plant life.

The coal and oil with which we heat our homes comes from under the earth. These fuels are actually the fossilized remains of vegetation that grew eons ago—on energy provided by the same sun that shines upon us today.

The author is especially enamored of, or perhaps just knowledgeable about, photovoltaic solar cells. Most of the book is devoted to how they work, their production, uses in space, applications on earth, school projects using them, and an appendix on where to buy them and the small motors they can run. This book seems unique among solar energy books in *not* discussing our present dependence on non-renewable energy sources (except in the section quoted above), or their depletion (except for brief mention in the Foreward contributed by Hubert Humphrey), or the environmental advantages of a switch to solar energy. The long and fascinating history of solar applications is barely exposed at all, and its future seems to be limited to using better solar cells. Quite a number of school projects are described, including a solar cell and motor operated Sun Tracker—most projects are from kits available from manufacturers.

I don't think this book begins to approach the quality of Franklyn Branley's *Solar Energy* or D.S. Halacy's paperback *Solar Science Projects*, which really explains how to make useful things from common materials.

—Roger Douglass

Solar Energy
John Hoke
1968; 82 pp

$3.45

from: Franklin Watts, Inc., 730 Fifth Ave.,
New York, New York 10019

SOLAR AND AEOLIAN ENERGY: PROCEEDINGS OF THE INTERNATIONAL SEMINAR AT SOUNION, GREECE, 1961

Here is almost an extension of the proceedings of the 1961 UN Conference in Rome, but with some emphasis on assessments and applications for Greece and other Mediterranean countries. Papers are in English or French. If you have a serious interest and some knowledge of a particular topic, it might be worthwhole to look through this book at a library sometime.

The topics and type of treatment range widely: there are a couple of papers on extracting water from humid air by condensation on rocks, one on hydroponic agriculture, one on concentrating palm and sugarcane juices by solar energy, several on the growth of algae in a "waste stabilization pond" for sewage treatment, water reclamation and algae production for feed or for fuel, and papers on the whole range of solar and wind energy applications. A valuable feature of this book is the inclusion of rather extensive discussion following some of the sessions.

—Roger Douglass

Solar and Aeolian Energy: Proceedings of the International Seminar at Sounion, Greece, 1961
Ed. by A. G. Spanides and A. D. Hatzikakidis
1964; 491 pp

Out of Print

distributed by:
Plenum Press
New York, NY

WIND AND SOLAR ENERGY: PROCEEDINGS OF THE NEW DELHI SYMPOSIUM

A very small but quite international conference, sponsored by UNESCO's Advisory Committee on Arid Zone Research, was the impetus for this book. Many of the papers dealt with sun and wind power in India. There's a report on wind power in Denmark and a fairly technical paper on wind power plant designed in Germany. Dr. V. Baum described solar energy investigations in the USSR (which were apparently dropped later) and F. Trombe described solar concentrators and furnaces in France.

One interesting paper estimated in detail the energy needs of an arid zone agricultural community of 40-50 families, and suggested ways they might be satisfied by wind power, solar heat and a small source of combustible vegetation. This paper interested the sponsoring Committee to the extent of recommending that the Director-General encourage the establishment of one or more such communities. The other recommendation was to establish a design for a simple standard pyrheliometer and stimulate its use in more widespread collection of data on solar insolation. It would certainly be nice if both recommendations had been acted upon

—Roger Douglass

P.S. I've been looking at this book in the Stanford Research Institute Library—a co-sponsor of the Arizona Solar Conferences of 1955. I notice that between 1959 and 1973 no one had checked this book out. But now almost all solar energy books are absent and this one was checked out four times in the last year.

Wind and Solar Energy: Proceedings of the New Dehli Symposium
1956;

Out of print

SOLAR ENERGY FOR PACIFIC NORTHWEST BUILDINGS

Here Prof. Reynolds describes Henry Mathew's home at Coos Bay, Oregon which receives an estimated 60% of its heat from solar collectors.

Prof. Reynolds also presents the results of his efforts to collect and evaluate solar climatic data for the cloudy northwest and shows graphs comparing available solar heat with house heating requirements in the Eugene - Corvallis area. Monthly maps of "percent of possible sunshine" throughout Oregon show large regional variations, so they can offer solar designers only qualitative guidance at best. The needed data for solar design is simply non-existant for most of the northwest.

As a first step toward further efforts to design with nature, there are "timetable charts" showing expected temperature, humidity, sky cover, and wind speed and direction at Eugene throughout the day and year. Pictures indicate the use of trees and vines for seasonal sun control for buildings.

—Roger Douglass

Solar Energy for
Pacific Northwest Buildings
John S. Reynolds
1974; 58 pp
$3.00

from:
The Center for Environmental Research
School of Architecture and Allied Arts
University of Oregon
Eugene, Oregon 97403

HANDBOOK OF FUNDAMENTALS (1972) APPLICATIONS (1974)

Large, definitive books published by the American Society of Heating Refrigerating and Air-Conditioning Engineers, Inc.

In the *Handbook of Fundamentals*, Chapter 17, "Thermal Insulation and Vapor Barriers," and Chapter 22, "Air-Conditioning Cooling Load," are of primary interest to the experimenter.

Chapter 59 of *Applications* is another article on solar energy by John Yellott. It is somewhat similar, but of more depth, than his article beginning on page 4 of the *Energy Primer*.

Handbook of Fundamentals (1972)
$33.00

Applications (1974)
$42.00

from:
ASHRAE (Sales Dept.)
345 East 47th Street
New York, NY 10017

HOW TO DESIGN AND BUILD A SOLAR SWIMMING POOL HEATER

A well done book on the physics, economics, and construction techniques of building a solar pool heater out of copper. The how-to-do-it

---

details are very complete.

How to Design and Build a Solar Swimming
Pool Heater
Francis de Winter
1974; 54 pp
free

from:
Copper Development Association
405 Lexington Avenue
New York, NY 10017

SOLAR ENERGY WARM AIR HOUSE HEATER

Here the Meinels' describe how to build several varieties of warm air heaters. Simple do-it-yourself plans are given for collector construction, various configurations of collector placement, and rock or water filled plastic bottle heat storage. Their designs are readily adaptable to mobile homes.

The bottles in the storage bin are spaced about 1 inch apart to allow the air from the fan to circulate readily. Open spaces are provided at each end of the bin to allow the air to distribute better into the various channels and levels of the bin. The bin is divided into channels and levels for structural reasons. Also, the weight of water in the stack of bottles, plus the temperature of about 160ºF, would cause the bottles to collapse slowly into spherical balloons. This is prevented by supporting each layer of bottles with a plywood floor resting on bricks which also form the channels.

Solar Energy Warm Air House Heater
Aden B. Meinel and Walter B. Meinel
1974; 20 pp
$5.00

from:
Helio Associates, Inc.
8230 E. Broadway
Tucson, Arizona 85710

SOLAR ENERGY

Informatics researchers combed through back issues of *Solar Energy* Journal and *Geliotekhnika, Proceedings of the UN Conference on New Sources of Energy, Introduction to the Utilization of Solar Energy* and many other titles to come up with a world perspective, by topic, of solar hardware. The sections on solar history and solar water heating around the world are excellent, and Russian solar activities are very completely documented. It is not a solar hardware how-to-do-it cookbook, but it might introduce you to many different approaches to solving your solar heating problem.

Solar Energy
1974; 473 pp
Order No. AD-778 846/6WE

$9.75 hardcopy

$2.25 microfiche

from:
National Technical Information Service
U.S. Department of Commerce
P.O. Box 1553
Springfield, Virginia 22151

LIVING WITH THE SUN

In 1957, the Association for Applied Solar Energy sponsored an international architectural competition to design a solar-heated residence. Not to exceed 2,000 sq. ft. or $30,000, the residence to be designed was for the "typical" family of two adults and two children.

If you're good at understanding architectural drawings, this book might give you several solar design ideas. Sixty pages of single family houses designed for the Sundown Ranch Estates in Arizona can become tedious, however.

Living with the Sun
1958; 78 pp
$10.00

from:
Microforms International Marketing Corp.
Fairview Park
Elmsford, New York 10523

SOLAR POWER

CRITERIA FOR THE PRELIMINARY DESIGN OF SOLAR-HEATED BUILDINGS

. . . is a manual for architects and builders and attempts to provide answers to many of the questions we are asked about solar house heating. This is a first edition. We hope to update it several times a year, adding charts and tables that will be useful to those working on the designs of solar heating systems.

Looks good for a start, has lots of practical installation advice.

Criteria for the Preliminary Design of
Solar-Heated Buildings
E. M. Barber and D. Watson
1974; 55 pp
$10.00

from:
Sunworks Inc.
669 Boston Post Road
Guilford, Connecticut 06437

FEDERAL SOLAR ACTIVITIES

There is a great deal of Federal interest in solar energy. The following reports give a good overview; your local library should be able to get copies for you to review.

H.R. 11864 Solar Heating and Cooling Demonstration Act of 1974,
Background and Legislative History
Subcommittee on Energy
Committee on Science and Astronautics
February 1974
(Serial L)

Solar Energy for Heating and Cooling
Subcommittee on Energy
Committee on Science and Astronautics
June 1973
(No. 13)

**Solar Energy Research:
A Multidisciplinary Approach**
Subcommittee on Energy
Committee on Science and Astronautics
December 1972
(Serial Z)

Bumper stickers shown on this page may be ordered for $0.50 each from Environmental Action of Colorado, 1100 14th Street, Denver, Colorado, 80202.

SOLAR ENERGY DIGEST

William Edmondson publishes the best, most up-to-date solar energy newsletter in the business, even though I strongly disagree with the $27.50 subscription rate for 12 issues. In spite of the price, the serious solar researcher will find SED the best way to keep current on state-of-the-art. Edmondson's been around the solar field a long time and seems to have good connections, hence good input.

SED comes regularly as clockwork, mailed by Ms. Edmondson and reproduced on bright yellow paper. It covers a broad range of solar related activities—from windmills to the cost and availability of rocks for a rock bed heat storage system. I think SED will grow with time into a combination newsletter and scholarly journal.

Solar Heated Buildings: A Brief Survey is now distributed by SED. Written by Wm. A. Shurcliff, the man whose book helped stop the SST disaster, it summarizes by state technical data on solar buildings that did exist, do exist, or are expected to exist very soon. The 4th Edition (July 1, 1974) includes notes and diagrams on 58 structures. A must if you're into solar heated structures.

Solar Energy Digest
Monthly
$27.50 per year

Solar Heated Buildings: A Brief Survey 1974; 36 pp	from: Solar Energy Digest P.O. Box 17776 San Diego, CA 92117

$5.00

SOLAR ENERGY THERMAL PROCESSES

If you're looking for a heavy mathematical treatment of solar energy theory, here it is. Written for engineers and scientists, it assumes a working knowledge of calculus. Excellent reference lists end each of the 15 chapters, and Appendix A is problems, "provided for those who may wish to use this as a textbook."

Solar Energy Thermal Processes
J.A. Duffie & W.A. Beckman
1974; 386 pp

$16.95

from:
John Wiley & Sons, Inc.
One Wiley Drive
Somerset, NJ 08873

PROJECT INDEPENDENCE: SOLAR ENERGY

A mind-boggling array of charts, scenarios, costs and timetables that lend credence to the early development and use of solar energy.

Project Independence Blueprint
Final Task Force Report
Solar Energy
1974; 554 pp
Stock No. 4118-00012

$6.20

from:
Superintendent of Documents
U.S. Government Printing Office
Washington, D.C. 20402

SOLAR ENERGY RESEARCH AND INFORMATION CENTER, INC.
Solar Energy Industries Association

If you write them for information, you get subscription rates for their newsletters, the *Solar Energy Washington Letter* and *Solar Energy Industry Report*. You get 26 approximately 4-page issues of each, plus four bonus issues of *Special Bulletin*, for $95.00 a year.

Operating at the same address is the Solar Energy Industries Association. The objectives of this group include, among others;

1. To foster and accelerate development and marketing of solar energy conversion systems through public, governmental, and industry communications.
2. To maintain an orderly industry with convenient access to components, systems, and other resources as the industry grows.
3. To advise opinion leaders in government, industry, the scientific community and other key publics.
4. To establish standards of nomenclature and measurements.
5. To identify and encourage responsible leadership personnel for service to the entire industry and in the public sector.
6. To encourage rising standards of performance, reliability and ethics.

Minimum annual dues are $200. The Association is compiling a *Directory of Membership and Solar Energy Industry Resource and Capability Guide.*
Solar Energy R & I Center, Inc. or
Solar Energy Industries Association
1001 Connecticut Avenue
Washington, D.C. 20036

SOLAR ENERGY SOCIETY OF AMERICA

This group is not to be confused with the well-established ISES. Here are a few paragraphs from their introductory letter:

Please consider the following an announcement and a personal invitation to you as a member of the International Solar Energy Society to become a Charter Member of the SOLAR ENERGY SOCIETY OF AMERICA.

The Society is seeking the support of the membership of the ISES to be the virtual technological backbone of its official journal slated for mid 1974 with a goal of over 100,000 subscribers by year end.

The journal will be a professional, informative publication aimed at the laymen of America. Its editorial and pictorial material will draw heavily from the scientific community, with subject matter spanning the earth and beyond, from biology to mechanics, and all other areas related to solar energy concepts and systems.

The journal will provide a communication interchange to bridge the gap between the solar energy information that abounds today and the practical application of that information. The Society will serve its members nationwide by being a central and vast reservoir of knowledge. An outstanding roster of advisors, who are prominent scientists, academicians, technologists and industrialists will help guide our efforts.

All of this dedicated to bringing the utilization of Solar Energy to reality in our national economy.

$25.00

Solar Energy Society of America
P.O. Box 4264
Torrance, CA 90510

A PRACTICAL SOLAR ENERGY HEATING AND COOLING SYSTEM, TB 73-10156

THE DEVELOPMENT OF A RESIDENTIAL HEATING AND COOLING SYSTEM USING NASA-DERIVED TECHNOLOGY

DEVELOPMENT OF A SOLAR-POWERED RESIDENTIAL HEATING AND COOLING SYSTEM

SOLAR SELECTIVE COATING ON ALUMINUM

The first of these is a two page NASA technical brief saying that solar heating and cooling using selective flat-plate collectors, water for thermal storage, and an ammonia/water absorption air conditioner is technically and economically feasible. A request for additional detailed information concerning TB 73-10156 yielded a copy of the second title above, a report from Lockheed-Huntsville to NASA-MSFC dated November 1972. This report describes a rather sophisticated analysis of flat-plate collectors (perhaps the most accurate to date), studies possible phase change materials for heat storage (they later decided sensible heat storage using water was best), examines systems selection and optimization of conditions for running an absorption heat pump, and describes a computer performance study of an "optimized" system using the NASA-developed collector and Huntsville weather and solar data.

A later request for added information regarding TB 73-10156 yielded a report dated May 10, 1974 bearing the third title above. Its main concern is comparing calculated with tested performance for the NASA collector, which is a selective-coated Roll-Bond® aluminum tube-in-sheet with wire-mesh-supported Tedlar

cover sheets. This study is preliminary to a system prototype trial at Marshall Space Flight Center. Three office trailers will simulate a residence to be heated and cooled using a 1967 model Arkla lithium bromide/water absorption air conditioner. Perhaps a suitable ammonia model wasn't available.

The final title above is a description of an electrolytic deposition process for making a selective-black surface on aluminum. NASA has applied for a US patent on this process, but they apparently are willing to license its use at no charge. The process can give a solar absorptivity as high as 0.93 and a thermal emissivity as low as 0.06. This is a "nickel-black" type of coating similar to that developed by Tabor and used on galvanized iron solar water heaters in Israel, so it should be fairly resistant to deterioration with time. Although the process only involves immersion and electrolysis in chemical baths, it's a multi-step process and close process control together with the development of a "knack" would undoubtedly be necessary for good results. So it's not a do-it-yourself operation for very many of us. It is really this selective coating that makes possible fairly efficient collector operation at the $200^\circ - 240^\circ F$ temperatures required by absorption air conditioners. For use in solar heating only, the selective coating isn't at all necessary.

—Roger Douglass

A Practical Solar Energy Heating and Cooling System, TB 73-10156

The Development of a Residential Heating and Cooling System Using NASA-Derived Technology

Development of a Solar-Powered Residential Heating and Cooling System

Solar Selective Coating on Aluminum

All of the above titles are available from:
Technology Utilization Office
Marshall Space Flight Center
Code A&PS-TU
Marshall Space Flight Center, Alabama 35812

WEATHER

We all talk about the weather a lot, but how many of us know where to get good information concerning it? For a start we can turn to the National Climatic Center in Asheville, North Carolina. NCC is the largest climatological data facility of the Environmental Science Services Administration (ESSA), which in turn is part of the National Oceanic and Atmospheric Administration (NOAA), which in turn is part of the U.S. Department of Commerce. (NOAA is often pronounced Noah, as in Noah and the Ark.) Formed in 1970, NOAA brought together the functions of ESSA, the bureau of Commercial Fisheries, Marine Game Fish Research Program, Marine Minerals Technology Center, National Oceanographic Data Center, National Oceanographic Instrumentation Center, National Data Buoy Development Project, National Sea Grant Program and elements of the U.S. Lake Survey. The Federal government works in strange and wonderous ways.

NOAA publications are detailed in *Selective Guide to Climatic Data Sources.* I would recommend this book to people trying to determine what weather information is available for their area. It is confusing in its details at first, but persevere and it will eventually make sense. If you order this book, ask for an updated price list. And if you order *from* this book, send your order for everything but the *Climatic Atlas of the United States* (see review in the wind chapter) to NOAA, even though it tells you to mail orders to the Superintendent of Documents, US Government Printing Office. NOAA has been fast and efficient in responding to my requests while the GPO hasn't always been so good.

For a good, cheap overview of solar radiation in Langleys by months for the entire U.S., order *Mean Daily Solar Radiation, Monthly and Annual.* It's a double-sided map with one large summary chart of numerical solar radiation data. A sampling of NOAA publications by title follows:
Climatological Data
Climatological Data, National Summary
Local Climatological Data
Hourly Precipitation Data
Monthly Climatic Data for the World
Climatic Guide
Average Precipitation in the United States
Daily Normals of Temperature and Heating
  Degree Days
Heating Degree Day Normals
Sunshine and Cloudiness at Selected Stations
  in the United States

Selective Guide to Climatic Data Sources
1969; 94 pp

$1.00

Mean Daily Solar Radiation, Monthly and
1964; 16" x 22"   **Annual**

$0.10

from:
Environmental Data Service
National Climatic Center
Federal Building
Asheville, North Carolina 28801

SOLAR PRODUCT MANUFACTURERS

The Library of Congress is compiling a list of "solar product manufacturers." I have no idea when it will be ready or how complete it will be, but they will put you on the mailing list for a copy when it is ready. Free

Reference Section
Science & Technology Division
Library of Congress
10 First St., S.E.
Washington, D.C. 20540

SOLAR ENERGY: ITS TIME IS NEAR

One point needs emphasis: no breakthroughs are needed to make solar energy feasible. All that is required is to engineer solar energy systems which are less costly than current designs by a factor of 1.5 to 4 depending on the type of application—except that considerably greater cost reductions will be necessary to make practical photovoltaic solar plants.

It is fair to say that the engineering problems to be solved in making solar energy practical are considerably simpler than those of the breeder reactor and far simpler than those which must be solved in devising a practical fusion reactor. Yet it is also fair to say that a substantial research and development program, together with a vigorous implementation program, will be required to confirm that solar energy may in fact provide a significant portion of the nation's future energy needs.

This latter statement is particularly true if the US energy "need" continues to grow exponentially into the next century. In fact, his final projection is that a total US solar investment of $300 billion (about a thousand 1973 dollars per capita) by the year 2000 would only mean that solar energy is carrying 13 per cent of the load at that time.

The solar applications upon which Mr. Morrow bases his projections are: solar home heating, shopping center or industrial plant (why not community?) sized solar-powered total-energy systems, and land based solar-thermal central power plants. These systems are described, and their costs estimated, in some detail. But the basic point is that fuel costs are going to rise faster than the capital costs of solar energy apparatus, so those solar systems which are not economic now soon will be. Mr. Morrow's estimates were based on 1972 fuel costs and interest rates, so they are already obsolete.

Mr. Morrow did not suggest this, but if the Federal Power Commission were to suspend the franchises that prohibit anyone but the big power companies from selling electricity, his projections indicate that by 1980 small local total-energy plants could be selling heat and electric power from the sun at competitive rates.
                                    —Roger Douglass

Solar Energy: Its Time Is Near
Walter F. Morrow, Jr.
Technology Review, Vol. 76, No. 2
December 1973; pp. 30-43

$1.50   ($10/year, 8 issues, US)

from:
Technology Review
Room E19-430
Massachusetts Institute of Technology
Cambridge, Massachusetts 02139

SOLARWIND

Solarwind is a brand new newsletter on solar and wind energy. Their first sample issue totaled 6 pages, reviewed some solar and wind energy formulas, contained a full-page picture of a Windworks windmill, and carried one page of ads and information on how-to-order future copies. All this cost one dollar. They plan to publish six issues per year for $4.50. Solarwind looks like a publishing redundancy as long as we have *Alternative Sources of Energy* Newsletter.

Mallman Optics and Electronics
836 South 113
West Allis, Wisconsin 53214

HELIOTECHNOLOGY

Heliotechnology is the English title of the Russian journal *Geliotekhnika.* Their solar

energy journal, published by the Academy of Sciences UzbSSR, is a very technical magazine and is for the serious specialist in the field. There are six issues per volume.

Allerton Press, Inc.
150 5th Avenue
New York, NY 10011

HARDCOPY
Vols. 1-9 (1965-1973) at $110.00/volume
(Allerton does not provide microfiche or microfilm versions. There is a 5% discount on all orders for a full set of back volumes.)

National Technical Information Service
U.S. Department of Commerce
P.O. Box 1553
Springfield, Virginia 22151

HARDCOPY
Vols. 1-2 (1965-1966) at $6.00/issue
(NTIS does not provide microfiche versions.)

SOLAR ENERGY UTILIZATION COMPENDIUM

The Western Research Application Center (WESRAC), University of Southern California, is publishing a compendium listing almost 2,500 citations and abstracts relating to solar energy. The ultimate literature reference?

Solar Energy Utilization Compendium

$50.00

from:
WESRAC/USC
809 West 34th Street
Los Angeles, CA 90007

SOLAR ENERGY JOURNAL

Back issues of *Solar Energy*, the Journal of the ISES, can be purchased from:

Microforms International Marketing Corp.
Fairview Park
Elmsford, New York 10523

HARD COPY
Vols. 1-11 (1957-1967) at $10.00 per volume
Vols. 12-13 (1968/69-1970/71) at $28.00 per volume
Vols. 14-15 (1972-1973) at $30.00 per volume
Complete Set Vols. 1-15 (1957-1973) $204.00

INTERNATIONAL SOLAR ENERGY SOCIETY

ISES is the association of people interested in solar energy. There are no membership requirements. For your membership fee, you get *Solar Energy*, the excellent quarterly journal of the ISES; *Solar News and Views*, an occasional newsletter of U.S. Chapter activities; and *ISES News*, the occasional newsletter of the International organization. Pergamon Press in England prints *Solar Energy*, but because of economic problems there, delivery has been a little erratic.

ISES membership has been exploding in the last year, and there's no reason why you can't help it continue to grow. Join the ISES and support the dissemination of solar energy research results.

$20.00

International Solar Energy
Society, c/o Dr. W. Klein,
Sec./Treas.,
Smithsonian Radiation
Biology Laboratory
12441 Parklawn Dr.,
Rockville, Md. 20852

SOLAR HEATING PROJECT AT NAVAL AMMUNITION DEPOT, HAWTHORNE, NEVADA

Wouldn't it be wonderful if this year a low cost home and hot water solar heating unit were made available to homeowners? Why isn't it available this year?

If technological welfare were not so prevalent in this country, solar heating and cooling of homes could be in mass existence now. All too many universities, research groups, and corporations are on technological welfare; therefore, technology is retarded. True research is a path to knowledge and the solution of problems. The research stratagem, on the other hand, is an end in itself whose main purpose is to sustain the research workers in a comfortable way of life. Keeping funds generated is more important than solving the problem. In fact, the corruption of research called the research stratagem is spreading rapidly.

But, at the Naval Ammunition Depot, Hawthorne, Nevada, in spite of technological welfare, two homes were heated this past winter with solar heat.

We became interested in alternate sources of energy last fall when the energy crisis affected us. Our people read and studied material, then talked to several authorities and experts in the field of alternate energy resources.

We have 625 civilian and military homes to heat as well as industrial, production, storage, and office buildings. The fuel crisis came to a head for us on Tuesday, December 11, 1973, when our supplier of propane fuel (most of our homes are heated by propane) called and stated he would no longer supply us with fuel after Friday, December 14. He had a fixed price contract and was losing $5000 per week. Bankruptcy was facing him as a small businessman. We did get the contract changed to include an escalation clause, but with one stroke of the pen we tripled our fuel cost. Consequently, on December 14 we decided we would make our test or demonstration of solar heating this winter.

Via the phone we talked to many of the experts and authorities. Our problem was simply stated: "We want to be heating two homes with solar energy by the first of February." After all the talk and all we had read, the excuses given for not being able to help us were amazing. Excuses were as follows: "Our simulation program isn't quite complete." "We won't have our collector completely designed for another year." "We haven't gathered enough data yet." "We need a six month feasibility study." And so on. Several groups visited us at Hawthorne but still the same excuses were given. Finally, on December 21, Dr. Jerry Plunkett of Materials Consultants Inc., Denver, Colorado visited us. He stated he had a design ready and would install two units. Remember, this was on Friday, December 21. The ground breaking occurred on January 3 and the official ribbon cutting on January 29. However, we had been heating the two homes for a week before that. Christmas holidays and a snow storm slowed the project by one week.

When we first started researching the possibility of using solar heat, the money figures scared us. One hundred, two hundred, three hundred thousand dollars for a feasibility study. One hundred fifty thousand—three hundred thousand for installation. It just didn't seem good economics to invest two or three hundred thousand dollars on a heating unit or even $30,000 for an $18,000 government home. In fact, we only had $17,000 to spend on solar heat for the two homes. The project ended costing $15,000 or $7,500 per home.

Besides the economic restraint other restrictions were imposed upon us:

a. Energy consumption of ancillary machinery and equipment had to be less than the energy generated in terms of heating. The conversion and storage of solar energy was to be less expensive in terms of BTU's and dollars, a double-barreled objective.

b. Navy housing restrictions required that the collectors be placed 120 feet behind the houses.

c. Two homes had to be heated by February 1, 1974, therefore, materials had to be used that were available. For example, mylar was used as a cover because it was immediately available. The main frame was made of wood, again because it was available.

The point is, all the materials used in the system were off-the-shelf items available to anyone. No exotic materials or pieces of equipment were used.

As another example, car radiators were used for heat exchangers. We used aluminum cross cut sections from beer cans for absorber panels.

A cursory explanation of the system should be given at this point in layman's terms:

a. The collector is a flat plate collector facing directly south at a 55° angle.

b. The collector is 45' by 15' or 675 square feet.

c. The solar radiation passes through the plastic covering (two layers) and heats the black backing surface which in turn heats the ambient air.

d. The air is now hot. Next, we have to get the heat from the air to the home when needed (the average air temperature was from 170°F to 200°F). The lower left hand corner of the collector panel contains a blower fan and two car radiators. The fan circulates the air to the right in a manifold at the top. The air then comes down the far left module heating the water in the heat exchangers. The hot water (approximately 170°F) is circulated from the heat exchangers to tanks buried behind the collector.

e. The tanks (2100 gallon) are storage units for the hot water where the heat can be stored for later use at night or during extended periods of cloudiness.

f. The collector is the heart of the system. It captures and transmits the heat from the sun. All interior surfaces are painted a dull black to maximize absorption of the sun's energy. Solar collection efficiency is improved by adding an absorber layer consisting of wire mesh painted dull black. For experimental purposes we also made panels with cut cross sections of used beer cans between wire mesh.

g. The hot water in the banks is transported to the house through 3/4" pipe and the exact opposite takes place from the collector. Hot water is converted to hot air through a heat exchanger (car radiator) placed in the cold air intake of the home's regular forced air furnace system. The home's regular forced air system is then used to distribute the heat.

It might be important to mention here that at Hawthorne the temperature during December through February and most of March is below freezing every night and even below zero at times.

You might think the finished collector looks a little crude. We think that it does and it reminds us of the Wright Brothers' first airplane. But, like the Wright Brothers' first airplane, if they had waited to design the 747 we still would not be off the ground. Today, the airplane is off the ground and beyond the sound barrier because someone made the first move; and that is what we decided to do—MOVE! Our system is not the optimal system. In no way are we saying this is the final solution to the solar heating problem, but we're a lot closer to the solution because we spent $15,000. How many groups have spent $15,000 or a lot more just writing a proposal? As a user of the system we're happy. It's heating the homes. In fact, we found the humidity and comfort level to be better than our regular forced air system.

Building such a system involved no physics or new technology, we used standard procedures and materials. We term it "sophisticated plumbing." The same solar concept has existed for hundreds of years, but as witnessed by the funding figures, as previously stated, many universities and research groups need millions of dollars and years to reinvent the wheel. We've talked to a great many young people and they want to do something, they want to move, but those in authority and control are on technological welfare. They just don't know what they can do until the government tells them or hands them their welfare check.

What we want is an operational system with off-the-shelf material at a price every homeowner can afford. Our $7,500 experimental model cost too much. With mass production we believe it can be lowered to $2,000.

Finally, we cannot give enough praise to Dr. Jerry Plunkett who gave us a system instead of excuses. Also, Captain E. J. Kirschke, Commanding Officer at NAD Hawthorne, without whose approval, leadership, and guidance the project would not have been possible.

—R. R. Dempsey
W. A. Wallace

PATENTS
To all to whom these Presents shall come— Greetings

The issue of patents for new discoveries has given a spring to invention beyond my conception.
—Thomas Jefferson

The word patent is derived from litterae patentes which means "open letters." "Open letters" doesn't seem to have anything to do with manufacture or technology, but it does reflect the intention of the framers of our patent system, which was to insure that new inventions and technology became publicly available. In return for making a new process or invention public, the inventor secures the sole right to use or assign his invention and collect royalties for a period of seventeen years after the patent is issued. In protecting the rights of the inventor, the patent system creates an incentive for new invention for the benefit of the public. After a patent expires, the patent becomes public domain and it may be manufactured and used by anyone.

An important by-product of the US patent system is the vast research facility it has created. Patents contain a wealth of information, and while use of the invention is the exclusive property of the inventor, use of the information is not. The United States Patent Office will send you a copy of any patent for only $0.50, you can pay someone to conduct a search for you ($150 on up), you can visit a regional patent library, or you can visit the Search Room, U.S. Patent Office, Crystal Plaza, 2021 Jefferson Davis Highway, Arlington, Virginia.

Patents in the Search Room, some 4 million of them, are arranged by type of invention. The first step when you get to the patent library is to consult the Manual of Classification to find the class and sub-class codes for the type of invention you want. Solar collectors, for instance, are found under Class 126, STOVES AND FURNACES, and Sub-Class 271, HEATERS, SOLAR, WATER. Once you have these numbers, it is simply a matter of finding the apppropriate stacks of patents on the shelves.

If it is just general information you are looking for on a type of invention, it is best to look through the groups of patents arranged by class and sub-class. But if you want specific information on a single patent, it is easier to find it among the microfilm patents that are arranged by number. To use the microfilm files, you must know either the name of the inventor of the patent number. There is a card catalog listing inventors alphabetically which will give you the patent number and the class and sub-class designations. With the patent number, you can go directly to the microfilm cabinets, retrieve the patent and read it on one of the reader-printers in the Search Room.

Unlike most libraries, you are expected to reshelve the patents when you are finished with them. Like most libraries, you are expected not to rip them off. The patents are in piles, not in bound volumes, so it is easy to run off with them. It is just as easy to make yourself a copy on machines provided for that purpose. On many patents, it becomes cheaper to order a complete patent. The Search Room is mostly used by attorneys investigating the patentability of new inventions, and it is assumed that these professionals are scrupulously honest. Eventually the Search Room may be limited to the exclusive use of attorneys if the general public is found incapable of viewing these patents as a national treasure to be protected and preserved for the benefit of all its citizens. I was told by a Patent Office employee that about 5% of all patents are missing, and this limits the useability of the collection for complete patent searches.

About two dozen public libraries in major cities throughout the country have printed copies of all the patents, arranged numerically. They are:

Albany, NY	University Library
Atlanta, GA	Georgia Tech Library (incomplete)
Boston, MA	Public Library
Buffalo, NY	Buffalo & Erie County Public Library
Chicago, IL	Public Library
Cincinnati, OH	Public Library
Cleveland, OH	Public Library
Columbus, OH	Ohio St. Univ. Library
Detroit, MI	Public Library
Kansas City, MO	Linda Hall Library (incomplete)
Los Angeles, CA	Public Library
Madison, WI	St. Historical Society
Milwaukee, WI	Public Library
Newark, NJ	Public Library
New York, NY	Public Library
Philadelphia, PA	Franklin Institute
Pittsburgh, PA	Carnegie Library
Providence, RI	Public Library
St. Louis, MO	Public Library
Stillwater, OK	Oklahoma A&M Library
Sunnyvale, CA	Public Library (beginning 1962)
Toledo, OH	Public Library

Many other libraries subscribe to the Patent Official Gazette which records the text of patents issued in a given year. It would be very time consuming to do a complete search in most libraries because the patents are not stored by classification. But if you know either the name of the patentee (be careful not to confuse this with the assignee) or the patent number, it is easy to find what you want in the Gazette. Libraries that have the Gazette or a set of patents should also have the Index of Patents. This lists the patentees and, starting in 1955, the patent numbers arranged by classification. Prior to 1955 there was just a list of patentees and a list of inventions.

You might want to observe one caution in looking at patents. The Patent Office makes every effort to see that patents are granted on inventions which are useful and which work, but this does not insure that a patented device has actually been built and tested. Be cautious and don't always take them at face value; with this in mind, you can still learn a lot from patents.

So far we have only considered retrieving information from the patent files. If you think you have a patentable idea and want to pursue the subject further, read General Information Concerning Patents and send for additional publications listed in it. If you're really serious about securing a patent, read Ideas, Inventions,

and Patents. This is a detailed book on how to develop and protect patents. If you want a more hands-on book that takes you beyond the patenting process into managing, manufacturing and selling your ideas or hardware, read Inventor's Handbook.

The patenting process generally takes a minimum of $1000 and several years wait. Here it is best to hire a good patent attorney—this is one person who can save you a lot of headaches. Even if you do not want to exploit your idea, it may make sense to patent it in the public interest. You can save a few dollars in fees and prevent someone else from ripping off the world with the idea. If your idea relates to "energy," it is quite possible your application may get special (faster) consideration.

—Gary Hewitt
Portland, Oregon

General Information Concerning Patents
1973; 43 pp
and
Obtaining Information From Patents
1973; 4 pp

One copy each free on request

$0.50 ea for Patents
$1.00 ea for Plant Patents
$0.20 ea for Trademarks
from:
Commissioner of Patents, Wash., D.C. 20231

Ideas, Inventions, and Patents
Robert A. Buckles
1957; 270 pp
$12.50

from: John Wiley & Sons, Inc., 1 Wiley Dr.
Somerset, NJ 08873
or: 1530 S. Redwood Rd., Salt Lake City, UT 84104

or: WHOLE EARTH TRUCK STORE

Inventor's Handbook
T. W. Fenner and J. L. Everett
1969; 309 pp
$8.50

from: Chemical Publishing Co., Inc. 200 Park Ave. S
Dept. 542, New York, NY 10003

or WHOLE EARTH TRUCK STORE

DISTILLATION

SOLAR DISTILLATION AS A MEANS OF MEETING SMALL-SCALE WATER DEMANDS

A well-designed, durable, basin-type solar still will cost in the neighborhood of $1 per square foot, produce 0.1 gallon of fresh water per squart foot on a good day, and average 25 gallons per square foot per year production in a favorable climate. This book describes designs of large stills that have been built, discusses materials and economics, and gives detailed mathematical theory of operation. There are 30 figures, 6 tables, 29 references and a bibliography. Personal survival stills

are not discussed. Combinations of solar with other heat input and fresh water production with other functions receive very limited treatment. *Solar Distillation. . .* was written by solar still experts from around the world.
—Roger Douglass

Solar Distillation As A Means Of Meeting Small-Scale Water Demands
1970; 86 pp
Sales No. E.70.11.B.1
$2.50

from:
Sales Section
United Nations
New York, NY 10017

or WHOLE EARTH TRUCK STORE

Varishade®is "a coating that shades when dry but is practically transparent when wet."

Three ounces of Sun Clear® will cover approximately 400 square feet of flexible plastic and will cost $3.00+.

Solar Sunstill, Inc.
from:
Solar Sunstill, Inc.
Setauket, New York 11733

VITA GREEN FARMS

3 to 7 gallon per week standard unit
3 ft x 4 ft collector, do-it-yourself installation.

Vita Green Farms
$200.00 plus tax and shipping
from:
Vita Green Farms, P.O. B. 878, Vista, CA 92083

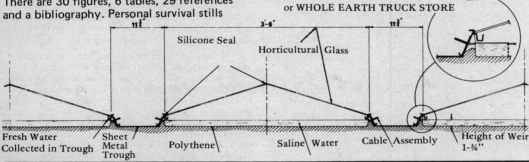

Fresh Water Collected in Trough | Silicone Seal | Horticultural Glass | Sheet Metal Trough | Polythene | Saline Water | Cable Assembly | Height of Weir 1-¾"

SUN STILL SURVIVAL KIT

Kit contains 25 sq. ft. of plastic, a 42 inch drinking straw, collapsible water container, plastic liner for polluted water and instructions. Dig a hole, place cup at bottom, cover the hole with plastic, and watch the water drip into the cup.

Sun Still Survival Kit $2.49
from:
Dick Cepek, 9201 California Ave., South Gate, CA 90280

HOW TO MAKE A SOLAR STILL (PLASTIC COVERED)

Hard facts, bill-of-materials, detailed drawings for a four foot wide by any length solar still. Basic, good.

How to Make a Solar Still (Plastic Covered)
1973; 13 pp; Do-It-Yourself-Leaflet L-1 **$1.00**

SIMPLE SOLAR STILL FOR THE PRODUCTION OF DISTILLED WATER

This is a description of a simple solar distillation unit designed primarily for use in service stations with the object of providing distilled water for automobile batteries. Distilled water is very necessary for battery maintenance, especially in warm and arid regions. The still should produce under normal operating conditions an <u>average</u> of three litres of distilled water per day.

Simple Solar Still for the Production of Distilled Water
1967; 6 pp; Technical Report No. T 17 **$1.00**

PLANS FOR A GLASS AND CONCRETE SOLAR STILL

In 1969, Brace built a 200 gallon per day still in Haiti. This report is the plans and specifications for that still. If you're in the market for a 50 foot by 75 foot still made from concrete, butyl, rubber, glass and silicone glass sealant, here's the answer. Very clear and understandable drawings.

Plans for a Glass and Concrete Solar Still
1972; 8 pp + 2 drawings;
Technical Report No. T 58   **$4.00**

from:
Brace Research Institute
Macdonald College of McGill University
Ste. Anne de Bellevue
Quebec, Canada H9x 3M1

When you pay Brace Research Institute by check or money order, remember to add a $0.25 handling fee.

SOLAR SUNSTILL, INC.

Sun Clear® is "a non-toxic, sprayable coating that converts the normal hydrophobic (nonwettable) surface of all plastics and many metals to a permanent hydrophilic (wettable) condition. Dripping is eliminated in greenhouses and up to 50% more light is transmitted through the treated plastic." This sounds ideal for plastic covered stills.

SUNWATER COMPANY

Complete automatic system delivered and installed in Southern California.
1 gallon per day $380.00
1½ gallon per day $420.00
2 gallons per day $465.00
Do-It-Yourself installation.

Sunwater Company
from:
Sunwater Co., 1112 Pioneer Way, El Cajon, CA 92020

For further information on solar distillation, see the fourteen articles that appeared in Vol. VI, UN NEW SOURCES OF ENERGY (1961), the two articles that appeared in Vol. 14, No. 3 (February 1973) of SOLAR ENERGY Journal, the nine articles that appeared in Vol. 14, No. 4 (March 1973) of SOLAR ENERGY Journal, or contact the Sea Water Conversion Laboratory, University of California, Berkeley, CA 94720. The movie WATER FROM THE SUN (see Audio-Visual section) is also educational.

DRYING

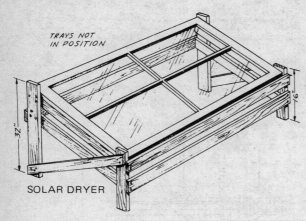

TRAYS NOT IN POSITION

32"

SOLAR DRYER

HOME STORAGE OF VEGETABLES AND FRUITS

Another book on canning, freezing, curing and drying. While the drying chapter is not as complete as that of the other two drying books mentioned here, it does give basic plans for various types of dryers—solar, oven, stove, and electric.

Home Storage of Vegetables and Fruits
Evelyn V. Loveday
1973; 152 pp
$3.00

from:
Garden Way Publishing Company
Charlotte, Vermont 05445

or WHOLE EARTH TRUCK STORE

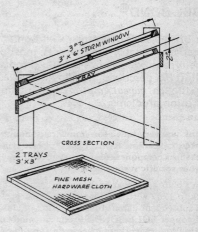

3 FT.
3' × 6' STORM WINDOW
TRAY
CROSS SECTION
2 TRAYS
3' × 3'
FINE MESH
HARDWARE CLOTH

A NATURAL CONVECTION SOLAR CROP DRYER

A new type of solar dryer consisting of a flat plate collector, a drying cabinet and a dehumidifier has been developed for various types of crop drying. A sloped flat plate collector heats the air and passes it by natural convection into a drying cabinet where it removes water from the fresh crop. The cooled moist air then falls to the bottom of the drying cabinet and is pulled through the dehumidifier and back into the base of the flat plate collector by the upward convection draught generated by the collector. Water is removed from the system as a liquid and the system operates without any mechanical aid.

A Natural Convection Solar Crop Dryer
O. St. C. Headley and B.G.F. Springer
10 pp
free

from:
Department of Chemistry
University of the West Indies
St. Augustine, Trinidad

'SOLAR-ELECTRIC' CROP DRYER PROGRESS REPORT

SOLAR HEAT FOR DRYING SHELLED CORN

In late 1973, the moisture content of 2,800 bushels of shelled corn was dropped from 20% to 14% using 4794 KwH of solar assisted electrical drying, as opposed to the 12,000 - 14,400 KwH that would normally be used with just electrical drying. Plastic covered solar collectors were added to the outside of an 18 foot diameter corn bin, with a 7½ HP auxiliary fan to provide circulation. This paper tells how they did it. A simple straightforward scheme that worked. I think Mr. Peterson is doing some of the most exciting dryer research work in the country.

'Solar-Electric' Crop Dryer Progress Report
Wm. H. Peterson
1973; 10 pp
free

Solar Heat for Drying Shelled Corn
Wm. H. Peterson
1973; 14 pp
Paper No. NC73-302
free

from:
Coop. Ext. Service
Col. of Agric. & Biol. Sciences
South Dakota State University
Brookings, South Dakota 57006

HOW TO MAKE A SOLAR CABINET DRYER FOR AGRICULTURAL PRODUCE

Hands-on plans for a small dryer. See John Yellott's article for further details.

How to Make a Solar Cabinet Dryer for Agricultural Produce
1973; 11 pp
Do-It-Yourself Leaflet L-6
$1.00

from:
Brace Research Institute
Macdonald College of McGill University
Ste. Anne de Bellevue 800
Quebec, Canada

When you pay Brace Research Institute by check or money order, remember to add a $0.25 handling fee.

My wife, Dian, recommends that you see the following for proven drying procedures and other helpful hints.

STOCKING UP

A thorough book on all aspects of food preservation. Written with the usual Rodale care for the life-giving values of food. The drying section is basic, simplified, with some good charts. With some adapting, it could be a guide for solar drying.

Nothing is added, and only water is taken away. You can dry food from your garden with what was once common knowledge. Drying is not difficult, but to have a good dried product you must follow directions carefully. The faster you work, the higher will be the vitamin content of the dried food, and the better the flavor and cooking quality. In the drying process, most of the water content is, of course, removed. On a pound-for-pound basis, the dried food then has a substantially increased concentration of many nutrients, especially minerals. However, there is a loss of some vitamins, most notably, vitamins C and A. These two are usually significantly lowered in drying and subsequent storage, and this fact should be kept in mind when considering drying as a means of preservation.

Stocking Up
1973; 351 pp
$8.95

from:
Rodale Press, Inc., Book Division
33 East Minor
Emmaus, Pennsylvania 10849

or WHOLE EARTH TRUCK STORE

DRY IT—YOU'LL LIKE IT

A recipe book of drying foods. Gourmet from page one, like dry-your-own birthday cake and zucchini chips for dips. Yummy.

The authors contend that 110°F is the maximum drying temperature for any plant drying task. Written for use with a dryer utilizing a thermostatically-controlled, wall-type heater with a circulating fan, the information presented could be adapted to your solar dryer needs.

Dry It—You'll Like It
G. MacManiman
1973; 64 pp
$3.95

from:
Living Foods Dehydrators
P.O. Box 546
Fall City, Washington 98024

or WHOLE EARTH TRUCK STORE

PUTTING FOOD BY

In addition to thorough discussions of canning, freezing and curing, *Putting Food By* has an excellent chapter on drying. Procedures, equipment, a few paragraphs on solar dryers, and lots of practical tips on drying fruits, vegetables, herbs and meats. This is the only book that talks about bacteria growth and control in the food drying process. It thoroughly evaluates dryer tray materials, including the problems presented by food acidity.

Putting Food By
R. Hertzberg, B. Vaughan and J. Greene
1973; 372 pp
$4.50

from:
Stephen Greene Press
Brattleboro, Vermont 05301

or WHOLE EARTH TRUCK STORE

For more information on hardware, see the 5 articles on solar drying in Vol V, UN *New Sources of Energy* (1961), the article by G.O.G. Lof in Vol. 6, No. 4 (1962) of *Solar Energy* Journal, and occasional other articles in the same publication.

COLLECTORS
ROLL-BOND®

For off-the-shelf collectors, Roll-Bond® flat plates are probably the cheapest, most durable tube-type products mass-produced today. John Yellott has described them in his article. Remember, though, *caveat emptor* when it comes to corrosion problems.

Gentlemen:

Thank you very much for your recent inquiry and interest concerning ROLL-BOND® plate-type heat exchanger components for use as solar energy collectors in your specific system design.

Olin's plate-type heat exchanger innovation dates back to 1952 with development of the processes and subsequent patent for production of aluminum and copper ROLL-BOND® Products commencing in 1955. Product marketing began with production of "Tailor-Made" ROLL-BOND® panels for use as evaporators in non-frost-free refrigerators. To date, the household refrigeration industry remains our largest customer, although our products have proven successful in various other applications ranging from ice makers to space radiator panels for thermal control heating and cooling the Apollo spacecraft Command Module.

At the present time, Olin Brass is the sole manufacturer of ROLL-BOND® panels in the U.S.A. Presently we have the capabilities of producing approximately 1,200,000 square feet monthly (in addition to our regular business) and in a short period of time (approximately 90-120 days) could increase production by an additional 600,000 square feet per month. Our present plant is well adapted to the production of Solar Energy Collector panels. We have excess rolling capacity and with a minimum of capital expenditure could expand the limiting facilities to greatly increase our capacity of finished product.

* *

OLIN ARTICLE FB-7610
Size: 17" x 50" (.060" gauge)
Material: Alloy 1100 Aluminum, 2-Side Inflated, Square Sheared to Size, TiO$_2$ Stopweld
Finish: "B" (Standard Mill)
Connectors: Two (2) heliarc welded to panel edges, including caps for shipping (Size: 1/2" O.D. x .050" wall x 3" long)
PRICING:
Quantity	Unit Price
1 to 20 pieces	$20.00 each

PLUS $15.00 PACKING CHARGE PER SHIPMENT

Note: This particular design is considered a "typical" part for use as a solar collector; therefore, a "special" run of parts was produced for retention and ordering as a STOCK ITEM in small quantities. Shipment could be made with as little as a 1 to 3 day notice.

Information on the Roll-Bond® products is available from the manufacturer:

Olin Brass/ Roll-Bond Products, East Alton, Ill. 62024

ECONOCOIL

An old line heat exchanger manufacturing company has discovered that their products can be painted black and used as solar collectors. Their products seem to be well made and durable. Prices are negotiable, based on order size.

GENERAL SPECIFICATIONS:
1. Allowable operating pressure: up to 75 PSIG
2. Thickness: approx 22 ga. = approx .029"
3. Material: carbon steel or stainless steel
4. Weight: approx. 55 lbs for 2' x 10' size
5. Finish: supplied as welded with paint to be applied by others
6. Pressure drop: usually less than 5 PSI for usual low flow rates in this service
7. Carbon steel is generally considered suitable for closed recirculating systems using glycol or treated water
8. Stainless steel is ideal for swimming pool water and for once through systems such as heating tap water

Tranter Manufacturing, Inc., 735 E. Hazel Street, Lansing, Michigan 48909

REVERE COPPER AND BRASS

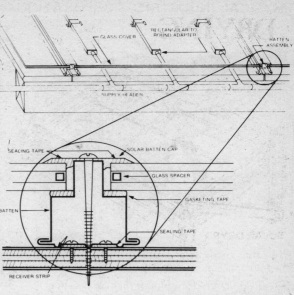

The Revere Solar Energy Collector is an extension of the established Revere System of Laminated Panel Construction which consists of copper sheet laminated to a plywood core to make an easily-installed copper composite building panel.

The solar collector has a flat, blackened copper surface which absorbs the sun's heat and transfers it to a fluid which is circulated through the panels in rectangular tubes. To convert the Revere laminated panel to a solar collector, a copper batten is added to the standard 2' x 8' panel. The batten, which snaps into a receiver strip, supports one or two layers of glass or other transparent material. Each solar collector panel uses from two to five tubes depending on efficiency requirements.

Revere Solar Energy Collectors are supplied with simple adapter fittings to facilitate the connection of the rectangular tubes to conventional round copper water tubes.

Revere Copper & Brass, Inc., POB 151, Rome NY 13740

PPG INDUSTRIES, INC.

Basically our collector is designed similar to our Twindow and metal pan spandrel unit which has been exposed to the environment for a number of years in vertical glazing applications. It contains 2 panes of 1/8" Herculite K glass. We have chosen 1/8" Herculite K for both the collector panes to not only provide maximum resistance to windload, hail impact, snow load and vandalism but also to provide maximum thermal shock resistance to the inner pane. The absorber plate is aluminum Roll-Bond® painted with a black PPG Duracron enamel which has an absorption of approximately 95%. The absorber panel ratio is 1. The sealants which we have currently chosen to use with the collector extend the operation of the collector to at least 300° F. Other sealants which should provide a higher temperature capability are currently being evaluated. The collector is vented through desiccant-containing chambers which we believe is necessary to prevent pressure build-up and the effects of moisture. We are providing 2½" of exposed Thermafiber or fiber glass insulation on the back of the absorber plate. The collector thickness less insulation is 1—3/8" thick and weighs 4.8 lbs./ft.^{2} without fluid. We are attempting to standardize on approximately 34—3/16" x 76—3/16" outside dimensions of the unit for commercial applications. The cost of this unit is $5.80/ft^2.

If I can provide any further information, please contact me.

R. R. Lewchuk
Project Manager
PPG Industries, Inc.
One Gateway Center
Pittsburgh, PA 15222

ENERGEX CORPORATION

Energex was one of the first companies to get into aluminum Roll-Bond® collector technology. The last I heard they had given up on aluminum Roll-Bond® because they could not control corrosion. They are supplying copper Roll-Bond® assemblies now, I hear, and they also sell a finned-tube collector, Type FT, which consists of a series of copper tubes with aluminum fins pressed on them. The advantage here is that the working fluid is in contact with more corrosion resistant copper.

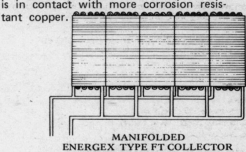

MANIFOLDED
ENERGEX TYPE FT COLLECTOR
SERIES-PARALLEL CONNECTED

Energex Corporation
5115 S. Industrial Road
Las Vegas, Nevada 89118

GARDEN WAY LABORATORIES

Garden Way is one of many smaller producers of collector assemblies using the Roll-Bond® plate. I think they are just now (mid-1974) getting production underway. Their prices should be competitive.

Garden Way Laboratories
Charlotte, Vermont 05445

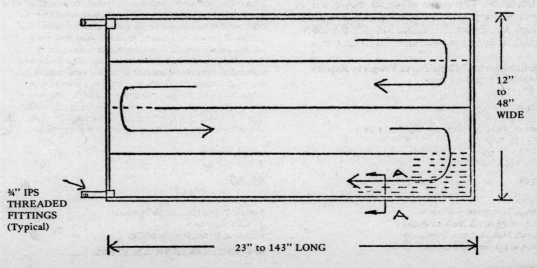

¾" IPS THREADED FITTINGS (Typical)

12" to 48" WIDE

23" to 143" LONG

PHYSICAL INDUSTRIES CORPORATION

PIC offers many solar products. Among others, they are:

Selectively coated aluminum-plate and copper tube water heating panels. Each panel weighs 65 lbs. and sells for $165.00, FOB Lakeside, California.

No. 1 Steam Generator Kit (shown). Filled with 70°F water on a chilly January day in San Diego, this unit developed 155 lbs. of steam pressure in 20 minutes. The price is $48.30, postpaid in the USA.

To go with the Steam Generator Kit is the Stuart-Turner long throw model steam engine. Price is $52.85, postpaid in the USA.

PIC people have been working on solar energy since 1953. Jack Hedger, President, is working on a heat engine using heat tanks of eutectic salts for fuel.

Physical Industries Corporation
P.O. Box 357
Lakeside, CA 92040

SUNPOWER INC.

William T. Beale is Associate Professor of Mechanical Engineering at Ohio University, as well as President of Sunpower. Sunpower is selling small solar water pumps to research groups for $780.00. They are developing less expensive commercial versions for sale in late 1974. Persons interested should send them a stamped, self-addressed envelop with a description of the intended use and performance requirements.

Sunpower Inc.
Route 4, Box 275
Athens, Ohio 45701

SOLAR ENERGY DEVELOPMENT INCORPORATED

Solar Energy Development Incorporated is currently concerned with the development and manufacture of flat plate evacuated collectors for use in the mid-west region. Our standard size is 1½" x 36" x 78" and we also make up special sizes which are limited by the available glass sizes.

Due to the fluctuation in cost of materials we are unable to give a general quote. As of June 1, the cost of a collector was $9.85/sq. ft.

We also do consulting and contracting, and will also do design for specific systems. Communes and cooperatives are encouraged to contact us for information on environmentally and ecologically proper energy systems. We use a total systems approach geared to the needs of the group.

Nicholas S. Macron, President
Solar Energy Development Inc.
1437 Alameda Avenue
Lakewood, Ohio 44107

ENVIRONMENTAL DESIGNS

We are presently developing a high efficiency flat plate solar energy collector, using water as the heat transport medium. This collector uses a selective surface and can achieve .90 absorbtivity and .10 emissivity. Initial tests result in outlet temperatures in the 200°F range at 1 gallon per minute flow rate. It will be marketed as an integral unit with housing, insulation, weather cover, and standard inlet and outlet pipe fittings.

We hope to be in production this fall, and anticipate a selling price of $10.00 per square foot. Initial sales will be from this office.

Our metal fabrication, electronic and engineering facilities enable us to also provide related solar energy recovery equipment, such as water storage tanks and automatic control systems.

environmental designs

Gary Ford, Manager
Environmental Designs
A Division of Steelcraft Corp.
P.O. Box 12408
Memphis, Tennessee 38112

SOLARSYSTEMS, INC.

On February 23, 24, and 26, 1974, Solarsystems, Inc. operated a production model of a vacuum-selective flat plate solar collector. The test data accumulated during these runs culminated 2½ years of R&D work, and made possible the decision to start mass production and sale of collectors immediately.

The collector tested is a vacuum-selective flat plate collector. The collector module is 4'-0" x 8'-0" for a total area of 32 square feet and contains a flat plate absorber with an effective surface area of 24 square feet.

The vacuum level during normal operation was 15 mm of Hg. This vacuum level effectively eliminates all of the convection heat losses from the absorber. The selective coating on the absorber was determined from test data taken from 10" x 10" samples to have an emissivity of .15 to .20 and an absorptivity of .90.

Solarsystems, Inc.

Solarsystems, Inc.
1515 W.S.W. Loop 323
Tyler, Texas 75701

POWELL BROTHERS, INC.

Our No. 12 Solar Collector Panel consists of three aluminum strips, each 6 inches wide by about 45 inches long. These strips are formed in a hydraulic press and die to fit tightly around an aluminum tube that is 1/2 inch in diameter and 12 feet long.

This makes a finished panel 135 inches long by 5½ inches wide, or a total of 5.35 square feet. Each strip after forming is then etched on the surface and has bonded to it a special black heat-absorbing coating that will last for years, and assures you of a high efficiency heat collector capable of collecting about 1000 BTU of heat per hour under a bright sun.

* *

INTRODUCTORY PRICES: NO. 12 POWELL SOLAR COLLECTOR PANELS (Approx. 5½" wide x 12 ft.; Minimum Purchase: 8 Panels)

In quantity of		
	8 - 15 panels	$7.30 each
"	16 - 31 panels	6.70 each
"	32 - 47 panels	6.20 each
"	48 - 63 panels	5.85 each
"	64 and over	5.50 each

Special hose for connecting the panels together is available at $.25 per foot.
Powell Bros.,Inc., 5903 Firestone Blvd.,
South Gate, CA 90280

UP-AND-COMING

Other companies that are getting it on to sell solar collectors are listed below. They should have their acts together by late 1974 or early 1975.

Brown Manufacturing
P.O. Box 14546
Oklahoma City, Oklahoma 73114

Corning Glass Works
Corning, New York 14830

A vacuum insulated cylindrical collector made from glass (what else did you expect . . .). The advantages are light weight, durability and low cost.

Emerson Electric Co.
8100 W. Florissant
Saint Louis, Missouri 63136

Energy Systems, Inc.
634 Crest Drive
El Cajon, CA 92021

General Industries
2238 Moffett Drive
Fort Collins, Colorado 80521

Itek Corporation
Optical Systems Division
10 Maguire Road
Lexington, Massachusetts 02117

Itek has developed a solar panel using water as a heat transfer medium. It has an average efficiency of 55% with an average input of 200 Btu/sq. ft. and has been tested in New England for over a year. It will produce water temperatures of 230°F at ambient outside temperatures below freezing.

Sunwater Company
1112 Pioneer Way
El Cajon, CA 92020

Unitspan, Inc.
6606 Variel Avenue
Canoga Park, CA 91303

E. K. Swanson Engineering
5615 South Jolly Roger Road
Tempe, Arizona 85283

Solergy
150 Green Street
San Francisco, CA 94111

Solar Directory $15.00

from: Environmental Action of Colo., U. of Colo.
1100-14th St., Denver, Colorado 80202

EDWARDS ENGINEERING CORP.

They sell system components—collectors, heat transfer and storage units, and heat pumps.

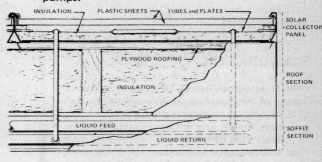

1—SOLAR COLLECTORS

The Solar Collector Panels are 2 feet or 3 feet in width and of any specified length to fit the building design. The Panels are so designed that they will take the place of the normal roofing material such as the shingles. The Panels consist of 1 inch of aluminum covered fibre glass insulation, heat absorbing aluminum plates, copper or aluminum tubes, one or two layers of transparent plastic sheeting, and an aluminum frame for fastening and holding the parts to the roofdeck.

Edwards Engineering Corp.
Pompton Plains, New Jersey 07444

SUNWATER COMPANY

Solar pool heaters.

Sheets of aluminum 3' x 10' are coated black to pick up solar heat. The coating is silicone rubber, which gives it extremely long life, as it resists sunlight, heat, water, and chemicals. To the under side of the aluminum sheet are bonded small copper tubes, which carry the water to be heated. The tubes are soldered together in standard pipe fittings at opposite corners. Several such panels, joined together by inlet and outlet manifolds, make up the solar heat collector.

Solar air heaters.

The heater units consist of sheet metal boxes about 6" deep x 24" wide x 96" long. They are insulated on the back and sides, have a porous black absorber material in the center, and are covered with one layer of glass. Cold air enters the bottom, is warmed in contact with the solar heater interior, and rises, like smoke in a chimney, out the top. Each unit or module of this size will deliver about 3500 BTU's per hour at noon, so that ten or a dozen of them will deliver as much heat as an ordinary 50,000 BTU fuel fired heater.

* *

The solar air heating panels are tentatively priced at $95 each. It is presumed that the owner will normally arrange for the construction of the storage and ducting himself. A complete system, depending on many factors, might cost anywhere from $1000 to $4000. The heaters are highly resistant to weather, and there is absolutely nothing to wear out for decades on end.

Solar domestic water heaters.

The solar heat absorber consists of a bed of water pipes made of plastic, reinforced with fiberglass. They are 4—3/4" outside diameter, and come in three standard lengths, 80", 10', and 15'. Each 1—1/2 lineal feet of pipe contains one gallon of water. The pipes are covered with two transparent covers, normally glass. At the outlet end, one of the pipes is additionally covered by partial thermal insulation, to help retain a useful amount of heat overnight. A pressure relief valve is supplied, in case excessive temperature produces steam pressure.

* *

PRICE

Size, in gallons internal capacity	Number and length of tubes	Price With glass	Without glass
10	2 ea. 80"	$200	$165
20	3 ea. 10'	300	250
30	6 ea. 80", or		
	3 ea. 15'	400	330
40	6 ea. 10', or		
	4 ea. 15'	500	415
50	5 ea. 15'	600	495

Sunwater Co.
1112 Pioneer Way
El Cajon, CA 92020

SUNWORKS INC.

Everett Barber is Assistant Professor at Yale's School of Architecture, as well as President of Sunworks. Sunworks is providing 36 collectors for a house in Connecticut, enough to provide 70% of the annual heat requirement. Heat will be stored in a water tank 5' in diameter and 12' high on the first floor of the house. In addition to double glazing, solar controls on windows, and heat recovery from the fireplace stack, this particular house will have 3" of polyurethane foam sprayed on the *outside* of its concrete block walls. Insulation on the outside of masonry construction reduces inside temperature extremes better than insulation on the inside. I feel good about the things Sunworks are into.

Sunworks, Inc.
669 Boston Post Road
Guilford, Connecticut 06437

SELECTIVE RADIATION SURFACES

Through a special electro-plating process, we have massed and formed layers of sub-skins or metal films to achieve these preferred conditions. The sub-skins are composed of various metals, each performing a duty and all are readily available and inexpensive by today's standards, two traits which make it a unique process. The order in which we placed the various metal skins and the crystaline structure are the two keys to why this surfacing works. The plating process is thermatically and electrically controlled to give the most desirable forms of crystalization in the various metal skins.

The heat retention properties of our product make it 100 percent more effective than a black bodied surface. Therefore, a solar collector can be either twice as powerful or half its present size and retain its full power.

Selective Radiation Surfaces
P.O. Box 8364
San Jose, CA 95155

Another company into thin films is:
Optical Coating Lab.,Inc., P.O.Box 1599,
Santa Rosa, California   95403

AAI CORPORATION

AAI was one of four firms that did a series of showy, super-fast school conversions to solar heating for the NSF early in 1974. They sell a collector with 2 layers of reflective, convection reducing hexagonal cells under glass. As I understand it, they've been a little slow in getting information out while they firm up their patent position. AAI offers complete installation services, from initial site survey to start-up.

AAI Corp., P.O. Box 6767,
Baltimore, Maryland 21204

INTER TECHNOLOGY CORPORATION

Inter Tech was another firm contracted by the NSF to convert a school to solar heating early in 1974. The collector system they designed for the Fauquier High School in Virginia measures 126' x 26' with 105 collector assemblies in it. It looks like the bleachers for a small-town high school football field, only without the seats. The active area of the collector covers 2,415 sq. ft. Four gallons of water storage per sq. ft. of collector are provided underground, where the tanks lose only about 1°F per day at 150°F. Inter Tech designed the intricate control system, also.

Inter Technology Corp.
Box 340
Warrenton, Virginia 22186

OBELITZ INDUSTRIES INC.

We have tailored plans for various solar heating situations: homes, water heaters, food dryers, lumber dryers, distillation installations, saline to fresh water evaporators and similar engineering and design services. We are developing standard designs. However, prices will vary with time.

I believe relatively simple approaches to solar utilizations are practical now. Further, many dollars will be wasted by both bureaucratic and academic over-kill, when most installations could be accomplished with simple state-of-the-art engineering.

–J. J. Hoblitzell

Obelitz Industries Inc.
P.O. Box 2788
Seal Beach, CA 90740

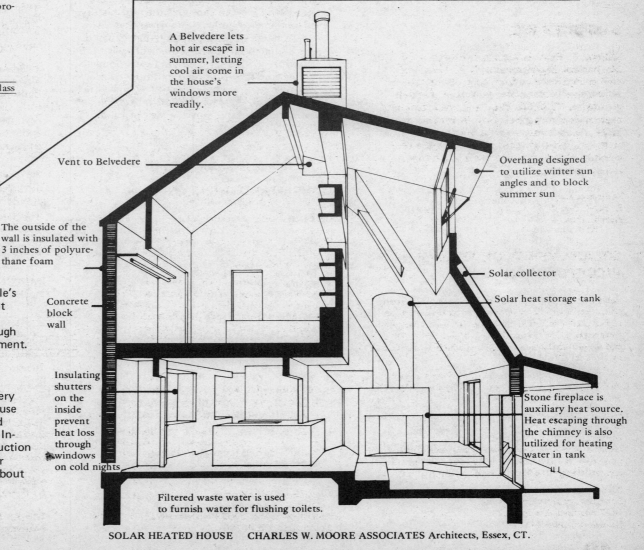

A Belvedere lets hot air escape in summer, letting cool air come in the house's windows more readily.

Vent to Belvedere

Overhang designed to utilize winter sun angles and to block summer sun

The outside of the wall is insulated with 3 inches of polyurethane foam

Concrete block wall

Solar collector

Solar heat storage tank

Insulating shutters on the inside prevent heat loss through windows on cold nights

Stone fireplace is auxiliary heat source. Heat escaping through the chimney is also utilized for heating water in tank

Filtered waste water is used to furnish water for flushing toilets.

SOLAR HEATED HOUSE   CHARLES W. MOORE ASSOCIATES Architects, Essex, CT.

WATER HEATING

FUN & FROLIC, INC. ———➤

Manufacturers of the Solarator water heater, a flexible PVC collector. Connections are by friction-fit 3/4" garden hoses. I'm not convinced of the durability of these units in the long run. They claim "over 40,000 installations on pools and other uses like green houses, cottages, boats and campers."

Solarator distributors are:

Fun & Frolic, Inc.
P.O. Box 277
Madison Heights, Michigan 48071

Solar Systems Sales
180 Country Club Drive
Novato, CA 94947

FAFCO

Solid, tough ABS plastic panels that heat swimming pool water. FAFCO is the leader in plastics technology as applied to solar water heating. They sell simple systems geared to the do-it-yourselfer, or you can have a distributor put in a system for you.

In order to heat your pool effectively with solar energy, it is necessary to have sufficient solar panel area exposed to the sun. In Northern California we recommend a minimum of half the area of the pool in solar panels, i.e., a 600 square foot pool would need 300 square feet of panels. The panels should be inclined at approximately 25° from the horizontal and face south for optimum efficiency. The panels can be easily installed on a roof, fence, or rack structure in a backyard, field, or hillside.

The FAFCO Solar Pool Heater has been carefully designed so that the homeowner can assemble the system himself or have a local contractor, plumber, or carpenter do the work. Each system is shipped with all the necessary fittings and clamps plus a detailed instruction manual.

FAFCO representatives are:

FAFCO Inc. (home office)
138 Jefferson Dr.
Menlo Park CA 94025

FAFCO L.A.
2388 Westwood Blvd.
Los Angeles, CA 90064

Swimming Pool Owners Co-Op
5984 Amaya Drive
La Mesa, CA 92041

Honikman Solar Heaters
927 N. Kellogg Avenue
Santa Barbara, CA 93111

Tradewinds Inc.
3366 North Dodge Blvd.
Tucson, AZ 85716

Solar Heaters Inc.
3536 W. Peoria Avenue
Phoenix, AZ 85029

Solar Energy Products
14928 North Florida Ave.
Tampa, FL 33612

SOLAR HEATER
FOR SWIMMING POOL

Flatten 120' of 1/2" copper tubing to 3/8" and squeeze it in a zig-zag pattern between two 4' x 8' aluminum sheets. Mount in a wood frame and cover with 1/8" Plexiglass. Plans are brief, but reasonably complete. The author doesn't tell how well Plexiglass holds up in the sun.

Solar Heater for Swimming Pool, 1974, 4pp
$3.00
from: Soltech Industries, 6702 Marilyn Dr.,
Huntington Beach, CA 92647

THE HEATING OF
SWIMMING POOLS

This study tells everything you ever wanted to know, or might ever want to know, about solar heating pools. It's an engineering treatise on desired temperatures for swimming (including theory of human comfort), the energy balance of unheated and heated pools, types of low-temperature solar water heaters (theory and performance curves—including types with open water channels), recommendations for planning and installing, and heating cost estimates. It includes 24 figures, 8 tables and 26 technical references. Sheridan's preface even serves to capsulize the past history of solar energy applications generally: "The research work on which this report is based was commenced to give a quick answer to the question of whether it would be economical to heat the then proposed, but now completed, Olympic pool at the University of Queensland. In the event, the decision not to heat the pool was influenced more by the lack of funds than my quick answer."

—Roger Douglass

The Heating of Swimming Pools
Norman R. Sheridan
1972; 63 pp
Solar Research Notes No. 4
Free

from:
Department of Mechanical Engineering
University of Queensland
St. Lucia, Queensland, 4067
Australia

HOME HEATING
SOLAR HEAT PANELS

Plans for a simple do-it-yourself air heating collector system. Simplified tables help you calculate heat loss from a conventional house. Drawings show how to install an air heater under ground-floor windows or on the roof. Kind of expensive for what you get.

Home Heating Solar Heat Panels
1973; 14 pp
$6.95

from:
Solar Concepts
P.O. Box 462
Independence, CA 93526

SOLAR WATER HEATING
IN SOUTH AFRICA

This report makes a nice companion piece to "Low Temperature Engineering Application of Solar Energy;" covering a lot of the same material on flat plate collectors, but with additional practical information that will compliment any solar energy library.

Although the title refers to solar heating in South Africa, it would be foolish to pass up this publication. It is a softbound research report put out by the National Building Research Institute of the Council for Scientific and Industrial Research. Its jam-packed pages include a section evaluating the relative performance of nine different flat plate collector designs (compared on the basis of a three week performance testing program), a description of each design, and accompanying pictures and diagrams. Each design can be built in a home workshop without special tools or exotic materials. The efficiency of each design is compared and the advantages and disadvantages discussed. The author does an excellent job of explaining thermosiphon circulation and reverse flow, and also draws attention to the many practical problems involved in designing and constructing solar water heater systems.

This book is a *must* for anyone seriously interested in solar water heating for low temperature applications. Just remember when reading this book that South Africa is a southern hemisphere country, so don't panic when it tells you to point your collectors north.

—Larry Hassett

Solar Water Heating in South Africa
D.N.W. Chinnery
1971; 79 pp
Research Report 248
$3.00

from:
The Director
National Building
Research Institute
C.S.I.R.
P.O. Box 395
Pretoria, 0001
South Africa

HOT WATER

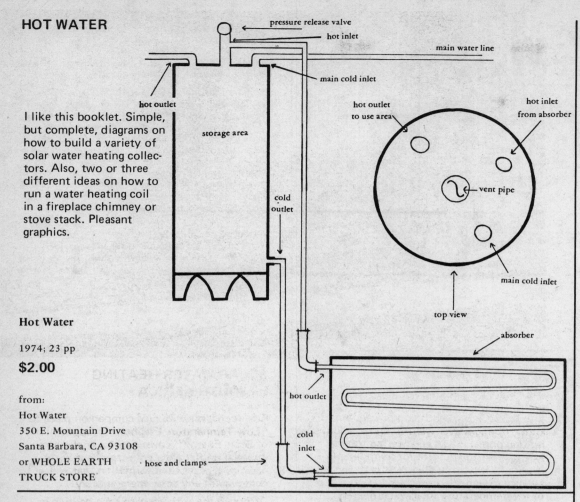

I like this booklet. Simple, but complete, diagrams on how to build a variety of solar water heating collectors. Also, two or three different ideas on how to run a water heating coil in a fireplace chimney or stove stack. Pleasant graphics.

Hot Water

1974; 23 pp

$2.00

from:
Hot Water
350 E. Mountain Drive
Santa Barbara, CA 93108
or WHOLE EARTH
TRUCK STORE

SOLAR-PAK SYSTEMS
GLOBAL DYNAMICS ENTERPRISES

Both of these firms sell plans to build collectors to heat water and/or your house. I think both are way overpriced for what you get.

Plans for the Solar-Pak Systems 7 pp **$7.00**
from: Solar-Pak Systems, P.O.B. 23585,
Tampa, Florida 33622

How to Heat Your Home $10.00
1974; 14 pp
from: Global Dynamics Enterprises, P.O.B. 711,
Lebanon, Missouri 65536

How to Build a Solar Water Heater $1.00
1973; 11 pp; Do-It-Yourself-Leaflet L-4

Use corrugated steel (galvanized) and an old steel drum to build your water heater. Good plans, but details are not always readable.

**How to Heat Your Swimming Pool
Using Solar Energy $1.00**
1973; 4 pp; Do-It-Yourself Leaflet L-3

An open trough, no glass, no insulation design.

The need for a large area of solar collector is the main deterrent to pool heating and, in fact, probably the only situation in which solar pool heating will be economically attractive is where a nearby sloping roof area is available. This roof might be over a grandstand or other sitting area, over a pump-room or over the change rooms. Where such a roof exists, then there is no doubt that the cheapest and most satisfactory pool heating system would be with solar energy.

from:
Brace Research Institute
MacDonald College of McGill University
Ste. Anne de Bellevue
Quebec, Canada H9X 3M1

Remember to add a $0.25 handling fee when paying Brace by check or money order.

ILLUSTRATED SOLAR ENERGY GUIDE OF FLAT-PLATE COLLECTORS FOR PRACTICAL HOME APPLICATION

Lots of diagrams on how to plumb various domestic water heating systems. If you're still unsure of how it's done, maybe reading this will help.

Illustrated Solar Energy Guide of Flat-Plate Collectors for Practical Home Application
1974; 24 pp

$2.00

from:
EI & I Associates
P.O. Box 37
Newbury Park, CA 91320

1. Cylindrical heat collector/water tank
2. Cylindrical guide
3. Inner "glass house"
4. Outer "glass house"
5. Annular space between collector (1) and (2)
6. Insulating air spaces
7. Cold water inlet
8. Hot water outlet
9. Vent pipe allowing trapped air to escape

The SAV design employs a simple cylindrical geometry. It is really a series of cylindrical elements around a common axis. The central tank is both heat collector and storage vessel in one. The remainder of the air spaces that make up the collector provide a "glass house" heating and insulation effect.

When the water in the narrow annular space (5)formed by the heat collector (1) and the cylindrical guide (2) heats up in the sun's rays, a relatively rapid circulation begins. This, a thermosyphonic action, is vigorous, due to quick heat transfer and reduced heat loss due to the insulating envelopes (3) and (4) built around each unit.

FRED RICE PRODUCTIONS

FRP is exclusive manufacturer and distributor of SAV Cylindrical Solar Water Heaters. Stephen A. Vincze, a New Zealander by adoption, invented the system shown. Each unit holds 12 U.S. gallons and sells for $189.95, FOB Los Angeles.

Fred Rice Productions
6313 Peach Avenue
Van Nuys, CA 91401

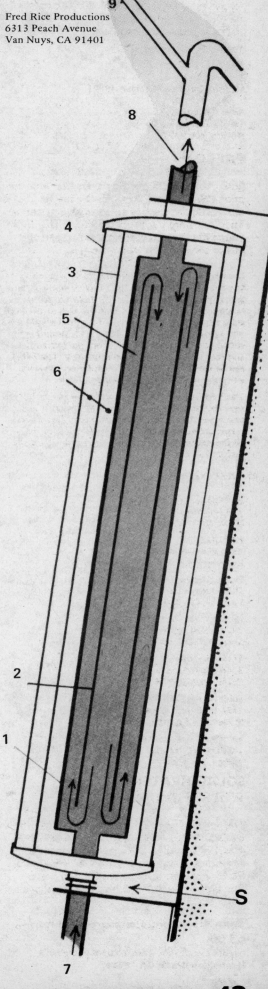

SKYTHERM PROCESSES & ENGINEERING

I think Harold Hay has designed the simplest, neatest solar heating system around. Out-of-sight, figuratively and literally. John Yellott's article describes the principles. Skytherm will be glad to design a shelter for you.

Skytherm Processes & Engineering
2424 Wilshire Boulevard
Los Angeles, CA 90017

SOL-THERM CORPORATION

Formerly known as the Solar Water Heater Division of Silves, Ltd.

This standard unit is adaptable as an add-on to your existing domestic water heater—be it gas, oil or electrically heated. The unit can also be used as a standalone for an isolated farmhouse, your summer cottage, and many other places.

Separate collectors are available for such uses as commercial water heating in conjunction with forced circulation systems, swimming pool water heating, space heating, and other medium and large scale applications. The same collectors can be used in conjunction with glycol for various heat transfer applications. Modifications to suit special conditions will be handled by our Engineering Department upon request.

The retail price for a standard domestic water heater is $495—FOB New York. The price is subject to change without prior notice except for firm quotations. Included are a 32-gallon storage tank with 1.5 kw thermostatically controlled electric heating element, two flat collectors, a mounting frame for a flat roof, and the in-system piping between the collectors and the tank.

The standard gravity-flow solar heater must be drained under freezing conditions to prevent damage to the pipes.

Sol-Therm Corp.
7 West 14th Street
New York, NY 10011

For additional information on solar water heaters, see the 12 articles in Vol. 5 (Solar Energy:II) of U.N. *New Sources of Energy*, or *Solar Water Heaters*, CSIRO Division of Mechanical Engineering Circular No. 2 (1964) Melbourne, Australia.

DAYLIN SUNSOURCE

When you're a half-billion dollar a year marketing organization and you want to get into the solar energy business, what do you do? In Daylin's case, they went to Israel and bought the Miromit company lock, stock, and collectors. Now able to import over 3,000 panels per month, with production expected to increase to 30,000 units per month in a year, Daylin SunSource is selling complete do-it-yourself water heating packages in southern California, Arizona, Colorado and Texas. Their system uses proven galvanized steel panels with the Tabor selective surface. In the southwest, check out the local Angels or Handy Dan store.

Absorber Panel
   Absorber Coating: Tabor "Selective Black" (Absorbtance greater than 90%, emittance less than 18%)
   Covering: Single layer glass
   Insulation: 2" Rockwool
   Plumbing: Horizontal manifold/vertical transfer pipes
   Size: 1 meter x 2 meters x 10 cm
   Weight: Approximately 100 pounds
Storage Tank
   Capacity: 26, 40, or 66 gallons standard
   Size: 24" dia x 3, 4, or 5 feet high
   Weight: 65 to 85 pounds
   Insulation: 2" Fiberglass
   Lining: Glass with magnesium anode
   Mounting: Vertical
   Boost Heater: Gas or electric
System
   Typical residential system—2 panels and 1-40 gallon tank
   Standardized efficiency: 46% (note black paint 36%)
   Nominal Water Temperature: 140°F
   Storage Time: 24 hours min. (10° loss)
Pay Off Period: 1 to 3 years (depending on fuel costs)
Code compliance: Design complies with Uniform Plumbing Code and Southern Building Code congress plumbing requirements.

Daylin Sunsource
9606 Santa Monica Blvd.
Beverly Hills, CA 90210

SOLAR ENERGY ENGINEERING

SEE sells plans for a solar water heater ($5.00) and a solar air heater ($5.00). I haven't seen the plans.

Solar Energy Engineering
P.O. Box 17177
Orlando, Florida 32810

TEDLAR

Thank you for your inquiry concerning "Tedlar" PVF film. The literature which you request is enclosed.

Prices, widths and put-ups for 400BG20TR "Tedlar" are discussed in the price list. The tensile strength of this film is about 13,000 lbs./sq. inch of cross-section, which means that a force of over 50 lbs. is required to break a 1" wide tape. The elongation-at-break of the film is about 250%. The film transmits about 92-94% of the total solar energy incident normal to the surface, with the main losses caused by surface reflection. After five years exposure in Florida, it retains about half its original strength and toughness and about 95% of its original transmission. The film can be heat sealed to itself or bonded by adhesives.

In fastening the film, the stress should be distributed as evenly as possible and puncture of the film should be avoided. All plastic films have relatively low resistance to tear propagation, and it is desirable to avoid starting tears.

Wind flutter should be avoided both because of the noise and because it causes film to fatigue, which can result in failure. In general, the narrower the span the better, and with spans over 1—1/2 to 2 feet you may find it worthwhile to support the film in some way to reduce the span.

If we can be of further help, please let us know.

E.I. DuPont deNemours & Co.
Film Department
Specialty Markets Division
Wilmington, Delaware 19898

SUNBURST, INC.

Sunburst, Inc. will be producing a one piece (collector and tank) unit to heat and store hot water. The unit will have an electric booster for supplemental heating. The unit should market for approximately $500.

Sunburst, Inc.
70 N.W. 94th Street
Miami Shores, Florida 33150

BASIC DESIGNS, INC.

Originators of the Sun Shower, a 2½ gallon black plastic bag with a 30" hose and small shower head attached. Fill it with water, flop it in the sun and in a few hours, hot water. Weighing only 12 ounces empty, it sounds like fun to carry on a camping trip.

Sun Shower
$6.95

from:
Basic Designs Inc.   or
3000 Bridgeway   WHOLE EARTH
Sausalito, CA 94965   TRUCK STORE

SPACE HEATING

SOLAR HOUSE PLANS

Harry Thomason believes that people can build their own solar houses. He has built four himself during the last 15 years and has more cumulative hours of solar heating experience than anyone else in the world. These plans are just detailed drawings for his first house, built in 1958 near Washington, D.C. (Descriptions of later houses can be found in *Popular Mechanics*, June 1973, among many other places.) The first winter (1959) was mild, and he only spent $4.65 for oil for supplementary heat. Thomason holds many patents (he is a Patent Attorney—his doctorate is in law) and you will need to buy a license to use his ideas. If you want an easy-to-build-from-standard-materials, proven solar heating system, it's probably worth it.

Thomason's solar collectors are sheets of black painted corrugated aluminum, with water running down the corrugations. The first house initially had clear polyethylene film over the collector, and glass over that. But the polyethylene disintegrated after a few years and he rebuilt the collector without it. Most everyone else finds two panes of glass the economic optimum for covering a solar house collector, but Thomason uses only one. Heat is stored in a 1,600 gallon steel water tank surrounded by 50 tons of 2"–4" rocks. The "experts" would say his solar system is overdesigned—too much collector and too much storage. But their own solar houses have been complicated and expensive failures and Thomason's has provided reliable solar heat for 15 years. It has probably paid for its construction cost by now (approximately $2,500 in 1958) through fuel saved over the years. But Thomason has not provided detailed engineering cost/performance evaluations on his houses and the solar experts tend to overlook his accomplishments.

There is no discussion in this 30-odd page booklet of how to adapt his plans to suit different climates. There is not even a mention of how much heat this particular house requires and how much the sun provides at various times of the year. There is a map showing "heating degree days per sunshine hour" from which an idea can be obtained about how different parts of the country compare for ease of solar heating. But this booklet will not help you to design a solar heating system in the sense of being able to predict how well it will heat a house in your locale.

The plans show how to connect a conventional air conditioner to cool the rocks at night and use stored "coolness" to cool the house by day. This saves money because the air conditioner is more efficient by night and uses cheaper off-peak electricity. If you live in a dry region with clear night skies, you can cool the rocks and keep the house cool in the summer by running water over the roof at night—much simpler and cheaper than using an air conditioner. Thomason's plans and systems are all oriented toward automatic thermostat control of air temperature in the house but complications are kept to a minimum.

—Roger Douglass

Solar House Plans
Harry E. Thomason, J.D.
Harry Jack Lee Thomason, Jr.
1972; 36 pp
Order No. 9440

$10.00

from:
Edmund Scientific Co.
150 Edscorp Building
Barrington, New Jersey 08007

THOMASON SOLAR HOMES, INC.

Dr. Thomason is now offering seminars for people interested in using his "Solaris" system of house heating. A 2-day primary seminar is offered for $200. After this encounter, if TSH, Inc. thinks you're qualified to carry on in this field of building, they will invite you back for a 3-day seminar ($500). If you pass this hurdle, you get a "Certificate of Attendance" and permission to build one or two solar houses for sale, *if* you guarantee your work. TSH, Inc. will then observe you and your crew build, and if all is well, they will give you a "Certificate of Competency." Dr. Thomason wants to keep his name clean and protect potential buyers, hence all the precautions. For further information, write:

Thomason Solar Homes, Inc.
6802 Walker Mill Road, S.E.
Washington, D.C. 20027

ARKLA INDUSTRIES INC.

Arkla Industries Inc. used to go under the name of Arkla Air Conditioning Co., a subsidiary of Arkansas-Louisiana Gas Company, as close as I can figure the geneology. Arkla is successor to Servel, Inc., the folks that made the gas-fired refrigerators so common years ago.

Thank you for your inquiry. Arkla Industries Inc. is presently involved in modifying a few obsolete, water cooled, small tonnage lithium bromide units for solar operation. The modifications are being made in the Engineering Model Shop and the units are destined for special research experiments only. These units are not commercially available. Solar operated residential units for general use will require redesign for this purpose.

A water fired 25 ton unit, the WF-300, for commercial application will be available soon.

Dr. Philip Anderson
Vice President, Engineering
Arkla Industries, Inc.
P.O. Box 534
Evansville, Indiana 47703

UNIVERSITY OF FLORIDA

For years, the Solar Energy Laboratory at the University of Florida has done important work on solar heating and cooling. Here is a list of the Lab's publications.

L–83 "Practical Applications of Solar Energy" by Farber and Reed (Nov 56) $0.50
L–127 "Tests Prove Feasibility of Solar Air Conditioning" by Eisenstadt, Flanigan and Farber (Nov 60) $0.55
L–170 "Crystals of High-Temperature Materials Produced in the Solar Furnace" by Farber (Feb 64) $0.50
B–18 "Domestic Solar Water Heating in Florida" by Hawkins (Sept 47) $1.80
T–439 "Solar Energy—Conversion and Utilization" by Farber (July 69) $0.75
T–456 "Supercharged and Water Injected Solar Hot Air Engine" by Farber (Jan 70) Combined with T–457. (included in T–456 is T–457).
T–457 "Design and Performance of a Compact Solar Refrigeration System" by Farber (Jan 70) $2.30
TPR–9 "Solar Energy Studies" (Feb 60). Includes five articles on the topics of solar water heating, refrigeration systems and solar absorbers. $1.75
TPR–14 "Solar Engines" by Farber and Prescott (Jul 65) $0.85
TPR–15 "The Direct Use of Solar Energy to Operate Refrigeration and Air-Conditioning Systems" by Farber (Nov 65) $0.50

(Add 15% for foreign mailing. Send check or money order with order; there is no billing or processing of purchase orders.)

Engineering Information & Publications Office
331 Joseph Weil Hall
University of Florida
Gainesville, Florida 32611

Solar Heated Buildings: A Brief Survey
1974; 36 pp

$5.00

from:
Solar Energy Digest
P.O. Box 17776
San Diego, CA 92117

For a good non-technical summary of solar heated houses, see Popular Science, *March, 1974, pp.78.*

UNIVERSITY OF DELAWARE

SOLAR ONE is open to the general public for viewing on Fridays (4 p.m. – 6 p.m.) and Saturdays (10 a.m. – 12 noon). Special group tours can be arranged by special appointment.

Institute of Energy Conversion
University of Delaware
Newark, Delaware 19711

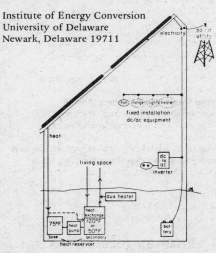

SOLAR ONE is a systemized house which converts sunlight directly into heat and electric power. When light strikes the solar panels on the roof, DC electricity is generated by the Cadmium Sulfide (Cds) Solar Cells. In addition, the sunlight heats these solar cells. Air is forced through the solar collectors and is heated by contacting the back of the hot solar cells. Additional black surface panels are provided to boost the heat further.

Ductwork conducts the hot air through a storage system containing eutectic salts. As the air passes over the eutectic salt, heat is transferred to the salt and causes it to melt at 120°F, absorbing a large amount of heat known as "Heat of Fusion." In this way heat can be stored in a much smaller volume (6 ft x 6 ft x 6 ft) than in heated rocks or water. During the evening and night hours when the house cools down, its air is circulated through the eutectic salt containers and now "extracts" this heat of fusion from the salt. The process starts over again when the sun begins to shine. When there is not enough sunshine to heat the house to comfortable temperatures, a heat pump is used to amplify the heat. In this way solar energy can be utilized for house heating even during cloudy winter days.

The use of Cadmium Sulfide Solar Cells and the generation of electricity as well as heat is what distinguishes SOLAR ONE from other solar structures that have been built in the past.

CONCENTRATING COLLECTORS

HAND FABRICATING LARGE PLANE SEGMENTED SOLAR ENERGY CONCENTRATING MIRRORS

A straight-forward booklet on making a master mold of any diameter and laying up fiberglass on the mold. Glass mirror segments are then cemented in place on the fiberglass. The author stresses two good points—start out small and work up, and be careful so you are not blinded, *permanently*, by the intense concentrated solar energy. The "blueprints" he includes with the booklet are dittoed and can be very difficult to read.

**Hand Fabricating Large Plane Segmented
Solar Energy Concentrating Mirrors**
1974; 12 pp
$2.00
from:
Sun Systems
716 Main Street
Berlin, Pennsylvania 15530

SOLAR SYSTEMS

Solar Systems, a division of the Kender Corporation, is a developer and manufacturer of solar panels, storage facilities, heat transfer hardware and complete systems.
Solar Systems
323 Country Club Drive
Rehoboth Beach, Delaware 19971

ALUMINIZED MYLAR

Our aluminized Mylar is commercial polyester or aluminized polyethylene terephthalate film.

Basically, aluminized film is used in cryogenic (super-insulation systems) or other applications where high reflectivity is desired. The reflectance of the decorative or general purpose type aluminized Mylar is approximately 85%.

The aluminum coating is vacuum deposited onto the film in a vacuum chamber. The actual metal deposit is 99.9% pure aluminum. The actual metal thickness (1×10^{-6} inches) is approximately 2 OHM/SQ. which is determined by measuring the D.C. electrical resistance of the deposited metallic film, and by an empirical formula equating the electrical resistance to thickness of the film in ANGSTROMS. Measurement of the electrical resistance provides a useful method for determining the thickness of vacuum evaporated metallic films.

Prices start at about $0.20/sq. ft. for .00025 inch thick aluminized mylar in small quantities. On the West Coast, it's distributed by:

Transparent Products Corp.
1727 W. Pico Blvd.
Los Angeles, CA 90015

or

1328 Mission Street
San Francisco, CA 94103

or

3414 N.E. Klickitat Street
Portland, Oregon 97212

RAM PRODUCTS

Ram sells Plexi-View® acrylic mirrors in two thicknesses, 1/8" and 1/4". Clear mirrors start at $2.39 per sq. ft. (1/8" thick)) and $2.94 per sq. ft. (1/4" thick) in 4' x 8' sheets. Many people are testing Plexi-View® mirrors for solar installations, but results are unknown.

Ram Products
1111 North Centerville Road
Sturgis, Michigan 49091

DON JOHNSON'S REFLECTORS

The aluminum parabola they sell is 48" in diameter and has a focal length of approximately 18". The steel parabola is 49" in diameter. Aluminum units are $48.00; steel, $38.00, FOB Minneapolis, Minnesota. Prices subject to change (aren't they all?).

DJ & A also sells a complete cooker, consisting of a Scotchcal covered aluminum reflector, grill, and stand for $95.00

Donald Johnson&Assoc., 2523 16th Ave.S.,Mpls.,MN55403

ALZAK ALUMINUM

Alzak is a brand name for an aluminum reflector material manufactured by Alcoa. It comes in a highly polished or a diffuse finish. The highly polished variety costs at least $1.50 per sq. ft. in 2' x 6' x .020" sheets, and that's for large quantities (180 sheets).

Aluminum Co. of America
Lighting Industry Sales
1501 Alcoa Building
Pittsburgh, Pennsylvania 15219

WORMSER SCIENTIFIC CORPORATION

The use of the proprietary Falbel pyramidal optical system reduces the size, and hence the weight and cost of the flat plate collector required by a factor of 2X to 6X. This reduces the overall cost of the solar energy system by factors of 1.6 to 2. It also greatly simplifies the integration of the system with structures of conventional architectural design and minimizes the effect on the esthetic appearance of the building.

A full scale experimental prototype of the pyramidal optics solar energy collection system has been built and initial tests have been performed which have proven the feasability of the system.

Wormser Scientific Corp.
88 Foxwood Road
Stamford, CT 06903

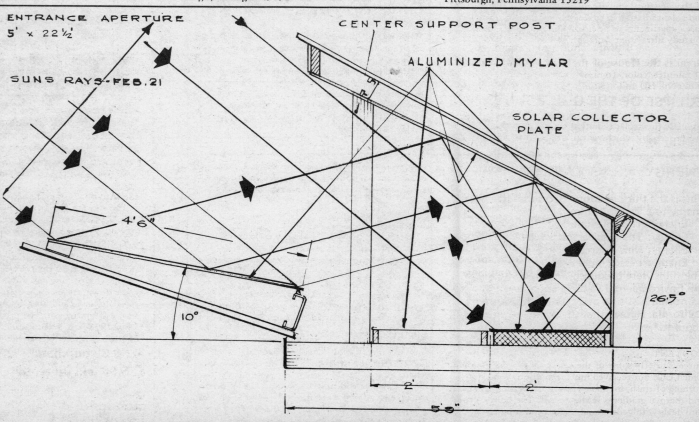

TYPICAL SECTION THRU CONSTRUCTION SHOWING CENTER SUPPORT AND DOOR IN AN OPEN POSITION.

AUDIO-VISUAL

If one picture is worth a thousand words, then a good movie must be worth a zillion words. I've found some of these films to be very valuable in teaching the concepts of alternative energy sources. If you do rent a film, book it early-demand is high, and waits can be long.

WATER FROM THE SUN

Coober Pedy is an opal-mining town in South Australia. In 1966 a still covering almost two acres was constructed there to provide a reliable supply of domestic water from the saline water that was abundant in the area. *Water From the Sun* shows the construction of the Coober Pedy still and uses animated diagrams to show how a solar still works.

Water From the Sun
1967; 15 minutes, color, 16 mm

SOLAR WATER HEATING

Prepared by Australia's governmental research organization, the CSIRO, this film explains the design of a standard collector for a solar water heater, and outlines the principles involved. An excellent film for classroom or solar energy workshop use. The print I saw had a scratchy soundtrack, but the film itself was still worth-

while.

Solar Water Heating
1964; 13 minutes, color, 16 mm

DESIGN FOR CLIMATE

In designing buildings with an agreeable indoor climate, today's architects and engineers must devise ways of controlling a number of natural "elements," including solar heat, sun and sky glare, wind, rain and noise.

This film looks at some of these problems, and shows how research results can help designers solve most of them on the drawing board, long before construction begins.

Design for Climate
1967; 21 minutes, color, 16 mm

free rental

from:
Office of Counsellor (Scientific)
Embassy of Australia
1601 Massachusetts Avenue
Washington, D.C. 20036

SOLAR SLIDE SET

If you want an understanding of the significant work Steve Baer and his Zomeworks people are pursuing, here's the answer. The slides are sharp, the color is generally good, and the written descriptions are complete. Learn and teach beadwall construction, drum heat storage, and skylid operation.

Solar Slide Set
1974; 21 slides, color

$12.00 purchase

from:
Zomeworks Corporation
P.O. Box 712
Albuquerque, New Mexico 87103

POWER ON THE DOORSTEP

Power on the Doorstep is Program No. 14 in the United Nations television series, *International Zone.* Many television stations around the country have prints in their permanent possession; write the UN to find out who near you has one. As I understand it, this film was made after the Rome alternative energy conference of 1961. I haven't seen it, it's probably quite dated, but maybe it should be resurrected. If you get a chance to see it, please send a review to *Alternative Sources of Energy* Newsletter. That way we'll all know if it is any good.

Power on the Doorstep

write:
Chief, Visual Services
Radio and Visual Services Division
United Nations
New York, NY 10017

NASA FILMS

The National Aeronautics and Space Administration, during its laps in the space race, produced dozens of films as a public service. Most of them are flying-through-space documentaries, but there are a few relating to solar energy that are fun to watch. Peter Clark at Village Design in Berkeley turned me on to these films—we viewed them one night at one of the Village's public "Energy Film Festivals." Here's a few of the best. Write NASA for a catalog of films available.

Great is the House of the Sun

Atop Mount Haleakala, the "House of the Sun," Dr. Waler Steiger and his colleagues from the University of Hawaii study the effects of the airglow phenomena and solar radiation in space, while other scientists prepare experiments to be flown aboard space satellites to study ultraviolet radiation.

Great is the House of the Sun
21 minutes, color, 16 mm
Order No. HQ 144

ECLIPSE OF THE QUIET SUN

Explains how solar radiation energy effects Earth, and the process by which we can harness that energy.

Rare study of a total eclipse in Canada.

Eclipse of the Quiet Sun
27 minutes, color, 16 mm
Order No. NAV 010

THE CASE FOR REGENERATION—LIVING IN SPACE

Introduces the concepts of regenerative life support. Shows what is needed to provide men with clean fresh air, drinkable water, food, personal hygiene, waste disposal, temperature and humidity control.

The Case for Regeneration—Living in Space
12 minutes, color, 16 mm
Order No. HQa 131

free rental

from:
Write or call "NASA Public Affairs Office" at the NASA installation, listed below, nearest to you.
   Washington, D.C. 20409
   Greenbelt, Maryland 20771
   Hampton, Virginia 23365
   Kennedy Space Center, Florida 32899
   Marshall Space Flight Center, Alabama 35812
   21000 Brookpark Road, Cleveland, Ohio 44135
   Houston, Texas 77058
   Moffett Field, California 94035

THE AGE OF THE SUN

Through filming actual installations and the use of animated graphics, we learn a little about solar space heating and cooling, solar space satellites, photovoltaics, thermal electric generation, ocean thermal and wind energy conversion, and anaerobic fermentation. Architect Richard Rittelmann, Economist Milton Searl and Congressman Mike McCormack are interviewed. I haven't seen this film, but I've heard it's good. Write for more information and complete rental requirements.

"......Anyone interested in purchasing or renting a print of 'The Age Of The Sun' should write me here at Glen/Kaye Films. Schools and educators should contact Sterling Educational Films, 241 East 34th Street, New York, N. Y. 10016, and refer to 'Energy: Harnessing The Sun' which is another version of the same film, slightly re-edited to be more appropriate for educational use......."

Sincerely,

Douglas R. Kaye, Producer

The Age of the Sun
1974; 21 minutes, color, 16 mm

$260.00 purchase
$35.00 and up rental

from:
Glen/Kaye Films
100 East 21st Street
Brooklyn, NY 11226

ENERGY: NEW SOURCES

This is the third in a four film series examining energy use. The four films are:
   Energy: The Dilemma
   Energy: The Nuclear Alternative
   Energy: New Sources
   Energy: Less is More
The films were produced in cooperation with the Environmental Quality Laboratory, California Institute of Technology, Pasadena, California. Here's what Churchill has to say about it.

CONTENT
Surveys briefly some of the potential sources of energy which have not received much attention: wind, tides, burning of trash, methane from trash or animal wastes, and thermal gradients in the oceans. The body of the film deals with geothermal, fusion and solar energy. The possibilities of solar cells, solar panels for hot water and temperature control of buildings, and solar heat for

generation of electricity are considered. Discussed also is the national policy which has led to neglect of these sources in favor of nuclear energy.

OBJECTIVES
Persons viewing the film will:
   Understand society's need to develop cleaner, alternative sources of energy.
   Obtain information on various new sources of energy and the problems and potentials of developing them.
   Realize that it takes time to develop new energy sources and that we will have to work on them now if we want to have them in the future.

Energy: New Sources
1974; 20 minutes, color, 16 mm

$250.00 purchase
$21.00 rental

from:
Churchill Films
662 North Robertson Boulevard
Los Angeles, CA 90069

LOOSE ENDS

THE STRONG SOLAR FURNACE

Made by Strong Electric Division of Holophane, this 14" parabolic mirror comes with an adjusting bracket, coarse and fine focusing devices, a sample holder and base. It sells for $100.00, FOB New York.

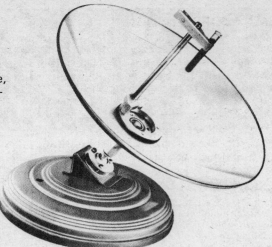

Science Kits, Inc.
777 East Park Drive
Tonawanda, NY 14150

THE POTENTIAL OF DIRECT SOLAR ENERGY IN PLANNING

The purpose of this bibliography is, then, to call attention to literature—past and present—which deals with the potential of utilizing direct solar heat in planning our cities and in redeveloping older, lower-income urban areas. It is hoped that the literature compiled and presented here will be of interest to researchers, economists, futurists, politicians, students, etc., as well as to planners and environmentalists.

The Potential of Direct Solar Energy in Planning
1973; 13 pp
Exchange Bibliography No. 476
$1.50

from:
Council of Planning Librarians
Post Office Box 229
Monticello, Illinois 61856

HONEYWELL

Honeywell has jumped into solar energy "head first." They've been researching trough-like concentrating collectors with the University of Minnesota, they converted a Minnesota junior high school to solar heating for the NSF, and they've built a transportable lab to gather solar heating and cooling data.

The laboratory consists of two units. A 45-foot semi-trailer houses the solar-heating equipment and a complete weather station. A second unit, a 12-by-50-foot "office" van, represents the building to be heated and supplied with hot water by sun power. The office van contains educational panels on solar energy for local briefings and seminars.

The energy collection system for the laboratory consists of 625 square feet of solar panels covered by a transparent "greenhouse" of tempered glass and plastic. Each of 64 panels contains a solar energy absorbing subpanel through which water is circulated and is heated up to approximately 200°F. The hot water then is transferred to storage tanks for use by the laboratory's conventional heating system. The two 475-gallon storage tanks hold enough heated water to warm the laboratory, approximately the size of a small home, to 70°F for 24 hours.

During the extensive data gathering and test period the laboratory will be operated by Honeywell for the National Science Foundation in northern climates for solar heating data gathering and experiments.

Honeywell, Inc., Aerospace & Defense Grp. PR, 2600 Ridgeway Pkwy., Minneapolis, MN 55413

SOLAR ENERGY OUTFIT

For science teachers and other experimenters.

$125.00

from:
Educational Materials & Equipment Co.
P.O. Box 17
Pelham, New York 10803

SOLAR EDUCATION

Several universities offer courses on solar energy. A brief survey follows.

Youngstown State University
Department of Electrical Engineering
410 Wick Avenue
Youngstown, Ohio 44503

The EE Department offers a full-time solar energy option at both the undergraduate and master's level. The first engineering school in the country to offer this program, as I understand it.

University of Colorado
Center for Management and Technical Programs
P.O. Box 1928
Boulder, Colorado 80302

CU periodically offers a 3-day course on solar heating and cooling systems. Generally, the faculty includes Richard Crowther, Dr. Lof, Dr. Kreith and Dr. Kreider. Register early because this course is popular, even at $250 tuition for 3 days.

University of Wisconsin—Extension
Department of Engineering
432 North Lake Street
Madison, Wisconsin 53706

Their 5-day course is designed for engineers getting into solar energy and assumes some background in heat transfer and thermodynamics. Dr. Duffie and Dr. Beckman are the usual instructors for this $350 program. Send for information on the dates of the next session.

George Washington University
Continuing Engineering Education Program
Washington, D.C. 20006

Dr. Thomason teaches a five day ($425) course on solar energy, centered around his successful "Solaris" system. Send for information.

California Institute of the Arts
School of Design
24700 McBean Parkway
Valencia, CA 91355

The School of Design offers BFA and MFA degrees in Environmental Design, including work on solar heating and cooling, energy conservation, wind power, etc. The faculty has built a solar powered hot air ballon, a Fresnel concentrating collector, various flat plate collectors, a solar pool heater, and a heliodon for simulated sun-angle studies. New projects are always under way.

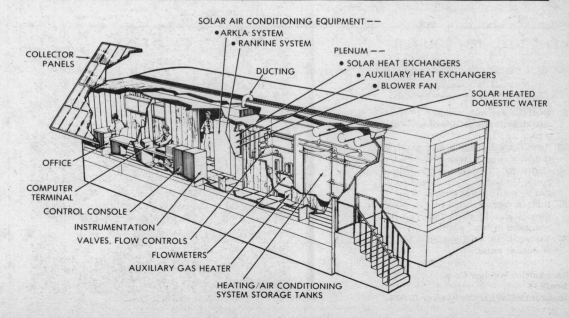

SOLAR AIR CONDITIONING EQUIPMENT ——
● ARKLA SYSTEM
● RANKINE SYSTEM

PLENUM ——
● SOLAR HEAT EXCHANGERS
● AUXILIARY HEAT EXCHANGERS
● BLOWER FAN

COLLECTOR PANELS

DUCTING

SOLAR HEATED DOMESTIC WATER

OFFICE

COMPUTER TERMINAL

CONTROL CONSOLE

INSTRUMENTATION

VALVES, FLOW CONTROLS

FLOWMETERS

AUXILIARY GAS HEATER

HEATING/AIR CONDITIONING SYSTEM STORAGE TANKS

DESERT SUNSHINE EXPOSURE TESTS, INC.

Suppose you've got a brand new solar product that you'd like to spring on the universe. But first you'd like to test it and see how it holds up in the sunlight. Where do you go to test it under controlled conditions? To Desert Sunshine, that's where. Located in the Sonora Desert 40 miles due north of Phoenix at 2,000 feet above sea level, their test site averages 4,000 hours of sunshine a year (11 hours average per day). They have all sorts of test equipment, lots of room and real knowledge about solar technology.

Desert Sunshine Exposure Tests, Inc.
Box 185 Black Canyon Stage
Phoenix, Arizona 85020

KALWALL CORPORATION

Kalwall sells 2 thicknesses of clear fiberglass "Sun-Lite" sheeting, .025 and .040 inches. The .025" material weighs .2 lbs./sq.ft. and the .040" thick material weighs .3 lbs./sq.ft., which is 1/8th the weight of a sq. ft. of double strength glass. They claim Regular Sun-Lite should last 7 years, while Premium Sun-Lite should last 20 years. If exposed to temperatures above 140°F for very long, the material yellows a bit and loses 10-12% of its solar transmittance. It has high resistance to impact and thermal shock. Initial light transmission for thin Sun-Lite Regular is approximately 95%, for thin Sun-Lite Premium, 93%.

Prices start at $0.25/sq. ft. for thin Regular and $0.35/sq. ft. for thin Premium. Minimum order size is $10, FOB Manchester, New Hampshire.

Kalwall Corporation
P.O. Box 237
Manchester, New Hampshire 03105

DOUBLE GLAZED WINDOWS

DUAL GLAZING

...Two panes of glass enclose 2-5/8" vented air space to reduce heat loss through glass by more than 50%. Glass is neoprene gasket glazed for easy replacement and most effective sound insulation.

1. Dual Glazing with enclosed airspace (vented to outside) eliminates 50% of heat loss through glass.
2. True Thermal break in vent and frame virtually eliminates drafts and condensation . . . helps control room temperature and humidity. Composite U value of .55 compares to .81 for sealed glazing with typical aluminum frame.
3. Built-in venetian blind reduces solar heat gain through glass by up to 70%. Blind is virtually concealed in "up" position.
4. Tests indicate an elimination of more than 55% of outside noise.

The Amelco Window Corp.
Box 333
Hasbrouck Heights, New Jersey 07604

CHEMAX CORPORATION

Chemax sells several varieties of hardening and non-hardening thermal cements. The hardening varieties provide better heat transfer, but they don't cope with thermal expansion as well. Prices run in the $12-14 a gallon range. Chemax has a world-wide distributor network.

If you try some of their products on a solar installation, keep good records and let the rest of us know how everything works out.

Chemax Corporation
211 River Road
New Castle, Delaware 19720

THERMON

Thermon offers two product lines of interest.

The first is a half dozen varieties of thermal cement. They claim their cements "provide a superior conductive medium . . . still unduplicated in the industry." Prices run $12-14 a gallon.

The other product line is "Heet Sheets," de-oxidized copper (99.98% pure) plate heat exchangers. Standard sizes are from approximately 2' x 2' to 2' x 8'. Each sheet is top rated at 150 psig and 375°F. Thermon does not offer these with a selective surface, but I suspect these would be good absorbing surfaces.

Thermon Manufacturing Co.
100 Thermon Drive
San Marcos, Texas 78666

DEKO-LABS

Deko-Labs sells two models of solar heating circulating pump temperature controllers. Model TC-1 is for commercial installations, Model TC-2 is for do-it-yourselfers. These are solid state devices with heavy duty mechanical relays and a variety of options regarding sensor functions. Basic prices are about $69 for the TC-2, $85 for the TC-1.

Deko-Labs
Box 12841
Gainesville, Florida 32604

TC-1 CONTROLLER

Familiar to us all, regardless of our race or our religion, sits a God given power in the sky, the SUN. With man's intelligence we can harness this free and never ending energy which I believe will grow a love for the human race, and build a lasting peace here on our planet Earth. Immediate development of solar energy will be a giant step into a clean and a healthy future. I, the undersigned, am a lobbyist for sun power.

Signature	Address
Date	City State Zip

LOBBYIST FOR SUN POWER

Ms. Marge Hayden is a woman with a cause. She believes in solar energy. She believes in it so much that she has been instrumental in having over 100,000 people sign petitions worded like the coupon. If you agree with her, sign the coupon, tear it out and mail it to Ms. Hayden.

Lobbyist for Sun Power
Ms. Marge Hayden
36 Autumn Lane
Attleboro, Massachusetts 02703

SOL-A-METER

Matrix claims these are weatherproof solar radiometers intended for rugged field construction use. All models use silicon photovoltaic cells as sensing devices. Their basic Mk1—G unit sells for $195.00, the top-of-the-line Mk14E-RDS with 12 volt recorder sells for $1,155.00, FOB Mesa, Arizona

Matrix Inc.
537 South 31st Street
Mesa, Arizona 85204

See the November 27, 1973 (Vol. 182A, No. 4114A) issue of *Science* magazine, p. 116, for a list of other pyranometer and pyrheliometer manufacturers.

SKYLIDS

Skylids are insulated louvers which are placed inside a building behind or beneath skylights, glass roofs, clerestories or vertical windows. They open during sunny weather and close by themselves during very cloudy periods and at night. When the skylids are closed they are an effective thermal barrier, greatly reducing heat losses through glazed openings, thus allowing one to have large glass areas which let solar heat and light into the building during the day without having large heat losses through these glass areas at night.

Skylids have the additional property of allowing one to regulate, by a manual override, the amounts of heat and light which a skylight admits into a room.

The essence of the skylid is its simplicity. The louvers move themselves by the shifting weight of the freon. The skylid powers itself; opening when the outside cannister is warmer than the inside and closing when the inside cannister is warmer. The skylid requires no electricity or outside power.

Unit No.	Length	Width	No. of Panels	Price
10 - 3	122"	68"	3	$340.00
10 - 2	122"	46"	2	240.00
8 - 3	98"	68"	3	300.00
8 - 2	98"	46"	2	220.00
6 - 3	74"	68"	3	260.00
6 - 2	74"	46"	2	200.00
4 - 3	50"	68"	3	220.00
4 - 2	50"	46"	2	180.00

Zomeworks Corp.
P.O. Box 712
Albuquerque, New Mexico 87103

SPECTROLAB

The National Weather Service has contracted with Spectrolab to supply Spectrosun Model SR-75 Pyranometer s for up-grading their solar radiation data stations around the country. Units cost $1,030.00 each, FOB Sylmar, California.

Spectrolab
12500 Gladstone Avenue
Sylmar, CA 91342

SOLAR COOKING

Solar Steam Cooker
1972; 13 pp
Do-It-Yourself Leaflet L-2
$1.00

The solar collector always contains water, about one cup of water being added each evening to replace the water that has boiled away. Steam is produced within an hour of sunrise and will continue to be produced for the rest of the day as long as the sun shines on the ° collector, i.e. almost until sunset. Thus it is possible to cook both the mid-day meal and the evening meal. Food left in the cooker will remain hot for several hours after sunset.

The solar cooker is a slow-cooking device, and is best suited for foods that require long slow boiling, such as stews, cereals and vegetables.

The construction of the solar cooker is simple with much margin for adaption to locally available material, therefore, the following fabrication instructions serve mainly as a guide to general proportions. It shows, for example, the approximate amount of metal surface and proportionate length of pipe needed for an efficient solar collector and the suggested size of the steam cooker. The dimensions of the collector and cooker may be somewhat altered to adapt to standard sizes of locally available materials. Suggestions are made throughout the text for possible material substitutes.

Brace Research Institute
MacDonald Campus of McGill University
Ste. Anne de Bellevue
Quebec, Canada H9X 3M1

Remember to add $0.25 handling fee when paying Brace by check or money order.

DESERT RESEARCH INSTITUTE

DRI is part of the University of Nevada system. They planned to build a solar heated and cooled building for its Desert Biology Laboratory. Originally budgeted to cost $350,000 for the basic shell, with another $300,000 for solar climate control and associated equipment, the bids came in over 2X the basic budget. The last I heard, their active President, John M. Ward was scouring the countryside for funds. I hope he finds them; Nevada's a great place to utilize solar energy.

Desert Research Institute
Reno, Nevada 89507

SOLAR ENERGY

You'll probably find these delightful reading whether you want to learn the basics of solar energy or not. Baer says in the introduction, "I have been trying to write a book on solar energy for some time, I even have some chapters mostly completed. Why not write a chapter for each issue of the *Tribal Messenger*—it could be an informal first draft . . . who wouldn't like to think of himself as an author? Besides, look at the stuff people read. So why not? And if the pieces I write are not for you—well, it isn't as if we sold you a roof that leaks or a car with a bum transmission."

Baer uses his fertile imagination well in explaining solar energy. He presents his observations of what technology is doing to man's priorities (the hierarchy of attention given in a drive-up liquor store is usually car, telephone, human customer), and reports his reactions to such things as a $200,000 grant to A.D. Little, Inc. to study a plan to orbit a huge satellite which would collect sunlight and beam the energy to earth as microwaves.

Why not build a second sun that can beam its energy right through the clouds—and at night too. Why not build a sun that you own? Think of it.

Why settle for a sun that goes out at night and is interrupted by clouds? Why be dependent on a sun with an uncertain past? Who owns that things anyway?

Why not build one yourself and know how and why it works? Never mind that it only relays the other sun's energy. Why not have a sun that you can control from a console like a stereo set or TV set? Why not have a sun that is your friend? That you can turn off and on. Why not make a sun that would burn up other people if they were bad—you could decide if they were bad and your sun, controlled by your console, could take care of the rest. Why go backwards in work with solar energy so that you end up like an old farmer farming the sky worrying about the weather. Why not transform the sun itself into a commodity, like a big tank of propane?

Baer makes his points with lots of other short scenarios and flights of fancy as well as down to-earth practical proposals such as non-mechanical "ice ranch" to produce at least six feet of ice per winter from shallow ponds of water in Albuquerque. The harvest would be worth at least $125,000 an acre—produced without electricity. He has an uncommon amount of common sense, and his views and ideas on the human-scale use of solar energy to create simple, liveable houses are excellent. Even if Baer's own Drum-Wall-in-a-Zome house doesn't appeal to you, the principles are sound and simple and well explained and deserve wide application.

—Roger Douglass

Solar Energy
Steve Baer
1973; 30 pp
$3.00

from:
Zomeworks Corp.
P.O. Box 712
Albuquerque, New Mexico 87103

GLASTEEL® INC.

Glasteel sells two grades of fiber reinforced plastic panels surfaced with DuPont's Tedlar®. Panels come flat or in corrugated sheets. Their principal market is greenhouses. Prices by quotation.

Glasteel®
1516 Santa Anita Avenue
South El Monte, CA 91733
or
2200 W. Emerson Place
Seattle, Washington 98199

DRUM WALL PLANS
BEADWALL PLANS
SOLAR WATER HEATER PLANS

The drum wall plans show various arrangements for building a cheap and effective solar heat collection and storage wall out of 55 gallon drums filled with water. They detail the construction of an insulated door to close over the drum wall at night to reduce heat loss to the outdoors. There's a lot of text too, discussing how it works, suggesting experiments with a drum collector, showing how much solar heat to expect per sunny day, explaining the economics of drum wall house heating, and so on. It's very well written—everything is there. And it's honest—"No one knows how long the drums will last; the drums bong as they change temperature; in very cloudy climates it will not provide heat; a drum wall makes the most sense if you are willing to let your house temperature fluctuate over a fairly wide range."

The Beadwall (patent applied for) is an alternative to using insulated doors or shutters to reduce heat loss thru a window or window wall at night. It's a system for blowing insulating styrofoam beads into or out of the space between two parallel sheets of glass or fiberglass. The plans detail Zomework's development and demonstration of the idea along lowest-possible-cost, do-it-yourself lines. Complete plans for a small Beadwall greenhouse are included. For $15 you will be licensed to build up to 144 square feet of beadwall window. In addition to providing good insulation/sun control, "the beadwall is also very beautiful as the beads flow in and out of the clear window."

The solar water heater plans are just as nice. They start by showing how to reduce the heat required for a shower by preheating incoming cold water with the used warm shower water. Just run the cold water through a coil on the shower floor before it goes to the water heater. The plans explain how the heater works, why water circulates by thermosiphon action, how to measure or calculate the flow, all the ins and outs of building and using a successful system with a copper or steel collector. The 4' x 8' collector should heat at least 30 gallons of water by 80° (from 50° to 130°F) on a clear winter day. An anti-freeze system is described for use in freezing weather. "Solar hot water gets you cleaner, makes you happier, rests your bones, and cures impotence. If you don't believe it, ask someone who uses it."

—Roger Douglass

Drum Wall Plans
1974; 2 – 2' x 3' sheets
$5.00

Beadwall Plans
1974; 7 – 2' x 3' sheets
$15.00

Solar Water Heater Plans
1974; 2 – 2' x 3' sheets
$5.00
from:
Zomeworks Corp.
P.O. Box 712
Albuquerque, New Mexico 87103

or WHOLE EARTH TRUCK STORE

SOLAR SENSORS

Jack Scovel has been producing solar heating pump control devices for a decade. His units are now solid state construction and they sell for $95.00, FOB Fairfax, Virginia.

J.S. Scovel, 420 Berritt St., Fairfax VA 22030

WINSTON "CRAB'S EYE" COLLECTOR

A very efficient "concentrating" flat plate collector has been invented by Dr. Roland Winston, a physicist at the University of Chicago. Just now beginning large scale development with the help of an AEC grant, Winston's collector sounds very promising. It has been claimed that the Winston collector is capable of ten times as much energy concentration as the general level of sunlight, without diurnal tracking of the sun.

A new principle for collecting and concentrating solar energy, the ideal cylindrical light collector has been invented. This development has its origins in detecting Cherenkov radiation in high energy physics experiments. In its present form, the collector is a trough-like reflecting wall light channel of a specific shape which concentrates radiant energy by the maximum amount allowed by phase space conservation. The ideal cylindrical light collector is capable of accepting solar radiation over an average 8-hour day and concentrating it by a factor of ~10 without diurnal tracking of the sun. This is not possible by conventional imaging techniques. The ideal collector is non-imaging and possesses an effective relative aperture (f-number) = 0.5. This collector has a large acceptance for diffuse light. In fact, the efficiency for collecting and concentrating isotropic radiation, in comparison with a flat plate collector, is just the reciprocal of the concentration factor.

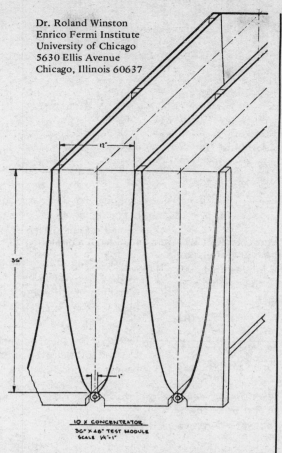

Dr. Roland Winston
Enrico Fermi Institute
University of Chicago
5630 Ellis Avenue
Chicago, Illinois 60637

10 X CONCENTRATOR
36" X 48" TEST MODULE
SCALE 1/4"=1"

THE ELECTROMAGNETIC SPECTRUM

Large colorful wall charts showing details of the electromagnetic spectrum from 10^{-14} to 10^{10} centimeters wavelength. I recommend the $5.00 chart—it's a lot more readable.

The Electromagnetic Spectrum
28" x 41"

$5.00

11" x 15"

$1.50

from:
Westinghouse Printing Division
Forbes Road
Trafford, Pennsylvania 15085

ENERGY FROM THE SUN

If you live in an area served by the Bell Telephone System, call up the local business office and see if they can still get you *Energy from the Sun*, Bell System Science Experiment No. 2. Included with this free package is a 90-page booklet telling you how to build a silicon solar cell out of the rest of the goodies in the kit. The booklet itself is very good in explaining solar insolation and the principles of helio-electricity. This kit is no play toy—small amounts of very dangerous chemicals are necessary. Good for high-school science projects.

SOLAR CELLS

See the December, 1974 issue of *Popular Science* for a good rundown on "Solar Cells." The article gives cost forecasts, development timetables, and info on manufacturing methods now being tested.

SUNDIALS

Waugh's book is an introduction to how sundials work and how they are constructed. He comes across as a man who understands time.
—T.G.

Sundials
Albert E. Waugh
1973; 228 pp

$3.50

from:
Dover Publications, Inc.
180 Varick Street
New York, NY 10014

or WHOLE EARTH TRUCK STORE

SUNDIALS

Sundials for sale! Prices range from $7.00 to $300.00.
—T.G.

Catalogue Free

from:
Sundials
New Ipswich
New Hampshire 03071

HELPERS

Solar Energy Company
810 18th Street, N.W.
Washington, D.C. 20006

SEC acts in a design and advisory capacity, as well as selling a wide variety of alternative energy products.

Solar Energy Research Corp.
Route 4, Box 26B
Longmont, Colorado 80501

Solar consultants and manufacturers. Builders of the largest solar heated greenhouses in Colorado.

Solar Home Systems
38518 Oak Hill Circle
Willoughby, Ohio 44094

Joseph Barbish believes in neutralizing as much of the heating load as possible, and then designing passively to cut the heating and cooling load even further. He's set up for commercial consulting, but he'll field an occasional question from do-it-yourselfers. He's done his homework on solar collectors.

Solar Power Supply Inc.
Route 3, Box A10
Evergreen, Colorado 80439

An enthusiastic group of talented young professionals, Solar Power Supply is anxious to inform you of current activities in the field of natural energy utilization. Our work includes applied research and development, consulting services, educational programs, product manufacture and marketing.

Soltec
P.O. Box 6844
Denver, Colorado 80206

Soltec is a small, new firm set up to offer a variety of services, including solar systems design and consulting and installation of solar life-support (SLS) systems. Rick Speed, who has written several articles on solar energy, is President.

Total Environmental Action
Box 47
Harrisville, New Hampshire 03450

Bruce Anderson started his own design and consulting firm last year. His book, Solar Energy and Building Design, should be out soon—I'm looking forward to seeing it. Sensitive designers interested in total life style change.

HELIO-DYNAMICS, INC.

HELIO-DYNAMICS has been involved in solar energy research and development for more than 20 years from which has evolved a line of solar equipment as follows:

Solar heating panels (.89m x 3.69m.) with single glazing for low temperature applications such as swimming pools. Each panel weighs 16 Kg. and is 80% efficient when ambient is 20°C. with 10 liters per minute flowing through panel. Panels have been installed in systems since 1960 and are operating with negligible reduction in thermal conversion.

Solar hot water systems for domestic use with storage. A system with two panels (approx. 6.43 sq. mtr.) as described above with double glazing produces on the average 386 liters of hot water at 56°C. rise when ambient is 13°C. with 455 liters storage.

Solar Air Conditioning Chiller and Air Handling Units; Chiller and collector system are integrated to provide a compact unit of high efficiency. A unit of approx. 13.37 sq. mtrs. produces 9,072 Kg-cal/hr. with an insolation of 1.47 Langleys with a wind of 12.07 Km/Hr. Another unit of larger size will produce 15,876 Kg-cal/hr. with the same conditions. As an alternative, units will generate hot water for domestic use.

Helio-Dynamics, Inc.
518 South Van Ness Avenue
Los Angeles, CA 90020

WATER

HARNESSING THE POWER OF WATER

Robin Saunders
Mechanical Engineer

Most everyone has witnessed the destruction caused by torrential floods, the subtleties of weathering or erosion, the power of wave motion, the strength and mystique of grand rivers, or the gentleness and swiftness of small streams. The power of water has the capacity for destruction and useful work.

Essentially water power is a form of solar energy. The sun begins the hydrologic cycle by evaporating water from lakes and oceans and then heating the air. The hot air then rises over the water carrying moisture with it to the land. The cycle continues when the water falls as precipitation onto the land, and the potential energy of the water is dissipated as the water rushes and meanders its way back to the lakes and oceans.

The potential of water at an elevation above sea level is one of the "purest" forms of energy available. It is almost pollution free (when not contaminated) and can provide power without producing waste residuals. It is relatively easy to control and produces a high efficiency. From 80% to 90% of controlled water energy can usually be converted to useful work. This is dramatic when compared with the 25% to 45% efficiencies of solar, chemical and thermal energy systems. As a result, large and small rivers around the world have been dammed and waterwheels and water turbines installed to capture the energy of water.

Here, we will be concerned with small hydro-plants that can service the needs of individuals and small communities. In many cases even very small streams can be harnessed to produce power. The power that can be developed at a site is calculated as the rate of flow of water (measured in cubic feet per minute) multiplied by the "head" or vertical distance (measured in feet) the water drops in a given distance. It is these two quantities which must first be measured to see if they are adequate to develop a hydro-plant.

Most hydro-power installations will require the construction of a dam. A dam can increase the reliability and power available from a stream. It can also provide a means by which to regulate the flow of water and can add to the elevation of the water (by making it deeper) thus providing greater head to operate the wheel or turbine.

Both waterwheels and turbines deliver their power as torque on a shaft. Pulleys, belts, chains or gear boxes are connected to the shaft to deliver power to such things as grinding wheels, compressors, pumps or electric generators.

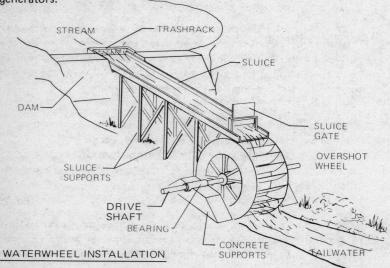

WATERWHEEL INSTALLATION

Waterwheels are the old-style, large diameter, slow turning devices that are driven by the velocity of the weight of the water. Because they are slow turning they are more useful for producing mechanical power for grinding and pumping than electrical power. The mechanical power can be connected by pulleys and belts to drive saws, lathes, drill presses and other tools. Waterwheels can provide a small amount of electric power (up to 10 HP) but it involves complex and expensive "gearing up" to produce the necessary speeds to actuate an electric generator.

Water turbines are preferable for producing electricity from the stream. Turbines generally are small diameter, high rpm devices that are driven by water under pressure (through a pipe or nozzle). When coupled with a generator, even relatively small turbines can provide electricity for most homestead needs.

Economics

Perhaps the greatest stumbling block to utilizing water power will be cost. Purchasing a manufactured waterwheel or turbine will obviously be more expensive than building your own. (In the Reviews/Water section a few companies and their relative costs are reviewed.) However, only a few of the many different types of waterwheels and turbines should be attempted by the home-builder. This includes most of the lower technology waterwheels but only one of the turbines. The Banki Turbine can with some time and perhaps some technical assistance be home-built. The Pelton Wheel and the Reaction Turbines are probably best left to the manufacturer. A home-built unit could be inefficient as well as downright dangerous. The cost of the waterwheel or turbine is only a portion of the over-all cost of installing a hydro-power system. Building dams also costs money. Here, the expense can be small if you use indigenous materials but if concrete and steel reinforcing are used the cost can be much greater. Then comes the expense for pipe or sluice to carry the water to the wheel or turbine. Depending upon the amount of flow and the distance involved this could be a very minor expense or a considerable one.

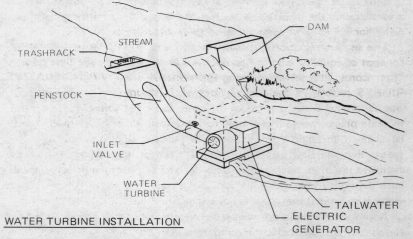

WATER TURBINE INSTALLATION

Probably the largest expense besides the wheel or turbine itself will be the gears or pulleys, the shafting and the electrical generator. A 1 KW generator should be obtainable for under $200 new and considerably less if surplus or used. A new 10 KW unit should start in the $800 range. The pulleys, drive belts and chains or gears needed to "gear up" the power of the waterwheel or turbine should be rather inexpensive.

The cheapest electrical generating hydro-power system that could be installed, dam, generator, turbine and all would cost a minimum of $500, and more likely $1,000. On the other end of the scale, a manufactured turbine, with dam and piping being constructed by the owner could cost from $3,000 to $10,000.

It is difficult to determine the long range cost of building or buying a hydro-plant, as opposed to hooking up with the local utility company. At present it is probably cheaper to go with the utility. But as the age of cheap utilities and the promise of something-for-nothing from nuclear power is disappearing, building an independent power source will become a more economical investment.

Environmental Considerations

Waterwheels and turbines in and of themselves have a negligible effect on the environment. However, the damming of a river or stream, a necessity with most installations, has an important and sometimes irrevocable effect upon the long-term ecological balance of that particular environment. Certainly dams can create a better environment for some animals and plants, and they can and do prevent natural disasters such as floods and severe erosion. But it is important to know that by building a dam, you are also creating a pond or lake where a stream or river used to exist; that you are flooding an already existing river ecosystem, encouraging the accumulation of silt, and perhaps providing a breeding ground for mosquitoes. The resulting pond or lake behind a dam also usually raises the water table behind the dam (as a result of seepage) and lowers it below the dam. Innumerable other changes are effected by the construction of a dam, and it is generally fair to say that the larger the dam the greater the changes. It is therefore of primary importance to foresee the ecological impact of installing a hydro-plant, and if necessary, to forego that particular site plan or the entire project.

WATER RIGHTS

Water is subject to a complex array of laws and regulations concerning its use. Wherever you may settle, some rules and regulations about water will surely follow. This is particularly true in the west and southwest states where arid conditions mean that almost all water that flows needs to be used by someone. Generally in the U.S. there are two types of water rights associated with property: Riparian rights and Appropriative rights.

RIPARIAN RIGHTS were originally brought to the United States through English common law. These laws were easily adapted as water laws for the eastern and midwestern U.S., where the supply of water was similar to that in England. Riparian rights are usually defined in the following way: The owner of any land that contains or is adjacent to a water course has a common law right to "reasonable use" of the natural flow. This right is shared equally by all other properties along the water course. And each is subject to the equal rights of all other riparian properties, or in some states, the higher priority of upstream users. This "reasonable use" means sharing the available water for domestic use, and then using excess water for irrigation of commercial crops or watering livestock.

The usual distinction between riparian and appropriative users is the concept of equality among riparian users as compared to the time priority "first come, first served" among appropriative users. APPROPRIATIVE RIGHTS evolved in the arid portions of the country where little rainfall and periods of drought forced a different tactic for controlling water use. In these places, water that is used for other than domestic purposes has to be claimed through a legal process to establish appropriation use. This means that the first person to make a claim on the water can have the exclusive use of as much as he/she needs; later settlers up and down stream have the right to the use or claim of any water left over. The theory is that water is so limited that there is not enough to share.

Appropriative rights are the exclusive law in Montana, Idaho, Wyoming, Nevada, Utah, Colorado, Arizona, New Mexico and Alaska. The states neighboring this drier region have a mixture of both riparian and appropriative rights; Washington, Oregon, California, North and South Dakota, Nebraska, Kansas and Texas.

The usual procedure for appropriative rights (assuming there is enough extra water available) requires public notice and perhaps a public hearing. If your claim is challenged, and it is important enough to warrant going to battle over the issue, a lawyer may be necessary (be sure to find one who knows about these matters; not many do).

Some older properties have mining or manufacturing claims that are listed by use of the water, rather than by a specific quantity of water appropriated. These may be listed as simply the amount of water required to operate a certain number of machines, or for certain processes that require water for washing or sluicing. In some areas these rights may still be on the books and tied to the property rights. To properly research these rights is a job for an historian (this should be part of the title search when purchasing a piece of property).

The local water districts and state water resource departments each has its own set of rules and rituals to obey in obtaining a dependable supply of water. Study them carefully; in many cases they can be circumvented though it is usually best to follow the proper procedures and establish a legal claim for your supply of water.

Once the claim has been filed, you must show ability to exercise the claim for appropriation (similar to mining and homesteading claims). This is usually done by filing a statement with the state's Department of Water Resources, of quantities and schedules of water removed. It may even be wise to file a report of how much is removed under the riparian rights; this can insure the supply in case someone upstream should attempt to cut it off.

Any local soil conservationist or Resources Conservation District (an agency of the U.S. Department of Agriculture) can usually be helpful in supplying information and assistance, not only concerning water rights problems, but also about dams, reservoirs and soils in the area. In addition, you should check with your local authorities and possibly file plans for your dam with them.

Water rights laws are some of the *most* involved around. There have been volumes of court discussions concerning the relative priorities of public, private, industrial, irrigation, hydro-electric, mining and navigational needs. Not only are they complicated, but water rights are often highly localized . . . differing considerably from state to state, county to county and city to city. In California, for example, there are such additional rights, besides the riparian and appropriative as: ground water, prescriptive, developed, surface, consumer, Pueblo, spring water, combinations, governmental, and used water. The rule then should be to investigate the laws and the local regulations before planning use of any water, either for irrigation, general water supply, or power.

MEASURING AVAILABLE WATER POWER

Assuming that you have overcome any legal, economic or environmental problems on your property you can now begin planning your hydro-power plant by calculating how much power is available from your stream. The amount of horse-power possible is determined by; (1) what quantities of water are available (the flow), and (2) what the drop or change in elevation (the head) along the water course is.

Measuring Flow

The volume of water flowing is found by measuring the capacity of the stream bed and the flow rate of the stream. Accurate measurements of the water flow are important for decisions about the size and type of water power installation. You will want to know; (a) normal flow and (b) minimun flow. If a unit is built just on the basis of normal flow measurements, it may be inefficient or even useless during times of low flow. If it is built just on the basis of minimum flow measurements, which usually occur during the late summer, the unit may produce considerably less power than possible. All water courses have a variation of flow. There are often daily as well as seasonal differences. The more measurements you make throughout the year, the better estimate you will have of what the water flow really is. Once you know the stream's varying flows, a system can be built to operate with these flows.

The Small Stream

$$Q = \frac{V}{S}$$ where
Q = flow rate in cubic feet per second (cfs)
V = volume of bucket in cubic feet
S = filling time in seconds   (Eq. 1)

The easiest way to measure the flow rate of a small creek or stream with a capacity of less than one cubic foot per second is to build a temporary dam in the stream. Channel all of the water flow into a pipe or trough and catch it in a bucket of known volume. Measure the time it takes to fill the bucket and use Eq. 1 to find the flow rate.

The Medium Stream: The Weir Method

$Q = T \times W$ where
Q = flow rate in cubic feet per second
T = flow value in cubic feet per second *per foot of width of the weir*, read from a standard table (Table I)
W = width of the weir in feet   (Eq. 2)

The weir method is used for measuring flows of medium streams with a capacity of more than one cubic foot per second. Basically a kind of water meter, a weir is usually a rectangular notch of definite dimensions, located in the center of a small dam. By measuring the (1) depth of water going over the weir and referring to standard tables, and measuring (2) the weir width, the volume of flow can be accurately calculated.

In order for standard tables to apply, the weir must be constructed of standard proportions. Before you build the dam, measure the depth of the stream at the site. The depth of the weir notch "H" (see Fig. 1A) must equal this. The weir notch must be located in the center of the weir dam (see Fig. 1B) with its lower edge at least a foot above the downstream water level. The opening must have a width at least three times its height (3H), and larger if possible. The notch will then be large enough for the water to pass through easily to measure the large flows, and yet not too large so that it cannot also accurately measure the small flows.

The three edges of the opening should be cut or filed on a 45° slant downstream, to produce a sharp edge on the upstream side of the weir. The sharp edges keep the water from becoming turbulent as it spills over the weir, so that measurements will be uniform.

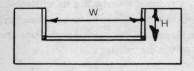

FIG. 1A WEIR

W SHOULD BE ABOUT 3 TIMES H. THE THREE SIDES ARE CUT TO A 45º BEVEL; SHARP EDGE PLACED UPSTREAM

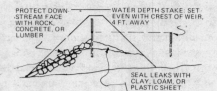

FIG. 1C WEIR DAM CROSS-SECTION

The weir dam need not be permanent, although if left in, it is convenient for continuously monitoring stream flow. The temporary dam can be made simply from logs, tongue and groove lumber, scrap iron, or the like. The dam must be perpendicular to the flow of the stream. And, when the weir is installed, be certain that the sides are cut perpendicular to the bottom, and that the bottom is perfectly level.

All water must flow through the weir opening, so any leakage through the sides and bottom of the dam must be sealed off. Side and downstream leakage can be stopped with planks extended into the banks and below the bed of the stream. Upstream leakage can be sealed off with clay or sheet plastic.

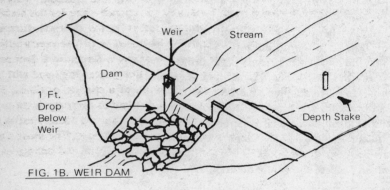

FIG. 1B. WEIR DAM

The accepted method of measuring the water depth over the weir notch (in lieu of putting a ruler in the weir notch) is to drive a stake in a spot accessible from the bank and at least four feet upstream from the weir. The reason for placing the stake at this distance is that the level of the water begins to fall as it nears the weir, where the water forms a crest. Four feet is a safe distance away from the weir to avoid measuring this lower water.

Pound the stake down until the top of the stake is exactly level with the bottom of the weir opening. A level can be established by placing a plank between the bottom of the weir opening and the stake, and using a carpenter's level. To measure the "head" (depth) of water flowing over the weir, allow the stream to reach its maximum flow through the weir, and place a ruler on the stake. Then directly measure the depth in feet of water over the stake.

Having measured the depth of the water, refer to the Flow Rate Weir Table (Table I) for the flow rate for that depth labelled "H" for Head. The flow rate in Table I is given in cubic feet per second for each foot of width of the weir. It is necessary to multiply the flow rate by the width of the weir in feet, to find the actual flow rate. For example: If the depth (H) of the water is 1 foot then the given flow rate from Table I is 3.26. To find the flow over a weir that is 4 feet wide, multiply 4 x 3.26 which equals 13.04 cubic feet per second.

The Large Stream: Float Method

The following method is not as accurate as the previous two. It is impractical to dam a larger stream and measure it for preliminary study, but with large amounts of water, a precise measurement is probably not so important.

TABLE I – FLOW RATE WEIR TABLE

Table for rating the flow over a rectangular weir.
Flow (Q) is in cubic feet per second per foot of width of the weir.
Multiply the flow value given times the width of the weir in feet to find the actual flow rate.

H, head (feet)	Q, flow (cfs)	H, head (feet)	Q, flow (cfs)	H, head (feet)	Q, flow (cfs)	H, head (feet)	Q, flow (cfs)
.05	.037	1.05	3.51	2.05	9.37	3.05	16.66
.10	.105	1.10	3.76	2.10	9.71	3.10	17.05
.15	.193	1.15	4.01	2.15	10.05	3.15	17.45
.20	.297	1.20	4.27	2.20	10.39	3.20	17.84
.25	.414	1.25	4.54	2.25	10.73	3.25	18.24
.30	.544	1.30	4.81	2.30	11.08	3.30	18.65
.35	.685	1.35	5.08	2.35	11.43	3.35	19.05
.40	.836	1.40	5.36	2.40	11.79	3.40	19.46
.45	.996	1.45	5.65	2.45	12.14	3.45	19.87
.50	1.17	1.50	5.93	2.50	12.51	3.50	20.28
.55	1.34	1.55	6.23	2.55	12.87	3.55	20.69
.60	1.53	1.60	6.52	2.60	13.23	3.60	21.10
.65	1.72	1.65	6.83	2.65	13.60	3.65	21.53
.70	1.92	1.70	7.13	2.70	13.97	3.70	21.95
.75	2.13	1.75	7.44	2.75	14.35	3.75	22.37
.80	2.34	1.80	7.75	2.80	14.73	3.80	22.79
.85	2.57	1.85	8.07	2.85	15.11	3.85	23.22
.90	2.79	1.90	8.39	2.90	15.49	3.90	23.65
.95	3.02	1.95	8.71	2.95	15.88	3.95	24.08
1.00	3.26	2.00	9.04	3.00	16.26	4.00	24.52

$$Q = A \times V \quad \text{where}$$

Q = flow rate in cubic feet per second (cfs)

A = average cross-sectional flow area in square feet
D(depth) X W (width)

D = the average depth of the stream

$$\frac{(d_0 + d_1 + d_2 + d_3 + \ldots d_n)}{n}$$

which is the sum of the depths at n stations *of equal* width, divided by n

W = the width of the stream

V = the velocity in feet per second of a float

(Eq. 3)

Choose a length of stream that is fairly straight, with sides approximately parallel, at least 30 feet long (the longer the better), that has a relatively smooth and unobstructed bottom. Stake out a point at each end of the length, and erect posts on each side of the bank at these points. Connect the two upstream posts by a level wire or rope (use a carpenter's line level). Proceed the same way with the downstream posts (see Fig. 2).

Divide the stream into at least five equal sections along the wires (the more sections, the better), and measure the water depth for each section. Then average the depth figures by adding each value and dividing by the number of values. For example, if you have 7 readings of equal width, add $depth_0 + depth_1 + depth_2 + depth_3 + depth_4 + depth_5 + depth_6 + depth_7$ and divide by 7. Since Fig. 2 shows d_0 and d_7 at the edge of the stream, their depths are zero, they are not included in the calculation, and the sum of the values is divided by 5. For other situations, Eq. 4 should be used.

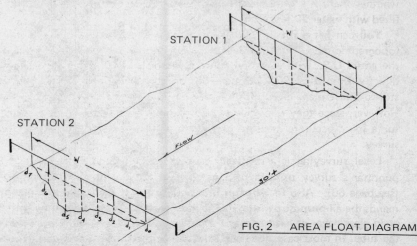

FIG. 2   AREA FLOAT DIAGRAM

$$A = \frac{(d_0 + d_1 + d_2 + d_3 + \dots d_n)}{n} \times (W)$$

where   A = average cross-sectional flow area in square feet

d = the depth at each reading

n = the number of readings taken along the

(Eq. 4)   stream's width

W = the width of the stream

Now to find the stream's cross-sectional area, multiply the average value of the depth times the stream's width (the length of the wire or rope as in Eq. 4.)

Remember that you are trying to find the average area of a section of the stream, so you must take the value of (A) for each station, add them together and divide by two.

Your next step is to measure the stream's velocity in order to determine Q (the stream's flow rate). Make a float of light wood, or use a bottle that will ride awash. A pennant can be put on the float so that its progress can be followed easily. Now set the float adrift, in the middle of the stream, upstream from the first wire. Time its progress down the stream with a stop watch, beginning just when the float passes the first wire, and stopping just as it passes the second wire. Since the water does not flow as fast on the bottom as it does on the surface, you must multiply your calculations by a coefficient to give you a more accurate estimate of the stream's velocity.

$$V = \frac{D}{T} \times .8$$ where   V = velocity in feet per second (fps)

D = distance in feet

T = time in seconds

(Eq. 5)   .8 = coefficient

Having determined the area and velocity of the stream, Eq. 6 gives the flow rate of the stream.

$$Q = A \times V$$ where   Q = flow rate (cfs)

V = velocity (feet per second)

(Eq. 6)   A = cross-section area in square feet

Measuring Head

The "head" or height of fall of the water determines what kind of waterwheel or turbine you will choose. Commonly, this distance is measured in feet. Head produces a pressure . . . water pressure. Basically the weight of the water at a given head exerts a pressure that is proportional to that head . . . the greater the head the greater the pressure. Pressure is usually measured in pounds of force per square inch (psi). Pipes, fittings, valves and turbines may be rated either in head or psi. The relationship between the two if you need to know head, and the equipment is rated in psi and vice versa, is:

1 ft. head = .433 psi   .water weighs 62.4 lbs. per cubic foot

.there are 144 square inches (in^2) per square foot

.thus $\frac{62.4 \text{lbs/ft}^3}{144 \text{in}^2 /\text{ft}^2} = .433$ psi/ft of head

An elevation of head will produce the same pressure, no matter what the volume or quantity of water is in that distance. If the head or depth of water is 20 feet the pressure of that water will be (20 x .433) = 8.7 psi whether there is a whole reservoir of water 20 feet deep or a 2 inch pipe filled with water 20 feet high.

You can get a rough estimate of head on your land from a detailed topographic map. The U.S. Geological Survey prints topographic maps of the entire U.S., with elevation contour intervals of 40'. They are available directly from the USGS (see page 68) or from some local sporting goods stores. These maps are useful for making note of particularly choice sites. However, since they only give an approximation of slopes and elevations, for a more accurate measure of head it will be necessary to take a level survey.

Level surveying is a relatively easy process. A good description of a poorman's survey using a carpenter's level can be found in *Cloudburst* (see page 66). Also included in that publication is a critique that recommends the all-purpose hand level. The hand level is a metal sight tube with a plain glass cover at each end and a prism, cross hair, and spirit level inside the tube. In most cases the hand level will be the simplest and least expensive way to go. More expensive and elaborate instruments are available (a surveying transit or a surveyor's level) but they will probably not be needed for these basic measurements.

Measuring the vertical difference in elevation between point A and point B.

    1. Basic Eyeball Method with Handlevel: How High is Your Eye?

    Measure the distance standing upright from the bottom of your feet to the middle of your eye. Stand at the lower point (point B) and sight through the level at the top of an object or at the ground next to an object so you know where to go next. Go stand at that spot and sight again, always working towards point A. With a pole in the ground at point A the elevation of the final sighting can be marked and subtracted from the total. By simply multiplying the elevation of the eye by the number of sightings (minus the extra elevation in the last sighting) the vertical elevation change from point A to B is determined.

    2. With surveying Rod and Handlevel

    Attach a tape measure to a pole with the zero end at the bottom. Have one person hold the rod while another sights through the handlevel. This does require some conversation between the "rod-man" and the "instrument man" about where the "level point" is on the rod and what the value of that point is.

    The instrument man must tell the rod man where the level point is on the rod (indicated with a pointing finger) and the rod man must read off and write down the value on the tape of that point. The instrument man stays put while the rod man moves on towards point B to some notable point where a new reading is taken. Then the instrument man "leap-frogs" downhill past the rod for a new reading and so forth. Add up the differences of readings for each time the instrument man moves past the rod man; the total of these differences will be the elevation change from point A to point B.

    The head is then the change in elevation between point A and point B. It is desirable to obtain the greatest amount of head possible. This can be accomplished in several ways. First, you can choose a site for the turbine where the greatest drop in the stream occurs in the shortest distance. Secondly, the amount of head can be increased with the construction of a dam (see Dams). Most hydro-power systems will require a dam anyway, and the higher the dam can be built, the greater the head will be. Finally, the head may be increased by the use of a channel or sluice. The channel or sluice will be downstream from the dam to carry the water to a place where a steeper drop occurs. Other determining factors must be considered in trying to realize the greatest amount of head. The most basic are cost, property lines, construction laws, soil condition and pond area in back of the dam.

Calculating Power

We can define power as the ability to do work. In order to determine if the hydro-power installation will meet your needs, the amount of available power must be calculated. The amount of this power is proportional to the head available and the flow rate of the water. Waterwheels and water turbines generate mechanical power (however, turbines are usually hooked up to an electrical generator, and the mechanical power generates electrical power). The mechanical power is usually measured in horsepower.

$$THP = \frac{Q \times H}{8.8}$$ where   THP = theoretical horsepower

Q = flow rate in cubic feet per second (cfs)

H = head in feet

(Eq. 7)   8.8 = correction factor for the units

Eq. 7 illustrates the theoretical horsepower available from the head and flow of a stream. Eq. 8 below refines the calculation of this available power. There are losses in the amount of head due to friction in the channel or pipe which carries water from the dam to the wheel or turbine. Thus, actual head is the amount of head loss (due to friction) subtracted from the total head available. A discussion of the head loss in pipes and canals can be found in the Channels, Sluices and Pipes section.

Another loss factor that Eq. 8 accounts for is the efficiency of the devices (turbine, generator, and any mechanical connection between the two: belts, gears, chains, pulleys) used to harness the power. In the case of water power, efficiency is an indicator of the conversion performance of the machinery used to harness the water power. It is usually measured as a percentage. Each machine or device will have its own efficiency percentage, and they must be multiplied together in order to obtain the over-all efficiency:

$$NHP = \frac{Q \times H \times E}{8.8}$$

where   NHP = net horsepower

           Q = flow rate in cubic feet per second

           H = actual head in feet

           E = efficiency of all the devices multiplied

                 times one another

                 (i.e. 75% X 85% X 80%)

(Eq. 8)   8.8 = correction factor for the units

DAMS

In developing water power, dams are needed for three functions: (1) to divert the stream flow to the waterwheel or turbine, (2) to store the energy of the flowing stream, and (3) to raise the water level (head) to increase the available power. In addition to being used to help develop power, a dam may be useful in providing a pond for watering livestock, for fire protection or for irrigation needs. However, keep in mind the possibility of ecological harm involved in damming a stream, and forego the construction if necessary.

There are four basic criteria for deciding possible sites for the dam and powerhouse: (1) the ease of building the dam, considering the width of the stream and the stability of the soil; (2) maximizing the amount of possible storage volume behind the dam without damaging the ecological balance; (3) minimizing the distance to a good powerhouse site in order to lower the difficulty and the expense of moving the water; and at the same time (4) finding a place where the greatest amount of head is available.

Once a site has been chosen the size and type of dam needed will largely depend upon the stream course and surroundings as well as your needs for power. An assessment must be made of basic requirements for power (both mechanical and electrical) and some estimate of future needs. This could be as simple as adding up the power needs for lighting and refrigeration, but could also include assessing needs for machinery, power tools, or appliances. Essentially then, the size and type of dam will depend upon the size and type of waterwheel or turbine that will be needed to fill power needs, and also upon the flow rate of the stream, the head available, the local restrictions on size and permanency, and the money available.

Diversion Dam

When there is a creek with a continuous flow and a natural drop that together will provide sufficient power for your needs, a small diversion dam will suffice. This can simply be a log placed up against some projecting rocks, with rocks, gravel and earth placed upstream to stop the underflow. Even a temporary dam of a few rows of sandbags will serve well (at least until the first flood comes) and can be cheaply and easily replaced. All that is necessary is a sufficient dam to divert the water into a sluice or pipe intake which carries the water to the turbine (see Channels, Sluices and Pipes).

Small diversion dams have the advantage of easily "washing out" during large flows thus preventing possible damage downstream which the washing out of a larger more permanent dam might cause. Also, diversion dams may be useful for running some of the stream's water into an off-stream storage location.

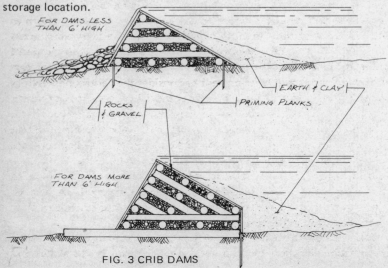

FOR DAMS LESS THAN 6' HIGH

EARTH & CLAY

PRIMING PLANKS

ROCKS & GRAVEL

FOR DAMS MORE THAN 6' HIGH

FIG. 3 CRIB DAMS

The need for storage is one of the dam's primary functions, but during times of large flow or flood can cause potentially dangerous situations. Normally the water would be stored directly behind the dam in the stream's course. However, if a diversion were used to divert the water to a side canyon or hollow, the need for storage would be met, while avoiding the danger of a flood washout. When large flows occurred the diversion dam could either be easily taken down or allowed to wash out by the stream's force; both situations leaving the off-stream storage facility full and intact. When the large flow subsided, the dam could simply be rebuilt.

Low Dams of Simple Construction

These can be built by adding to the diversion dam's structure. Instead of one log, use several stacked together log cabin style, or like a corn-crib —hence the term "crib dam." The crib dam (see Fig. 3) consists of green logs or heavier timbers stacked perpendicular to each other, spaced about 2 or 3 feet apart. These should be spiked together where they cross, and the spaces in between filled with rocks and gravel. The upstream side, especially the base, should be covered with planks or sheets of plastic to prevent leakage, and then further covered with earth or clay to seal the edges. Priming planks should be driven into the soil approximately two to three feet deep at the upstream face to limit the seepage under the dam (particularly on porous soils). Priming planks are wooden boards, preferably tongue and groove, with one end cut to a point on one edge. They are driven into the soil so that the long pointed side is placed next to the board that was previously driven. Then as each successive board is driven into the soil it is forced up snug against the preceding board as a result of the angle of the bottom cut.

PRIMING PLANKS

The downstream face of the dam must be protected from erosion or undercutting wherever water will spill over. This is most important at a time of large flows! The spillways can be made of concrete, lumber, or simply a pile of rocks large enough to withstand the continual flow. Crib dams can be built with the lower cross-timbers extended out to form a series of small water cascades downstream. Each cross-timber step should be at least as wide as it is tall.

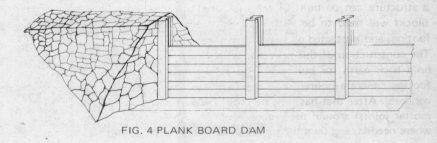

FIG. 4 PLANK BOARD DAM

Earth-Fill Dam

This is the cheapest kind of dam if earth moving equipment is available. Sometimes these can be small gravel dams (under 5 feet) that can wash out with each season's flood, and can be rebuilt when necessary. For larger earth dams (in California anything more than 6 feet high or 5 acre feet or storage) a registered civil engineer will have to be consulted, and some soil studies should be made to determine the method of construction. For more information on the structure, placement, and suitability of earth fill dams, see the USDA Handbook No. 387, "Ponds for Water Supply and Recreation," page 67.

Plank Board Dam

Much like a plank-board overflow spillway, a small dam can be constructed from wooden planks supported by posts set in a concrete foundation (see Fig. 4). The posts can be wood 4 x 4's (or larger) with steel channel or angle-iron attached to the sides, or the posts could be steel I-beams set directly in the foundation. The wooden planks can be dropped into the steel slots to form as much of a dam as is needed (up to the height of the posts). The upstream face of a plank board dam will often need to be sealed with plastic sheeting to prevent leakage. The planks (2 x 6 or larger) can be either added or removed to vary the height of the dam and can be completely removed during the flood season.

Rock Masonry Dam

With a plentiful supply of rocks and stone nearby, a good rock masonry dam can be built of uncut rock laid in cement mortar. This style should be built with a base at least 8/10 the height. With a masonry dam more than 8 feet high some engineering consultation would be important (and may even be required). Many soil factors can threaten the stability of the dam.

Concrete Gravity Dam

One of the more common building materials for containing water is good old concrete. A 1925 USDA Bulletin: "Power for the Farm From Small Streams," recommends a mixture of one part Portland cement, 2 parts sand, and 4 parts gravel or broken stone. Large boulders can be thrown in, but they should be well set in the concrete and should not exceed 30% of the total volume. The dam with dimensions shown in Fig. 5 should not be more than 50 feet long.

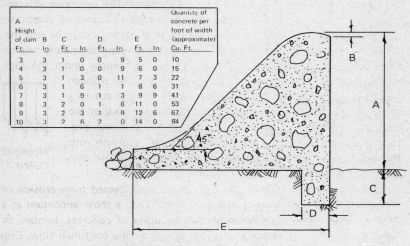

A Height of dam Ft.	B Ft.	B In.	C Ft.	C In.	D Ft.	D In.	E Ft.	E In.	Quantity of concrete per foot of width (approximate) Cu. Ft.
3	3		1	0	0	9	5	0	10
4	3		1	0	0	9	6	0	15
5	3		1	3	0	11	7	3	22
6	3		1	6	1	1	8	6	31
7	3		1	9	1	3	9	9	41
8	3		2	0	1	6	11	0	53
9	3		2	3	1	9	12	6	67
10	3		2	6	2	0	14	0	84

FIG. 5 CONCRETE GRAVITY DAM

Concrete Block Dam

For simpler construction, and considerably less volume of concrete mix, a structure can be built of manufactured standard concrete blocks. The blocks will need to be reinforced with re-bar, placed on a firm concrete footing, and protected on the downstream face with a pile of sizable rocks. The construction of this type dam is very similar to retaining walls used to hold back earth for buildings. The re-bar must be placed first, then the footing concrete poured, and the first row of blocks placed on the wet concrete. After that has set, the other rows of blocks can be placed (with mortar joints) around the vertical bars; the horizontal bars can be placed where needed, and then the holes in the block should be filled with poured concrete.

LARGE AND SMALL FLOWS

The process of developing a water power installation is complicated by variations in the quantity of stream flow. Large flows can wash out dams, destroy waterwheels and turbines and create dangerous situations downstream. It is important to know what the possible large flows for the particular stream will be and how best to prepare for them.

The maximum expected flow in a stream cannot always be measured directly; it could happen at 3 am on a cold rainy night. Nor can flows be determined by the regular high-water marks along the banks, or by old timers who remember the "big rains of ought-8." The "Big Flood" for a particular drainage will come as the result of the right combination of strength and intensity of an exceptional storm as well as the soil conditions, moisture content, vegetation, and the physical structure of the drainage area around that stream. Hydrologists, local flood control people, soil conservation agencies, or water districts can often offer assistance in predicting the flood flows for small drainages. Another source, where these agencies are not available, is a US Department of Agriculture handbook (No. 387) "Ponds for Water Supply and Recreation" (see page 67).

For all types of dams there must be some provision to handle the maximum flows that can come with a severe rain storm; otherwise the sides, foundation, and the structure of the dam can be weakened. This is particularly true for earth dams, since any flow that exceeds the capacity of the spillway will erode the dam with frightening ease. As this would occur at a time when the stream is already at flood stage, the added volume of water from a washed out dam could be exceptionally dangerous downstream and the owner of the dam could be legally liable for the damage.

With small dams, especially earth dams, the best way for large flows to safely pass downstream may be to allow them to wash out the dam. With larger dams this method may be impractical, costly and dangerous. In these situations it will be necessary to use a culvert or weir for the large flows to pass through.

An opening can be made with a large culvert placed through the dam. The *Water Measurement Manual*, page 67, will aid in determining the capacity for a given length and size of pipe. The face of the dam should be protected from the downstream outflow of the culvert, or, if you have one long enough, the culvert can be extended beyond the footing of the dam to the natural stream course. The problem with pipes and culverts is that they are easily plugged by brush and trash. They must be watched almost continuously during storms or the water back-up may overflow the dam. Because of this problem, culverts do not make good spillways; so, there should be some additional spillway provided. However, pipes and culverts can be useful to control the flow rate downstream, a simple "gate valve" (of a sort) can be made by placing a piece of plywood over the upstream end of the pipe. The flow rate can then be controlled by adjusting the plywood to allow the proper opening.

A sufficient flood flow capacity can be provided by one or more rectangular openings in the dam. These could be built like large rectangular weirs to provide a continuous measure of the flow rate, as well. (Use Table I to find the size weir required to handle the flood flows). Such an opening would not be easily plugged by trash, and the flow could be regulated by placing planks flat across the upstream side of the opening to raise the spill level.

Plank board dams are well suited to handle floods. During times of large flow the planks may simply be removed to allow more water to pass downstream (see Dams).

Small flows do not present the potential danger that large flows do. They may, however, be of insufficient quantity to operate the waterwheel or turbine. Although it may be desirable to store water behind the dam in order to gain a larger flow for the wheel or turbine, it may not be possible or necessarily advisable. Water right laws in many cases will prohibit halting the flow downstream even if you plan to let it flow later in the same day. Also, during times of low flow, the intermittent storage and release of water will cause some erosion in the stream course above and below the dam. In short, it is probably best to design your hydro-power installation to operate at the minimum seasonal flow rate, rather than attempting storage during that time. This suggestion should not be taken as advice against storage of water during times of normal or average flow, but here too, care should be taken and the laws should be investigated.

CHANNELS, SLUICES AND PIPES

Every hydro-power installation (with the possible exception of an undershot wheel) will require a means to carry the water from the stream to the waterwheel or turbine. In most cases a dam will have been constructed and the task will be to take all or part of the water and run it to the wheel or turbine. In many cases there will be a considerable distance from the dam to the turbine and it will be important to consider the various possibilities and compare the costs of both materials and labor. Most of the lower technology waterwheels will be best serviced by an open channel or sluice. The Pelton wheel, Banki, Propeller, Kaplan and Francis turbines will almost always require piping. Discussion of how each of these units operate will follow in the Waterwheels and Water Turbines section.

Basically, there are two ways to move water from one location to another—either with unpressured flow along an open channel (e.g. a canal, sluice or a natural stream) or with flow under pressure contained in a pipe. Each has advantages in the appropriate situation.

A canal is simply a ditch dug out along the ground, that will maintain a nearly constant elevation (with a very gradual down grade slope) and carry water at a low velocity with a minimal amount of head loss. The head loss will be the same as the loss of elevation along the canal.) The size (i.e. the cross-section area) of the canal that will be required to carry a given amount of flow will depend on the roughness of the canal, the amount of vegetation growing in the canal and the slope of the canal. Canals are more often used for irrigation than for a hydro-power plant, although the two needs, power and agriculture will often be compatible—a dam and canal can divert water for both purposes. In short, a canal will move water with a minimum of both cost and head loss.

The sluice is really another type of open channel. The difference being that a canal is usually dug out of the ground, whereas a sluice is an elevated structure or open box channel, somewhat like the old Roman aqueduct or gold-miners flume. They are useful for carrying water over or around obstacles where a ditch would be impractical (e.g. rocky ground, side canyons, or very steep hillsides). The overshot water wheel requires a sluice to carry the water out over the structure of the wheel.

The sluice itself can be made from wood or metal. The sluice must be supported by a strong structure. Remember that water weighs 62.4 lbs. per cubic foot, so a 2' x 4' box channel would have to carry *500 lbs. per foot of length*, or each four feet of sluice would hold a ton of water!

Channel Flow

There are several objectives in channel design: to (1) move the water with as little head loss as possible; this means a gradual slope, slower velocity, and an adequately large channel; (2) do the job as cheaply as possible, avoiding any undue construction complications, and keeping the channel as small and as short as possible; and (3) move as much water as is available within the above constraints. Some compromises must be made along the way, since it is unlikely that all these criteria can be met in any one design.

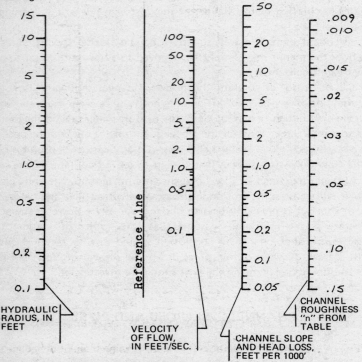

FIG. 6A CHANNEL FLOW NOMOGRAPH

USE OF THE NOMOGRAPH: Draw a straight line from the appropriate value for "n" through the velocity of flow desired, to Reference line; this sets the pivot point. Then a second line is drawn from the hydraulic radius (determined by the size and shape of the channel) through the pivot point to the head loss scale; this gives the slope required to overcome the head loss in a given channel for water moving at a given rate.

To find the channel size and slope needed to meet the above requirements involves the use of a "Channel Flow Nomograph" (Fig. 6A). The two following methods will describe how to use it. In order to avoid complications in the examples, we are assuming a uniform channel cross-section, a steady flow rate of water, and a constant slope along the channel.

Method Number One involves the use of a chart called a "nomograph" (Fig. 6B) to determine the required slope of the channel. First, determine the amount of water that must be diverted to the channel; this depends on the amount of flow available from the stream, and the wheel or turbine requirements (see Waterwheels and Water Turbines). Now consult Table II

to find the maximum allowable velocity for the water to move through the channel. For example, if the flow is 1 cfs, and the channel were dug in soil with about 40% clay content, the maximum water velocity without causing erosion in the channel would be 1.8 feet per second.

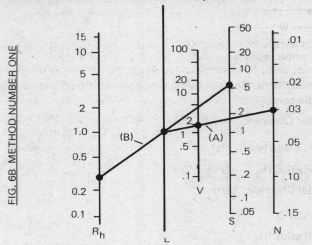

The next value that needs to be known in order to work with the nomograph is the channel roughness (n). This is also read directly from Table II and in this example would be .03.

Last, we must find the hydraulic radius in feet. The hydraulic radius is equal to a proportion of the channel through which the water flows. The first step is to find the minimum channel cross-sectional area that is required to carry the stream's flow (see Eq. 9).

$$A = \frac{Q}{V}$$

where A = cross-section area of the channel in square feet
Q = flow in cubic feet per second
V = maximum water velocity in feet per second
(Eq. 9) before erosion begins (from Table II)

Continuing with our "example" stream, using Eq. 9, "A" would equal 1 cfs divided by 1.8 fps or 0.56 ft². Once the channel area is figured, the channel shape is chosen. The shape is largely a function of the materials found or used. Channels made of timber, masonry, concrete or rock should have walls constructed perpendicular to the bottom (see Fig. 7). The water level height should be one half of the width. Earth channels should have walls built at a 45° angle (see Fig. 8). Design them so that the water-level height is one half that of the channel width at the bottom.

CHANNEL ROUGHNESS

TABLE II

Composition of channel wall	Maximum water velocity (ft/sec) before erosion begins	Channel roughness (n)
fine grained sand	0.6	0.030
coarse sand	1.2	0.030
small stones	2.4	0.030
coarse stone	4.0	0.030
rock	25.0	0.033
earth:		
sandy loam, 40% clay	1.8	0.030
loamy soil, 65% clay	3.0	0.030
clay loam, 85% clay	4.8	0.030
soil loam, 95% clay	6.2	0.030
100% clay	7.3	0.030
earth bottom with rubble sides	(use one of above factors for earth)	0.033
concrete with sandy water	10.0	0.016
concrete with clean water	20.0	0.016
wood	25.0	0.015
metal	no limit	0.015

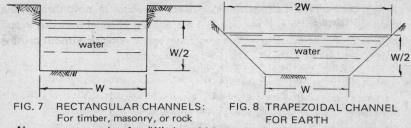

FIG. 7   RECTANGULAR CHANNELS:
For timber, masonry, or rock

FIG. 8   TRAPEZOIDAL CHANNEL
FOR EARTH

Now we must solve for (W) the width across the bottom of the channel which will enable us to find the hydraulic radius, the last value we must know to use the nomograph.

For Rectangular Channels: Timber, Masonry, Concrete or Rock Lined

$$\text{Area} = \frac{W^2}{2} \qquad \text{so } W = \sqrt{2A}$$

Hydraulic Radius (R_h) = $(0.25)(W)$ \qquad (Eq. 10)

For Trapezoidal Channels: Earth

$$\text{Area} = (.75)(W^2) \qquad \text{so } W = \sqrt{\frac{A}{.75}}$$

Hydraulic Radius (R_h) = $(0.31)(W)$ \qquad (Eq. 11)

To find the (W) of our example stream, use $W = \sqrt{\frac{A}{.75}}$. We know A = .56 ft², then $W = \sqrt{\frac{A}{.75}} = \sqrt{\frac{.56}{.75}} = 0.86$ ft. Now the hydraulic radius can be calculated using the formula $R_h = (.31)(W)$. $R_h = (.31)(.86) = 0.27$. The hydraulic radius is then .27 ft.

To continue with the example, we have found the flow (1 cfs), the velocity (1.8 fps), the channel roughness (.03), and the hydraulic radius (.27 ft) and now need to find, using the nomograph, the channel slope required to move 1 cfs at a maximum velocity of 1.8 fps.

Using the nomograph (Fig. 6B), locate the point .03 on the *channel roughness* scale (N) and locate 1.8 fps on the *velocity* scale (V). Draw the line (A) through these two points to the *reference line* (L). Then locate the .27 on the *hydraulic radius* scale (R_h). A second line (B) drawn from .27 through the point at which line (A) intersects the reference line will intersect the *channel loss/head loss* scale (S) at approximately 7.6. The channel slope/head loss is then 7.6 feet per thousand feet. Evaluating this outcome to see if this is the channel to construct will depend upon the length of the channel and the amount of head needed to operate the wheel or turbine.

In most cases the head loss and slope found in this manner will be too great for the requirements of the site, and so some redesign will be necessary. To redesign for a lesser, more gradual slope, a larger channel (with a larger hydraulic radius) will be necessary to move the same amount of water since the velocity would then be less.

Method Number Two begins with an assumed velocity much less than the maximum allowable. If we use the same flow rate, 1 cfs, it might be logical to choose a velocity of 0.5 fps. The channel area can then be found using Eq. 9. The example would require an area 2 ft². The corresponding hydraulic radius for a trapezoidal earth channel would be 0.51 calculated using $(0.31) \times \sqrt{2 \text{ ft}^2} / .75$.

Using the nomograph (Fig. 6C) and plugging in the appropriate values gives a channel loss/head loss of only .25, a drop of about 3 feet per thousand feet of channel length.

If the slope is still too great, the channel design can be changed by: (a) assuming a slower velocity, with either a larger channel or a smaller flow, or (2) reducing the channel roughness by removing vegetation or otherwise "smoothing out" the channel.

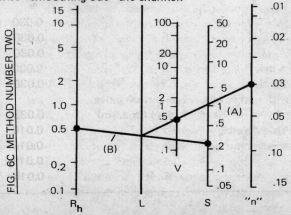

Pipe Flow

The other alternative for water flow, besides the open channel flow, is the pressure flow of water contained in a pipe. This type of flow could exist over a very wide range of conditions: from the large volume of low pressure water flowing in a culvert (as under a road) to the small volume, high pressure flow of water in a pipe. Both cases can be analyzed with the pipe flow nomograph (Fig. 9). It is important to find the proper diameter and strength of pipe to handle the required flow without undue expense or excessive head loss. Although water pipe is expensive (particularly the high pressure steel pipe) it is the only way to deliver water under pressure.

Pipe flow nomographs are used to find head flow loss in pipes. The use of the nomograph in Fig. 9 is relatively easy. One line is drawn through the proper values on the flow rate (Q) scale and pipe size (D) scale, and will indicate the water velocity in the pipe and the corresponding head loss per 100 feet of pipe.

For example, to use a 4" steel pipe to move a flow of 1 cfs, draw a line from the 4" mark on line "D" on the nomograph through 1.0 cfs on the "Q" line. This will give a value on the head loss line "H_L" of 20 feet of head loss per 100 feet of pipe. In most instances this would be too prohibitive a loss, and so some larger pipe would be required. To use a 6" pipe for the same flow rate (1 cfs) would mean a head loss of only 3 feet per 100 feet. This is a much more reasonable size of pipe for the 1 cfs flow.

This nomograph (Fig. 9) is only for the use of steel pipe. Steel is relatively rough compared with other kinds of pipes, with a roughness coefficient (C) of 100. It is possible to find the head loss and velocity in pipes other than steel (as long as the flow rate "Q" and pipe diameter are known). By finding the C value of the pipe (Table III) and using Eq. 12, the velocity, flow rate and head loss can be found.

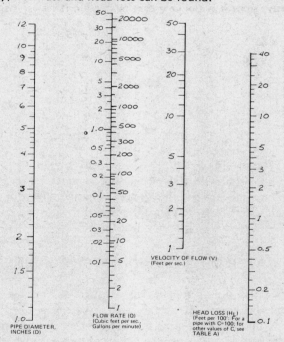

FIG. 9   NOMOGRAPH FOR HEAD LOSS IN STEEL PIPE (C=100)

$V = (V_N)\dfrac{C}{100}$ where

(Eq. 12A)

V = velocity of water through a pipe other than steel

V_N = velocity of water read from nomograph, when Q and D are known

C = pipe roughness coefficient (Table III)

$Q = (Q_N)\dfrac{C}{100}$ where

(Eq. 12B)

Q = flow rate of water (cfs) through pipe other than steel

Q_N = flow rate value read from nomograph

C = pipe roughness coefficient (Table III)

$H_L = (H_{LN})\left(\dfrac{100}{C}\right)^{1.85}$

where

(Eq. 12C)

H_L = head loss per 100 feet of pipe

H_{LN} = head loss read from nomograph

C = pipe roughness coefficient (Table III)

To take $\dfrac{100}{C}$ to the 1.85 power, it is necessary to use logarithms. Either consult a friend, textbook or slide rule for assistance.

For example, using a new pipe lined with bitumastic enamel, and the same flow rate (1 cfs) and diameter pipe (6 inches) then:

$$V = 5 \text{ (fps)} \left(\frac{145}{100}\right) = 7.25 \frac{\text{feet}}{\text{second}}, \text{ a faster V, as a result of smoother pipe}$$

$$Q = (1 \text{ cfs}) \left(\frac{145}{100}\right) = 1.45 \text{ cfs}$$

$$H_L = (3\text{ft}) \left(\frac{100}{145}\right)^{1.85} = (3)(.512) = 1.54 \text{ feet per 100 feet}$$

TABLE III PIPE ROUGHNESS TABLE
VALUE OF C* FOR USE WITH PIPE-FLOW NOMOGRAPH

Pipe	C*
New tar-coated	130
New cement-lined	150
New cast-iron, pit cast	120-130
New cast-iron, centrifugally cast	125-135
Cement lining, applied by hand	125-135
Bitumastic enamel, hand brushed	135-145
Bitumastic enamel, centrifugally applied	145-155
Ordinary tar-dipped cast-iron, 20 years service in inactive water.	110-125
Ordinary tar-dipped cast-iron after long service with severe tuberculation	30-40
Ordinary tar-dipped cast-iron; average tuberculation;	
new	135
5 years old	120
10 years old	110
15 years old	105
20 years old	95
30 years old	85
40 years old	80
New bituminous enamel-lined	150
Transite	140+
Poly-vinyl chloride (PVC)	130

*C is a smoothness coefficient which gives a numerical value for how smooth the pipe and fittings are. A rougher pipe with a lower value increases the head loss in the pipe.

WATER WHEELS AND WATER TURBINES

So far we have been discussing ways to measure available water power, build dams and construct channels and sluices. Now we shall turn our attention to the actual devices, the waterwheels and turbines that turn water power into useful work. The choice of turbine or wheel is probably the biggest decision in building a hydro-power plant. The main factors that will determine your choice are:

1. *Flow rates:* minimum to be available, maximum to be utilized and maximum to be routed through the dam.

2. *Available head:* elevation difference in feet or meters between head waters and tail waters.

3. *Site sketch:* an elevation or topographic map with dam and power locations indicated.

4. *Soil conditions:* determines the possibility of erosion and the size and slope of a canal; also a consideration in dam construction.

5. *Pipe length:* required from dam or end of canal to powersite.

6. *Water conditions:* clear, muddy, sandy, acid, etc.

7. *Tailwater elevation:* the maximum and minimum water level immediately below the turbine.

8. *Air temperature :* annual maximum and minimum, particularly amount of exposure to freezing temperatures.

9. *Power generation:* a waterwheel if you want mechanical energy, or a turbine for electrical energy, and how much of each type of energy is needed.

10. *Cost/Labor:* pre-packaged vs "home-built."

11. *Materials:* use of native or purchased materials to suit the design and use.

12. *Maintenance:* some assessment of reliability and ease of repair.

We will discuss those waterwheels and water turbines that are appropriate for the small scale projects that individuals and communities might reasonably consider. There are really too many designs, devices and inventions associated with hydro-power to describe in this limited space. Furthur research has led us to conclude that construction instructions for wheels that may be "home-built" are adequately treated in other publications. Consequently we will not take the time here to rehash what is already available, and the reader should refer to p. 69 *Reviews/Water* section. For the more technically minded, the discussion of each wheel and turbine has *some* detailed and geometric coverage of construction.

WATERWHEELS

Waterwheels are particularly useful for generating mechanical power. This power is taken off the center shaft of the wheel and usually connected, via belts and pulleys, to machinery. Waterwheels generally operate at between 2 and 12 revolutions per minute (rpm) and are appropriate for slow speed applications such as turning grinding wheels, pumping water and sometimes running lightweight machinery and tools (i.e. lathes, drill presses and saws). Waterwheels may be used to generate electric power but because of the slow rotational speeds, difficulties are often encountered. Waterwheels will operate in situations where there are large fluctuations in the flow rate. The changing flow will bring about a change in the rpm of the wheel.

Undershot Wheel

The most basic design (and simplest concept) in waterwheels is the old-style undershot wheel. The earliest design for the undershot wheel was a simple paddle wheel, immersed in the stream flow, that splashed along with the current. This sort of wheel powered the fountains of Louis XIV's Palace of Versailles. A number of undershot wheels, each 14 meters in diameter, powered the fountain's pumps with an overall efficiency of only 10%.

The refinements that were developed to improve the efficiency of the undershot wheel included better controls on the water in order to increase the velocity of the water as it hit the paddles, and to limit the amount of water so the paddles would not get bogged down in the backwater.

Since the really significant loss of energy in the paddle-type undershot wheels came from the shock and turbulence as the water hit the flat paddles, around 1800 the shape of the paddles was changed to reduce this loss. The end result of this change, the curved blades of the Poncelet undershot wheel, is still the last word in the design of the undershot waterwheel.

Poncelet Wheel

These "low-technology" wheels are best suited for heads ranging from three feet up to ten feet and flows ranging from three cubic feet up to whatever is available. They generally operate at a low rpm (for example 7.4 rpm for a 14 foot diameter wheel with a six foot head) as determined using the appropriate formula from Table IV. Poncelet wheels usually develop a high torque; this coupled with their low rpm make them best suited for mechanical work rather than electrical generation. Poncelet wheels are usually made of wood with reasonably heavy timbers being used for the spokes. The buckets or vanes are usually made of sheet-steel.

A well designed Poncelet wheel utilizes the impulse of the water jet as it strikes the vanes at the bottom of the wheel. The vanes are curved so that they allow the water to enter the buckets with a minimum of shock (which would cause some energy loss). The water then "runs up" the curve of the bucket vane, exerting a force on the wheel. As the energy of the water is transferred to the wheel and the wheel rotates, the water falls back and drops from the wheel to the tailwater with nearly zero velocity. The Poncelet is 70% to 85% efficient.

The diameter of the wheel is largely a matter of preferred use and limitations in materials, usually with a minimum diameter of 14 feet up to a maximum of four times the head. For the same output the smaller wheels will turn much faster and with less torque than the larger wheels.

TABLE IV WATERWHEEL AND WATER TURBINE SPECIFICATIONS

Wheel or Turbine Type	Range of head (feet)	Wheel or runner diameter (feet)	Optimum rpm	Efficiency %	Ability to handle changing: Q flow	H head	Technology of construction	Materials
WATERWHEELS								
Undershot Wheel	6'-15'	(3)(H)	$\frac{42.1\sqrt{H}}{D}$	35-45%	good	fair	low	metal/wood
Poncelet Wheel	3'-10'	2H-4H (>14')	$\frac{42.1\sqrt{H}}{D}$	60-80%	good	fair	medium	metal/wood
Breast Wheel	6'-15'	(H)-3(H)	dependent on design less than overshot	40-70%	good	fair +20%H	low	metal/wood
Overshot Wheel	10'-30'	(.75)(H)	$\frac{41.8}{\sqrt{D}}$	60-85%	good	none	low	metal/wood
WATER TURBINES								
Michell (Banki)	15'-150'	1'-3' +	$\frac{862\sqrt{H}}{D, in}$	60-85%	good	good	medium	welded steel
Pelton Wheel	50'-4000'	1'-20'	$\frac{76.6\sqrt{H}}{D}$	80-94%	good	fair	medium/high	steel, cast iron or bronze
Francis	100'-1500'	1'-20'	dependent on design	80-93%	poor	poor	high	cast or
Kaplan	14'-120'	2'-30'	50-220	80-92%	poor	good	high	machined
Propeller	8'-200'	2'-30'	50-220	80-92%	poor	poor	high	steel

H = head in feet
D = diameter of wheel in feet

The bottom of the sluice under a Poncelet wheel must be made in a close-fitting breast for an arc of 30° (15° on either side of bottom-dead center) see Fig. 10. *Breast* or *breast works* may be defined as a structure that is formed to fit close to the rim of the waterwheel, usually intended to help the wheel retain water in its buckets. A breast should be made of concrete or other easily-formed durable materials. It should fit as close as possible to the wheel but not so close that the wheel could rub or bind as it rotates. The tailrace beyond the breast should be deepened and widened to insure that the backwater does not hinder the rotation of the wheel.

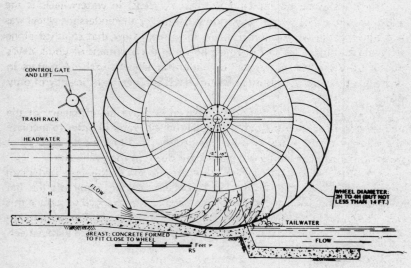

FIG. 10 PONCELET WHEEL

Breast Wheel

Breast wheels can be used for heads between 5 and 15 feet; however, since they are not quite as efficient as overshot wheels for similar heads, they are generally only considered for heads under 10 feet. They are more difficult to construct than the other types of basic water wheels, in that they require a close-fitting breast works (similar to the one pictured in Fig. 10) to keep the water in the buckets along the lower half of the wheel. These breast works further complicate matters since the wheel must be protected from rocks, logs, and debris, to prevent the wheel being jammed and damaged.

When the water enters the wheel at about the elevation of the center shaft, it is considered a "breast wheel;" when the entrance is below the center shaft, the wheel is a "low-breast;" when above, it is a "high-breast."

From late 19th and early 20th century records of American and European practice (still pretty much the state-of-the-art for these wheels) it is evident that the efficiency will vary with the type of breast wheel: about 35% to 40% for low-breast wheels, little better than a simple undershot; about 45% to 55% for midrange; and for "high-breast," about 60% to 65%, approaching that of the overshot wheels.

Not only do breast wheels have complicated, curved breastworks and entrance gate, but the buckets must be "ventilated" to allow air to escape to the next higher bucket as each fills. It seems that considering the operating inefficiencies, maintenance problems, and difficulty of construction, it would make more sense to build an overshot wheel. And for the same effort in design and construction, a Poncelet wheel can give a higher efficiency than the medium or low-breast wheels.

Overshot Wheel

Overshot wheels have traditionally been used for falls (heads) of 10 to 30 feet. They have sometimes been used with higher falls, but because of the size of the wheel needed, there are usually more practical ways to harness the energy. In an overshot wheel, a small portion of the power is a result of the impact of the water as it enters the bucket. Most of the power is from the weight of the water as it descends in the buckets. The wheel should be designed so that the water enters the buckets smoothly and efficiently so that the greatest amount of power is produced with the least amount of waste. The efficiency of this wheel, if well constructed is anywhere from 70% to 80%.

When the supply of water is small, during dry times, the wheel still operates, even though the buckets are only partially filled. This, of course, reduces the power output, and yet the efficiency is increased since less water spills from a less-full bucket. The corollary to this would seem to be that a wheel with an excess carrying capacity would operate at a higher efficiency. However, this increases the construction cost and usually the efficiency gained is not worth the extra expense.

Fig. 11A shows an overshot wheel with curved steel buckets. The water, controlled by the sluice gate at G, flows along a trough or sluice, A, to a drop at the crown of the wheel at C. The end of the sluice is slightly curved toward the wheel and placed such that the water enters at (or slightly after) the vertical center-line of the wheel. The sides of the sluice are extended just enough to fill several buckets at a time, without losing water over the sides of the wheel.

The supply of water as it is regulated by the sluice gate, is usually limited to under an 8 inch depth (see Fig. 11A). In most cases this flow would be controlled by hand, although with a little mechanical ingenuity, the gate could be regulated by an automatic governor.

Overshot Construction

Suppose that the total fall or head available is 20 feet. To insure that the centrifugal force from the water in this head filling the buckets will not cause too much spilling, the rim speed, U, should not be too great. The rim speed is the velocity of the outer edge of the wheel, usually expressed in feet per second. One value for U has been given in an engineering handbook (c. 1930) as U = 2D. With the curved buckets in common usage (as shown in Fig. 11A), a better value of U = 1.55√2D, where D is the diameter of the wheel.

As a first approximation, assume the wheel diameter is 16 feet. Then U = 1.55 (√2 x 16) = 8.8 feet per second. The rim velocity should be between 50% to 70% of the velocity of the water, the best being about 65%. If the rim speed is much faster than this, the back of the buckets will tend to "throw" the water out and away from the wheel.

For our example in which the rim speed is 8.8 feet per second, the velocity of the water entering the buckets would be 8.8 ÷ 65% = 13.5 feet per second.

The headwater behind the sluice gate required to produce this velocity is:

$$h = \frac{v^2}{2g}$$

where h = head in feet (at the sluice gate)
v = velocity of water entering buckets in feet per second
(Eq. 13)   g = acceleration of gravity, 32.2 feet per second[2]

Then, $h = \frac{13.5^2}{2 \times 32.2} = 2.82$ feet. Because of loss of velocity in the sluice and gate due to friction, another 10% should be added to the 2.82 feet to give a required gate head of about 3.1 feet. At best, only half of this velocity is useful work, i.e. contributing to the torque of the wheel. The rest, say 1.6 feet, is lost in the turbulence as the buckets fill.

At this point the initial estimate of wheel diameter can be evaluated. The sum of gate head (3.1 feet), wheel diameter and tailwater clearance (about .5 feet, sufficient so that the wheel does not "hit" the tailwater and get slowed down while it is rotating), should be the total head difference between headwater and tailwater. In this case the total head of 20 feet, minus the gate head (3.1 feet), wheel diameter (16 feet), and tail water drop (about .5 feet), leaves only .4 foot error in the initial estimate of wheel diameter. This is well within the accuracy of the design.

The 16 foot example wheel would operate best at about 10 rpm (from Table IV). Some care should be taken to keep the wheel running at the design rpm by manually regulating the flow with the sluice gate.

Once the wheel diameter and the rim speed are known then the rpm can be calculated with Eq. 14.

$$rpm = \frac{(U)(60)}{C}$$

where   rpm = revolutions per minute
U = rim speed in feet per second
C = wheel circumference in feet (π diameter)

(Eq. 14)

It is necessary to determine the volume of the buckets that is available to be filled with each revolution of the wheel. An approximate formula for this is a product of the area of the buckets (the width times the depth) times the circumference of the wheel at mid-depth of the buckets (that is π times the diameter of the wheel minus half the depth of the buckets).

Volume per revolution = π[(D - b)] x [(width of buckets) X (depth of buckets)]

(Eq. 15)

The buckets are only assumed to be partially full, because a full fill would cause losses due to spilling with no net power gain. Assume then that wooden buckets will be filled approximately 50% and metal buckets approximately 67%. The flow (Q) needed to fill these buckets at the optimum rpm can now be determined using:

Q = (volume per revolution) x (rpm) x (% fill)   where q = flow in cfm

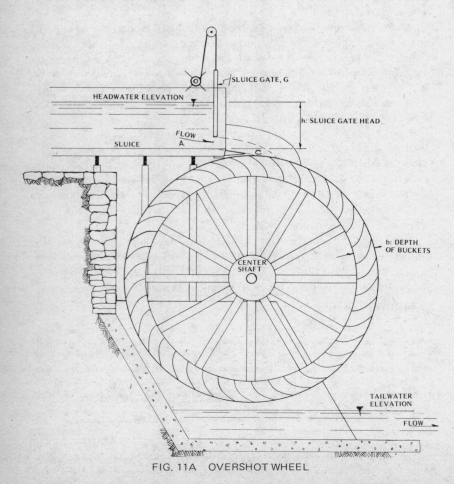

FIG. 11A   OVERSHOT WHEEL

The particular depth chosen for the buckets is rather subjective. One source says the depth should be ".3√D to .5√D where narrower wheels are desired." Another says simply that "spacing and depth should be the same" and the spacing should be ".10 inch to .18 inch."

From the usual practice in the 19th century, it seems that a reasonable number of buckets for a wheel should be about 2.5D (where D is in feet). This has to be a whole number so that the buckets are equally spaced around the wheel. The spacing, s, would be $s = \frac{\pi D}{n}$ where n = number of buckets. Or, to find the angle in degrees between each bucket, divide the full circle, 360° by n.

To find curvature of the buckets for an overshot wheel (see Fig. 11B), set the distance J to K equal to 1/3 b. and the distances L to M equal to (1.2) times the circumvential pitch or bucket spacing, S. A bucket chord line is drawn from M to K with a point, R, found near to K (the length of K to R is about 1/4 the length of J to K). The center of the arc from R to M is set at 0 on a line that is offset 15° from the radius. The arc from M to R should be "rounded" into the radial line J.K.

During construction of this wheel, the job of placing the buckets would be much easier with a template or jig already cut to the exact bucket curvature. If the jig were set up to include the center of the wheel, it could be moved rather quickly around the wheel to indicate the placement of each bucket.

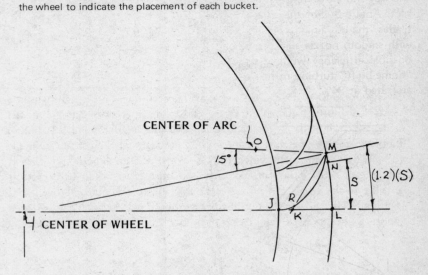

FIG. 11B   OVERSHOT WHEEL: BUCKET CONSTRUCTION

WATER TURBINES

Water turbines are used for producing either direct current (D.C.) or alternating current (A.C.) electricity. Turbines can be classified into two types; (1) impulse, and (2) reaction. Impulse turbines include the Michell (Banki) and Pelton types. They are vertical wheels that utilize the kinetic energy (or momentum) of a jet of water which strikes the buckets or blades. The buckets or blades are so shaped that they turn the flow of water through as near 180° as possible and move at a speed which results in the spent water falling straight to the bottom of the wheel housing, which is mostly full of air. The Michell (or Banki) turbine is simple to construct, while the Pelton wheel is more complicated.

Reaction turbines are horizontal wheels that are moved at high speeds. Unlike the impulse wheels, they are encased in a housing which is completely filled with water, and the continuation of the outlet below the machine results in the formation of a slight vacuum, which both increases the total head and reduces turbulence. These are really too "high-tech" to consider "home-building" and should be purchased from a manufacturer.

Michell Turbine (Banki Turbine)

There is some confusion in this country about the origin of this style water turbine. In the early part of this century an English engineer, A.G.M. Michell, wrote a discussion of the "cross-flow" turbine. Later European references usually mention Michell as the source. It was, however, a paper by Donat Banki, "Neue Wasserturbine," that introduced the concept to America. A study published in 1949 by the Oregon State College (now the University) included a "free translation" of Banki's paper, along with their test results (see page 68). Subsequent references to this type turbine usually have called it a Banki Turbine, although the European manufacturers list their products as the "Michell cross-flow turbine."

The Michell turbine is probably the best choice for most small hydropower installations. It is fairly simple to construct, requiring some welding, simple machining and a few amenities in the workshop. The steel parts can be cut from stock sheet and standard steel pipe. The design is essentially the same for a very wide range of flows and head. For installations with variations in flow rates, the rotational speed for top efficiency will remain the same (for a constant head) over a range of flows from 1/4 of the flow to full design flow. A 12'' diameter wheel with a head of 15 feet will operate at about 280 rpm. One speed change of approximately 6.5:1 will give the rpm necessary to generate A.C. power. A flow of 0.9 cfs would be required for one horsepower output at this head.

The *Michell Construction* section has a brief description of the theory of this unique turbine; further, more technical discussion can be found in the Oregon State study. Basically there are two parts, a nozzle (Fig. 12A) and a turbine runner (Fig. 12B). The drum-shaped runner is built of 2 discs connected at the rim by a series of curved blades. The rectangular nozzle squirts a jet of water at an angle of approximately 16° across the width of the wheel; the water flows across the blades to their inner edge, flies across the empty space within the drum, strikes the blades on the inner side of the rim and exits from the wheel about 180° from the first point of contact. About 3/4 of the power is developed in the first pass through the blades, the remaining 1/4 in the second pass. With a well designed set-up with smooth nozzle surfaces, as well as thin, smooth blades, the maximum possible efficiency would be 88%; the Oregon State test in 1948 with a "home-built" turbine managed a respectable 68%; the German machines are rated at 84%.

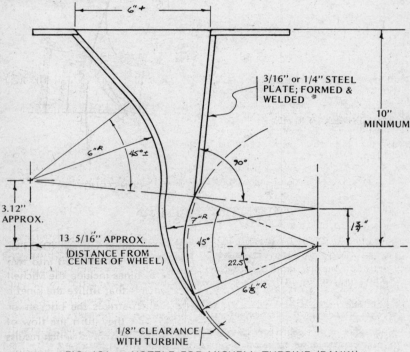

FIG. 12A   NOZZLE FOR MICHELL TURBINE (BANKI)

The cost of materials to construct a Michell turbine is really rather insignificant, especially when compared with the other types of manufactured water turbines. The big expenses will be for the electrical generating equipment, the piping, and, should you need it, the cost of having some machine shop put the wheel together. The Michell turbine is undoubtedly the best power source (where the head is appropriate, in the range of 15 feet to about 100 feet) for the limited budget and those with a desire to be able to do-it-themselves. No other wheel or turbine is quite as versatile, easy to build, and still useful for power generation.

Michell Construction

The following data is for construction of a 12'' diameter wheel. The dimensions for wheel diameter and blade curvature can be changed proportionately for larger wheels though the angles will remain the same.

The end plates are 1 foot diameter discs, cut from 1/4 inch sheet steel, with keyed hubs welded in to fit a suitable sized shaft (this is dependent on power requirements). The blades are cut from standard 4 inch steel water pipe (wall thickness is .237 inch). Each blade is cut for a 72° arc; this can be measured at 1/5 the circumference of the pipe (for a 4'' pipe the distance along the arc would be 2.83 inches, or .236 feet). Each length of pipe suitable for blade pieces will make only 4 blades (each piece 1/5 the pipe's circumference); since there is some loss of material with each cut, there would not be enough left over after 4 blades and 5 cuts to allow a 5th blade.

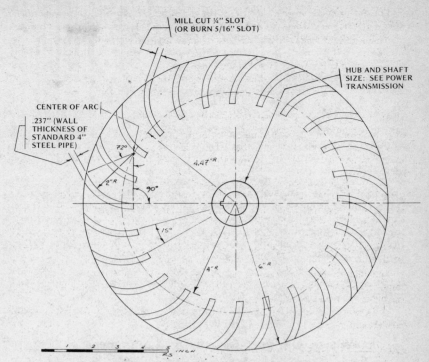

FIG. 12B   12'' WHEEL WITH 24 BLADES FOR MICHELL TURBINE

The length of each blade must be 3/4 inch longer than the inside width of the wheel (W_2) to allow enough to stick out beyond each side plate for a 1/8 inch welding tab. The slots on the side plates can be cut with a welding torch. This should require about a 5/16 inch wide cut. For a more accurate job, the slots could be milled out with a .25 inch mill-bit, assuming a milling machine is available. Every center-of-radius for the arc of each cut will fall on a circle of 4.47 inch radius as measured from the center of the wheel (again, this is for a 12 inch wheel). If the wheel is to have 24 blades, each blade will be placed every 15 degrees around the wheel (i.e. every 360/24 degrees); and so, each center-of-radius will be 15 degrees apart around the 4.47 inch radius circle. Once the centers are located for the arc of each blade slot, the arcs are drawn at 2 inch radii, and the slots can be cut.

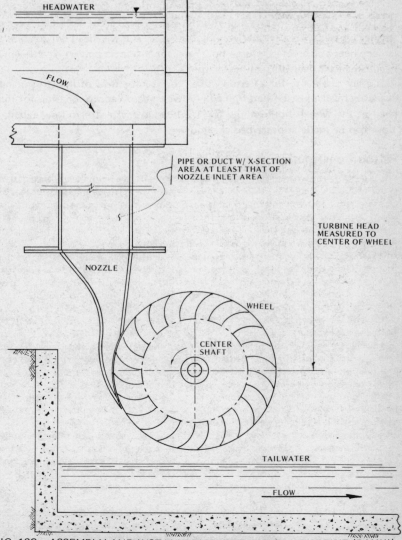

FIG. 12C   ASSEMBLY AND INSTALLATION FOR MICHELL TURBINE (BANKI)

For constant speed regulation (something essential for running an A.C. generator), a slide gate valve would have to be added to the nozzle, plus a centrifugal governor to actuate the valve. (This little mechanism could cost as much as all the other materials combined.) For high heads, the entrance works would be connected directly to a pipe.

Design equations for Michell Turbine:

(Eq. 16)   Width of nozzle = $W_1 = \dfrac{(210)(Q)}{(D)(H)}$

(Eq. 17)   Inside width of turbine = $W_2 = W_1 + 1$ inch

(Eq. 18)   Length of blades = $W_2 + 3/4$ inch

(Eq. 19)   Optimum rpm = $\dfrac{(862)(\sqrt{H})}{(D)}$

where Q = flow rate in cubic feet per second
     D = wheel diameter in inches
     H = head at the wheel in feet
     W_1 = outside width of turbine runner
     W_2 = inside width of turbine runner

The specific details of assembly of the wheel and nozzle can be best understood from the drawings (Figs. 12A, 12B and 12C).

PELTON WHEELS
Written with the Assistance of Guy Immega

The Pelton wheel is an important type of impulse water turbine because with an adequate head it can develop a high rpm useful for A.C. power generation. A Pelton wheel is usually small in diameter with specially shaped bucket cups mounted on the perimeter. Water is directed into the cups by a nozzle. Characteristically, a Pelton wheel requires a very high head of water (over 50 feet), delivered at a small volume of flow through a pipe. This makes the Pelton wheel particularly useful for a small mountain stream. A Pelton wheel turns at high speed (up to 1000 rpm) which makes it attractive for use as a power source for electrical generators (which usually require 1800 or 3600 rpm). The efficiency of a Pelton wheel with polished cups can be up to 93%.

The selection of Pelton wheels is dependent upon the site available, and the power required. With a higher head, the power can be obtained from a smaller wheel, with a smaller volume flow rate. A lower head will require a larger wheel at a greater volume flow rate, for the same power. At the same head, smaller wheels turn at higher rpm's.

To lay out a site for a Pelton wheel, the volume flow of the stream and available head must be determined. A "worst case" approximation for the head at the wheel should allow for 1/3 head loss; the stream flow calculations can be made as described previously.

Pelton Construction

Aside from the wheel itself, the most important part in a Pelton wheel installation is the feed pipe. Generally, to obtain a high head of water, many hundreds of feet of pipe are required. With this length of pipe, a primary concern is the friction of the water flowing in the pipe. Pipe friction is generally expressed in loss of head per 100 feet of pipe. If the pipe feeding a Pelton wheel is too small, then the pressure of water at the nozzle is reduced (effective head reduced).

Friction will be great in a narrow pipe. As the pipe diameter gets larger, the friction in the pipe decreases. But at some point, the high cost of a large diameter pipe outweighs the advantage of less friction. The general rule-of-thumb is that "maximum power-per-dollar invested is extracted from a pipe at 1/3 head loss. . ." This means that a 1/3 head loss gives the highest efficiency at the lowest price. Pipes with diameters allowing less than 1/3 head loss are more "efficient," but are prohibitively expensive.

Head loss may be determined by the use of the pipe flow nomograph (Fig. 9). For instance, suppose the pipe feeding a Pelton wheel must be 100 feet long and will have a static head of 200 feet. (Static head is the pressure inside a pipe filled with water, when the water is not flowing; in this case the pressure is equal to 200 feet of head.) Then the maximum tolerable head loss is 1/3 of 200 feet, or 66 feet. That leaves 134 feet of effective head at full flow. Expressed differently, the head loss must be less than 6.6 feet per 100 feet of pipe.

Suppose also that the stream is less than 6 inches wide and 6 inches deep, and the volume flow is about 32 cfm (.534 cfs), and that the entire stream is fed into the pipe. From the pipe flow nomograph, a 4 inch pipe is found to be more than sufficient to carry the flow, within the allowed 1/3 head loss.

Equation 20 is for finding the speed of the jet of water at the nozzle.

$V = \sqrt{2gH}$ where V = nozzle velocity, when maximum power is taken from the feeder pipe
     g = acceleration of gravity, 32 feet per second^2
(Eq. 20)   H = effective head at full flow

The nozzle size is set by either the design flow rate of the system or the capacity of the wheel, whichever is less. At any point in the pipe or nozzle, the flow is a product of the velocity of the water through a particular cross-section.

Q = (V)(A)   where Q = flow
     V = velocity
     A = cross-sectional area   (Eq. 21)

Since the nozzle velocity is known from Eq. 20, and the design flow (Q) is known, the theoretical nozzle opening can be found:

T.A. = $\dfrac{Q}{V}$ where T.A. = theoretical nozzle opening (area) in inches squared
     Q = flow in cfs   (Eq. 22)
     V = velocity in feet per second

With the above example, the area = $\dfrac{.534}{92.6}$ (144 inch^2/feet^2) = .83 inch^2

However, to find the actual flow through a given nozzle the theoretical area must be divided by a "nozzle coefficient" (C_n). C_n is .97 for a plain nozzle without controls. To find the necessary area for delivering the design flow:

Area required = $\dfrac{\text{theoretical area}}{C_n}$

A = $\dfrac{.83}{.97}$ = .855 inch^2 (Eq. 23)

Then, using simple geometry, the radius and diameter of the proper nozzle can be found.

r = $\sqrt{\dfrac{A}{\pi}}$ where r = radius of the nozzle in inches
     A = area required for delivering the design flow

then r = $\sqrt{\dfrac{.855}{3.14}}$ = .522 inch

And since diameter = 2 x radius, D = (2) x (.522) = 1.044 inch   (Eq. 24)

The 4 inch feed pipe we selected on the basis of pipe flow will be more than adequate for this 1 inch diameter nozzle.

When the nozzle is delivering water so that the wheel can achieve maximum power, the rim speed of the wheel will be 1/2 the velocity of the nozzle jet.

U = .5 V   where U = rim speed of the wheel (Pelton wheel)
     V = velocity of the jet of water from the nozzle   (Eq. 25)

In the case of the 12 inch wheel with a 1 inch nozzle, the circumference of the wheel is: C = πD, or C = $\pi \dfrac{12 \text{ inches}}{12 \text{ in/ft}}$ = 3.14 feet.

From Eq. 20 V = $\sqrt{2gH}$, we know that with the available head of 134 feet, the nozzle jet velocity will be 92.6 feet/second. Therefore, from Eq. 24, the rim speed will be half the velocity, or 46.3 feet/second.

To find rpm use Eq. 14 (from Overshot wheels):

rpm = $\dfrac{\text{rim speed}}{\text{circumference}}$ = $\dfrac{46.3 \text{ ft/sec}}{3.14 \text{ ft/revolution}}$ = 14.74 $\dfrac{\text{revolutions}}{\text{second}}$ x $\dfrac{60 \text{ sec}}{\text{minute}}$ = 885 rpm

If the wheel is overloaded, the speed will be slower and the power will drop. If the wheel is underloaded, the speed will be greater, but water will be wasted.

SCALE MODEL OF A PELTON WHEEL: Showing nozzle on right and pulley on left. Normally the cups on the wheel would be notched in the center so that water shooting out the nozzle would hit more than one cup at a time.

Reaction Turbines: Francis Wheel, Kaplan Turbine, Propeller (and others)

Some people may come into possession of one of this class of reaction turbines. These consist of a number of curved and convoluted vanes or runners arranged around a central shaft. The water flowing through these vanes causes the wheel to rotate by the "reaction" or pressure of the water. These turbines require careful engineering to operate properly and must be purchased from a manufacturer rather than be home-built.

Reaction turbines are usually designed for a limited range of flow and head conditions, and are not suitable for other than their design specifications. They are very efficient when properly regulated for load and flows (up to 93%) and turn at a high rpm. The high rpm makes them ideal for driving an electrical generator. Because of their shape and structure they are expensive, but it is possible to find used or surplus turbines at bargain prices (be sure to check the specifications of head and flow as the turbine may be useless if it doesn't fit the situation).

The only knowledge that is needed for installing a turbine of this class is its rating for head and flow rate, operating speed, and of course all the basic information about the site at which the turbine will be placed.

The James Leffel Company manufactures a complete package unit for small hydro-power sites (see page 69). Leffel's design, a Hoppe turbine, a variation of the Francis is available for heads of 3 to 25 feet with an electrical output of 1 to 10 kw.

POWER TRANSMISSION

In many cases the power available from a hydro-power installation will not supply the amount of power desired. In those cases it will probably be necessary to re-define your needs or fill them on a priority basis. Some needs can also be filled by another source of power. It is thus useful to think in terms of an integrated power systems approach from the outset.

It is probably pretty obvious that the operating speeds of the water wheels and turbines will not exactly match the speeds required to drive the generator or compressor. The common design of A.C. generators requires a particular rpm in order to produce the proper voltage and frequency of electricity. For the 60 cycle frequency common in the U.S. and Canada, the minimum input of a two-pole generator is 3600 rpm. Four pole generators are slightly more expensive, but operate at 1800 rpm. Six and eight-pole generators are also available (with proportionately slower operating speeds of 1200 rpm and 900 rpm) but these are specialty items that can be hard to find and are quite expensive besides. Even the speediest turbine of them all, the Pelton wheel, would require a head of more than 2000 feet to drive a 12 inch wheel at the 1800 rpm that is needed for a four-pole A.C. generator.

At the other extreme in power sources, the overshot wheel would turn at about 10 rpm (for a 16 foot wheel); the gearing up to get the speed necessary for electric generation would require a gear ratio of over 1-to-100. This sort of speed change would, in itself, cause some considerable loss in the overall efficiency of the system.

D.C. generators and alternators are available throughout the world for use in autos. They can operate at most any rpm above their minimum (that is, something faster than about 700 rpm); also, they are usually equipped (in an auto) with some sort of voltage regulator to avoid overcharging the batteries. This sort of flexibility in operation, along with their ready availability and their bargain prices, make them attractive for use in small scale generating plants (for windmills, as well as waterwheels). The D.C. technology developed for automotive systems can be applied for some household uses: D.C. storage batteries, light bulbs, radios, tape players and small motors are available. The biggest problem in converting a household to D.C. use are those motors in appliances and power tools. Most are designed for the common 60 cycle A.C. power source at 120 volts and would be completely useless for a 12 volt D.C. power supply.

Most installations use belts and pulleys to transfer the power from turbine to generator and, at the same time, obtain the needed rpm along the way. Larger installations, or those with high torques (like the waterwheels) need to have some sort of metal gearing or drive chains to handle the loads. Ready-built gear boxes and speed changers are usually available at surplus or used machinery dealers. And, of course, the neighborhood auto junk yard has a plentiful supply of rear axles, already complete with roller bearings and wheel mounting bolts. These can be arranged to provide a gear ratio of from 3:1 to almost 9:1. (Of the three rotating parts, that is, the two wheels and one drive shaft connection, one must be fixed in order for power to be transferred through the other two.) To check the gear ratio of any gear box in question merely turn one shaft and count the resulting turns of the other shaft.

Glossary

axial flow	A term for hydraulic machinery, pumps, turbines, in which the water flows parallel to the power shaft (axis of rotation) as in a propeller pump.
center of curvature	That spot where the point of the compass is stuck when drawing an arc or circle.
cfm.	Water flow rate, cubic feet per minute.
cfs.	Cubic feet per second.
control gate	See gate.
design flow	That flow rate for which the turbine is designed.
fps = feet/second	Velocity in feet per second. Also: (fps)(60) = feet/minute - feet per minute.
flume	An old term for a wooden or metal box channel: an aqueduct.
gate	In a sluice or canal, a structure of vertical sliding boards or metal that controls the flow of water (as in a "watergate").
gpm.	Gallons per minute (there are 7.48 gallons in each cubic foot).
head	The elevation of water that is available and so, a measure of the energy of the water. In some cases the pressure in a pipe may be indicated by the head in feet of water. The law of conservation of energy in water flow is given by the equation:

$$\frac{v^2}{2g} + \frac{P}{\alpha} + \begin{array}{c}\text{(elevation)}\\ \text{in feet}\end{array} = \text{a constant along a continuous flow.}$$

v = velocity in feet/second
2g = 64.34 feet per second^2
α = 64.4 lbs. per cubic foot
P = pressure in lbs. per square foot

headwater	The static head (without velocity) usually behind a dam, sluice, or weir.
HP	Horsepower. A measure of power, equivalent to 745 watts.
hydraulic radius	A concept used in analysis of water flow in channels. Equal to the cross-section area of the flow divided by the wetted perimeter.
penstock	A pipe to carry water to the turbine, usually under a high pressure.
percent grade	% Grade. The slope of ground, creek, or canal—in feet per 100 feet or meters/100 meters. (Not the same as the channel flow equations "s.")
psi	Pounds per square inch. A pressure measurement, equivalent to .433 foot of head (of water).
Q	Symbol for flow rate, usually in cubic feet per second or liters per second.
radial flow	For hydro machinery, pumps and turbines; where the water flows radially out from the power shaft; as in a centrifugal pump, or radially as in a Francis wheel.
radius of curvature	The distance from the center of curvature to the arc.
rim speed	The velocity of a point on the rim of a rotating wheel or turbine = (rpm)(2π)(radius).
rpm	Rotation, revolutions per minute.
slope	In channel flow calculations: slope, s = feet of drop per 1000 feet of horizontal distance (or meters drop per kilometers).
tailrace	The channel that carries the tailwater flow.
tailwater	The water surface elevation immediately downstream of a waterwheel or turbine (see various wheel illustrations).
torque	Something that produces or tends to produce rotation or torsion and whose effectiveness is measured by the product of the force and the perpendicular distance from the line of action of the force to the axis of rotation.
tuberculation	The pits and lumps of rust and corrosion in steel and cast-iron pipe.
weir	An exact opening (rectangular, triangular, or trapezoidal) used to accurately measure water flow rates.
wetted perimeter	A concept used in flow analysis. It is that portion or length of the channel cross-section that is in contact with the flow (measured perpendicular to the flow). For a circular pipe flowing full, the wetted perimeter would equal the circumference of the pipe.

REVIEWS/WATER

SENSITIVE CHAOS

Fluids in motion. The beauty and strength, motion, flow, grace and harmony of water and wind. ALIVE. A theoretical look at the inter-relationship of nature and human beings using movement as the common denominator. Opinionated and presumptuous in spots, Schwenk hammers away at the aliveness and biosimilarity of nature and human beings.

—T.G.

Sensitive Chaos
Theodor Schwenk
1965; 231 pp

$10.00

from:
Rudolph Steiner Press
35 Park Road
London, England N.W.1

or WHOLE EARTH
TRUCK STORE

The ray has assimilated the movement of the waves into its fin movements (after Hesse-Doflein)

SURVEYING & SURVEYING TOOLS

"Surveying is the art of measuring and locating lines, angles and elevations on the earth's surface." It is also the method used to stake out those territorial claims that are so important to the animal in man. **Surveying** is a standard handbook for surveyors; it is also used as a text for college courses and would be sufficient for a self taught course in land surveying.

Besides the knowledge of how to survey the tools, good tools help make a survey successful. Most of the companies which make surveying tools make good ones. Two that are well known among licensed land surveyors are Berger and Lietz. Berger is the smaller of the two but has all the basics necessary for most successful survey work. They also send a free booklet on request entitled, "How to use transits and levels for faster more accurate building." Lietz has the complete line of accessories, including machetes, technical books and drafting equipment—that is, everything from the first reconnaissance, through the brush down to the final drawing of the finished project.

—Robin Saunders

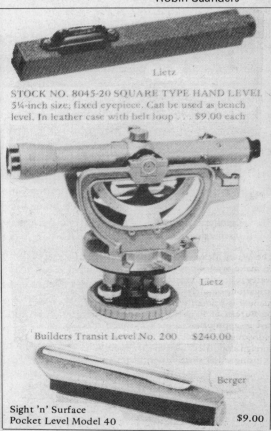

STOCK NO. 8045-20 SQUARE TYPE HAND LEVEL. 5¼-inch size; fixed eyepiece. Can be used as bench level. In leather case with belt loop . . . $9.00 each

Builders Transit Level No. 200 $240.00

Sight 'n' Surface
Pocket Level Model 40 $9.00

Lietz
829 Cowan Road
Burlingame, CA 94010

Berger Instruments
Div. of High Voltage Engineering Corp.
37 Williams Street
Boston, MA 02119   **Catalogue free**

VOLUNTEERS IN TECHNICAL ASSISTANCE

VITA is a non-profit corporation that provides information and technical assistance to groups involved with projects around the world. Much of their assistance is directed to unindustrialized nations. Their expertise is "low-tech" engineering technology predominantly in the areas of water and water resources, agriculture and food, home improvement, sanitation, construction and communication. The *Low Cost Development of Small Water Sites* pamphlet ($1.00) has basic information on measuring head and flow as well as information on various types of waterwheels and turbines.

—T.G.

Publications List and
Information Available from:

VITA
3706 Rhode Island Ave.
Mt. Rainier, Maryland 20822

VILLAGE TECHNOLOGY HANDBOOK
Revised 1970. 400 pages; $7.00
$12.00 Air

Stocking Spare Parts for a Small Repair Shop
1964. 7 pages; $.25

How to Salt Fish
1966. 9 pages; $.25

Making Building Blocks with the CINVA-Ram
Block Press. A Supervisor's Manual
1966. 23 pages; $.65

Low Cost Development of Small Water Power
Sites 1967. 43 pages; $1.00

Hydraulic Ram for Village Use
1970. 9 pages; $.25

Low Cost Windmill for Developing Nations
1970. 45 pages; $1.00

Study of VITA-USA Program Impact
1970. 75 pages; $3.00

Health Records System
1971. 20 pages; $.60

How to Perform an Agricultural Experiment
1971. 23 pages; $1.00

CLOUDBURST

A practical handbook for rural survival. A teaching book with experience and ideas on building and using tools, saunas, curing fish, chicken house, domes, compost shredder, juice press and more. Forty pages devoted to waterwheels including one of the more "recent" available articles on the subject— a 1947 Popular Science reprint entitled "Harnessing the Small Stream."

Vic Marks who edited this book lives with his friends in British Columbia. Through Cloudburst Press they have a few other books in the works, including two on mushroom growing and gathering, a garden/cookbook and CLOUDBURST II.

—T.G.

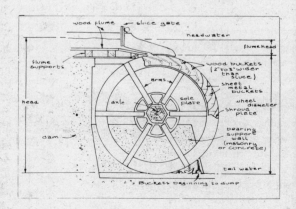

Cloudburst
Vic Marks, editor
1973; 128 pp

$3.95

from:
Cloudburst Press
Box 79
Brackendale, B.C.
Canada

or WHOLE EARTH
TRUCK STORE

Surveying
C. B. Breed and A. J. Bone
1942, 1971; 495 pp

$9.95

from:
John Wiley & Sons
605 Third Avenue
New York, NY 10016
or WHOLE EARTH
TRUCK STORE

USE OF WEIRS AND FLUMES IN STREAM GAUGING

WATER MEASUREMENT MANUAL

Since water is such a precious commodity, some sort of accounting is usually necessary for measuring and metering the distribution of the wealth. This is particularly true for those situations where a large volume of water must be purchased from some local water utility, (e.g. irrigation) or for a community of water users to meter each individual outlet. These are needs that require some accuracy in measurement; but there is no need to resort to expensive mechanical devices. These two books discuss those means or "artificial controls" that can be used to measure the water flow rate with a great deal of accuracy and a minimum of expense and maintenance. The World Meteorological Organization book is primarily concerned with stream flow measurement made with open flow weirs and flumes. The Water Measurement Manual is a standard in the water resources business; it catalogues all sorts of possibilities for flow measurement with pipes, gates, and orifices as well as the standard weirs and flumes. For the money and the information the Water Measurement Manual is really the best bargain.

—Robin Saunders

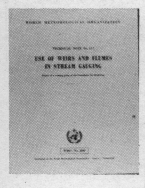

Cipolletti weir in a permanent bulkhead discharging under free-flow conditions.

The Water Measurement Manual has been prepared to make available to designers, system operators, and water users the information needed for measuring irrigation, municipal, and industrial waters. The manual is primarily intended for personnel working on Bureau of Reclamation projects. However, it is just as appropriate for use by other groups or individuals, either in the United States or in foreign countries, who are engaged in designing or using water distribution facilities.

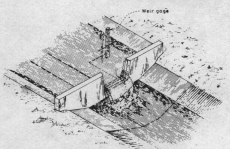

Use of Weirs and Flumes in Stream Gauging: Technical Note No. 117, 1971, 55 pp **$4.50**

from: World Meteorological Org. Publications Ctr. P.O. Box 433, NY, NY 10016

Water Measurement Manual: Bureau of Reclamation, 1967; 323 pp **$2.50**

from: Sup't of Documents U.S. Gov. Printing Office Washington, D.C. 20402 or WHOLE EARTH TRUCK STORE

SMALL EARTH DAMS

Dam building is a very involved undertaking. This circular endeavors to supply you with practical suggestions which may be of assistance to you. It is up to you to fit them together as they apply to your situation.

About 20,000 small earth dams have been built on California farms in the last 25 years and more are being built all the time. While many of the early dams were built primarily as stock-watering ponds, farmers are also deriving benefits from their reservoirs in the way of irrigation water and even recreational purposes.

But dams have disadvantages too. They are expensive to build; they require labor and more expense to maintain properly; they may increase the nearby mosquito population.

So perhaps a dam would be a good investment for you; perhaps not. This circular discusses: The Laws Involved; Selection of a Site; Construction Details; Maintenance Practices; Management Practices.

DESIGN OF SMALL DAMS

This is the definitive text on the design and construction of earth fill dams. The dams discussed and illustrated are medium sized or large by most standards. With considerable information on ecological impacts, soil geology, soil placement, construction techniques and the like this book has become part of the reference library of most civil engineers working in the field.

—Robin Saunders

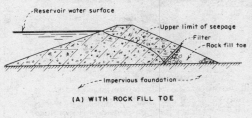

(A) WITH ROCK FILL TOE

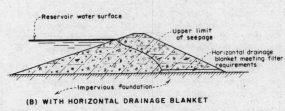

(B) WITH HORIZONTAL DRAINAGE BLANKET

Figure 114. Modified homogeneous dam.

Design of Small Dams Dept. of the Int. 1973; 816 pp

$12.65

from: Sup't of Documents U.S. Gov. Printing Off. Washington, D.C. 20402

or WHOLE EARTH TRUCK STORE

Small Earth Dams Circular 467 Lloyd N. Brown 1965; 23 pp **Free**

from: California Agricultural Extension 90 University Hall, U.of Ca. Berkeley, Ca. 94720

PONDS FOR WATER SUPPLY AND RECREATION

The demand for water in the US has increased rapidly over the years. The USDI has put out this handbook to satisfy those farmers, ranchers, and other country folks who want to provide for themselves rather than wait for "that big irrigation project proposed for '84." The stated concerns are for irrigation, fishing, recreation, fire protection, and wildlife habitat; of course, the same sort of dam can be used for a water-power reservoir (the USDI doesn't mention that possibility).

They do, however, include most all the information that you need to know to build your own earth-fill dam (for whatever purpose), including: assessing the needs for water; preliminary site studies; drainage areas required for various size ponds; regional climates and storm run-off; requirements for inlet works and over-flow spillways; various construction techniques; and sealing the ponds to limit seepage. Some of the most useful information is the basic course in do-it-yourself hydrology to estimate the storm run-off and average annual stream flows that the reservoir will have to handle. The discussion is really for large farm ponds and reservoirs and the construction methods are really for those with some heavy equipment that can move a lot of dirt. However, the basic hydraulics discussed are just as important for any size or shape of dam.

—Robin Saunders

Selecting a suitable site for your pond is important. Preliminary studies of any site are needed before construction. If you are considering more than one site, study each one in order to select the most practical and economical site.

From an economic viewpoint, locate the pond where the largest storage volume can be obtained with the least amount of earthfill. A good site usually is one where a dam can be built across a narrow section of a valley, the side slopes are steep, and the slope of the valley floor permits a large area to be flooded. Such sites also minimize the area of shallow water. Avoid large areas of shallow water because of excessive evaporation and the growth of noxious aquatic plants.

Ponds for Water Supply and Recreation; Agriculture Handbook No. 387, Soil Conservation Service, U.S. Dept. of Agriculture, 55 pp

$1.25

from: Sup't of Documents U.S. Gov. Printing Office Washington, D.C. 20402 or WHOLE EARTH TRUCK STORE

HANDBOOK OF APPLIED HYDRAULICS

If you were going to build Hoover Dam or supply Chicago with water this is the book you would use to find out how. —T.G.

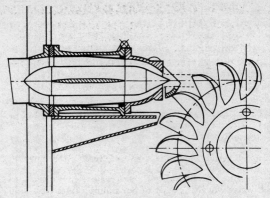

Straight-flow-type nozzle with internal needle servomotor for Pelton-type impulse turbine.

Handbook of Applied Hydraulics, C.V. Davis and K.E. Sorenson, 1969, 1584 pp, 978 illustrations

$39.50

from:
McGraw-Hill Book Company
330 W. 42nd St.
N.Y., N.Y. 10036

OSSBERGER-TURBINENFABRIK

Seems to be the only company in the world which manufacturers the Michell (Banki) cross-flow turbine. They have units producing from 8.5 KW up to 220 KW and build each unit in accordance with the local conditions. These units are probably better suited for the small community rather than the individual. Share the cost and the power.
—T.G.

OSSBERGER 542

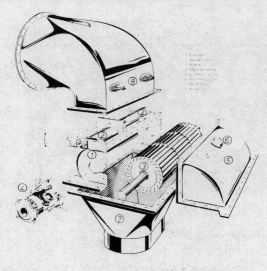

Miniature power stations like this 8.5 kVA plant in Marianhill (South Africa) are, despite their modest output, completely self-contained, automatic hydro-electric generating sets which are only shut down once a year for a change of oil and grease. Year in, year out, day and night, they deliver any power needed—at constant voltage and frequency, of course. No matter whether only one small lamp is burning or whether full power is demanded, the set always supplies the right amount of power. If all loads are disconnected, the set continues to run at no-load speed, ready at any time to instantly generate the power required when loads are connected.

Information Free
from:
Ossberger-Turbinenfabrik
D-8832 Weissenberg i. Bay, P.O. Box 425
Bayern, Germany

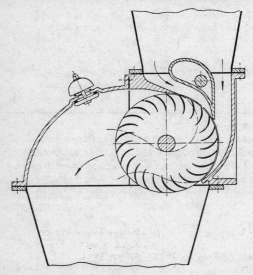

Patented OSSBERGER cross-flow
Vertical admission

JUDD DISTRIBUTING COMPANY

The Judd Distributing Company and General Store say that they are distributing a water turbine with a maximum 3 KW output for a cost between $400 and $1000. They also have a catalogue of their other wares. They are friendly folks. Write them for more information.
—T.G.

Judd Distributing Company and General Store
8600 Lake City Way, N.W.
Seattle, Washington 98115

THE BANKI WATER TURBINE

This paper covers a study made in 1948 for a "typical" installation of the Banki or Michell cross-flow turbine. The test on this simply constructed water turbine produced 2.75 horsepower at 280 rpm using 2.22 cfs at 16ft. of head: a resulting efficiency of 65%. As the authors state this is only a first try, and by no means the best efficiency for this type of turbine (though quite respectable). The first half of the article is a loose translation of the original paper by Donati Banki "Neue Wasser turbine" — an involved discussion of the theory of hydraulics of the turbine, including the vector analysis of the water flow, blade angles, curvature, and speed (strictly technical stuff).

The second half is a brief discussion of the test set-up and the results, including variations of horsepower and efficiency at different speeds and flow rates.

This is apparently the only complete discussion of the Banki or Michell turbine available in the states. It is interesting to note the prediction that, "...there is a distinct place for the Banki turbine in the small turbine field" has not been realized in this country in the 25 years since the paper was published.
—Robin Saunders

Banki water turbine built in Oregon State College Hydraulics Laboratory.

The Banki Water Turbine: Bulletin No. 25, C.A. Mockmore, Fred Merryfield 1949; 30 pp

Free (1st copy)

$.40 (2nd & ea. additional copy)
from:
Oregon State Univ.
Engineering Exp. Sta.
Corvallis, Ore. 97331

U.S. GEOLOGICAL SURVEY

Geological surveys of the U.S. Mostly large scale. Often individual studies of rivers, National Parks, earthquake areas, soil studies, etc. Their standard topographic maps are 7½ minute and 15 minute maps which sell for $0.75 postpaid. They also have maps covering larger areas. Free for the asking are state maps showing what smaller area topo maps are available and a useful pamphlet "Topographic Maps" which explains how to read all the numbers and curved lines.

All maps available from: Distribution Sect., U.S. Geological Survey, Federal Center, Denver, Colo. 80225. Also from: Local centers. Check the phone book in larger cities.

JAMES LEFFEL (Company founder)

LEFFEL

As far as we can tell Leffel is the only company in the USA that has been manufacturing small hydroelectric units for any length of time (over 100 years). They also manufacture big units.

Their small units, called Hoppes, run on a maximum of 25 ft. of head and a maximum output of 10 KW. With those maximum specifications the unit costs approximately $7200 including turbine and generator but no piping, F.O.B. factory. Cost increases as the amount of head decreases; so to get 10 KW out of 15 ft. of head would cost considerably more.

When we made our inquiry, they had a small Pelton wheel "in stock." Using a head between 200 and 300 ft. the unit cost approximately $3000.

In requesting information, ask for a Pamphlet A which explains how to measure head and flow, etc., and Bulletin H-49 which describes the workings and different models of the Hoppes unit.

—T.G.

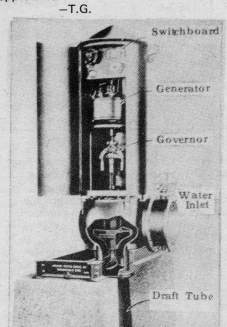

Cutaway Section Showing Governor Control Valve.

Leffel Information Free

The James Leffel Company, Springfield,Oh. 45501

PUMPS AND POWER LTD.

Pumps and Power manufactures small-scale Pelton wheels. Starting at fifty feet of head a basic wheel with housing but without a generator or piping runs approximately $2400 F.O.B. Vancouver.

—T.G.
(suggested by Guy Immega)

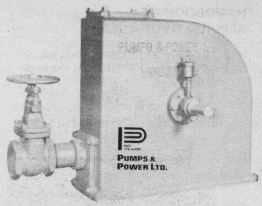

Dear Sir: March 1, 1974

In replying to your letter of February 25th, you are correct that Pumps & Power Limited does still manufacture, but on a very limited scale, impulse (Pelton) water wheels. A copy of our Bulletin Data W29-10-57 is enclosed along with a questionnaire form and a table of useful information that we send out to prospective purchasers.

Our Type 'B' wheel is manufactured in four sizes; any one of which is available in either single or double nozzle construction. Our market for these small wheels is very limited but for your information, one of the last ones we sold was a complete small 5 KW plant shipped to West Samoa in the South Sea Islands.

In addition, we do have patterns and design for much larger wheels custom built to meet specific needs and design criteria. Our market for these larger wheels is practically now non-existent as the Province where such large quantities of electrical energy might be required, is well serviced by hydro transmission lines.

No, we do not see a resurgence in water wheel sales due to the so-called energy crisis.

We hope that this information will be of some assistance to you.

Yours very truly,
Pumps & Power Limited

DATA REQUIRED

In order to engineer a PARAMOUNT Type 'B' Waterwheel or Hydro-electric Installation, the following information is required:
  a) Horsepower or Kilowatts to be produced?
  b) Static head or fall measured vertically from source to wheel?
  c) Length of penstock (pipeline) measured from source to wheel? Size of penstock and material (steel, wood, plastic) if already installed?
  d) Quantity of water available in U.S. or Imperial gallons per minute, or cubic feet per second, measured at both maximum and minimum flow

Where (d) is not known we will advise quantity needed to develop desired power and also advise the correct size of pipeline that must be used to convey the needed quantity of water.

Pumps and Power, 1380 Napier Street,
P.O.Box 2048, Vancouver 6, B.C.

PRIMARY SOURCES (PUBLICATIONS) FOR ADDITIONAL INFORMATION ON WATER POWER

	Head and Flow	Dam	Channels,Sluices	Poncelet	Breast	Overshot	Michell (Banki)	Pelton	Reaction Turbines	Power Transmission
LOW-COST DEVELOPMENT OF SMALL WATER-POWER SITES. From: VITA (see page 66)	Yes	Yes	Yes	Minimal	No	Minimal	Yes	Minimal	Minimal	Minimal
CLOUDBURST (see page 66)	Yes*	Yes*	No	Yes	Yes	Yes	Yes†	No	No	Minimal
YOUR OWN WATER-POWER PLANT. from: Popular Science 1947. Reprinted in the Mother Earth News issues No. 13 & No. 14 (see page 186)	Yes	Yes	No	No	No	Yes	No	Yes	No	Minimal
HYDROPOWER x from: Wadebridge Ecological Centre 73 Molesworth St. Wadebridge, Cornwall, England ± 1.50 postpaid	Yes	Yes	Yes	Yes	No	Minimal	No	Yes	No	Minimal

*reprinted from: YOUR OWN WATER-POWER PLANT (Pop. Sci.)
†reprinted from: LOW-COST DEVELOPMENT OF SMALL WATER-POWER SITES (VITA)
x The most recent good overview of small scale water power was written in 1947 (YOUR OWN WATER-POWER PLANT). This article which originally appeared in Popular Science is still the best place to begin reading, researching and understanding the workings of a small hydro-power plant.

Water in the Service of Man
H.R. Valentine
224pp; 1967
Penguin Books (out of print)

Windmills and Watermills
John Reynolds
196pp; 254 illus; 1971; reprint 1974
Praeger Publishers
111 Fourth Ave.
New York, N.Y. 10003
$8.95

Power From Water
T.A.L. Paton & J.G. Brown
210pp; 1961
Leonard Hill (books) London
(out of print)

COMMUNITY WATER SYSTEMS

Some friends in Big Sur California could have used this one when they were expanding an old 1930 water supply system to service a dozen new homes. They miscalculated the pipe size, got a trickle out of the kitchen sink and had to dig up a thousand feet of the wrong size pipe.

Included are basic explanations and practical data on population densities, water use, wells and sources of supply, distribution systems, water quality, and cost accounting for residential as well as industrial applications. Although the approach is mainly to simplify the planning procedure of large and small scale public water systems for those unfamiliar with the workings, the book may even prove useful to those civil engineers working in this field who find themselves too close to the subject to see the easy approximations.

—Robin Saunders

Pipe Discharges in Gallons Per Minute for Different Diameter Pipe for Known Lengths and Under a Pressure of 40 Pounds Per Square Inch

Pipe Size Inches	Length of Pipe in Feet							
	100	200	300	400	500	600	700	800
1½	100	64	52	44	40	37	36	35
2	200	130	100	86	76	70	66	64
2½	300	210	160	140	120	110	105	100
3	600	410	325	290	250	235	220	205
4	1,200	730	580	490	410	380	350	330
6	3,200	2,400	1,700	1,450	1,300	1,180	1,090	1,000
8	7,100	4,700	3,600	2,900	2,600	2,300	2,100	2,000
10	13,000	8,200	6,200	5,200	4,400	4,000	3,600	3,300
12	18,500	11,200	8,800	7,300	6,300	5,600	5,100	4,800

Cut-Away of AWWA Valve Showing Wedging Mechanism   Hub Ends   Flanged Ends

Community Water Systems, Joseph S. Ameen, 1960, 214 pp

$7.50

from:
Technical Proceedings
P.O. Box 5041
High Point, N.C., 27262
or WHOLE EARTH TRUCK STORE

DOWSING

Moses is said to have been the first dowser— with a little help from his friend.

Both *Dowsing* and *The Beginner's Handbook of Dowsing* are "how to" books. *Dowsing* in pamphlet form gives more information especially on different types of dowsing rods. It is also cheaper, and its author has more of a professional dowsing background. The handbook is considerably better illustrated with most of the basic stuff in it. Both sources refer to the American Society of Dowsers Inc., Danville, Vermont 05828, a non-profit educational and scientific organization. They publish a quarterly journal—"The American Dowser." —T.G.

PLANNING FOR AN INDIVIDUAL WATER SYSTEM

For those who like their education with a bit of visual aids, this book has plenty of multi-colored pictures, charts, and even a few cartoons to lighten the subject. In spite of the slick approach, the information is all very relevant for those installing their own water supply system. Much emphasis is placed on water quality, both how to prevent contamination and how to use the methods of water treatment.

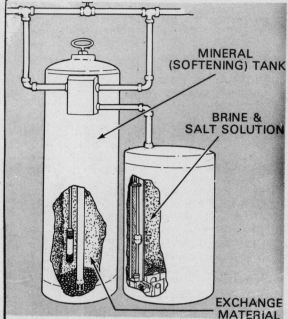

MINERAL (SOFTENING) TANK

BRINE & SALT SOLUTION

EXCHANGE MATERIAL

Dowsing
Gordon Maclean, Sr.
1971; 46 pp

$1.00

from:
Gordon Maclean, Sr.
30 Day Street
South Portland, Maine 04106

The Beginner's Handbook of Dowsing
Joseph Baum
1974; 31 pp

$2.95

from:
Crown Publishers Inc.
419 Park Avenue South
New York, N.Y. 10016

or WHOLE EARTH TRUCK STORE

This same organization has several other instructional manuals for farm related vocational training; mostly things like tractor repair manuals, electrical maintenance, and so forth. One that looks particularly interesting is an 80 page piece on "Understanding & Measuring HorsePower" ($3.55).

—Robin Saunders

Planning for an Individual Water System, 1955, 1973; 155 pp

$5.95

from:
American Assoc. for Vocational Instructional Materials, Engineering Ctr. Athens, Georgia 30602
or WHOLE EARTH TRUCK STORE

WATER SUPPLY AND WATER WELLS

In many areas of the world ground water is in plentiful supply. Searching for it is usually a matter of consulting geologic maps, learning about existing wells in the area and looking for surface evidence such as streams and ponds. Designing, drilling and maintaining the well and water system must be done carefully and with an understanding of the processes. It is not an easy task to develop a useable and ecological water supply.

The *Water Well Manual*, a reprint of a U.S. Department of State publication *Small Wells Manual*, covers the area of finding water, well drilling and maintenance more than adequately.

For more information especially on "power" drilling methods, a useful but out of print publication from the USGPO is *Well Drilling Operations* (check your local library).

A final suggestion is *Water Supply for Rural Areas*, a World Health Organization book. This is probably the most complete book of the three in covering water supply. It discusses many health related aspects of water, hand dug wells, pumping systems and also construction of small dams.

I suggest using the *Water Well Manual* for its information on wells and *Water Supply for Rural Areas* for its information on developing a good overall water supply system. Both do the job.

—T.G.

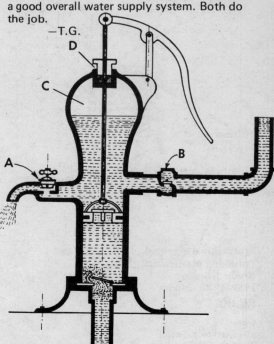

Hand-Pump Flexibility in Use

Water Well Manual
U.P. Gibson & R. D. Singer, 1969, 1971; 155 pp.
$6.00
from: Premier Press
P.O.B. 4428, Berkeley, California 94704
or WHOLE EARTH TRUCK STORE

Water Supply for Rural Areas, E.G. Wagner & J. Lanoix, 1959, 339 pp
$9.00
from:
Q Corp, World Health Organization, 49 Sheridan Ave., Albany, N.Y. 12210
or WHOLE EARTH TRUCK STORE

PROFESSIONAL PLUMBING

PLUMBING MATHEMATICS

We all know that plumbers cost a lot by the hour; at those rates it wouldn't take long to pay for the price of this book. It is very complete, not only what to do, but even considerable amounts of practical advice on procedures and potential problems. How to install everything from Roman baths, furnaces and gas pipes to the plumbing system for an entire house. This book written by a former plumbing inspector even includes useful math basics for plumbers.

—Robin Saunders

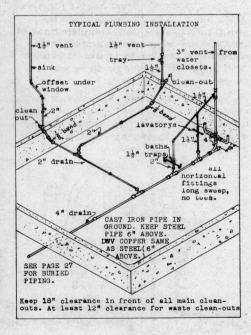

Professional Plumbing Illustrated, and Plumbing Mathematics Simplified
Arthur J. Smith
1959, 1972; 243 pp
$6.00
from:
Mrs. Arthur J. Smith
4037 Golf Drive
San Jose, California 95127

IRRIGATION PUMPING PLANTS

Basically about sizing, designing, and installing pumping plants for irrigation systems. Also, gets into some handy stuff on trouble-shooting and maintenance problems that are part of the regular operation of pumps and their motors.

—Robin Saunders

Irrigation Pumping Plants
U.S.D.A.
1959; 70 pp
$0.45
from:
Superintendent of Documents
U.S. Government Printing Office
Washington, D.C. 20402

WHOLE MOTHER EARTH WATER WORKS

WHAT?
We are manufacturing a low priced Hydraulic Ram of a very simple and easy to duplicate design. It is not and will not be patented. Our rams are priced from $125 to $274 depending on the fall. We are also giving away free, a lower quality ram to anyone who has need of it. We also offer advice and are trying to serve as a "switchboard" to connect people who need help with water systems, with people who can volunteer to help them.

WHY?
We know what it is like to carry every drop of water you use. We are trying to become an energy producer (in a round-about way) rather than an energy consumer. We are trying to make a living because there is no other work here.

HOW?
With faith and borrowed money. We have sold most of the first rams we made (one each). What problems are developing are fast disappearing. What we see for the future: we hope to be out of debt by 1975 and off food stamps by 1976.

Edward Barberie
Managing Engineer
Whole Mother Earth Water Works
Green Spring, West Virginia 26722

HYDRAULIC RAMS— VITA, RIFE, VULCAN

Volunteers in Technical Assistance publishes a pamphlet, "Hydraulic Ram for Village Use" (1970, 9 pp, $0.25). It contains good instructions on how to build a hydraulic ram.

The Rife Company manufactures three different types of rams. Costs run between $300 and $3000 (FOB factory) with drive or intake pipe sizes from 1¼" to 8". Rife claims to have received more than 10,000 inquiries from having been reviewed in the Last Whole Earth Catalog. We at the Truck Store haven't heard any complaints.

Green and Carter Ltd. manufacturers the Vulcan ram. With drive pipe size from 1¼" to 7" their rams cost a bit less than Rife's but the shipping expense from merry ole' England will certainly make up the difference.
—T.G.

HYDRAULIC RAM: AN ENGINEERING BELIEVE-IT-OR-NOT

The principles behind the successful operation of a hydraulic ram are engineering facts of life that I always have found difficult to believe. By means of air pressure, built up by the weight and velocity of the water, a stream of falling water manages automatically to pump a good part of itself to a height of 25 feet for each foot that it falls. Given a flow of not less

FINDING AND BUYING YOUR PLACE IN THE COUNTRY

After a year of selling books on buying land to people who come to us at the Whole Earth Truck Store, this is the first one I can recommend with a clean conscience. With chapters on looking for land, climate, water rights, legal information, escrow, the contract, financing your purchase and much more. It's a damn good book.

—T.G.

Purchasing land should be done as carefully as selecting the person you will share it with. The more land you see, the more you will learn about differences in value and about your expectations. Try to keep an open mind when land hunting. Many people find that, after seeing many kinds of places, they choose a different type of environment than they had originally sought. Take your time and approach your search with a relaxed but probing attitude. Even if you are not ready to actually buy land at the present time you should begin looking, since it takes time to find the right place and you want to find out as much information as you can about country property before you buy.

Finding and Buying Your Place in the Country,
Les Scher, 1974; 393 pp
$6.95
from: Collier-Macmillan Publishing Co., Inc.
866 Third Ave., NY NY 10022
or WHOLE EARTH TRUCK STORE

than 1½ gallons per minute from a spring, creek, or artesian well, and—for example— a fall or "head" of four feet, you could elevate part of the flowing water to a tank 100 feet above the ram. These facts suggest that hydraulic rams ought to be an important factor in water-supply systems in many rural areas—and they are.

Information free

Rife Hydraulic Engine Mfg. Co.
Box 367
Millburn, N.J. 07041

Green & Carter Ltd.
Vulcan Iron Works
Kingsworthy
Winchester
Hampshire
England

WATER POWER

This is the trade magazine of the hydroelectric industry—"the Big Stuff." It's all about water, water, water, water, and dams, dams, dams. Many of the articles are technical—some not, and are useful basic information. Each issue is chock full of ads from the companies which make big generators, turbines, dams, valves, transformers, etc. —T.G.

NAMES AND ADDRESSES OF WATER TURBINE MANUFACTURERS

ACEC SA, BP 4, B-6000 Charleroi, Belgium.

Allis-Chalmers Corporation, Hydro Turbine Division, York, Pennsylvania 17405, USA.

Alsthom, Société Generale de Constructions Electriques et Méchaniques, 38 Avenue Kieber, 75784 Paris, Cedex 16, France.

Alsthom Helleniki, 7 Stadiou Street, Athens, Greece.

Maschinenfabrik Andritz AG, 8045 Graz-Andritz, Austria.

Asgen SA, via N. Lorenzi 8, 16152 Genoa, Cornigliano, Italy.

Ateliers des Charmilles SA, 109 rue de Lyon, CH-1211 Geneva 13, Switzerland.

Sociedad Espanola de Construcciones Babcock & Wilcox, Bilbao, Spain.

Barber Turbine and Foundries Ltd, PO Box 370, Meaford, Ontario, Canada.

Bardella Borriello Eletromecanica SA, Av. Prof Elestino Bourroul 276, 02710 Sao Paulo, Brazil.

Bédard Girard Ltd, 117 Lagauchetiere Street West, Montreal 128, Quebec, Canada.

Bell Maschinenfabrik AG, 6010 Kriens, Switzerland.

Bingham-Willamette Co. 2800 Northwest Front Avenue, Portland, Oregon, USA.

Boving & Co (Anz) Pty Ltd, St. James's Bldg. 121 William St, Melbourne, Victoria 3000, Austrlia.

Boving & Co Ltd, Villiers House, 41-47 Strand, London WC2N 5LB, U.K.

BVS, 157 Cours Berriat, Cedex 275, 38 Grenoble Gare, France.

CKD-Blansko, Narodni Podnik, Blansko, Czechoslovakia.

Clyde Carruthers, 140 Arthur Street, N. Sydney, New South Wales, Australia.

Creusot Loire, 15 rue Pasquier, Paris 9e, France.

Dominion Engineering Ltd, PO Box 220, Montreal 101, Canada.

Drees & Co GmbH, 4760 Werl (Westf.), Postfach 43, West Germany.

Ebara Mfg Ltd, Asahi Bldg, 6-7 Ginza, 6-chome, Chuo-ku, Tokyo 104, Japan.

Energomachexport V/O, Moscow V-330, Ul. Mosfilmovskaja 35, USSR.

Escher Wyss Ltd, 8023 Zurich, Switzerland.

Franco Tosi SpA, Legnano, Milan, Italy.

Fuji Electric Co. Ltd., 11 Yurakucho-1 chome, Chiyoda-ku, Tokyo, Japan.

Ganz Mavag, Budapest 8, Monyves Kalman krt. 76, Hungary.

General Electric Co. International Sales Div., 159 Madison Ave, NY NY 10016, USA.

GIE, via Algardi 4, Milan, Italy.

Gilbert, Gilkes and Gordon Ltd, Canal Iron Works, Kendal, Westmoreland, U.K.

Heavy Electricals (India) Ltd, Bhopal, India.

Hitachi Ltd, New Maru Bldg, Marunouchi, Chiyoda-ku, Tokyo, Japan.

Ingra, Zagreb, PO Box 02487, Yugoslavia.

C. Itoh & Co Ltd, Central PO Box 117, Osaka, Japan.

C. Itoh & Co Ltd, Montreal, Canada.

James Leffel & Co (The), Springfield, Ohio 45501, USA.

Jeumont Schneider, 5 Place de Rio de Janeiro, Paris 8e, France.

Jyoti Calor-Emag Ltd, Baroda 390003, India.

KMW, Karlstadt, Sweden.

Kvaerner Brug AS, Box 3610, Oslo, Norway.

Leningrad Metal Works, Zavod, Leningrad, USSR.

Titovi Zavodi Litostroj, Ljubljana, Rjakovicera 36, PO Box 308/Vi, Yugoslavia.

Marine Industries Ltd, 1405 Peel Street, Montreal 110, Quebec, Canada.

Maschinenfabrik B. Maier, 4812 Brackwede (Westf.), Brockhagener Strasse 14/20, Postfach 320, West Germany.

Mason Brothers Engineering Ltd, Auckland, New Zealand.

Mecanica Pesada SA, rio Branca 81-21 andar, Rio de Janeiro, Brazil.

Mitsubichi Heavy Industries Ltd, 5-1 Marunouchi, 2-chome, Chiyoda-ky, Tokyo 100, Japan.

Neyrpic, Avenida Roque Senz Pena 570, Buenos Aires, Argentina.

Neyrpic, Cedex 75, 38 Grenoble Gare, France.

Neyrpic Espagnol, Avenida Jose Antonia, 191-217, Cornalla de Llobregat, Barcelona, Spain.

Nisso Iwai, 2-chome, Chiyoda-ku, Tokyo, Japan.

Nohab AB, S-461 01 Trollhattan, Sweden.

Ossberger Turbinenfabrik, 8832 Weissenburg (Bayern), West Germany.

Riva Calzoni SpA, 20144 Milan, via Stendhal 34, Italy.

Skodaexport, Prague 1, Vaclavake N. 56, POB 492, Czechoslovakia.

Sorefame, Apartado No. 5, Amadora, Portugal.

Sulzer Brothers Ltd, CH-8401 Wintherthur, Switzerland.

OY Tampella, Engineering Works, Tampere, Finland.

Tokyo Shibaura Electric Co Ltd, Producer Goods Export Division 1-6, 1-chome, Uchisaiwaicho, Chiyoda-ku, Tokyo 160, Japan.

Ateliers de Constructions Mecaniques de Vevey, CH-1800 Vevey, Switzerland.

Voest AG, Muldenstrasse 5, A-4020 Linz, Austria.

Voith GmbH(J.M.), D-7920 Heidenheim, Postfach 45, West Germany.

Voith SA (J.M.), Av. Paulista 2444 CJ/42, Brazil.

Waagner-Biro AG, Margaretenstrasse 70, Postfach 60, A-1051 Vienna, Austria.

Water Power 12 issues per year **$26.00 per year $10.50 students $2.45 single issue** from: Subscription Manager, I.p.c. Business Press Ltd., Oakfield House, Perrymount Rd., Haywords Heath, Sussex RH16 3DH, U.K.

TIDAL POWER

The book is compiled from the contributions to the 1971 International Conference on the Utilization of Tidal Power. It is perhaps the most comprehensive statement of state-of-the-art harnessing of tidal power on a large scale; and, as such it is a highly technical tome. The subjects covered include construction techniques, corrosion problems, environmental problems, pumped storage operations, math-models of operations, sedimentation problems and the economics of it all. As one contributor puts it in his introduction, "Tidal power should be recognized as a special source of energy, requiring special technology for its development. Approaching tidal power as saltwater river hydro-power is bound to cripple the development of the appropriate technologies." A point that is repeatedly made in the papers presented is that often tidal projects are rejected as being too expensive, and too "unsure," when the real problem is the lack of information and research. There are, of course, certain requirements of geology and geography that have to be met for any tidal power location to be feasible. But even with obvious restraints it is estimated that Canada could supply as much as 15% of its total national power needs with renewable tidal power.

—Robin Saunders

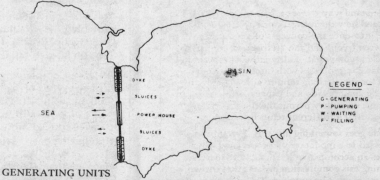

UNDERGROUND
PUMPED-STORAGE SECTION

TIDE MILLS

Early records indicate that tide mills were being worked along the Atlantic Coast of Europe, notably in Great Britain, France and Spain by the 11th century. One such installation in the Deben Estuary, in Great Britain, was mentioned as early as 1170 in the records of the Parish of Woodbridge. This is believed to be still in operation. Tidal energy was widely used in coastal areas where the tides attained a sufficient range to the middle of the 19th century. Part of the water supply of London in 1824 was provided by 20 ft. diameter waterwheels installed in 1580 under the arches of London Bridge. A tidal power installation for pumping sewage was still in use in Hamburg in 1880. Other installations have been reported throughout this era in Russia, North America, and Italy. Some of the old structures were of impressive size. A tide mill in Rhode Island built in the 18th century used 20 ton wheels 11 ft. in diameter and 26 ft. in width.

GENERATING UNITS

The energy potential in a tidal power development is exploited under low to very low heads. The only turbine types which are adaptable to such plants are the axial flow, high specific speed types including the Kaplan, bulb, straight flow and tube designs.

* * *

Tidal power development does not, of itself, represent a pollution source, but creation of an impoundment could aggravate an existing problem or create a problem where one did not previously exist. Factors that would increase pollution potential would be decreased dilution due to reduced tidal exchange, increased temperatures, and reduced dissolved oxygen concentrations due to decreased re-aeration rates. A pollutant that, in the absence of an impoundment, was removed without nuisance by dilution and tidal exchange, might well be a problem if its concentration was higher and less dissolved oxygen was available to meet the demands of decomposing micro-organisms. The problem would be worse if settleable material was deposited, because of low velocities, in stratefied deep water with an initially low dissolved oxygen concentration. Benthic organisms could be smothered and the water made intolerable for fish.

Tidal Power T. J. Gray & O. K. Gashus; 1972; 630 pp **$28.00** from: Plenum Press, 227 West 17th Street, New York, NY 10011 or WHOLE EARTH TRUCK STORE

HEAT PUMPS AND REFRIGERATORS

The usual hydro-power installation will be for generating electricity; this is the form of energy that is usually most useful for doing work, and the easiest to handle and distribute to fill the most needs. There are some situations, however, where it would make more sense to connect the machinery to be driven directly by the water turbine. This avoids some of the losses inherent in converting the water's energy into work then into electric energy, and then back again into work. Something like 30 to 50% can be lost in the typical small installation.

One of the applications for such a direct connection of a water turbine (or, for that matter, a wind mill as well) is to run a heat pump or refrigeration system.

A heat pump is a device which transfers thermal energy or heat from a "cooler" region to a "warmer" one. The direction of energy transfer is contrary to the normal flow. Heat naturally flows from the warmer region to a cooler region. We can reverse this natural tendency, if we supply some additional energy (usually in the form of work).

A refrigerator is an elementary heat pump. Energy is continually removed from the refrigerated space and "pumped" to a region of higher temperature—your kitchen. Work is supplied to run the compressor. A heat pump is simply a refrigerator which can operate in "two directions," enabling us to heat or cool a given space with the same equipment.

The attractiveness of a heat pump arises from the relatively small amount of work required to transfer a given amount of thermal energy (or heat). Under favorable conditions, three or four units of energy can be transferred for every unit of energy supplied as work. This means that we can supply a dwelling with three or four units of heat by investing only one unit of work—say from a hydro unit, windmill, or utility line. It seems that you are getting something for nothing, and, in fact, you are!

Suppose you lived in a small, one-room dwelling exposed to outside air temperatures of 40° F. In principle, you could heat that room using a modified refrigerator. You would do it in the following way. First, remove the refrigerator door. Then place the refrigerator next to an open door or large, open window with the "cold space" exposed to the outside air and the heat coils on the inside. If you sealed up the cracks properly and supplied the appropriate electrical input, the room temperature would rise.

To understand why the room is warmed, we need to understand how the refrigerator operates. To do this, we introduce the concepts of a working fluid (often freon) and the "refrigeration cycle." The cycle is composed of alternating compression and expansion processes with intermediate opportunities for the working fluid to absorb or give off heat. The compression and expansion processes are important, since they permit the fluid to absorb and reject heat at different temperatures.

The cycle goes something like this: Freon gas is compressed to a moderately high pressure which produces an accompanying temperature increase. It is during this compression process that the work for the cycle must be supplied. The high temperature freon gas (typically around 140° F) is then circulated through pipes which are exposed to the room air. Since the freon is hotter than the room air, energy is transferred into the room until the freon gas cools and condenses to a liquid. As we said before, the amount of energy transferred into the room is several times that put into the compressor. To find out where this "extra" energy comes from, we must follow the cycle further. Immediately after condensation, the freon liquid is still at a high temperature and pressure. The temperature of this fluid can be reduced significantly (below 0° F) by reducing the pressure suddenly. This pressure reduction is accomplished with an inexpensive expansion valve. The low pressure freon, which is now a mixture of liquid and gas, is then circulated through a pipe exposed to the outside air. Here the freon takes energy from the "cold" outside air. It can do this easily since the freon temperature is well below 0° F! This is where the

"extra" energy is obtained. The key point is that the outside air contains energy which can be used to heat the room—you merely need a device to collect it.

The cycle is completed as the cold freon collects enough energy from the outside air to vaporize completely. The resulting gas is then fed back into the compressor to start a new cycle. It is often useful to think of this gas as a "carrier" for the energy collected from the outside air, and that the compressor "conditions" the fluid so that the energy can be delivered to the room at a higher temperature. It should be realized that the energy used to operate the compressor eventually enters the room as heat. Thus, if three units of energy are collected from the outside air, and one unit of energy is supplied from a mechanical or electrical source to run the compressor, four units of energy will be transferred into the house.

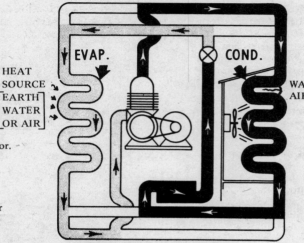

HEATING CYCLE OF A HEAT PUMP

The term Coefficient of Performance (COP) is often used in heat pump and refrigeration literature. This is simply the ratio of energy delivered to the room divided by work input to the compressor. The higher the COP, the better. In the example above, the COP would be 4.0, since four units of energy were supplied for each unit of work inputed. A COP of two to four is common for units operating with moderate outside temperatures (30 to 40° F). However, the COP decreases as the outside temperature falls, and manufacturers' specifications should be consulted to obtain the exact COP for the outside temperatures anticipated in a particular locality.

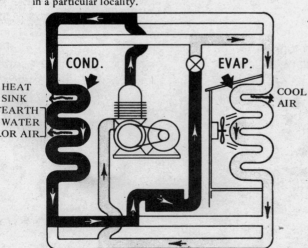

COOLING CYCLE

A new heat pump, which can be used both to heat and cool a living space costs about $2500. Typically such units include automatic controls for humidity and temperature. The main disadvantage of a heat pump is, obviously, the high initial cost. In the long run however, heat pumps will save money since fuel bills will be significantly lower than those incurred with gas or electric heat. This is especially true in light of the most recent increases in the cost of natural gas.

Heat pumps suffer from two major problems. First, the COP is reduced significantly in severe climates. Sometimes this can be remedied by switching to another chemical in the freon family which has different thermal properties. However, one should obtain qualified help before embarking on such an

expensive proposition. A second problem involves the tendency for ice to form on the "cold" coils and severely degrade the operation. Manufacturers claim to have solved this problem on newer units, but again, you should seek a qualified opinion if you live in a particularly humid location.

To summarize, a heat pump is a fairly sophisticated device which can save considerably on fuel costs for heating. The unit can easily be reversed for cooling in the summer. Commercial units have a high initial cost, but are economical in the long run due to fuel savings. In principle, heat pumps can be constructed with parts from commercial-size refrigeration units, but considerable expertise is required. Home construction is not a job for beginners!

Straight refrigeration systems are much more common and can easily be adapted to particular situations. Cheap refrigeration systems can be obtained from restaurant supply houses or institutions. These usually have belt driven compressors (originally driven by an electric motor, of course). These motors are usually in the range of ½ to 4 horse power. Considering the usual efficiencies of electric generators and motors, it would take 1.5 to 2 times that size in waterwheel generated electric power. Even if an electric generating installation is being built, the saving in power by attaching a direct drive refrigeration system is significant enough that it should be given serious consideration, particularly with the larger units.

We began this discussion by introducing the advantages of hooking the compressor in a heat pump or refrigerator directly to a water turbine or windmill. Saving the efficiency lost by not turning mechanical energy into electric and then the electrical energy back into mechanical seems to be self-evident without the need for further elaboration. However, the advantages of using a heat pump should be considered regardless of whether the compressor receives its energy input from mechanical or electrical sources; though in this case mechanical is certainly preferable.

—Robin Saunders and Harry Whitehouse

graphics from:
Heat Pumps for Heating and Cooling Homes
$.25

from:
Superintendent of Documents
U.S. Government Printing Office
Washington, D.C. 20402

EXPLORING MECHANICS

A basic physics text written by a high school physics teacher. For someone with little or no understanding of pressures in fluids, vectors, power and work, torque, fluids in motion or physics of the atmosphere. This is introductory material. Depth is shallow but the scope is broad enough to include a lot of energy-related physics basics.

—T.G.

Exploring Mechanics
Alexander Efron
1957; 181 pp

$4.95

from:
Hayden Book Company, Inc.
50 Essex Street
Rochelle Park, New Jersey
07662

or WHOLE EARTH
TRUCK STORE

WIND

Wind is another form of energy, created by the sun; the heating of our atmosphere during the day and its absence cooling the night sky. It's like breathing—that's it, the earth breathes. Wind is the reaction of our atmosphere to the incoming energy from the sun. Heat causes low pressure areas and the lack of heat results in high pressure areas. This process causes the wind.

It seems ironic that probably the oldest and most constant character of the universe, e.g., massive movements of energy, heating to cooling (entropy), the motion of our atmosphere is suddenly rediscovered as a "new source" of energy. History tells us that next to agriculture, it is very possible that wind may have been one of the first sources harnessed by man.

Our main concern regarding wind energy is that it is not as constant and/or predictable as, say, the sun. There are many solutions to this problem, but usually the situation is managed by a *storage system* designed to have the energy available at the time it is needed or desired. Yet, on the other hand, one might look at this concern in a different perspective and not see it as a problem at all, but simply as a challenge to our ability to adapt. If we are truly aware of our capabilities to adapt or adjust, then we also realize our limitations. It should be noted that we have adapted to our lifestyles most effectively considering we inhabit the planet in so many numbers. So that the problem with *wind* is not predictability, but it is *our* ability to respond.

Our dependent, real and intimate relationship with the biosphere can no longer afford to be overlooked. Wind systems are visual indicators of amounts of energy used, and therefore assist us in understanding this *environmental relationship*. The right perspective of this situation is important, for then and only then are we able to design our part of the environment, without selling short our individuality or our abilities.

All things in life change, as does the Sun, the Wind, the Water, and all living things in accordance with them.

ENFIELD - ANDREAU
WIND TURBINE

Living things dance with their surroundings,
  and so
    our ways also
     will see.
The evolution of life is the act of creation
  and its particularity
    its distinction
  is its movement,
    its visibility.
The way, itself
  will define it
    in the process
These systems should do as well!

ALL THIS IS POSSIBLE, AND IN THE STARRES AND WINDES. . .
—William Shakespeare

The one nice thing about the correct approach, or the right question to a situation is that the *answers* always reveal themselves as if they were always there.

—T.W.

Wind Synergy Technique*

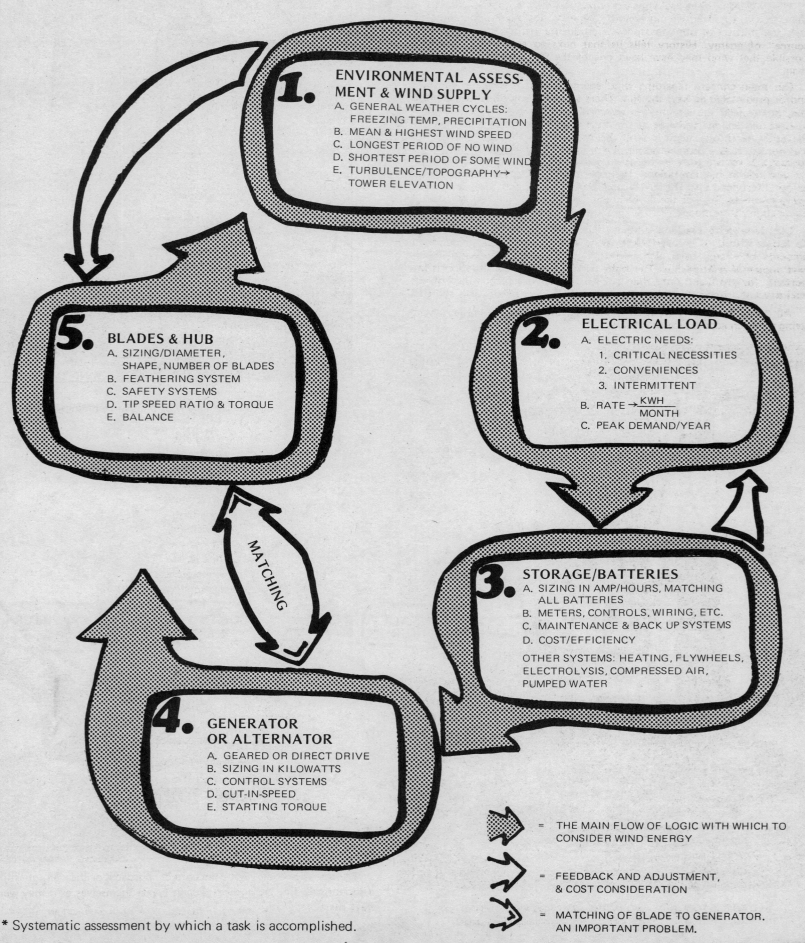

1. ENVIRONMENTAL ASSESS-
MENT & WIND SUPPLY
A. GENERAL WEATHER CYCLES:
FREEZING TEMP, PRECIPITATION
B. MEAN & HIGHEST WIND SPEED
C. LONGEST PERIOD OF NO WIND
D. SHORTEST PERIOD OF SOME WIND
E. TURBULENCE/TOPOGRAPHY→
TOWER ELEVATION

5. BLADES & HUB
A. SIZING/DIAMETER,
SHAPE, NUMBER OF BLADES
B. FEATHERING SYSTEM
C. SAFETY SYSTEMS
D. TIP SPEED RATIO & TORQUE
E. BALANCE

2. ELECTRICAL LOAD
A. ELECTRIC NEEDS:
1. CRITICAL NECESSITIES
2. CONVENIENCES
3. INTERMITTENT
B. RATE → $\dfrac{\text{KWH}}{\text{MONTH}}$
C. PEAK DEMAND/YEAR

MATCHING

3. STORAGE/BATTERIES
A. SIZING IN AMP/HOURS, MATCHING
ALL BATTERIES
B. METERS, CONTROLS, WIRING, ETC.
C. MAINTENANCE & BACK UP SYSTEMS
D. COST/EFFICIENCY

OTHER SYSTEMS: HEATING, FLYWHEELS,
ELECTROLYSIS, COMPRESSED AIR,
PUMPED WATER

4. GENERATOR
OR ALTERNATOR
A. GEARED OR DIRECT DRIVE
B. SIZING IN KILOWATTS
C. CONTROL SYSTEMS
D. CUT-IN-SPEED
E. STARTING TORQUE

= THE MAIN FLOW OF LOGIC WITH WHICH TO
CONSIDER WIND ENERGY

= FEEDBACK AND ADJUSTMENT,
& COST CONSIDERATION

= MATCHING OF BLADE TO GENERATOR.
AN IMPORTANT PROBLEM.

* Systematic assessment by which a task is accomplished.

Wind Energy Conversions

WIND → MECHANICAL → ELECTRIC

BETZ THEOREM 59.3% MAXIMUM

SLOW SPEED

MODERATE SPEED (GENERATOR)

MATCH BLADE TO GENERATOR

CONSIDERATIONS
1) WEATHER
2) SPEED (MEASUREMENT), HIGHEST, AND MEAN
3) LONGEST PERIOD OF NO WIND
4) SHORTEST PERIOD OF SOME WIND
5) TURBULENCE/TOPOGRAPHY→TOWER ELEVATION
6) SITE LOCATION

USE
ELECTRICAL
ELECTROLYSIS (H_2)
RESISTANCE HEATING

USES
PUMP
GRIND
CIRCULATE
COMPRESS

MECH.

BLADES → CONTROLS → HARDWARE → TOWERS

WIND PLANT MATERIALS

FABRIC
WOOD
METAL
FIBERGLASS
PLASTIC
RUBBER
ETC.

CONSIDERATIONS

STRESS
STRENGTH

TEMPERATURE

EFFICIENCY
COST

MAINTENANCE

VIBRATION

FRICTION

DEGRADATION

BLADES

DESIGN
(A) LIFT VECTOR
(B) PITCH
(C) CHORD
(D) ANGLE OF ATTACK
(E) LENGTH

TYPE

Propeller   Savonius
Darrieus   Magnus

WIND SPEED (FT/SEC)
TIP SPEED (REV/SEC)

DIAMETER

BALANCING

TORSION, BENDING MOMENT, TRACKING

CONTROLS

HOUSING

DIRECTING INTO WIND
(A) VANE (UP-WIND)
(B) COWLING (DOWN-WIND)
(C) WIND ROSE

SPEED GOVERNING

BRAKES

AIR BRAKES

FLYBALLS

BLADE FEATHERING
(A) TEETERING
(B) GIMBALED
(C) HINGLESS
(D) FULLY ARTICULATED
(E) HELICAL
(F) RADIAL
(G) CONING

HARDWARE

GEARS
(A) SIZE OF FACES)
(B) RATIOS

BEARINGS

BUSHINGS

DIRECT DRIVE

LUBRICANTS

BELTS, CHAINS, ETC.

SPRINGS

CABLE

TOWERS

DESIGN
3 LEGS
4 LEGS
OCTAHEDRON
HELICAL

MATERIALS
ANGLE STEEL
PIPE
WOODEN
GUIDE WIRES
CEMENT BASE
CONCRETE BLOCK
CONCRETE

ALIGNMENT

ELECT.

GENERATOR or ALTERNATOR
(D.C.)   (A.C.)

→ STORAGE BATTERIES → CONTROLS → INVERTERS D.C. TO A.C.

BRUSHES OR SLIP RINGS

NUMBER OF FIELD POLES

PHASES (1, 2, 3)

A.C. TO D.C. WAVE RECTIFICATION

"CUT IN SPEED"
SIZE AND SHAPE
PERMANENT MAGNET
INDUCTION

VOLTAGE
CURRENT   WATTS

STORAGE BATTERIES

RATING (AMP HOUR)

CHEMICALS AND CHARACTERISTICS

LEAD ACID   NI-CAD

NUMBER OF CYCLES

RATE OF CHARGE & DISCHARGE, DEPTH OF CHARGE

MATCHING SET

OTHER STORAGE SYSTEMS
FLYWHEELS
COMPRESSED (AIR OR GAS)
HYDRO STORAGE, MAIN POWER GRID

CONTROLS
REGULATOR

BREAKERS & FUSES

GROUNDING

LIGHTNING ARRESTERS

WIRING (A) SIZING
(B) A.C. & D.C. SYSTEM DIFFERENCES

SLIP RINGS

INVERTERS D.C. TO A.C.

ROTARY OR STATIC

WAVE FORM

CONTINUOUS DUTY

IDLING AMPS

EFFICIENCY

FLOW CHARTS
The items discussed in the above chart may be used either in the building, designing or purchasing of wind driven generators; it is suggested that any additions one finds could be written in, thus making the chart even more useful.

WIND DRIVEN GENERATORS
BY
James Sencenbaugh
Electrical Engineer

INTRODUCTION

Perhaps the primitive horizontal windmills of 10th century Persia were the first attempt at harnessing wind. This mill, with its sails revolving on a vertical axle mounted in a square tower, was used to grind corn. Diagonally opposed slots in the walls ducted air to the enclosed sail assembly. Tradition tells of the prisoners of Genghis Khan introducing the mills into the East. Horizontal mills became commonplace throughout China, where they were used primarily for irrigation. At the end of the 12th century, mills could be found throughout Northern Europe. By the late 13th century they were in use in Italy, but almost 200 years later the windmill was still unknown in Spain. German crusaders driving through Asia Minor probably instituted the technique in this region. Design from this period on varied greatly and improvements developed independently in many countries.

Unlike windmills which use the wind directly for mechanical energy, a modern wind driven generator extracts energy from the wind and converts it into electricity. A complete wind driven system consists of a: (1) tower to support the wind generator, (2) devices regulating generator voltage, (3) the propeller and hub system, (4) the tail vane, (5) a storage system to store power for use during windless days, and (6) an inverter which converts the stored direct current (D.C.) into regulated alternating current (A.C.) if it is required. An optional backup system, such as a gas or diesel generator, is used to provide power through extremely long calm periods.

With the invention of automobiles and the development of their electrical systems, small D.C. generators of low output and moderate speed input became available on a large scale. Changes in wiring enabled these early generators to be used in the first wind driven designs. At the same time, the rapid increase in aeronautical research led to intensive investigation on airfoil and (propeller) blade design. With this background, the wind driven generator came into its own as the first form of free private electrical power generation. It was first sold as an accessory to battery powered radios. The Zenith radio corporation offered a small 200 watt windplant at a reduced price when bought with one of their battery powered radios. It was during this period that the Wincharger Co. of Sioux City, Iowa was reported to have been turning out 1000 units per day. The wind driven generator field bloomed in the late 1920's and 30's and at its peak over 300 companies were formed throughout the world. A large number of varied designs were available, from a down-wind 1800 watt Win Power to the 3000 watt Jacobs unit. The introduction of the Rural Electrification Agency (REA) in the United States brought a cheaper, more convenient method to have larger amounts of electricity, and wind plants all but disappeared. Jacobs finally closed its doors around 1956 and Wincharger now only makes the original 200 watt 12 volt D.C. model designed in the 1930's.

At present there are only six *major* manufacturers of wind driven generators in the world. Two are in the United States: Dynatechnology (Wincharger) and Bucknell Engineering (bought by Precise Power Corporation). Both build very small 200 watt units on a limited production basis. Dunlite of Australia (which builds plants marketed by Quirk's) manufactures two basic models: a D.C. generator type and a brushless alternator type. Elektro G.M.B.H. of Winterthur, Switzerland offers a complete line of windplants from 50 to 6000 watts. Aerowatt of Paris, France, builds a number of excellent wind plants designed for commercial and marine applications, but their prices are extremely high. Last is Lübing Maschine Fabrik of Barnstorf, West Germany. They primarily build water pumping windplants, but do offer a small 400 watt, 24 volt unit.

The most economical windmill is one which furnishes the kilowatt-hr at the lowest cost. The production of energy by windmills at a favorable cost is made difficult by the fact that the wind is an intermittent source of energy. During a large part of the time it blows too little to produce any useful output and other times it is of such velocities as to cause potential damage to the windplant.

The actual power available from the wind is proportional to the cube of the windspeed. In other words, if the windspeed is doubled, you will

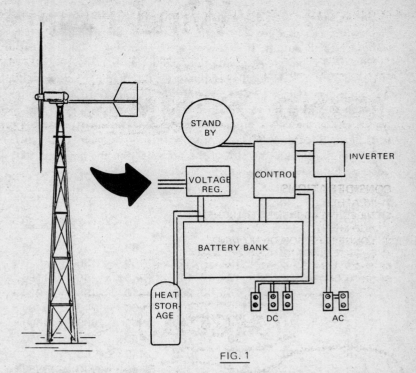

FIG. 1

IN THIS SYSTEM, THE WIND DRIVEN GENERATOR CHARGES A BATTERY BAN from which DC power is taken directly for use or inverted, making AC for appliances like T.V., and radios. Excess power runs a heating storage system.

get eight times as much power (Cube Law). Another fundamental principle governing windmill design is that it is theoretically impossible in an open-air windplant to recover more than 59.26% (A. Betz) of the kinetic energy contained in the wind. If the prop itself is 75% efficient, and the generator 75% efficient, then 33.34% of the kinetic energy of the wind may be converted into electricity. The other important factor to point out is that the amount of energy captured from the wind by a windplant depends on the amount of wind intercepted; that is, the disk area swept by the blades. A well designed windplant irrespective of the number of blades decelerates the whole horizontal column of air to one-third its free velocity. These facts and the nature of wind currents generally restrict the designer to the most common wind velocities of 3 to 10 meters per second (6.7 to 22.3 mph).

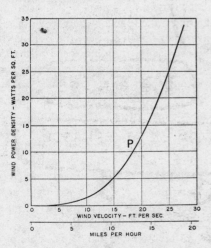

FIG. 2. THEORETICAL POWER DENSITY OF WIND

$$P = K \cdot A \cdot V^3$$

Unit of Power P	Unit of Area A	Unit of Velocity V	Value of K
Kilowatts	Square feet	Miles per hour	0·0000053
Kilowatts	Square feet	Knots	0·0000081
Horse power	Square feet	Miles per hour	0·0000071
Watts	Square feet	Feet per second	0·00168
Kilowatts	Square metres	Metres per second	0·00064
Kilowatts	Square metres	Kilometres per hour	0·0000137

WIND FORMULA TABLE 1: Where P= Power in Kilowatts, K= Constant (Air density and other conversion factors), A= Area swept, and V= Wind Velocity.

Table 2 will give an appreciation for the principles involved in wind-plant design. A 6 foot diameter prop, operating at 70% efficiency in a 20 mph wind, can produce 340 watts. This shows the relationship between windspeed and output. If the wind speed is doubled, you will get eight times as much power. Also note the relationship between propeller diameter and output. Keeping the results for the 6 footer in mind, let us double the prop diameter to 12 feet and note the output at 10 and 20 mph. At 10 mph the 12 footer can produce up to 170 watts and at 20 mph, 1360 watts. Hence the power output from the 12 feet diameter prop is 4 times that of the 6 footer, or *power is proportional to the square of the diameter of the prop*. Double the size of the propeller and the power output will increase by a factor of four.

Propeller Diameter in Feet	Wind Velocity in mph					
	5	10	15	20	25	30
2	0.6	5	16	38	73	130
4	2	19	64	150	300	520
6	5	42	140	340	660	1150
8	10	75	260	610	1180	2020
10	15	120	400	950	1840	3180
12	21	170	540	1360	2660	4600
14	29	230	735	1850	3620	6250
16	40	300	1040	2440	4740	8150
18	51	375	1320	3060	6000	10350
20	60	475	1600	3600	7360	12760
22	73	580	1940	4350	8900	15420
24	86	685	2300	5180	10650	18380

TABLE 2. WINDMILL POWER OUTPUT IN WATTS, assuming 70% efficiency

ENVIRONMENTAL ASSESSMENT

It is not enough just to know these fundamental principles before deciding to build or buy a windplant. Your choice of site must be assessed to see if a windplant will give you equitable returns, in addition to the positive environmental effects.

Consider the following conditions at the site on a *frequency* and *intensity* basis: rain, freezing temperatures, icing, sleet, hail, sandstorms, and lightning. The life and longevity of a wind plant, as well as its structural design and cost, depend on the completeness of your weather assessment. (Note: Most manufactured wind systems are "tropic-proofed;" be sure to check this if buying a system.)

In order to determine the usable output (Kw-hrs. per month) produced by a particular size wind driven system, the output characteristics of the windplant and the average yearly wind speed at the site must be known. The average yearly winds at a location can be obtained from the National Weather Bureau records center, U.S. Weather Bureau, Federal Building, Asheville, N.C. 28801. They carry statistical data for the U.S. for the last 50 years. Although they might not have information for your exact location, they should have records of a city or area very near. This information is a good start for estimating if the winds in your area are suitable for wind power. Another source of wind information will be your local airport. The next step should be the purchase of an anemometer (wind gauge) to estimate local wind conditions. A small hand held unit is available from Dwyer for $6.95 (see page 99). There is also a more expensive remote reading anemometer by Taylor of Rochester, N.Y., for about $75.00 (see page 99). The transmitter assembly can be mounted on a T.V. type mast at the height the wind plant is to be installed.

Another means of assessing local wind velocities is by using the Beaufort scale (Table 3). If readings are taken with regularity and then compared to the local Weather Bureau data, the scale is a very accurate and inexpensive way of measuring wind speed. Readings should be taken every day at the same times for accurate results (typically four times a day). Data should be taken for at least one month, and preferably longer, to determine mean average wind speed. Determining the longest period of no wind and the shortest period of some wind annually are two calculations that will be very helpful in figuring storage systems and back-up system requirements. If the test results show that there is over a 10 mph wind average on an norm of 2 to 3 days per week, you have an adequate site for wind power. The site findings should be compared to official Weather Bureau data for

sites nearby to see if they correlate with the 10 year monthly averages for that area.

Effect Caused by the Wind		Beaufort		Speed	
On Land	At Sea	Number	Description	(m/sec)	(miles/hr)
Still: smoke rises vertically	Surface mirror-like	0	Calm	0–0.2	0–1
Smoke drifts but vanes remain still	Only ripples form	1	Light air	0.3–1.5	1–3
Wind felt on face, leaves rustle, vane moves	Small, short wavelets, distinct but not breaking	2	Light breeze	1.6–3.3	4.7
Leaves and small twigs move constantly, streamer or pennant extended	Larger wavelets beginning to break, glassy foam, perhaps scattered white horses	3	Gentle breeze	3.4–5.4	8–12
Raises dust and loose paper, moves twigs and thin branches	Small waves still but longer, fairly frequent white horses	4	Moderate breeze	5.5–7.9	13–18
Small trees in leaf begin to sway	Moderate waves, distinctly elongated, many white horses, perhaps isolated spray	5	Fresh breeze	8.0–10.7	19–24
Large branches move, telegraph wires whistle, umbrellas hard to control	Large waves begin with extensive white foam crests breaking, spray probable	6	Strong wind	10.8–13.8	25–31
Whole trees move; offers some resistance to walkers	Sea heaps up, lines of white foam begin to be blown downwind	7	Stiff wind or moderate gale	13.9–17.1	32–38
Breaks twigs off trees; impedes progress	Moderately high waves with crests of considerable length; foam blown in well-marked streaks; spray blown from crests	8	Stormy wind or fresh gale	17.2–20.7	39–46
Blows off roof tiles and chimney pots	High waves, rolling sea, dense streaks of foam; spray may already reduce visibility	9	Storm or strong gale	20.8–24.4	47–54
Trees uprooted, much structural damage	Heavy rolling sea, white with great foam patches and dense streaks, very high waves with overhanging crests; much spray reduces visibility	10	Heavy storm or whole gale	24.5–28.4	55–63
Widespread damage (very rare inland)	Extraordinarily high waves, spray impedes visibility	11	Hurricane-like storm	28.5–32.6	64–72
	Air full of foam and spray, sea entirely white	12	Hurricane	32.7–36.9	73–82

TABLE 3. THE BEAUFORT SCALE

The relative wind velocity prevailing in any location determines what size of wind generator is best suited for that region. Table 4 shows a sample region having annual average velocities of 10 mph or greater. Note that the 10 mph average wind is made up of many low winds and a few high winds. A 6 mph wind is generally considered to be the lowest wind for any practical use. In terms of energy available, 12 to 25 mph is the range of higher winds providing good power conversion. The relationship between the wind and power available to a wind generator can be exemplified by the detailed study that was made of wind records at Dayton, Ohio. Data was taken from 1936 to 1943, covering a 7 year period. In each month two groups of winds exist. First, there are the frequent or *prevalent winds* ranging from 5 to 13 mph. Second there are the *energy winds* which blow less frequently, ranging from 13 to 23 mph. A quick glance at Table 4 will give a clue to the energy winds. The prevalent winds blow 2–1/2 times more frequently than the more vigorous energy winds; for example, 5 days prevalent as opposed to 2 days of the energy winds. But because the energy varies with the cube of the velocity, the energy winds produce 3/4 of the total power. A windmill utilizing the prevalent winds must be twice the diameter of a windmill running *only* on the energy winds, if each is to produce the same amount of electricity per month.

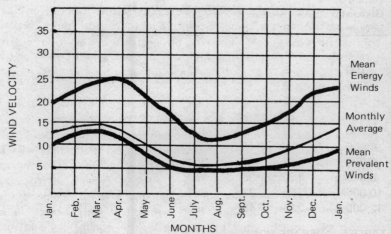

TABLE 4. The curves represent averages of 13 "frequency" and "energy" charts compiled from Weather Bureau records.

Tower design and installation are as important as site selection. A support must be built that is strong enough to handle loads from the dead weight of the generator assembly itself, as well as the thrust loads developed from the propeller at the highest anticipated windspeed. Most commercial towers are designed for a wind loading of at least 140 mph, and then a generous safety factor is added. Manufacturers discourage the installation of these larger units on home roofs because the loads on a 12 or 14 foot diameter prop are so powerful in winds over 45 mph that they could cause serious structural damage to the rafters, or even send the plant crashing down through the roof. A six or eight foot diameter prop on a wood frame structure can cause noise to be transmitted throughout the structure, even though the plant is balanced and running smoothly. This noise, which resembles a low howl or groan, can bother even the most sound sleeper.

The best location for a wind plant is as high as economically possible to reach undisturbed air. Placing a windplant a minimum of 30 to 40 feet above the ground (not on a roof!) will greatly increase the amount of power available to the swept area. Ideally the plant should be placed 15 to 20 feet above all obstacles within a 500 foot radius because surrounding objects have a very disturbing effect on the air and cause whirling eddy currents that greatly effect plant performance.

TURBULENCE/TOPOGRAPHY → TOWER ELEVATION

A hill or ridge of high ground lying in the path of the wind will have a considerable influence on the wind. Remember, also, that the winds blow *parallel* to the ground, not perpendicular to gravity. Obtaining a topographical map from the U.S.G.S. will enable you to estimate any turbulence due to topography. Tall trees behind a wind plant, as well as trees in front, interfere with a wind plant's operation. Most commercial wind plants are designed so that they can be installed 500 to 600 feet away from the point where power is required, so there is leeway for avoiding obstacles.

LOAD

The next assessment which needs to be made is how much power your appliances will actually require. The more accurately you figure these needs, the lower your storage costs become. The storage system expense is a direct result of the load. Figure *all* electrical needs:

1. Critical needs (e.g. refrigerator)
2. Convenience needs (e.g. electric blanket)
3. Intermittent needs (e.g. power saw)

Construct a chart, as shown below, listing the devices in use, hours per day each is in use, and the number of watt-hours each device requires.

Appliances	Watt Rating	Hours/Day in Use	Watt-Hr./Day
4 light bulbs	100 each	6	2400
1 stereo	80	4	320
1 percolator	480	1	480
1 sewing machine motor	30	1	30
List of Appliances (see page 83)		total	3230

Nominal Output Rating of Generator in Watts	Average Monthly Wind Speed in mph					
	6	8	10	12	14	16
50	1.4	3	5	7	9	10
100	3	5	8	11	13	15
250	6	12	18	24	29	32
500	12	24	35	46	55	62
1,000	22	45	65	86	104	120
2,000	40	80	120	160	200	235
4,000	75	150	230	310	390	460
6,000	115	230	350	470	590	710
8,000	150	300	450	600	750	900
10,000	185	370	550	730	910	1090
12,000	215	430	650	870	1090	1310

TABLE 5. AVERAGE MONTHLY OUTPUT IN KILOWATT-HOURS

1. From the table find the average wind speed vs. generator rating to determine Kw-hr./month output. Let's assume the wind-generator is operating in an area with 10 mph average winds and that the generator rating is 4 Kw: from the table we find the expected monthly output to be about 200 Kw-hr./month (the table gives the figure 230, but we'll work with a more conservative figure). To find out how many Kw-hr. per day of electricity we could use (i.e. the *use rate*) with a 200 Kw-hr./month supply from the wind, divide the power available for the whole month (kw-hr./month) by the days in the month (30):

$$\frac{200 \text{ Kw-hr./month}}{30 \text{ days}} = 6670 \text{ watt-hr./day}$$

This is an excellent planning figure to design around when you are trying to estimate the number of watts consumed by devices, appliances, etc. to be used each day. In this example, with a windplant of the given size and average winds of 10 mph, you have 6670 watt-hrs. per day available to you.

2. The next step is to find the capacity in kw-hr. of the battery system in use. Assume a battery capacity of 270 amp/hrs. at 115 volts. Watts in the system is found by multiplying amps by volts. Therefore, 115 volts x 270 amp/hrs. = 31,050 watt-hours or 31.050 Kw-hrs.

3. Find the number of days you could expect to operate, assuming no wind, with 6670 watts/day load, from a 31,050 watt-hour storage system.

$$\frac{31,050 \text{ watts}}{6670 \text{ watts}} = 4.66 \text{ days}$$

Roughly, you could operate for at least four days directly from the batteries, with no input from the wind generator or the stand-by unit.

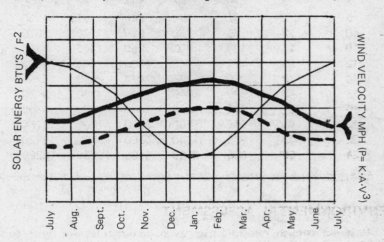

TABLE 6. COORDINATED WIND ELECTRIC DEMAND

Peak electrical demand could be coordinated with the peak energy period. This situation does not exist everywhere, but where it does it should be utilized.

Power company output is typically 60 cycles per second alternating current (A.C.). A battery storage system is direct current(D.C.). All resistance and heating devices (e.g., light bulbs, toasters) and universal motors (having brushes) can run on A.C. or D.C. The following require A.C. only; they will not operate on D.C:

1. Fluorescent lights (unless rewired),
2. Devices with transformers (e.g., televisions, radios, tape decks),
3. Appliances with standard induction motors.

If D. C. power is inadvertently supplied to an A.C. appliance, there is a high probability that the appliance will be destroyed.

BATTERY AND STORAGE SECTION

The most difficult and important calculation to make is the sizing of your storage system. Although there are many sophisticated and perhaps exotic methods of energy storage presently in development which could be used in this application, the most reliable at present is the lead acid storage battery. This battery still represents the cheapest practical method of electrical energy storage available for the individual user of wind power. Because the wind itself is an intermittent source of energy, a battery storage system must be capable of storing power through long, windless periods with reasonable efficiency at moderate cost.

Batteries used in wind plants are designed for repeated cycling over a period of many years. Their construction allows them to go repeatedly from a fully discharged to a fully charged state without damage. Some designs can withstand approximately 2000 complete cycles. These batteries are commonly known as stationary or houselighting batteries and are available in sizes from 10 amp/hr. to 8000 amp/hr. The normal voltage of the system is determined by the number of cells in series (each cell is approximately 2 volts), but the amount of storage capacity is determined by the plate thickness and area.

These batteries have thicker plates than the standard automobile battery and employ separators made of glass fiber material. The structural integrity

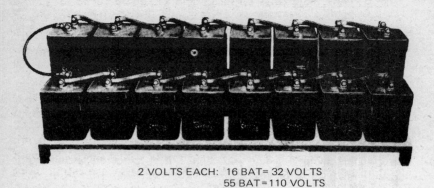

2 VOLTS EACH: 16 BAT = 32 VOLTS
55 BAT = 110 VOLTS

CAR BATTERY — 6 VOLTS

FIG. 3 SIZE AND VOLTAGE DIFFERENCES BETWEEN CAR BATTERY AND LIGHTING PLANT BATTERIES

of these cells is much greater, and large amounts of reserve space between the bottom of the plates and the case is common. This allows a large amount of area for material to collect without any damage from internal shock or shorting. Golfcart batteries have similar characteristics. Gould P B220, a 6 volt-220 amp cell, and Trojan P J217, a 6 volt-217 amp cell, can be used with reasonable success (see page 99).

A battery on charge is not a fixed or static potential, and is subject to change in its voltage and current output characteristics with changes in light, temperature elevation, etc. Simple testing methods compensate and adjust for these changes.

One important thing to remember is that when a battery is charging and discharging, there is a change not only in its amperage but also in its voltage level. Figure 4 shows that the battery voltage rises slowly until it reaches the 80-85 percent capacity-returned point, rises sharply between about 2.3 and 2.5 volts per cell (the gassing point where H_2 is created), and then flattens out at about 2.6 volts when the battery is fully charged. This sharp rise in voltage, during which only a small part of the charge is returned, is a characteristic of a lead acid cell and does create some design and operational problems. To return the last 15 percent of the charge in a reasonable time the charge voltage must increase by about 20%, or 0.5 volts. The high charge voltage required to complete the charge process may be unattainable because of the operating voltage of appliances. The current charge rate (amps) should be reduced at the gassing point 2.6 volts/cell to below the 20 hours rate. $(\frac{270 \text{ amp/hr}}{20 \text{ hr}} = 13.5 \text{ amps})$. This should be done by the electronic control and regulating system in your windplant.

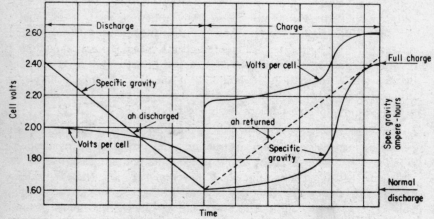

FIG. 4. TYPICAL VOLTAGE AND GRAVITY CHARACTERISTICS DURING A CONSTANT RATE DISCHARGE AND RECHARGE.

BATTERY CAPACITY

The nominal rated capacity of most lead acid batteries is taken at 8, 10

or 20 hour discharge rates down to a cell voltage of 1.85 volts per cell. At higher discharge rates the capacity is reduced, while at lower discharge rates the available capacity is increased. Figure No. 5 illustrates the change in capacity with the rate of discharge. At the 12 hour rate, for example, a nominal 500 amp hour capacity battery has an available capacity of 550 amp hour, or 110%, down to a discharge voltage of 1.85 volts per cell. The capacity taken out of the battery is approximately 1040 amp hr. and about 83% of the total available capacity. This limitation on the extent of discharge is to ensure that the battery is not worked excessively and to provide a reserve capacity, which will greatly extend the life of the battery.

One of the key factors in guaranteeing the life of the battery system is the regularity of maintenance. It is vital that the electrolyte level in all batteries is maintained. This is done by adding distilled water to each battery when needed. All batteries must have tight connections to minimize (1) corrosion, (2) unequal voltage per cell, and (3) reduced capacity. The battery set must be an originally matched set. Do not mix batteries of different ages. Batteries should be located a few inches off the floor and away from the wall to permit good air circulation. For more exact information on batteries write the battery companies in your area.

A new battery does not become fully active until used the equivalent of about 30 complete cycles, because the plates are somewhat hard and do not absorb and deliver the full current. On a battery of 400 amp/hr. capacity this break-in period requires a few months with an average load.

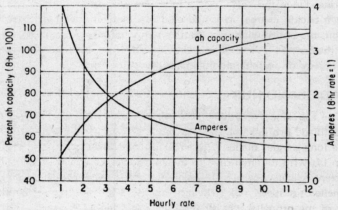

FIG. 5. CAPACITY-RATE CURVE BASED ON 8-HR. RATE

An important component in your overall electrical system is the wire. The correct size of wire for a given current must be accurately calculated. Keep in mind that D.C. travels through the wire and A.C. travels on the surface. This is important to know because fuses, circuit breakers, and switches for high current D.C. are different than for A.C. (D.C. outlets will have a polarity. Check when the system is wired to be sure they are correct.)

GENERATOR OR ALTERNATOR

The combined data of electrical needs and the size of the storage system necessary (which is based on the average wind speed) will determine the generator size necessary for your system. The last critical matching problem will be that of the blades to the generator.

Since propeller speed seldom exceeds 300-400 rpm, especially in the larger diameters, this calls for a low-speed generator designed to match the torque and horsepower output parameters of the prop in use. Dunlite compromises a bit by using an alternator which develops maximum output at 750 rpm, corresponding to a prop speed of only 150 rpm. Hence a 5:1 step-up gear is used. Elektro on the other hand utilizes all direct drive with the exception of the larger 6000 watt unit, which is geared. All major manufacturers are now using a multi-poled alternator which produces alternating current. An alternator is used for two reasons: (1) it operates at a lower cost than a comparable wattage D.C. generator, and (2) perhaps the most favorable factor, the high current is taken directly from the stator coils (see Fig. 6) and not through brushes as in a D.C. generator. Eventually the brushes wear down and need replacement.

One of the major cost factors in a modern wind system is the low speed continuous duty alternator or generator. Conventional alternators generally are designed for high rotational speeds (1800 to 3600 rpm), being driven by a gasoline engine, and therefore cannot be used for wind driven systems. Wind driven generators require a low cut-in speed. By using direct drive or a very low gearing ratio such as in the Dunlite unit, losses are kept to a

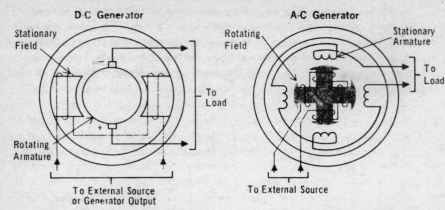

D-C Generator

Stationary Field

Rotating Armature

To Load

To External Source or Generator Output

A-C Generator

Rotating Field

Stationary Armature

To Load

To External Source

The d-c generator has a rotating armature and a stationary field. Voltage for its field can be obtained either from an external source or from the generator's own output

The a-c generator has a stationary armature and a rotating field. Voltage for its field must come from an external source, called an exciter

FIG. 6. AN AC GENERATOR AND A DC GENERATOR

minimum and overall machine efficiency remains relatively high. The design of direct drive generators is materials efficient and the low rotational speed keeps wear to a minimum.

Special electronic regulators are designed as part of generating systems to control the amount of current delivered to the batteries at a safe charging rate. Once the batteries are fully charged, the alternator will put out only a trickle charge, as is the case for the Dunlite unit. In the Elektro design, the entire windplant shuts down when the voltage regulator registers the battery cell voltage is above a predetermined level. This prevents any chance of overcharging the battery.

BLADES AND HUB

The efficiency of your entire wind system depends on what type of prop (blade profile) you use. All modern wind driven systems use two or three long slender blades with an airfoil section designed to produce maximum lift with minimal drag in the rpm range for which it operates. These efficient blades operate at a high tip speed ratio, which is the ratio of propeller tip speed (U) to wind velocity (V). The outstanding characteristic of the propeller-windmill is that at a given wind speed it rotates 5 to 10 times faster than a conventional multi-bladed windmill of the same size. The propeller type excels in lightness of construction, reduction of gearing difficulty, and is the only type of windmill through which direct generator drive can be accomplished. A higher tip speed ratio means higher rpm for a given wind speed, and higher rpm generally means more power output.

It is critical that the balance of the blade and hub system and its tracking are precisely adjusted. Static balancing insures equal mass distribution at all points in the rotation system. The procedure is fairly simple for two blade systems but becomes increasingly complex as more blades are added. Three dimensional configurations, such as Savonius rotors, are even more difficult. The figures below may be of some help.

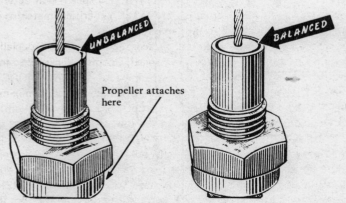

UNBALANCED

BALANCED

Propeller attaches here

FIG. 7. A METHOD DEVELOPED BY THE ARMY FOR BLADE BALANCING

Dynamic balance is very difficult to achieve. The main concern is to prevent vibrations. Therefore all blades must be identical in their lift or reaction components. Tracking means that the blades follow each other in exactly the same plane of rotation. The blade tips should track within 1/8", if possible, and should be no closer than one foot to the tower. The better the tracking the less the vibration.

Fig. 8 shows the relative tip speed ratio and power curves for various propeller types and VERTICAL AXIS rotors (SAVONIUS). The Figure shows the advantages of the propeller type windplant (curves 3,4,5,6,8 & 11) over the Savonius type plant (curves 1,7,9 &10). Also see "Additional Notes and Thoughts" (page 84) for more information on the Savonius Rotor.

One has the choice of whether to use two or three blades. It is generally a decision based on economics and the relative output of the generator to be used. Although a two-bladed prop will run at a slightly higher aerodynamic efficiency than a similarly designed 3-bladed prop, it is seldom used in commercial plants with generator ratings above 2000 watts output. This is because the three-bladed prop provides the extra starting torque necessary to overcome difficulties found in lower winds, fluxing and eddying. They run slightly smoother when orienting to changes in wind direction. In comparison, it was found early in wind-generator design that the two-bladed system is "choppy" when the tail vane shifts during wind direction changes. When the blades are straight up and down they have no centrifugal resistance to the tail movements. When the blades are parallel to the ground the resistance is maximum. However, it is interesting to note that the Elektro two-bladed wind plants do not exhibit this trait since the variable pitch weight arms are placed at 90 degrees to the blade element and, in terms of balance, the assembly "looks" like a 4-bladed prop during rotation. Hence wind direction changes are very smooth.

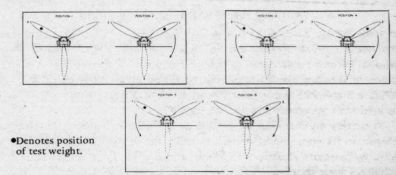

• Denotes position of test weight.

KNIFE EDGE BALANCING METHOD REQUIRES A PAIR OF PERFECTLY ALIGNED AND LEVELED EDGES OF HARD STEEL, A SPINDLE AND A HOIST

Once maximum power is developed at the rated windspeed of the generator (typically in the 16 to 25 mph range), excess power developed by the prop is potentially destructive and must be controlled. There are as many methods of overspeed control as there have been manufacturers of windmills, and each system has its own merits and disadvantages. The airbrake or airspoiler was used by several manufacturers during the 1920's and 30's on small diameter machines and is still used on the 200 watt unit built by Dynatechnology. Two small sheet metal vanes, resembling barrel slats, were placed at 90 degrees to each prop about the center axis of the hub. Springs held the vanes in normal position until centrifugal force pulled the vanes outward, diverting air away from the prop and thus decreasing rpm. This system was successful for small diameter units. Airbrakes are undesirable for larger scale operations since they throw heavy loads onto the entire structure.

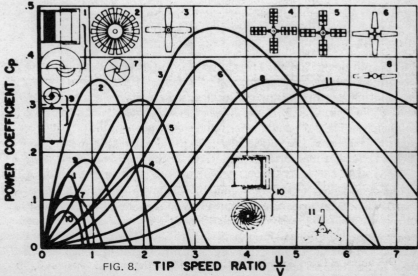

FIG. 8. TIP SPEED RATIO $\frac{U}{V}$

POWER COEFFICIENT C_P

FIG. 9   "NORMAL"   "GOVERNING"

Quirk's, built in Australia, used a system in its early years which was similar in operation to the prairie windmills. The generator and prop assembly was mounted off axis from the supporting tower. The thrust developed by the prop would push the generator assembly around the tower axis, against a tail hung by gravity, at a design windspeed. Thus, the prop would turn partially sideways from the oncoming wind, slowing the prop down. A popular method among the home-built units in the 1920's was the use of a pilot vane set parallel to the prop. The arm of the vane was equal in distance to the radius of the propeller, and the area exposed to oncoming air would help to push the prop and generator assembly out of the wind. The disadvantage of these types of swinging systems is that they induce gyroscopic vibration and eliminate the power supply at the very time when the best winds are available. However, well designed systems are able to operate directly into the airstream and then be activated at a predetermined windspeed. More sophisticated designs utilize a feathering principle (which regulates the propeller rpm by changing the angle of attack (pitch)) at high wind speeds. Pitch regulation is *attractive* since it holds the energy absorption nearly constant at all wind velocities, and allows continuous power output in high winds without inducing stress. Both Elektro and Quirk's utilize centrifugal force to act upon a set of spring-loaded weights to change pitch. Noting the Elektro diagram (Fig.10) it can be seen that the weights work on a direct line of centrifugal force and hence the actual density of the weight element itself is about 1 lb. For the two-bladed units, the assembly is designed to begin changing pitch (feathering) at about 400 rpm propeller speed. At this speed there is about 25 lbs. of centrifugal force on the weight arm itself. Quirk's utilizes a component of centrifugal force to act upon its weights, which are placed out from the prop shaft itself.

FIG. 10. CONTROL-PROPELLER HUB OF HEAT-TREATED NON-CORROSIVE LIGHT METAL WITH REGULATING MEMBERS, ADJUSTING MOVEMENT ON TAPEROLLER AND NEEDLE BEARINGS, EASY TO LUBRICATE, PROTECTED FROM WEATHER, NO RISK OF ICE-BUILDING. (ELEKTRO)

This positioning, and the lower prop speed of 150 rpm, results in the necessity of a 4 lb. weight at the end of each arm. Both systems are very successful in the control of any overloading, and can maintain safe rpm into winds of hurricane force. However, even though these units are stressed for 80 mph winds, the manufacturer still recommends that the propeller be stopped manually and/or rotated sideways to the wind. Most models have a brake control at the bottom of the tower for this purpose. Special wind-plants by these companies are available to operate unattended in winds up to 140 mph. Quirk's uses the conventional windplant, fitted with smaller diameter propellers (generally 10 ft. diameter). The latter, being shorter in arm length and with added internal stiffeners, allows the unit to operate head-on into high winds. Elektro prefers to shut down the plant completely, and has an optional high speed control package which can be added to the standard plants.

Hopefully the multitude of systems to come will be designed around some basic criteria like "Safety, Reliability, and Cost," in that order. These are important considerations particularly for those wishing to build their own design. A real understanding of the force and magnitude of the wind serves to reinforce the need for these criteria. Many a wind system has been literally swept away.

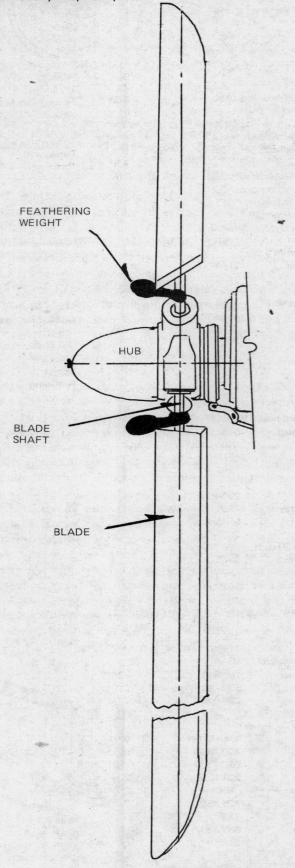

FIG. 11 QUIRK'S FEATHERING SYSTEM

One marvelous feeling that comes to you from taking these responsibilities, that is realizing the ability-to-respond, is the gathering of the sense of freedom. The individual benefits of these renewable energy systems represents only one part of the picture. Along with emoting their sense of ecological satisfaction, they provide a positive direction towards self-determination. A rare thing these days.

All (things) are possible. And in the stars and winds . . .

COMPOSITE OF KILOWATTHOUR RATINGS FOR VARIOUS APPLIANCES

(PRE–ENERGY CRISIS ESTIMATES)

Name	Watts	Hrs/Mo.	KWHRS/Mo.
Air conditioner, central			620*
Air conditioner, window	1566	74	116*
Battery charger			1*
Blanket	190	80	15
Blanket	50-200		15
Blender	350	3	1
Bottle sterilizer	500		15
Bottle warmer	500	6	3
Broiler	1436	6	8.5
Clock	1-10		1-4*
Clothes drier	4600	20	92*†
Clothes drier, electric heat	4856	18	86*†
Clothes drier, gas heat	325	18	6*†
Clothes washer			8.5*
Clothes washer, automatic	250	12	3*
Clothes washer, conventional	200	12	2*†
Clothes washer, automatic	512	17.3	9*
Clothes washer, ringer	275	15	4*†
Clippers	40-60		½
Coffee maker	800	15	12
Coffee maker, twice a day			8
Coffee percolator	300-600		3-10
Coffee pot	894	10	9
Cooling, attic fan	1/6-3/4HP		60-90*†
Cooling, refrigeration	3/4-1½ ton		200-500*
Corn popper	460-650		1
Curling iron	10-20		½
Dehumidifier	300-500		50*
Dishwasher	1200	30	36*
Dishwasher	1200	25	30*
Disposal	375	2	1*
Disposal	445	6	3*
Drill, electric, ¼"	250	2	5
Electric baseboard heat	10,000	160	1600
Electrocuter, insect	5-250		1*
Electronic oven	3000-7000		100*
Fan, attic	370	65	24*†
Fan, kitchen	250	30	8*†
Fan, 8"-16"	35-210		4-10*†
Food blender	200-300		½
Food warming tray	350	20	7
Footwarmer	50-100		1
Floor polisher	200-400		1
Freezer, food, 5-30 cu.ft.	300-800		30-125*
Freezer, ice cream	50-300		½
Freezer	350	90	32*
Freezer, 15 cu.ft.	440	330	145*
Freezer, 14 cu.ft.			140*
Freezer, frost free	440	180	57*
Fryer, cooker	1000-1500		5
Fryer, deep fat	1500	4	6
Frying pan	1196	12	15
Furnace, electric control	10-30		10*
Furnace, oil burner	100-300		25-40*
Furnace, blower	500-700		25-100*†
Furnace, stoker	250-600		3-60*†
Furnace, fan			32*†
Garbage disposal equipment	1/4-1/3 HP		½*
Griddle	450-1000		5
Grill	650-1300		5
Hair drier	200-1200		½-6*
Hair drier	400	5	2*
Heat lamp	125-250		2
Heater, aux.	1320	30	40
Heater, portable	660-2000		15-30
Heating pad	25-150		1
Heating pad	65	10	1
Heat lamp	250	10	3
Hi Fi Stereo			9*
Hot plate	500-1650		7-30
House heating	8000-15,000		1000-2500
Humidifier	500		5-15*
Iron	1100	12	13
Iron			12
Iron, 16 hrs/month			13
Ironer	1500	12	18
Knife sharpener	125		¼*
Lawnmower	1000	8	8*†
Lighting	5-300		10-40
Lights, 6 room house in winter			60
Light bulb, 75	75	120	9
Light bulb, 40	40	120	4.8
Mixer	125	6	1
Mixer, food	50-200		1
Movie projector	300-1000		
Oil burner	500	100	50*
Oil burner			50*
Oil burner, 1/8 HP	250	64	16*
Pasteurizer, ½ gal.	1500		10-40
Polisher	350	6	2
Post light, dusk to dawn			35
Power tools			3
Projector	500	4	2*
Pump, water	450	44	20*†
Pump, well			20*†
Radio			8
Radio, console	100-300		5-15*
Radio, table	40-100		5-10*
Range	8500-1600		100-150
Range, 4 person family			100
Record player	75-100		1-5
Record player, transistor	60	50	3*
Record player, tube	150	50	7.5*
Recorder, tape	100	10	1*
Refrigerator	200-300		25-30*
Refrigerator, conventional			83*
Refrigerator-freezer	200	150	30*
Refrigerator-freezer 14 cu.ft.	326	290	95*
Refrigerator-freezer, frost free	360	500	180*
Roaster	1320	30	40
Rotisserie	1400	30	42*
Sauce pan	300-1400		2-10
Sewing machine	30-100		½-2
Sewing machine	100	10	1
Shaver	12		1/10
Skillet	1000-1350		5-20
Skil Saw	1000	6	6
Sunlamp	400	10	4
Sunlamp	279	5.4	1.5
Television	200-315		15-30*
TV,BW	200	120	24*
TV, BW	237	110	25*
TV, color	350	120	42*
TV, color			100*
Toaster	1150	4	5
Typewriter	30	15	.5*
Vacuum cleaner	600	10	6
Vacuum cleaner, 1 hr/wk			4
Vaporizer	200-500		2-5
Waffle iron	550-1300		1-2
Washing machine, 12 hrs/mo			9*
Washer, automatic	300-700		3-8*
Washer, conventional	100-400		2-4*
Water heater	4474	89	400
Water heater	1200-7000		200-300
Water pump (shallow)	½HP		5-20*†
Water pump (deep)	1/3-1 HP		10-60*†

AT THE BARN

Name	Capacity HP or watts	Est. KWHR
Barn cleaner	2-5 HP	120/yr.*
Clipping	fractional	1/10 per hr.
Corn, ear crushing	1-5 HP	5 per ton*
Corn, ear shelling	¼-2	1 per ton*†
Electric fence	7-10 watts	7 per mo.*†
Ensilage blowing	3-5	½ per ton
Feed grinding	1–7½	½-1½ per 100 lbs.*†
Feed mixing	½-1	1 per ton*†
Grain cleaning	¼-½	1 per too bu*†
Grain drying	1-7½	5-7 per ton*†
Grain elevating	¼-5	4 per 1000 bu*†
Hay curing	3-7½	60 per ton*
Hay hoisting	½-1	1/3 per ton*†
Milking, portable	¼-½	1½ per cow/mo.*†
Milking, pipeline	½-3	2½ per cow/mo.*†
Sheep shearing	fractional	1½ per 100 sheep
Silo unloader	2-5 HP	4-8 per ton*
Silage conveyer	1-3 HP	1-4 per ton*
Stock tank heater	200-1500 watts	varies widely
Yard lights	100-500 watts	10 per mo.
Ventilation	1/6-1/3 HP	2-6 per day*† per 20 cows
IN THE MILKHOUSE		
Milk cooling	½-5 HP	1 per 100 lbs. milk*
Space heater	1000-3000	800 per year
Ventilating fan	fractional	10-25 per mo.*†
Water heater	1000-5000	1 per 4 gal
FOR POULTRY		
Automatic feeder	¼-½ HP	10-30 KWHR/mo*†
Brooder	200-1000 watts	½-1½ per chick per season
Burglar alarm	10-60 watts	2 per mo.*
Debeaker	200-500 watts	1 per 3 hrs.
Egg cleaning or washing	fractional HP	1 per 2000 eggs*†
Egg cooling	1/6-1HP	1¼ per case*
Night lighting	40-60 watts	10 per mo. per 100 birds
Ventilating fan	50-300 watts	1–1½ per day*† per 1000 birds
Water warming	50-700 watts	varies widely
FOR HOGS		
Brooding	100-300 watts	35 per brooding period/litter
Ventilating fan	50-300 watts	¼–1½ per day*†
Water warming	50-1000 watts	30 per brooding period/litter
FARM SHOP		
Air compressor	¼–½ HP	1 per 3 hr.*
Arc welding	37½ amp	100 per year.*
Battery charging	600-750 watts	2 per battery charge*
Concrete mixing	¼-2 HP	1 per cu. yd.*†
Drill press	1/6–1 HP	½ per hr.*†
Fan, 10"	35-55 watts	1 per 20 hr.*†
Grinding, emergy wheel	1/4–1/3 HP	1 per 3 hr.*†
Heater, portable	1000-3000 watts	10 per mo.
Heater, engine	100-300 watts	1 per 5 hr.
Lighting	50-250 watts	4 per mo.
Lathe, metal	¼–1 HP	1 per 3 hr.
Lathe, wood	¼–1 HP	1 per 3 hr.
Sawing, circular 8"–10"	1/3–1/2 HP	1/2 per hr.
Sawing, jig	1/4–1/3 HP	1 per 3 hr.
Soldering, iron	60-500 watts	1 per 5 hr.
MISCELLANEOUS		
Farm chore motors	½–5	1 per HP per hr.
Insect trap	25-40 watt	1/3 per night
Irrigating	1 HP up	1 per HP per hr.
Snow melting, sidewalk and steps, heating—cable imbedded in concrete	25 watts per sq. ft.	2.5 per 100 sq. ft. per hr.
Soil heating, hotbed	400 watts	1 per day per season
Wood sawing	1–5 HP	2 per cord

Symbol Explanation
*AC power required
†Normally AC, but convertible to DC

Notes: Lighting in this table is assumed to be incandescent—if flourescent, the wattage bulbs consume the same power but deliver 3 times as much light—flourescent bulbs also require AC, but can be converted to DC.

These figures can be cut by 50% with conservation of electricity.

1) Sources for this table represent a conglomerate of several separate tables taken from:

a) Northern States Power Co., Mpls, Mn
b) University of Minnesota, Agricultural Extension Service
c) Seattle City Light, Seattle, Washington
d) Energy Conservation Techniques, National Bureau of Standards
e) Garden Way Labs
f) Henry Clews
g) Real Gas and Electric

SAVONIUS ROTOR

A detailed look at the graph "TORQUE COEFFICIENTS OF 11 WINDMILLS" and Fig. 8 show the relationship of SAVONIUS type mills to the propeller type. The other graphs show a comparison of regular and modified SAVONIUS rotors. The changes in efficiency (coefficient of lift CL over coefficient of drag CD) by modifying the blade shape, are shown in graph No. 1.

This information plus the inherent problems with Bearings and Balancing, put the SAVONIUS rotor in a better perspective from a design and life-of-the-system stand point. The life of the system is not usually viewed as an economic problem, but we find in the long run it is an important parameter. It becomes obvious that dependable, long term economic electrical power from the wind is best provided by the propeller type designs. The best application of the SAVONIUS rotor is for pumping and grinding (slow speed, medium torque uses).

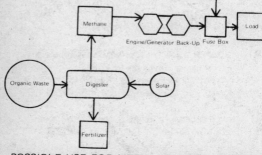

VERTICAL-AXIS DOUBLE SAVONIUS WINDMILL-TYPE F-13 OF THE SOVIET WIND ENERGY INSTITUTE

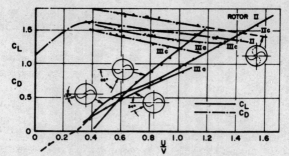

GRAPH 1 MODIFIED SAVONIUS

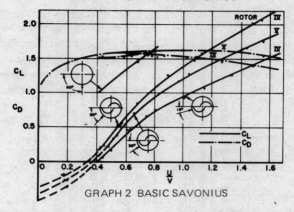

GRAPH 2 BASIC SAVONIUS

Roman Numerals Coordinate & identify CL & CD for each rotor.

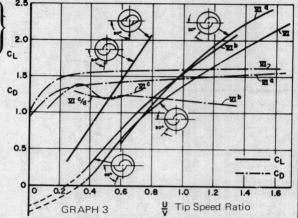

GRAPH 3 $\frac{U}{V}$ Tip Speed Ratio

AERODYNAMIC PERFORMANCE OF A COLLECTION OF BASIC AND MODIFIED SAVONIUS ROTORS THROUGH POWER EXTRACTION (BRAKED). U/V RANGE UP TO U/V MAX.

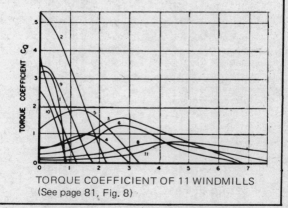

TORQUE COEFFICIENT OF 11 WINDMILLS
(See page 81, Fig. 8)

RULES OF THUMB

1. Air is 800 times less dense than water.
2. Use a two battery system where possible, lead antimony or lead calcium and pure lead (only loses 15% maximum of charge).
3. You should be able to get by with an inverter rated between one quarter and one half the wattage rating of your wind generator.
4. Never let the rate of discharge of a battery in amperes exceed 15% of the amp-hour rating.
5. A general rule is that batteries should never be discharged below 20% of rated charge.
6. When using bearings use tapered roller bearings or thrust bearings for turn table.
7. Motoring of the generator sometimes helps icing problems/shut down in sleet.
8. Question, what is the largest helicopter blade design?
9. Look for compound winding in the generator.
10. A blade is always spilling power.
11. The quality of a battery is the function of the softness (paste to lead ratio) of the plates.
12. Armature equals amperage, field equals voltage.
13. The base of a tower should be in the ground a minimum of 5 feet.
14. The tower cap should be 15 feet higher than the tallest object within 500 feet.
15. Never use bearings or gears in a feathering mechanism.
16. Grease is cheaper than steel.
17. Trees grow.
18. Plumb your tower, perfectly and square.
19. An overdesigned tower is better than an underdesigned tower.
20. Wind blows parallel to the ground—not perpendicular to gravity.
21. Vibrations kill bearings.
22. Back up systems should equal wind generation output.

ADDITIONAL NOTES AND THOUGHTS

Wherever there is a high standard of living, there is also a low standard and the cost of these high standards is usually paid for by future generations.

Ideally one who knows freedom understands the responsibility and gravitates toward self-sufficiency, self-perpetuation and realizes self-determination.

What the life cycle is costing.

Compressors should compress gases, not "air."

Junk cars will always be a resource.

Information→ Knowledge → Power → Money. The more you know, the less you pay.

—T.W.

"Wind, water and solar power are running to waste."
— 1903 DAILY CHRONICLE, 1/14

AEOLUS — THE GOD OF WIND
BOREAS — THE NORTH WIND
NOTUS — THE SOUTH WIND
EURUS — THE EAST WIND
ZEPHYR — THE WEST WIND

POSSIBLE USE FOR METHANE GAS SINCE THE AMOUNT OF GAS IS USUALLY SMALL, AND PERIODS OF NO WIND MAY ALSO BE SHORT.

"THE DEW IMPEARLED WINDS OF DAWN"
—TENNYSON

A partial list of wind generator companies in the U.S.A. 1910-1970
—T.W.

Air Electric	Air Charger
Win Charger	Delco
Paris-Dunn	Western Electric
Jacobs	Nelson
Wind Power	Allied
Rural Lite	Miller
Air King	Aerodyne
Wind King	Zenith

ELECTRICAL THOUGHTS
ON
WIND DRIVEN GENERATORS

Donald Marier
Editor ASE Newsletter

The basic principle of a generator is that electric power is produced when a conductor moves through a magnetic field (Fig. 6). By increasing the magnetic field strength of a generator, the power output is increased proportionally. Voltage output can be stepped up by increasing the number of armature windings or by increasing the speed of the generator. For example, by doubling the number of turns in an armature, the generator will put out twice the voltage at the same speed as before, since the number of wire conductors crossing the magnetic field per unit time has been doubled. The current output is limited by the size of the wire used. See page 81.

Generators of vastly different physical size can have the same power rating. This is why the speed at which the generator puts out a certain power should be specified.

There are great differences in quality and cost between a generator rated at 3000 watts at 200 rpm and one rated at 3000 watts at 2000 rpm.

The blades (propeller) of a wind plant generally do not turn faster than about 200 rpm. (The speed of the blade tips is between 4 and 8 times the speed of wind.) Most electric motors and generators are built for speeds of from 100 to 4000 rpm, with 1800 and 3600 rpm being standard speeds for A.C. motors. A good share of wind designs in the past have used gears for matching the low speed of the blade to a relatively high speed generator. Besides the wear the gears are subject to, high speed generators can break down faster than direct slow speed generators.

In direct drive systems the gearing (so to speak) is electrical. The generator is designed to give its maximum output at the same speed as the blade system gives its maximum output. This results in a long-lived, reliable system, but uses more copper and steel.

The direct drive system can be used with either a D.C. generator or with an alternator. Old Jacobs' wind generators were a sturdy, direct drive design. Unfortunately, most were the 32 volt design which is not compatible with modern 100 volt equipment. (I am presently re-building one for 110 volt operation...) See page 105.

The generator, along with the storage system is the most important part of the wind plant. From the day it is put up, the generator will be turning more or less continuously for years.

Most often, people have used car alternators in their homebuilt windplants. But car alternators are not well suited for wind generators as they are high speed devices and are very inefficient. (A D.C. car generator takes much less horsepower from the car's engine than an alternator.) When alternators were first used widely in cars, the industry promoted the myth that they charge better at low engine speeds, and that alternators had some inherent characteristic which made this possible. Actually the industry converted to alternators because of economics. They found that alternators were a higher speed device which needed less construction materials and had a shorter life. A D.C. generator could not function at the speeds at which alternators turn. The "trick" of the car alternator is that the pulley ratio is higher than with generators, allowing the alternator to be operated at top engine speeds . . . (10,000 ALT. rpm).

To show the difficulties of making a direct drive unit out of a car alternator, consider the following example. Assume the alternator will generate 1000 watts at 3000 rpm and that it is wound with 12 turns per coil of number 16 wire. To rewind the alternator for the speed range of the blades, cut the speed by a factor of 16 to 187 rpm. This would mean using 128 turns of number 28 wire per winding and the power output would be 62 watts. Obviously the only way to use a high speed alternator is with a gear or belt design. The disadvantage of this set-up is that its lifetime will not be very long.

Many people ask whether a wind system would be compatible with their present appliances, motors and tools. First it should be pointed out that when you change to a wind system, you will be changing the way you live Many of the solar house designs to date have tried to duplicate exactly the characteristics of fossil fuel houses so the "public would accept the design." The result in the past was that these designs were often overly complicated and expensive . . .

The same applies to wind systems. There are two options—to use the D.C. voltage from the batteries directly or to convert the D.C. to A.C. with a rotary or electronic inverter. The D.C. system is simpler and cheaper in that no inverter is needed. Any heating element device such as light bulbs and irons will work equally well on A.C. or D.C. Most power tools can run on A.C. or D.C.—that is, tools using universal motors (they have brushes) and using A.C./D.C. switches. Electronic devices such as stereos can be run off of small A.C. inverters. The main problem is to find a refrigerator or freezer which will run on D.C. Refrigerators made in the last 15 or 20 years have sealed units. Before that, they had belt drive compressors allowing the use of any type motor. Commercial units still can be obtained with belt drive compressors. Also the recreational vehicle industry is now producing refrigerators which will run on A.C., D.C., or gas. They are expensive, but a used market should be developing soon. D.C. motors are not easily available, but car generators can be rewound for 110 or 32 volt operation and used where a 1/4 or 1/3 hp motor is needed. If you can't purchase one locally see page 100.

NOTES:

Winnie Redrocker has some information on high speed alternator use in ASE No. 15.

Martin Jopp of Princeton, Minnesota, has 55 years experience with motors and generators. He used a set of car batteries for his windplant for two years while waiting to find a set of used lighting plant batteries for storage. (See "Some Notes on Windmills in ASE No. 12, October 1973.)

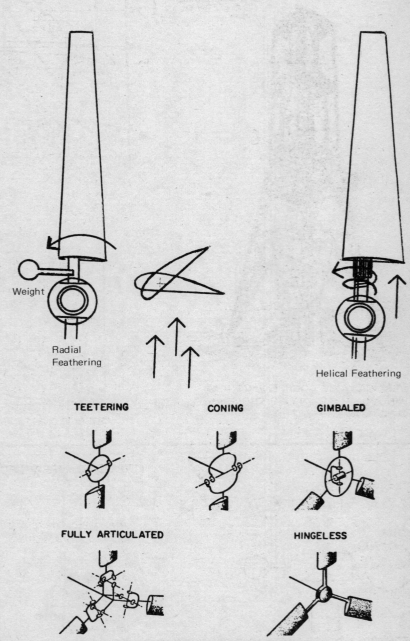

Weight

Radial Feathering

Helical Feathering

TEETERING   **CONING**   **GIMBALED**

FULLY ARTICULATED   **HINGELESS**

FIG. 12 TYPICAL ROTOR HUB CONFIGURATIONS
& FEATHERING SYSTEMS

RECYCLED WIND GENERATOR

The basic design (below) shows the components necessary for building a small, working wind generator from purchased ("off the shelf") and/or recycled materials.

FEATHERING: The system is modified from a windplant built by Paris-Dunn Co. of Iowa in the 1930's and 40's. Its main advantage is that it eliminates most of the typical speed-governing problems (i.e. loading and vibration) using a simple feathering device. It uses a spring and hinge that allow the propeller and generator to feather when wind speeds become so high (see photos on next page).

WIND PLANT MATERIALS: The plant is constructed mostly with nuts and bolts, so only some drilling and cutting (but no

welding) is required. A wide choice of materials is possible, depending on your imagination and what is available. There are many variations and "tradeoffs" possible in the design.

BLADES: The Clark "Y" airfoil is a blade which is easy to carve, and fairly efficient (a tip-speed ratio of 8). It could be carved from hardwood, and the leading edges covered with copper foil for longer life. Care should be taken not to carve the trailing edge so thin that it will split. Construction instructions can be found in ASE Newsletter No. 14, pp. 10-13. (Note that the LeJay Manual has a layout for a Clark "Y" with a tip-speed ratio of 3 or 4.) Cut the prop from 2"x6"x8" hardwood stock. Other high tip-speed ratio airfoils may also be used.

GENERATOR: A good generator to convert to windplant use is a Delco unit that comes from International Harvester.

2900 Z Stock	Rewind
600 Watts	300 Watts
at 1925 rpm	at 962.5 rpm
18 slots in Armature	18 slots
36 bar commutator	36 bars
number 12 wire	number 15 wire
8 turns/slot in armature	16 turns/slot in armature

The way one rewinds or gears the generator determines the amperage and voltage output. If you rewind the armature with twice as many turns per slot (for example, from 8 turns of No. 12 wire per slot (stock) to 16 turns of No. 15 wire per slot), you achieve the necessary voltage to comply with battery and appliance requirements (12V). This output can then be attained at a slower speed (962 rpm), which the prop will reach in approximately a 25 mph wind. Note that the wire size has been reduced from 50 amps to 25 amps. 12 volts x 25 amps = 300 watts.

TOWER: The tower could be a standard windmill tower, or Hans Meyer's Octahedron Tower, which is very nice and is materials efficient (page 97).

Consult the remaining pages in this section for additional information. Further information on small wind plants will be available from future Alternative Sources of Energy and New Alchemy Institute Newsletters.
—T.W.

Fig. 1 Hub   Fig. 2 Frame
Fig. 3$_A$ Slipring Assembly   Fig. 3$_B$ Sliprings
Fig. 4 Turntable   Fig. 5 Rear View of Gen.
Fig. 6   Manual Pull-Out

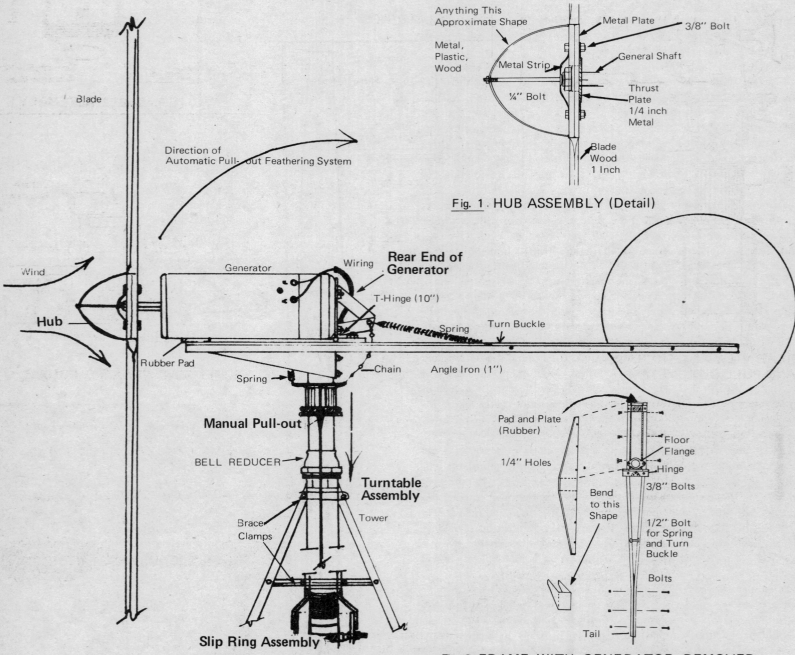

Fig. 1 HUB ASSEMBLY (Detail)

WIND-DRIVEN GENERATOR (Side View)

Fig. 2 FRAME WITH GENERATOR REMOVED (TOP VIEW)

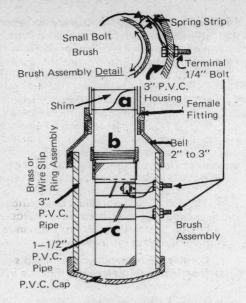

Brush Assembly Detail

- Spring Strip
- Small Bolt
- Brush
- Terminal 1/4" Bolt

- Shim
- 3" P.V.C. Housing
- Female Fitting
- a
- b
- Bell 2" to 3"
- Brass or Wire Slip Ring Assembly
- 3" P.V.C. Pipe
- c
- 1-1/2" P.V.C. Pipe
- Brush Assembly
- P.V.C. Cap

Fig. 3A SLIP RING ASSEMBLY AND HOUSING (DETAIL)

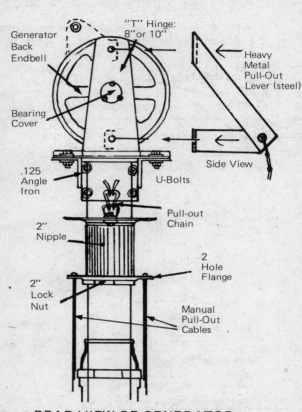

- Generator Back Endbell
- "T" Hinge: 8" or 10"
- Heavy Metal Pull-Out Lever (steel)
- Bearing Cover
- Side View
- .125 Angle Iron
- U-Bolts
- Pull-out Chain
- 2" Nipple
- 2 Hole Flange
- 2" Lock Nut
- Manual Pull-Out Cables

Fig. 5 REAR VIEW OF GENERATOR AND PULL-OUT SYSTEM

- Connecting Lead Wires
- PVC (Plastic) Pipe and Fitting
- Pipe Wall
- Hole for Insert
- Thin Brass
- B Type
- Brass Insert Lock
- c
- Wire Wound Tightly
- Hole
- C Type
- Hole

Fig. 3B SLIP RINGS *

*Slip rings B or C type may be used.

- 1-1/2 Floor Flange (2 or 4 Hole)
- T Hinge 10"
- Space if Needed
- Generator
- 3/8 Bolt
- 3/8" Bolt
- U-Bolts
- Pull-Out Chain
- Light Return Spring
- Bolt
- 2" Floor Flange (4 Hole)
- 2" Pipe Nipple
- Movable 2 Hole Floor Flange Bored Out
- Nut or Flange (2 Hole)
- Pull-Out Cable or Wire
- 1-1/2 Pipe

Fig. 6 MANUAL PULL-OUT ASSEMBLY (Side View)

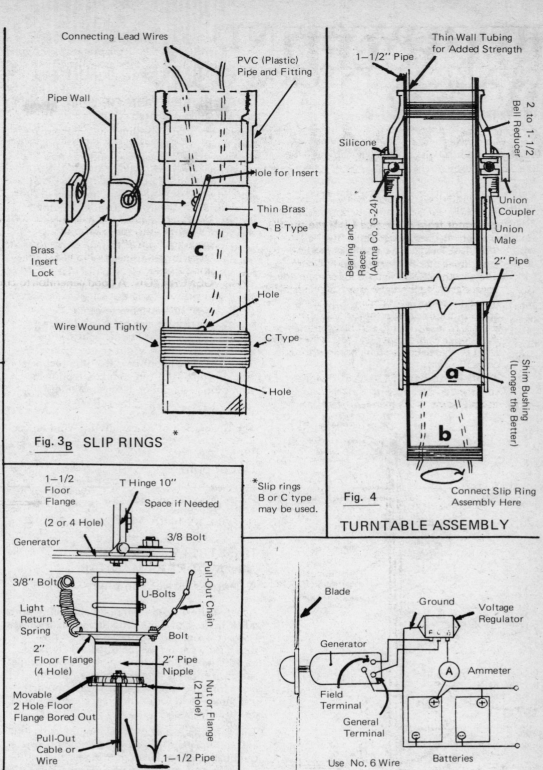

- Thin Wall Tubing for Added Strength
- 1-1/2" Pipe
- 2 to 1-1/2 Bell Reducer
- Silicone
- Union Coupler
- Union Male
- Bearing and Races (Aetna Co. G-24)
- 2" Pipe
- Shim Bushing (Longer the Better)
- a
- b
- Connect Slip Ring Assembly Here

Fig. 4

TURNTABLE ASSEMBLY

SCHEMATIC WIRING DIAGRAM

- Blade
- Ground
- Voltage Regulator
- Generator
- Ammeter
- Field Terminal
- General Terminal
- Batteries
- Use No. 6 Wire

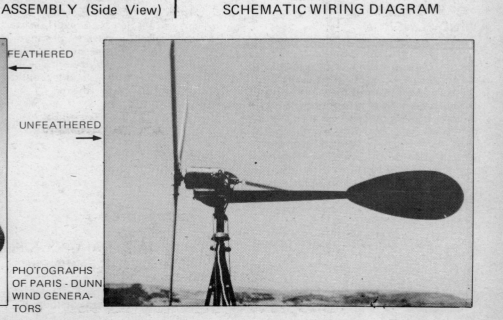

FEATHERED

UNFEATHERED

PHOTOGRAPHS OF PARIS - DUNN WIND GENERATORS

REVIEWS/WIND
GENERAL INFORMATION

POWER FROM THE WIND

To the lay reader or the scientist, the value of Putnam's book is its laudable logic and elucidation. He writes with candor and cognizance of the conception, design, financing, erection, viability and shortcomings of the first experimental windmill.

The actualization of wind-turbines as a power source is interesting and here, supplemented with excellent drawings, charts and graphs, is an informative, highly readable basis for expanded research.

The surprise of this text is that it is such enjoyable reading. Beyond the mysteries of science, Putnam reflects the enthusiasm of all who collaborated on the project and he relates technical data so lucidly it is easily understood.

—Connie Meade

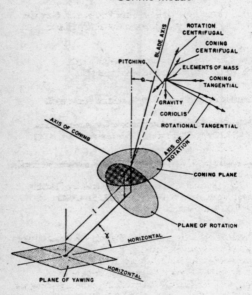

Power From the wind
P. C. Putnam
1948; 223 pp

$9.95

from:
Van Nostrand Reinhold Co.
450 West 33rd Street
New York, NY 10001

or WHOLE EARTH TRUCK STORE

WIND POWER

At any price this is the best, most concise description of wind energy on an individual user scale available. Some of the language used is difficult at times, but there is a glossary to help, plus a list of references, and a list of consultants for system planning and engineering. The book covers a very important item, which is a back up system for short periods of no wind. There are many places across the country where a back up system is needed. A major part also discusses assessing one's electric needs called the "Demand Analysis," including sample calculations and cost accounting.

—T.W.

Wind Power
Charles D. Syverson, P.E.
John G. Symons, Jr. Ph.D.
1973; 19pp

$3.00

from: J.G. Symons, Jr., PH.D., Box 233, Mankato MN

THE GENERATION OF ELECTRICITY BY WIND POWER

Almost everyone working in wind energy research has probably read this book, and most of the articles in magazines and journals usually get their grounding from it. It is highly recommended reading. The best bet would be to try to get a copy through your local library and xerox it. Golding's book is considered a classic and is a thorough survey of wind energy. He covers taking wind data with no use of instruments, the history of windmills and how to do surveys of local sites. He also discusses different types of mills, blades, and generators, and the *economics* of wind generators, and compares them to other energy sources. He also has a good sense of the need for international cooperation and communication about these systems. One very nice thing about it is its 1955 technical jargon, which isn't too complex (about the level of high school or 1st year of college.)

—T.W.

The Generation of Electricity by Wind Power
E. W. Golding
1955; 318 pp

Out of print

published by:
Philosophical Library, Inc.
15 East 40th Street
New York, NY 10016

THE STREET FARMERS WINDWORKERS MANUAL
A People's Power Pamphlet

A tasty little 16-page pamphlet containing some quick basics and some solid design plans. Bruce Haggart wrote and illustrated this sensible, sober, jolly packet which discusses Dynamos vs. Alternators, maintenance and power storage, and then submits an absolutely wizard set of plans for a cheap junky-funky water-pump attachment and for an airscrew generator built out of bicycle parts.

This Britisher is a devil at rejasing (reusing junk as something else). Dead bikes and mopeds are cannibalizable for bearings and gear shafts. Front forks and handlebars can serve as rotating shaft mounts.

This'll get you itching to try your hand. Nothing mysterious here. Quoting Haggart: ". . . as you can't sell the wind, consider anything you can build yourself from scrap materials and that gives you light and power to be alchemic rather than efficient. Do it and see, but don't expect to run factories off them."

—Gar Smith

The Street Farmers Windworkers Manual
Bruce Haggart
1974; 16 pp

$0.50

from:
Peace News
5 Caledonian Road
London N1

STANDARD HANDBOOK FOR MECHANICAL ENGINEERS

Safety, Reliability, & Cost—Wind Energy is more complex and hazardous, in a technical manner, than other systems like solar heat and methane. SHME helps immensely in answering the difficult technical questions. It's a must, particularly if you are trying to build your own plant.

—T.W.

Marks Standard Handbook for Mechanical Engineers
Ed. Theodore Beaumeister
1963, new edition 1974;
1200 pp, with 6 pp on wind power by E. M. Fales with formulas and tables

$31.00

from: McGraw-Hill
1221 Avenue of the Americas
New York, New York 10020

or WHOLE EARTH
TRUCK STORE

WIND POWERED MACHINES

In the book are presented the basic problems connected with the selection of layouts, calculations and parameters of wind machines, their energy-producing character, technical and economic indices. Methods of optimal matching of wind engines with working machines, calculations for strength, and construction and automation of wind machines are analyzed in detail. A description is given of the set up of domestic and foreign wind installations for various purposes. Discussion of wind as a source, the theories of wind machines and aerodynamics are presented. The uses of machines are presented according to zone.

The book is intended for engineers, designers, workers and mechanics connected with utilization of wind energy and agriculture.

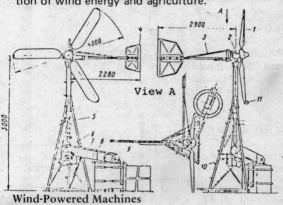

Wind-Powered Machines
Y. Shefter, 1972; 288 pp
by: Mashinostroyeniye Press, Moscow, RUSSIA
from: N.T.I.S. **$8.95**

IS THERE A PLACE FOR THE WINDMILL IN THE LESS DEVELOPED COUNTRIES?

Progress of common man, in any of the less developed countries, depends on his getting control of more energy.

This is a good overview of wind energy, its economics and problems in less developed countries, and also applies to this country.

You will find discussions of the following: windmill use, windmill vs. other systems, use of output, and a listing of windmill manufacturers and their characteristics.

—T.W.

Is There a Place for the Windmill in the Less Developed Countries?
Working Paper Series No. 20
M. F. Merriam
1972; 20 pp

Free

from:
The East-West Center
1777 East-West Road
Honolulu, Hawaii 96822

ELECTRIC POWER FROM THE WIND

The best and cheapest source of information on wind energy. Check other sources for more information on batteries, inverters and their problems, etc.—but a very good place to start reading. —T.W.

Electric Power From the Wind
Henry Clews
1973; 29 pp

$2.00

from:
Solar Wind Company
P.O. Box 7
East Holding, Maine 04429

or WHOLE EARTH TRUCK STORE

GOVERNMENT SPONSORED WIND ENERGY R&D

In 1973 NSF funded work at Oklahoma State University on a 10 kilowatt field-modulated generator that would produce an output frequency independent of the shaft speed. There was also a grant to R. Powe at Montana State University to evaluate the idea of a ring of cars on a track, each bearing a vertical airfoil or sail.

1974 NSF grants went to Robert Wilson for a state-of-the-art review of the aerodynamics of wind systems (this should be completed by August, 1974) and to Thomas Sweeney to assist the final development of the Princeton Sailwing Rotor. A 6-12 kilowatt Sweeney-type plant should be marketed by Grumman Aerospace Corp. by the fall of 1974, and plans for a do-it-yourself unit will also be available.

NASA, in conjunction with NSF, is building a 100 kw at 18 mph wind generator at NASA's Plum Brook test area at Sandusky, Ohio. The NASA design involves a variable-pitch 125 ft. rotor downwind from the tower. NSF plans 0.5 Mw and 2 Mw "Proof-of-Concept" windmills in the future.

—Roger Douglass

GOVERNMENT REPORTS

These reports are available from:
National Technical Information Service
U.S. Department of Commerce
P.O. Box 1553
Springfield, Virginia 22151

Wind Energy Conversion Systems, Workshop Proceedings, Held at Washington, D.C. on 11-13 June 1973
Joseph M. Savino
1973; 267 pp; $6.50

This is How You Can Heat Your Home With a Little Windmill
Leo Kanner Associates
1974; 13 pp; $3.00

Exploitation of Wind Energy
H. Christaller
1974; 12 pp; $3.00

Wind Energy Conversion Systems
J. M. Savino
1973; 270 pp; $15.50

H2-O2 Combustion Powered Steam-MHD Central Power Systems
G.R. Seikel, J.M. Smith, & L.D. Nichols
1974; 14 pp; $3.00

Status of Wind-Energy Conversion
R. L. Thomas and J. M. Savino
1973; 9 pp; $4.00

Analysis of the Possible Use of Wind Power in Sweden. Part 1: Wind Power Resources, Theory of Wind-Power Machines, Preliminary Model 1 and 10 Mw Wind Generators
B. Soedergard
1974; 55 pp; $5.75

Exploitation of Wind Energy
Hans Christaller
1974; 10 pp; $3.00

Influence of Wind Frequency on Rotational Speed Adjustments of Windmill Generators
Ulrich Hutter
1973; 16 pp; $3.00

The Development of Wind Power Installations for Electrical Power Generation in Germany
U. Hutter
1973; 29 pp; $3.00

The Influence of Aerodynamics in Wind Power Development
E. W. Golding
1961; 48 pp; $4.00

Windmill Generator for the Bumblebee Buoy
D. M. Brown
1972; 19 pp; $3.00

Utilization of Wind Power by Means of Elevated Wind Power Plants
F. Kelinhenz
1973; 30 pp; $3.00

WIND POWER POTENTIAL IN SELECTED AREAS OF OREGON

If you're planning to build a windcharger in Oregon this book will be of limited use but it lists sources and individuals which would supplement anyone's data-lust. Commissioned by several of the Peoples Utility Districts in Oregon, Report No. PUD 73-1 is concerned with monolithic windplants able to kick out a thousand-plus kws.

Oregon State U's Department of Atmospheric Sciences apparently would be a good place to consult for wind statistics in the Oregon Coast. They monitor stations from Astoria to Yaquina and from Mt. Hebo to Winchester Bay.

The trippy part of this 63-page booklet is the back half. The task force tries to determine what it would cost today to build an equivalent of the famous Putnum aerogenerator that stood on Grandpa's Knob, Vermont, in the early 1940's. This plant produced 1250 kw in a mean average breeze of 17 mph. It had a blade diameter of 175 feet. Putnam's 1940's engineering cost breakdown, printed along with a 1973 budget, shows engineering costs are up from $159,400 to $462,800 and construction costs are up from $306,538 to $1,051,493 (with the rotor taking 60% of the manufacturing costs!) The study assumes 100 such units producing 1500 kilowatts. Over a period of 20 years the cost of electrical energy from these plants averages out to $.010 per kwh. This is economically competitive but the $700/kw "installed-cost" is too steep an initial price. However, the report concludes, this is based on a design that is 30 years old. The study, then, substantiates the prospects for the newest generation of windplant designers.

—Gar Smith

Wind Power Potential in Selected Areas of Oregon
E. Wendall Hewson, et al
1973; Report No. PUD 73-1

free

from:
Oregon State University
Corvallis, Oregon 97331

VITA REPORTS

All available from:
Volunteers in Technical Assistance
3706 Rhode Island Avenue
Mt. Rainier, Maryland 20822

Low Cost Windmill for Developing Nations
Dr. Hartmut Bossel
1972; 40 pp; $1.00

Helical Sail Design
report number 1131.1
$0.75

Savonious Rotor Plans
report number 1132.1
$0.75

The following reports are not reviewed but are useful additional sources of information.

Canadian National Aeronautical Establishment Report Low Speed Aerodynamics

A Wind Tunnel Investigation of a 14 ft. Diameter Vertical Axis Windmill   LTR-LA-105
P. South & R. S. Rangi
1972; 17 pp; cost unknown

U.S. Federal Power Commission. Fitting Wind Power to the Utility Network; Diversity, Storage, Firm Capacity, Secondary Energy
Percy H. Thomas, retired.
Washington, 1954. 24 p. TJ825.U515

U.S. Federal Power Commission. The Wind Power Aerogenerator, Twin-Wheel Type; A Study
Percy H. Thomas. Washington, Office of the Chief Engineer, Federal Power Commission, 1946. 77 p. TJ825.U52

The U.S. Energy Crisis: Some Proposed Gentle Solutions, Presented Before the ASME and IEEE
W. E. Heronemus
reprinted in Congressional record (daily ed)
Feb. 9, 1972, 92d Cong., 2d sess., v. 118: E1043-1048.

Windmills in the Light of Modern Research
A. Betz
U.S. National Advisory Committee for Aeronautics, Aug. 1928. 29 p. (Technical Memorandum no. 474)
TL507.U57 no. 474

Studies on the Utilization of Wind Power in India
P. Nilakantan and R. Varadarajan
(Bangalore National Aeronautical Laboratory, 1962.)
Technical Note, no. TN-WP-11-62) TL 504.B35
no. TN-WP-11-62, etc.

U.S. War Production Board. Office of Production Research and Development
Final report on the wind turbine. Research conducted by New York University, College of Engineering, Engineering Research Division. Washington, 1946, 278 p. (Its W.P.B. 144) PB 25370

A New Propeller-Type, High-Speed Windmill for Electric Generation
E. N. Fales
ASME Transactions, Vol 19, Paper AER-50-6, 1928.

Ramakumar, R. and others. Wind Energy Storage and Conversion System for Use in Underdeveloped Countries
from:
Intersociety Energy Conversion Engineering Conference
4th, Washington, D.C. 1969. Proceedings. New York, American Institute of Chemical Engineers, 1969.
p. 606-613. TK2896.155 1969

The Windmill: Its Efficiency and Economic Use
Edward Charles Murphy
from:
Washington, U.S. Gov't Print. Off.
1901.2 v (U.S. Geological Survey. Water-supply and irrigation paper no. 41-42) TJ825.M96

U.S. Congress. House. Committee on Interior and Insular Affairs
Production of power by means of wind-driven generator. Hearings, Eighty-second Congress, first session, on H.R. 4286. September 19, 1951.
Washington, U.S. Govt Print. Off., 1952.41 p.
HD171.A18A32 82d, 1st no. 16

U.S. Federal Power Commission
Aerodynamics of the wind turbine, adapted for use of power engineers, prepared by Percy H. Thomas. Wasington, Office of the Chief Engineer, Federal Power Commission, 1949.80 p. TK1541.U54

U.S. Federal Power Commission. Electric Power From the Wind; a Survey
Percy H. Thomas. Washington, Office of the Chief Engineer, Federal Power Commission, 1945. 57 p.
TK2081.U54

...ational Symposium on Molinology, ...d, Denmark, 1969

Transactions of the 2. International symposium on Molinology, Denmark, May 1969. By Shmuel Avitsur and others; edited by Anders Jespersen. Lyngby, Danske Mollers Venner, Brede Baerk, 1971. 590 p. TJ823.157 1969

Proceedings of the New Delhi Symposium on Wind and Solar Energy, 1956

from:
United Nations Educational and Cultural Organization (UNESCO)
c/o Department of State, Washington DC 20520
The following titles are from the table of contents:
   (1)   Wind machines—J. Juul
   (4)   Planning and balancing of energy of small-output wind power plant—U. Hutter
   (5)   The economic utilization of wind energy in arid areas—E. W. Golding

United Nations Conference on New Sources of Energy, Proceedings solar energy, wind power and geothermal energy, Rome, August 21-31, 1961, Vol. 7, Wind Power $16.00

United Nations Document E/Conf. 35/8,
United Nations, New York, NY
The following titles are from the table of contents:

LIST OF TABLE OF CONTENTS

Proceedings of Conference, Rome 21-31 August 1961
Volume 7, Wind Power
U.N. Publication
The following titles are from the table of contents:
 (1) Studies of wind behavior and investigation of suitable sites for wind-driven plants — Golding.
 (2) Measurement of the characteristic parameters of wind power for the selection of favourable sites for wind-driven generators (summary) — Argand.
 (3) Speculative methods in wind surveying — Ballester.
 (4) Prospecting for wind power with a view to its utilization — Barasoain, Fontan.
(5) Wind measurements in Southern Argentina and remarks on wind and solar energy in that country — Cambilargiu.
(6) Wind flow over hills, in relation to wind power utilization — Frenkiel.
(7) Wind measurements — Jensen.
(8) Some aspects of site selection for wind power plants on mountainous terrain — Lange.
(9) Wind measurement in meteorology (summary)
(10) Some aspects of wind profiles — Petterssen.
(11) Wind power resources of India with particular reference to wind distribution — Ramakrishan, Venkiteschwaran.
(12) Wind measurement techniques — Sanuki.
(13) Study of wind behaviour and investigation of suitable sites for wind-driven plants — Sollman.
(14) Wind measurements in relation to the development of wind power — Tagg.
(15) Survey of existing wind info.—World Met. Org.
(16) The design and testing of wind power plants— Vadot.
(17) Regulating and control system of an experimental 100 kW wind electric plant operating parallel with an AC network — Armbrust.
(18) Experiences with wind-driven generators with propeller behind a mast of streamline section (summary) — Cambilargiu.
(19) Classical designs of small drainage windmills in Holland, with considerations on the possibilities of their improvement and adaptation in less developed countries — Havinga.
(20) The aerodynamic layout of wing blades of wind-turbines with high tip-speed ratio — Hutter.
(21) Design of wind power plants in Denmark — Juul.
(22) Wind power plants suitable for use in the national power supply network — Kiss.
(23) Wind turbines of new design in Japan — Moriya, Tomosawa.
(24) Considerations on a natural aspect of the harnessing of wind power (summary) — Santorini.
(25) A wind-driven electrical generator directly coupled into an AC network—the matching problem — Sterne, Fragolania.
(26) Small wind-electric plant with permanent magnetic generator — Villinger.
(27) Testing of the Gedser Wind Power Plant — Askegaard.
(28) Various relationships between wind speed and power output of a wind power plant — Clausnizer.
(29) Test methods applied to the Andreau-Enfield 100-kW wind-driven generator at Grant Vent (summary) — Delafond.
(30) The testing of a wind power plant — Morrison.
(31) Recent developments and potential improvements in wind power utilization — Hutter.
(32) Wind power plant in Eilot — Frenkiel.
(33) Experience with Jacobs wind-driven electric generating plant, 1931-1957 — Jacobs.
(34) Small radio, powered by a wind-driven bicycle dynamo — Stam, Tabak, van Vlaardingen.
(35) Adaptation of windmill designs, with special regard to the needs of the less industrialized areas — Stam.
(36) Operation of Allgaier type (6-8 kW) wind electric generator at Porbandar, India — Venkiteshwaran.
(37) A method for improving the energy utilization of wind-driven generators, and their operation with conventional power sets — Walker.
(38) Utilization of random power with particular reference to small-scale wind power plants — Walker.
(39) Developments and potential improvements in wind power utilization — Arnfred.
(40) Windmill types considered suitable for large-scale use in India— Nilakantan, Ramakrishan, Venkiteshwaran.
(41) Problems of automatic coupling of a wind-driven generator to a network (summary) — Delafond.
(42) Recent developments and potential improvements in wind power utilization for use in connection with electrical networks in Denmark — Juul.
(43) Economy and operation of wind power plants — Juul.

CLIMATE

WEATHER

The book is possibly the cheapest, best, most lucid, communicative little book about weather there is.

—T.W.

Of all aspects of the natural world, weather is outstanding in its beauty, its majesty, its terrors, and its continual direct effect on us all. Because weather involves, for the most part, massive movements of invisible air and is concerned with the temperature and pressure changes of this almost intangible substance, most of us have only a limited understanding of what weather is all about. This book will help you to understand it and also to understand, in some degree, how weather changes are predicted.

Weather
Paul E. Lehr
1965; 160 pp

$1.25

from:
Golden Press
Western-Publishing Co.
1220 Mound Avenue
Racine, Wisconsin 53404

or WHOLE EARTH TRUCK STORE

CLIMATIC ATLAS OF THE U.S.

Very good and necessary information, expands and makes you aware, in another sense, of your environment. Is not very localized in terms of a particular plot of land, but a good place to start for a general look at the climate throughout the U.S. Two hundred seventy one climatic maps, 15 tables, covering mean temperature, snowfall, precipitation, wind speed, solar radiation, etc.

—T.W.

Climatic Atlas of the U.S.
1968; 80 pp

$4.25

from:
Superintendent of Documents
U.S. Government Printing Office
Washington D.C. 20402

or WHOLE EARTH TRUCK STORE

PREVAILING DIRECTION AND MEAN SPEED
OF WIND ANNUAL

UNDERSTANDING OUR ATMOSPHERIC ENVIRONMENT

This book's emphasis is on understanding, that is, on providing one with the physical explanation of atmospheric phenomena. As such, its purpose is twofold: to give you a deeper appreciation of this part of the universe, which we experience so intimately and continuously, and to impart an awareness of some of the laws of physics and the way in which they are applied.

—T.W.

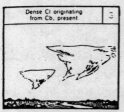
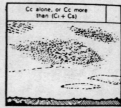

EXAMPLES OF THE C_h FAMILY OF CLOUD TYPES

Understanding Our Atmospheric Environment
Neiburger, Edinger, Bonner
1973; 193 pp

$10.95

from:
W. H. Freeman & Company
660 Market Street
San Francisco CA 94104

or WHOLE EARTH TRUCK STORE

THE ENCYCLOPEDIA OF ATMOSPHERIC SCIENCE AND ASTROGEOLOGY

Expensive but amazing book intended for high school to Ph.D. Time Saver. This is a book you might not buy but maybe your local library will. The book is mainly directed to "earth scientists" which we are all to one extent or another. The idea of it is to provide speedy access to basic facts and ideas, and has many references so you're not at a "dead end."

—T.W.

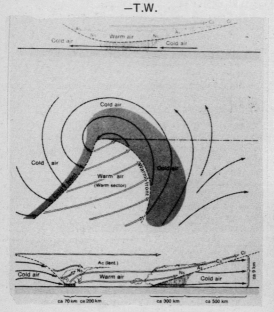

IDEALIZED WAVE CYCLONE MODEL: UPPER- Vertical cross section north of wave cyclone; MIDDLE: Representation of frontal wave and streamlines on surface weather map; LOWER: Vertical cross section through warm sector. Shading shows area of current precipitation.

The Encyclopedia of Atmospheric Science and Astrogeology
Ed. Rhodes W. Fairbridge
1967; 1200 pp

$38.50

from:
Van Nostrand Reinhold Publishing Corp.
450 W. 33rd Street
New York, NY 10001

THE WINDS, ORIGINS & BEHAVIOR OF ATMOSPHERIC MOTION

This book says the same thing as *Sensitive Chaos*, (see 266), but puts it in mathematically useable form—if you can understand the math. What the book has to say for the most part, however, is basic and readable.

The study of flows of the earth's fluids forms a great part of the science called geophysics; the atmosphere and its motions. The book covers basic and technical information about the wind, its character, vortices, turbulence, force, patterns, and measurement give a good understanding of the magnitude that the wind possesses.

—T.W.

The Winds, Origins & Behavior of Atmospheric Motion
George Hidy
1967; 174 pp

$3.95

from:
Van Nostrand Reinhold Co.
450 West 33rd Street
New York, NY. 10001

CLOUDS ASSOCIATED WITH THE SIERRA WAVE IN THE LEE OF THE SIERRA NEVADA RANGE IN CALIFORNIA. The lowest cloud reaches an alt. of 6 k m. . The middle one is a lenticular cloud located along the crest of the lee wave at 10 km. The upper one is another lee wave cloud at 13 km.

THE SELECTION & CHARACTERISTICS OF WIND POWER SITES

All ERA reports, including this one which costs $24.00, are very expensive, but the information is good. The report describes in very technical detail the development and successive stages, of a wind survey covering the British Isles area suitable for large-scale generation of wind power. Methods are shown for making a wind velocity survey and in employing the results to form a reasonably reliable estimate of wind potential. Also discussed is the relationship between *estimated* and *actual* output.

—T.W.

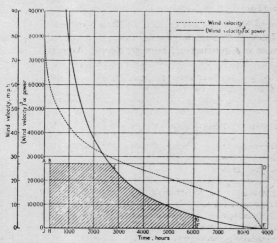

VELOCITY AND POWER-DURATION CURVES TYPICAL OF AN EXCELLENT SITE

Method of Selection
1. Meteorological Records
2. Study of Maps
3. Inspection of Sites
4. Technique of Site Selection

The Selection & Characteristics of Wind Power Sites
The Electric Research Association
E. W. Golding & A. H. Shodhart C/T 108
1952; 32 pp

$24.00

from:
E.R.A.
Cleeve Road, Leatherhead
Surrey KT22 7SA
England

STORAGE (Electricity, Air, Water, and Heat)

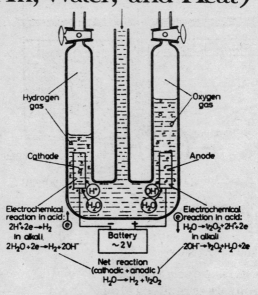

ELECTROLYSIS OF WATER

ELECTROCHEMICAL SCIENCE

Want to understand batteries? This book is the best I've seen for it tries to explain, in a simple and largely qualitative way, the most important ideas of electrochemical science. It is not a specialized discipline. On the contrary, it is an interdisciplinary area which studies the behavior of electrified interfaces wherever they arise—in chemistry, materials, science, energetics, biology, engineering and so on. The book also has a good theory on how we got where we are. A bit technical.

—T. W.

Electrochemical Science
J. O'M. Bockris & D. M. Drazic
1972; 300 pp

$20.50

from:
Barnes & Noble Books
10 E. 53rd Street
New York, NY 10022

"This book is small, but the message it is written to convey is large: an environment unpolluted by power generation, in which we can live in the future, is possible through an electrically based technology."

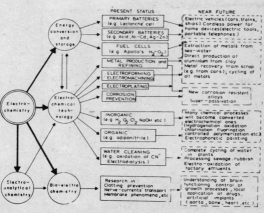

THE ELECTROCHEMICAL FUTURE

TERIES AND ENERGY SYSTEMS

The size and characteristics of a battery system is the most important and difficult part of the wind plant to assess. I'd say this book covers the subject most completely.
—T.W.

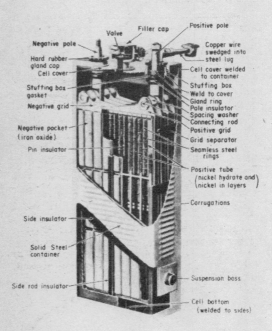

GENERAL CONSTRUCTION OF THE EDISON CELL.

Batteries and Energy Systems
C. L. Mantell Ph.D.
1970; 221 pp
$15.00

from:
McGraw-Hill Book Co.
1221 Avenue of the Americas
New York, NY 10020

or WHOLE EARTH TRUCK STORE

COMPRESSED AIR

Compressed air as a storage system could be useful if your needs require mechanical to mechanical energy, though you should remember that compressors have to overcome the first and second laws of thermodynamics and thus are inefficient. People with information on compressed air as a wind system storage device are listed below:
Hans Meyer
Windworks
Box 329, Rt. 3
Mukwonago WI 53149

International Technical
Box 340
Warrenton, Virginia 22186

Alternative Sources of Energy
Rt. 2, Box 90A
Milaca, MN 56353
Issue No. 14: May, 1974

FLYWHEELS

Many ramifications both economic and practical are not known about Flywheels at this point in time. Very high technology.
—T.W.

Sources of information:
Science Magazine
"Energy Storage" (1),
May 17, 1974 (II), May 24, 1974
Wind Energy Conversion Systems,
Workshop Proceedings, Wash. D.C.
(see page 89)
Popular Science Magazine
Scientific American Mag.

WATER STORAGE IN RESERVOIRS

This is a very well established technique of hydro-plant storage on a large scale.

The main problem is *evaporation losses* and *complexity* so it could be a good secondary storage system for small scale, but as a primary storage it is not likely. Of course all of this is broken down to needs and your particular environment (i.e. land, climate, local costs). Ideally you'd want to use the same equipment for generating and for pumping (Fig. 2) and endemic materials work best in the long run. "What is life cycle costing?" "All systems work well if they are matched to the environment."
—T.W.

HEAT STORAGE SYSTEM

A bit misgiven but a partial assessment of the current state-of-the-art and problems of wind energy—a good solution if you can use it.
—T.W.

Wind Power
1973; 24 pp
FREE

from:
Energy Unlimited, Palmer, Mass. 01069

BATTERY STORAGE

Battery companies are the best sources of information on batteries. (See page 99.)
—T.W.

HYDROGEN

Hydrogen is inexpensive, about half the current price of gasoline for equivalent usable energy. It's clean; water is the only emission. It's plentiful, even eternal, the most abundant element in the universe and on earth. It's safe; N.A.S.A. tests rate it safer than gasoline. It's adaptable; to almost any internal combustion application. An entire economy could be based upon hydrogen as a universal fuel.
—Carl A. MacCarley
UCLA Hydrogen Research

Electrochemisty of Cleaner Environments
J. O. M. Brockris, Ed.
"Hydrogen Economy"
D. P. Gregory and G. M. Long
1972

$22.50

From:
Plenum Press
New York, New York

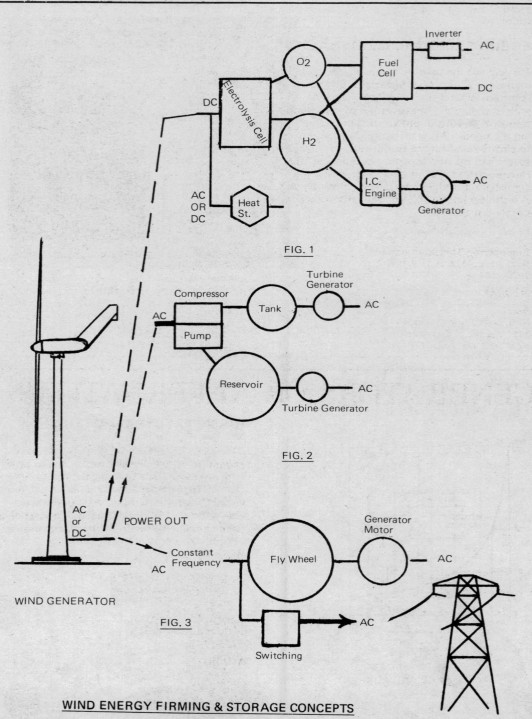

FIG. 1

FIG. 2

FIG. 3

WIND GENERATOR

WIND ENERGY FIRMING & STORAGE CONCEPTS

WIND ENERGY
Its Utilization in Isolated Regions of the Americas (½ to 100 kw)

Presented at the inter-American meeting organized by the AAAS and the Mexico National Council for Science and Technology, Science of Man in the Americas Session on "non-Nuclear Energy for Development" at Mexico City on June 22, 1973.

I met Christian Bettignies at this conference, and I guess the analogy of "in every dark cloud there is a silver lining" applies. The report is the most current international overview I've seen. And he now has up-dates. Most of the things he mentions in the paper he has been involved in.

—T.W.

Wind Energy
C. Bettignies
1972; 50 pp

$2.00

from:
Northern Engineering Center
Ecole Polythechnique
2500 Ave Marie Guyard
Montreal 250 P.O.
Canada

ENGINEERING THERMODYNAMICS

Throughout the text, the value of a systematic method in analyses is emphasized. Such an approach is absolutely essential. A lack of understanding the fundamentals of engineering frequently results in one starting problems "in the middle." It is the author's intention to clearly establish the tie between the macroscopic and the microscopic viewpoints at an early stage and provide the reader with a full appreciation of the importance of both views. A technical book, college level, uniformly and simply put together.

—T. W.

Engineering Thermodynamics
W. C. Reynolds & H. C. Perkins
1970; 584 pp

$10.00

from:
McGraw-Hill Book Company
1221 Avenue of the Americas
New York, NY 10020

FOUNDATION OF THE THERMODY-NAMIC THEORY OF GENERALIZED FIELDS
Essays in Natural Philosophy

Technical but beautiful.
—T. W.

"We are to admit no more causes of natural things than such as are both true and sufficient to explain their appearances. To this purpose the philosophers say that Nature does nothing in vain, and more is in vain when less will serve; for Nature is pleased with simplicity, and affects not the pomp of superfluous causes."

—Isaac Newton

"The only justification for our concepts and system of concepts is that they serve to represent the complex of our experiences; beyond this they have no legitimacy . . ."

—Albert Einstein

Foundation of the Thermodynamic Theory of Generalized Fields
Mahmoud A. Melehy
1973; 255 pp $15.00

from:
Mono Book Corp.
6747 Whitestone Road
Baltimore MD 21207

DIRECT ENERGY CONVERSION
2nd Edition

Very highly technical. Nothing on wind energy but goes into all the other "new energy sources," has a good chapter on storage systems of all types. A very good up-to-date section on fuel cells is also included.

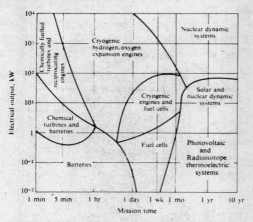

VARIOUS TYPES OF SYSTEMS IN A POWER-TIME CONTINUUM SHOWING THOSE REGIONS WHERE EACH SYSTEM APPEARS TO HAVE AN ADVANTAGE (in both weight and other factors) COMPARED TO ALL OTHERS.

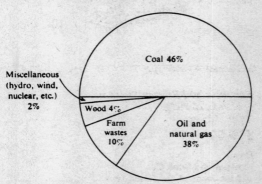

PRESENT USE OF NATURAL ENERGY RESOURCES.

Direct Energy Conversion
Stanly W. Angrist
1969   350 pp

$15.95

from:
Allyn & Bacon, Inc.
Rockleigh, New Jersey 07647

or WHOLE EARTH TRUCK STORE

GENERATORS OR ALTERNATORS

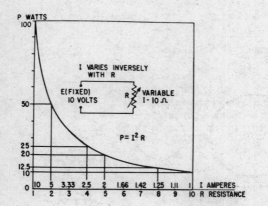

GRAPH OF POWER RELATED TO CHANGING RESISTANCE AND CURRENT

BASIC ELECTRICITY

The most important thing, it appears, is to communicate, especially today, and in order to commune-icate, both parties must understand the language and use it. *Basic Electricity* is just what it says, Basic. However, it goes beyond this, but only through understanding and communicating in a very special manner, Logic. "People should do as well!"

—T.W.

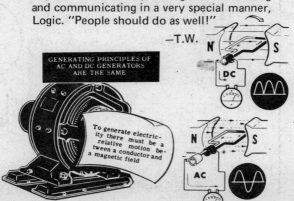

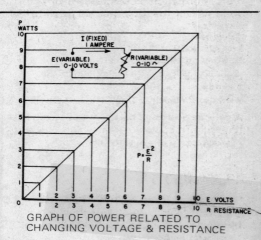

GRAPH OF POWER RELATED TO CHANGING VOLTAGE & RESISTANCE

Basic Electricity
Vol. 1-5, 6 & 7
Van Valkenburgh, Hooger & Neville, Inc.
1953; 700 pp

$13.75

from:
Hayden Book Co.
50 Essex Street
Rochelle Park, N.J. 07662
or WHOLE EARTH TRUCK STORE

BASIC ELECTRICITY

Basic Electricity was written for the Navy by the Navy to make available the fundamental information about electricity. The text is basic and not too technical, but requires the understanding of *basic* algebra—there are hundreds of illustrations that make it easy to read the pictures and find most of the information you need. It also covers the components of D.C. generators, and A.C. alternators, and motors.

—T.W.

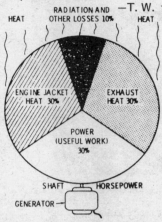

SUMMARY OF BASIC FORMULAS
Adjacent to each quantity are three segments. Note that in each segment, the basic quantity is expressed in terms of two other basic quantities, and no two segments are alike.

Basic Electricity
Bureau of Naval Personnel
1970; 490 pp

$3.50

from:
Dover Publishing Inc.
180 Varick Street
New York, N.Y. 10014

or WHOLE EARTH TRUCK STORE

ELECTRIC GENERATING SYSTEMS

The purpose of this text is to discuss the application of engine generating systems to standby, portable, marine and mobile power needs. The book attempts to bridge the gap between books on engines, electricity, generators, and instruments, with reference particularly to ONAN generators. It has a glossary and index. An excellent book but mostly concerned with generators currently available "off the shelf." All of these are high RPM units when compared to the wind generator range of 0 to 200 RPM. Overall a very useful book.

—T. W.

Electric Generating Systems
Loren J. Mages
1970; 374 pp

$5.95

from:
Theodore Audel & Company
4300 West 62nd Street
Indianapolis, Indiana 46268

or WHOLE EARTH TRUCK STORE

ELECTRIC MOTOR TEST & REPAIR

The book is <u>not</u> a college-level theory-ridden textbook. It is a workshop handbook, written in a highly useable form. What the book undertakes is covered in a logical and complete manner. For those who wish to rebuild motors, generators, etc., it is a welcome addition to your book shelf. It is the most practical book for <u>learning</u> the information on testing and rewinding small horsepower motors of every type, and most large basic motors AC & DC. Basic motors and generators are very similar.

—T. W.

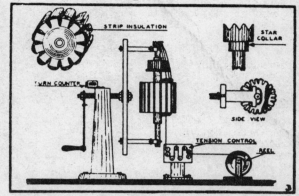

DETAIL OF SIMPLE HAND-OPERATED WINDING MACHINE

Electric Motor Test & Repair
Jack Beater
1966; 160 pp

$6.95

from:
TAB Books
Blue Ridge Summit, PA 17214

or WHOLE EARTH TRUCK STORE

MECHANICAL (Blades & Towers, Etc.)

WIND FORCES IN ENGINEERING

Freedom equals responsibility. There are, in every country, numerous codes relating to wind loads on structures. The intention of this book is to give the designers a method of calculating wind loads from basic experiments and principles. It is difficult to compare codified rules and is unnecessary. A designer should, if he considers a code applicable:

1. Consult the ruling Code of Practice, and calculate his design loads.
2. Work out the wind loads from basic data in this book and associated references.
3. Select the greater of the two loadings.

No code covers the complete range of wind and structures. Most codes are many years old, and only provide an approximate answer; the best codes acknowledge this.

—T.W.

Also suggested reading for Towers: *On the Estimation of Wind Loads for Buildings and Structural Design.*" Proc. Inst. Civ. Engrs. 25,1963 by C. Scruton and C. W. Newberry

Wind Forces in Engineering
Peter Sachs
1973; 390 pp

$36.00

from:
Pergamon Press, Inc.
Maxwell House, Fairview Park
Elmsford, New York 10523

THEORY OF WING SECTIONS

The wing sections or their deviations described in this book continue to be the most commonly used ones for airplanes designed for both sub and supersonic speeds, and for application to helicopter rotor blades, propeller blades, and high performance fans.

This book is intended to serve as a reference for engineers and is a resource to anyone studying at high technical levels. It includes a summary of air foil data. A knowledge of integral calculus and elementary mechanics is helpful, but if you take time to read it very carefully it is a valuable book. It does contain all aerodynamic information you'd need for designing windmill blades. It starts off hot and heavy but give it and yourself a chance to "sync in."

—T.W.

Theory of Wing Sections
Ira H. Abbott & A. E. Von Doenhoff
1959; 693 pp

$5.00

from:
Dover Publishing Inc.
180 Varick Street
New York, NY 10014

INTRODUCTION TO THE THEORY OF FLOW MACHINES

Introduction to the Theory of Flow Machines
A. Betz, 1966; **Out of Print**

Pergamon Press, Inc., Maxwell House, Fairview Park, Elmsford, NY 10523

AERODYNAMIC THEORY

Aerodynamic Theory
W. F. Durand, editor
1963, 6 volumes, 2177 pp total

Out of Print
published by:
Dover Publ.Inc., 180 Varick St., N.Y., NY 10014

WINDMILL TOWER DESIGN

Discussion of reinforced concrete and block-masonry towers.

—T.W.

Windmill Tower Design
F. Montesano and A. Fernandez
1973; 92 pp   Brace Research Institute

LeJAY MANUAL

This marvelous manual from 1945 is still around, and loaded with useful information for the small scale home builder. The end of the book has a glossary, a discussion of wind electric plants and useful knowledge of electricity and batteries. There are 50 plans for devices from bug catchers to electric scooters. A definite bargain for the price. Might be considered the wind plant hotrodders manual.

—T.W.

LeJay Manual, 1945, 44pp **$1.70**
from: LeJay Mfg. Co., BellePlaine MN 56011

OCTAHEDRON TOWER

Hans Meyer, Windworks, Rt. 3, Box 329, Mukwonago, Wisconsin 53149

WINDMILLS AND MILL WRIGHTING

"Millwright; a builder and repairer of wind, water, and other mills." In this all-inclusive lucid text on windmills there is a glossary of windmill terms, an incredible folding plan of a windmill and its working parts, and many photographs and line drawings of windmills. It also describes vividly the life of the miller during high winds, like the wooden break catching fire from too high wind speeds. This is the finest book on the subject and is recommended for anyone working on or thinking about wind energy.

—T. W.

Windmills & Millwrighting
Stanley Freese
1957; 200 pp
$7.95

from:
Great Albion Books
Pierce Book Co., Inc.
Cranbury, New Jersey 08512

1. Brick Pier
2. Main-Post
3. Cross-Tree
4. Quarter-Bar
5. Retaining strap
6. Heel of main-post

7. Centering Wheels
8. Crown-Tree
9. Side-Girt
10. Brace
11. Cap-Rib

12. Steps or Ladder
13. Weather-Beam
14. Wind-Shaft
15. Tail-Beam
16. Sail-Stock

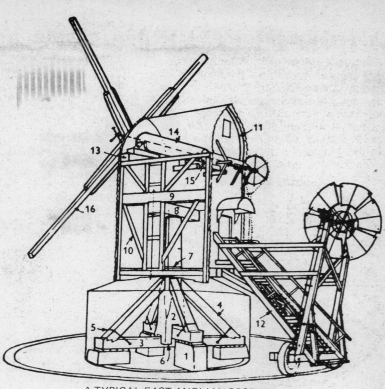

A TYPICAL EAST ANGLIAN POST-MILL.

WATER PUMPING WINDMILLS

AERMOTOR WATER SYSTEMS

DEMPSTER INDUSTRIES INC.

from:
Dempster Industries Inc.
P.O. Box 848
Beatrice, Nebraska 68310

HELLER—ALLER COMPANY: BAKER WINDMILLS

The *Original* **BAKER** RUN-IN-OIL **WINDMILL**

from:
The Heller-Aller Co.
Corner Perry & Oakwood
Napoleon, Ohio 43545

Distributor:
O'Brock Windmill Sales
Rt. 1- 12th Street
North Benton, Ohio 44449

AERMOTOR PUMPING CAPACITY								
Diameter of Cylinder (Inches)	15 MPH Capacity per Hour, Gallons		Total Elevation in Feet					
			SIZE OF AERMOTOR					
	6 Ft	8-16 Ft	6 Ft	8 Ft	10 Ft	12 Ft	14 Ft	16 Ft
1¾	105	150	130	185	280	420	600	1,000
1⅞	125	180	120	175	260	390	560	920
2	130	190	95	140	215	320	460	750
2¼	180	260	77	112	170	250	360	590
2½	225	325	65	94	140	210	300	490
2¾	265	385	56	80	120	180	260	425
3	320	470	47	68	100	155	220	360
3¼		550			88	130	185	305
3½	440	640	35	50	76	115	160	265
3¾		730			65	98	143	230
4	570	830	27	39	58	86	125	200
4¼		940			51	76	110	180
4½	725	1,050	21	30	46	68	98	160
4¾		1,170				61	88	140
5	900	1,300	17	25	37	55	80	130
5¾		1,700				40	60	100
6		1,875		17	25	38	55	85
7		2,550			19	28	41	65
8		3,300			14	22	31	50

from:
Aermotor Water Systems
Broken Arrow, Oklahoma 74012

WIND ELECTRICS

AEROWATT S.A.
37, Rue Chanzy, 75-Paris 11ᵉ
France

TABLE I AEROWATT WIND-BLOWN GENERATORS
MAIN CHARACTERISTICS **minus storage costs**

	$1935. 24 FP 7	$3105. 150FRP7	$4565. 300FP7	$8375. 1100FP7	$18860 4100FP7
Wind speed at start of charge m/s (Miles/Hr.)	4	(6.7)3	3	3	4
Nominal wind speed m/s (Miles/Hr.)	7	(15.7)7	7	7	7.5
Nominal power watts	28	130	350	1125	4100
Nominal output voltage-volts	24	24	110	110 220/380	110 220/380

Aerowatt's machines are very expensive but are exceptional in design. The generator is a 3 phase A.C. permanent magnet type which starts charging in 6 mph winds and reaches full output at 15 mph.

BUCKNELL ENGINEERING
10717 Rush Street
So. El Monte
California 91733

12 Volt 200 Watt Wind Plant

Thank you for your inquiry on our wind generator. Due to the great demand for this literature, we find it necessary to request a $3.00 charge for the literature and handling. This package includes cover letter, technical write-up, wind velocity chart, drawing of unit, and company brochure.

The package of information will be sent Third Class mail within the United States and Canada unless you include additional postage for First Class or Air Mail as follows: $0.16 for First Class and $0.22 for Air Mail. (In the event of a postage change, rates will be $0.20 for First Class and $0.26 for Air Mail.)

Please made check or money order payable to Patricia Feiner—who is the secretary to the company and responsible for this service. Upon receipt of this payment, the material will be promptly mailed. Be sure to include your name and address in legible handwriting-preferably printed. Also include your zip code.

Thank you,

W. H. Bucknell

WINCO DYNATECH. ,INC.
P.O. Box 3263
Sioux City, Iowa 51102

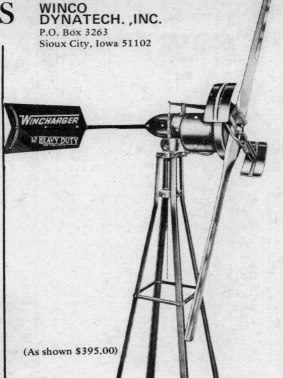

(As shown $395.00)

Capacity (Watts)	200
Approximate maximum amps	14
Approximate maximum volts	15
Generator Speed Range (RPM)*	270/900
Governor Type	22" air brake

DUNLITE ELECTRICAL CO.
Division of Pye Ind.
21 Frome St., Adelaide 5000
Australia

Three-blade wind-driven power plant, with automatic, variable-pitch propeller.

WIND DRIVEN GENERATORS

DUNLITE Model "L," 1000 Watt, 32 or 36 Volt sliprlng Windplant, metal 3-bladed full-feathering propeller, Diotran voltage regulator and control panel. Ideal for charging electric battery powered vehicles!

DUNLITE Model "M", 2000 watt, Brushless windplant, available in 24, 32, 48, and 115 volts. Diotran voltage regulator and control panel. **Complete system $6,350.00.**

ELEKTRO G. m. b. H.
St. Gallerstrasse 27
Winterthur, Schweiz

Brushless 3 phase alternator-type wind generator with rectified D.C. manufactured by ELEKTRO G.m.b.H. of Winterthur, Switzerland.

Model	Tropic Encased Unit	Rated Output In Watts	Rated Windspeed MPH	Voltages Available
W 50	Yes	50	39	6, 12, 24
W250	Yes	250	40	12, 24, 36
WV05	*	750	20	(12), 24, 36, 48, 65
WV15G	*	1200	23	(12), 24, 48, 115
WV25G	*	1800	22	(24), 36, 48, 65, 115
WV25/3G	*	2500	23	(24), 36, 48, 65, 115
WV35G	Yes	4000	24	48, 65, 115
WVG50G	*	6000	26	65, 115

Model	Propeller Diam. Ft.	No. Blades	Relative Cost of System(DC)
WV15G	9ft. 10in.	2	$5800
WV25G	11ft.6in.	2	5800
WV25/3G	12ft.6in.	3	6500
WV35G	14ft.5in.	3	8400
WVG50G	16ft.5in.	3	9500

$1500 for inverter (DC/AC)

*Tropic encased model available at extra cost.

ELECTRO MODEL WV 15 G 1200 WATT 110 VDC WINDPLANT.

WVG50G

ENAG s.a.
Rue de Pont-l'Abbe
Quimper (Finistere)
France

Two-Bladed Eolienne 24/30 Volts - 400 Watts $1,587
(as shown)

Three-Bladed Super Enag Eolienne 24/30 Volts - 1200 W
Complete with propeller and instrument panel $2.287
(as shown)

Three-Bladed Super Enag Eolienne 110 Volts - 2500 W
$4,164
(as shown)

INDUSTRIAL INST. LTD.
Stanley Rd., Bromley BR2 9JF, Kent, England
Mr. Kirylok. .4 KW to 4 KW; 1 KW machine available.
Main business is inverters.

'LUBING'
Maschinenfabrik, Ludwig Bening
2847 Barnstorf, P.O. Box 171, Germany

Lubing, is a geared 1 to 5.5 step up alternator,
brushless type, 3 phase 24 volt D.C. or 12 volts
on request, very beautifully packaged system.

USSR ENERCGOMASHEXPORT
35 Mosfilmovskaya UI, Moscow V 330

USSR INSTITUTE FOR FARM ELEC-
TRIFICATION I-U VESHNIAKOVSKI
Prc. Dom Moscow J-456: Numerous machines from
½ to 25 KW.

DOMENICO SPERANDIO & AGER
Via Cimarosa 13-21
58022 Folloncia (GR) Italy

GARBINO 12 V 250W
TURBINE 24V 500W
MONSONE 48V 1000W

PLANS & KITS

WINDWORKS
Windworks sells plans for a 12 volt system; a comprehensive bibliography covering most topics regarding
wind energy, a free hand-out, and they are also
"happy to try and answer specific questions."

Windworks
Box 329, Route 3   Plans $12.00
Mukwonago, WI 53149   Bibliography $3.00

BOTH THESE WINDMILLS USE OCTAHEDRON TOWERS

SENCENBAUGH WIND ELECTRIC
Sencenbaugh Wind Electric
P.O. Box 11174   KIT—$1400.00
Palo Alto, CA 94306   includes: stub tower
                        generator, control & blades

1000 WATT 12-VOLT WIND GENERATOR

SIMPLIFIED
WIND POWER SYSTEMS
FOR EXPERIMENTS

The section on simplified aero dynamics
of wind mill blade design is the main
thrust through out the book. It offers
information not found easily in other
places, and has good material on hybrid
designs. The author is an aerospace
engineer, with a good feel for what he is talking
about.
73 pages

$8.00
from:
Jack Park
Box 4301
Sylmar, Calif. 91342

HOMECRAFT
C.C. Melotz sells plans for a number of funky
wind devices from the Savonius to the propeller type.

Homecraft, 2350 W. 47th St., Denver, Colo. 80211

PRINCETON SAILWING
The Princeton Windmill Program has developed a
sailwing wind turbine suitable for generating
electricity, and recently licensed it to an aircraft
company for development. Information is available:

A booklet: "The Princeton Windmill Program" is
$1.00 from:
Forestal Campus Library
Princeton University
Princeton, NJ 08540

Information regarding possible purchase of a
machine should be sent to:
Mr. William Carl
Grumman Aircraft Corp.
Plant 30/Department 300
Bethpage
Long Island, NY 11714

Plans for the machine are being prepared (no
price yet). Write:
Flanagan's Plans
2032 23rd Street
Astoria, NY 11105

(Plans and Kits, Cont'd)

WINDY TEN

Sells plans for an incredible replica of a Dutch wind-mill which also produces electricity. A sight to behold!

Windy Ten
Box 111
Shelby Michigan 49445

WIND SPINNERS/EARTH MIND

A 'nuts 'n bolts' approach to wind/electric systems.

By golly, somebody at last has done a good job of spelling out what is involved in making a wind electric system yourself. The design is for the well-known Savonius Rotor ("S" rotor), which is not a particularly efficient type, but is easy to build. The author is honest about it all, and gives a commendable amount of numbers and tables necessary to figure out expected performance for this and other machines. He also discusses the toughest riddle of the S rotor: how to get it up on a tower where the wind is and yet keep things simple. Altogether it seems to be very complete information and you could actually make a workable machine from these instructions.

Earth Mind   — J. Baldwin
2651 O'Josel Drive
Saugus, CA 91350
$7.50

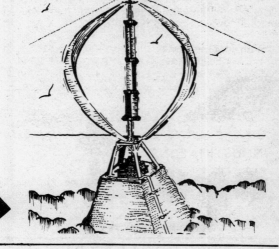

DARRIEUS HOOPE WITH SAVONIUS ROTOR.
This shows advantageous use of the Savonius rotor. The design is being explored by NASA and also by Oklahoma State University.

MANUFACTURERS ★★★

Wind Energy Distributors

	AEROWATT	ELEKTRO X	ENAG	LUBING X	DUNLITE QUIRKS	WINCO WINCHARGER	AGER	BUCKNELL
Budgen & Assoc. 72 Broadview Ave. Pointe Claire 710 Quebec, Canada								
Energy Alternatives Box 223 Leverett, MA 01054					X	X		
Environmental Energies Inc. 21243 Grand River Detroit, MI 48219		X			X			
Garden Way Laboratories Charlotte Vermont 05445	X	X			X	X		
Independent Power Developers Box 618 Noxon, Montana 59853					X			
Low Impact Technology 73 Molesworth St. Wadebridge Cornwall, England		X	X		X	X		
Penwalt Automatic Power 213 Hutcheson St. Houston, Texas 77003	X							Hutter Machine WE-10 6 KW, 10 Meters
Real Gas and Electric Co. Box A Guerneville, CA 95446		X			X	X		
Sencenbaugh Wind Electric Box 11174 Palo Alto, CA 94306		X			X			Kit
Solar Energy Company 810 18th St. N.W. Washington, D.C. 20006	X					X		
Solar Wind Co. R.F.D. 2 East Holden, Maine 04429		X			X	X		
Windlite Box 43 Anchorage Alaska 99510		X			X	X		

WIND HARDWARE

ANEMOMETERS

Reviewed below are anemometers from three different companies: Inexpensive (Dwyer), moderate (Taylor), and finest available (Bendix). The remaining companies are listed as additional sources of wind speed measuring devices.

Dwyer Instruments, Inc.
P.O. Box 373
Michigan City, Indiana 46360

Dwyer makes 2 interesting weather instruments. One is a hand held wind meter which you can align with the wind and read the speed in either of 2 scales, 2-10 MPH or 4-66 MPH. The other can be mounted permanently with the indicator placed indoors. Its cost is $24.95.

Taylor Instruments
Arden, North Carolina 28704

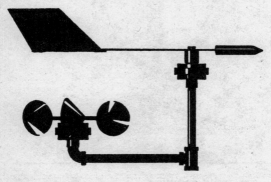

Full range of weather measuring instruments. Least expensive anemometer $85.00 with 60' of lead in wire, also rain gauges. The instruments are designed with the non-professional in mind and are attractive.

Bendix Environmental Science Division
1400 Taylor Avenue
Baltimore, Maryland 21204

The Bendix Environmental Science Division is an advanced development, engineering and manufacturing organization providing components, products and systems. Our products are high quality, competitively priced and reliable. Our product line is constantly being expanded and new catalog sheets will be provided to everyone on our mailing list.

The Bendix Aerovane® Wind Data System is unexcelled in performance, reliability, and service life. You want it they've got it. Its cost is $1220.00.   —T.W.

Climet Instruments Co.
1620 West Colton Avenue
P.O. Box 1165
Redlands, California 92373

Kahl Scientific Instrument Corporation
Box 1166
El Cajon, San Diego, California 92022

Davis Instrument Mfg. Co., Inc.
513 East 36th Street
Baltimore, Maryland 21218

Aircraft Components
North Shore Drive
Berton Harbor, Michigan 49022

Danforth
Division of the Eastern Co.
Portland, Maine 04103

Meteorology Research Inc.
Box 637
Altadena, California 91001

Robert E. White Instruments, Inc.
33 Commercial Wharf
Boston, Massachusetts 02110

Texas Electronics Inc.
5529 Redfield Street
P.O. Box 7151 Inwood Station
Dallas, Texas 75209

Maximum, Inc.
8 Sterling Drive
Dover, Massachusetts 02030

INVERTER COMPANIES

STATIC

Gulton
13041 Genise Avenue
Hawthorne, CA 90250

Lorain
1122 F. Street
Lorain, Ohio 44052

Creative Electronics
3707 W. Touhy Avenue
Chicago, Illinois 60645

Globe
5757 N. Green Bay Avenue
Milwaukee, Wisconsin 53201

Wilmore
Box 2973
W. Dunham Station
Dunham, North Carolina 27705

Basku
603-5th
Highland, Illinois 60645

Interelectronics
100 U.S. Highway 303
Congers, N.Y. 10920

Systron-Donner Corp.
889 Galindo
Concord, CA 94518

STATIC INVERTER

Emhiser Rand Industries
7721 Convoy Court
San Diego, CA 92111

300 and 500 watt transistorized square wave inverters with 6, 12, 24 and 36 or 48 volt inputs. Efficiency up to 80%, frequency regulation +1%.

Price $1.50 to $1.25/watt

Load demand at no extra cost

Dynamote Corporation
1130 Northwest 85th
Seattle, Washington 98117
(206) 784-1900

Manufacture SCR static inverters all with demand load provision. Primarily for RV/mobile communications market. Voltage input ranges of 12, 24, 32 and 36 volts with outputs of 120 Va to 1000 Va respectively.

New company—no specifications, prices or delivery time quoted.

Topaz Electronics
3855 Ruffin Road
San Diego, CA 92123
(714) 279-0831

Topaz Electronics is known throughout the computer industry for their work with uninterruptible power systems. They manufacture a complete line of sine-wave (Quasi-Square) inverters in ranges from 250 to 10,000 watt output. SCR commutating output with ferro-resonant filter and capacitor shaping network.

Frequency 50 - 60 hz +1% of fixed frequency
75% efficiency typical at full load
Net price $3 to $1.37/watt depending on size of inverter.

Delivery time: in stock to 6 weeks

Demand load at extra cost.

NOVA Electric Manufacturing Company
263 Hillside Avenue
Nutley, N.J. 07110
(201) No. 13434

Manufactures complete line of single and three phase inverters from 125 to 3000 Va. All transistor in design. Nova uses a high frequency audio keying so that relatively small iron core components are required. Claim quieter operation than SCR inverters. Efficiency of 75 to 80% at full load
Regulation of +1%
Net price $2.15 to $1.29/watt depending on size of inverter

Delivery time: 6 weeks

Demand load at extra cost.

ROTARY

Electro Sales
100 Fellsway West
Somerville, Massachusetts 02149

Ganter Motor Co.
2750 W. George Street
Chicago, Illinois 60618

Surplus Stores

Northwestern Electric
1752 N. Springfield Avenue
Chicago, Illinois 60647

BATTERY COMPANIES

Bright Star
602 Getty Avenue
Clifton, NJ 07015

Burgess Div. of Clevite Corp., Gould
P.O. Box 3140
St. Paul, MN 55101

Delco-Remy
Division of GM
P.O. Box 2439
Anderson, IN 46011

Eggle-Pichen Industries
Box 47
Joplin, Missouri 64801

ESB Inc.
Willard
Box 6949
Cleveland, OH 44101

Exide, 5 Penn Ctr., Plz.
Phila. PA 19103

Ever Ready
Union Carbide Corp.
270 Park Avenue
New York, NY 10017

Globe-Union
5757 N. Greenbay Ave.
Milwaukee, WI 53201

Gulton
212 T Dorham Avenue
Metuchen, NJ 08840

Keystone Battery Company
16 Hamilton Street
Saugus, Massachusetts 01906

Marathon Battery Company
8301 Imperial Drive
Waco, Texas 76710

RCA
415 S. 5th Street
Harrison, NJ 07029

Surrette Storage Battery Co., Inc.
Box 711
Salem, Massachusetts 01970

Batteries Mfg. Co.
14694 Dequindu
Detroit, Michigan 48212

C & D Batteries Eltuce Corp.
Washington & Chewy Street
Conshohocken, PA 19428

Gould Inc.
485 Calhoun Street
Trenton, NJ 08618

Mule Battery Company
325-T Valley Street
Providence R.I. 02908

Delatron Systems Corporation
20370 Rand Road
Palatine, Illinois 60067

BLADES

Gurnard Mfg. Corp.
100 Airport Rd.
Beverly, Mass. 01915

Senich Corp.
Box 1168
Lancaster, PA 17609

GENERATORS

Kato
3201 3rd Avenue N.
Menkato, Minnesota 56001

Onan
1400 73rd Avenue NE
Minneapolis, Minnesota 55432

Winco of Dyna Tech.
2201 E. 7th Street
Sioux City, Iowa 31102

Kohler
421 High Street
Kohlen, Wisconsin 53044

Howelite
Rendale and Nelson Streets
Port Chester, New York 10573

McCulloch
989 S. Brooklyn Avenue
Wellsville, New York 14895

Sears and Roebuck

Winpower
1225 1st Avenue East
Newton, Iowa 50208

Ideal Electric
615 1st Street
Mansfield, Ohio 44903

Empire Electric Company
5200-02 First Avenue
Brooklyn, New York 11232

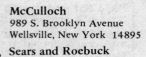

ONAN GENERATOR

TOWERS

Advance Industries
2301 Bridgeport Drive
Sioux City, Iowa 51102

Eldon Arms
Box 7
Woodman, Wisconsin 53827

THOMAS REGISTER 1974 has five pages of tower manufacturers. Check your local library.

Additional information on two unique towers is available. The Octahedron tower from Windworks (see page 97) made of 1 1/8" electrical conduit and a concrete or concrete block tower design from Brace Research Institute (see page 94).

DC—MOTORS

The best source for fractional to five horsepower direct current motors. Five horsepower to five hundred horsepower available on order.

—T.W.

Reliance Electric Co.
24701 Euclid Ave.
Cleveland, Ohio 44117

RESEARCH GROUPS

GROUPS AND CONSULTANTS

REDE
Rede Library
Box 307
Providence, Rhode Island 02901

Research and Design Institute, REDE, is a non-profit design science agency. REDE's present work with wind energy systems makes use of the American Wind Turbine multi-blade design. There appears to be many ways of tapping the energy from this relatively slow speed, high torque design. Under the direction of Ronald Beckman, the group is pursuing the research of solar and integrated systems as well as wind.

Max's Pot
Maximum Potential Building Systems
6438 Bee Cave Rd.
Austin. Texas 78746

The following photos and drawings are form the work done by this group. For more information, see Integrated Systems.

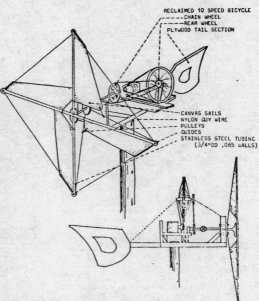

RECLAIMED 10 SPEED BICYCLE
CHAIN WHEEL
REAR WHEEL
PLYWOOD TAIL SECTION

CANVAS SAILS
NYLON GUY WIRE
PULLEYS
GUIDES
STAINLESS STEEL TUBING
(3/4"OD .065 WALLS)

Wind Energy Society of America
1700 East Walnut
Pasadena, California 91106

A non-profit corporation concerned with information dissemination on wind energy, directed toward the Academic community.

—T.W.

American Wind Energy Association
21243 Grand River
Detroit, Michigan 48219

Environmental Energies, Inc., Association consists of manufacturers, distributors and people interested. Write for more information.

—T.W.

Syverson Consulting
2007 Roe Crest Drive
N. Mankato, MN 56001

Wind Power
Box 233
Mankato, MN 56001

California Environmental Energy Services
6105 Sonoma Mountain Road
Santa Rosa, CA 95404

Otis James
c/o K and M Consultants
Box 513 Hopkins
Minnesota 55343

In 1975 they will completely describe five existing wind generator systems along with pictures and component parts analysis. What they offer now is a Wind Generator Constructor's Handbook.

Montana Project
Dr. Ralph Powe
Montana State University, Bozeman, Montana

Montana State University conceived a sail-powered car running on a 5 mile circular railroad-like track, driving generators to feed the system or to connect directly to high lines.

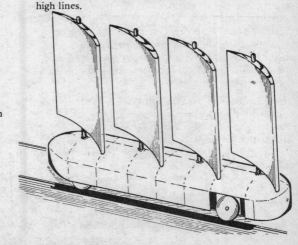

New Alchemy Institute East
P.O. Box 432
Woods Hole, Mass 02543

MADURAI TYPE SAILWING WINDMILL: An eight meter diameter prototype sail wing windmill was erected Feb-March 1973 on a small farm owned by T.O. Heineman in a dry hill region of Madurai district, Tamilnadu. It lifted three hundred pounds to a height of twenty feet in one minute in a slight breeze. This was accomplished by a rubber rope passing over a six-inch pulley on the horizontal drive shaft.

This sail wing windmill is made of a one meter diameter bullock cart wheel to which three bamboo poles are lashed in a triangular pattern with overlapping ends. Each bamboo pole forms the leading edge of a wing, and a nylon cord stretched from the outer tip of the pole to the rim of the wheel forms the trailing edge. A stable and light weight airfoil results from stretching a long narrow triangular cloth sail "sock" over that bamboo-nylon frame. This wing configuration, a hybrid of low-speed eight bladed jib-sail wings and high speed two-bladed aerodynamic sail wings, produces high starting torque at low wind speeds. The bullock cart wheel is attached at the hub to the end of an automobile axle shaft which rotates in two sets of ball bearings. The shaft and bearing assembly is mounted horizontally on top of a ball bearing turntable.

The principal limiting factor is the availability of the steel turntable. This is the only component that cannot be assembled in an Indian village. A machine shop is required. The turntable consists of two circular steel plates separated with a raceway of ball bearings and held together with a ring of eight bolts which encircle the bottom plate. A dust cover or 2 large "O" rings should be incorporated to provide dust protection to the bearings. The services

of a village wheel wright cum blacksmith are required for production of the oxcart wheel and mounting the wheel on the turntable shaft, the sails are manufactured on a standard sewing machine. The occasional presence of one person is required for operation. The Windmill is intended for the direct use and operation by its owner-builder.

Marcus Sherman
Madurai, India

NASA
Lewis Research Center
Cleveland, Ohio 44135

NASA/NSF mod-zero 125 ft. dia. windmill is expected to produce 100 KW. NASA is also working on the Darrieus Hoope for individual power requirements. For further information: Mr. Ron Thomas or Mr. Joseph M. Savino, address above.

Project Ouroboros
School of Architecture, Univ. of Minn.
Minneapolis, MN 55455

A 5 KW, off the shelf, 15 foot blade wind generator. Design coordinated by Alan Sondak. For further info see Integrated Systems.

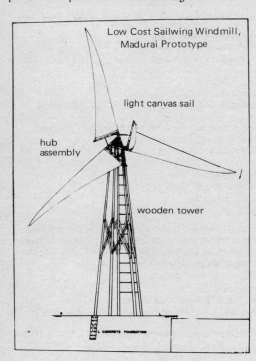

Low Cost Sailwing Windmill, Madurai Prototype

light canvas sail

hub assembly

wooden tower

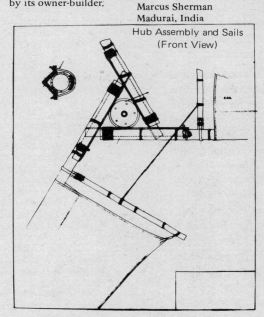

Hub Assembly and Sails (Front View)

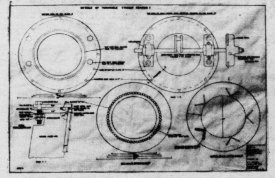

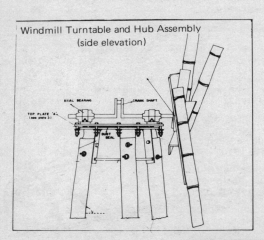

Windmill Turntable and Hub Assembly (side elevation)

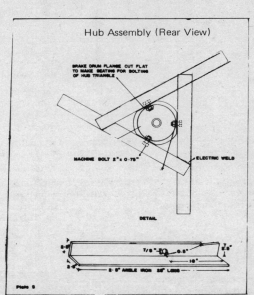

Hub Assembly (Rear View)

LOW COST SAILWING WINDMILL, MADURAI. PROTOTYPE

BRACE RESEARCH INSTITUTE
Macdonald College of McGill University

T. Lawand

The information service of the Brace Research Institute was more of a happening than anything else. We had always exchanged technical and scientific papers with other research institutes both at home and abroad. As well, we had supplied organizations in developing countries with leaflets and information on a gratis basis—for this is part of the mission of the Institute in helping developing countries, particularly arid areas, in increasing their productivity.

As a result of a letter appearing in the first Whole Earth Catalog, in which it was erroneously reported that we would give out free leaflets on solar and wind energy, water supply, desalination, greenhouse agriculture and Appropriate Technology, we received a flood of requests. In order to discourage this, we issued a price list feeling that most of the requestors were not serious in their search for this information. To our surprise an extremely high percentage answered, and sent money for these leaflets. It then became obviously apparent that nobody was filling this need and offering this service. Hence, we took a limited number of our leaflets, drawings, plans and specifications as per the attached price list of leaflets in English, French, Spanish and Arabic, and offered them in the next edition of the Whole Earth Catalog. We thought the matter would die there, but is quite apparent that many people, and not just by any means just young people refer to the Whole Earth Catalog. From then original out-of-date prices have been quoted and re-quoted, completely without our solicitation all over the world. We receive requests from over 75 countries in a multitude of currencies and languages. In principle, we do not charge needy organizations, individuals from the developing areas of the world, or indeed wherever they may be. We do feel, however, that it is not unreasonable to help pay for this service by charging a nominal amount to to people and organizations in developed or industrialized areas.

It is obviously quite important that this task be taken over someday by organizations which can handle this in a more businesslike way. In the meantime we will try and continue this role until it can be effectively shown that it is no longer necessary and is redundant. In the interim we ask those people who utilize this service to bear with us. We must occasionally raise our prices as inflation hits everyone. Also on some occasions when businessmen and professionals in particular, always for some reason or other, resident in the United States of America send threatening letters, generally directed to the Principal of this University, because they have not received their leaflets, which may have been lost in the mail, etc., then we feel that we should cancel this service. We have not, because of the many letters of support and thanks we have received from people, again often resident in the United States, encouraging us to continue this task. At times they send us small donations which we are very grateful to receive, and for which we have no mechanization to extend our thanks.

BRACE RESEARCH INSTITUTE

List of available publications from the Institute.
Due to inflation we have had to increase our basic price.

L. 1	How to Make a Solar Still (Plastic Covered), by A. Whillier and G. T. Ward, 9 pp., January 1965. Revised February 1973.	$1.00
L. 2	How to Make a Solar Steam Cooker, by A. Whillier, 6 pp., January 1965. Revised October 1972.	$1.00
L. 3	How to Heat your Swimming Pool using Solar Energy, by A. Whillier, 2 pp., January 1965. Revised February 1973.	$0.50
L. 4	How to Build a Solar Water Heater, by D. A. Sinson and T. Hoad 10 pp., February 1965. Revised February 1973.	$1.00
L. 5	How to Construct a Cheap Wind Machine for Pumping Water, by A. Bodek, 12 pp., February 1965. Revised February 1973.	$1.00
L. 5F	French version of L. 5.	$0.50
L. 6	How to Make a Solar Cabinet Dryer for Agricultural Produce, by T. A. Lawand, 9 pp., March 1966. Revised March 1973.	$1.00
L. 8	Como Construir un Desecador Solar para Productos Agricolas: Spanish translation of L. 6 by T. A. Lawand and M. A. Nevot, 11 pp., March 1966.	$1.00
L. 9	Comment Construire une Cuisiniere Solaire à Vapeur—French translation of L. 2, by Paul Bastien and Van-Vi Tran, 7 pp., March 1969.	$1.00
L. 10	Comment Fabriquer un Séchoir Solaire pour Produits Agricoles—French translation of L. 6, by T. A. Lawand, 11 pp., February 1973.	$1.00
T. 17	Instructions for Constructing a Simple 8 sq. ft. Solar Still for Domestic Use and Gas Stations, by T. A. Lawand, 6 pp. Revised September 1967.	$1.00
T. 19	Appareil Simple de Distillation Solaire pour la Production d'Eau Distillée—French translation of T. 17, 6 pp., January 1965.	$1.00
T. 58	Plans for a Glass and Concrete Solar Still, by T. A. Lawand and R. Alward, 9 pp., December 1968. Revised October 1972.	$4.00
T. 85	Production Drawing for Solar Cabinet Dryer by O. Goldstein, June 1973.	$2.00
L. 7	T.20 Arabic versions of L. 6 and T. 17 respectively. each	$1.00

Please send a postal money order or if you send a cheque, please add 25 cents for handling charges. Kindly make cheques payable in Canadian currency.

Precise Power Corporation
John Roesel, Box 1905, Bradenton, Florida 33506

Mr. Roesel is working in conjunction with Dr. Hughes of OSLU on constant-frequency field modulated generators for a new system to feed wind power directly into "AC" power lines. The latest thing we hear from John is a revolutionary engine/generator plant (see Popular Science October 1974).

ERA
Electrical Research Association
List of publications available. If a lot of it interests you, you should consider becoming a member.

LIST OF ERA PUBLICATIONS

			U.S. Member Price	U.S. Non-Member Price
1.	Trans. /IB703	Lines of development of rural wind-power plants. K. Schenfer and A. Ivanov, "Elektrichestvo," No. 5, pp. 21-22, May 1941.	$4.50	$9.00
2.	Trans. /IB1015	Stability of a synchronous generator driven by wind-power and working on a power system. V. V. Andrianov, "Elektrichestvo," No. 10, pp. 26-32, October 1949.	4.50	25.50
3.	Trans. /IB1025	Investigation of the possibilities of utilization of wind-power. J. Juul, "Elektroteknikeren," Vol. 45, pp. 607-635, 22 October 1949.	7.20	72.00
4.	Trans. /IB1027	New designs of wind-power generators. J. Batria, "Elektrotech. Obzor," Vol. 38, pp. 582-585, November 1949. (Translation of main parts only), 10 pp.	4.50	15.00
5.	Trans. /IB1046	Experimental data on models of devices for accumulating wind energy in space. R. Vezzani, "Elettrotecnica," Vol. 35, pp. 488-493; December 1948.	4.50	24.00
6.	Trans. /IB1051	The asynchronous generator and its use in wind-power station. F. Kasper, "Elektrotech. Obzor," Vol. 34, No. 4 pp. 60-63; No. 5-6, pp. 81-89, 1945.	6.00	58.50
7.	Trans. /IB1052	The present state of planning and erection of large experimental wind-power stations. V. R. Sektorov, "Elektrichestvo," No. 2, pp. 9-13, 1933.	4.50	19.50
8.	Trans. /IB1064	On the regulation of slow-running wind-power generators. I. D. Mogilnitskii, Paper of the Lenin Academy of Agricultural Sciences, No. 5, pp. 36-40, 1950.	4.50	10.50
9.	Trans. /IB1072	Elastic power transmission in wind power installations. B. Ganger, H. V. Institute of Karlsruhe Technical High School, March 1974. 12 pp.	4.50	18.00
10.	Trans. /IB1161	Parallel operation of a wind power station with a powerful grid. V. M. Andrianov and D. N. Bystritskii, "Elektrichestvo," No. 5, pp. 8-12, 1951.	4.50	12.00
11.	Trans. /IB1249	Regulation of the output of a wind power station. V. M. Andrianov and A. I. Pokataev, "Elektrichestvo," No. 6, pp. 19-24, 1952.	4.50	16.50
12.	Trans. /IB1266	Electrical problems raised by the utilization of wind power. G. Lacroix, "Bull. Soc. Franc. Elect.," Vol. 10, pp. 211-215, April 1950.	4.50	13.50
13.	Trans. /IB1283	Modern wind-power utilization. G. R. Seidel, "Der Elektrotechniker," Vol. 4, pp. 61-66, March 1952.	4.50	25.50
14.	Trans. /IB1305	Experience in the utilization of wind power for electric power generation. A. Asta, "Ricerca Scientifica," Vol. 23, No. 14, pp. 537-558, April 1953.	4.50	31.50

			U.S. Member Price	U.S. Non-Member Price

15. Trans. /IB1334 Achievements of Soviet wind power engineering. E. M. Fateev and I. V. Rozhdestvenskii, "Vestnik Mashinostroeniya," No. 9, pp. 24-27, 1952. (From a translation into German, "Energietechnik," Vol. 3, pp. 53-56, February 1953. 4.50 16.50

Vol. 3, pp. 53-56. February 1953. 4.50 16.50

16. Trans. /IB1371 Wind power stations working in connection with existing power systems. A. Kroms, "A.S.E. Bull.," Vol. 45, No. 5, pp. 135-144, 6 March 1954. 4.50 33.00

17. Trans. /IB1381 Theory and calculation of a wind turbine. G. D. Mattioli, Padua, October 1944. 4.50 43.50

18. Trans. /IB1760 Electrical Power supply by wind power to the 10cm Schoneberg (Eifel) Radio Link and experience gathered with its operation. G. Rosseler, "Nachirichtentech. Z. (N.T.Z.)," Vol. 12, pp. 352-360, July, 1959. 4.50 31.50

19. Trans. /IB2158 Development, testing and operation of a 200 Kw wind power station in Denmark. Report of the Windpower Committee of the Association of Danish Electricity Undertakings. (OEF). Copenhagen 1962. 15.00 75.00

1. C/T101 Large-scale generation of electricity by wind power—Preliminary report. E. W. Golding. 1949. 15 pp. $6.00 $12.00

2. IB/T4 The aerodynamics of windmills used for the generation of electricity. L. H. G. Sterne and G. C. Rose. 1951. 12 pp. 6.00 12.00

3. C/T104 Wind- and gust-measuring instruments developed for a wind-power survey. H. H. Rosenbrock and J. R. Tagg. 1951. 10 pp. 3.00 9.00

4. C/T105 An extension of the momentum theory of wind turbines. H. H. Rosenbrock. 1951. 10 pp. 2 illustration sheets 6.00 12.00

5. C/T106 The design and development of three new types of gust anemometer. H. H. Rosenbrock. 1951. 37 pp. 12.00 24.00

6. C/T108 The selection and characteristics of wind-power sites. E. W. Golding and A. H. Stodhart. 1952. 32 pp. 12.00 24.00

7. C/T110 The utilization of wind power in desert areas. E. W. Golding. 1953. 11 pp. 6.00 12.00

8. C/T111 The economic value of hydrogen produced by wind power. A. H. Stodhart. 1954. 8 pp. 3.00 9.00

9. C/T112 The use of wind power in Denmark. E. W. Golding and A. H. Stodhart. 1954. 16 pp. 1 illustration sheet 6.00 12.00

10. C/T113 Vibration and stability problems in large wind turbines having hinged blades. H. H. Rosenbrock. 1955. 53 pp. 15.00 30.00

11. C/T114 An experimental study of wind structure (with reference to the design and operation of wind-driven generators). M. P. Wax. 1956. 24 pp. 9.00 18.00

12. C/T115 Wind data related to the generation of electricity by wind power. J. R. Tagg. 1957. 52 pp. 15.00 30.00

13. C/T116 The testing of wind-driven generators operating in parallel with a network. D. E. Villers. 1957. 22 pp. 9.00 18.00

14. C/T117 The development of a method for measurement of strains in the blades of a windmill rotor. J. G. Morrison. 1957. 28 pp. 9.00 18.00

15. C/T118 The combination of local energy resources to provide power supplies in underdeveloped areas. E. W. Golding. 1956. 21 pp. 9.00 18.00

16. C/T119 A preliminary report on the design and performance of ducted windmills. G. M. Lilley and W. J. Rainbird. 1957. 65 pp. 7 Illustration sheets. 22.50 37.50

17. C/T120 Windmills for electricity supply in remote areas. G. Gimpel and A.H. Stodhart. 1958. 24 pp. 9.00 18.00

18. C/T122 The automatic operation of a medium-sized wind-driven generator running in isolation. Preliminary report. J. G. Walker. 1960. 14 pp. 6.00 12.00

19. C/T123 Wind Driven Generators. The difference between the estimated output and actual energy obtained. J. R. Tagg. 1960. 7 pp. 2 illustration sheets. 3.00 9.00

20. IB/T22 The windmill today. G. Gimpel. 1958. 11 pp. 6.00 12.00

21. W/T16 The potentialities of wind power for electricity generation (with special reference to small-scale operation). E. W. Golding and A. H. Stodhart. 1949. 26 pp. 9.00 18.00

THESE PUBLICATIONS AND MANY OTHERS ARE AVAILABLE FROM THE PUBLICATION SALES DEPARTMENT.

ERA
Cleeve Road
Leatherhead Surrey KT22 7SA
England

UNIVERSITIES (partial list)

**University of Massachusetts
Amherst, Mass. 01002**

The projects at U of M are headed by William E. Herconemus whose main concept is off-shore wind power systems, the idea of anchoring towers off the New England coast, tapping the wind energy, then electrolizing seawater to produce hydrogen.

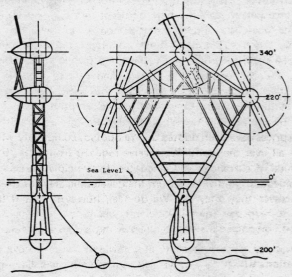

Cambridge
See Integrated Systems

A list of all manufacturers of windmills for both water pumping and electricity production by Gerry E. Smith $1. From University of Cambridge, Department of Architecture, Technical Research Division, 1 Scroop Terrace, Cambridge CB2 1PX, England.

Brown University
Prospect Street
Providence, Rhode Island 02912

One of the many groups doing research on the vertical axis darrieus hoope.

**University of Hamburg
School of Naval Architecture**
University of Hamburg
Hamburg, W. Germany

The energy crisis has brought up very much interest in wind-propulsion for merchant ships. During the last years there was done a lot of research work in the Institute concerning wind forces on ships and especially the properties of a new sailing ship concept based on modern aerodynamics and structural technology. Mr. Wilhelm Prolss is the inventor of this new propulsion system called "Dynaship."

Energy for the Future— The Oklahoma State University Effort

This is now NSF/RANN supported and might be a Proof of Concept —as Mitre recommends. This is more wind than it is solar.

Since 1961, an interdisciplinary team of Engineers at Oklahoma State University has been developing a family of energy systems which could operate from inter- mittent sources of energy, such as solar radiation and wind energy, and utilize a mechanism of energy storage to insure that the input and output energy rates can be made relatively independent of one another. The research effort anticipated the ultimate end of inexpensive and domestically available hydrocarbon fuels, and sought to develop power systems which utilize sources of energy that are essentially non-polluting, non-depleting, and widely distributed over the surface of the earth.

Energy for the Future—The Oklahoma State University Effort
1974; 180 pp

$5.00

A book from Engineering Energy Lab,
College of Engineering,
Oklahoma State University
Stillwater, Oklahoma 74074

INDIVIDUALS

Mr. Walter Schoenball
4S, Ch. M. Duboule
1211 Geneve, Switzerland

Noah double-rotor wind power plant (prototype) was installed on the German west coast in July, 1973. Basic data of this experimental unit is as follows: rotor diameter 36 ft., 5 blades for each of the two contrarotating propeller systems; nominal speed of each rotor 71.4 RPM, 380 Volts, maximum electrical output, 70KW.

The main advantages in comparison to other experimental windplants are the absence of gearboxes and other power transmitting devices. The high relative speed as a result of the contra-rotating propeller system keeps its size and manu-facturing costs within reasonable limits. We under-stand, however, this wind plant has met with an accident.

—T.W.

TWIN ROTOR

Judi Johnston
Rt. One Box 49
Stevensville, Montana 59820

Judi sent in these pictures on a friend's windplants. All in all very impressive.

—T.W.

MAGNUS TYPE SAVONIUS ROTOR

John McGeorge
11 Ells Street
Norwalk, Connecticut 06850

John has designed and developed an 18 Ft. dia., 3-blade wind machine of 2.5 KW output. The machine is now under test and although it has not been designed for commercial production, it has inter-esting innovations. Designed after the Gedser Mill, the unit was built to produce maximum power at 1- MPH average wind speed. The blades are designed to stall at approximately 20 MPH to prevent over-speeding.

—T.W.

HOME-MADE WIND PLANT

Mr. Lyman E. Greenlee
P.O. Box 47
Pennsboro, West Virginia 26415

Mr. Greenlee's patents had a 650 watt 32 volt windcharger which ran their small farm where Lyman grew up. He has some very useful information on wind energy. He now has two auto engines running on hydrogen. By the end of this year, he hopes to have:

1. A car running on hydrogen
2. A wind generator making the gas
3. Storage systems
4. Plans for home construction for all these things, plus a listing for parts which are hard to find locally.

Mr. Greenlee has a degree in chemistry and is a former high school physics teacher.

—T.W.

Jim De Korne
Box 5
El Rito NM 87530

Jim is working integrating wind with solar energy to run a greenhouse. Also has 3000 W Jacobs.

—T.W.

Willard D. Gillette
P.O. Box 241
Brunswick ME 04011

Willard D. Gillette has built an experimental wind machine that runs a rather small rotor inside an aerodynamic shroud containing field coils. There are magnets in the rim of the rotor. He thus achieves a high rate of relative motion between the two without having to resort to gears, brushes, or enormous blades. The machine is thus lighter and more efficient than others, and requires less material. Speed is governed by turning on more field coils as the wind picks up, thus giving the dynamo more work to do, hence keeping down the speed of the rotor. Smart! Professionals (only, please) may discuss things with him by writing. The rest of us will have to wait and see.

—Jay Baldwin

Lee Johnson
OMSI Energy Center
4015 S.W. Canyon Road
Portland, OR 97221

John Burgess
134 Hobart Avenue
San Mateo, California 94402

John has built a 660 watt/12 volt in 5 MPH wind, 4 blades, 10 feet diameter propellers made from aluminum pipe 8 inches wide, using a Chrysler alternator, stepped up 10 to 1 using "V" belts.

—T.W.

Dr. Ulrich Hutter
Universitat Stuttgart
7 Stuttgart-Vaihinga
Pfaffenwldring
West Germany

Dr. Hutter, a leading pioneer in the development of modern wind power plants is an expert in aeronautical design. He has contributed greatly to the development of efficient and beautiful high speed wind motors.

—T.W.

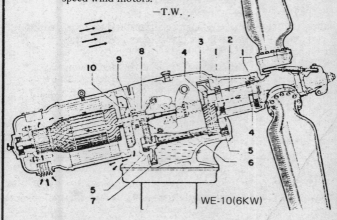

WE-10(6KW)

1. MAIN BEARING
2. MAIN SHAFT
3. MAIN GEAR
4. BEARING LOCK
5. INTERMEDIATE BEARING
6. INTERMEDIATE SHAFT
7. INTERMEDIATE GEAR
8. PINION GEAR
9. THRUST BEARING
10. OIL SEAL

1940 JACOBS 1800 WATT, 32 VOLT WIND GENERATOR

JACOBS GOVERNOR WITH
CONNECTING GEAR REMOVED

JACOBS CONNECTING GEAR WITH
BLADE GEAR (NOTICE THE WEAR).

ECLIPSE WINDMILL

ALLIED GOVERNING DEVICE, AN EXCELLENT DESIGN.

WINCHARGER GOVERNING DEVICES, ONE OF MANY THEY PRODUCED.

The cost of a wind system that provides energy at our present rate of consumption is prohibitively expensive for a single family alone. It is as much a waste of materials as our present rate of consumption is a waste of energy. There is a definite *economy of scale* with wind systems. That is, the larger the system (up to a certain point), the more favorable the ratio of the cost of materials to the energy received. Sharing these costs and benefits with other families or small groups is economic, efficient, and energy conserving.

Wind has both a potential and kinetic form of energy. It is the kinetic form which we harness and the security in the potential energy which we seek. The Wind section, along with other sections in this book, offers some ideas, concepts and methods which contribute to a standard of living that provides an opportunity to further understand the human situation, without destroying the environment. The movement of the universe is creation.

BIOFUELS

BIOFUELS COMMENTS

BioFuels are, as the name implies, renewable energy sources from living things. They are to be distinguished from *fossil fuels* which are also of biological origin, but which are non-renewable. All biofuels are ultimately derived from plants, which capture the sun's energy, convert it to chemical energy by photosynthesis, and in the process of being eaten or decayed, pass this energy onto the rest of the living world. In this sense, then, all forms of life, their byproducts and wastes, are storehouses of solar energy ready to be eaten, burned or converted into various organic fuels.

The following *BioFuels Section* is divided into six parts: *Biomass Energy, Agriculture, Aquaculture, Methane Systems, Alcohol* and *Wood*. For various reasons we have given special attention to some of these subjects and played down others. For example, *biomass energy* is a complex subject involving the dynamics of biology, photosynthesis, ecosystems, bio-conversion process, etc. All we can do in our limited space is skim the top, oversimplify concepts and hopefully give an overview for the rest of the BioFuels section.

With respect to *agriculture*, so much has been written about the why and how of composting, organic farming/gardening, natural pest control, etc., that we have only included a partially annotated bibliography, a few overview comments and some pertinent book reviews as a *primer* to renewable strategies for agriculture . . . from the backyard to the urban lot to the farm.

The same can be said for *methane systems*, which have enjoyed recent popularity in a variety of places from industry to feedlots to municipal waste plants to the backyard. A wide range of information about digester designs, methane gas and sludge utilization is now available in both popular and technical books and articles. And here, too, rather than describe the nitty-gritty of "how-to-do-it" (requiring more space than we've got) we have simply tried to cull out the information that has helped us to understand the principles, problems and designs involved.

On the other hand, *aquaculture* is not so familiar. Although fish farming is big business in some places, there is really very little information about ways to manage fish ponds and small fish farms using simple materials, ecological techniques and local resources (including solar and wind power). But as food scarcities increase in the years to come, aquaculture will likely become more popular as an alternative source of animal protein and market item for local food economies. Dominick Mendola has outlined the background and basic ecological strategies for small aquaculture operations. With the help of Bill McLarney he has also annotated much of the pertinent information available in the field of aquaculture to help get things started.

As far as *alcohol* is concerned, we have real mixed feelings about its production and use as a practical biofuel for individuals and small groups. Interest in alcohol as a fuel source seems to crop up periodically during hard times . . . like today for example. But the legal restrictions controlling the production of ethyl alcohol and the technical problems associated with producing methyl alcohol seem overwhelming in terms of small scale operations. We've presented a brief overview of alcohol as a renewable energy resource in the hopes that the ethanol laws will become more flexible and methanol distillation technology more accessible and practical.

One spin-off from the energy "crisis" has been a renewed interest in *wood* as a fuel. From suburban woodlots to National Forests, scars of recent harvests are now a common sight. And in the marketplace firewood is nearly as expensive as coal. Because wood is such an exploitable biofuel, we felt that reasonable space ought to be devoted to a discussion of its efficient use.

A final thought about BioFuels. The harnessing of solar, wind and water power is basically a mechanical problem of capture, conversion and storage. The harnessing of BioFuel energy, on the other hand, is also a *biological problem* that must be sensitive to the chemistry, nutrition and ecology of living systems. It's hard to find people who are skilled or inspired in both disciplines of engineering and biology . . . of mechanical forces and life forces. This is why the building of a digester, a still, an efficient greenhouse, a fish pond or even an ecologically designed truck garden requires a special integration and "bringing together" of varied talents, skills and people. And this is why the utilization of BioFuels should be a top priority in organizing local efforts and designing for local needs.

ABOUT REFERENCES LISTED IN BIOFUELS

Many of the references listed in the BioFuels section were written during a simpler, more humanistic and more decentralized time, i.e., prior to pesticides, rural electrification, over-sized waste treatment plants, etc. Other information comes from periods of war, depression and other times of scarcity when there was a strong premium placed on self-sufficiency and survival technologies. Many of these references are out of print or hard to get.

Today, impending hard times have precipitated a rash of new "how-to and why" books, doomsday survival manuals, homecraft guides, expensive new-age textbooks and esoteric symposia from the "concerned" technical bureaucracy. Everywhere there is information, from the past *and* the present. We have found that if you try hard enough, virtually all of it is available in one way or another: libraries, cooperative purchases, copy shops, out-of-print bookstores and a publishing industry that is generally responsive to demands for republication. We needn't get hung up on books . . . simply use them as tools. Note:

WORDS GUIDE
EXAMPLES MOVE   —R.M.
BUT THERE IS NO SUBSTITUTE FOR DOING IT

BIOMASS

BIOMASS ENERGY
by Richard Merrill

Every day, over 200 times more energy from the sun falls on our planet than is used by the U.S. in one year. About half of this energy is reflected back into space (Fig. 1). Most of the sunlight that finally penetrates the atmosphere ends up charging the great heat, wind and water systems of the biosphere. The rest (only 1/10 of 1%) is captured by green plants, algae and a few kinds of bacteria and converted by photosynthesis into the chemical energy of protoplasm. The plants are then eaten by other creatures who incorporate this chemical energy into their bodies.

All plant matter is called *biomass*, and the energy that is released from biomass when it is eaten, burned or converted into fuels is called *biomass energy*. Microbes, plants, trees, animals, vegetable oils, animal fats, manure garbage, even fossil fuels, all represent forms of biomass energy that can be produced, cultivated or converted in a variety of ways for human needs.

Compared to solar, wind and water devices, plants are very inefficient at converting solar energy into useful forms of energy. But only plants can convert solar energy into chemical energy; only plants can produce the fuel that sustains life. We can build fancy solar collectors and wind generators, but with all of our science and sophisticated gadgets, we still don't know how to construct a plant, or even how to produce a practical method of artificial photosynthesis. Biomass is the oldest and most fundamental source of renewable energy. And all we can do is grow with it, we can't build it.

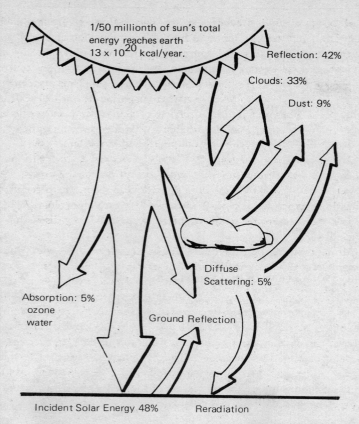

1/50 millionth of sun's total energy reaches earth 13 x 10²⁰ kcal/year.

$1/50$ millionth of sun's total energy reaches earth 13×10^{20} kcal/year.

Reflection: 42%

Clouds: 33%

Dust: 9%

Diffuse Scattering: 5%

Absorption: 5% ozone water

Ground Reflection

Incident Solar Energy 48%   Reradiation

FIG. 1   AVERAGE DISPOSITION OF SOLAR ENERGY IN THE BIOSPHERE. EVERY DAY NEARLY 100 TIMES MORE ENERGY FALLS ON THE EARTH'S SURFACE THAN IS USED BY THE U.S. IN ONE YEAR.

Photosynthesis is more than just the basic process by which solar energy is converted into chemical (biomass) energy. It has also been one of the driving forces in the creation of the biosphere itself. Theory has it that for millenia following the cooling of the earth, organic molecules evolved in shallow seas from the ingredients of the primitive atmosphere (methane, hydrogen, ammonia and water). In time, some of these early compounds were able to reproduce and to subsist by "eating" other organic molecules. Other forms of proto-life survived, not by eating each other (which had its obvious limitations), but by evolving methods of using outside solar energy to synthesize their food from carbon dioxide and simple materials, i.e. by "photo"-synthesizing what they needed to maintain and propagate themselves. This was perhaps the most important step in organic evolution; for the first time one biological group could pass the vast and renewable resources of solar energy onto the rest of the living world. Equally im-

I. BASIC PHOTOSYNTHESIS FORMULA:

$$CO_2 + H_2 \xrightarrow[\text{chlorophyll}]{\text{solar energy}} (CH_2O) + 2x + H_2O$$

carbon dioxide   hydrogen supply   biomass energy (carbohydrate)   element

II.   GREEN ALGAE AND HIGHER PLANTS

$$CO_2 + H_2O \longrightarrow (CH_2O) + O_2$$
oxygen

III.   SULFUR BACTERIA

$$CO_2 + H_2S \longrightarrow (CH_2O) + S + H_2O$$
hydrogen sulfide   sulfur

IV.   SOME ALGAE AND BACTERIA

$$CO_2 + H_2 \longrightarrow (CH_2O) + H_2O$$
hydrogen

V.   PURPLE BACTERIA

$$CO_2 + CHO + H_2O \longrightarrow (CH_2O) + H_2 + H_2O$$
organic material

TABLE I GROSS EQUATIONS FOR DIFFERENT KINDS OF PHOTOSYNTHESIS. GREEN PLANTS ARE BY FAR THE MOST IMPORTANT CONTRIBUTOR TO THE ENERGY BUDGET OF THE BIOSPHERE.

portant was the fact that photosynthesis led eventually to the accumulation of oxygen and ultra-violet absorbing ozone in the atmosphere. This radically altered conditions for life on earth and probably triggered the explosive evolution of animal life and the eventual colonization of the land. Today the process of photosynthesis provides us with all of our oxygen, all of our food and most of our energy. Its importance cannot be overemphasized, although it is often forgotten.

Actually, organisms have evolved several ways to photosynthesize (Table I). But because water is so abundant, *green plant* photosynthesis is far and away the most important contributor to the energy budget of the biosphere. Likewise, other forms of life that don't get their energy directly from the sun have evolved a variety of methods for getting the energy and materials they need to survive (Table II).

I. LIFE FORMS BY THE WAY THEY OBTAIN ENERGY
  A. Phototrophs (energy from sunlight)
    Algae, Higher Plants, some Bacteria (green, purple)
  B. Chemotrophs (energy from chemicals)
    1. LITHOTROPHS (inorganic chemicals)
       some bacteria
    2. ORGANOTROPHS (organic chemicals)
       Animals, Fungi, Most Bacteria

OR

II. LIFE FORMS BY THE WAY THEY OBTAIN ENERGY AND CARBON
  A. Autotrophs (energy from non-living sources, carbon from CO_2)
    1. PHOTOSYNTHETIC (energy from light) . . . "A" above
    2. CHEMOSYNTHETIC (energy from inorganic chemicals) . . . "B1" above
  B. Heterotrophs (energy and carbon from organic chemicals) . . . "B2" above

TABLE II   THE CLASSIFICATION OF LIFE FORMS ACCORDING TO THE WAY THEY OBTAIN ENERGY AND CARBON. ONLY TWO SOURCES OF ENERGY ARE AVAILABLE: SOLAR ENERGY AND BIOMASS ENERGY. LIKEWISE ONLY TWO SOURCES OF CARBON ARE AVAILABLE: CARBON DIOXIDE AND, AGAIN, BIOMASS.

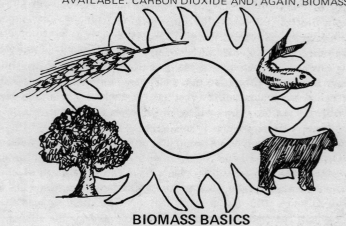

BIOMASS BASICS

To better understand the fundamentals of biomass production we need to define a few terms. The easiest way to do this is to trace the patterns of energy and materials as they pass through a simple community of plants and animals. As an example, we can take a hypothetical 1 acre pasture of grass and foraging cows.

The amount of solar energy falling on the field will vary greatly according to latitude and climate. For a typical mid-latitude area the average amount of incident solar energy is between 1 and 4 billion kilocalories per acre per year (kcal/acre/yr).** For our purposes we can take the lower value. Of this amount about 99% (990 million kcal/yr) is lost immediately from the grass plants by reflection and evaporation. The rest (10 million kcal/yr) is converted into plant tissue and is called the *gross primary productivity (GPP)*. The GPP does not represent the accumulated biomass since the plants must use some of their own energy to maintain themselves. In our pasture example, about 75% of the GPP (7.5 million kcal/yr) is actually converted into grass biomass and becomes available as food for the cows.[1,2] This is called the *net primary producitivity (NPP)*. The NPP

**A kilocalorie, or 1000 calories, is the amount of heat needed to raise one kilogram of water (about a quart) one degree centigrade. It is equal to 3.96 BTU.*

is the measure of accumulated biomass available for food, fuel or conversion. The rest of the GPP not converted to plant biomass is radiated as unusable heat by respiration.

$$\underset{\substack{\text{Gross Primary Productivity} \\ \text{(solar energy assimilated} \\ \text{by plants)}}}{10 \text{ million kcal/yr}} = \underset{\substack{\text{Net Primary Productivity} \\ \text{(biomass, yield or food} \\ \text{energy)}}}{7.5 \text{ million kcal/yr}} + \underset{\substack{\text{Respiration} \\ \text{(heat energy)}}}{2.5 \text{ million kcal/yr}}$$

Now assume that the cows only eat about 1/2 of the available grass in the pasture.[2] This means that the amount of biomass eaten by the cows represents (1% x 75% x 50%) = .38% or less than 1/2 of one percent of the solar energy falling on the field. In our example, this amounts to 3.8 million kcal/yr and is called the *gross herbivore producitivity*. In general about 90% of this food energy is lost as cow respiration and manure, leaving only about 10% as cow meat (380,000 kcal = 180 lbs of beef protein). This biomass is called the *net herbivore productivity*.

We can expand our simple community by assuming that if the cows were left to fend for themselves some would die naturally and decay in the pasture while others would fall prey to local predators. The predators, in turn, would lose about 90% of the cow flesh energy to respiration and wastes, converting only about 10% into their bodies as *net carnivore productivity*.

The passing of energy and nutrients from their source in plants through a series of organisms is called a *food chain*. So far we have been talking about a simple grass-cow-predator food chain. We can also refer to all animals feeding in the same level of the food chain as being in the same *trophic level*. In the pasture, grass-eaters like cows and gophers would be in one trophic level and cow-eaters like wolves and people would be in the next "higher" trophic level. We can now make some generalizations about biomass production:

Solar Efficiency of Biomass Production

Compared to mechanical systems, plants are very inefficient at converting solar energy into available (chemical) energy (Table IV). We can determine photosynthetic efficiency by comparing the chemical energy stored in plant tissue (either gross or net productivity) with the solar energy received by the plant. For our pasture/cow example we assumed an efficiency of 1% which is within the range of most crops and plants (Table V).

There are two major reasons why plants are so inefficient at converting solar energy. First, plants tend to put their maximum growth into short periods during favorable times of the year. If efficiencies are measured over the entire growing season, values will be much lower than if they are measured during peak growing periods (Table V).

Secondly, plants are simply unable to use most of the sunlight available to them. On land, from 70-80% of the incident light is reflected or absorbed by physical things other than plants.[3] We can get an idea of what happens to the remaining light energy from an elegant study done on an acre of corn during a 100 day growing season.[4] The study showed that 44.4% of the light received by plants was used to evaporate the 15 inches of rainfall received during the season: 54% was converted directly to heat and lost by convection and radiation, and the minute quantity remaining (1.6%) was actually converted into the tissues of the corn plants. About 33% of this gross productivity was used in respiration leaving 1.2% of the available light energy as corn biomass (Table III).

	Glucose (lbs)	kcal. (million)	Solar Efficiency
INCIDENT SOLAR ENERGY		2.043	
PRODUCTIVITY			
Net (N)	3040	25.3	1.2%
Respiration	930	7.7	0.4%
Gross (G)	3970	33	1.6%
Production efficiency = N/G			76.6%

TABLE III   ENERGY BUDGET OF AN ACRE OF CORN DURING ONE GROWING SEASON (100 DAYS). 76.6% OF THE SOLAR ENERGY ASSIMILATED IS PUT INTO BIOMASS. FROM REF. 4

The fact that a portion of plant productivity is used for plant maintenance suggests another measure of solar efficiency for plants: the *production efficiency*. This is defined as the rate of energy lost during respiration to the net productivity.

		% Efficiency		
		Of Process	To Heat	To Electricity
I.	BASIC PHYSICAL CONVERSIONS			
	A. STEAM → MECHANICAL ENERGY	10-30		
	B. MECHANICAL → ELECTRICAL			80
	C. STEAM → ELECTRICAL			A.xB.= 8-25
II.	SOLAR - PHYSICAL CONVERSIONS			
	A. LOW TEMPERATURE SOLAR			
	1. Solar energy → hot water		20	
	B. HIGH TEMPERATURE SOLAR			
	1. Solar heaters, cookers, reflectors		50-80	
	2. Solar reflector → steam		40-60	
	3. "I-C" above			8-25
	4. Solar → steam → electricity			3-15
	C. SOLAR → ELECTRICITY (PHOTOCELLS)			
	1. Cadmium sulfide			5
	2. Silicon			12
	D. WIND			
	1. Wind → mechanical	44		
	2. "I-B" above			80
	3. Wind → mechanical → electrical			35
III.	SOLAR - BIOLOGICAL CONVERSIONS			
	A. FOOD CHAINS			
	1. Solar energy → plant chemical energy[1]	0.3-3.0		
	2. Plant energy → herbivore energy	5-10		
	3. Herbivore → carnivore energy	5-15		
	B. WOOD			
	1. Solar energy → forest wood	0.5-3.0		
	2. Wood → heat (steam)		60-80	
	3. "I-C" above			8-25
	4. Solar → steam → electrical			.04-.8
	C. BIOGAS (DIGESTION)			
	1. Solar → plant[1]	.3-3.0		
	2. Biomass → biogas[2]	40-70		
	3. Biogas → heat		75	
	4. Biogas → heat → mechanical[3]	25-40		
	5. "I-B" above			80
	6. Organic waste → electricity (via biogas)			.02-.5
	D. ALCOHOL (DISTILLATION)			
	1. Fruits, grains → ethanol	75		
	2. Wood → ethanol	65		
	3. Biomass waste → methanol	55		

TABLE IV   EFFICIENCIES OF SOLAR ENERGY CONVERSION SYSTEMS: COMPARING THE BIOLOGICAL WITH THE MECHANICAL

*Not including process heat

	% of Gross Productivity	% of Net Productivity
EXPERIMENTAL		
LABORATORY		
Algae (Chlorella)	20-35	
Dim light experiments	15-20	
FIELD		
Chlorella silt ponds	3.0	
Sewage ponds	2.8	
CULTIVATED CROPS		
PEAK OF SEASON		
Sugar beets, Europe	7.7	5.4
Sugar cane, Hawaii	7.6	4.8
Irrigated corn, Israel	6.8	3.2
DURING SEASON		
Sugar beets, Europe	2.2	
Rice, Japan		2.2
Sugar cane, Java		1.9
Corn, U.S.	1.6	1.3
Water hyacinth	1.5	
Tropical forest plantation	0.7	
ECOSYSTEMS		
Annual desert plants (peak)	6-7	
Tropical rain forest	3.5	
Freshwater springs, Florida	2.7	
Polluted bay, Texas	2.5	
Coral reef	2.4	
Beech forest, Europe	2.2	1.5
Scots pine, Europe		2.4
Oak forest, U.S.	2.0	.91
Perennial herb, grass		1.0
Cattail marsh	0.6	
Lake, Wisconsin	0.4	
Broomsedge community	0.3	
BIOMES		
Open ocean	0.09	
Arctic tundra	0.08	
Desert	0.05	
BIOSPHERE		
Land		0.4
Sea		0.2

TABLE V   PHOTOSYNTHETIC EFFICIENCY OF VARIOUS PLANTS, CROPS, AND ECOSYSTEMS. (SEE TEXT FOR EXPLANATION)

Production efficiencies range between 85% (natural grasslands) to 29% (tropical rainforests). Generally speaking plant communities tend to fall into three groups (Fig. 2): (1) Those with high net productivity and low respiration. Included here are plants that have been selected for putting weight on fast, e.g., crops, weeds, young plants and vegetation in the early stages of ecological succession. (2) Those with low net productivity and low respiration. These are plant communities in marginal areas where water (desert), light (arctic) or nutrients (mid-ocean) are limited. (3) Those plants with low productivity and high respiration. These include mature ecosystems (old forests, coral reefs), polluted waters and other situations where the energy cost of maintenance is high. Note here for example that the older a woodlot gets, the less efficient it is in converting solar energy into wood.

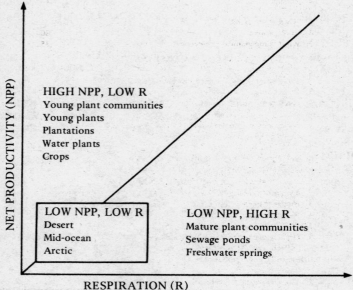

FIG. 2   THE RELATIONSHIP BETWEEN ENERGY GAINED IN
NET PRIMARY PRODUCTIVITY AND ENERGY LOST TO
RESPIRATION FOR VARIOUS PLANT COMMUNITIES.

Whereas plants convert about 75% of their gross productivity into biomass, animals, being mobile and feeding sporadically, are far less efficient. As a general rule about 90% of the available energy is lost at each exchange point between animals in the food chain.[5,6] In other words, the more removed an animal is from a plant diet, the more plant biomass it takes to maintain it. At the present time, over 80% of all U.S. grains are fed to livestock. Much of this valuable food energy is lost in cow respiration and feces (some of it could be retrieved by treating the manure as a resource rather than a waste). Obviously there is a great deal to be said for eating more vegetable proteins in one's diet and less meat, i.e. for eating closer to the bottom of the food chain.[7]

Energy Subsidies in Biomass Production:

High photosynthetic and production efficiencies in crops are maintained with large outside energy inputs (fertilizers, supplemental foods, irrigation,

cultivation). Anything that reduces the energy cost of internal self-maintenance of a biological system is called an *energy subsidy*.[8] For example, modern agriculture is only productive because of a large energy subsidy of fossil fuels (see Agriculture Section). In terms of producing from its own internal energy supplies, modern agriculture is not efficient at all.

The Distribution of Biomass in Biological Systems

Energy flows through a biological community only once and is not recycled but is transformed into heat and ultimately lost to the community. Only the continual input of new solar energy keeps the community running. On the other hand, all matter is ultimately recycled through decomposers (mostly microbes) which break down complex organic molecules into simple materials to be used again by the plants. Thus in all biological systems . . . pastures, fish ponds, truck gardens, woodlots or the entire biosphere . . . *matter cycles and energy flows* (Figs. 3 and 4).

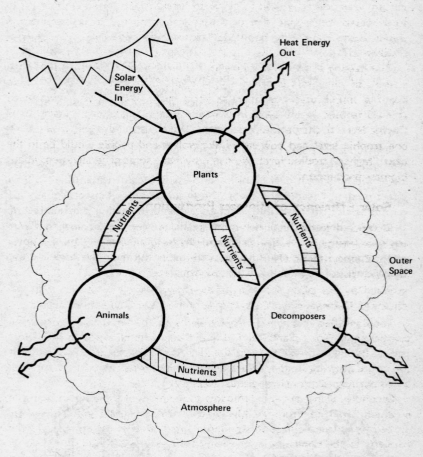

FIG. 3   RECYCLING OF NUTRIENTS AND FLOW OF ENERGY IN THE
BIOSPHERE. VIRTUALLY ALL MATERIALS ARE RECYCLED IN
THE BIOSPHERE, BUT ONLY A SMALL PORTION OF INCOMING
SOLAR ENERGY IS STORED AT ANY ONE TIME. EVENTUALLY
ALL BIOMASS ENERGY DISSIPATES INTO OUTER SPACE AS HEAT.

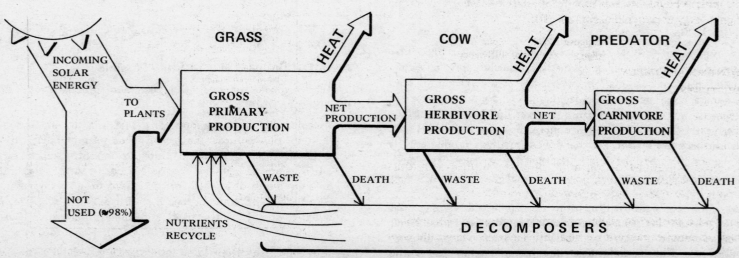

FIG. 4   RECYCLING OF NUTRIENTS AND FLOW OF ENERGY IN AN ECOSYSTEM FOOD CHAIN (GRASS, COW, PREDATOR). SEE TEXT.

For the efficient conversion of matter and energy back into the life cycle, ecosystems are organized into a biological hierarchy that can be shown graphically as *ecological or trophic pyramids*. The base of the pyramids are the abundant biomass of plants. Since energy and biomass are lost as they pass along the food chain, animals near the base of the pyramid (plant eaters) are more numerous (in terms of biomass, energy content and numbers) than the animals above which eat them (Fig. 5).

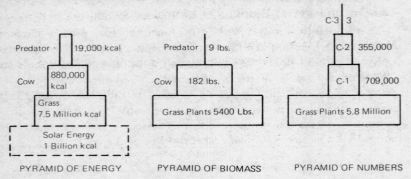

FIG. 5   THREE KINDS OF ECOLOGICAL PYRAMIDS BASED ON THE FOOD CHAIN OF A 1 ACRE FIELD OF GRASS OVER 1 YEAR. PYRAMIDS OF ENERGY AND BIOMASS ARE FROM GRASS/COW ECOSYSTEM DESCRIBED IN TEXT. PYRAMID OF NUMBERS IS FROM DATA PRESENTED BY ODUM 1971 (REF. 8), WHERE: C-1=PRIMARY CONSUMERS (HERBIVOROUS INVERTEBRATES); C-2=SECONDARY CONSUMERS(CARNIVOROUS SPIDERS AND INSECTS); C-3= TERTIARY CONSUMERS (MOLES AND BIRDS).

This concept helps us to understand the distribution of biomass in a biological system. For example, under normal conditions, we know that there will be a great deal more insect pests in a garden than there will be insect predators feeding on them. If a pesticide kills all insects equally (as most do), it will have the effect of actually increasing the number of pests . . . unless, of course, more pesticides are used. Knowing about ecological pyramids is also important in the biological design of a polyculture pond (see Aquaculture Section), the pasturing of livestock and the management of other cultivated ecosystems.

BIOMASS PRODUCTION AND CONVERSION

Productivity Units

Primary productivity is the rate at which biomass is "fixed" by photosynthesis per unit area per unit time. It is usually expressed as dry organic matter in grams per square meter per day or per year ($g/m^2/day$; $g/m^2/yr$); kilograms per hectare per year (kg/ha/yr); pounds per acre per year (lb/acre/yr); metric tons per hectare per year (mT/ha/yr); short tons per acre per year (sT/acre/yr) or in terms more familiar and practical such as bushels per acre per season, lugs per tree, etc. Often productivity is measured in grams of carbon per square meter per day or year ($g\text{-}C/m^2/day$). As a general rule of thumb, about 45% of the weight of dry organic matter is carbon.

Biomass can also be converted to energy units and expressed as calories per square meter per day ($cal/m^2/day$), or kilocalories per square meter per day or year ($kcal/m^2/day$; $kcal/m^2/yr$). Converting biomass into energy units comes in handy when you are considering the energy budgets of natural ecosystems and agriculture, or the efficiencies of

bio-conversion processes. For "ball-park" estimates, 1 gram dry weight of organic matter is equivalent to 4-5 kcal of energy (1400-1750 kcal/lb or 5500-6900 Btu/lb). For more precise biomass to energy conversions see Table VI.

		SOLID	LIQUID	GAS	
	kcal/g	BTU/lb	BTU/gal	BTU/ft^3
FOSSIL FUEL				
COAL				
bituminous	9.2	13,100		
anthracite	8.9	12,700		
lignite	4.7	6,700		
COAL COKE	9.1	13,000		
CRUDE OIL		18,600	138,000	
FUEL OIL		18,800	148,600	
KEROSENE		19,810	135,100	
GASOLINE		20,250	124,000	
LP GAS		21,700	95,000	
COAL GAS				450-500
NATURAL GAS (Methane)		21,500	75,250	1050
PROPANE		21,650	92,000	2200-2600
BUTANE		21,250	102,000	2900-3400
BIOFUELS				
CARBOHYDRATES				
sugar	3.7-4.0	5300		
starch/cellulose	4.2	5800		
lignin	6.0	8300		
PROTEIN				
grain/legume	5.7-6.0	8050		
vegetable/fruit	5.0-5.2	7025		
animal/dairy	5.6-5.9	7850		
FATS				
animal	9.5	13,100		
vegetable oil	9.3	12,800		
MICRO-ALGAE	5.0-6.5	9500		
WOOD				
oak, beech	4.1	5650		
pine	4.5	6200		
all woods	4.2	5790		
BRIQUETS	8.1	11,500		
ALCOHOL				
methanol		8600	67,000	
ethanol		12,000	95,000	
BIOGAS (60% CH$_4$)				600-650
METHANE		21,500	75,250	1050
MISC. "WASTES"				
municipal organic refuse	2.8-3.5	4000-5000		
raw sludge	2.7-5.3	3700-7300		
digested sludge	2.7-5.0	3800-6900		
paper	5.5	7600		
glass	5.6	7700		
leaves	5.2	7100		
dry plant biomass	5.6	8000		
MISC. ANIMALS				
insect	5.4			
earthworm	4.6			
mammal	5.2			

TABLE VI   ENERGY VALUES OF VARIOUS FOSSIL FUELS AND BIOFUELS (ref. 9-12).

Amount of Biomass Theoretically Possible

We can estimate the theoretical maximum productivity of biomass in the following way[13];

    Assume that: a) The amount of available light imposes the upper limit to total photosynthesis and hence to productivity. b) Photosynthesis is limited to the visible region of the light spectrum (.4-.7 microns)** c) The average amount of solar radiation falling on a given area of average air mass during the growing season (June-Sept.) is 500 cal/cm^2/day, and that of this, 222 cal/cm^2/day is attributed to the visible spectrum. Maximum productivity: If we make allowances for inactive absorption (10%), plant respiration (33%), inorganic materials in the plant.

**1 micron (u)=one-millionth of a meter.

(8%) etc., the theoretical maximum net productivity is around 77 grams/m²/day = 687 lbs./acre/day = 34sT/acre/100 days = 125 sT/acre/hr. As we shall see, even under ideal conditions (controlled laboratory pilot experiments and farming situations where high-yield crops are grown year around), the best we can hope for is around 25-35% of this theoretical maximum.

Net Productivity of the Biosphere

According to Fogg[19] if one year's yield of the earth's photosynthesis were amassed in the form of sugar cane it would form a heap over 2 miles high and with a base 43 miles square! A more precise estimate of our planet's productivity is around 175 billion dry tons per year (14). This figure is made by adding up the estimated productions of the major environments of the biosphere (Table VII). Note that 2/3 of the total productivity is generated on land . . . 1/4 by tropical forests alone. About 5% of the land productivity is due to agriculture, and about 0.5% of the total productivity is consumed as human food and livestock fodder. Interestingly enough, agricultural systems generally do not appear to be any more productive than many natural ecosystems.

Biome	Area 1 Million Square Miles	Average Net Primary Productivity Tons/Acre/Year	World Total Net Primary Productivity 1 Billion Dry Tons/Year
LAND			
Extreme (desert, ice)	9.3	.1	.1
Tundra	3.1	.6	1.2
Boreal forests	4.6	3.6	10.6
Temperate forests	6.9	5.8	25.8
Woodlands, shrublands	2.7	2.7	4.6
Grasslands:			
Temperate	3.5	2.2	5.0
Savannah	5.8	3.1	11.6
Desert scrub	6.9	.3	1.4
Tropical forests	7.7	8.9	44.1
TOTAL	50.5	27.3	104.4
AVERAGE		3.21	
Cultivated land:			
Mechanized	1.5	5.3*	5.1
Unmechanized	3.8	1.3*	3.3
TOTAL	5.3	6.6	8.4
AVERAGE		2.46	
FRESHWATER			
Lakes and streams	0.8	2.2	1.1
Swamps and marshes	0.8	8.9	4.4
TOTAL	1.6	11.1	5.5
AVERAGE		5.37	
MARINE			
Open ocean	125.9	.4	44.8
Coastal areas	13.1	.9	7.5
Upwelling areas	0.2	2.7	.3
Estuaries and reefs	0.8	8.9	4.6
TOTAL	140.0	12.9	57.2
AVERAGE		0.63	
BIOSPHERE TOTAL	197 Million Square Miles	1.39 Tons/Acre/Year	175.5 Billion Dry Tons/Year

TABLE VII GROSS ESTIMATES OF THE BIOMASS PRODUCTIVITY OF THE BIOSPHERE. Data culled from various sources (ref. 8, 14-18). * = including non-edible portions.

The energy equivalent of 175 billion dry tons of biomass is about 550 quadrillion (5.5×10^{17}) kcal. If we assume an annual insolation for our planet of 6×10^{20} kcal, we can then conclude that every year the biosphere fixes a little less than 1/10 of one percent of the solar energy falling on the earth's surface. Looked at another way, we can compare the average net productivity values of the major environments of the biosphere (Table VII) and note what a small fraction of the theoretical productivity (125sT/acre/hr) they represent. Again we see how inefficient plants are at converting solar energy to biomass, but emphasize how indispensable this "inefficient" process is to human survival.

Biomass Conversion

Solar energy remains trapped in plants until it is released at the time of being eaten, burned or decayed. We can distinguish between using green plants or organic wastes as raw materials for biomass conversions (Fig. 6). In the case of the former, growing crops means that nutrients must be recycled in order to maintain the fertility (productivity) of the land or waters. If nutrients can't be recycled they've got to be brought in from outside...often at great expense and energy. This is one reason for linking waste producing operations (e.g., livestock, sewage plants, methane digesters) with agriculture, algae ponds and other crops...to close the cycle.

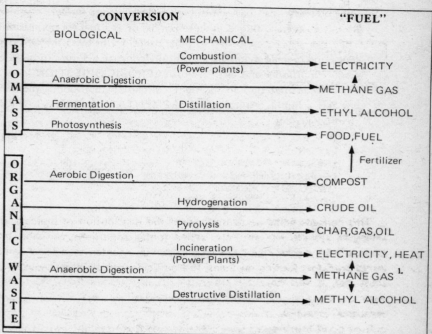

FIG. 6 BIOMASS CONVERSION PROCESSES

[1.]Anaerobic digestion also produces a liquid fertilizer, "sludge."

Although there are a variety of ways to convert plants directly into organic fuels, impending food shortages suggest that alternative fuel production may not be the wisest use of land and crops. Organic wastes, on the other hand, are produced all around us. Although they are still generally considered as a problem rather than a resource, there is little doubt that organic wastes will have to be used more and more as a raw material for conversion and recycling. Each year the U.S. produces over 870 million dry tons of discarded organic matter. Conservatively, about 16% of this (136 million tons) can be easily collected with even today's priorities (Table VIII). Virtually all of this "waste" can be converted in a variety of ways to fuels and fertilizers:

HIGH—TECH CONVERSIONS (Requiring high temperatures, pressures or corrosive chemicals, i.e., causing a relatively high impact on the local environment):

a) Pyrolysis: The heating of organic wastes (200-900°C) in the absence of air at atmospheric pressure to produce gas (500BTU/ft³; oil (120,000BTU/gal.) and char (700-1200BTU/lb) all of which are combustible. The amount of energy recovered from the byproducts of pyrolysis is equal to 75-98% of the energy subsidy, i.e., there is a new energy loss for the process[21]

b) Hydrogasification: Direct gasification of organic wastes (especially manure) with hydrogen at high temperatures (500-600°C) and pressures (1000 psi) to produce substitute pipeline gas (methane, ethane). About 6000 ft³ of gas is produced (6 million BTU) per ton of dry organic matter. The hydrogen is generated from the residual char from the hydrogasification.

c) Hydrogenation: Conversion of organic wastes to oil by treatment with carbon monoxide and steam under pressure (2000-6000psi) at high temperatures (300-400°C). The net yield of low sulfur oil (16,000BTU/lb) is about 1.3 barrels per ton of dry organic waste.

d) <u>Destructive Distillation</u>: The heating of high-cellulose organic wastes (wood and refuse) and the distillation of liquid residues to produce methyl alcohol.

e) <u>Acid Hydrolysis</u>: The treatment of wood wastes with heat and acid to produce sugars for fermentation/distillation to ethyl alcohol.

LOW—TECH CONVERSIONS (i.e., processes with a relatively low impact on the local environment)

Organic wastes can be used directly as a livestock fodder, as a fertilizer (e.g., sewage sludge in algae ponds) or as a fuel for combustion. They can also be converted to other useful forms by COMPOSTING (decaying organic materials in carefully constructed piles to produce a soil conditioner and fertilizer); ANAEROBIC DIGESTION (decaying organic materials in air-tight containers to produce methane gas and a liquid fertilizer) and FERMENTATION/DISTILLATION to ethyl alcohol.

Source	Waste Generated	Readily Collectable
Agriculture		
Crops and food waste	390	22.6
Manure:		
Cattle	172.0	
Hogs	11.0	
Sheep	1.6	
Poultry	9.5	
	194.1	26.0
Urban		
Refuse	129	71.0
Municipal sewage solids	12	1.5
Industrial wastes	44	5.2
Logging and wood manufacturing	55	5.0
Miscellaneous	50	5.0
Total	874.1	136.3

TABLE VIII AMOUNTS (1 MILLION TONS) OF DRY, ASH-FREE ORGANIC WASTES PRODUCED IN THE UNITED STATES IN 1971. ADAPTED FROM REF. 20

Energy Plantations & High-Yield Biomass

One spin off from the "energy crisis" has been an interest in growing high-yielding plants in "energy plantations" and burning the biomass in conventional power plants to generate electricity. For example one proposal[22] describes how 100-650 square miles of rapidly growing trees could fuel a 1 million kilowatt electrical power plant. Another idea[23] calls for the growing of sea kelp in offshore waters of California and Peru in areas extensive enough to produce 1.8 billion dry tons of marine algae per year. This biomass would then be digested and converted to 12 trillion BTU of methane energy annually (17% of current U.S. demands).

According to proponents, the energy plantation has a few advantages over other sources of fuel[24,25]: 1) A favorable impact on our balance of payments and foreign relations (i.e., produced domestically). 2) A favorable impact on the environment (unlike strip mining and nuclear power plants). 3) Since biomass is low in sulfur it has an advantage over coal as a fuel. 4) Energy plantations generate a renewable supply of energy.

There are, however, major problems with the energy plantation concept: 1) It means that large land areas will be converted into single crop stands (monocultures) which are notoriously susceptible to disease and pest outbreaks. The ecological instability inherent in high-yield monocultures is rarely considered as part of the "cost" of large scale farming operations...whether they are producing for food or fuel. 2) It implies that large areas of land or offshore waters will be controlled by the limited interests of energy companies. 3) By centralizing energy production, the energy plantation perpetuates the need for elaborate transmission grids and tends to ignore the great potential of decentralized power generation, i.e., producing the energy where it is needed. 4) And finally, the idea of producing crops for anything but food is going to become increasingly difficult to justify in the years to come.

One interesting aspect of the energy plantation studies has been an evaluation of some high yielding plants that could conceivably be used as part of a local food/energy economy. According to Alich and Inman[25] the following land plants appear to have the most potential for biomass production (we have noted some additional advantages):

FORAGE GRASSES: Sudangrass (*Sorghum vulgare*); napiergrass (*Pennisetum purpureum*); silage corn (*Zea mays*); and forage sorghum (*Sorghum vulgare*). Sorghum is especially appealing since it is a perennial and can produce a ratoon crop (shoots from the roots of harvested plants). It is also generally more heat and drought resistant than corn and requires less water for normal growth.

KENAF (*Hibiscus cannabinus*): An annual plant of the Malvacea family with a stalk of 50% cellulose. Kenaf yields especially well when irrigated.

EUCALYPTUS: Native of Australia. One of the most productive trees in the world, *Eucalyptus* thrives under a variety of conditions, its flowers serve as an important source of nectar for honey bees, it sprouts profusely from cut stumps and it is very pest resistant.

SHORT ROTATION HARDWOODS: Several species of trees can be harvested at 1-3 year intervals in closely-spaced plantations. In this way the entire above ground portion of the tree can be used. In the case of many of the hardwoods, the young plants are able to regenerate themselves rapidly from the cut stump by sprouting (sycamore, poplar, sweetgum, ash) or by root sprouts (alder).

SUNFLOWER (*Helianthus annus*): There are several advantages to sunflowers: they are high-yielding, hardy and produce an edible seed that can also be extracted for its oil. The flowers seem to be a good refuge and food source (nectar and pollen) for a variety of beneficial insects (predators and parasites of crop pests). The stalks can be burned or used as silage. The Russians have succeeded in crossing the sunflower with the Jerusalem artichoke (*Helianthus tuberosus*) which produces large underground tubers that are good to eat.

In addition:

COMFREY (*Symphytum asperrimum*): A high-yielding perennial plant of the Borage family. Comfrey has one of the highest protein contents (21%) of any plant known. It is also one of the few plants that concentrates vitamin B-12. Its flowers are an important source of nectar, and its leaves have well known medicinal properties.

It is important to remember that the value of a plant is usually measured as a trade off between quality and quantity. For example, modern high yield grains are often low in protein content, susceptible to disease or reduced in some other *QUALITATIVE* way. The crops discussed above are no exception and they should always be grown with this trade off firmly in mind.

A few additional points: Solar Physical conversions (pyrolysis, solar cells, solar boilers, wind generators etc.) are several times more efficient at converting solar energy to organic fuels or electricity than are conversions which include photosynthesis as a part of the process. However, photosynthesis is, and is likely to remain, the <u>only</u> practical process by which solar energy can be converted into chemical energy. Only plants can produce carbon fuels without an expensive electrochemical process as part of the system.

The capacity and efficiency of biomass systems are limited, but within those limitations they are potentially the cheapest and wisest source of renewable chemical energy.

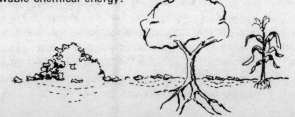

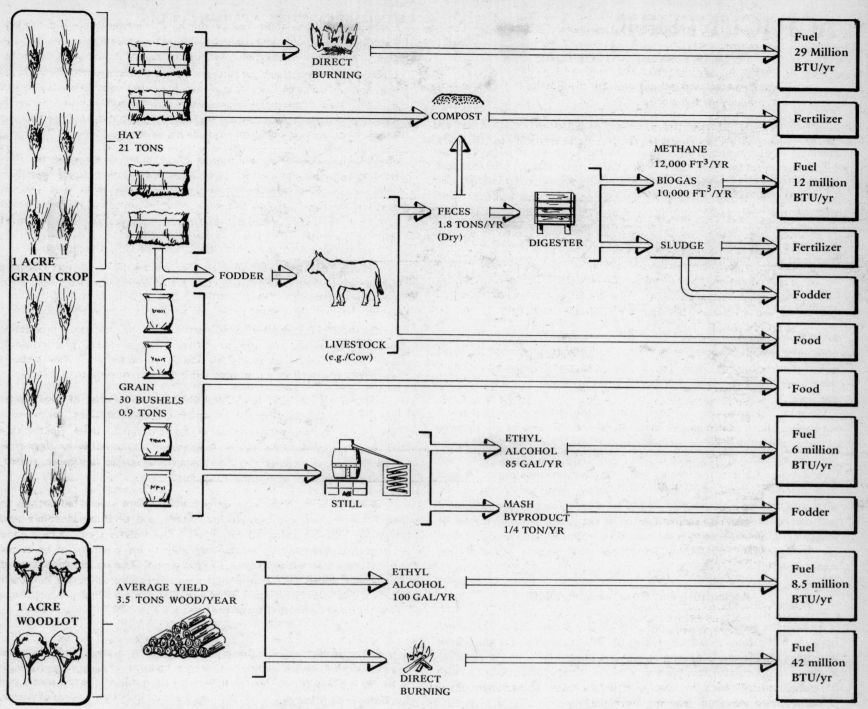

END PRODUCTS AND ROUGH ENERGY EQUIVALENTS OF VARIOUS BIOMASS CONVERSIONS FROM A 1 ACRE GRAIN FIELD AND WOODLOT.

References Cited:

[1]Golley, F.B. 1960. ENERGY DYNAMICS OF A FOOD CHAIN OF AN OLD-FIELD COMMUNITY. Ecol. Monogr. 30: 187-206.

[2]Love, M.L. 1970. THE RANGELANDS OF THE WESTERN UNITED STATES. "MAN AND THE ECOSPHERE" Sci. Amer., Feb., 1970.

[3]Rabinowitch, E. and Govindjee. 1969. PHOTOSYNTHESIS John Wiley, New York.

[4]Transeau, E.N. 1926. THE ACCUMULATION OF ENERGY BY PLANTS Ohio Journal of Science, 26:1-10.

[5]Slobodkin, L.B. 1962. ENERGY IN ANIMAL ECOLOGY. In: "Advances in Ecological Research", J.B. Cragg (ed.), Academic Press, New York.

[6]Kozlovsky, D.G. 1968. A CRITICAL EVALUATION OF THE TROPHIC LEVEL CONCEPT. I: ECOLOGICAL EFFICIENCIES. Ecology, 49:48-59.

[7]Lappe, F.M. 1971. DIET FOR A SMALL PLANET. Ballantine Books, Inc. New York.

[8]Odum, E.P. 1971. FUNDAMENTALS OF ECOLOGY. W.B. Saunders Co., Phil.

[9]Cohen, L.J. and J.F. Fernandes. 1968. THE HEAT VALUE OF REFUSE. Mech. Engin., Sept. 1968: 47-51.

[10]Fair, G.M. & E.W. Moore. 1932. HEAT AND ENERGY RELATIONS IN THE DIGESTION OF SEWAGE SOLIDS. I. THE FUEL VALUE OF SEWAGE SOLIDS. Sewage Works Journal, 4:242.

[11]Golley, F.B. 1961. ENERGY VALUES OF ECOLOGICAL MATERIALS. Ecology 43: 581-584.

[12]Merrill, A.L. and B.K. Watt. 1955. ENERGY VALUE OF FOODS---BASIS AND DERIVATION. USDA Handbook No. 74.

[13]Loomis, R.S. and W.A. Williams. 1963. MAXIMUM CROP PRODUCTIVITY: AN ESTIMATE. Crop Science, 3:67-72.

[14]Whittaker, R.H. 1970. COMMUNITIES AND ECOSYSTEMS. The Macmillan Co., Toronto.

[15]Rodin, L.E. and N.I. Bazilevich. 1965. PRODUCTION IN TERRESTRIAL VEGETATION. (ed., G.E. Fogg). Oliver and Boyd, London

[16]Ryther, J.H. 1963. GEOGRAPHIC VARIATION IN PRODUCTIVITY In: "The Sea", vol 2, M.M. Hill (ed.), Interscience, New York.

[17]Vallentyne, J.R. 1965. NET PRIMARY PRODUCTIVITY AND PHOTOSYNTHETIC EFFICIENCY IN THE BIOSPHERE. In: "Primary Productivity in Aquatic Environments". C.R. Goldman (ed.), Univ. Calif. Press, Berkeley.

[18]Westlake, D.F. 1963. COMPARISONS OF PLANT PRODUCTIVITY. Biol. Rev. 38: 385-425.

[19]Fogg, G.E. 1968. PHOTOSYNTHESIS. American Elsevier Publ. Co., Inc., N.Y. 116 pp.

[20]Anderson, L.L. 1972. ENERGY POTENTIAL FROM ORGANIC WASTES: A REVIEW OF THE QUANTITIES AND SOURCES. U.S. Dept. Inter., Bureau of Mines, Info. Circular 8549

[21]Cremtz, W.L. 1973. OIL FROM AGRICULTURAL WASTES. In: "Proceedings International Biomass Energy Conference. (SEE REVIEWS).

[22]Szego, G.C. and C.C. Kemp. 1973. ENERGY FORESTS AND FUEL PLANTATIONS. Chem. Tech., May 1973.

[23]Szetela, E.J. et al 1974. EVALUATION OF A MARINE ENERGY FARM CONCEPT. United Aircraft Research Labs. 400 Main St., Hartford, Conn., 06108.

[24]Szego, G.C. and C.C. Kemp. 1974. THE ENERGY PLANTATION. Inter-Technology Corp., P.O. Box 340, Warrenton, Va. 22186.

[25]Alich, J.A. and R.E. Inman. 1974. EFFECTIVE UTILIZATION OF SOLAR ENERGY TO PRODUCE CLEAN FUEL. Stanford Research Institute, National Science Foundation, "Research Applied to National Needs". NTIS, PB-233 956/2WE, $5.00.

AGRICULTURE

ENERGY AND AGRICULTURE

Richard Merrill

Agriculture is the means by which solar energy becomes our food energy. For thousands of years before farm machinery, pesticides, chemical fertilizers, etc., a great deal of human labor was required to grow food. But even in these "primitive" times more energy was available from the food than was required to grow it. Today, the tools of agriculture depend almost entirely on the high-energy inputs of fossil fuels (natural gas, petroleum, diesel, gasoline, LP gas, aviation fuel, etc.), and, the need for fossil fuels in agriculture is increasing every year. This is due not only to the demands of a rising population, but also to the demands of more sophisticated applications of power and chemicals to food production (Fig. 1). In fact we are rapidly approaching a time (some argue that we are already there) when more energy will be required to produce our food than is obtained from it.

What is not often appreciated is that an agriculture nurtured by a single non-renewable resource is not only extremely vulnerable, but also, eventually, non-renewable itself: "What happens to food costs as fossil fuels become scarcer?," and, indeed: "What happens to agriculture when the oil wells and gas fields run dry?" These are important questions for our times.

Looking back we can now see that for the last few generations we have simply been exchanging finite reserves of fossil fuels for our supplies of food and fibre. Obviously this trade-off can't continue indefinitely. Soon we will have little choice but to adopt farm technologies that use a diverse base of alternative energy supplies. These include organic wastes to supplement chemical fertilizers, renewable forms of energy (solar, wind, and organic fuels) to help supply rural power needs, and integrated pest control programs to reduce the use of pesticides. Without the use of solar/wind/biological energies as back-up systems in the production of our food, modern agriculture could very well become self-defeating rather than self sustaining.

Agriculture and Our Changing Diets

During the last two generations, the yields of most major U.S. crops have increased from 200-400% (Table I). The reason for this abundance is simple: intensive oil energy has replaced human labor as the principle input of crop production. Today virtually every phase of agriculture depends on fossil fuels in one form or another[1]. In fact agriculture consumes more petroleum than any other industry[2].

	1930	1940	1950	1960	1970
GRAINS:					
Rice	1.05	1.15	1.19	1.71	2.31
Corn	.57	.81	1.07	1.53	2.00
Sorghum	.30	.38	.63	1.11	1.42
Barley	.57	.55	.65	.74	1.02
Wheat	.42	.46	.50	.78	.93
Rye	.35	.35	.34	.55	.73
SUGAR BEETS	11.9	13.4	14.6	17.2	18.8
TOBACCO	.39	.52	.63	.85	1.06
SOYBEANS	.39	.49	.65	.71	.80

TABLE I.   AVERAGE YIELD OF U.S. MAJOR CROPS. VALUES GIVEN IN TONS (USDA Agricultural Statistics, 1971)

Some recent studies have examined the energy budget of various U.S. crops in an attempt to show patterns of energy consumption in agriculture. One way to do this is to add up the energy inputs involved in crop production (Fig. 2), and then to compare this total with the amount of energy provided by the yield of the crop. The ratio of yield energy to input energy (call it the "energy efficiency") is then used to reveal trends in the way energy is consumed in agriculture, or to compare the energy efficiencies of different crops.

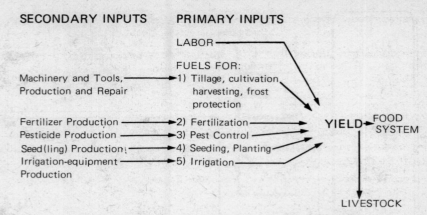

FIG. 2   MAJOR INPUTS OF ENERGY INTO AGRICULTURE.

Pimentel[3] measured the energy budget of the U.S. principal crop . . . corn. He showed that the energy efficiency has started to decline in recent years (Table II shows 3 of the 6 years measured). This alone has a profound effect on other food industries since corn supplies most of the livestock feed in this country. As the efficiency continues to decline, the price of meat will continue to rise.

Input	1945	1959	1970
Labor	12,500	7,600	4,900
Machinery	180,000	350,000	420,000
Gasoline	543,400	724,500	797,000
Nitrogen	58,800	344,400	940,800
Phosphorus	10,600	24,300	47,100
Potassium	5,200	36,500	63,000
Seeds for planting	34,000	60,400	68,000
Irrigation	19,000	31,000	34,000
Insecticides	0	7,700	11,000
Herbicides	0	2,800	11,000
Drying	10,000	100,000	120,000
Electricity	32,000	140,000	310,000
Transportation	20,000	60,000	70,000
TOTAL INPUTS	925,500	1,889,200	2,896,800
CORN YIELD (OUTPUT)	3,427,200	5,443,200	8,164,800
KCAL RETURN/INPUT KCAL	3.7	2.9	2.8

TABLE II.   ENERGY EFFICIENCIES OF U.S. CORN PRODUCTION PER ACRE. Data are in Kilocalories. After Pimentel et. al, 1973 (Ref. 3).

Another study[4] examined the energy budget of all major field crops, vegetables, fruits and livestock produced in California. Because California is by far the largest producer of farm products in the country, the study has broader significance.

There were two major results. First, there was an accounting of the energy consumed by the different fossil fuels and agricultural inputs (Table III). Natural gas accounted for 53% of all the energy consumed, followed by diesel fuel (18%). The production, distribution and application of fertilizer accounted for nearly 15% of the total energy inputs.

Fertilizer production is so heavily geared to fossil fuel inputs that prices can only rise with increasing prices of petroleum products. It takes 8 million kilocalories of energy to make one ton of ammonia fertilizer[10]. The cost of natural gas as a raw material (source of hydrogen) and fuel (to fix atmospheric nitrogen) accounts for 60% of the manufacturing costs of ammonia, and ammonia now supplies 90% of all fertilizer nitrogen.

A second result was a list of the energy efficiencies of different crops (Table IV). In terms of energy, grains are among the most efficient of crops to produce, processed raw foods are the least efficient and raw fruits and vegetables are intermediate. In general, raw fruits and vegetables seem to require about as much energy to grow as they provide. Similar results have been obtained for crops grown in England[5].

So despite the high yields of modern farm technology, there does not always appear to be an obvious net return of energy to society. The benefits of solar energy fixed in our foods are increasingly being offset by the subsidy of fossil fuel energy needed to produce them. In fact, as far as energy is concerned, our agriculture is far less efficient than other forms of agriculture using more labor and less technology[6-9].

| Category | Energy Source (In Millions of Units) | | | | | | Total |
	Natural Gas Therms	Electricity KWH	Diesel Fuel Gallon	Gasoline Gallon	LP Gas Propane Butane Gallon	Aviation Fuel Gallon	Million BBLS Crude Oil
Field crops	364.784	464.681	96.400	19.477	2.381	–	9.34
Vegetables	165.999	358.193	38.792	25.031	4.441	–	4.62
Fruits and nuts	127.168	410.773	26.158	12.602	3.296	–	3.39
Livestock	107.111	1,460.966	46.443	7.813	12.261	–	4.19
Irrigation	40.618	7,177.441	6.531	.487	4.521	–	5.16
Fertilizers	305.748	579.362	6.738	3.529	1.114	–	5.87
Frost protection		40.501	60.003	6.854	.904	–	1.63
Greenhouses	102.700	83.427	–	–	–	–	1.82
Agr. aircraft	–	–	1.072	1.607	–	8.994	0.25
Vehicles (farm use)	–	–	10.447	117.798	–	–	2.77
Others	–	–	–	–	23.711	–	0.39
TOTAL	1,214.128	10,575.344	292.584	195.198	52.629	8.994	
Equivalent (Million bbls crude oil)	20.93	6.21	7.06	4.17	0.86	0.19	39.43

TABLE III. FOSSIL FUEL REQUIREMENTS FOR DIFFERENT ASPECTS OF AGRICULTURE. Data are for California (1971), from Ref. 4.

Commodity	Crop Caloric Content (A) 1,000 kcal/ton	Fuel and Electrical Energy Input (B) 1,000 kcal/ton	A/B* (Efficiency)
Field Crops			
Barley	3,166.1	479.0	6.6
Beans (dry)	3,084.4	2,683.1	1.2
Corn	3,338.4	1,027.3	3.3
Rice	3,293.1	1,289.3	2.6
Sorghum, Grain	3,011.8	1,188.8	2.6
Sugar	3,492.6	6,654.2	.5
Wheat Flour	3,020.9	563.3	5.4
		Average	3.2
Raw Vegetables and Fruits			
Beans, Green	1,115.8	2,048.0	.5
Broccoli	290.3	1,178.6	.2
Carrots	381.0	359.8	1.1
Cauliflower	244.9	986.4	.2
Celery	154.2	351.5	.4
Lettuce	163.3	484.3	.3
Melons	235.9	636.6	.4
Onions	344.7	390.3	.9
Potatoes	689.5	325.4	2.1
Strawberries	335.6	727.6	.5
Tomatoes	199.6	262.2	.8
Apples	508.0	401.1	1.3
Apricots	462.6	840.4	.6
Grapefruit	371.9	1,165.5	.3
Grapes	607.8	576.9	1.1
Oranges	462.6	1,089.5	.4
Peaches	344.7	471.6	.7
Pears	553.3	964.2	.6
Plums	598.7	1,650.9	.4
		Average	.7
Canned Vegetables and Fruits			
Beans, Green	870.9	3,021.5	.3
Tomatoes	190.5	1,138.9	.2
Apples	371.9	1,397.8	.3
Grapefruit	272.2	1,797.7	.2
Grapes	462.7	1,115.3	.4
Pears	417.3	1,734.1	.7
		Average	.3
Frozen Vegetables and Fruits			
Beans, Green	925.3	2,856.1	.3
Broccoli	254.0	1,911.2	.1
Cauliflower	199.6	1,619.8	.1
		Average	.2
Dried Fruits and Nuts			
Almonds	5,424.9	7,086.7	.7
Prunes	3,120.7	4,447.1	.7
Walnuts	5,697.1	10,745.6	.5
		Average	.6

*A/B = RATIO OF: CALORIC CONTENT/FUEL AND ELECTRICAL ENERGY. (The larger the number, the greater the efficiency.)

TABLE IV. THE ENERGY EFFICIENCIES OF DIFFERENT CALIFORNIA CROPS (1972). From Cervinca et al. (Ref. 4).

There are strong implications in the fact that the principal raw material of agriculture is a dwindling resource. As oil prices go up, food prices go up. This applies especially to farm products that require heavy energy inputs like processed foods and animal protein. In fact meat may become so expensive in the future that it will be replaced by vegetable protein in the diets of many people; for many it already has. As pointed out in the *biomass* section, from 80-90% of the food-energy eaten by animals is lost as metabolic heat. This is why it takes so much more energy to produce animal protein than it does plant protein** (Fig. 3).

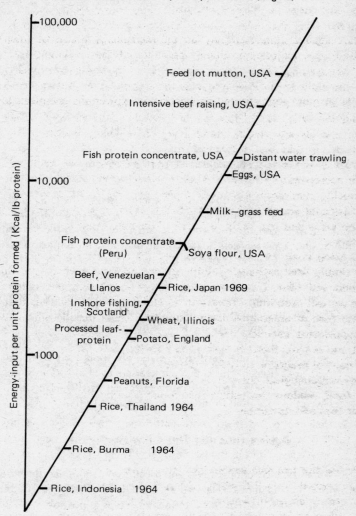

FIG. 3 TYPICAL ENERGY SUBSIDIES IN MODERN PROTEIN PRODUCTION. From Slesser (1973). Ref. 12.

It should not be inferred that because of the "energy crisis" we are all likely to become vegetarians. One of the hardest things for people to change is their diet. Furthermore, sources of good vegetable protein like soybeans and hard grains are also becoming hard to get as the United States implements its basic 1970's foreign policy of using domestic crops to reduce the balance of payments deficit and to barter for oil and natural gas on the foreign market. Inevitably, scarcities of fossil fuels (whether real or political) will lower the quality of food for most people, especially the poor...unless, of course, we begin producing some of our own food at the local level and with local resources.

The Food System and Our Changing Living Habits

Agriculture is just the starting point of a complex food industry that involves production, transportation, marketing, plus domestic storage and cooking. In 1963, food-related activities consumed about 12% of the total U.S. energy budget[13], or the equivalent of about 240 gallons of gasoline per person (Table V). Assuming that a well fed person eats about 1 million kilocalories of food energy per year (29 gallons of gasoline), we can see that the energy needed to put food on our table is nearly 8 times more

**In the U.S. it takes about 6500 kcal. to produce one pound of beef or about 38,000 kcal per pound of protein[11]. In contrast, one pound of corn (fed to the cattle) requires only 500-650 kcal to produce[3,4].

than the energy we get from our food. Or put another way, one actually eats 8 times more energy per day than is contained in the food eaten. If we considered all the energy lost in converting plants to animals; running vehicles; processing, cooking and storing food; etc., the figure would become even higher. *The further removed we are from our food sources, the more energy we consume when we eat.*

SOURCE	MILLION BTU'S	HEAT EQUIVALENT GALLON GASOLINE	% OF TOTAL
Agriculture	5.8	43.0	18
Food Processing	10.6	78.5	33
Transportation	0.9	6.7	3
Wholesale & Retail Trade	5.2	38.5	16
Domestic	9.9	73.3	30
Cooking	3.91		
Refrigeration, Freezing	4.61		
Appliance Production	.66		
Travel for Food	.72		
TOTAL	32.4 million BTU's per person per year	240 gal. gasoline	100.0%

TABLE V.   ENERGY REQUIREMENTS OF FOOD-RELATED ACTIVITIES IN THE UNITED STATES (1963). Adapted from Ref. 13.

A more detailed breakdown of the energy used in the U.S. food system is shown in Table VI. Both Tables V and VI reveal something interesting. About 1/3 of the energy that goes into providing us with food is consumed domestically. This suggests that a great deal can be done to change our habits and activities in order to deal with the increasing costs and declining quality of our food. A few suggestions:

1. Start a food garden; your own in your backyard, or a community project. In many U.S. cities, municipal and industrial land is being loaned for community gardens. When you grow your own food, use methods that don't require large inputs of fossil fuel energy (e.g., pesticides, chemical fertilizers, elaborate tools etc.) Over half of the pesticides used in the U.S. each year are used in and around cities[16], and each year people use more chemical fertilizers on their urban lawns than are used in the entire country of India.

2. Change your diet to more natural and raw foods, and less meat. This would reverse a trend in our diets that has been interrupted only a few times in the last 50 years (Table VII).

3. Organize food cooperatives and local food economies; develop urban/rural food alliances. Help to get food directly from nearby producer to consumer with as few intermediate steps as possible.

4. Support small independent and neighborhood food stores near to home. Support small farmers in their attempt to grow for markets in your area.

More and more pressure is being put on farmers to produce food for the demands of both a rising population and expanding global markets. The existence of large-consuming factory farms will probably be a part of our food system for some time to come whether they are fueled by oil or nuclear power. But it needn't be an either/or situation. Everywhere people want more control over their lives, institutions and resources. An agriculture using the resources and wastes of the surrounding region and producing for local markets is one of the most important ways that a society can provide for itself.

COMPONENT	1947	1958	1970	(1970) % of Total
On Farm				
Fuel (direct use)	136.0	179.0	232.0	
Electricity	32.0	44.0	63.8	
Fertilizer	19.5	32.2	94.0	
Agricultural steel	2.0	2.0	2.0	
Farm machinery	34.7	50.2	80.0	
Tractors	25.0	16.4	19.3	
Irrigation	22.8	32.5	35.0	
Subtotal	272.0	356.3	526.1	24.2
Processing Industry				
Food processing industry	177.5	212.6	308.0	
Food processing machinery	5.7	4.9	6.0	
Paper packaging	14.8	26.0	38.0	
Glass containers	25.7	30.2	47.0	
Steel cans and aluminum	55.8	85.4	122.0	
Transport (fuel)	86.1	140.2	246.9	
Trucks and trailers (manufacture)	42.0	43.0	74.0	
Subtotal	407.6	542.3	841.9	38.8
Commercial and Home				
Commercial refrigeration and cooking	141.0	176.0	263.0	
Refrigeration machinery (home and commercial)	24.0	29.4	61.0	
Home refrigeration and cooking	184.0	257.0	480.0	
Subtotal	349.0	462.4	804.0	37.0
Grand Total	1028.6	1361.0	2172.0	100.0

TABLE VI.   ENERGY USE IN THE U.S. FOOD SYSTEM. From Steinhart (1974), Ref. 14. Values: 10^{12} kcal.

	FRUITS		VEGETABLES			MEATS
	FRESH	PROCESSED	FRESH	PROCESSED		
				Canned	Frozen	
1920	130	17	196	18	—	160
1925	121	18	190	25	—	163
1930	119	19	197	28	—	153
1935	134	22	198	26	—	139
1940	138	34	198	34	.6	166
1945	133	34	217	43	1.9	178
1950	107	43	170	41	3.2	177
1955	95	49	155	42	5.9	192
1960	90	50	150	43	7.0	195
1965	80	48	141	47	8.0	204
1970	80	55	141	51	9.6	230

TABLE VII.   PER CAPITA CONSUMPTION OF FRESH AND PROCESSED FOODS IN THE U.S. (Retail-weight equivalent in pounds). U.S.D.A. Statistics (1971)

References Cited

[1] Perelman, M. 1972. FARMING WITH PETROLEUM. Environment 14:8-13.

[2] Committee on Agriculture, House of Representatives. 1971. FOOD COSTS... FARM PRICES: A COMPILATION OF INFORMATION RELATING TO AGRICULTURE. 92nd Congress, 1st Session, Washington D.C.

[3] Pimentel, D., et al. 1973. FOOD PRODUCTION AND THE ENERGY CRISIS. Science, 182:443-449.

[4] Cervinka, V., W.J. Chancellor, R.J. Coffelt, R.G. Curley and J.B. Dobie. 1974. ENERGY REQUIREMENTS FOR AGRICULTURE IN CALIFORNIA, California Department of Food and Agriculture, Sacramento, Calif. (with University of California, Davis.)

[5] Blaxter, K. 1974. POWER AND AGRICULTURAL REVOLUTION. New Scientist 61 (885): 400-403.

[6] Black, J.N. 1971. ENERGY RELATIONS IN CROP PRODUCTION—A PRELIMINARY SURVEY. Annals Appl. Biol. 67(2): 272-278.

[7] Rappaport, R. 1971. THE FLOW OF ENERGY IN AN AGRICULTURAL SOCIETY. Sci. Amer. 225: 117-132.

[8] Cottrell, F. 1955. ENERGY AND SOCIETY. McGraw-Hill, New York.

[9] Heichel, G.H. 1973. COMPARATIVE EFFICIENCY OF ENERGY USE IN CROP PRODUCTION. Conn. Agric. Exp. Sta., Bulletin 739, New Haven.

[10] Muller, R.G. 1971. AMMONIA, PROCESS ECONOMICS. Program Report, no. 44, Stanford Research Institute.

[11] Slesser, M. 1973. ENERGY ANALYSIS IN POLICY MAKING. New Scientist, 60 (870): 328:330, 1 Nov., 1973.

[12] Slesser, M. 1973. HOW MANY CAN WE FEED? Ecologist, 3(6): 216-220.

[13] Hirst, Eric. 1973. ENERGY USE FOR FOOD IN THE UNITED STATES, Natural Science Foundation Environmental Program, Oak Ridge, Tenn. Gov. Printing Office.

[14] Steinhart, J.S. and C.E. Steinhart. 1974. ENERGY USE IN THE U. S. FOOD SYSTEM. Science, 184: 307-316.

[15] Merrill, R. 1974. TOWARDS A SELF-SUSTAINING AGRICULTURE. In: "Radical Agriculture", Harper and Row (In Press).

[16] Environmental Protection Agency. 1972. THE USE OF PESTICIDES IN SUB-URBAN HOMES AND GARDENS, AND THEIR IMPACT ON THE AQUATIC ENVIRONMENT. EPA/ Gov. Print. Office, Washington D.C.

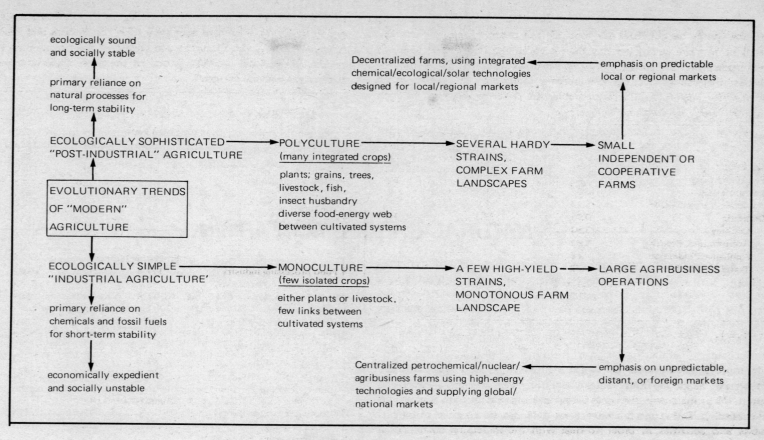

COURSES FOR FUTURE AGRICULTURES

AGRICULTURE: REVIEWS AND INFORMATION

The agriculture review section is divided into the following parts: FOOD AND PEOPLE; NATURAL GARDENING AND FARMING; SOILS AND SOIL FERTILITY; CROP ECOLOGY; NATURAL PEST MANAGEMENT; MIXED CROPS AND COMPANION

PLANTING; PROPAGATION. No attempt is made to discuss any of these subjects in detail, but only to present an overview and list some of the groups/articles/books where details can be found.

FOOD AND PEOPLE

*The world can provide for every man's need
But not for every man's greed.*

—Gandhi

Millions are starving in the Third World, and at home the time approaches when it will be cheaper to eat oil than food. Meanwhile about all we can do is move further down the food chain and do what we can to right the imbalance of food and people.

The following are a few of the many, many items written recently about food and people:

The Borgstrom Triad: All written by Georg Borgstrom and published by Macmillan Co., New York.

HUNGRY PLANET (1965, revised 1972). Overview of the balance between people and food.

TOO MANY (1969). Concentrates on the biological constraints facing human society in quest for food.

FOCAL POINT: A GLOBAL FOOD STRATEGY (1971). Focuses on six starving areas of the world: Mexico, Java, Egypt, the Caribbean (yes, the Caribbean), Pakistan, and Bangladesh. Concludes that UN rhetoric can't be eaten. Meanwhile, the U.S. continues to take 95% of Mexico's shrimp harvest. Borgstrom cites three areas as possible world food bastions . . . New Zealand, Canada and Argentina. Good ideas about better food storage and distribution (and not JUST yield), more rational settlement patterns and internationalization of the seas. But his ideas about compulsory birth control on a global scale still seem hard to swallow.

Lappe, Frances. 1971. **DIET FOR A SMALL PLANET.** Ballantine Books, New York. 301 pp. $1.50. Now in its 14th printing, the first rational outline for high protein meatless cooking. Charts, facts and recipes.

Brown, Lester. 1974. **THE NEXT CRISIS? FOOD.** Foreign Policy, No. 13, Winter 73-74. 333 pp. Good overview of world food problem. Some paraphrased comments on ways to relieve the stress:

1) Poor nations deserve special rights of access to food supplies. . . Financial aid will be necessary to enable poor nations to maintain minimum reserve stocks. . .

The U.S. must devise new food aid legislation which ensures that needed levels of food aid are available to needy countries whether or not commercial surpluses exist at the time. 2) Creation of an internationally-managed world food reserve; either a centrally-managed food bank or the FAO plan of coordinated national reserve policies proposed in 1973. 3) Slowing population growth. 4) Support of agriculture in food-short countries that gives special attention to the role of small farms. . . There is growing evidence that in many developing countries . . . small farmers, at least those with tools, health and education . . . engage in more intensive cultivation and generally average considerably higher yields per acre than do large farmers . . . The United States would be wise to help build an atmosphere of international cooperation rather than conflict and competition in an area in which we, more than any other nation, hold the key to a more stable and equitable world system—the world food market.

Ehrlich, A. and P.R. Ehrlich. 1974. **FOOD.** The CoEvolution Quarterly. Summer, 1974. pp. 21-40. (Box 428, Sausalito, Calif.) Another overview, but with lower-level conclusions. To wit:

Suppose all efforts to help the United States cope with a world of scarcity prove futile, and severe food shortages, along with other disruptions, develop. To prepare for this contingency, not all of your efforts at changing the future should be invested in social and political action; you should also be taking steps beforehand to reduce your dependence on the services provided by our complex society. One side of the coin of self-sufficiency is to be prepared for the unexpected. Americans tend not to believe in disasters, natural or otherwise. Consequently, they are forever being caught by surprise—and usually quite unprepared.

Obviously, one key to self-sufficiency is to have supplies on hand of everything you need to survive. There is no need to engage in panic buying whenever scarcity is forecast. If you hear that a bread shortage is coming next week, we don't recommend rushing to the store to buy ten loaves. We hope, rather, that you already have enough flour, yeast and powdered milk in your pantry to make your own bread, if necessary. Remember the great toilet paper panic?

If you have any storage facilities at all—a reasonably dry basement is ideal, but even a small closet can hold a surprising amount—you can gradually accumulate and put by enough food and supplies to tide your family over for a period of time during an emergency or to compensate for shortages. The Mormons as a regular practice keep enough supplies on hand for a year. This may not be practical for you, but enough food and water to survive for two to four weeks, plus emergency light and heat sources are within the reach of all but the poorest. Moreover, buying ahead is a hedge against inflation.

Food stores can be built up gradually by buying perhaps ten or twenty per cent more than you need each time you visit the supermarket. If you plan carefully, most of the food can be used up and replaced as part of your regular consumption, thus avoiding overlong storage. Canned and even dehydrated foods deteriorate over time, so it is wise to date everything, even cans, as you buy. As much as possible, you should try to store foods that your family now likes and eats often. If they don't like a food now, they won't like it any better in an emergency, even if nothing else is available.

For what length of time you should prepare to be self-sufficient is up to you. The time will, of course, be dictated by such factors as your life-style, where you live, the storage capacity of your home, and what you can afford. Arranging to be independent for a week is relatively easy; storing up supplies for a year is much harder. You will have to decide for yourself what sort of emergencies you are most likely to have to face and make your plans accordingly. Planning for self-sufficiency may seem in some ways disloyal to the rest of society. But in times of serious trouble, how society survives will in large measure depend on how well its individual people can take care of themselves.

We would only add that you also try growing some of your own food wherever and whenever possible. Buying processed foods for times of emergency is not self-sufficiency. It is survival at the expense of energy outside your sphere.

NATURAL GARDENING/FARMING

Just as a grassland matures into a forest, a garden or field of crops matures in its own way through the years. When crops are first planted in a new area, especially if it has been fallow for a while, soil nutrients are often out of balance, weed seeds are plentiful, and local pests are apt to cause problems until you get to know their life histories. However, with each passing year, soils become richer and cleaner and the local environment becomes a familiar backdrop to the dynamics of the field or garden.

It's during the first year or two of a garden that people generally get discouraged. Weeds and bugs can take over quickly in an "immature" piece of land. Also, there is a tendency for people who are just starting out to celebrate the planting and the harvest, but to ignore the vital tasks of maintenance in between. A food-garden should be viewed as a dynamic habitat which, if given steady (not necessarily heavy) attention, will mature through the seasons. That is, it will return more and more food relative to the labor needed to produce it.

There are three parts to a self-renewing garden scene: soil fertilization, pest management, and crop propagation. Natural fertilizers (compost, green manures, rock minerals, etc.) are discussed in virtually every organic gardening book. Natural pest management is described to some degree in most of the books. But the practical aspects of plant propagation seem to be left to speciality books, most of which are out of print (see page 127 of the *Primer*). We are told how to compost and get rid of aphids, but not how to breed locally adapted varieties of crops. This seems to be the weak link in any really complete natural gardening book. This is why we have placed so much emphasis on the subject of propagation in this section.

Scores of books have been written about organic/bio-dynamic/ecological gardening and farming techniques, philosophies, and experiences. They all have one thing in common: they are general. No book can give you all the answers . . . unless of course you write it yourself for your own backyard, vacant lot or field. Ideally each region, community or city should have its own reference book for food production that describes local conditions of climate, pests, soils, adapted crop varieties, sources of organic materials, etc. In the meantime, maybe some of the books listed below will help things get started. Whenever possible, we have grouped or keyed the references according to whether they are advanced, technical, and esoteric (A); popularized material with technical support (B); or simple and elementary (C). We have listed important books that are out of print (OOP) in the hope that pressure will be brought to bear to bring them back. Other reference keys: Government Printing Office (GPO); National Technical Information Service, Springfield, Va. (NTIS).
—R.M.

General Ecology

Kormondy, E.J. 1969. CONCEPTS OF ECOLOGY. Prentice-Hall, Inc. Englewood Cliffs, N. J., 209 pp. (C)
MacFadyen, A. 1957. ANIMAL ECOLOGY. Isaac Pitman & Sons Ltd., London. 344 pp. (B) A simple ecology text by a soil biologist.
Odum, E.P. FUNDAMENTALS OF ECOLOGY. W.B. Saunders Co., Philadelphia, 574 pp. (B) One of the best ecology textbooks, from populations to ecosystems, natural to cultivated situations.
Whittaker, R.H. 1970. COMMUNITIES AND ECOSYSTEMS. Macmillan Co., N. Y., 162 pp. (B)

Gardening

Darlington, J. 1970. GROW YOUR OWN. Bookworks, Berkeley, Calif. 87 pp. (C) Very simple introduction to backyard organic gardening.
Foster, C.F. 1972. THE ORGANIC GARDENER. Vintage Books, N. Y. 234 pp. (C) Forty-three years of experience and advice. Good drawings, references, and some great ideas.
Heckel, A. (ed.). 1967. PFEIFFER GARDEN BOOK. Bio-Dynamic Farming and Gardening Assoc., Stroudberg, Pa. 200 pp. (C) Classic introduction to backyard bio-dynamic gardening.
Kramer, J. 1972. THE NATURAL WAY TO PEST-FREE GARDENING. Charles Scribner's Sons, N. Y. 118 pp. (C) Well-balanced between pest control and soil fertility. Talks more about the why and what than the how. Good list of organic merchants nationwide.
O'Brien, R. Dalziel, 1956. INTENSIVE GARDENING. Latimer Trend & Co., Plymouth. 183 pp. Details of labor intensive cultivation of organic vegetables. Quite a different approach than HOW TO GROW . . .
Ogden, S. 1971. STEP-BY-STEP TO ORGANIC VEGETABLE GROWING. Rodale Press, Emmaus, Pa. 182 pp.(C) A very good "how-to" book of one organic grower's methods.
Philbrick, J. & H. 1971. GARDENING FOR HEALTH AND NUTRITION. Steiner Publications, Blauvelt, N. Y. 93 pp. (C) The most succinct introduction to bio-dynamic gardening.
Rodale, R. (ed.). 1971. THE BASIC BOOK OF ORGANIC GARDENING. Ballantine Books, N. Y. A more concise version of earlier books. A very good introduction.
Rodale, J.I. (ed.). 1961. HOW TO GROW VEGETABLES AND FRUITS BY THE ORGANIC METHOD. Rodale Press, Emmaus, Pa. A classic reference book of organic technique. Mostly testimonials that seem relevant to Eastern U.S. But for first approximations it is quite valuable.
Rodale, J.I. (ed.). 1959. THE ENCYCLOPEDIA OF ORGANIC GARDENING. Rodale Press, Emmaus, Pa. A book can be judged by how often it's used. This book gets used an awful lot. Outdated in the area of natural pest control, but a valuable reference book.
Rodale, J.I. 1945. PAY DIRT. Rodale Press, Emmaus, Pa. 245 pp. Rodale's first and perhaps best book. Now in its 14th printing.
Sunset Books. 1967. SUNSET WESTERN GARDENING BOOK. Lane Books, Menlo Park, Calif. 449 pp. East or West, this is the most useful book we have found for everyday gardening advice. Beautifully organized, cross-referenced in encyclopedic fashion. The growing zone maps for the Western states ought to be expanded for the entire U.S. (Non-organic).
Sunset Books. 1971. GUIDE TO ORGANIC GARDENING. Lane Books, Menlo Park, Calif. 72 pp. An excellent PRACTICAL guide to methods and tools.
Tyler, H. 1972. ORGANIC GARDENING WITHOUT POISONS. Simon and Schuster, N. Y. 224 pp. Good photos, well rounded between soil fertility and pest control.

Farming

Allen, F. 1971. MAKING A GO OF ORGANIC FARMING: SOME COMMERCIAL CONSIDERATIONS. Rodale Press, Emmaus, Pa. 28 pp. $0.50.
Bromfield, L. 1947. MALABAR FARM. Ballantine Books, N. Y. 470 pp. (C) The first book to read if you want to run a farm without chemicals and with the cycles of life. A personal account.
Corley, H. 1967. ORGANIC FARMING. Faber and Faber. London. 200 pp. (B) Biography describing experiences on 185 acre farm in the upper Thames Valley. Good composting information.
Hainsworth, P. 1954. AGRICULTURE: A NEW APPROACH. Faber & Faber, Ltd., London. 248 pp. (B) One of the best sources for documenting the validity of organic farming techniques. Evidence culled from many places.
Howard, A. 1947. THE SOIL AND HEALTH: A STUDY OF ORGANIC AGRICULTURE. Devin-Adair (now Schocken Books, N. Y., 1972). 307 pp. (C) A classic overview by a pioneer in organic soil fertility. Good practical stuff from years of experience, but the other half of the problem (pests) is taken too lightly.
King, F.H. 1911. FARMERS OF 40 CENTURIES: PERMANENT AGRICULTURE IN CHINA, KOREA AND JAPAN. Rodale Press, Emmaus, Pa. 441 pp. (C) $7.95. Classic treatise of aboriginal farming in the Far East. Organic recycling at the epitome of cultural developmment. Valuable photos of early rural China.
Pfeiffer, E. 1940. BIO-DYNAMIC FARMING AND GARDENING. Anthroposophic Press, N. Y. 240 pp. (C) THE introduction to bio-dynamic farming techniques.
Steffen, R. et al. 1972. ORGANIC FARMING: METHODS AND MARKETS. Rodale Press, Emmaus, Pa. 124 pp. Testimonials of organic farmers, some techniques, marketing problems, directory of organic farmers in U.S. Superficial but handy.

OUT OF PRINTS TO BRING BACK

Sykes, Friend. 1949. HUMUS AND THE FARMER. Rodale Press. Emmaus, Pa. 392 pp. (B) (OOP)

Sykes, Friend. 1959. MODERN HUMUS FARMING. Faber & Faber Ltd., London. 270 pp. (B)

Turner, Newman. 1955. FERTILITY PASTURES AND FERTILITY ACRES. Faber & Faber. London. 39 pp. (OOP) The herbal ley (pasture) as the basis of soil fertility. Valuable stuff for the beginning farmer. It should be reprinted.

Turner, N. 1951. FERTILITY FARMING. Faber & Faber, Ltd. (24 Russell Square), London. 264 pp. (OOP)

U.S. Dept. Agriculture. 1938. SOILS AND MAN. USDA Yearbook for 1938. (GPO) (OOP) After the dustbowl of the mid-thirties, the USDA sent scientists and technicians into rural America. A survey in 1934 of 2 million acres was taken with regards to erosion, soil fertility depletion, etc. The results of the survey are published as the yearbook. Most of the book emphasizes organic materials and methods. This book is absolutely essential for the serious organic agriculturist. It is without equal in its depth of treatment and source of data. Write the USDA and demand that it be reprinted.

Groups and Periodicals

ACRES, USA. monthly newspaper, 10227 East 61st St., Raytown, Mo. 64133 ($5.00/yr). The only practical organic farming periodical in this country. It is geared to midwest conditions, but has valuable information for everyone. Articles, organic merchants, and most important, a political base for what the movement is all about. Highly recommended.

BIO-DYNAMIC AGRICULTURAL ASSOCIATION, Broome Farm, Clent, Stourbridge, Worcs. England. English equivalent of the U.S. Bio-Dynamic Association. Bi-annual magazine (STAR AND FURROW), lending library, and advice. Membership for U.S. is £ 2.00/yr.

BIO-DYNAMIC FARMING AND GARDENING ASSOCIATION. R. D. 1, Stroudsburg, Pa. 18360. Numerous publications including BIO-DYNAMIC QUARTERLY ($4.00/year). Write for list.

GARDEN WAY PUBLISHING COMPANY, Charlotte, Vt. 05445, phone (802) 425-2171. Garden Way has been around for some time. Their publications are some of the most practical survival and how-to manuals around. At the present they are expanding into small scale machinery and alternative energy devices. Great people to deal with. Write and ask for their doings. Also ask about their soil testing program.

HENRY DOUBLEDAY RESEARCH ASSOCIATION, Bocking, Braintree, Essex, England. Newsletter and publication upon request. As they call it: "the keenest, most practical and helpful compost-gardener's association in the world." Seeing some of their information and newsletters, they seem to come as close as any to practical, non-mystifying information.

INTERNATIONAL FEDERATION OF ORGANIC AGRICULTURE MOVEMENTS (IFOAM), "Nature et Progres", 3 chemin de la Bergerie, 91700 Ste-Genevieve-des-Bois, France. Putting together a network of information for and of organic farming movements and groups throughout the world.

NATURAL ORGANIC FARMERS ASSOCIATION. RFD 1, Plainfield, Vt. 05667. Membership is $10.00/year. They have a newsletter and would probably be into giving advice on problems of farming, marketing, food, etc. Give and you shall receive.

ORGANIC GARDENING AND FARMING MAGAZINE, Rodale Press, Emmaus, Pa. 18049 (monthly, $5.85/year). "O. G." has been around since 1942. The magazine is only part of the Rodale Press which publishes numerous books and articles on food, health, gardening and other self-sufficient spin-offs. The name of the game for them is information and for this they are top rate.

OZARK ACCESS CATALOG, Box 506, Eureka Springs, Ark. 72632. $5.00/yr. Practical information on gardening, house building and other survival things.

RURAL RESOURCES AND INFORMATION, P. O. Box 684, Toppenish, Washington 98948. A loose and easy regional newsletter with something for everyone. They ask for donations instead of subscriptions. That usually doesn't last long. Write to them. They started out well.

SCIENTIFIC HORTICULTURE. Journal of the Horticultural Education Association. Birkbeck College, Malet St., London WC1E 7AX. £3.50/year once per year. Two to three hundred page journal on technical/ecological aspects of gardening and small farming methods, usually organic.

THE SMALLHOLDER. (An exchange of ideas and information of interest to country people living in Canada west of the Rocky Mountains). $3.00/year for 12 issues. Good stuff even if you live east of the Rockies.

THE SOIL ASSOCIATION. Walnut Tree Manor, Haughley, Stowmart, Suffolk, England IP 14 235. Founded in 1946 to promote organic husbandry. The "Haughley Experiments" (now run by Pye Institute) are the longest running organic farming experiments around. They publish a bi-monthly magazine sent free to members ($12.00/year).

HOW TO GROW MORE VEGETABLES

An excellent "how-to" book for growing a great deal of food in a very small area, while conserving resources and water. The method combines two European horticultures: biodynamic techniques, developed in Europe in the 1920's; and French Intensive techniques begun in the 1890's outside Paris. The biodynamics contributes raised beds, companion planting and organic manures. The French Intensive contributes close-spacing techniques which reduce weeds and hold water.

It's easy to get impatient with this method . . . it is *labor* intensive. But as you gradually work your soil for a few seasons, it just gets easier and easier, and the results can be rather amazing. The book gives step-by-step details, and the best 'moon planting' description I've seen. The section on companion planting is a rehash of old stuff and should be updated.

If you have a small plot of land, and a reasonable amount of labor, this book and this method will be a valuable tool for you.

P.S. *Also available:* Preliminary Research Report on 1972 yeilds at Ecology Action Test Garden, mini-farm economic potentials, and some world wide implications. 22 p. $2.00. *In preparation:* Research Report on 1973 and 1974 results.

—R. M.

How to Grow More Vegetables . . .
(than you ever thought possible on less land than you can imagine)

John Jeavons
1974; 82 pp.

$4.00

from:
Ecology Action of the Midpeninsula
2225 El Camino Real
Palo Alto, Calif. 94306

SOILS: BIOLOGY AND FERTILITY

Soil Fundamentals

Soil is perhaps the most complex ecosystem in the biosphere. In many ways, less is known about it than the surface of the moon. Soil consists of both the living and the dead, the geological and the biological. Microbes, animals, minerals, water, and gases all interact in a dynamic balance of life and death. The soil isn't just a medium for holding plants upright. It's also a habitat for many living things, whose related activities feed the plants. And it is this biological energy in the soil that can be tapped to fertilize crops and give us food.

Some of the larger soil animals are familiar: insect larvae, earthworms, etc. are worm shaped or otherwise equipped for burrowing. Other animals like sow bugs and ground beetles live on top of the soil under refuges.

Far richer in species and numbers are the microbes that don't have to make their spaces, but which live in the tiny pores between bits of soil. Although they escape our eyes, soil microbes —algae, fungi, and bacteria— make up the bulk of living matter and form the energy foundation upon which all other members of the soil community ultimately depend. Most soil microbes live inside other animals or in the film of moisture that lines the hollows of the soil.

Soil is the product of two processes: the decomposition of rock (biological and by natural weathering) and the decay of plant and animal life. The combination of these processes determines the ability of soils to support plant life. As organic matter decays, it gives off acids that release nutrients held in a complex form in rock minerals (mostly clay). This is why the best natural fertilizer is a combination of manure or compost and finely ground rock mineral fertilizers (limestone, dolomite, rock phosphate, rock granite, etc.). As usual, the geological and the biological form the optimum symbiosis.

The formation of *humus* is the most important component of soil fertility. The process begins with large soil animals eating decaying organic debris that has been partly broken down by certain bacteria. Other kinds of bacteria continue the breakdown in the intestines of the soil animals. As the excretion of the large soil animals are eaten by smaller animals, it becomes progressively finer and richer in nutrients that plants can take up through their roots. This "soil manure" is called *humus*. Just as cows give manure from plants they eat, so soil animals give manure *(humus)* from the soil's organic matter that they eat.

Humus serves a variety of purposes in the soil: 1) It provides nutrients. 2) It helps to release nutrients from rock materials. 3) It holds water in the soil. 4) It stimulates beneficial soil fungi such as *mycorrhiza* (symbiotic root fungi) and predatory forms that prey on the nematodes. 5) Decaying organic matter releases carbon dioxide that can be used by plants during photosynthesis. 6) It provides trace minerals typically lacking in chemical fertilizers. Trace minerals (e.g., boron, manganese, copper, cobalt) are the building blocks of enzymes and vitamins that help plants to resist disease. 7) To some degree (and there is controversy here) humus provides antibiotics to plants that also help them to resist disease. All of these processes operating in concert from the one main source . . . humus . . . serve to promote a healthy soil and healthy plants.

Humus can be made by gathering up local organic wastes into "compost piles" and letting the materials decay into humus. By putting the pile together carefully and with attention to detail, a rich fertilizer and soil conditioner can be produced.

The increasing cost of chemical fertilizers has placed a premium on organic wastes in rural areas. Where livestock operations used to give manure away, now they are selling it. However, in the cities, organic residues are still considered a waste rather than a resource. Go to your local dump and watch it being thrown away . . . by the ton! About 30% of all the solid waste generated in the home is capable of being composted. Unfortunately most of this still goes down garbage disposals or into trash cans. This is too bad, because there is plenty of good information available about ways to fertilize with local organic wastes. It only takes a little time and change of habit.

—R.M.

BEGINNING BOOKS

Farb, Peter. 1959. LIVING EARTH. Harper & Row, N. Y. 178 pp. Simple introduction to the ecology of the soil.

Kohnke, H. 1966. SOIL SCIENCE SIMPLIFIED. Balt Publ. Lafayette, Indiana. 77 pp.

Kuhnelt, W. 1961. SOIL BIOLOGY. Rodale Press, Emmaus, Pa. 397 pp. Draws on work mostly from European soils, but still very good for general descriptions of soil properties and adaptations of soil animals. Good bibliography.

Ortloff, H. and H.B. Raymore. 1972. A BOOK ABOUT SOILS FOR THE HOME GARDENER. William Morrow & Co., Inc., N. Y. 189 pp.

Russell, E.J. 1957. THE WORLD OF SOIL. Fontana, c/o Watts, Franklin, Inc., N. Y. 237 pp. Clear and smooth descriptions by an expert.

Russell, E.J. 1950. LESSONS ON SOIL. Cambridge Univ. Press, Cambridge. 133 pp. Great learning guide . . . for schools, for anyone.

Schaller, F. 1968. SOIL ANIMALS. Univ. Mich. Press, Ann Arbor. 145 pp. Brief outline of soil ecosystems, emphasizes larger soil animals. Introductory.

Schatz, A. 1972. TEACHING SCIENCE WITH SOIL. Rodale Press, Emmaus, Pa. 133 pp.

INTERMEDIATE BOOKS

Albrecht, W. A. 1958. SOIL FERTILITY AND ANIMAL HEALTH. Fred Hahue Printing Co., Webster, Iowa. 232 pp. A vital book on soil fertility, livestock health, and human disease.

Balfour, E. B. 1950. THE LIVING SOIL. Devin-Adair, N. Y. 270 pp. One of the first to document organic technique with research evidence (albeit weak). A classic in soil biology/fertility relationships.

Bridges, E.M. 1970. WORLD SOILS. University Press, Cambridge. 89 pp. Patterns of soils in the world. Superb color plates of soil profiles.

Buckman, H.O. and N.C. Brady. 1974. THE NATURE AND PROPERTIES OF SOILS. Macmillan Co., N. Y. 639 pp. Best college text on soils. It even has "humus" in the index.

Davies, Nancy et al. 1973. SOIL ECOLOGY. Prentice-Hall, Englewood Cliffs, New Jersey. 197 pp. Learning ecology through the soil. Textbookish, but simple . . . top rate.

Eyre, S.R. 1963. VEGETATION AND SOILS. Aldine Publishing Co., Chicago. 328 pp. How plants effect soils and human settlements and vice versa.

Garrett, S. 1963. SOIL FUNGI AND SOIL FERTILITY. The Macmillan Co., N. Y. 165 pp. Overview by an expert.

Jackson, R.M. and F. Raw. 1966. LIFE IN THE SOIL. St. Martin's Press, N. Y. 59 pp. Authors from Rothamsted discuss soil ecology and ways of studying it. Good stuff.

Parkinson, D. et al. 1971. METHODS FOR STUDYING THE ECOLOGY OF SOIL MICRO-ORGANISMS. IBP Handbook No. 19, Blackwell Scientific Publ., Oxford. 116 pp.

Rodale, R. (ed.). 1961. THE CHALLENGE OF EARTHWORM RESEARCH. Soil and Health Found., Emmaus, Pa. 102 pp. Modern research on earthworm ecology. Top bibliography.

Russell, E. and J. Russell. 1961. SOIL CONDITIONS AND PLANT GROWTH. John Wiley & Sons, Ltd. N.Y. 688 pp. First published in 1912, now nine editions later it is still a classic.

U.S. Dept. of Agriculture. 1957. SOILS. USDA Yearbook, 1957. Gov. Printing Office, Washington D.C.

Waksman, S.A. 1952. SOIL MICROBIOLOGY. John Wiley & Sons, Inc., N. Y. 356 pp. (OOP) Classic textbook still of MUCH value.

ADVANCED BOOKS

Burges, A. 1958. MICRO-ORGANISMS IN THE SOIL. Hutchinson, London. More recent and ecologically oriented than Waksman's SOIL MICROBIOLOGY.

Doekson, J. and J. van der Drift (ed.). 1963. SOIL ORGANISMS. North Holland Publ. Co., Amsterdam. Current research on the biology and ecology of soil life and ecosystems.

Gray, T. and S. Williams. 1971. SOIL MICROORGANISMS. Hafner Publ. Co., N. Y. 240 pp.

Gray, T. and D. Parkinson (ed.). 1968. THE ECOLOGY OF SOIL BACTERIA. Univ. Toronto Press, Canada. Anthology of technical papers.

Harley, J. 1959. THE BIOLOGY OF MYCORRHIZA. Leonard Hill, London. 233 pp. A bit out of date, but lays out the biology of beneficial root fungi.

Krasil'nikov, N.A. 1958. SOIL MICRO-ORGANISMS AND HIGHER PLANTS. NTIS, Washington D. C. 474 pp. $4.75. English translation of Russian works in soil science; top rate for relations between soil microbes and higher plants.

McLaren, A. and G. Peterson. 1967. SOIL BIOCHEMISTRY. Edward Arnold, London. 509 pp.

Parkinson, D. and J. Waid (ed.). 1960. THE ECOLOGY OF SOIL FUNGI. Liverpool Univ. Press, England. 324 pp. Technical anthology. Good on mycorrhiza.

Pauli, F. 1967. SOIL FERTILITY: A BIODYNAMIC APPROACH. Adam Hilger, London. 204 pp. Semi-technical book for soil researchers. Humus can be studied in the context of science as a whole.

Humus and Soil Fertility

Allison, F. E. 1973. SOIL ORGANIC MATTER AND ITS ROLE IN CROP PRO—DUCTION. Elsevier Scientific Publishing Co., New York. $52.00. Author from the USDA. Good up-to-date overview of organic farming methods. A bit hard on the organic approach in general. Outrageous price.

Kononova, M.M. 1961. SOIL ORGANIC MATTER: ITS NATURE, ITS ROLE IN SOIL FORMATION AND IN SOIL FERTILITY. (Second English Ed.), Pergamon Press, New York. 544 pp. (A) A technical bible of Russian humus science.

Waksman, S.A. 1938. HUMUS. Williams & Williams Co., Baltimore. 526 pp. (OOP) (B). Definitive up to its time. No popular sequel yet.

Composting

Billington, F.H. 1955. COMPOST FOR GARDEN PLOT OR THOUSAND-ACRE FARM. Faber & Faber, London. (B) (OOP)

Breidenbach, A.W. 1971. COMPOSTING OF MUNICIPAL SOLID WASTES IN THE UNITED STATES. (EPA, GPO) (SW-47r). 101 pp. (B) Best popular overview of municipal composting. Conclusion: in the U.S. it is not yet economically practical. So what else is new?

Bruce, M. 1967. COMMON SENSE COMPOST MAKING BY THE QUICK RETURN METHOD. Faber & Faber, London. (C) Method of backyard composting designed during WWII for victory gardens in England. Great practical "how-to" book.

COMPOST SCIENCE, (bimonthly magazine, $6.00/year.) Rodale Press, Emmaus, Pa, , 18049. Best journal in the country on organic waste recycling. Describes both experiences and research in a popular style with technical back-ups. Too bad there isn't a comparable journal for all natural farming.

Dindal, D.L. 1972. ECOLOGY OF COMPOST: A PUBLIC INVOLVEMENT PRO—JECT. Office of Public Service, State University of New York, Syracuse. 12 pp. (C) Great little pamphlet ($0.10) for getting anyone started.

Gainesville Municipal Waste Conversion Authority, Inc. GAINESVILLE COMPOST PLANT: FINAL REPORT ON A SOLID WASTE MANAGEMENT DEMONSTRA—TION. NTIS, Pb-222 710. 237 pp. (B) Example of the struggles of a municipal composting operation.

Golueke, C. 1972. COMPOSTING: A STUDY OF THE PROCESSES AND ITS PRINCIPLES. Rodale Press, Inc., Emmaus, Pa. 110 pp. (B) Principles, technology, health aspects, home composting methods . . . it's all here in a truly fine book about composting.

Golueke, C.G. et al. 1954. A CRITICAL EVALUATION OF INOCULUMS IN COMPOSTING. Applied Microbiology, 2(1): 45-53.

Gotaas, H.B. 1956. COMPOSTING. SANITARY DISPOSAL AND RECLAMATION OF ORGANIC WASTES. World Health Organization. From: The American Public Health Association, 1740 Broadway, New York 10019. 205 pp. (B) Loaded with general information. Focuses on intermediate (villages, small towns) and large scale applications.

Hortenstine, C. and D.F. Rothwell. 1973. COMPOSTING MUNICIPAL REFUSE AS A SOIL AMENDMENT. EPA/NTIS, PB-222 422. 62 pp. (B)

Koepf, H.H. 1966. COMPOST: WHAT IT IS, HOW IT IS MADE, WHAT IT DOES. Bio-Dynamic Farming and Gardening Assoc., R.D. 1, Stroudberg, Pa. 18360. 18 pp., $0.55.

McGauhery, P.H. 1971. AMERICAN COMPOSTING CONCEPTS. EPA, GPO (SW-2r). 23 pp. (C). Brief popular overview.

Poincelot, R. 1972. THE BIOCHEMISTRY AND METHODOLOGY OF COMPOSTING. The Connecticut Agricultural Experiment Station, New Haven, Conn. 06504 (A) One of the most concise descriptions of the technical aspects of composting. Lots of references (169) and lots of facts.

RECLAMATION OF MUNICIPAL REFUSE BY COMPOSTING. Technical Bulletin No. 9. Series 37. Sanitary Engineering Research Project. Univ. Calif., Berkeley. June 1953. 89 pp. (A) Technical, but with some useful hints that can be culled from controlled experiments.

Rodale, J. (ed.). 1969. THE COMPLETE BOOK OF COMPOSTING. Rodale Press, Emmaus, Pa. 1007 pp. (C) Despite the title and length, the book is far from complete. Useful in places.

Schatz, A. and V. Schatz. 1971. TEACHING SCIENCE WITH GARBAGE. Rodale Press, Emmaus, Pa. (C) Simple and direct ways of teaching scientific principles and importance of waste recycling at the same time.

Snyder, W.C. et al. 1972. BIOLOGICAL CONSEQUENCES OF PLANT RESIDUE DECOMPOSITION IN SOIL. EPA-NTIS, PB-221 113. 136 pp. (A) The other side of the coin. Toxicity of decomposing plant wastes on seedlings and roots of field crops.

Tietjen, C. and S. Hart. 1969. COMPOST FOR AGRICULTURAL LAND? Journal Sanit. Engin. Div. of P.A.S.C.E. 95 (SA2): 269-287. (B)

Compost Privies (Waterless Toilets)

"dein eigenes scheisse stinkt nicht"
—Albert Einstein

The hard times we face bring back old ideas with new approaches. The compost privy is just such an idea. Human excrement and organic household waste are deposited in a container, but instead of being filled over like the old privy, these wastes are composted *aerobically* (not digested), removed from the container and recycled on local land. The compost privy takes the place of the toilet, the septic tank and the garbage can.

The basic design component is a large sloping tank 8-10' long and about 8' high, that is connected to toilet and kitchen garbage inlets. The tank also has vents and a vent pipe which carries away odors, water vapor and carbon dioxide while bringing oxygen to the decomposing material. It is separated into chambers. The upper chamber receives the toilet wastes, and the rest of the chambers receive organic garbage or serve as holding places for the finishing compost. The combined wastes decompose as they settle down the inclined bottom of the tank. By the time the material reaches the bottom it has been converted to humus.

ADVANTAGES:

1) The compost privy can be used where sewer hookups or septic tanks are unavailable or not practical.
2) The compost privy saves water normally flushed down the toilet. About half the annual domestic water consumption (7,000-10,000 gallons per person) is saved each year.
3) The use of a compost privy eliminates the largest pieces of waste travelling through pipes. This means that you can use 2" waste pipe instead of 4" in a house, thereby saving money on plumbing. Because there is no need for water traps (more money saved), water pipes can drain clear after use, thus reducing the possibility of freezing.
4) The compost privy returns valuable nutrients and humus to the soil. Between 1 and 2 cubic feet of humus, safe to use in a garden, are produced from each person's excreta in a year.
5) The compost privy allows you the use of the squatting position, which is the healthiest posture for defecation.

LIMITATIONS:

1) The compost privy does not receive "gray" water (water from sinks, showers, etc.). However, this can be diverted into the garden, recycled through a solar still, or emptied into a sump pit and leaching lines.
2) The idea of a compost privy conflicts with the vast majority of local health codes.
3) The compost privy requires considerable floor space, and may be hard to incorporate into existing structures.

If you want to experiment around with a compost privy, you can either buy one or build one. The only one on the market in this country is the Clivus Mulstrum.

The Clivus Mulstrum (meaning "inclined compost room") originated in Sweden. The United States franchise for the Clivus is now owned by Abby Rockefeller (can you dig it!). Units are totally enclosed fibreglass tanks going for about $1500.00. People who have worked with them claim they are very difficult to incorporate into existing houses, and that the 20' air vent often conflicts with local building codes. For more information write:

CLIVUS-MULSTRUM USA
14A Eliot St.
Cambridge, Mass. 02138

Other people have simply used the basic design principles and built their own. One proven design is available from the Farallones Institute and can be built "by amateur builders using common materials and common tools for less than $100." In this design, wastes do not slide down an inclined plane, but simply pile up. The mound of waste must be turned every month or so, and every six months it is shifted to another compartment. For plans and an enjoyable rap write:

Composting Privy
Technical Bulletin No. 1
Farallones Institute
Point Reyes Station, Calif. 94946
($2.00)

As far as the health aspects of composting human excrement, the consensus (Golueke, Gotaas, Scott, and various technical papers) is that most fecal-borne diseases caused by bacteria (typhoid, cholera), protozoans (amoebic dysentery), worm eggs, and other gut parasites are destroyed within fourteen days in a well-heated compost pile by either heat

or antibiotic agents. The big unknown, however, seems to be the survival of disease viruses, which are incredibly hard to detect, let alone identify. There seems to be no evidence one way or the other on whether pathogenic viruses survive compost heat.

COMPOST PRIVY BIBLIOGRAPHY

Berry, W. 1973. A COMPOSTING PRIVY. Organic Gardening and Farming Magazine. Dec. 1973, pp. 88-97. Some useful hints plus a discussion of health aspects by Clarence Golueke.

Golueke, C. & H. Gotaas. PUBLIC HEALTH ASPECTS OF WASTE DISPOSAL BY COMPOSTING. American Journal of Public Health. 44(3): 339-348

Hills, Lawrence. 1972. THE CLIVUS TOILET: SANITATION WITHOUT POLLUTION. Compost Science, May-June 1972.

Rodale, Robert. 1971. GOODBYE TO THE FLUSH TOILET. Compost Science, November-December 1971.

Scott, J.C. 1952. HEALTH AND AGRICULTURE IN CHINA. Faber & Faber, London. 279 pp. A fantastic account of composting experiments in China using night soil. A very valuable book for anyone interested in composting human wastes.

Shell, G.L. and J.L. Boyd. 1969. COMPOSTING DEWATERED SEWAGE SLUDGE. U.S. Dept. of Health, Education, and Welfare. (GPO) 28 pp. (C)

Swanson, C. 1949. PREPARATION AND USE OF COMPOSTS, NIGHT SOIL, GREEN MANURES AND UNUSUAL FERTILIZING MATERIALS IN JAPAN. Agronomy Journal, 41(7): 275-282.

Wagner, E.G. and J.N. Lanoix. 1958. EXCRETA DISPOSAL FOR RURAL AREAS AND SMALL COMMUNITIES. World Health Organization, Geneva. Many useful designs for privies including compost privies. Important review of health aspects of human wastes.

Wiley, J.S. 1962. PATHOGEN SURVIVAL IN COMPOSTING MUNICIPAL WASTES. Journal, Water Poll. Cntrl. Fed., 34(1): 80-90.

Green Manure Notes

by
Samuel and Louise Kaymen
NATURAL ORGANIC FARMERS ASSOCIATION
PLAINFIELD, VT. 05667

The term green manure refers to the practice of incorporating young green plants into the soil. These plants are usually grown with the single purpose of being used as a soil improver. This practice is usually applied to plots or fields that are in a planned system of rotation. The green manure crops can be annuals, biennials or even perennials planted at almost any time of the year depending on the rotation system and the crop chosen. On the basis of their time of seeding and their occupation of the land, green manure crops are used quite differently. One useful succession that works well in New England is oats and Canada field peas, early spring, then one or two crops of buckwheat between late spring and late summer, then winter rye and hairy vetch planted in the fall. The rye and vetch occupy the ground throughout the winter and are considered a cover crop, i.e. they prevent the topsoil from being washed away by rains. The rye and vetch are allowed to grow some in the spring and are dug into the soil when about 9-12 inches high.

Rye and vetch are planted on land that has a food crop all summer. Many people seed rye into the corn crops at the time of the last cultivation and use it to cover the soil all winter. Some use buckwheat during the summer in between the food crop rows. Some crops are planted in the spring with a spring grain crop, such as a slow growing clover with spring wheat. After the wheat is harvested, the clover may be incorporated into the soil or allowed to winter over and incorporated in the next spring. There are many specific reasons for using green manures:

1. *The addition of organic matter* as food for the life of the soil.
2. The ability of legume crops to *accumulate atmospheric nitrogen* is another important function.
3. Another reason to grow green manure crops is to *conserve water soluble elements* needed for plant growth. A crop of rye, clover or buckwheat could pick up the various elements and hold them in plant form until they are needed.
4. Many crops, especially deep-rooted ones such as alfalfa, sweet clover and ragweed, *concentrate needed plant nutrients* from the subsoil. Their subsequent decay releases those deep gathered elements in the topsoil. This permits the use of these elements by succeeding shallow-rooted crops.
5. The *solubility of* calcium, phosphorous, potassium, magnesium and other *elements is increased* through the effect of the organic and inorganic acids produced as a result of the decomposing organic matter of green ma-

nures.

6. Green manure crops *improve the subsoil* by penetrating deeply. As the roots decay, numerous channels are formed which facilitate the circulation of air and the movement of water up and down in the soil.

7. The *protection of the surface soil* is often considered one of the most important functions of the green manure crop. On sloping land the soil is protected from water erosion, and light soils are protected from wind erosion.

Now let's assume you have a piece of abused, exploited and mismanaged earth. One way to get going is to make use of the weeds that grow there naturally, since their very function is to improve the soil. But, left to nature, it would take a long time. We can speed up the process by incorporating the weeds into the topsoil. Then allow the weeds to germinate and grow again. Always dig in the weed crop at the time when it is young, green and succulent so it will decompose very rapidly.

If your piece of earth has a little grass growing with the weeds then you *don't* have to "weed fallow" the first season. You can start immediately with the first green manure crop to use on poor land . . . buckwheat. This wonderful plant has the ability to make use of minerals in the soil better than most other plants. It accumulates calcium, and is an effective competitor with weeds. You should broadcast it at about 100 lbs per acre, or ¼ lb for 100 square feet. Sow buckwheat after July, for it likes to make its flowers in cool moist weather. When it is about 10% in bloom, dig it in.

After buckwheat the next green manure to be used is winter rye and hairy vetch. The vetch is a legume and fixes atmospheric nitrogen. It is also a vine and will climb up the ryegrass. The mixture should be Balbo rye (125 lbs/acre) and vetch (60 lbs/acre).

The final green manure to use, after your soil has received the benefits of the above, is sweetclover, either white or yellow (15-20 lbs/acre). Sweetclover can accumulate over 200 lbs of nitrogen per acre, the highest of any legume. That was its primary use in agriculture in the early part of this century, before cheap nitrogen fertilizer came along. With the price of fertilizer going up, sweetclover may again resume its role.

GREEN MANURE BIBLIOGRAPHY

Alther, R. and R.O. Raymond. 1974. GREEN MANURE: A GUIDE FOR THE HOME GARDENER. Garden Way Publishing Co., Charlotte, Vt. 36 pp. (C) $2.00. A really fine description of a dying art. The "Chart of Green Manure Information" is priceless.

Lipman, J.G. 1927. GREEN MANURING. PRINCIPLES AND PRACTICES. John Wiley & Sons. 356 pp. (OOP) (C)

Rogers, T.H. and J.E. Giddens. 1957. GREEN MANURE AND COVER CROPS. USDA Yearbook, 1957. pp. 252-257.

Willard, C.J. and E.E. Barnes. 1959. EXPERIMENTS ON THE USE OF SWEET-CLOVER FOR GREEN MANURE. Ohio Agric. Exp. Sta. Res. Bull. No. 839. 32 pp.

Fertilizers

If you want to buy rock mineral or organic fertilizers, there are many companies around the country that sell them. Shipping costs are very high, and they can only get higher. Check with local suppliers first: nurseries, feed companies, garden supply houses, etc. Otherwise, lists of natural fertilizer companies are given in the classified section of Organic Gardening and Farming Magazine, and Acres monthly newspaper.

FERTILIZERS BIBLIOGRAPHY

Andrews, W.B. 1947. THE RESPONSE OF CROPS AND SOILS TO FERTILIZERS AND MANURES. W.B. Andrews, State College, Mississippi. (OOP) Good early summary of chemical vs. organic fertilizers as regards to yield.

Blake, M. 1970. DOWN TO EARTH: REAL PRINCIPLES FOR FERTILIZER PRACTICE. Crosby Lockwood & Son, Ltd. London. 93 pp. (B) Chemical and organic fertilizers can be mixed and used in a truly beneficial way.

Ministry of Agriculture, Fisheries and Food. 1971. TRACE ELEMENTS IN SOILS AND CROPS. Proceeding of a Conference, Soil Scientists of the National Agricultural Advisory Service. Technical Bull. 21. Her Majesty's Stationery Office, London. 217 pp. (A)

Organic Gardening and Farming. 1973. ORGANIC FERTILIZERS: WHICH ONES AND HOW TO USE THEM. Rodale Press, Inc., Emmaus, Pa. 129 pp. (C) A good, simple, practical book.

Stephenson, W.A. 1968. SEAWEED IN AGRICULTURE AND HORTICULTURE. Faber & Faber, London. 231 pp. (B) Definitive!

Stiles, Walter. 1951. TRACE ELEMENTS IN PLANTS AND ANIMALS. (2nd ed.), Cambridge Univ. Press, Cambridge,England.

Taft, D.C. and C.D. Burris. 1974. PHOSPHATE CONSUMPTION AND SUPPLY. Garden Way Laboratories, Charlotte, Vt. 05445. 9 pp. (C) There is no known substitute for phosphate rock. It is probably one of the major limiting resources on this planet.

CROP ECOLOGY

Plant Basics

Bailey, L.H. 1915. FARM AND GARDEN RULE-BOOK. Macmillan Co., N.Y. (OOP) Easily one of the more valuable books one can own. Should be reprinted.

Elliott, J.H. 1958. TEACH YOURSELF BOTANY. The English Universities Press Ltd., London. 214 pp. (B) Combine this with Fogg's book and you've got what you need to know about plants.

Fogg, F.E. 1963. THE GROWTH OF PLANTS. Penguin Books. Baltimore, M.D. 288 pp. (B) Photosynthesis, plant biology/chemistry/ecology, and the rhythms of growth and flowering . . . it's all there. Great introduction.

Fogg, F.E. 1968. PHOTOSYNTHESIS. American Elsevier Publ. Co., N.Y. (B) Elegant and simple while staying deep into the subject.

Galston, A.W. 1961. THE LIFE OF GREEN PLANTS. Prentice-Hall, Englewood Cliffs, N.J. One of the best introductory books on plant science.

Harrington, H.D. and L.W. Durrell. 1957. HOW TO IDENTIFY PLANTS. The Swallow Press Inc., Chicago. 203 pp. (C) If you want to collect seeds or plants, take this book as a back up to your local plant key. Explains all the fancy words.

Hayward, H. 1967. THE STRUCTURE OF ECONOMIC PLANTS. Hafner Service. Detailed anatomy of 16 cultivated plants: corn, hemp, onion, alfalfa, wheat.

Janick, J. et al. 1969. PLANT SCIENCE: AN INTRODUCTION TO WORLD CROPS. W.H. Freeman, San Francisco. 269 pp. (B) Classic textbook of the foundations of world crop production. Illustrations unmatched.

Jaques, H.E. 1958. HOW TO KNOW THE ECONOMIC PLANTS. Wm. C. Brown Co., Publ. 174 pp. (C) One of the "Picture Key Series".

Magness, J. et al. 1971. FOOD AND FEED CROPS OF THE UNITED STATES. Bulletin 828, New Jersey Agric. Exper. Station, New Brunswick. 255 pp. (C) Handy reference for all major crops grown in the U.S.

Rickett, H.W. 1957. BOTANY FOR GARDENERS. Macmillan Co., N.Y. 236 pp. (C) Simple coverage of the basic principles of botany using cultivated plants.

Shurtleff, M.S. 1966. HOW TO CONTROL PLANT DISEASES IN HOME AND GARDEN. Iowa State Univ. Press, Ames. 649 pp. (B) Probably the best book to have, although no color plates.

Sprague, H.B. 1964. HUNGER SIGNS IN CROPS. McKay Co., Inc., N.Y. 390 pp. (B) Color photos, keys and text allow first approximations to nutritional deficiencies in common temperate crops.

United States Department of Agriculture. 1960. INDEX OF PLANT DISEASES IN THE UNITED STATES. Agric. Handbook No. 165, Gov. Print. Office, Washington D.C. 531 pp. Known diseases of cultivated plants and range of occurrence.

Truck Crops

Hills, L. 1971. GROW YOUR OWN FRUITS AND VEGETABLES. Faber & Faber, London.

John, G.F. 1968. BEST IDEAS FOR VEGETABLE GROWING. Rodale Books, Inc. Emmaus, Pa. (C) Compilation of testimonials by O. G. & F. editors.

Jones, H.A. and T.R. Joseph. 1928. TRUCK CROP PLANTS. McGraw Hill Co., N.Y. (OOP) A well-known old source of data on propagation, cultivation, manuring, storage, diseases, etc. Pre-chemical ideas.

Knott, J.E. 1957. HANDBOOK FOR VEGETABLE GROWERS. John Wiley & Sons, Inc. 245 pp. (C) $8.00. Mostly tables and charts of every aspect of vegetable biology. One of the most useful reference books you can own.

MacGillivray, J.H. 1952. VEGETABLE PRODUCTION. The Blakiston Co., N.Y. 397 pp. (B)

MacGillivray, J.H. 1968. HOME VEGETABLE GARDENING. California Agricultural Exper. Sta., Extension Serv., Circular 449. 31 pp. (C)

Riotte, L. 1974. THE COMPLETE GUIDE TO GROWING BERRIES AND GRAPES. Garden Way Publishing Co., Charlotte, Vt. 144 pp. (C)

Robbins, A.R. 1974. TWENTY-FIVE VEGETABLES ANYONE CAN GROW. Dover Publications, Inc., N.Y. 216 pp. (C) Reprint of 1942 book. Biology, horticulture, harvest, storage, uses of them all.

Rodale, J.I. et al (eds.). 1969. BEST IDEAS FOR ORGANIC VEGETABLE GROWING. Rodale Books, Inc. Emmaus, Pa. 197 pp. (C)

Shewell-Cooper, W.E. 1967. THE COMPLETE VEGETABLE GROWER. Faber & Faber, London. 288 pp. (C) Geared to English conditions, but one of the best introductions and reference books on vegetables.

Sunset Books. 1970. VEGETABLE GARDENING. Lane Books, Menlo Park, Calif. 72 pp. (C) Simple, practical and visual.

Wester, R. 1972. GROWING VEGETABLES IN THE HOME GARDEN. Home and Garden Bulletin No. 202, USDA, Gov. Printing Office, Washington D.C. 49 pp. (C)

Tree Crops

Alther, L. 1973. NON-CHEMICAL PEST AND DISEASE CONTROL FOR THE HOME ORCHARD. Garden Way Publ. Co., Charlotte, Vt. 24 pp. (C) Very brief introduction.

Hesler, L.R. and J.H. Whetzel. 1920. MANUAL OF FRUIT DISEASES. Macmillan Co., N.Y. 460 pp. (B) (OOP)

Horn, H. 1971. THE ADAPTIVE GEOMETRY OF TREES. Princeton Univ. Press, Princeton, N. J. 144 pp. (B) Things to consider before laying out an orchard.

Horticultural Education Association Fruit Committee. 1960-61. THE POLLINATION OF FRUIT CROPS. Scientific Horticulture 14:126-150; 15:83-122. (England). Trees arranged in orchards according to the way they are pollinated. Hard to find this kind of information.

Martin, S.R. 1965. HOW TO PRUNE FRUIT TREES. R. Sanford Martin, 9703 La Canada Way, Sunland, Calif. 90 pp. (C)

Pfeiffer, E. 1957. THE BIODYNAMIC TREATMENT OF FRUIT TREES, BERRIES, AND SHRUBS. Bio-Dynamic Farming and Gardening Assoc., Stroudberg, Pa. 30 pp. (C)

Smith, J.R. 1953. TREE CROPS: A PERMANENT AGRICULTURE. Devin-Adair, Old Greenwich, Ct. 408 pp. (C) Cultivating neglected but productive trees as an economically/ecologically viable agriculture.

Southwick, L. 1972. DWARF FRUIT TREES FOR THE HOME GARDENER. Garden Way Publ. Co., Charlotte, Vt. 118 pp. (C)

Sunset Books. 1972. PRUNING HANDBOOK. Lane Books, Menlo Park, Calif. 96 pp. (C)

TREES, "The Yearbook of Agriculture" 1949. USDA Gov. Printing Office, Washington D.C.

Wittrock, G. 1971. THE PRUNING BOOK. Rodale Press, Inc., Emmaus, Pa. 172 pp. (C)

Youngmand, W.H. and C.E. Randall. 1972. GROWING YOUR TREES. The American Forestry Association, 1319. 18th St., N. Y., Washington D.C. 20036. 88 pp. (C) Before you plant any non-food tree . . . read this. How, why and where to grow what.

NATURAL PEST MANAGEMENT

Pesticides are poisons that kill pests: insecticides (insects), herbicides (weeds), and fungicides (plant disease). Although little is known about the extent to which pesticides have been used, a great deal is known or suspected about their abuses. Suffice it to say that pesticides have been used so much on farmlands and around cities (50% are used in cities) that they must now be considered an integral part of our biological systems: present in our bodies, flowing with the rivers, drifting in the air and falling with the rain. After a generation of unrestrained use, pesticides have produced —and are still producing—serious side effects to public health, wildlife, soil life, and the balance of natural ecosystems. The FULL consequences of these effects are as yet unknown and remain for future generations to discover.

Besides their dangers, pesticides commonly fail to control pests. There are at least three reasons for this: 1) Pests often become resistant to pesticides. 2) Pesticides cause outbreaks of secondary pests. 3) For various ecological reasons, pesticides tend to free pests from control by their natural enemies. All these factors produce a series of ecological backlashes that cause farmers to use larger doses of more toxic pesticides at greater economic, environmental and energy costs.

The use of pesticides will probably remain an integral part of agriculture for years to come. But their *unrestrained use as an end in themselves* can only benefit the petrochemical companies, and not agriculture or the environment in which it operates.

There are two alternative strategies to the use of pesticides: 1) The use of safe pesticides in a controlled way. 2) The use of techniques that don't use pesticides at all. The prerequisite for better pesticide use is accurate pest monitoring. By keeping a regular account of the numbers of pests, pesticide application can be planned more rationally, giving adequate control with a few well-timed applications. Often a crop is vulnerable to attack for only a relatively short period. Massive applications at regular intervals is a consuming, not a rational, approach to pesticide use. Another way is the use of selective poisons which kill the target pest but are harmless to natural enemies. Finally, there is a whole host of non-persistent botanical pesticides derived from wild plants: Ryania, rotenone, pyrethrum and many more yet unknown. Most research is done to find more lethal chemicals, rather than less persistent but more specific ones.

Alternatives to pesticides are based on a more rigorous understanding of the term "pest control". A "pest" is not anything that crawls in the field. A pest is any creature whose numbers jeopardize the crops being grown. "Control" doesn't mean total eradication (impossible anyway), but rather keeping a potential pest below a certain level. In order to work, alternatives to pesticides should do three things: 1) They should be capable of keeping pests at a harmless density. 2) They should not cause pests to develop resistances. 3) They should work with and not against the controls provided by natural enemies of pests.

There are several methods of pest control that fulfill these requirements to one degree or another. Sex-scent attractants, baits, light traps, sterile-male radiation, resistant crop varieties, and "soft" pesticides have all been used alone or as part of an integrated control program. But these tactics are based on one narrow strategy: *discouraging the pests*. A more permanent and stabilizing method is based on *encouraging the natural enemies* of pests, their predators, parasites and diseases. In other words: controlling pests biologically, rather than chemically. Listed below are some aspects of biological control that are currently being studied or practiced:

1) Finding natural enemies suitable for specific pests and environments. Most familiar are the predatory insects . . . the bugs that eat bugs. These include certain beetles, lacewings, mantises and dozens of other less familiar species. More numerous and effective in controlling pests are the parasitic wasps, such as trichogramma. These tiny insects deposit their eggs in the soft bodies of pests or their eggs. More recent discoveries include a few types of insect diseases. Bacteria such as milky spore disease on boll weevils and tobacco budworms, and *Bacillus thuringiensis* ("Biotrol", "Thuricide", "Parasporin") have been marketed and recommended for use against caterpillars. Also under consideration at the present are some fungi and virus diseases. All of these diseases are specific to certain insects and harmless to other animals.

2) Some private businesses have begun rearing large numbers of natural enemies under artificial conditions (insectaries). Several kinds of natural enemies have been raised successfully and sold to the public by the insectaries or by distributing companies. In a few cases farmers have formed cooperative insectaries to serve the needs of several farms.

3) New ecological techniques are also being developed for nurturing natural enemies that occur naturally in the fields. What is not generally appreciated is that methods of biological control are usually most effective in a cultivated habitat that itself is diverse. Planting several kinds of crops simultaneously or rotating crops in a specific way gives natural enemies more options for survival and makes them more effective at controlling pests. This subject is discussed in more detail in the following section.

Controlling insect pests by using their natural enemies is not so much a technology as it is an understanding of ecology. All animals are kept from overrunning the countryside by their natural enemies. The process goes on all around us, although we are likely to take it for granted. Natural enemies are small, relatively rare and don't kill bugs as fast as chemicals. Instead, there is a lag time between peak numbers of pests and the time when their enemies can respond and bring their numbers down. The whole key to using predators, parasites and disease to combat pests is a fundamental understanding of ecology and some patience. No simple answers exist to problems of pest control, whether in the backyard garden or field. What is clearly needed is an approach that looks to each pest situation as a whole and then comes up with a program that integrates the different alternatives outlined above. This integrated approach is nothing more than reacting to a biological problem in a holistic way with basically biological tools.

—R. M.

BASIC BOOKS

Brooklyn Botanic Garden Record. 1966. HANDBOOK ON BIOLOGICAL CONTROL OF PESTS. Brooklyn Botanic Garden, N. Y. 97 pp. One of the best places to start for learning about the subject. Many photos.

Cox, J. 1974. HOW TO USE BIOLOGICAL CONTROLS EFFECTIVELY. Organic Gardening and Farming Magazine. Feb. 1974. pp. 76-82. Twenty-five points by experts on how to select and use beneficial insects in the garden . . . on the farm.

Olkowski, H. 1971. COMMON SENSE AND PEST CONTROL. Consumers Cooperative of Berkeley. 4805 Central Ave., Berkeley, Ca. 52 pp. Probably the best place to start if you want to manage your household/garden with respect to "pests". Simple, Clear, Beautiful.

Olkowski, H. & W. Olkowski. 1974. INSECT POPULATION MANAGEMENT IN AGRO-ECOSYSTEMS. In: "Radical Agriculture," R. Merrill, (ed.), Harper and Row. (In Press).

Philbrick, J. and H. Philbrick. 1963. THE BUG BOOK: HARMLESS INSECT CONTROLS. Garden Way Publ. Co., Charlotte, Vt. 143 pp.

Rodale, J.I. 1966. THE ORGANIC WAY TO PLANT PROTECTION. Rodale Press, Emmaus, Pa. 355 pp. Principles of non-chemical pest control. Troubleshooting text geared to 1) crop, and 2) pest, what it is and how to subdue it.

Van den Bosch, R. and P. Messenger. BIOLOGICAL CONTROL. Intext Educational Publishers, N. Y. 180 pp. Great non-technical introduction for layman.

INTERMEDIATE BOOKS

Clausen, C.P. 1940. ENTOMOPHAGOUS INSECTS. McGraw-Hill, N. Y. 688 pp.
Overview biology of insects that eat insects. An oldie but a goodie.
Clausen, C.P. 1956. BIOLOGICAL CONTROL OF INSECT PESTS IN THE CONTINEN-
TAL UNITED STATES. USDA Tech. Bull. 1139 151 pp.
DeBach, P. 1974. BIOLOGICAL CONTROL BY NATURAL ENEMIES. Cambridge
Univ. Press, London. 323 pp.
Hunter, B. 1971. (2nd ed.) GARDENING WITHOUT POISONS. Berkeley Publ. Co.,
N. Y. 352 pp. Factual book of non-chemical pest control. Good introduction.
National Research Council. 1969. INSECT-PEST MANAGEMENT AND CONTROL.
Publ. 1695. Washington D.C. 420 pp. Good practical manual including info on
surveying techniques and cultural control.
Swan, L. 1964. BENEFICIAL INSECTS. Harper and Row, N. Y. 429 pp. Simple cover-
age of bio-control and biologies of predators and parasites.

ADVANCED BOOKS

Burges, J.D. and N. Hussey. 1971. MICROBIAL CONTROL OF INSECTS AND MITES.
Academic Press, N. Y. 861 pp. Technical anthology on the use of diseases to control
pests.
DeBach, P. (ed.). 1964. BIOLOGICAL CONTROL OF INSECT PESTS AND WEEDS.
Reinhold Publ. Co., N. Y. 844 pp. Great overview of history and basic concepts.
Anthology by all the experts.
ECOLOGICAL ANIMAL CONTROL BY HABITAT MANGEMENT. 1969. Tall Timbers
Research Station, Proceeding of Conference, TTRS, Tallahassee, Fla. (2 vols.) Tech-
nical, but of value to farmer seeking cultural and integrated control methods.
Huffaker, C.B. 1971. BIOLOGICAL CONTROL. Plenum Press. N. Y. 511 pp. Easy
up-to-date textbook coverage of subject by pioneer researcher.
National Academy of Sciences. 1969. PRINCIPLES OF PLANT AND ANIMAL PEST
CONTROL. Vol. 3. "Insect Pest Management and Control". NAS, WAshington D.C.
Rabb, R.L. and F. Gutherie (ed.). 1970. CONCEPTS OF PEST MANAGEMENT. North
Carolina Univ. Press, Raleigh. 242 pp. Technical, but excellent information on the
ecology behind integrated control.

Identifying Insects, and Pest Problems

Borror, D.J. and R. White. 1970. A FIELD GUIDE TO THE INSECTS OF AMERICA
NORTH OF MEXICO. Houghton Mifflin Co., Boston. (C) Best introductory guide
to insect identity. Color plates and keys to get them to "family".
Borror, D.J. and D. DeLong. 1971. (3rd ed.). AN INTRODUCTION TO THE STUDY OF
INSECTS. Holt Rinehart and Winston, N. Y. 812 pp. One of the better textbooks
to families of insects.
Davidson, R.H. and L.M. Peairs. 1966. (6th ed.) INSECT PESTS OF FARM, GARDEN
AND ORCHARD. Wiley.
Herrick, G. 1925. MANUAL OF INJURIOUS INSECTS. Henry Holt & Co., N. Y. 489
pp. (B) (OOP) Valuable pre-pesticide information. Good life-history stuff on pests.
Metcalf, C.W. et al. 1962. DESTRUCTIVE AND USEFUL INSECTS; THEIR HABITS
AND CONTROL. McGraw-Hill, N. Y. 981 pp. (B) The best book for identifying
pest problems from the way the plant looks. GREAT troubleshooter.
Pictured Key Nature Series. HOW TO KNOW THE IMMATURE INSECTS: INSECTS;
BUTTERFLIES; BEETLES; GRASSHOPPERS. William C. Brown and Co., Dubuque,
Iowa. Illustrated keys to insects you might find in the garden, on the farm.
Swan, L.A. and C.S. Papp. 1972. THE COMMON INSECTS OF NORTH AMERICA.
Harper and Row, New York. 750 pp. $15.00.
U.S. Department of Agriculture. 1971. INSECTS AND DISEASES OF VEGETABLES
IN THE HOME GARDEN. USDA Home and Garden Bulletin. No. 46. Gov. Printing
Office, Washington D.C. 50 pp. (C) Good photos, drawings, simple descriptions . . .
forget the chemical advice.
Wescott, C. 1973. THE GARDENER'S BUG BOOK. Doubleday and Co., Inc., Garden
City, N. Y. 689 pp. (B) A "must" reference for identifying pests, their life histories,
and what they eat . . . with chemical advice.
Zim, H. 1966. INSECT PESTS. Golden Press, N. Y. 160 pp. (C) Grade-school level, but
can get anyone started. Top rate color drawings.

Insect-Control Dealers, Insectaries

The following companies supply biological control agents. Write the
companies and ask for information about prices and availability, and the
techniques of using the living things they sell. Don't buy anything until you
are ready to use it.

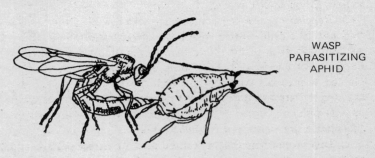

WASP
PARASITIZING
APHID

Bio-Control Co., Rt. 2, Box 2397, Auburn, Calif. 95603. Ladybug beetles gathered
in the Sierras from winter colonies; sometimes mantis cases.
Biotactics, 4436 Elora Court, Riverside, Calif. 92503. Phytoseiulus (predator
of red spider mites).
Agrilite Systems, 404 Barrier Building, Columbia, S.C. 29201.
California Green Lacewings, Inc., 2521 Webb Ave., Alameda, Calif. 94501. Lace-
wing fly eggs.
Eastern Biological Con. Co., Rt. S Box 379, Jackson, New Jersey 08527.
Ecological Insect Services. 15075 W. California Ave., Kerman, Calif. 93630. Con-
sultation and control for farms and gardens.
Peter Escher, Threefold Farm, Spring Valley, N. Y. 10977. Ryania, a botanical
spray which kills worms in fruits and is useful for many other pests.
Fairfax Biological Laboratory, Clinton Corners, N. Y. 12514. "Doom", trade name
for milky spore disease.
Gothard, Inc., P.O. Box 370, Canutillo, Tex. 79835, Specializes in trichogramma
wasps, mantis egg cases.
Hopkins Agricultural Chemical Co., Box 584, Madison, Wisconsin 53701. Ryania.
International Mineral and Chemical Corp., Crop Aid Products, Dept. 5401, Old
Orchard Road, Skokie, Ill. 60076. Thuricide, trade name for Bacillus thuringiensis.
Mincemoyer's Nursery, R.D. 5, Box 379, New Prospect Road, Jackson, N. J. 08527
Mantis egg cases, both native and Chinese..
Rincon-Vitova Insectaries, Inc., P. O. Box 95, Oak View, Calif. 93022. Phytoseiulus,
a predator of red spider mites, and other control insects.
Thompson Hayward Chemical Co., Box 2382, Kansas City, Kansas. 66110. Biotrol,
trade name for Bacillus thuringiensis.
The Vitova Co., Inc., Biological Control Division, P. O. Box 745, Rialto, Calif.
92376. Lacewings (larvae or young adults); two kinds of trichogramma; parasites
for fly maggots and armyworms.

Resistant Varieties

Atema, H. 1974. A PRELIMINARY STUDY OF RESISTANCE IN 20 VARIETIES OF
CABBAGES TO THE CABBAGE WORM BUTTERFLY. Journal No. 2, New Alchemy
Institute, Box 432, Woods Hole, Mass. (B)
Cox, J. 1973. INSECT RESISTANT VARIETIES: TOOLS FOR THE GARDENERS.
Organic Gardening and Farming Magazine, May 1973. pp 85-90. (C)
Painter, R.H. 1968. INSECT RESISTANCE IN CROP PLANTS. University Press of
Kansas, Lawrence. 520 pp. (B) On the method of finding resistant plants. Covers
the field. Some useful varieties listed.
Radcliff, E.B. and R.K. Chapman. 1966. PLANT RESISTANCE TO INSECT ATTACK
IN COMMERCIAL CABBAGE VARIETIES. Journal of Economic Entomology, 59(1):
116-120. (A) An example of some handy stuff being tucked away in technical
journals.

MIXED CROPS AND COMPANION PLANTING

In wildlife communities there is a wide variety of plants growing together in the same area that form a natural plant association. These plants
are able to co-exist because they complement each other's requirements,
provide direct benefits to each other, or make demands on resources at different times. Some thrive in direct sunlight, others live in the shade provided by larger plants; some have shallow roots, while others penetrate
deeply; some grow quickly and can be harvested early, making room for
slower growing forms; some serve as food for natural enemies that in turn
feed on pests of other plants. All available space is used at all times by an
array of differently adapted plants.

The possible combinations of cultivated plants helping or harming one
another are far too numerous to describe here in detail. A few obvious
kinds of mixed cultures may be familiar:

Intercropping: These are the well-known space-saving combinations . . .
fast and slow-growing plants, shallow and deep-rooted ones, tall and shade-
loving crops, vines and supporting plants, etc. These combinations increase

the dimensions of the garden by exploiting available space.

Rotation: Some plants may leave behind beneficial conditions for other
plants that follow. Nitrogen-fixing legumes (peas, beans, vetch, clover,
etc.) planted before a major crop are the most familiar example. Also heavy-
feeding crops (potato, cabbage, corn) can be followed by light-feeding
crops.

Companion crops: Crop patterns and local environments can be modified so as to favor beneficial insects already in the field, or to discourage
the presence of pests. Changes might include the cultivation of plants that
provide food for natural enemies or that discourage the invasion of pests,
and the maintenance of uncultivated areas or permanent refuges. Some examples are listed below.

a. Flower crops: The nectar and pollen of many flowers provide food
for adult beneficial insects. In orchards, for example, wildflowers can nur-
ture populations of parasitic wasps and thereby reduce certain pests. Research in Russia has shown that, when the weed *Phacelia* was planted in

orchards, a parasite of the tree's scale pest thrived in the orchard by subsisting on the nectar of the weed. Another Russian study showed that, when small plots of umbellifers (a family of plants) were planted near vegetable fields in a ratio of 1 flower plant to 400 crop plants, up to 94% of the cabbage cutworms were parasitized. Flowers of crop-plants such as the cabbage family, legumes and sunflowers can also serve as alternative food sources for beneficial insects.

b. Repellent crops: Most insects are selective as to the kinds of plants they eat. It is believed that insects are attracted to the odors of "secondary" substances in plants rather than to the food value of the plant itself. Experiments have shown that odors given off by aromatic plants interplanted with crops can interfere with the feeding behavior of pests by masking the attracting odor of the crops. Repellent crops so far described include various pungent vegetables *(Solanum, Allium)* and aromatic herbs *(Labiatae, Compositae and Umbelliferae).*

c. Trap crops: Some plants can be used to attract pests away from the main crop. With careful monitoring these "trap" crops can provide food in the form of large numbers of pests, which then attract their own natural enemies. For example, when alfalfa strips were interplanted with fields of cotton, the Lygus bug (a serious pest in California) migrated away from the cotton and into the alfalfa. With their concentrations of Lygus bugs, the alfalfa plots then provided a food source for several predatory insects in the area. Trap crops of alfalfa may also have applications in walnut and citrus orchards and bean fields. In the coastal climate of California, brussels sprouts, which attract large numbers of aphids, can serve as winter insectaries for parasitic wasps. When aphids attack other crops in the spring, the wasp populations, having fed on aphids during the lean winter, are large enough to respond quickly and control the aphids.

d. Hedgerows and Shelter Belts: For centuries hedgerows have been planted between field crops to slow down winds. Uncultivated land also affects the distribution and abundance of insects associated with nearby crops. Wild plant stands can provide alternative food and refuge for pests and their natural enemies alike. In England, where much farming is done near wild vegetation, pest problems are generally less severe than in the United States where monoculture farming persists.

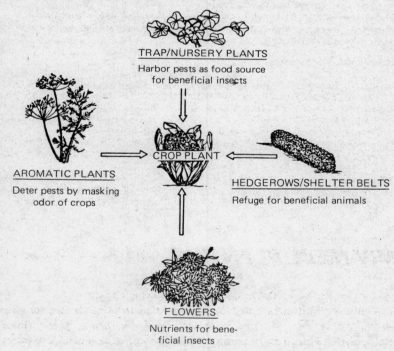

TRAP/NURSERY PLANTS
Harbor pests as food source for beneficial insects

AROMATIC PLANTS
Deter pests by masking odor of crops

CROP PLANT

HEDGEROWS/SHELTER BELTS
Refuge for beneficial animals

FLOWERS
Nutrients for beneficial insects

FIG. 4 SOME POSSIBLE COMPONENTS AND PLANT INTERACTIONS OF A DIVERSE CROPPING SYSTEM. Based on a garden model of "companion planting" arrangements.

Many other kinds of plant relationships can be cultivated to advantage. Some "component" species probably serve more than one beneficial function. Repellent herbs, for example, also produce food-rich flower heads, as do many trap crops. Garden models (Fig. 4) exist for a variety of mixed cropping schemes, and these undoubtedly could be tested and applied on a larger scale. Interest, however, will probably remain focused on monocultures until the "costs" of pesticides and poor farm management exceed the "costs" of ecological designs.

Interplanting the farm landscape with trees, hedgerows and other perennial stands, together with rotations, strip cropping and mixed stands will serve to promote stability and effective natural pest control. But diverse landscapes and mixed farming methods *per se* will not create stability. Sometimes diversity decreases pest damage, other times it may increase it. The web of possible plant/animal relationships is immeasurably complex, and each situation and crop ecosystem is unique. In other words, the right kind of diversity must be established, and we can only know that by practical experience in local areas and ecological studies of the agricultural environment.

—R.M.

GENERAL BOOKS/ARTICLES

Allen, R. 1974. DOES DIVERSITY GROW CABBAGES? New Scientist, 29 Aug., 1974. (B)

Cox, J. 1972. HOW TO PLANT A COMPANION GARDEN. Organic Gardening and Farming Magazine, Feb., 1972. pp. 50-55; (C)

Dethier, V. 1947. CHEMICAL INSECT ATTRACTANTS AND REPELLENTS. Blakiston Co., Phil. (B) (OOP) Discusses the mechanisms behind plants that attract and repel insects.

Dethier, V.G. 1970. CHEMICAL INTERACTIONS BETWEEN PLANTS AND INSECTS. In: "Chemical Ecology", E. Sondheimer and J.B. Simeone (ed.), Academic Press, London. (B) Semi-technical overview of the subject.

Merrill, R. 1972. ECOLOGICAL DESIGN IN THE ORGANIC GARDEN: COMPANION PLANTING AND NATURAL REPELLENTS. Organic Gardening and Farming Magazine: April 1972, pp. 48-53. (B)

Philbrick, H. and R.B. Gregg. 1966. COMPANION PLANTS AND HOW TO USE THEM. Devin-Adair Co., N.Y. 111 pp. (C) Admittedly only a primer, the book is still the most complete compilation of formal experiments and casual observations of beneficial plant combinations for the home gardener.

Root, R. 1973. ORGANIZATION OF A PLANT-ARTHROPOD ASSOCIATION IN SIMPLE AND DIVERSE HABITATS: THE FAUNA OF COLLARDS (Brassica oleracea). Ecological Monographs, 43: 95-124. (A)

Scott, G. 1969. PLANT SYMBIOSIS. William Clowes and Sons, Ltd., London. (B)

TRAP PLANTS, REPELLENT PLANTS, FLOWERS AND HEDGES AS COMPANION CROPS

Brooklyn Botanic Garden. 1958. HANDBOOK ON HERBS. Brooklyn Botanic Garden, Brooklyn, N.Y. 96 pp. (C) A lot of books describe herbs as food and medicine. This seems to be the most concise book for telling you how to grow and identify them.

Fraenkel, G.S. 1959. THE RAISON D'ETRE OF SECONDARY PLANT SUBSTANCES. Science 129: 1466-1470. (B) Why plants put out odors that attract pests.

Leius, K. 1967. INFLUENCE OF WILD FLOWERS ON PARASITISM OF TENT CATERPILLARS AND CODLING MOTH. Can. Ent. 99: 444-446. Eighteen times as many tent caterpillars (pupae) parasitized in orchards with rich undergrowths of wild flowers as in orchards with poor floral undergrowths.

Leius, K. 1960. ATTRACTIVENESS OF DIFFERENT FOOD AND FLOWERS TO THE ADULTS OF SOME HYMENOPTEROUS PARASITES. Can. Ent. 92: 369-76. (B)

Stern, V. 1969. INTERPLANTING ALFALFA IN COTTON TO CONTROL LYGUS BUG AND OTHER INSECT PESTS. In "Tall Timbers Conference on Ecological Animal Control by Habitat Management," Proceeding, No. 1; 55-69. Tall Timbers Research Station, Tallahassee, Fla.

Tahvanainen, J.O. and R. Root. 1972. THE INFLUENCE OF VEGETATIONAL DIVERSITY ON THE POPULATION ECOLOGY OF A SPECIALIZED HERBIVORE, PHYLLOTRETA CRUCIFERAE. Oecologia (Berl) 10: 321-346. (A) Adult flea beetles more abundant on collards grown in monocultures than on those grown adjacent to natural vegetation. Mixed crops per se tended to "confuse" pests.

van Embden, H.F. 1964. THE ROLE OF UNCULTIVATED LAND IN THE BIOLOGY OF CROP PEST AND BENEFICIAL INSECTS. Scientific Horticulture, Vol. 17.

WEEDS

Agricultural Research Service (USDA). 1971. COMMON WEEDS OF THE UNITED STATES. Dover Publications, Inc. N.Y. 462 pp. (C)

Cocannouer, J. 1964. WEEDS: GUARDIANS OF THE SOIL. Devin-Adair Co., N.Y. 179 pp. (C)

Fogg, J.M. 1956. WEEDS OF LAWN AND GARDEN. Univ. of Pennsylvania Press, Phil. 251 pp. (C)

Hatfield, A.W. 1971. HOW TO ENJOY YOUR WEEDS. Collier Books, N.Y. 192 pp. (C)

Jaques, H. 1959. HOW TO KNOW THE WEEDS. Wm. C. Brown Co., Dubuque, Iowa. (C)

Pfeiffer, E. 1970. WEEDS AND WHAT THEY TELL. Bio-Dynamic Farming and Gardening Assn., Inc. Stroudberg, Pa. 96 pp. (C)

HARMFUL CROPS

Garb, S. 1961. DIFFERENTIAL GROWTH-INHIBITORS PRODUCED BY PLANTS. Botanical Reviews, 27:422-443. (B) Useful list of crops that inhibit each other.

Lawrence, T. and M.R. Kilcher. 1962. THE EFFECT OF FOURTEEN ROOT EXTRACTS UPON GERMINATION AND SEEDLING LENGTH OF FIFTEEN PLANT SPECIES. Canadian Journal of Plant Science, 42(2): 308-318. (A)

Whittaker, R.H. and P.P. Feeny. 1971. ALLELOCHEMICALS: CHEMICAL INTERACTIONS BETWEEN SPECIES. Science, 171: 757-770. (A)

Genetic Erosion and Monocultures

For millenia, people have domesticated wild species of plants and animals for food, selecting strains that were palatable and easy to grow. About 75 years ago, engineers began to develop controlled breeding programs by selecting crop varieties that were resistant to some of the diseases and pests that have plagued societies throughout history. These efforts continue today, but they have taken a back seat to the development of a few high-yielding and uniform crops which meet the demands of mechanical harvesters and a competitive market economy.

For several reasons the new genetic strategy has placed agriculture in its most vulnerable position ever, by forsaking biological quality for yield and appearance:

1) The genetic base for most major crops has become dangerously narrow. As farming practices rely more and more on a few productive varieties (Table I), the numerous strains once grown in and adapted to local communities are being abandoned. Changing land use patterns further reduce the diversity and distribution of genetic types, by destroying habitats of local wild plants. A genetic reserve is important because the evolutionary contest between diseases and cultivated plants is a continuous exchange of mutual adaptations; short-lived microbes mutate and recombine to new diseases while longer-lived crops struggle to adapt resistances. The development of resistant varieties is also a continuous process and needs a diverse genetic base from which to operate. Unfortunately, many of the old varieties of crops have been discarded irretrievably; new varieties represent only a small fraction of the gene pool once planted. This loss, although not well publicized and understood by the public, has serious implications for the availability of future food supplies.

2) Planting large areas in the same kind of crop encourages the spread of disease and pest outbreaks. When the monocultures are extended over broad geographic areas, as they are today in the United States, the potential for crop epidemics is compounded. This is precisely the condition that caused the great Irish potato famine of the 1840's and the U.S. corn leaf blight in the early 1970's when over 15% of the total U.S. corn crop was destroyed. These and other examples show that crop monocultures and genetic uniformity actually invite crop epidemic, increase pesticide use, and increase the potential for higher food costs and food shortages.

Unfortunately, the market economy rather than common sense determines whether a new crop variety is used. The farmer requires uniform crops for tending and mechanical harvesting. The middlemen require uniformity for processing and mass merchandising. The competitive market permits no alternatives. This dilemma was highlighted by the 1970 U.S. corn leaf blight and was described in a report issued by the National Academy of Sciences, which concluded that:

a) . . . most major crops are impressively uniform genetically and impressively vulnerable. b) This uniformity derives from powerful economic and legislative forces. c) . . . increasing vulnerability to epidemics is not likely to generate automatically self-correcting tendencies in the marketplace.

3) Most high-yield crops encourage the use of pesticides and synthetic fertilizers; in fact, they have actually been developed together with agricultural chemicals. This means that farmers are forced to use pesticides to protect their high yields and to stretch production potential. High-yield varieties are productive only because they are responsive to heavy doses of chemical fertilizers; they are ineffective without this input.

**   **   **   **

What is needed is a diversified breeding program which can continually breed new varieties of hardy, domestic stocks adapted to *local* conditions. In this way, a wide genetic reservoir for the selection process is maintained, and the patchwork of diverse crops establishes buffer areas against epidemics. In particular, as noted by Howard Odum: "We need to get livestock back onto the farm and develop varieties that can fend for themselves in reproduction, protect themselves from weather and disease, move with the food supply and develop their patterns of group behavior. We must conserve and develop further a wide variety of competitive plant species that can also provide a reasonable growth in unfertilized soils and resist pests and disease."

—R.M.

CROP	NUMBER OF POPULAR COMMERCIAL, OR CERTIFIED VARIETIES	MAJOR VARIETIES NO.	% OF CROP ACREAGE
Beans, snap	70	3	76
Cotton	50	3	53
Corn$_1$	197	6	71
Peanut	15	3	70
Peas	50	2	96
Potato	82	4	72
Rice	14	4	65
Soybeans	62	6	56
Sugar beet	16	2	42
Sweet potato	48	1	69
Wheat	269	9	50

TABLE I. The extent to which a few crop varieties dominate American agriculture. From: National Academy of Sciences. GENETIC VULNERABILITY OF CROPS. $_1$Released public inbreds only, expressed as percentage of seed requirements.

General Horticulture Information Sources

BROOKLYN BOTANIC GARDEN. 1000 Washington Ave., Brooklyn, N. Y. 11225. Extremely useful Garden and Horticultural Handbooks, priced from $1.25 to $1.60 on everything from soils and mulches to roses and dye plants.

THE NEW YORK BOTANIC GARDEN. Bronx, New York 10458. The library offers bibliographies on different plant subjects ALL FREE except for: "The Medicinal and Food Plants of the North American Indians." ($1.25).

HENRY DOUBLEDAY RESEARCH ASSOCIATION. 20, Convent Lane, Bocking, Braintree, Essex, England.

INFORMATION DIVISION, USDA Agricultural Research Service. Federal Center Building, Hyattsville, Md. 20782.

NORTH AMERICAN FRUIT EXPLORERS. Sec. Robert Kurle, 87th and Madison, Hinsdale, Ill. 60521. Publish North American Pomona quarterly, information and resources . . . advantages of personal exchange members and library.

SOIL CONSERVATION SOCIETY OF AMERICA, Plant Resources Division. Write to: D. E. Hutchinson, Chairman, Natural Vegetation Subcommittee, 5717 Baldwin Ave., Lincoln, Nebraska 68507.

UNITED STATES NATIONAL ARBORETUM. Washington, D.C. 20002. For plant identification problems or lists of specific kinds of plant sources (i.e. "Native Flower Sources").

U.S. NATIONAL HERBARIUM. Smithsonian Institution, U.S. National Museum. Washington, D.C.

NURSERY STOCK AND SUPPLY LOCATIONS

THE AMERICAN HORTICULTURAL SOCIETY. 901 N. Washington St., Alexandria, Va. 22314. If you cannot find plants you are looking for, the AHS can probably help. They also have an important sourcebook: DIRECTORY OF AMERICAN HORTICULTURE. ($5.00) that lists the major plant organizations and societies plus the agricultural extension services and experimental stations.

AMERICAN ASSOCIATION OF NURSERYMEN, INC. 835 Southern Building, Washington D.C. 20005.

BROOKLYN BOTANIC GARDENS (See Address Above). "1200 Trees and Shrubs, Where to Buy Them."

CALIFORNIA RARE FRUIT GROWERS. Star Route Box P, 919 3rd Ave., New York, N. Y. 10022. Seed exchange, lists of plant sources, lots of practical information, exchange between members, quarterly newsletter, dues $3.00.

COLLEGE OF AGRICULTURE, L. H. Bailey Hortorium, Mann Library Bldg., Ithaca, New York 14850. For specific plant . . . where to get . . . must have botanical name. Card catalog.

HERB BUYER'S GUIDE. Richard Hettern, Pyramid Communications, Inc., 919 3rd Ave., New York, N. Y. 10022 ($1.25).

HERB GROWER MAGAZINE. Falls Village, Conn. 06031. "The Marketplace" quarterly $5.00.

HERB SOCIETY OF AMERICA. 300 Massachusetts Ave., Boston, Mass. 02115. Sells a list of herb sources.

THE INTERNATIONAL PLANT PROPAGATORS' SOCIETY. John A. Wott, Sec./Treas. Dept. of Horticulture, Purdue University, Lafayette, Indiana 47907. More for specialists.

PLANT BUYERS' GUIDE. Massachusetts Horticultural Society (Ahrno H. Nehrling, Director of Publications), Bellman Publishing Co., Inc. Boston, Mass.

USDA FOREST SERVICE. Washington D.C. "Forest Tree Seed Orchards: A Directory of Industry, State and Federal Tree Seed Orchards in the U.S."

USDA SOIL CONSERVATION SERVICE. Northeast Regional Technical Service Center, Upper Darby, Penn. 19082.

WILSON SEED FARMS. Polk, Nebraska 68654. Much helpful information, list of commercial sources of native plants and seeds.

Propagation Bibliography

OVERVIEW

Burkill, I. H. 1953. HABITS OF MAN AND THE ORIGIN OF THE CULTIVATED PLANTS OF THE OLD WORLD. Proceedings of the Linnean Society of London, 164:12.

Frankel, O. and E. Bennett. 1970. GENETIC RESOURCES IN PLANTS . . . THEIR EXPLORATION AND PRESERVATION. (Inter. Biol. Progr., No. 11), Davis Co., Phil., Pa.

National Academy of Sciences. 1972. GENETIC VULNERABILITY OF MAJOR CROPS. NAS, Washington D.C.

Harlan, J.R. 1971. AGRICULTURAL ORIGINS: CENTERS AND NONCENTERS. Science, 174: 468.

Sauer, C. AGRICULTURAL ORIGINS AND DISPERSALS. MIT Press, Cambridge, Mass. 175 pp. (C)

Schwanitz, F. 1966. THE ORIGIN OF CULTIVATED PLANTS. Harvard University Press, Cambridge, Mass. 174 pp. (C)

Vavilov, N. J. 1949. THE ORIGIN, VARIATION, IMMUNITY AND BREEDING OF CULTIVATED PLANTS. Chronica Botanica 13(1-6). Waltham, Mass. (B) (OOP) A classic among classics.

GENERAL PROPAGATION

Bailey, L. H. 1967. (18th printing from 1896). THE NURSERY MANUAL. The Macmillan Co., N. Y. 456 pp. (B) Dated, but still in print and still a good place to start.

Brooklyn Botanic Garden. 1957. HANDBOOK ON PROPAGATION. Brooklyn Botanic Garden, Brooklyn, New York 11225. $1.25. (C) Great simple introduction.

Free, Montague. 1957. PLANT PROPAGATION IN PICTURES. Doubleday & Co., N. Y. 249 pp. $6.95.

Hartmann, H.T. and D.E. Kester. 1968. PLANT PROPAGATION: PRINCIPLES AND PRACTICES. Prentice-Hall, Inc., Englewood Cliffs, N. J. 702 pp. (B) Comprehensive and slightly technical, this is probably the most thorough popular book on plant propagation in print. A book with which to end . . . not start.

Mahlstede, John P. & E.S. Haber. 1957. PLANT PROPAGATION. John Wiley & Sons, Inc., New York. 410 pp. $10.25. Very good.

Prockter, Noel J. 1950. SIMPLE PROPAGATION. A BOOK OF INSTRUCTIONS FOR PROPAGATION BY SEED, DIVISION, LAYERING, CUTTINGS, BUDDING AND GRAFTING. W.H. & L. Collingridge Ltd., London, Transatlantic Arts, Inc., Forest Hills, New York. 144 pp. (C) (OOP)

van der Pijl. 1972. PRINCIPLES OF DISPERSAL IN HIGHER PLANTS. 2nd ed. Springer-Verlag. $12.60. (A)

Wright, R.C.M. 1956. PLANT PROPAGATION AND GARDEN PRACTICE. Criterion Books, New York. 192 pp. (B)

SEEDS

Adams, R.L. 1951. VEGETABLE AND FLOWER SEED INDUSTRY OF CALIFORNIA. Calif. Agricultural Experimental Station, Contribution, Giannini Foundation, Univ. of Calif., Berkeley. Most of the world's vegetable and flower seeds are grown in California.

Barton, Lela V. 1961. SEED PRESERVATION AND LONGEVITY. Leonard Hill Books Ltd., Interscience Publ. Inc., New York. 216 pp. (B) (OOP)

Cox, Joseph and George E. Starr. 1927. SEED PRODUCTION AND MARKETING. John Wiley & Sons, Inc. (OOP) How to grow seeds: explains production of vegetables (by family), field legumes (clovers, alfalfa, etc.), grasses (rye, timothy, etc.). Out of print, should be reprinted!

Harrington, James F. and D. E. Johnson. 1970. SEED STORAGE AND PACKAGING: APPLICATIONS FOR INDIA. National Seeds Corporation Ltd., (Rockefeller Foundation), New Delhi. 223 pp. (B)

Hawthorne, Leslie R. and Leonard H. Pollard. 1954. VEGETABLE AND SEED PRODUCTION. The Blakiston Co., Inc., New York. (OOP) Detailed information on commercial seed harvesting and breeding of vegetables (by family); written for commercial operations using mechanization, but information can be gleaned for small timers. No discussion of storage techniques. Should be reprinted!!

Knott, James K. 1962 (Rev. ed.). HANDBOOK FOR VEGETABLE GROWERS. Chap. 6, "Seed Production." John Wiley & Sons, Inc., New York.

Kozlowski, T.T. (ed.). 1972. SEED BIOLOGY. Vol. 1: "Importance, Development, Germination." Vol. 2: "Germination, Control, Metabolism, Pathology." Vol. 3: "Insects and Seed Collection, Storage, Testing and Certification." Academic Press, New York. Probably most significant recent work on all phases of seed propagation. Well worth the price (especially Vol. 3) if you're really into it. ($65.00 set).

Lobanov, V. Ya. 1967. QUALITY DETERMINATION OF SEEDS. Published for USDA and National Science Foundation by the Israel Program for Scientific Translations. NTIS.

Martin, A.C. and W.D. Barkley. 1973. SEED IDENTIFICATION MANUAL. Univ. of Calif. Press, Los Angeles. 221 pp. Photos (824), drawings, keys of seeds of cultivated and wild plants found in farmlands, wetlands and woodlands of North America.

Mayer, A.M. and A. Poljakoff-Mayber. 1963. THE GERMINATION OF SEEDS. Monograph Series on Pure and Applied Biology. Pergamon.

Roberts, E.H. (ed.) 1972. VIABILITY OF SEEDS. Syracuse Univ. Press, New York. 448 pp.

SEED WORLD MAGAZINE. Now out of print — old issues have much useful information. (327 So. La Salle St., Chicago, Ill.).

U.S. Dept. Agriculture. 1952. TESTING AGRICULTURAL AND VEGETABLE SEED. Handbook No. 30. Washington D.C. (GPO). Very valuable pamphlet.

U.S. Dept. Agriculture. 1942. STORAGE OF VEGETABLE SEEDS. USDA Leaflet 220. Gov. Printing Office, Washington D.C.

U.S. Dept. Agriculture. 1936. SEEDS. USDA Yearbook for 1936. Washington D.C., Gov. Printing Office.

PLANT GENETICS, BREEDING

Allard, R.W. 1960. PRINCIPLES OF PLANT BREEDING. Wiley, N. Y.

Briggs, F.N. and P.F. Knowles. 1967. INTRODUCTION TO PLANT BREEDING. Reinhold, N. Y.

Crane, M.B. and W.J. Lawrence. 1952. GENETICS OF GARDEN PLANTS. Macmillan. N. Y. (OOP)

Darlington, C.D. 1973. CHROMOSOME BOTANY AND THE ORIGINS OF CULTIVATED PLANTS. Hafner Publ. Co., New York. 231 pp. (B)

Lawrence, W.J. 1945. PRACTICAL PLANT BREEDING. Allen and Unwin. London.

Williams, W. 1964. GENETIC PRINCIPLES AND PLANT BREEDING. Blackwell Sci. Publ., Oxford, England. 504 pp. (A)

POLLINATION ECOLOGY

Free, J.B. 1970. INSECT POLLINATION OF CROPS. Academic Press, New York. 544 pp. (A)

Grout, R.A. 1953. PLANNED POLLINATION: AN AGRICULTURAL PRACTICE. Dadant & Sons, Inc., Hamilton, Ill. 23 pp (C)

Lovell, J.H. 1918. THE FLOWER AND THE BEE: PLANT LIFE AND POLLINATION. Charles Scribner's Sons, New York. 282 pp. (B) (OOP)

Meeuse, J.D. 1961. THE STORY OF POLLINATION. The Ronald Press,Co., New York. 243 pp. (B)

Mittler, T.E. (ed.). 1960. PROCEEDINGS OF THE FIRST INTERNATIONAL SYMPOSIUM ON POLLINATION. Copenhagen. Swedish Seed Growers Assoc., Stockholm. Lindhska Press, Orebro, Sweden. (A)

JOHNNY'S SELECTED SEEDS

Plant breeding in the U.S. today is directed towards satisfying the desires of 200 million Americans, the qualities most worked towards being uniformity, color, commercial adaptability, and yield. By working primarily with these aims in mind, often nice-looking produce is the result, but one must question if this direct genetic manipulation results in benefiting our natural world, and consequently our physical, mental, and spiritual health.

In questioning the direction of plant breeding today, we decided to take it a step further, and Johnny's Selected Seeds was born. Our work is directed by an understanding that good food is the basis of our well being, and quality seeds are the most fundamental step in creating good food. Our first catalog, for the 1974 gardening season, is the result of our efforts so far in growing and obtaining quality seeds from around the world. We'll be able to offer an increasing number of varieties as they are discovered and grown.

Following are some general indications for seed production of a few of the more common garden vegetables. If you would like some specific information, please write to us and we'll be glad to help out.

The first group of plants, following, are *self pollinated*, that is, fertilization of the ovaries occurs by way of the anthers in the same flower. Generally there is only a small degree of chance cross-pollination between varieties of this group, and different varieties of the same species can be kept relatively pure even when grown in close proximity.

1. Peas and Beans—Grow as usual, but allow for a 3-4 month growing period which they require for seed maturity. Normally when plants are mature they die and, being dry, the seeds are easily hand picked or threshed from the pods.

2. Tomatoes—Raise as normal. Select the plants and individual fruits which most appeal to you. Spoon out seeds with pulp into any non-metallic container, keep in a warm place, and stir twice daily. The resulting fermentation will reduce the jelly-like pulp to a thin liquid from which the seeds can easily be washed. Finally, spread seeds out to dry thoroughly.

3. Lettuce—In the North, plant in early spring, in the South and West Coast areas, plant in fall. After heading, seedstalks will form, producing flowers, and eventually seeds. Cut seedstalks, hang to dry, and simply shake out seeds.

Following are plants which are *pollinated by wind and/or insects*. Two varieties of the same species must be isolated to prevent crossing. At least one quarter mile is recommended between varieties to maintain purity, but 200 feet is generally enough distance. A small amount of interaction between varieties won't hurt, and the more diverse genetic makeup can be an aid to the strain's adaptability. Flowering of two members of the same species often does not occur simultaneously, and in such cases, there is no worry about crossing.

1. Cucumber—Select the desired plants and individual fruits, and let the fruit come to a gourd-like maturity on the vine. Extract seeds and pulp, and then process as with tomato seeds (above). When washing is completed, put seeds in a container and cover with water, stir, and let settle. Seeds which float are either immature or were not pollinated, and should be discarded.

2. Squash—Simply grow the fruits to maturity, extract seeds, remove pulp, and wash and dry. Fermenting is not necessary.

3. Beets—A biennial vegetable which must go through the winter, regardless of location, to produce flower

stalks and seed the following year from planting. In snowless areas, fall planting is suitable; in areas with freezing and snow, plant so that medium sized roots are grown before severe weather. In far northern areas a mulch for the winter is recommended to prevent possible winterkill. Mature seed is easily rubbed by hand from the seed stalks. Beets are prolific seed yielders, and a few plants will provide more than enough seed for the average gardener and friends.

4. Carrots—A biennial to be treated similarly to beets (above).

5. Sweet Corn—Plant early enough in the season to allow for maturity, which is evidenced by a browning of the husks and leaves, and a hardness of the kernels. As with all home seed growing, avoid hybrid varieties. Seed is probably best stored until needed on the cob.

6. Radishes—An annual member of the cabbage family which should be sown in the spring so that plants are well formed during the long day lengths of early summer which stimulate seedstalk formation. After flowering, seed pods will form, and when browning and drying occur, the whole plant may be gathered and the seeds beaten out or removed by hand from the pods. In selecting plants to be left in for seed, do not choose the first 20% or so of the plants which begin to go to seed, as this quick flowering or "bolting" characteristic is not desirable in radishes.

7. Cabbage—Another biennial, which flowers and produces seed the year following planting. In snowless areas seed may be sown in late summer or fall. In the North, plant so that a strong thick stem is formed before snow and/or frozen ground. (Heading is not necessary, but a strong stem is, or seedstalk formation will not occur in the following season. At least partial heading is desirable so that selection can be made.) Flowering will occur during late spring or early summer of the 2nd year, seed maturing towards fall. Harvesting is similar to radish seed, cabbage making the same kind of seed stalks and pods.

8. Melons—Remove seed from mature muskmelons and process by fermentation as described for tomatoes, above.

Here at *Johnny's Selected Seeds* we have a seed swapping program with home gardeners and farmers. If you have any special personal, family, or heirloom strains of vegetables, herbs, or cereals, and would like to share them with us and with other gardeners, we'll trade you one of our special things for one of your s. It's a great way to get some mighty nice varieties out of hiding, provides a lot of fun for all involved, and can result in these strains being available to many other gardeners by way of our increasing the seed and listing it in our catalog. Please get in touch with us if you have something which may be of interest.

Rob Johnston Jr.
JOHNNY'S SELECTED
SEEDS
N. DIXMONT, MAINE 04932

REDWOOD CITY SEED CO.

Man's existence depends solely upon plants; and modern society's foundations rest upon high-yield food plants. According to West German biologist Franz Schwanitz if man were still a hunter and gatherer the world could support only 30 million people. Through the development of high-yield food plants, however, more than 100 times this number inhabits the earth.

Since the development of agriculture some 6,000 years ago, man has made significant changes in wild plants in developing cultivated plants. He has eliminated "undesirable" characteristics from the genetic makeup of wild plants to make them more suited to his needs.

For example, in almost all important plants grown for their fruit and seeds, the natural mechanisms of seed dispersal are mostly lost. Wild plants depend heavily upon delayed germination for their survival. This insures that matured seed will not sprout with the last rains of autumn, when the seedlings would be wiped out by winter, snow or frost. For man's purposes, however, delayed germination is undesirable. It would require larger amounts of seed, as most of it would be consumed by rodents and birds during their long stay in the ground. Also, remnants germinating in later years would constantly infect new plantings. Therefore, man has developed plants whose seed germinate readily without regard to the season.

Cultivated plants have been bred specifically for cultivation: to thrive only in an artifically controlled environment (i.e. a well-cultivated, pest and weed free, heavily fertilized field in correctly-spaced rows). We now have a world full of cultivated plants which are not suited for existence in nature.

This extreme dependence on such a small number of plants is only recent. Not only is the number of plants small, but the diversity and greater base within each crop is narrowing.

For the home gardeners we can suggest many ways of dealing with these problems. *First* and most importantly, one should gain independence from commercial food distribution by putting as much land as possible into cultivation, from the backyard to open fields. Begin with a small number of crops; become familiar with their culture, and try different varieties to find the best one for your area. Barter with your neighbors for the vegetables you do not produce.

Secondly, grow plants only from non-hybrid seed. You must cross two parent plants to produce hybrids, and this must be done every year for hybrid seed. Non-hybrid seed is easily reproduced; you only have to let a few plants go to seed on their own accord, making sure that you grow only one type of vegetable at any one time in your garden to avoid crossing. A more important reason for growing non-hybrid plants is that once a variety falls out of general use, its genetic variation is lost forever—and with it goes man's ability to develop new strains of crops. Many non-hybrids have vanished irretrievably from the face of the earth in the last few decades. Instead of researching new application for old varieties, new hybrids are developed.

Thirdly, in relation to varieties which would be suited for specific areas, gardeners should turn their attention towards native and naturalized wild plants. These plants are in a position to compete with weeds, and are suited to the climate, requiring little if any cultivation. There are a great number of wild plants which would be excellent food sources if grown and collected: acorns, actinidia, wild beet, burdock, cattail, chufa, and sorrel, just to name a few.

Wild plants are usually utilized in developed nations only in times of poverty or famine; but everyone's survival may some day depend upon wild plant collection.

What we are doing at the Redwood City Seed Co. is to start to collect wild plant seeds and to offer non-hybrid vegetable seed inexpensively. We welcome anyone who can collect seeds of food, medicinal, or dye plants from their garden or the wild, and send us a list of these plants. We will then send a list of seeds for trade, our *Index Seminum*. We use botanical names only, and prefer that you list botanical names also.

We have a complete Catalog of Seeds for $.25 which has interesting histories on some of the plants offered, and fairly complete cultural instructions for each plant. Beginning autumn 1974 we will have a $.75 quarterly seed list which will supplement our catalog that lists mainly rare seeds and new items.

We are also in the process of putting together a book which describes various techniques that the home gardener can use to grow his-her own seeds in most major climates of the United States. Write for information.

Our address is:
REDWOOD CITY SEED CO.,
P.O. Box 361, Redwood City, California 94064
U.S.A. Mr. C. Dremann, Proprietor, 415-325-0339

A WORLD SEED SERVICE— J.L. HUDSON

We offer several thousand species and varieties of plants in our catalog, listed alphabetically by the Latin or botanical name.

We have attempted to offer seeds of sufficient variety to fill the many interests of our customers. We have a large selection of plants native to Australia, Europe (particularly alpine species), South Africa, Japan, India and the Himalayas.

During the next few years we will be concentrating more on the addition of important economic plants, (such as dye, medicinal, fiber, and wild food plants), with even less emphasis on hybrids than in the past.

We would like to urge people to grow their plants from seed, rather than buying nursery stock.

Our catalog is $.50. We regret that the cost of printing and mailing prohibits our sending copies to you free of charge. Our address is: A World Seed Service— J. L. Hudson, P.O. Box 1058, Redwood City, California 94064 U.S.A.

GENERAL INFORMATION

Merrill, R. (ed.) RADICAL AGRICULTURE. Harper and Row. (In Press). Anthology of articles by activists in rural restoration. Land Reform, Agribusiness, Urban/ Rural Alliances, New Technologies, etc.

Goldstein, J. 1973. THE NEW FOOD CHAIN: AN ORGANIC LINK BETWEEN FARM AND CITY. Rodale Press, Emmaus, Pa. A series of articles with a vision of cities and farms complementing each other instead of competing.

Allaby, M., and F. Allen. 1974. ROBOTS BEHIND THE PLOW. Rodale Press, Emmaus, Pa. A critical assessment of large-scale farming and a discussion of alternatives. A really fine book.

McWilliams, C. 1970. FACTORIES IN THE FIELD. Perregrine Press, Santa Barbara, Calif. The history of California agriculture and farm labor. Enough to blow you away.

Gardens For All, Inc. 1974. COMMUNITY GARDENING PROCEDURAL MANUAL. P. O. Box 164. Charlotte, Vt. 05445. The Garden Way Research Co. has considerable experience and information about organizing community gardens. Write them (same address).

COMMUNITY GARDEN NEWS. Emphasis on vacant lot gardens, school gardens, company/employee gardens, housing development gardens, gardens for the handicapped, and how cities can get programs under way. Write: Jean M. Davis, Suite G17, American City Bldg., Columbia, MD. 21044.

AQUACULTURE

AQUACULTURE: BRINGING IT HOME WITH THE NEW ALCHEMISTS

The art of culturing fish and shellfish for food has been a flourishing tradition in Asia for centuries. In many "polyculture" ponds several species of edible plants and animals are grown together with a degree of ecological sophistication unrivaled in animal husbandry. In the United States aquaculture has been limited to the growing of single cash crops (e.g., trout, catfish, oysters) in commercial ponds or coastal waters. There never has been much of an interest in an aquaculture that could work for small groups, farmers, or communities using local resources and ecological techniques in temperate North American climates.

However as our beef/oil economy continues to decay, more and more people are beginning to think about producing food at the local level for their families, collectives, neighborhoods, communities, etc. For some the old "Victory garden" will flourish on roof-tops and street corners, in backyards and vacant lots. For others the bounties of vegetables, herbs and fruits can be enhanced with animal protein supplied by a low energy, low cost, ecologically-sound aquaculture. In order to work, such a mini-fish farm must be suited to the needs and local resources of individuals and small groups with little in the way of money or land.

To this end the New Alchemy Institute (Box 432, Woods Hole, Massachusetts 02543) has been experimenting with various "backyard fish farms" for the past few years. So far the New Alchemists have been concentrating on five basic strategies in an attempt to develop a low-cost, indigenous aquaculture adapted to northern climates: (1) the use of ecological models from Asian polyculture ponds, (2) the use of inexpensive greenhouses over fish ponds to keep the waters warm, (3) the use of biological filters for the transformation of toxic substances into useful nutrients, (4) the use of solar/wind power to regulate the internal climate of the pond-greenhouses and to pump filtered water through the system, (5) the use of fertilizers and supplemental fish foods produced in local gardens and insect cultures. The New Alchemists have published numerous useful how-to-do-it pamphlets, books and articles on the philosophy/ecology/hardware of backyard fish farms (see Aquaculture, page 137). Because the following paper is written only as a perspective, we refer the reader to the New Alchemy Institute for the "nuts and bolts" stuff. However, as the New Alchemists themselves are the first to admit, very little is known about small aquaculture operations in temperate climates. We can put together information from esoteric articles, the experiences of a few aquaculturists, the records of perennial fish ponds in the tropics or even the pertinent fallout from commercial set-ups, but perhaps more than any other kind of food/energy system described in the *Primer*, aquaculture is still in our heads . . . it needs participants and the flow of our experiences.

—R. M.

AQUACULTURE
by Dominick Mendola

The purpose of aquaculture is to provide fish and shellfish protein for human diets. The need for a substantial increase in the world's supply of protein is obvious . . . as is the place of fish in human nutrition. What is not so obvious is why aquaculture is a beneficial means of food production, especially protein. The reason is because aquaculture is more akin to agriculture than to ocean fisheries since the means of production (water, land stock and equipment) are accessible to many people and resources can be controlled by individuals, small groups, or even entire communities.[1] Also, since many of the fish populations presently exploited by ocean fisheries have reached their maximum sustainable yields, aquaculture can help supply the additional needs of an increasing demand for fish products.[2]

There are definite advantages to culturing fish as a food source. For one thing fish are able to produce more protein per pound of food eaten than, say, a cow, chicken, or any other land animal (Fig. 1).

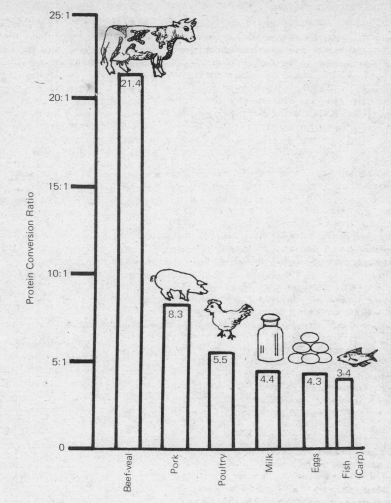

FIG. 1 POUNDS OF FEED GIVEN TO VARIOUS LIVESTOCK TO PRODUCE 1 POUND OF PROTEIN FOR HUMAN CONSUMPTION. REDRAWN FROM FIGURE OF LAPPÉ (REF. 3) AND DATA OF BARDACH ET AL (REF. 1).

There are two basic reasons for this: (1) Fish and shellfish live in a medium that has about the same density as their bodies and as a result they don't have to spend much energy supporting themselves against gravity. Thus, aquatic animals have a reduced skeleton and a greater ratio of flesh to bones . . . a definite advantage for a food species. (2) Fish and shellfish are cold-blooded, and their body temperatures are essentially that of their surroundings. Because of this they don't have to spend much energy maintaining warm body temperatures as do warm-blooded birds and mammals. This "saved" energy can go into the production of animal protein.

There are other advantages. Fish live in a three dimensional world where nutrients necessary for growth are distributed throughout a volume. So for a given area, aquaculture can yield more food than land-based animal husbandry.[4] For example, in an area once used for cattle grazing in Tanganyika, beef was produced at a rate of 9.8 pounds per acre per year (lbs/acre/yr). When this was replaced with aquaculture (with artificial feeding) fish production provided meat at the rate of about 2200 lbs/acre/yr.[5] Table I shows yields of selected aquaculture systems compared to typical land-animal husbandries.

As Table I indicates, there are different kinds of aquacultures; fresh water, brackish and marine. There are also a wide variety of animals (fish and shellfish) and plants (seaweeds, watercress, water lettuce, etc.) that are widely grown. We shall emphasize fresh water pond aquaculture that uses indigenous resources (simple materials, locally-grown fish foods and solar/wind power supplies). There are several reasons for this approach: (1) The methods and materials needed for this form of aquaculture are available to more people than for mariculture (farming the sea) or commercial aquaculture. (2) Costs can be kept low and human labor can provide the energy for construction and maintenance. (3) Many existing bodies of water can be easily converted to this form of aquaculture. (4) With small, self-contained fish operations one can easily control most of the inputs affecting the health, productivity and stability of the system. For example, many of the pollutants (pesticides, heavy metals and petroleum products) increasingly found in fish products can be eliminated or at least reduced with small aquaculture systems. However, even with local freshwater supplies one must consider the history of the use of toxic chemicals in the area. In fact it is always best to have water checked by a water quality laboratory since many toxins, especially pesticides, are slowly but surely finding their way into almost every supply of surface and ground waters in the U.S.[8,9,10,11] *

Aquaculture	Place	Culture/Feeding	Annual Yield* (lb/acre/yr)
FISH			
Largemouth bass, bluegill	U.S.	Polyculture/natural	225-400 (average)
Channel catfish	U.S.	Commercial ponds/artificial	2,000-3,000 (maximum)
Channel catfish	U.S.	Experimental, sewage ponds	3,600
Chinese carps	S.E. Asia	Polyculture/heavy fertilizer	6,300-8,000 (maximum) 2,700-3,600 (average)
Common carp	Poland	Sewage ponds	1,200
Common carp	Japan	Intensive ponds/heavy	4,500
Estuarine (Mullet)	U.S.	Tidal ponds/natural	185 (average)
Rainbow trout	U.S.	Flowing water ponds/heavy	60,000 (maximum)
Tilapia	Tropical world	Ponds/fertilization, feeding	2,000-5,500 (large fish) 18,000 (small fish)
Walking catfish (Clarias)	Thailand	Commercial/heavy feeding	88,000 (maximum)
SHELLFISH			
Sea mussel	Spain	Floating rafts	540,000 (with shell) 270,000 (meat)
Freshwater mussel	Alabama	Polyculture, experimental ponds	1,131 (with shell) 413 (meat)
Oyster	U.S.	Bottom culture, mechanical pest control	4,500 (maximum)
Oyster	U.S.	Bottom culture, chemical pest control	45,000 (maximum)
Oyster	Japan	Floating lines, no pest control	50,000 (average)
LAND HUSBANDRY			
Pasture beef	U.S.	Animals range free	50-200
Hogs	Malaysia	Natural forage	2,300-11,000
Chickens	U.S.	Cages/artificial feed	160,000

TABLE I   YIELDS OF SOME DOMESTIC FISH, SHELLFISH AND LAND ANIMALS. FROM REF. 4, 6 AND 7.

*In terms of energy production fish have a caloric value of about 1 kcal/gram of wet weight; e.g., the "Walking Catfish" produces about 4 million kcal/acre/year. For comparison, beef production yields only about 162,000 kcal/acre/year. (Ref. 10).

Many of the aquatic species that can be cultured for food are from tropical countries where aquaculture has been a way of life for centuries. Some of these animals can be imported or bought from distributors on this continent (see Reviews), and will thrive under artificially heated conditions. However, with a few notable exceptions (e.g., *Tilapia*) it is probably best to rely on temperate climate species, especially those found in the local area. (See Aquaculture appendix page 141, for list of some commonly available species together with their general habits.)

Ecological Food Production and Aquaculture

In nature it is common to see many kinds of plants and animals living together all with different habits. Generally speaking, in natural communities with a high degree of ecological diversity (i.e. with many kinds of plants and animals exchanging energy among themselves) like tropical rainforests or coral reefs, one usually finds a greater degree of stability than "simple" communities like pine forests or corn fields. With high ecological diversity there is less chance that disease or sudden changes from outside will destroy the integrity of the community or kill off individual species.[12,13]

In aquaculture, ecological diversity is called *polyculture*, where a variety of plants and animals, picked for their mutually beneficial interactions, are grown together in the same system (pond, tank or combina-

A few filter materials (e.g. polyurethane foam and activated carbon) have been used successfully to remove toxins from water solutions. However such filters are impractical in all but the smaller or commercial systems since they must be changed often or cleaned with organic solvents. Also, to be effective, the filters require a very slow flow rate.

tion). In ideal polyculture, large plants provide food for some fish, while microscopic floating plants (phytoplankton) serve as food for others. These plant-eating fish in turn serve as food for flesh-eating fish. All waste products are then eaten as detritus by certain other fish and shellfish. In this way, all available food niches are filled so that energy flow and nutrient recycling can proceed at a maximum rate. There are of course many possible combinations of fish and shellfish that are ecologically impossible as for example when a particularly voracious fish eats everything else in the pond. In other words, a lot of aquatic organisms living together *per se* do not produce ecological diversity. Only certain combinations can do that.

Once a proper polyculture system is found, it usually turns out to be synergistic, that is the growth of each individual species is enhanced beyond the point where it would be if it were raised separately in a monoculture. Put another way, polyculture assures that all food materials added to the system are completely used for growth. And herein lies the great advantage of polyculture over monoculture in aquatic food production systems.

Polyculture and the Sacred Carp

The polyculture model comes from the Chinese and Asian peoples who have been practicing the art of aquaculture for thousands of years. Today, in China, freshwater aquaculture provides at least 1.5 million tons of protein food every year.[14] As noted above, the Asian polyculture system is based on the belief that the pond is an ecosystem and that it should contain a variety of edible species for the maximum use of food and habitats.

The mainstay of the Asian polyculture pond is the Chinese Carp, of which there are several species (Fig. 2).

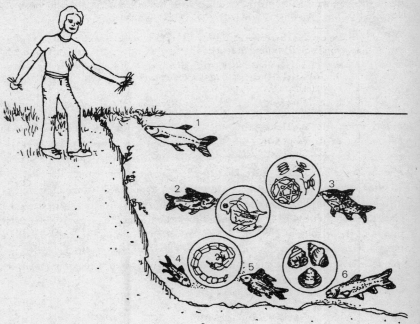

FIG. 2   FEEDING HABITS OF PRINCIPAL CHINESE CARP SPECIES. (1) GRASS CARP (CTENOPHARYNGODON IDELLUS) FEEDING ON LARGE FLOATING PLANTS. (2) BIG HEAD (ARISTICHTYS NOBILIS) FEEDING ON MICROSCOPIC ANIMALS (ZOOPLANKTON) IN MIDWATER. (3) SILVER CARP (HYPOPHTHALMICHTYS MOLITRIX) FEEDING ON MICROSCOPIC PLANTS IN MIDWATER. (4) MUD CARP (CIRRHINUS MOLITORELLA), AND (5) COMMON CARP (CYPRINUS CARPIO) FEEDING ON BOTTOM ANIMALS, DETRITUS AND CARP FECES. (6) BLACK CARP (MYLOPHARYNGODON PICEUS) FEEDING ON MOLLUSKS. FIGURE REDRAWN FROM BARDACH ET AL (REF. 1)

Typical yields from Chinese polyculture ponds average about 2400 lbs/acre/year, with some of the better ponds producing 4800-6400 lbs/acre/year.** Yields are increased by feeding manures, vegetable wastes and other organic materials to the ponds. These fertilize the water and increase the primary productivity (yields of plants). This excess food energy is then passed up the food chain to the carp.

Often the Asians situate their fish ponds at the bottom of a hill or sloping farmland, allowing natural drainage to carry the manures and agri-

**1 kilogram/hectare = 2.2 lbs/2.47 acres or about 1 lb/acre (actually 1 kg/ha = .89 lbs/acre).

cultural runoff into the pond (Fig. 3).

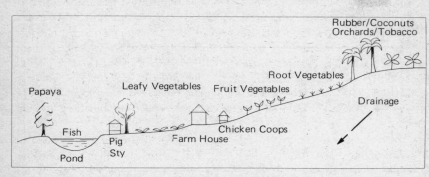

FIG. 3   AN INTEGRATED AQUACULTURE-AGRICULTURE SYSTEM USED
IN SINGAPORE. REDRAWN FROM BARDACH ET AL (REF. 1) AND
DESCRIPTION OF HO (REF. 6).

The Asians also use the pond water to irrigate (and fertilize) their crops.
At regular intervals the ponds are drained and the accumulated bottom
sludge is dug out and added to vegetable beds as compost.

Table II has been compiled to show various carp polyculture schemes
that have been tried throughout the world. These examples give an idea of
optimal conditions for the stocking, management and feeding of carp.

Simple Energy Budgets for Aquaculture

There doesn't seem to be any information or exact accounting of all
energy inputs into freshwater fish ponds. (But see the materials list for
the 3 backyard fish models built by the New Alchemists, in their Journal
No. 2). For now we have to be content with budgets based on labor inputs
for Asian pond operations.

Le Mare[7] described a very efficient 11 acre farm near Penang, Malaya on
which a tenant farmer kept pigs and fish, and tended a small diverse garden
and some rice fields. The pigs were bred, kept in a nursery, and then fattened
in pens. Some pigs were kept in sties on the banks surrounding a series of 8
small ponds (about 2 acres total). Daily the farmer allowed running water
to wash through the pig sties and carry the dung and excess pig food into
the ponds by a series of drainage ditches.

The ponds were about 3 feet deep and were stocked with various
Chinese carp (Common, Silver and Grass), in polyculture with *Tilapia
mossambica*. All ponds were planted with "water lettuce" *(Ipomea repens)*,
a floating aquatic plant suitable for pig food (21% protein—dry weight).
Under these conditions the water lettuce grew so rapidly that about 1100
lbs/day (wet weight), *in excess of that eaten by the carp*, were harvested
and added as a supplement to the pig food (broken rice, rolled and ground
oats, groundnut cake, copra cake, brain, fish meal, and cod liver oil) in a
ration of 1/3 water lettuce to 2/3 feed.

Production of fish during the first year was about 3200 lbs/acre. The
farm also produced 700 pigs (about 2700 lbs. of pig meat). The records of
production costs showed that the fish gave a higher proportional return
than the pigs because little labor and materials were spent tending the fish,
whereas a great deal of labor plus additional food was spent on the pigs.
In other words, the *energy subsidy* of the fish culture was lower than
for the pigs. Since the only inputs were human labor, we can easily estimate the time (energy) necessary to manage and harvest the 2 acres of
ponds from what we know of fish raising.

Species, Stocking Ratio		Treatment and Stocking Density	Yields and Survival
1. KWUNGTUNG PROVINCE, CHINA			
TENANT FARM, 1/5 ACRE			
a. Mud Carp	(Ref. 15)	Mud Carp—600 fingerlings (30 lbs.)	≈ 4000 lbs/acre/year
b. Grass Carp	(Ratio not given)	Grass Carp—200 fingerlings (14 lbs.)	
c. Big Head Carp		Big Head Carp—25 fingerlings (9 lbs.)	
d. Silver Carp		Silver Carp—25 fingerlings (9 lbs.)	
e. Black Carp		Black Carp—10 fingerlings (2 lbs.)	
f. Common Carp		Common Carp—25 fingerlings (2 lbs.)	
2. INDIA EXPERIMENTAL PONDS			
a. Grass Carp	(Ref. 16)	24,300-36,500 per acre	2590 lbs/acre/year
b. Silver Carp	(3:4:3)	Carp fry	80% survival
c. Common Carp		No feeding data	
3. ISRAEL, BRACKISH WATER PONDS			
a. Common Carp	(Ref. 17)	Variable stocking rates.	(estimated) 6250-8000 lbs/acre/year
b. Silver Carp		Ponds fertilized.	
c. *Tilapia aurea* Food habits unknown		Fish fed pelletized diet high in protein.	
d. *Tilapia nilotica* Plankton feeder?			
Omnivore or feeds on high plants			
(exact habits unknown)			
e. Grey Mullet (*Mugil* spp.)			
Plankton, benthic algae			
4. ROMANIA, 300 ACRE POND			
a. Common Carp	(Ref. 18)	1700, 570, 40 respectively lbs/acre	1750 lbs/acre/year
b. Silver Carp	(3:1:1)	Yearling fish, supplemental feeding	56% Common, 34% Silver, 10% Grass
c. Grass Carp			Food Conversion Ratio 3:1
5. ROMANIA, 300 ACRE POND			
Same as above	(Ref. 18)	2350, 1300, 160 per acre respectively.	2050 lbs/acre/year
	(14:8:1)	Supplemental feeding.	56% Common, 39% Silver, 5% grass
			Food Conversion 2.7:1
6. CHINA, 1½ ACRE POND			
a. Black Carp	(Ref. 15)	Black Carp—773 (844 g)	Total weight 11,800 lbs/year
b. Silver Carp		Silver Carp—2000 (23 g)	≈ 50% Blacks
c. Big Head		Big Head—400 (30g)	Net Production 100,000 lbs/year or
d. Bream (*Parabramu pekinesis*)		Bream—1214 (25 g)	6700 lbs/acre/year
Feeds on insects, worms, small fish		Grass Carp—110 (191g)	95.6% survival
e. Common Carp		Common Carp—1905 (26g)	
		Total 6402 (812 kg)	
		Fish (1800 lbs)	
4. BURMA, 3 REARING PONDS, 0.2 ACRES EACH			
a. Grass Carp	(Ref. 19)	1370-2035 2g fingerlings/acre	(After 6 months)
b. Silver Carp	(Variable)	Fed with mixture of rice bran, peanut cake,	Total production 1700, 1820, 1242 lbs/acre
		and chopped green vegetation. (Ratio 1:1:2)	Average production: Silver —868 lbs/acre
		7—11 lbs/day (quantity doubled after 3 months)	Grass—720 lbs/acre
			Survival: Silver 95%, Grass 97%

TABLE II   POND STOCKING DENSITIES, MANAGEMENT TREATMENTS AND YIELDS OF VARIOUS CARP POLYCULTURE SCHEMES

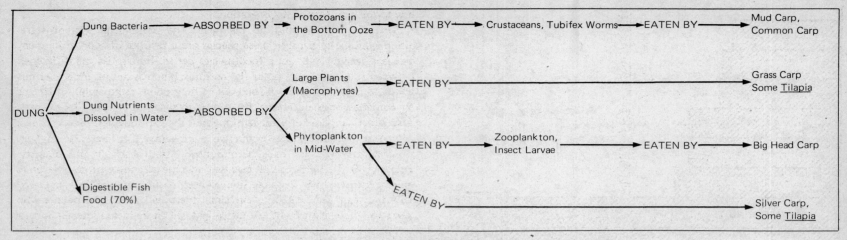

FIG. 4   THE CONTRIBUTION OF DUNG FERTILIZER TO THE DIFFERENT
FOOD CHAINS OF A POLYCULTURE FISH POND.

LABOR ENERGY INPUT
A. Assume that a person doing moderate work consumes about: 170 kcal/hr.
B. Assume that the farmer must spend about 500 hours per year tending and harvesting the fish from the 2 acres of ponds.
C. Therefore total labor energy expended is:
    500 hrs/year x 170 kcal/hour . . . . E = 85,000 kcal/year

FISH ENERGY OUTPUT (PRODUCTION)
D. Annual fish production from the 2 acres of ponds is: 3600 kilograms (7900 lbs)
E. Assume energy value of fish flesh to be:
    1 kcal/gram wet weight
F. Then energy value of total production is:
    (3600 Kg) x (1 Kcal/gram) . . . . P = 3,600,000 Kcal/year

ENERGY BUDGET OF MALAYSIAN POLYCULTURE FISH POND
    C/F . . . . . . 0.02 = 2% i.e. a labor energy subsidy of 2 Kcal is required for every 100 Kcal of fish produced

TABLE III   ENERGY BUDGET FOR POLYCULTURE FISH PONDS IN MALAY-
SIA. NOTE: THE PIG MANURE AND SPILT PIG FOOD THAT FER-
TILIZE THE PONDS ARE CONSIDERED AS BY-PRODUCTS OF THE
PIG PRODUCTION, AND FOR OUR PURPOSES HERE ARE NOT FI-
GURED IN THE ENERGY BUDGET. BASIC DATA FROM REF. 7

The value of 0.02 is an extremely low figure when compared to other methods of food production (see Fig. 2, page 115 of the *Primer*).

It is interesting to note that the pig dung serves as food for the fish in at least four important ways (Fig. 4). This illustrates the importance of organic fertilizers to the balanced diversity of the fish pond (i.e., more than just one food chain is supplied with food).

Taiwan is another Asian country where fish is an important part of the diet (63% of the animal protein eaten). Aquaculture in Taiwan covers the range from intensive coastal oyster farms to carp and *Tilapia* polycultures in inland ponds. The results of one study from Taiwan[20] are important because they suggest that under comparable conditions freshwater pond aquaculture has a higher return on energy/material investment than either pig farming or ocean fishing (Table IV).

Type of Husbandry	Kg*/Man Year Average	High	Kg/Hectare/Year** Average	High	U.S. $/Kg Average	Low
Brackish Water (Milk fish)	5,098	11,022	2112	2687	0.37	0.29
Freshwater Ponds (carp, Tilapia)	10,453	70,607	1537	2413	0.31	0.20
Shallow Sea (oysters)	45,575	--	1292	2096	0.16	0.10
Hog Farming	12,000	--	(see Table I)		0.43	--

* 1Kg = 2.2 lbs.
** 1 Kg/ha - .89 lbs/acre

TABLE IV   PRODUCTIVITY AND PRODUCTION COSTS FOR DIFFERENT
TYPES OF WATER AND LAND HUSBANDRY IN TAIWAN.
AFTER REF. 20

When compared in terms of protein production, the results stay relative-

ly the same. Shallow sea oyster farming is the most economical, followed by freshwater pond aquaculture (Table V). However, it is worth re-emphasizing the obvious: freshwater pond aquaculture is practical for many more people than is mariculture. And in this sense, it may be the most efficient means of animal protein production.

Product	Production Kg Protein/Man-Year Average	High	Cost U.S. $/Kg Average	Low	Protein %	Fat %
Brackish Water (Milk fish)	519	1,123	3.63	2.84	20	2
Freshwater (Carp)	1,148	7,759	2.80	1.81	22	9
Shallow Sea (Oyster)	4,552	--	1.60	--	10	4
Hog	757	--	6.81	--	8	41

TABLE V   ESTIMATED COST OF PROTEIN PRODUCTION IN TAIWAN.
FROM REF. 20

Using the same logic we did for the Malaysian fish-pig farm we can now estimate the energy budget of the Taiwan polyculture system (Table VI).

LABOR ENERGY INPUT
A. Assume the labor energy of a man-year to be:
    (8 hrs/day) (170 kcal/hr)(365 days/yr) . . . . . 496,000 kcal
FISH ENERGY OUTPUT (PRODUCTION
B. 23,000 lbs/man year* . . . . 10.5 million kcal
ENERGY BUDGET OF TAIWAN FISH FARMING
    A/B = .05 = 5%

TABLE VI   PARTIAL ENERGY BUDGET OF FRESH WATER POND AQUA-
CULTURE IN TAIWAN. AFTER REF. 20. BUDGET INCLUDES
MAINTENANCE ENERGY ONLY AND NOT SECONDARY INPUTS
LIKE: PRE-PLANNING, SITE CONSTRUCTION, PRODUCTION
ENERGY OF MATERIALS USED, FERTILIZERS, ETC.

Although these examples are for tropical countries, they do suggest that an aquaculture which is practiced with ecological techniques is an ex-tremely efficient means of obtaining protein for human nutrition. Also, aquaculture can thrive on waste products and need not depend upon grains which themselves can be used for human food.

As a final point of interest we can compare the energy budgets (protein ratios) of various foods produced in the U.S. (Fig. 5).

This information suggests that fish provide more animal protein per energy input than any other kind of U.S. food (compare to Fig. 1), even though most of the fish produced by the U.S. is from offshore fishing.

The Small Fish Farmer in the U.S.

We have given examples of pond aquaculture systems operated in the tropics. Now what about comparable systems for temperate latitudes . . . specifically the U.S?

First of all it is important to understand that the single most important

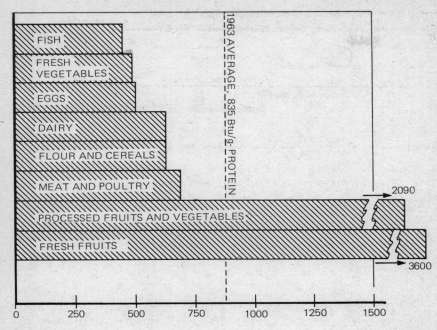

1963 AVERAGE, 835 Btu/g-PROTEIN

PROTEIN RATIO (Btu-primary energy/g - food protein

FIG. 5   PROTEIN RATIO OF VARIOUS FOOD GROUPS IN THE U.S.
PROTEIN RATIO = RATIO OF ENERGY INPUTS TO ENERGY
OUTPUTS (PROTEIN ENERGY). REDRAWN AFTER REF. 21.

factor with regards to fish production is water temperature. Being cold-blooded, fish and shellfish respond immediately to changes in temperature, generally growing better in warmer water. The tropics receive more solar energy (see Fig. 2, pp 26 of Primer) and have a warmer average climate than the higher latitudes. Thus aquatic organisms grow faster and for longer periods (year around) in the tropics than they do in temperate climates. Generally speaking, within the temperature range in which a fish can thrive, an increase of about $10°C$ can cause growth and metabolism to double. This relationship is also reversible. Growth rates can be cut in half for each $10°C$ drop in average water temperature. Below a critical temperature, of course, growth ceases altogether (e.g., when fish are over-wintering), and if the water temperature continues to fall, a lower *lethal limit* is reached.

As a result of this temperature relationship, natural or managed aquatic systems in most of the U.S. aren't very productive. This is why the majority of commercial aquaculture operations (except trout which thrive in cold waters), are located in the southern Gulf states.

The small farmer not living on the Gulf of Mexico, in the southwestern U.S. or southern California has few choices if he wants to raise fish for food in farm ponds. He is bound to choose an endemic species that can survive over winter, until summer when growth can resume. Since the growing season is so short (3-6 months in most of the U.S.) productivity is low compared to the tropics.

In the U.S. the traditional regime is the Largemouth Bass-Bluegill community. The bass is a predator and feeds only on smaller fish (including their own offspring) and invertebrates it can find in the pond. The bluegill feeds mostly on bottom animals. Because they eat mostly animals and not plants, bass-bluegill cultures rarely produce more than 400 lbs/acre/yr.

The same situation exists for the other traditionally cultured fish in the U.S. (catfish, trout and perch), which are basically flesh eaters growing only during the warm part of the year. When raised in small farm ponds without supplemental feeding, yields are very low. It is only when these fish are raised commercially that the yields increase substantially. Commercial trout and catfish are big business in the U.S., and like the rest of agriculture they have already been locked into the agribusiness syndrome. Monoculture is practiced with heavy overstocking and feeding with high protein trout and "cat chows." The ponds must be artificially aerated to keep the fish from dying. Plants are kept out of the system lest they foul up the "efficient" workings, and if they should happen to become established . . . herbicides are often used![14]

But even with chemical aids and technical "advances," American catfish farmers seldom produce more than 3000 lbs/acre/yr. Trout have yielded up to 60,000 lbs/acre/yr (Idaho trout farms), but the fish are very expensive due to the high cost of the operation.

There is another point to be made. The bass-bluegill system is traditional primarily because these species are a favorite of sport fishermen, and not because they are a food-species *per se*. Herein lies the difference between U.S. and Asian pond fish cultures. Whereas the Asians are serious about trying to get as much food out of their ponds as possible, Americans are content with an occasional fish dinner to augment their beef/pork diets. Also Americans are fairly squeamish about the fish they eat; very few seem willing to accept a more productive plant-eating fish like carp. In fact, most herbivorous fish have been dubbed "trash fish" in this country. Possibly these prejudices will give way in time as animal protein becomes more expensive. For example, per capita consumption of fish increased 15% between 1967-1970.[2] And since there will always be people who want to "grow their own" we just might see an increased interest in rural fish ponds.

According to Bill McLarney,[22] a 1 acre farm pond somewhere in rural America, with bass and bluegill, could produce 108 pounds of edible meat per year if the following management practices were followed: (1) Periodic harvesting of larger fish by partial draining and seining. This provides additional food for the remaining smaller fish. (2) Leaving about 25% of the small fish that remain after the last harvest (in mid-late fall), and a small breeding population of adult fish making the pond a perennial source of food. (3) Using proper skill in dressing the fish. McLarney quotes a 40% dressing loss for fish caught in Massachusetts ponds. With these precautions one could get over 100 pounds of edible fish meat per acre per year in a growing season of about 6 months.

Tending a large farm pond is only practical if you happen to live on a farm or other open space; but what about people with just a backyard. Are there fish rearing systems for them?

The Backyard Fish Farm

At the present time a small research group in Massachusetts, the New Alchemy Institute, is experimenting with different kinds of small scale aquaculture systems geared to individuals, families and small groups. The Alchemists have pioneered in methods of raising herbivorous fish in small ponds and tanks enclosed by greenhouses, and fueled with local resources.

The Alchemists' systems are modeled after Asian polyculture farms, but are adapted for northern climates. They have done this by: (1) Incorporating home-built solar heat collectors to add to the warming effect of the greenhouse and raise the water temperature of the ponds to $20°$–$30°C$. At these temperatures *Tilapia* and carps undergo rapid growth and reach harvestable size in as little as 10 weeks if given proper food. (2) Stocking, fertilizing and feeding with organic wastes and natural foods grown either near or right in the cultures. (3) Using biological filters for removing toxic materials, and wind energy for moving the filtered water. The systems are designed to be ecologically efficient without requiring large sums of money for their construction, or much time for their maintenance.

To date the New Alchemists have tested three basic aquaculture models (Figs. 6, 7, 8). Figure 9 shows their next planned project . . . The Ark. Journal No. 2 of the New Alchemy Institute has a complete description of all four set-ups. We will describe briefly one of their systems (the Mini-Ark). It illustrates the basic strategy behind backyard fish farming: to mimic the fish culture after a natural pond ecosystem.

Figure 8 shows the "Mini-Ark." Designed as a precursor to the Ark (Fig. 9), it is a closed recirculating system in three stages. A water pumping windmill made from simple materials (see Wind Section page 95 of *Primer*) circulates the water by pumping it from the lower fish pool to the upper pool where the water then flows back down through the middle and lower pools by gravity.

The *upper pool* is a purifying filter consisting of three separate compartments: a biological filter, an earth filter and an algae culture. Basically the entire filter pool takes the place of the earth-bottom of a natural pond or lake. The biological filter is a bed of crushed clam (Quahog) shells which provides a large surface substrate for the growth of nitrifying bacteria. These microbes convert the toxic waste materials produced by the fish (mostly ammonia) into nitrates and nitrites (NO_3 and NO_2). If allowed to accumulate, these toxins would either kill the fish directly or stunt their growth. Also the nitrates and nitrites are the form of nitrogen most pre-

COMPOST INSULATOR/HEATER
For Backyard Fish Farm Pool/Dome System

Cross section

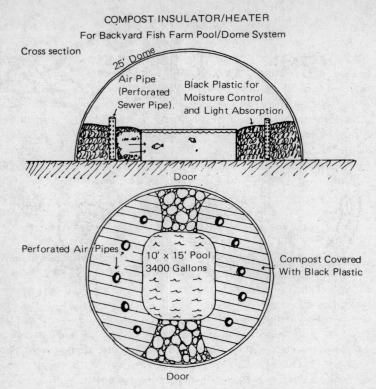

FIG. 6   A DOME-COVERED FISH POND FOR NORTHERN CLIMATES.
FROM THE JOURNAL NO. 2 OF THE NEW ALCHEMY INSTITUTE.

WARM WEATHER FISH CULTURE CYCLE

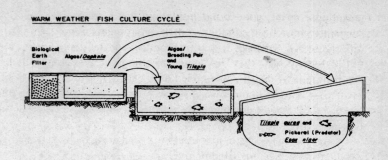

FIG. 7   A THREE-TIERED, FLAT TOP FISH RAISING COMPLEX.
FROM THE JOURNAL NO. 2 OF THE NEW ALCHEMY INSTITUTE.

FIG. 8   THE MINIATURE ARK: A WIND-POWERED, SOLAR-HEATED, COM-
BINED GREENHOUSE AND BACKYARD FISH FARM. FROM THE
JOURNAL NO. 2 OF THE NEW ALCHEMY INSTITUTE.

ferred and acceptable to plants.** Thus potentially harmful wastes are recycled into useful nutrients for the plants, which in turn feed the fish, etc. etc. The clam-shell filter does two other things: it traps suspended organic matter which tends to use up available oxygen, and it buffers the pH of the culture water.

The earth filter section consists of small water plants growing in dirt. The earth does two things: first, it provides trace elements vital to growing plants and animals; second, it inoculates the system with nitrifying bacteria for the biological filter. The aquatic plants growing in the earth bed contribute oxygen to the filter thus ensuring the life of the (aerobic) nitrifying bacteria even when wind and water circulation are poor.

The third compartment of the upper pool becomes rich with microscopic algae (phytoplankton) as the nutrients from the biological filter flow into this space. This rich "soup" is allowed to flow into the *middle pool* where tiny crustaceans (*Daphnia*) eat the phytoplankton and increase in numbers. The *middle pool* is periodically drained into the *bottom pool* where the *Daphnia* serve as food for juvenile fish growing there.

The *bottom pool* (8500 gallons) is the main culture pool for the fish. Presently the Alchemists are stocking species of *Tilapia* in polyculture. These fish grow well in the warm water (25°-30°C) made possible by the

---

**Recent research [23] has indicated that when raising herbivorous fish like Tilapia or Carp it may not be wise to include large water plants in the system since they remove large amounts of nutrients (especially nitrates and phosphates) which would otherwise be used by the phytoplankton for primary productivity.*

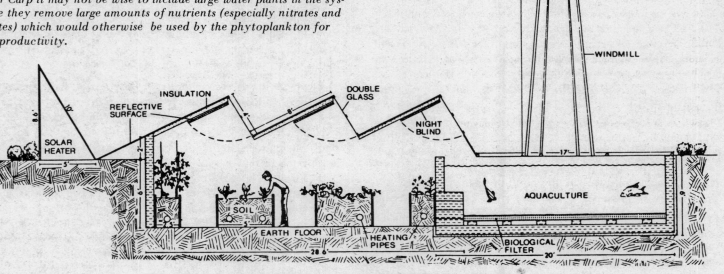

FIG. 9   THE ARK; A PROPOSED ADVANCED MODEL OF THE MINI-ARK.
FROM JOURNAL NO. 2 OF THE NEW ALCHEMY INSTITUTE.

greenhouse cover, good pond insulation and a solar collector. Since the Alchemists have been conducting their experiments as models for others to use, they have not been trying to produce especially high yields. However Bill McLarney feels that they might be able to harvest about 100 lbs/yr of fish from one of their dome ponds (3000 gallons). This is quite an improvement over natural non-managed systems when we consider that this pond is only 0.02 acres (remember the maximum 400 lbs/acre/yr for the bass-bluegill farm ponds).

There are many techniques used by the New Alchemists to increase fish productivity. They are listed here by way of summary:

1. Increase water temperature by using insulated pools, greenhouse structures with double insulating skins, solar water heaters, insulating night covers for the tanks and reflective panels which bring more heat into the pools.

2. Fertilize with manures to increase the primary productivity of the system.

3. Raise herbivorous fish which feed at the primary consumer level of the food chain and are thus more efficient at converting primary productivity (aquatic plants) to fish meat.

4. Polyculture . . . growing a variety of animal species that feed in different ecological niches and utilize different living habitats of the contained ecosystem (culture tank or pond).

5. Raise natural foods in or near the system for supplemental feeding (see Fig. 10). These foods may include midge fly larvae *(Chironomids)*, fly maggots, other insects caught by "bug lights" at night, earthworms, amphipods as well as plants such as garden weeds, vegetable wastes (especially carrot tops), grass clippings, etc. (See the bibliography at the end of this article for further information on the cultivation of natural animal foods for fish.) When animal protein is used as a supplement to the plant diets of herbivorous fish, especially in the early stages of growth, it enables the fish to grow faster and stay in better health than when they are fed strictly on plant materials. The New Alchemists have found that about 10% of the diet of *Tilapia* should be made up of animal foods. Animal protein also has a high conversion efficiency into fish flesh. In other words it takes less animal foods to produce a given amount of fish flesh than it does plant material (Table VII).

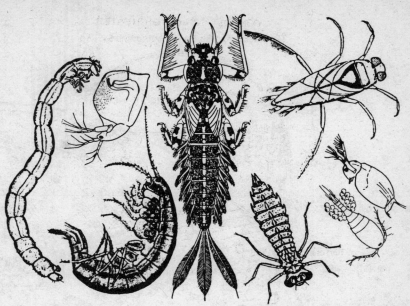

FIG. 10   AQUATIC INVERTEBRATES GROWN AS NATURAL FOODS FOR CULTURED FISH AND PRAWNS. CLOCKWISE FROM UPPER RIGHT: WATER BUG, CLADOCERON AND COPEPOD, DRAGONFLY NYMPH, GAMMARUS, CHIRONOMID MIDGE LARVAE, DAPHNIA, CENTER, MAGFLY NYMPH.

materials that have a long life and low energy cost.

8. Consideration of the cost-effectiveness of the system. Is it economical to build and maintain? The New Alchemists have taken pains to design for the homesteader or small group, but yet have not skimped on design. Their systems are designed to last and provide paybacks in terms of edible products for many years.

The Neighborhood Fish Farm

Another system worth mentioning is one that has been designed to serve the animal protein needs of a larger number of people, say a group of families or a community. It is derived from the greenhouse-polyculture schemes described above. It is a fairly large system and it emphasizes, in addition to fish production, shellfish culture and vegetable hydroponics.

The modular unit is shown in Fig. 12. It is a quonset-type greenhouse 100' by 30' that is equipped with double plastic walls, insulation on the north side and ends, and solar heat collectors alternated with clear double-wall sections on the south side. Inside are three large culture tanks (60' x 6' x 4') built of polyurethane foam, hand layed-up cement and fiberglass or wood (the tradeoffs on tank design haven't been completely explored as yet). Also smaller tanks for rearing natural foods and housing biological filters are included as partitions from the larger culture tanks. An area at one end of the greenhouse is set up for rearing juvenile animals and keeping breeding adults. Finally, associated with each main tank is a hydroponic growing compartment where the culture water from the main tanks (a "soup" of excellent fertilizer) is flushed through gravel beds planted with vegetable crops (Fig. 11).

Foods of Plant Origin		Household scraps	1
		Banana leaves	25·0
Lupine seeds	3-5	Guinea Grass	48·0
Soyabeans	3-5		
Maize	4-6		
Cereals	4-6	**Foods of Animal Origin**	
All cereals	5		
Potatoes	20-30	Gammarus	3·9-6·6
Maize	3·5	Chironomids	2·3-4·4
Cottonseed	2·3	Housefly maggots	7·1
Cottonseed cake	3·0	Fresh sea fish	6-9
Groundnut cake	2·7	Fish flour	1·5-3·0
Ground maize	3·5	Freshwater fish	2·9-6·0
Ground rice	4·5	Fresh meat	5-8
Oil palm cakes	6·0	Liver, spleen and abbatoir offals	8
Mill sweepings	8·0	Prawns and shrimp	4-6
Rice flour	8·0	White cheese	10-15
Manioc leaves	13·5	Dried silkworm pupae	1-8

Mixtures

Fresh sardine, mackerel scad, dried silkworm pupae	5·5
Liver of horse and pig, sardine, silkworm pupae	4·5
Silkworm pupae, silkworm feces, grass, soyabean cake, pig manure, night soil	4·1
Cortland Trout diet No. 6	7·1
Raw silkworms pupae, pressed barley, Lema and Gammarus	2·5

TABLE VII   CONVERSION RATES OF VARIOUS FOODS INTO FISH. CONVERSION RATE = WEIGHT OF FOOD/INCREASE IN WEIGHT OF FISH. THE LOWER THE NUMBER THE MORE EFFICIENT IS THE FOOD IN PRODUCING FISH FLESH. ADAPTED FROM HICKLING (REF. 15).

6. Periodic harvest of larger fish. This allows the remaining smaller fish to use the available food more efficiently.

7. Use of low-impact technology for building the equipment needed to run the fish farm. These include windmill pumps for circulating water, solar collectors for warming the pond water, wind generators and heating coils for heating the water during periods of cloudy weather, and use of building

Nutrient Rich
Effluent From
Prawn Tanks

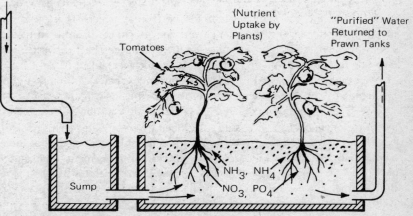

(Nutrient Uptake by Plants)

"Purified" Water Returned to Prawn Tanks

Tomatoes

Sump

NH_3, NH_4

NO_3, PO_4

FIG. 11   HYDROPONIC VEGETABLE GROWING TANK. ILLUSTRATES PURIFYING ACTION OF PLANTS ON NUTRIENT LADEN CULTURE WATER.

Among the many kinds of animals grown is the giant Malaysian fresh-

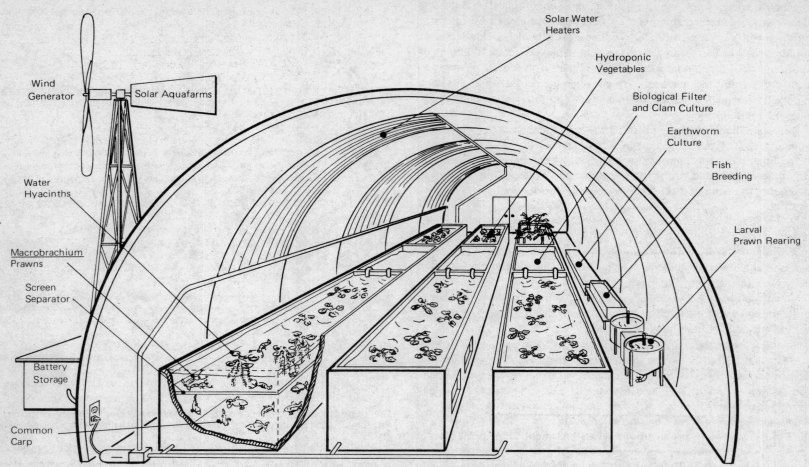

Labels on figure:
Wind Generator — Solar Aquafarms
Water Hyacinths
Macrobrachium Prawns
Screen Separator
Battery Storage
Common Carp
Solar Water Heaters
Hydroponic Vegetables
Biological Filter and Clam Culture
Earthworm Culture
Fish Breeding
Larval Prawn Rearing

FIG. 12 A 100' x 30' "AQUASOLARIUM" SOLAR-WIND POWERED AQUATIC FOOD PRODUCTION UNIT. AFTER A DESIGN OF D. MENDOLA, NEW ALCHEMY INSTITUTE—WEST AND S.A. SERFLING, SOLAR AQUAFARMS, DAVIS, CA.

water prawn (*Macrobrachium rosenbergi*). A relative of saltwater shrimp, this animal is especially suited to freshwater tank culture. It is fast growing (egg to adult in 7-9 months at 27°C), hardy, omnivorous, disease resistant, easy to breed and tasty. The Western New Alchemists have spent the last 2 years working with this animal and heartily recommend it. It is ideal for culture as human food since it has a high protein content (22% wet weight) and a high yield of edible meat (about 50%).

The females bear from 10,000 to 60,000 eggs (15,000 average). About 50 to 80% of these hatch as planktonic larvae. After spending about 30 days in special rearing vessels, the larvae "settle out" as bottom-crawling, diminutive versions of the adult animal. Survival from eggs to this post-larval stage is usually about 50% with good culture conditions.

The main culture tanks are partitioned horizontally to keep prawns in the top half and common carp in the bottom half. The top half is planted with floating aquatic plants (water hyacinths) whose fibrous roots serve as a habitat for the juvenile prawns. The hyacinths also act as hiding places for the adults, since the males are very aggressive towards each other (i.e. territorial) and tend to fight if allowed to come into contact.

Other methods have also been proposed to house the adult prawns, but these are primarily designed for intensive, high-yield commercial operations.

Common carp are kept beneath the horizontal screen. These feed on the rain of animal wastes coming from above. The carp are bred in the laboratory and stocked as juveniles in the subspace. The fish wastes are taken up by the water plants and the hydroponic vegetables.

After the water is passed through the hydroponic beds it is pumped into the biological filter beds and then back into the main culture tanks. A scheme is also being worked out where a portion of the culture water including organic debris is passed into a bed of fresh water clams (*Corbicula*). The bivalves filter out the detritus and use this food energy for their own growth. They multiply readily without any management, and can be periodically cropped to be fed back to the prawns or used for human food. Still another cycle involves some of the culture water passing into a tank where *Daphnia* are grown as food for the juvenile prawns.

The prawns must eat particulate materials. They will take almost any garden scraps chopped finely and are particularly fond of cooked rice and raw oats. Only supplemental amounts of these foods are needed, since a good portion of their food can be the clams and *Daphnia* cultured in the system.

The energetics of the prawn-carp operation are still being worked out by the west coast New Alchemists who plan on writing a workbook on it next year (Fig. 13, next page). What is known already, however, is that about 900 pounds of prawns (450 pounds of meat) and 400-600 pounds of fish meat per year can be harvested from a system whose initial costs (materials plus maintenance) average $1000 per year amortized over 10 years. This is a reasonable expenditure for a system that yields over 1000 pounds of edible meat . . . not to mention the unknown quantity of clams and vegetables.

* *

We have seen examples of backyard, neighborhood and farm-scale fish farms tailored for the American environment and modeled after natural aquatic ecosystems. Obviously any aquaculture set-up requires a certain amount of biological skill to construct and maintain. However, with time, patience and proper attention, we believe these schemes, or ones like them, can be made practical and serve as integral parts of a local food producing operation.

OBTAINING FISH AND SHELLFISH FOR AQUACULTURE

Some freshwater animals suitable for aquaculture are legally controlled in many states. For example, in California, it is illegal to import grass carp and the freshwater clam *Corbicula* across state lines, or to release these species into natural waters. In closed aquaculture systems (those recirculating the same water) you have control over species escaping into local streams, etc., and possibly upsetting their ecological balance. In open systems (those using water from local sources and releasing culture water into them) there is always a possibility of contamination. Tropical or sub-tropical species like *Tilapia* or *Macrobrachium* would probably not survive a winter in streams and rivers in most of the United States. Others adapted to cool waters might thrive. In any event it is probably best to check with your local Fish and Game Office. They can tell you the legal implications of growing a particular fish or shellfish for food. As far as obtaining *Tilapia*,

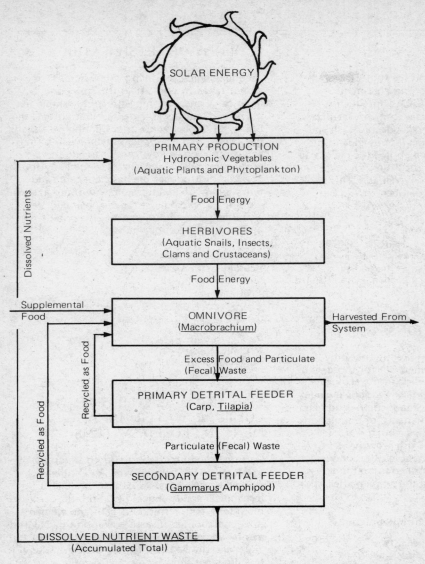

FIG. 13 ENERGY AND NUTRIENT FLOW SCHEME FOR A CLOSED-CYCLE POLYCULTURE SYSTEM DESIGNED FOR MAXIMIZING PRODUCTION OF FISH AND PRAWNS AND MINIMIZING ENERGY LOSSES

inquiries should be made with local aquarium stores, or by contacting one of the distributors listed below.

Sources for fish stocks:

Perry Minnow Farm
Rt. 1, Box 128-C
Windsor, VA 23487
(Israeli Carp)

J. M. Malone and Son Enterprises
P.O. Box 158
Lanoke, Arkansas 72086
(Grass Carp, Tilapia)

Finally, Journal No. 2 of the New Alchemist includes further information on how and where to obtain stocks of *Tilapia*. Journal No. 2 and other pamphlets on aquaculture (see below) can be obtained from:

New Alchemy Institute
Box 432
Woods Hole, Massachusetts 02543

NEW ALCHEMY AQUACULTURE PUBLICATIONS

1. AQUACULTURE BIBLIOGRAPHY
William O. McLarney. Includes references on polyculture and pond construction. Available from New Alchemy, or Readers' Service, Organic Gardening and Farming magazine. Emmaus, Pennsylvania 18049. Price $1.00
2. THE BACKYARD FISH FARM WORKING MANUAL FOR 1973
W. O. McLarney, ed. This first "how-to-do-it" manual for backyard fish farmers has been updated and much improved in a comparable article in The Journal of the New Alchemists No. 2.
3. WALTON II: A COMPLEAT GUIDE TO BACKYARD FISH FARMING
W. O. McLarney and J. H. Todd, 1974. It's all we have learned about raising fish under intensive and ecological conditions. An extensive treatment intended to assist those wanting to start raising low-cost, high-quality fishes. Includes sources of fish. The Journal of The New Alchemists No. 2. 1974. $6.00.

4. AQUACULTURE SERIES FOR ORGANIC GARDENING AND FARMING MAGAZINE (EMMAUS, PA 18049).
August 1971, W. McLarney Aquaculture on the Organic Farm & Homestead
November 1971, W. McLarney, The Fish Pond Revisited
January 1972, J. Todd and W. McLarney The Backyard Fish Farm
February 1972, W. McLarney Why Not Carp?
April 1972, W. McLarney Pond Construction: First Step to Successful Aquaculture
5. AQUACULTURE: THE FARMING AND HUSBANDRY OF FRESHWATER AND MARINE ORGANISMS
J. Bardach, J. Ryther and W. O. McLarney. John Wiley and Sons, 1972, 868 pages, $37.50. This is the definitive English language text in the field. NAI's McLarney was the primary contributor to the book. It's very expensive, but if you are going to commit yourself to aquatic farming, you will need to read it. Ask your library to buy it. The cost is largely in the plates and illustrations which add a lot of value to the text. See Reviews.
6. STUDIES OF THE ECOLOGY OF THE CHARACID FISH, BRYCON GUATEMALENSIS, IN THE RIO TIRIMBINA, COSTA RICA, WITH SPECIAL REFERENCE TO ITS SUITABILITY FOR CULTURE AS A FOOD FISH
W. O. McLarney. The Journal of The New Alchemists No. 1, $2.00, 1973. Yep, it's what it says it is!
7. THE ARK: A SOLAR HEATED GREENHOUSE AND AQUACULTURE COMPLEX ADAPTED TO NORTHERN CLIMATES
By several New Alchemists. The Journal of The New Alchemists No. 2, 1974, $6.00. Design and rationale for such a structure. All our aquaculture structures employ a variety of methods for trapping and storing the sun's heat. Discussion of these methods are in articles on aquaculture.
8. AQUACULTURE: TOWARD AN ECOLOGICAL APPROACH
W. O. McLarney, In: "Radical Agriculture," ed. Richard Merrill, Harper & Row (In Press).

REFERENCES CITED

[1] Bardach, J. E., J. H. Ryther, and W. O. McLarney, 1972. AQUACULTURE: THE FARMING AND HUSBANDRY OF FRESHWATER AND MARINE ORGANISMS. See reviews.
[2] Whitaker, Donald R., 1972. AQUACULTURE VERSUS LATENT RESOURCES. 17th Annual Meeting, Atlantic Fisheries Technology Conference, Annapolis, Maryland, October 22-25, 1972.
[3] Lappé, Frances M., 1971. DIET FOR A SMALL PLANET. Ballantine Books, Inc. New York.
[4] McLarney, W. O., 1971. AQUACULTURE ON THE ORGANIC FARM AND HOMESTEAD. Organic Gardening and Farming Magazine, August 1971.
[5] Schuster, W. H., G. L. Kesteven, and G. E. D. Collins. 1954. FISH FARMING AND INLAND FISHERIES MANAGEMENT IN RURAL ECONOMY. F.A.O. Fisheries Study No. 3. Rome, Italy.
[6] Ho, R., 1961. MIXED FARMING AND MULTIPLE CROPPING IN MALAYA. In: Proceedings of the Symposium on Land-Use and Mineral Deposits in Hong Kong, Southern China and Southeast Asia. S. G. Davis (ed.), Hong Kong University Press.
[7] LeMare, D. W., 1952. PIG-REARING, FISH-FARMING AND VEGETABLE GROWING. Malayan Agricultural Journal, Vol. 35, No. 3, pp 156-166, Kuala Lumper, Malaya.
[8] McLarney, William O., 1970. PESTICIDES AND AQUACULTURE. American Fish Farmer 1(10):6-7, 22-23.
[9] Woodwell, George M., P. P. Craigard, and H. A. Johnson. 1971. DDT IN THE BIOSPHERE: WHERE DOES IT GO? Science 174:1101-1107.
[10] Manigold, D. B. and J. A. Schulze, 1969. PESTICIDES IN WATER: PESTICIDES IN SELECTED WESTERN STREAMS. A PROGRESS REPORT. Pesticide Monitor Journal 3:124-135.
[11] Risebrough, R. W., 1969. CHLORINATED HYDROCARBONS IN MARINE ECOSYSTEMS. In: Chemical Fallout, M. W. Miller and G. C. Berg (eds.), Charles C. Thomas, Springfield, Illinois.
[12] Margalef, Ramon, 1968. PROSPECTIVES IN ECOLOGICAL THEORY. University of Chicago Press, Chicago, Illinois.
[13] Odum, Eugene P., 1971. FUNDAMENTALS OF ECOLOGY, 3rd edition, W. B. Saunders Company, Philadelphia, Pennsylvania.
[14] McLarney, W. O., 1974. AQUACULTURE: TOWARDS AN ECOLOGICAL APPROACH. In: "Radical Agriculture," R. Merrill (ed.), Harper & Row (in press).
[15] Hickling, C. F., 1971. FISH CULTURE. See reviews.
[16] Anon. 1968. F.A.O. AQUACULTURE BULLETIN. Vol. 1, No. 1, July 1968. F.A.O., Rome, Italy.
[17] Anon, 1971. F.A.O. AQUACULTURE BULLETIN, Vol. 4, No. 1, October 1971. F.A.O., Rome, Italy.
[18] Anon, 1967. Indo-Pacific Fisheries Council. Current Affairs Bulletin 50:25, 1967. F.A.O. Bangkok, Thailand.
[19] Anon, 1971. Indo-Pacific Fisheries Council. Occasional Paper 71/5, 1971. F.A.O. Bangkok, Thailand.
[20] Shang, Yung C., 1973. COMPARISON OF THE ECONOMIC POTENTIAL OF AQUACULTURE, LAND ANIMAL HUSBANDRY AND OCEAN FISHERIES: THE CASE OF TAIWAN. Aquaculture 2:187-195.
[21] Hirst, Eric, 1973. ENERGY USE FOR FOOD IN THE U.S. Oak Ridge National Laboratory Report No. ORNL-NSF-EP-57.
[22] McLarney, W. O., 1971. THE FARM POND REVISITED. Organic Gardening and Farming. November 1971.
[23] Rogers, H. H. and D. E. Davis, 1972. NUTRIENT REMOVAL BY WATER-HYACINTH. Weed Science 20(5):423-428..

A GUIDE TO THE STUDY OF FRESH-WATER BIOLOGY

A hip-pocket guide to the identification of fresh-water animals. A recognized classic, the fifth edition adds fish to the algae, protozoans, rotifers, molluscs, and insects (immature ones too) described in earlier editions. Excellent drawings illustrate the key characteristics of each organism, while a key-guide fills in the gaps for identification. Also included: materials for collecting in the field and methods of determining water chemistry. A valuable book for those learning to identify food organisms of cultured fish . . . and, of course, the fish themselves.

A Guide to the Study of Fresh-Water Biology
James Needham and Paul Needham
1962, 5th ed. (1st ed., 1938); 108 pp

$2.95

from:
Holden-Day, Inc.
500 Sansome Street
San Francisco, California 94111

TEXTBOOK OF FISH CULTURE: BREEDING AND CULTIVATION OF FISH

More information is included in this book for the would-be organic fish farmer than any other single book I've read. A major sourcebook for the breeding and cultivation of freshwater food-fish. Packed with drawings, tables and photos of culture hardware and systems presently in use throughout the world. There is also information on pond construction, maintenance and improvements, natural methods of increasing pond production, enemies and diseases of fish, harvesting of fish etc. The high price and lack of an index are drawbacks, but this book is a must for the serious aquaculturist.

Textbook of Fish Culture:
Breeding and Cultivation of Fish
Marcel Huet
1970; 436 pp

$27.00 (⌐ 12,50) plus shipping

from:
Fishing News (Books) Ltd.
23 Rosemount Avenue
West Byfleet, Surrey, England
or
110 Fleet Street
London EC4A2JL

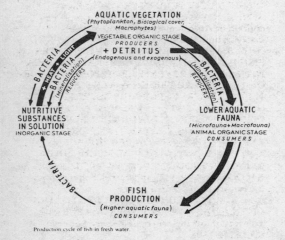

AQUATIC VEGETATION
(Phytoplankton, Biological cover,
Macrophytes)
VEGETABLE ORGANIC STAGE
PRODUCERS
+ DETRITUS
(Endogenous and exogenous)
BACTERIA
NUTRITIVE
SUBSTANCES
IN SOLUTION
INORGANIC STAGE
LOWER AQUATIC
FAUNA
(Microfauna+Macrofauna)
ANIMAL ORGANIC STAGE
CONSUMERS
FISH
PRODUCTION
(Higher aquatic fauna)
CONSUMERS
Production cycle of fish in fresh water.

FISH CULTURE

One of the finer books on the subject: well organized, full of illustrations and many references (312). Also: aquaculture history, pond construction and management, fertilizers, supplemental feeding and foods, brackish and sea water culture, stocking rates, yields, fish genetics, diseases etc. The photos (66) take you around the world in pond culture. The data on stocking rates are especially valuable. This book is cheaper than Huet or Bardach, et. al., but not as inclusive.

Fish Culture   from:
C. F. Hickling   Faber and Faber
1971 (2nd ed); 317 pp   24 Russell Square
⌐ 4,50 ($10.85 U.S.)   London WC1 England

GROWTH AND ECOLOGY OF FISH POPULATIONS

Definitely for the serious practitioner only . . . not a book for the beginner, but for those who want a deeper understanding of the ecological principles behind rearing fish. Sections include: growth processes in fish, food, competition and niches, growth and maintenance of populations, predator-prey relationships among fish, the trophic environment and fish growth, etc. Contains information not found in other books reviewed here. Well illustrated in textbook fashion, a little heavy on the mathematics.

Growth and Ecology of Fish Populations
A. H. Weatherley   from:
1972; 293 pp   Academic Press
                      111 5th Avenue
$13.50   New York, N.Y. 10003

AQUACULTURE: THE FARMING AND HUSBANDRY OF FRESHWATER AND MARINE ORGANISMS

Hailed as a "bible" by American aquaculturists, this comprehensive volume covers both freshwater and marine aquacultural practices. There are sections on general principles and economics, plus sections on culture methods and techniques for every major species being cultured throughout the world. These include: Common, Chinese and Indian carp; pike; perch; bass; Tilapia; mullet; eels; salmon and trout; pompano; yellowtail; marine flatfish; freshwater crayfish; crabs; scallops; mussels; abalone; squid; shrimp, lobster and frogs; seaweeds and edible freshwater plants. There are many references, excellent illustrations and photos showing the systems and apparatus in use for the different culture practices. Although the emphasis is towards commercial aquaculture, there is much information for the organic fish farmer. Recent printing of the paperback edition will bring this valuable sourcebook into the reach of all those interested in aquaculture.

Aquaculture: The Farming and Husbandry of
Freshwater and Marine Organisms
John E. Bardach, John H. Ryther
and William O. McLarney
1972; 868 pp

$37.50 hardback

paperback edition late 1974

from:
Wiley-Interscience
605 3rd Avenue
New York, NY 10016

ECOLOGY OF FRESH WATER

A concise guide to life in fresh waters. The author takes you on a field trip to a pond, a quiet canal and a running stream to sample the plants and animals in a manner that unfolds the beauty of the aquatic world. Chapter on aquatic plants has good drawings (usually hard to find), and chapter on energy transfer in aquatic ecosystems tells it like it is . . . and neatly too. The book introduces the basic concepts and terminology of aquatic ecology without getting esoteric . . . a real must for the beginner. Very well illustrated and referenced, the book fits in your hip pocket or satchel.

Ecology of Fresh Water
Alison Leadley Brown
1971; 129 pp

$4.00

from:
Harvard University Press
79 Garden Street
Cambridge, Massachusetts 02138

FISH AND INVERTEBRATE CULTURE: WATER MANAGEMENT IN CLOSED SYSTEMS

Definitely the first book to buy if you're ready to get *started* in fish farming. An excellent manual covering the necessities—biological, mechanical and chemical filtration, the carbon dioxide system, respiration, salts and elements, toxic metabolites, disease prevention by environmental control, laboratory tests, etc. A real "nuts and bolts" book for the culturist. Many fine drawings show water management hardware, water circulation and flow schemes, relevant biological and chemical cycles and water treatment procedures. The information is especially directed to the problems encountered in closed-system culture in tanks or small ponds, but the chemistry is also applicable to water management in larger systems.

Fish and Invertebrate Culture:
Water Management in Closed Systems
Stephen H. Spotte
1970; 145 pp   from:
$9.50   John Wiley & Sons, Inc.
                  1 Wiley Drive
                  Somerset, N.J. 08873

                  or 1530 South Redwood Road
                  Salt Lake City, Utah 84104

                  or WHOLE EARTH TRUCK STORE

Biological Filtration

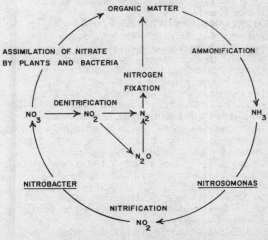

ORGANIC MATTER
ASSIMILATION OF NITRATE
BY PLANTS AND BACTERIA
AMMONIFICATION
NITROGEN
FIXATION
DENITRIFICATION
NO_3^- NO_2^- N_2 NH_3
N_2O
NITROBACTER   NITROSOMONAS
NITRIFICATION
NO_2^-

Figure 1. The nitrogen cycle.

BIBLIOGRAPHY: AQUACULTURE

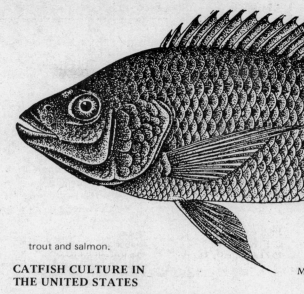

Tilapia mossambica Peters

BOOKS, SYMPOSIA AND GENERAL ARTICLES

Introductory Note: The literature on aquaculture is scattered among various obscure scientific and popular publications, many of them of rather poor quality. Literature dealing with the broad field of aquaculture is scarcer than writings on specific forms of the art. (Adapted from Aquaculture Bibliography of Bill McLarney, NAI-East).

Bardach, J.E. 1968. AQUACULTURE. Science, 161: 1098-1106. Brief world survey of aquaculture and its future.

Bardach, J. E. and J. H. Ryther. 1968. THE STATUS AND POTENTIAL OF AQUACULTURE. Vol. No. 1, Culture of Invertebrates and Algae, Vol. No. 2, Fish Culture. NTIS.

Borgstrom, G. (ed.) 1961. FISH AS FOOD. Vols. I & II. Academic Press, N.Y.

Eddy, Samuel. 1957. HOW TO KNOW THE FRESH-WATER FISHES. Wm. C. Brown Co., Dubuque, Iowa. Identification of the native fishes of North America.

FAO (Food and Agricultural Organization of the United Nations). 1966. FAO WORLD SYMPOSIUM ON WARM WATER POND FISH CULTURE. Hereafter—FAOWS. 123 papers by top aquaculturists from all over the world. Mostly in English.

Gerking, S. D. (ed.) 1967. THE BIOLOGICAL BASIS OF FRESHWATER FISH PRODUCTION. John Wiley & Sons, N.Y.

Hora, S. L. and T.V.R. Pillay. 1962. HANDBOOK ON FISH CULTURE IN THE INDO-PACIFIC REGION. FAO Fisheries Biology Technical Paper No. 14, 204 pp. Detailed treatment of Asian fish culture. Techniques of pond fertilization, polyculture stocking, etc.

Jones, W. 1970. COMMERCIAL FISH FARMING: HOW TO GET STARTED. American Fish Farmer 1(2):5-8.

Prowse, G. A. 1963. NEGLECTED ASPECTS OF FISH CULTURE. Indo-Pacific Fisheries Council, Current Affairs Bulletin. 36:1-9. Digestibility of algae, effects of different fertilizers on algae, pros and cons of natural aquatic plants as fish food, optimal size of ponds, genetic selection, etc.

Schaeperclaus, W. 1948. TEXTBOOK OF POND CULTURE. Fishery Leaflet No. 311, U.S. Dept. Inter., Fish and Wildlife Series, Wash. D.C.

U.S. Bureau of Sport Fisheries and Wildlife. 1970. REPORT TO THE FISH FARMERS, THE STATUS OF WARM-WATER FISH FARMING AND FISH FARM RESEARCH. Resource Publ. No. 83, U.S. Dept. Inter., Division of Fisheries Research, Wash. D.C.

MAGAZINES AND JOURNALS

AMERICAN FISH FARMER. P.O. Box 1900. Little Rock, Arkansas 72203 (monthly). Good coverage of aquaculture in this country and throughout the world.

AQUACULTURE. Elsevier Scientific Publishing Co., 52 Vanderbilt Ave., N.Y. Scientific articles on aquaculture . . . both freshwater and marine. Up to date research.

AUSTRALIAN FISHERIES. Fisheries Division of Australian Government, Public Services. Dept. of Primary Industry Canberra, A.C.T. 2600.

BAMIDGEH. (Bulletin of Fish Culture in Israel), Nir-David, D.N., Israel. (monthly). Scientific papers on fish culture in Israel and elsewhere (in English). Deals with carp, mullet and Tilapia. Israel has done quite a bit in fish culture in arid climates.

FAO FISH CULTURE BULLETIN, F.A.O. Rome, Italy. (Quarterly). Short reports on aquaculture development worldwide.

FAO PUBLICATIONS—REPRINTS. Available from: Unipub, Box 433, New York, NY 10016. Send for list of available titles under FAO headings.

FARM POND HARVEST. 372 South East Ave., Kankakee, Illinois 60901. (Quarterly). Mostly items on management of American farm ponds for sport and food fish production.

PROGRESSIVE FISH CULTURIST. Gov. Print. Office. (Monthly). Mostly hatchery culture of trout and salmon.

CATFISH CULTURE IN THE UNITED STATES

Introductory Note: The channel catfish is the most important aquacultural species in the United States. It may or may not be well suited to the homesteader, but they could conceivably become the first fish to be raised on a commercial scale, using organic methods, in this country. —B.M.

Allen, F. 1971. WEHAH FARM — RICE RAISERS THE RIGHT WAY. Organic Gardening and Farming 18(7):66-72. Contains a brief description of growing catfish in conjunction with rice.

AMERICAN FISH FARMER 2(3). This issue contains three good articles on the economics of catfish farming.

Brown, E. E., M. G. LaPlants, and L. H. Covey. 1969. A SYNOPSIS OF CATFISH FARMING. University of Georgia College of Agriculture Experiment Stations. Bulletin 69, 50 p.

CATFISH FARMERS OF AMERICA. The Catfish Farmer. The monthly official publication of the CFA. $6.00 per year from: Catfish Farmers of America, Tower Building, Little Rock, Arkansas 72201.

CATFISH FARMING. From: Agri-Books, Box 5001-AC, San Angleo, Texas 76901. $12.00.

Lee, J. S. 1971. CATFISH FARMING. Mississippi State University Curriculum Coordinating Unit for Vocational-Technical Education. State College, Mississippi 39761. 103 p. $2.00. Excellent detailed treatment of all phases of catfish culture.

Mahan, P. 1973. RAISING CATFISH IN A BARREL. Organic Gardening and Farming. Nov. 73:112-117.

Swingle, H. S. 1957. COMMERCIAL PRODUCTION OF RED CATS (SPECKLED BULLHEADS) IN PONDS. Proc. S. E. Ass. Game Fish Commissioners. 10:156-160. The only paper on the possibility of culturing bullhead catfish, which might, under some conditions, be more suitable to the homesteader than channel catfish.

Tiemeier, O. W. and C. W. Deyoe. 1967. PRODUCTION OF CHANNEL CATFISH. Kansas State University of Agricultural Experiment Station. Bulletin 508.

CARP CULTURE

Many good papers on carp culture also appear in Bamidgeh, the Bulletin of Fish Culture in Israel, and the serious reader should consult the annual indices for this journal. —B.M.

Alikunhi, K. H. 1966. SYNOPSIS OF BIOLOGICAL DATA ON COMMON CARP, Cyprinus carpio (Linnaeus) 1958, Asia and the Far East. FAO Fisheries Synopsis 31.1.

Backiel, T. and K. Stegman. 1966. TEMPERATURE AND YIELD IN CARP PONDS. FAOWS, FR: V/E-2.

Ehrlich, S. 1964. STUDIES ON THE INFLUENCE OF NUTRIA ON CARP GROWTH. Hydrobiologia 23(½):196-210.

Kirpichnikov, V. S. (ed.). 1970. SELECTIVE BREED-IND OF CARP AND INTENSIFICATION OF FISH BREEDING IN PONDS. Bulletin of the State Scientific Research Institute of Lake and River Fisheries. Vol. 61. 249 pp. NTIS.

Ling, S. W. 1966. FEEDS AND FEEDING OF WARM WATER FISHES IN PONDS IN ASIA AND THE FAR EAST. FR:III-VIII/R-2. Gives a good idea of the relative worth of various carp feeds.

Meske, C. 1968. BREEDING CARP FOR REDUCED NUMBER OF INTERMUSCULAR BONES, AND GROWTH OF CARP IN AQUARIA. Bamidgeh 20(4):105-119. Describes a highly intensive system of growing carp in a closed recirculating system, with spectacular yields.

Nair, K. K. 1968. A PRELIMINARY BIBLIOGRAPHY OF THE GRASS CARP. FAO Fisheries Circular 302, 155 pp.

Nambiar, K.P.P. 1970. CARP CULTURE IN JAPAN—A GENERAL STUDY OF THE EXISTING PRACTICES. Indo-Pacific Fisheries Council, Occ. Pap. 1970/1, 41 p. Fairly complete treatment of Japanese practices.

Sarig, S. 1966. SYNOPSIS OF BIOLOGICAL DATA ON COMMON CARP. Cyprinus carpio (Linnaeus) 1785, Near East and Europe, FAO Fisheries Synopsis 31.2.

Stevenson, J. H. 1965. OBSERVATIONS ON GRASS CARP IN ARKANSAS. Progressive Fish Culturist 27(4):203-206.

TILAPIA CULTURE

Introductory Note: Despite the great importance of Tilapia in fish culture, there is not extensive literature on these fishes. Below are listed a few publications which may be helpful. Many good papers on Tilapia culture also appear in Bamidgeh, the Bulletin of Fish Culture in Israel, and the serious reader should consult the annual indices for this journal.

—B.M.

Avault, J. S., Jr. E. W. Shell, and R. O. Smitherman. 1966. PROCEDURES FOR OVERWINTERING TILAPIA. FAOWS FR: V/E-3.

Chimits, P. 1957. THE TILAPIAS AND THEIR CULTURE, A SECOND REVIEW AND BIBLIO-GRAPHY. Fisheries Bulletin FAO 10:1-24.

Hickling, C. F. 1963. THE CULTIVATION OF TILAPIA. Scientific American. 208:143-152.

Lasher, C. W. 1967. TILAPIA MOSSAMBICA AS A FISH FOR AQUATIC WEED CONTROL. Progressive Fish Culturist 29(1):48-50.

Maar, A., M.A.E. Mortimer and I. Van der Lingen. 1966. FISH CULTURE IN CENTRAL EAST AFRICA. FAO, Rome. 158 p. Good, simple description of African methods, many of them involving quite small ponds.

Myers, G. S. 1955. NOTES ON THE FRESHWATER FISH FAUNA OF MIDDLE CENTRAL AMERICA WITH SPECIAL REFERENCE TO POND CULTURE OF TILAPIA. FAO Fisheries Paper No. 2:1-4.

Shell, E. W. 1966. RELATIONSHIP BETWEEN RATE OF FEEDING, RATE OF GROWTH AND RATE OF CONVERSION IN FEEDING TRIALS WITH TWO SPECIES OF TILAPIA, T. MOSSAMBICA AND T. NILOTICA. FAOWS FR:III/E-9.

Swingle, H. S. 1966. BIOLOGICAL MEANS OF IN-CREASING PRODUCTIVITY IN PONDS. FAOWS, FR: V/R-1. Tilapia-catfish combinations for culture in the United States.

Swingle, H. S. 1960. COMPARATIVE EVALUATION OF TILAPIAS AS PONDFISHES IN ALABAMA. Transactions of the American Fishery Society 89(2):142-148.

Uchida, R. N. and J. E. King. 1962. TANK CULTURE OF TILAPIA. Bulletin of United States Fish and Wildlife Service: 199(62):21-52.

BASS AND SUNFISH IN FARM PONDS

Introductory Note: Most state conservation departments and many university agricultural extension services have booklets on farm ponds which may be useful, particularly to neophytes.
—B.M.

Davison, V. E. and J. A. Johnson. 1943. FISH FOR FOOD FROM FARM PONDS. U.S. Department of Agriculture, Farmers' Bulletin 1938. 22 pp.

Davison, V. E. 1947. FARM FISH PONDS FOR FOOD AND GOOD LAND USE. U.S. Department of Agriculture, Farmers' Bulletin 1938. 29 pp

Etnier, D. A. 1971. FOOD OF THREE SPECIES OF SUNFISHES (Lepomis) AND THEIR HYBRIDS IN THREE MINNESOTA LAKES. Transactions of the American Fisheries Society 100(1):124-128. May be useful to anyone planning polyculture including sunfish.

Lewis, W. M. and R. Heidinger. 1971. AQUACULTURE POTENTIAL OF HYBRID SUNFISH. American Fish Farmer 2(5):14-16.

Ricker, W. E. 1948. HYBRID SUNFISH FOR STOCKING SMALL PONDS. Transactions of the American Fisheries Society 75:84-96.

Stockdale, T. M. 1960. FARM POND MANAGEMENT. Agricultural Extension Service, the Ohio State University. 24 pp.

TROUT

Bussey, G. 1971. HOW TO GROW TROUT IN YOUR BACK YARD (OR OTHER UNLIKELY PLACES). Available for $3.00 from Life Support Systems, Inc., Box 3296, Albuquerque, New Mexico 87110. Gene Bussey manufactures and sells closed recirculating systems which are claimed to make it possible to grow large numbers of trout—organically, if one wishes—at low cost on any scale from very small for individual use to a large commercial operation.

Lavrovky, V. V. 1966. RAISING OF RAINBOW TROUT (Salmo gairdneri Rich.) TOGETHER WITH CARP (Cyprinus carpio L.) AND OTHER FISHES. FAOWS, FR:VIII/E-3. That's right, they grow trout and carp together in Russia.

Scheffer, P. M. and L. D. Marriage. 1969. TROUT FARMING. U. S. Soil Conservation Service. Leaflet 552. GPO $.10. Should be read by would-be beginners of trout culture.

Borell, A. E. and P. M. Scheffer. 1966. TROUT IN FARM AND RANCH PONDS. U.S. Department of Agriculture. Farmers' Bulletin. No. 2154. 18 p. GPO $0.10.

AMERICAN CRAYFISH CULTURE

Introductory Note: Most of the available literature on crayfish culture deals with Louisiana species and methods. Techniques should be developed for crayfishes native to other parts of the country. Anyone seeking to do so should explore the purely biological literature on crayfish as well as the culture literature, paying particular attention to size, feeding habits, and reproductive habits of the species which are of interest.
—B.M.

Anonymous. 1970. CRAWFISH: A LOUISIANA AQUACULTURE CROP. American Fish Farmer 1 (9), pp. 12-15.

Fielding, J. R. 1966. NEW SYSTEMS AND NEW FISHES FOR CULTURE IN THE UNITED STATES. FAOWS FR: VIII/R-2.

Ham, B. Glenn. 1971. CRAWFISH CULTURE TECHNIQUES. American Fish Farmer 2 (5), pp. 5-6, 21 and 24.

Lacaze, Cecil. 1970. CRAWFISH FARMING. Fisheries Bulletin. No. 7. Louisiana Wild Life and Fisheries Commission, P.O. Box 44095, Capitol Station, Baton Rouge, Louisiana 70804.

POND POLYCULTURE

Introductory Note: Although polyculture is one of the oldest and most important methods of increasing fish pond productivity, there is little literature dealing with polyculture per se. What little there is deals mostly with Oriental systems, but it should be read by the serious aquaculturist, for these must serve as the models for analogous systems in North America.
—B.M.

Buck, D. Homer, Richard J. Baur and C. Russell Rose. 1973. AN EXPERIMENT IN THE MIXED CULTURE OF CHANNEL CATFISH AND LARGE-MOUTH BASS. The Progressive Fish Culturist. 35 (1):19-21.

Childers, W. F. and G. W. Bennett. 1967. EXPERIMENTAL VEGETATION CONTROL BY LARGE-MOUTH BASS—TILAPIA COMBINATION. Journal Wildlife Management 31:401-407.

Coche, A. G. 1967. FISH CULTURE IN RICE FIELDS, A WORLDWIDE SYNTHESIS. Hydrobiologia 30(1):1-44.

Prewitt, R. 1970. RAMBLING ALONG. American Fish Farmer 2(1):23-24. Brief discussion of the beginnings of polyculture in the U.S.

Sarig, S. 1955. CULTURE OF TILAPIA AS A SECONDARY FISH IN CARP PONDS. Bamidgeh, 7(3):41-45.

Tang, Y. A. 1970. EVALUATION OF BALANCE BETWEEN FISHES AND AVAILABLE FISH FOODS IN MULTISPECIES FISH CULTURE PONDS IN TAIWAN. Transactions of the American Fisheries Society 99(4):708-718. Technical discussion of Chinese carp polyculture in relation to feeding and fertilization.

Yashouv, A. 1969. MIXED FISH CULTURE IN PONDS AND THE ROLE OF TILAPIA IN IT. Bamidgeh 21(3):75-82.

Hashouv, A. 1958. ON THE POSSIBILITY OF MIXED CULTIVATION OF VARIOUS TILAPIA WITH CARP. Bamidgeh, 10(3):21-29.

FERTILIZATION

Ball, Robert C. 1949. EXPERIMENTAL USE OF FERTILIZER IN THE PRODUCTION OF FISH-FOOD ORGANISMS AND FISH. Michigan State College Agricultural Experiment Station Technical Bulletin 210, 28 pp.

McIntire, C. David and Carl E. Bond. 1962. EFFECTS OF ARTIFICIAL FERTILIZATION ON PLANKTON AND BENTHOS ABUNDANCE IN FOUR EXPERIMENTAL PONDS. Oregon Agricultural Experiment Station Technical Paper No. 1423, Corvallis, Oregon.

Swingle, H. S. and E. G. Smith. 1939. INCREASING FISH PRODUCTION IN PONDS. Transactions of 4th North American Wildlife Conference. American Wildlife Institute, Washington, D.C.

Swingle, H. S. 1947. EXPERIMENTS ON POND FERTILIZATION. Alabama Agricultural Experiment Station Bulletin 264, 34 pp. Auburn, Alabama.

Tanner, Howard A. 1960. SOME CONSEQUENCES OF ADDING FERTILIZER TO FIVE MICHIGAN TROUT LAKES. Transactions American Fishery Society 89(2):198-205.

Walny, Pawel. 1966. FERTILIZATION OF WARM-WATER FISH PONDS IN EUROPE. FAOWS, FR:II/R-7.

NATURAL FOODS

De Witt, John W. and Wendell Candland. 1970. THE WATER FLEA, DAPHINA, AS A COMMERCIAL FISH-FOOD ORGANISM FROM MUNICIPAL WASTE OXIDATION PONDS. Humbolt State College, Arcata, California.

McLarney, William O. 1974. AN IMPROVED METHOD FOR CULTURE OF MIDGE LARVAE (Chironomidae) FOR USE AS FISH FOOD. Journal of the New Alchemists 2:118-119.

Sorbeloos, P. 1973. HIGH DENSITY CULTURING OF THE BRINE SHRIMP, ARTEMIA SALINA. Aquaculture (1):385-391.

Spotte, Stephen. 1973. MAKING YOUR OWN FISH FOOD AND HOW TO RAISE EARTHWORMS AND BRINE SHRIMP FOR FISH FOOD. Chapter in: Marine Aquarium Keeping. Wiley-Interscience, New York.

U. S. Fish and Wildlife Service. 1962. FISH BAITS: THEIR COLLECTION, CARE, PREPARATION AND PROPAGATION. U.S.D.I. Fish and Wildlife Service, Leaflet Fl-28. Includes mealworms, bloodworms, earthworms, Hellgrammites and other aquatic forms, among others.

Yashouv, A. 1956. PROPAGATION OF CHIRONOMID LARVAE AS FOOD FOR FISH FRY. Bamidgeh 22(4):101-105.

Yount, James L. 1966. A METHOD FOR REARING LARGE NUMBERS OF POND MIDGE LARVAE—WITH ESTIMATES OF PRODUCTIVITY AND STANDING CROP. The American Midland Naturalist 76(1):230-238.

NUTRITION, GROWTH AND ENERGETICS

Davies, P.M.C. 1967. THE ENERGY RELATIONS OF CARASSIUS AURATUS (GOLDFISH)—III. GROWTH AND THE OVERALL BALANCE OF ENERGY. Comparative Biochemistry and Physiology 23:59-63.

Halver, John E. (ed.) 1972. FISH NUTRITION. Academic Press. New York.

Hastings, W. H. (e.a. 1966). WARMWATER FISH NUTRITION. U.S.D.I. Bureau of Sport Fisheries and Wildlife. Fish Farming Experimental Station, Stuttgart, Arkansas.

Mann, K. H. 1965. FISH IN THE RIVER THAMES. Journal Animal Ecology 34:253-75. Deals with metabolism and production of natural and culture situations.

Mann, Hans. 1961. METABOLISM AND GROWTH OF POND FISH. In: Borgotrom, G. (ed.) Fish as Food. Vol. I:82-89.

POND CONSTRUCTION

Delmendo, M. N. et. a. 1970. CONSTRUCTION OF PONDS FOR AQUACULTURE. Indo-Pacific Fisheries Council. Symposia 18-27 Nov. 1970. Paper No. IPFC/C70/SYM 26. FAO Bangkok 2, Thailand. Deals with larger ponds—as for commercial culture. Some general guidelines, useful to smaller systems.

Dillon, O. W., Jr. 1970. POND CONSTRUCTION, WATER QUALITY AND QUANTITY. Paper presented to the California Catfish Conference, Sacramento, California. January 20-21, 1970. Probably available from U.S. Soil Conservation Service, Fort Worth, Texas.

Mitchell, T. E. and M. J. Usry. 1967. CATFISH FARMING—A PROFIT OPPORTUNITY FOR MISSISSIPPIANS. Mississippi Research and Development Center, 787 Lakeland Drive, Jackson, Mississippi. 83 pp. Deals specifically with catfish farming, but the information on pond construction is among the best available. Probably some charge for this publication.

Renfro, G. Jr. 1969. SEALING LEAKING PONDS AND RESERVOIRS. U.S. Soil Conservation Service. SCS-TP-150. 6 p.

Vanicek, C. David and A. Wendell Miller. 1973. WARMWATER FISH POND MANAGEMENT IN CALIFORNIA. U.S. Department of Agriculture Soil Conservation Service Report No. M7-N-23056. GPO.

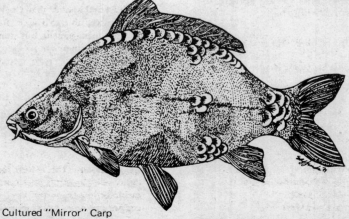
Cultured "Mirror" Carp

POPULAR FISH AND SHELLFISH SPECIES SUITABLE FOR SMALL-SCALE FRESH WATER POND CULTURE IN THE U.S.

Species	Feeding and Habits	Area of Origin/Culture	Temperature Range (°C) Optimum	Minimum	Comment
CYPRINIDS					
Common carp _Cyprinis carpio_	Eats attached algae, bottom detritus and benthic animals.	China/worldwide	18°-28°	13°	Can be polycultured
Mud carp _Cirrhina molitorella_	Eats attached algae, bottom detritus and benthic animals.	China/worldwide	20°-28°	13°	Can be polycultured
Grass carp _Ctenopharyngodon idella_	Eats large plants, floating and attached. Also grass clippings, weeds.	Amur river, China	23°-29°	13°	Can be polycultured
Big Head carp _Aristichthys nobilis_	Eats microscopic animals (Zoo plankton) in mid-water.	China	20°-28°	13°	Can be polycultured
Silver carp _Hypopathalmichthys molitrix_	Eats microscopic plants (phyto-plankton) in mid-water.	China	20°-28°	14°	Can be polycultured
Black carp _Mylopharyngodon piceus_	Eats bottom molluscs (snails, clams, mussels)	China	20°-28°	13°	Can be polycultured
CICHLIDS					
Tilapia heudeloti (or _microcephala_)	Eats large and maybe microscopic plants. Tolerates brackish water.	Coastal West Africa from Senegal to Congo	20°-30°	12°	All _Tilapia_ will breed in captivity.
Tilapia mossambica (Java Tilapia)	Eats mostly plankton, but also all plant material and some animal feed. Tolerates mild salinity.	East Africa/S.E. Asia, Japan, Latin America, U.S.	15°-30°	16°	Slightly aggressive to other species. Difficult with small carp in polyculture.
Tilapia nilotica (nile Tilapia)	Eats plankton and large plants.	Syria to East Africa/ throughout world.	15°-30°	16°	Little known.
Tilapia zillii	Eats only plants, mostly large. Used in weed control.	Equatorial East Africa/ throughout world	22°-26°	15°	Aggressive toward other species.
Tilapia aurea	Eats a variety; chopped plants, grain and animal foods.	West Africa	25°	13°	
SALMONID					
Rainbow trout _Salmo gairdneri_	Eats mostly aquatic insects. Needs high protein diet when fed artificially and lots of oxygen.	Pacific coast of North America	13°-20°	12°	Generally monoculture but possible for polyculture.
CENTRARCHIDS					
Bluegill _Lepomis macrochiris_	Eats mostly bottom animals, possibly algae	U.S. principal species stocked in farm ponds for angling.	20°-25°	10°	Eats young of other species. High reproduction causes stunting.
Redear Sunfish _Lepomis microlophus_	Eats bottom animals especially snails.	U.S. principal species stocked in farm ponds for angling.	20°-25°	10°	Eats young of other species. High reproduction causes stunting.
Largemouth bass _Micropterus salmoides_	Eats small fish and bottom animals. Stocked with sunfish in farm ponds, also bluegill (1 bass: 10 bluegill) needs lots of oxygen.	U.S. lakes and ponds	20°-30°	10°	Obligate carnivore—eats other fish and invertebrates.
Crappies and _Pomoxis Spp._	Eats bottom animals.	U.S. lakes and ponds. Stocked with bass.	20°-30°	10°	Very low reproduction. Used only in fish-out ponds.
MISCELLANEOUS FISH					
Bigmouth Buffalo _Ictiobus cyprinellus_	Eats plankton, bottom animals and detritus.	Popular in U.S. in early 1900's. Renewed interest in hybrids.	20°-25°	13°	♀ Black X ♂ Bigmouth = fast growing hybrid.
Smallmouth Buffalo _Ictiobus bubalus_	Eats plankton, bottom animals and detritus.				Stocked in catfish ponds
Black Buffalo _Ictiobus niger_	Eats plankton, bottom animals and detritus.				Also used in rice field rotations (900 lbs/acre in 18 months).
Channel catfish _Ictalurus punctatus_	Eats other fish and bottom animals.	U.S. rivers, lakes and ponds. Widely cultured. Survives freezing.	22°-28°	15°	Mostly grown in commercial monocultures. Not practical for small scale rearing.
Brown bullhead _Ictalurus nebulosus_	Eats other fish and bottom animals.	U.S. rivers, lakes and ponds	22°-28°	15°	Smaller and hardier than Channel catfish, but more susceptible to disease. Reproduce easily without management, but stunting and over-population can occur.
Yellow bullhead _Ictalurus natalis_	Eats other fish and bottom animals.	U.S. rivers, lakes and ponds	22°-28°	15°	
Black bullhead _Ictalurus melas_	Eats other fish and bottom animals.	U.S. rivers, lakes and ponds	22°-28°	15°	
SHELLFISH					
Red crayfish _Procambris clarki_	Scavenger: table scraps, detritus, etc. but needs some plants for best growth.	Southern U.S. to 35°N, into Southern California. Found in streams, creeks, lakes and flood control channels.	10°-30°	13°	Due to rapid growth, more suitable for growth than _Astacus_ or _Pacifastacus_. Use in polyculture with carps, bass, bluegill, etc.
Bivalve molluscs _Lampsilis_ spp. _Corbicula_ spp.	Live in bottom mud/ooze. Filter out plankton and floating detritus.	_Lampsilis_ in Mississippi Valley; _Corbicula_ introduced from Asia, now found in waterways of East and West coasts.	10°-30°	5°	_Lampsilis_ needs fish as host for parasitic young—drawback, _Corbicula_ does not. Do poorly in turbid or low O_2 water. Very susceptible to copper and other heavy metals. Good polyculture animals; improves O_2 supply for fish.

METHANE
BASIC PROCESS OF METHANE DIGESTION

When organic material decays it yields useful by-products. The kind of by-product depends on the conditions under which decay takes place. Decay can be *aerobic* (with oxygen) or *anaerobic* (without oxygen). Any kind of organic matter can be broken down either way, but the end products will be quite different (Fig. 1).

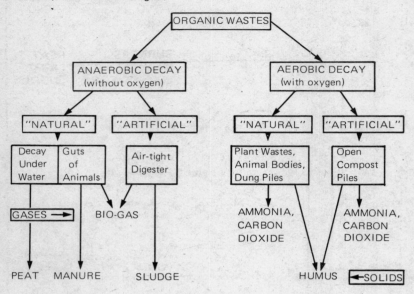

FIG. 1   END PRODUCTS OF ORGANIC DECAY.

It is possible to mimic and hasten the natural anaerobic process by putting organic wastes (manure and vegetable matter) into insulated, air-tight containers called *digesters*. Digesters are of two types: (1) *Batch-load digesters* which are filled once, sealed, and emptied when the raw material has stopped producing gas; and (2) *Continuous-load digesters* which are fed a little, regularly, so that gas and tertilizer are produced continuously.

The digester is fed with a mixture of water and wastes, called "slurry." Inside the digester, each daily load of fresh slurry displaces the previous day's load which bacteria and other microbes have already started to digest.

Each load of slurry moves in the digester to a point where the methane bacteria are active. At this point large bubbles force their way to the surface where gas accumulates. The gas is very similar to natural gas and can be burned directly for heat and light, stored for future use, or compressed to power heat engines.

Digestion gradually slows down toward the outlet end of the digester and the residue begins to stratify into distinct layers (Fig. 2).

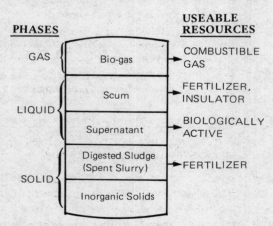

FIG. 2   LAYERING OF BY-PRODUCTS
IN THE DIGESTER

Sand and Inorganic Materials at the bottom.

Sludge, the spent solids of the original manure reduced to about 40% of the volume it occupied in the raw state. Liquid or dry sludge makes an excellent fertilizer for crops and pond cultures.

Supernatant, the spent liquids of the original slurry. Note that the fertilizing value of the liquid is as great as sludge, since the dissolved solids remain.

Scum, a mixture of coarse fibrous material, released from the raw manure, gas, and liquid. It resembles, more or less, the "head" of beer. The accumulation and removal of scum is one of the most serious problems with digesters. In moderate amounts, scum can act as an insulation. But in large amounts it can virtually shut down a digester.

Biogas, the gas produced by digestion, known as marsh gas, sewage gas, dungas, or bio-gas, is about 70% methane (CH_4) and 29% carbon dioxide (CO_2) with insignificant traces of oxygen and sulfurated hydrogen (H_2S) which gives the gas a distinct odor. (Although it smells like rotten eggs, this odor has the advantage of making leaks easy to trace.)

Biology of Digestion

The most important thing to remember is that digestion is a biological process which involves a series of reactions by two kinds of anaerobic bacteria feeding on the raw organic matter. *Acid-producing bacteria* break down the organic matter into simple materials (mostly acetic acids), and *methane-producing bacteria* convert the simple materials into methane. A successful digester depends on maintaining a balance between these two kinds of bacteria. This is achieved by regular feeding, proper pH (acid-base balance), an optimum temperature of 95° and a good quality of raw materials (for further information on this see the New Alchemy Newsletter).

Digestible Properties of Organic Matter

When raw materials are digested in a container, only part of the waste is actually converted into methane and sludge. Some of it is indigestible to varying degrees, and accumulates in the digester or passes out with the effluent and scum. The "digestibility" and other basic properties of organic matter are usually expressed in the following terms:

MOISTURE: The weight of water lost upon drying at 220° F until no more weight is lost.

TOTAL SOLIDS (TS): The weight of dry material remaining after drying as above. TS weight is usually equivalent to "dry weight." (However, if you dry your material in the sun, assume that it will still contain around 30% moisture.) TS is composed of digestible organic or "Volatile Solids" (VS), and indigestible residues or "Fixed Solids" (FS).

Volatile solids (VS): The weight of organic solids burned off when dry material is "ignited" (heated to around 1000° F). This is a handy property of organic matter to know, since VS can be considered as the amount of solids actually converted by the bacteria.

Fixed Solids (FS): Weight remaining after ignition. This is biologically inert material.

So if we had 100 pounds of fresh chicken manure, 72-80 pounds of this would be water, and only 15-24 pounds (75-80% Volatile Solids of the 20-28% Total Solids) would be available for actual digestion.

Manure Production

When you see a table that shows the amount of manure produced by different kinds of livestock, bear in mind that the amount on the table will probably not be the amount that is actually available from your animals. There are three major reasons for this: 1) Manure production varies with the size of the animal. 2) Not all of the manure produced is easily collected, and depends on the degree of livestock confinement. 3) The kind of manure that can be collected may be fresh excrement (feces and urine), excrement plus bedding, wet feces only, etc.

The Livestock Unit: Keeping in mind all the things that can affect the type and amount of manure that can be collected for digestion, we can assemble a general manure production table that shows *rough average amounts* of fresh manure, total solids and volatile solids produced by various livestock. The table enables us to get some idea of the relative production of readily available digestible material (VS) by different livestock (the "livestock unit"). Thus, on the average one large horse produces about 180 times as much digestible material per day as a laying chicken.

| | Wet Raw Manure * | | | Total Solids | | Volatile Solids | Livestock |
	lb/day	ton/yr	gal/day	lb/day	ton/yr	lb/day	Unit
Bovine							
Dairy Cow	1600 132	24	18	16.6	3.1	13.8	300-350
	1300 107	19.5	15	13.5	2.5	11.2	250-300
Dairy Heifer	1000 85	15.5	11.2	9.2	1.7	7.5	150-200
Beef Feeder	1000 60	11	7.5	6.9	1.3	5.9	150
Beef Stocker	500 45	8.2	5.2	5.8	1.0	4.8	120
Horse							
Large	1000 45	8.2	6.7	9.4	1.7	7.5	180-200
Medium	850 36	6.6	5.4	7.0		5.5	120-150
Pony			15.4	3.0		2.4	50-70
Swine							
Hog Breeder	500 25	4.6	3	2.2	0.4	1.6	40
Hog Feeder	200 13	2.4	2.2	1.2	0.22	1.0	25
	100 6.5	1.2	1.1	0.6	0.11	0.5	13
Wiener	15 1.0	0.2		0.1			
Sheep							
Feeder	100 4	0.7	0.8	1.0	0.18	0.8	20
Lamb	30 1.5	0.3		0.4		0.2	5
Fowl							
Geese, Turkey	15 .6	220 lb	.2 qt	.15	55 lb	.10	2.5
Ducks	6 .4	250 lb	.15 qt	.10	37 lb	.07	1.8
Broiler Chicken	4 .3	110 lb	.1 qt	.07	26 lb	.05	1.3
Laying Hen	4 .2	75 lb	.1 qt	.05	18 lb	.04	1.0

	Portion	Amount	% TS	TS/day	%VS	VS/day	Livestock Unit
Humans (150 lbs)	Urine	2 pt., 2.2 lb	6%	.13	75%	.10	6
	Feces	0.5 lb	27%	.14	92%	.13	
	Total	2.7 lb	11%	.27	84%	.25	

TABLE I MANURE PRODUCTION OF VARIOUS LIVESTOCK AND HUMANS. "Livestock Unit" = VS production relative to laying hens.

*Bulk density of raw manure = 34 ft^3/ton or 60 lb/ft^3, or 8 lb/gal with no flushing water.

USE	FT^3	RATE
Lighting	2.5	per mantle per hour
Cooking	8 - 16	per hour per 2 - 4" burner
	12 - 15	per person per day
Incubator	.5 - .7	ft^3 per hour per ft^3 incubator
Gas Refrigerator	1.2	ft^3 per hour per ft^3 refrigerator
Gasoline Engine*		
CH$_4$	11	per brake horsepower per hour
Bio-Gas	16	per brake horsepower per hour
For Gasoline		
CH$_4$	135 - 160	per gallon
Bio-Gas	180 - 250	per gallon
For Diesel Oil		
CH$_4$	150 - 188	per gallon
Bio-Gas	200 - 278	per gallon
*25% efficiency		

TABLE II USES FOR METHANE. Consumption of methane and bio-gas for different uses.

METHANE DIGESTERS: SOME BASIC QUESTIONS

With this very general background we are ready to ask a fundamental question about the use of digesters: Are methane digesters practical? Do we have the resources (easily available organic wastes, time and money) to build one? Will a methane digester provide us with enough gas or liquid fertilizer to make it worth our while to build and *maintain* one?

Are methane digesters practical? The answer has to do with scale and needs. On a large-scale, that is, in centralized waste treatment facilities (municipal, community or village), livestock operations, and food processing plants there is no doubt that anaerobic digestion is a sound way of recycling organic wastes. Increasing work is being done on digesters at this level all the time. On an intermediate scale (ranches, stables, large kennels, small livestock farms, etc.) the big trade-off is in the cost of the operation. On a small scale there seems to be real doubt whether digesters are really practical for anything except isolated homesteads or as educational tools.

Certainly there would be argument on this from people experimenting with small scale digester systems. But the common complaint among people who have tried to set up small digesters is that the amount of gas available is usually too small to justify the time and expense of building one.

Some operations we have seen actually use more energy (often electricity) heating their digester than the digester produces. Thus we are left with little more than a fancy, energy-consuming fertilizer machine. This may not be so bad if we believe that the fertilizer value of digester sludge is superior to manure . . . and there is reason to believe this. But it does rearrange our thinking about small scale digesters as to what their purpose really is: to produce gas, fertilizer or simply to handle waste?

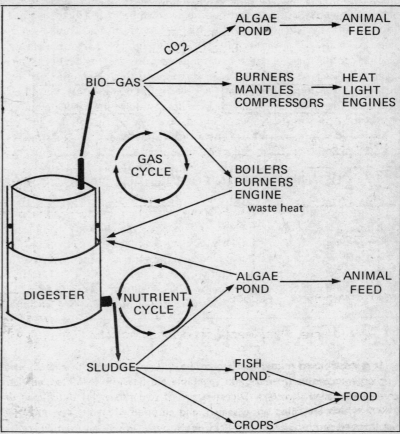

FIG. 3 THE POTENTIALS OF A DIGESTER SYSTEM.

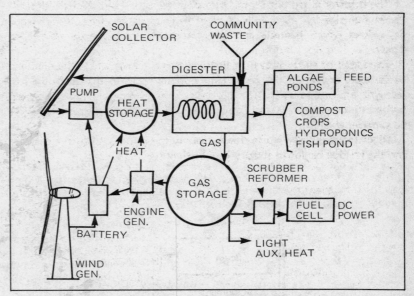

FIG. 4 THE POTENTIALS OF AN INTEGRATED RENEWABLE ENERGY SYSTEM USING A DIGESTER.

Let's look at a few facts. Suppose you had 60 laying hens and all of their manure available for digestion. From Table I we can see that 60 laying hens produce about 2½ lbs of VS per day. If we assume that 1 lb of VS can yield 5-7 ft^3 of methane gas, then 60 chickens will provide us with about 12-18 ft^3 of methane/day, enough to cook all the simple meals of a person for one day (Table 2). Notice also that it takes the wastes from 8 adults to provide enough gas to cook the meals of one person. If you think it is worth it . . . do it. In cases where people are willing to reduce their standard of living drastically, and have the time to maintain a digester, small digesters could be an asset and help to provide a small portion of the energy needs and a valuable fertilizer. But just because it produces energy, a digester is not necessarily worth building. Do some serious figuring first. Use Tables I and II as guidelines and refer to the books in the review section for more detailed information.

Once the decision has been made to build a digester two additional questions need to be asked: 1) With the organic wastes and resources at hand, what kind of digester should be built and how big should it be? 2) What is the best way of using the gas and sludge produced? The first question is explained in detail in the many books described in the review section. With regards to the second question, remember that a digester is just the heart of a system that produces fuel gas *and* fertilizer. These by-products can be used in a variety of ways (Fig. 3 and 4). Perhaps the biggest advantage to digesters is not so much that they produce fuel and fertilizer, but that they serve so well as back-up components to an integrated system. Their biological requirements for heat mean that digesters can be fed by the excess energies of solar and wind devices while at the same time they can use their own waste products as fuel. Digesters are literally the guts of an integrated energy system (see the article in the Integrated Systems section by Ken Smith for more detail on this subject).

USING BIO-GAS IN ENGINES AND CARS

One of the most popular myths about digesters is that they can supply enough methane energy to run automobiles. Stick the chickens in the back of the car and off we go. Again, let's look at a few facts.

First off, methane is 120 octane indicating that it can be used most efficiently in an engine with a high compression ratio like diesel (15:1) rather than a gasoline engine (8:1). Generally, a diesel will burn about 6500 BTU (for a good description of using bio-gas to power diesel engines see John Fry's book, page 65.)

In addition it is far more efficient to use methane in a stationary heat engine located near the digester so that waste heat can be recirculated back into the digester. It is inefficient to use methane in mobile heat engines (cars, trucks) because 75% of the available energy is lost as heat, and because the gas must be compressed so that it can be carried around easily. Thus the most efficient use of methane in engines is in stationary diesel engines located near to the digester.

But that's only part of the problem. Suppose your car gets 15 miles to the gallon. One gallon of gas is equivalent to about 140 ft³ of pure methane. Assume that one pound of volatile solids produces 5 ft³ of methane. In order to go just 15 miles in your car you would need about 28 pounds of volatile solids or the daily output of 10 ponies or 550 chickens or 100 people. And even if you have that lying around, 140 ft³ is equal to the volume of about twenty 50-gallon oil drums, so you would certainly have to compress the gas in order to carry it around with you . . . more energy. At 1000 psi it takes about 20% of the energy available after compression just to compress the gas. In order to liquefy methane, pressures in excess of 5,000 psi (or very cold temperatures) are needed. This means multiple compressors, expense and energy. You might be able to find some fancy storage device such as zeolite (an aluminum silicate crystal that absorbs various gases including methane) or perhaps you could store your methane in liquid propane like Harold Bates did (the fellow who started this whole myth about chicken-powered cars).

There are no panaceas or free lunches with renewable energy systems, certainly not methane digesters.

—R.M.

METHANE REVIEWS

MAX'S POT, DRUM BIO-GAS PLANT

Max's Pot has evolved from a simple oil drum vertical digester to a 2-drum solar heated horizontal digester, to its current digester system. The present bio-gas plant (still 50 gallon oil drums) consists of: 1) Four *holding tanks* for receiving human feces, kitchen wastes, animal manure, and garden wastes. 2) A *solar collector* for heating water which is circulated through coils in the digester, keeping it at an optimum 95° F. 3) *Storage drums* for storing the solar-heated water. 4) *Mixing drums* for mixing the wastes from the four holding tanks. 5) A *digester* made from three 50-gallon oil drums. 6) *Gas storage tanks*. Presently Max's Pot is putting together a brochure that not only explains the design of their bio-gas plant, but also gives information about performance specifications of materials used to build bio-gas plants (hand pumps, toilets, valves, oil drums, etc.) plus directions for sizing digesters in various climates of the United States. For general inquiries send self-addressed stamped envelope to:

Max's Pot, Drum Bio-gas Plant
Center for Maximum Potential
Building Systems
1974

$5.00

from:
Center for Maximum Potential
Building Systems
6438 Bee Caves Road
Austin, Texas 78746

METHANE

A general rap on methane systems with the usual considerations of sludge/gas use, types of digesters plus standard charts of raw materials/gas properties. Main discussion is interspersed with articles from U.S. and G.B. newspapers and magazines (e.g., *Compost Science*), a few ads for alternative energy hardware/groups in G.B. and 20 or so rough schematics and *brief* descriptions of a wide variety of batch and continuous digesters

(e.g., rotary, steel cage, spherical, batch-series), some quite imaginative. Especially interesting: an "auger" (helical) agitator and a circular digester for use in Yurts (adapted from the Golueke/Oswald waste water and algae-circular house design). Better for expanding the potentials of small-scale digester designs than for the actual building.

—R.M.

Methane
Steven Sampson, edited by Andrew MacKillop
1974; 71 pp

⊥ 1.60 (about $4.00)

from:
Wadebridge Ecological Centre (WEC)
73 Molesworth Street
Wadebridge, Cornwall, Great Britain

PRACTICAL BUILDING OF METHANE POWER PLANTS

L. John Fry is a pioneer methane digester builder. This book is the history and some details of the horizontal displacement digester that Fry developed and built using low-cost, labor-intensive techniques in South Africa.

This is a passive, "plug-flow" type system. In the case of a digester this means that organic material must move passively along the digester through succeeding steps of digestion. This ensures almost total digestion of the material, but it requires long detention times (30-40 days). Conventional sewage treatment digesters, using mechanical mixers, achieve 95-98% digestion in 15-20 days. The biggest trade-off between the two systems seems to be in tank size, e.g., a 20-day digester is 1/2 the cost of a 40-day digester. The plug-flow system seems reasonable where tanks are cheap or can be made with labor-intensive methods. The rapid mixing digester is a better choice where time and labor cost are major considerations. A small tank cost will justify additional mixing equipment cost, which promotes rapid digestion and prevents scum build-

ups.
Of special value in the book are 1) A generation of experiences with methane digesters *and* digester systems, from the simple to the complex. 2) Step-by-step designs for tested models built from simple materials (inner tubes, oil drums), plus a description of a 400 cubic foot concrete-building digester. 3) Plans for converting diesel motors to methane. 4) Ways of using sludge as a farmland fertilizer.

Some of the book is pulled from the New Alchemy newsletter which the author helped to write. The price is too bad, but for practical knowledge, you can't beat it.

—Ken Smith, Evan Brown

Practical Building of Methane Power
Plants for Rural Energy Independence
L. John Fry
1974; 96 pp

$12.00

from:
L. John Fry
1223 N. Nopal
Santa Barbara, CA 93102

or WHOLE EARTH TRUCK STORE

BIOFUELS CO.

We became involved in manure digestion as a means of increasing the efficiency of photosynthesis on my farm. While bio-gas is valuable, my research indicates that for every dollar's worth of output products, 60-90% is in the fertilizer and soil conditioning value of the effluent. Consequently the true value of methane digesters (at least in cold regions) is as a fertilizer producer. Aerobic composting is labor intensive, often smelly and buggy, and the wastes lose 50-75% of their nutrient potential while being oxidized. Anaerobic digestion avoids these problems and losses by presenting the nutrients in reduced rather than oxidized form. In this way plant nutrients are: 1) More readily assimilated by plant roots, 2) more readily absorbed or chelated by soil colloids (clay and humus), thus preventing leaching or volatilization, and 3) less prone to become fixed in unavailable chemical structures (like phosphorous or iron in alkali soils). Although gas quantity and quality vary directly with temperature, and retention times vary inversely, it seems from my controlled experiments run in gallon jugs kept at varying temperatures from 50° to 100° F, that the NPK of the effluent doesn't change much with temperature. What this seems to mean (especially in cold climates) is that if gas production would be so small as to not warrant fancy heating systems, the digestion process is still valuable because it produces a great fertilizer.

We are seeking to become consultants in cold region applications of anaerobic digesters to soil fertility programs. We now have plans for a "Model No. 2" digester . . . a cold regions, low-tech, operating fertilizer machine which can serve as an *initial involvement* in methane digestion and will provide sufficient gas for cooking *in the summer months* with no other heat than the sun, and compost and warm mixed water. For year around gas, and sufficient gas to be worth the 'gearing up' to regular use, a digester must be larger, insulated, buried and heated. The means of heating will determine the smallest size which is still economical. The plans for our elementary batch digester with no moving parts (for cold regions) are expected to cost $3.00. Please send a self-addressed stamped envelope for inquiries.

Bio-gas Plans

$3.00

from:
Biofuels Co.
George Oberst
Box 609
Noxon, Montana 59853

METHANE DIGESTERS FOR FUEL GAS AND FERTILIZER

"(This book) is highly recommended by this reviewer to anyone intent upon building a digester for biogas production . . . The chapter on the biology of the digestion process is written in a style both lucid and in a language intelligible to the non-specialist in biology. It is a valuable section in that it provides a rational basis for the design and operation of the digester . . . The section on design covers a wide variety of possible designs (actually only 3 . . . RM). Especially fascinating to this reviewer was the section on the 'innertube' digester."

—Clarence Golueke
Compost Science

INDEX—Introduction; Background; History; Biology of Digestion; Raw Materials; The Gas; Digester; Design; Using Gas; Using Sludge; Building a Sump Digester; Building an Innertube Digester; Necessity is the Mother of Invention; References (68).

* *

Starter brew can be generated in a 1 or 5 gallon glass bottle. Care must be taken to fill the bottle only about ¼ full with either (a) active supernatant from a local sewage works or (b) the runoff from the low point on the land of any intensive stock farm in your district. Fill ¼ more with fresh dung. Leave the other ½ of the bottle for fresh manure additions at weekly intervals. Never fill too near the screw cap, since foaming could block off the opening and burst the bottle. Of course, the screw cap must be left loose to keep the bottle from exploding, except when agitating the bottle. It is a peculiarity of methane brews that a slight agitation when adding material is beneficial, but that continuous agitation has an adverse effect.

Methane Digesters for Fuel Gas and Fertilizer
L. John Fry, Richard Merrill
1973; 46 pp

$3.00

from:
New Alchemy Institute West
P.O. Box 376
Pescadero, CA 94060

OR WHOLE EARTH TRUCK STORE

THE BIOMASS INSTITUTE

The Biomass Energy Institute was founded in Manitoba, Canada in 1971. The Institute's goals are "Accumulate, develop, classify and disseminate information on biomass energy, and to act as a coordinating body between business, government and the academic community to optimize the use of biomass energy."

The Institute sponsored an *International Biomass Energy Conference* in Winnipeg in May 1973, and the Proceedings have been published in a very informative book ($10.00 from the Institute). There is also a newsletter of activities (2-3 times per year) and a pamphlet: *The Renewable Biomass Energy Guidebook* ($2.00 from the Institute).

The Institute has organized a lot of people, proposals and ideas about biomass energy, e.g., a pilot (25 hog) digester, a prototype 1000 hog waste recycler, Institute of Algology, etc.

For information write:
Biomass Energy Institute
310-870 Cambridge Street
Winnipeg, Manitoba R3M 3H5

METHANE: FUEL OF THE FUTURE

Popular style, brief overviews of anaerobic process, digester design, etc., plus old and new ways of using gas and sludge (municipal, agriculture, *Methane in Developing Countries, Domestic Use* and *Transportation*). Good sections: *A Digester in Every Garden* (not practical without lifestyle changes): *Research Needs* and *References* (mostly in England). No practical designs, mostly descriptions, potentials and inspirations nicely put.

—R.M.

Methane: Fuel of the Future
Bell, Boulter, Dunlop and Keiller
1973; 86 pp

$1.60 paper (plus postage)

$4.50 cloth (plus postage)

from:
Andrew Singer
Bottisham Park Mill
Bottisham, Cambridgeshire
England

or WHOLE EARTH TRUCK STORE
$2.25 paper

RECYCLING TREATED MUNICIPAL WASTEWATER AND SLUDGE THROUGH FOREST AND CROPLAND

The Wastewater Renovation and Conservation Project was started at The Pennsylvania State University in 1962 to investigate the feasibility and environmental impact of disposal of treated municipal wastewater on land through spray irrigation. Since then the term 'Living Filter' has become more or less synonomous with the idea of spray irrigation of municipal wastewater on land.

This book is a symposium held at Penn State in August of 1972 to review current info related to the use of land for disposal of wastewater. It is the most complete book on the subject that I have seen. There are sections on: (1) properties of wastewater, (2) properties of soil to receive wastewater, (3) properties of wastewater during recycling, (4) properties of soil during recycling (especially valuable is an entire chapter on "Microbial Hazards of Disposing of Wastewater on Soil"), (5) responses of crops to wastewater, (6) systems design and economics and (7) examples of operating systems. As with

most symposia there are lots of numbers, references and some esoteric descriptions. Furthermore, municipal wastewater is not your average homestead/small farm digester sludge. But if you are serious about using your garden plot or farmland as a 'living filter' for digester effluent there is good information and much food for thought here.

—R.M.

Recycling Treated Municipal Wastewater and Sludge Through Forest and Cropland
William E. Sopper & Louis T. Kardos (editors)
1973; 479 pp

$16.50

from:
The Pennsylvania State University Press
215 Wagner Building
University Park, PA 16802

A HOMESITE POWER UNIT: METHANE GENERATOR

Gives a background and, for general design purposes, shows how to calculate digester and gas holder size plus loading rate. A bit pedantic in the algebra, nonetheless it gives detailed, step-by-step design specifications for a digester built and working in California (Fig. 5).

—R.M.

An estimating procedure is presented in Table 6 where total daily gas needs are calculated at 17.3 ft^3 while special weekly needs are 89.1 ft^3. Thus, every week, 106.4 ft^3 storage space is required. This example illustrates an important design constraint: The size of the gas holder is based essentially on that use which consumes gas at the greatest rate. This is a key factor in all systems which contain storage components.

* *

FIG. 5 A BATCH DIGESTER

The digester is a steel tank 66 inches long, having a diameter of 45 inches, located one foot above the ground on about a 5 degree incline in the direction of the 4 inch slurry exit valve (C). Since the unit was located in a moderate climate, the above ground digester used the heat from the sun for creating optimal temperatures. The incline toward the exit valve allows for easy slurry flow out of the digester. . . The loading apparatus is made of a drum (A), 22 inches in diameter and 34 inches high, to which a funnel (B), 22 inches in diameter at one end and 4 inches in diameter at the other, is attached. The loader is secured by way of a 4-inch galvanized union to a 4-inch gate valve (E) used as the continuous feed inlet to the digester. Extending 6 inches above the tank and attached to the valve (E) is a 4-inch diameter pipe (F) extending 2 feet into the tank. This pipe accepts new organic matter, empties directly into the existing slurry, and prevents the gas located in the upper part of the tank from escaping during loading operations.

A Homesite Power Unit: Methane Generator
Les Auerbach, Bill Olkowski, Ben Katz
1974; 50 pp

$5.00

from:
Les Auerbach
Alternative Energy Systems, Inc.
242 Copse Road
Madison, CT 06443

GOBAR GAS RESEARCH STATION . . . INDIA

In India cows roam free, manure is plentiful and energy and fertilizer are scarce. Usually cow dung and local forests are burned to the detriment of the land. In the early 1940's the India Agricultural Research Institute started a program to design and develop digesters that could provide families and small farmers with *both* fuel and fertilizer from cow manure ("Gobar"). Ram Bux Singh has pulled together information from his own work and that of his predecessors (e.g., Desai, Acharya, Khadi and Village Industry Comm.) in two semi-popular manuals: (1) *Bio-Gas Plant: Generating Methane from Organic Wastes* is a general introduction and synthesis of two earlier pamphlets. It gives a general background and history of methane research throughout the world together with rough schematic drawings and descriptions of five basic "gobar" plants that have been tested to operate under a variety of conditions (small digesters .. single and double chamber; large digesters .. single and double stage; batch digester with animal/plant waste mixture). The author describes ways of using the gas (light, heat, cooking, incubator, refrigerator, fan, water pump, rice huller, generator), and lists results of experiments with the different kinds/sizes of digesters operating at various times of the year. (2) *Bio-Gas Plants; Designs with Specifications* contains 48 pages of roughly drawn schematics and photos of different scaled digesters and gas holders for temperate and cold climates (including a privy digester). Not quite detailed nuts and bolts, but enough for first approximations. Digesters are built from bricks, cement, mortar and metal bracings. One could argue with the basic design of these digesters. Being vertical and buried in the ground they would seem to be hard to clean out when operating on a continuous feed. Also there is no provision for the elimination of scum. But they are simple and provide good models for the individual or small group working with easily available materials.

—R.M.

Dear Primer,

By now (June 1974) more than 7,000 Bio-Gas plants are operating in India and a target for the installation of 100,000 plants has been fixed by the Government in the fifth Five Year Plan. At present some plants are under trial which could be used in cold climate areas.

—Ram Bux Singh

Bio-Gas Plants: Generating Methane From Organic Wastes
1971; 71 pp

$5.00 (including air post)

Bio-Gas Plants: Designs with Specifications
Ram Bux Singh
1973; 54 pp

$7.00 (including air post)

both books from:
Gobar Gas Research Station
Ajitmal, Etawah (U.P.)
India

or WHOLE EARTH TRUCK STORE

METHANE BIBLIOGRAPHY

Information about methane digestion is scattered widely in many places: in agricultural/municipal/industrial waste-recycling literature, in specialized microbiology texts and journals, in popular magazines like *Compost Science* and in many recent alternative publications (see Reviews). Some of the most valuable research has come out of the Sanitary Engineering Research Laboratory (SERL) in Richmond, California. Unfortunately, much of their information is hard to come by. Another good source of technical information has been the series *Sewage Works Journal* (1928-1948); *Sewage and Industrial Wastes* (1949-1958) and now the *Journal of the Water Pollution Control Federation* (1959-present). *Sewage Works Journal* is especially valuable since it represents a science and technology of waste recycling before the trend to make treatment centers bigger and information more and more incomprehensible.

The following are but a *very* few of the key sources of information about methane systems. References are keyed in the following way: ASAE = American Society of Agricultural Engineers, St. Joseph, Michigan. ASCE = American Society of Civil Engineers. EPA = Environmental Protection Agency. GPO = Superintendent of Documents, Government Printing Office. SERL = Sanitary Engineering Research Laboratory, University of California, Berkeley, at Richmond, California. WPCF = Water Pollution Control Federation, 2900 Wisconsin Ave. N.W., Washington D.C. 20016.

METHANE DIGESTION: MUNICIPAL/INDUSTRIAL

Dept. of the Environment, 1965. SMALL SEWAGE WORKS OPERATORS' HAND-BOOK. HMSO Press, P. O. Box 569, London S.E. 1 9 NH. From: Pendragon House Inc., Palo Alto, Calif. 94301.

Fair, G.M. et al. 1968. WATER AND WASTEWATER ENGINEERING. Vo. 2, Wiley, N.Y. (A)

Geyer, J. 1972. LANDFILL DECOMPOSITION GASES. EPA, NTIS, PB-213 487, $3.75. Annotated bibliography of 48 articles about anaerobic gases generated by landfills.

Hawkes, H.A. 1963. THE ECOLOGY OF WASTE WATER TREATMENT. Pergamon Press, N. Y.

Imhoff, K. and G. Fair. 1956. SEWAGE TREATMENT (2nd ed.). John Wiley and Sons. N. Y. (B) Best semi-technical overview.

McCabe, B.J. and W.W. Eckenfelder. 1958. BIOLOGICAL TREATMENT OF SEWAGE AND INDUSTRIAL WASTES, Vol 2, Reinhold, N. Y.

MANUAL OF INSTRUCTION FOR WATER TREATMENT PLANT OPERATORS. New York State Dept. of Health. (From: HES, P. O. Box 7283, Albany, N.Y. 12201) Great tool!

Metcalf and Eddy, Inc. 1972. WASTEWATER ENGINEERING. McGraw-Hill, N. Y. 782 pp. (A) A technical overview; up to date.

Stander, G.J. et al. 1968. INVESTIGATION OF THE FULL-SCALE PURIFICATION OF WINE DISTILLERY WASTES BY THE ANAEROBIC DIGESTION PRO—CESS. CSIR Research Dept. No. 270, Bellville, S. Africa.

Young, J.C. and P.L. McCarty. 1969. THE ANAEROBIC FILTER FOR WASTE TREATMENT. Jour. WPCF, 41:R160-R173. Speeding up detention time with submerged 1" round stones. More surface area for bacteria. Works best with dilute soluble organic wastes (i.e., not manures).

METHANE DIGESTION: AGRICULTURAL WASTES

Baines, S. 1970. ANAEROBIC TREATMENT OF FARM WASTES. Proceedings, Symposium Farm Wastes, Univ. of Newcastle Paper 18 (Univ. of Wisc. Extension), pp. 132-137.

Cross, O. and A. Duran. 1970. ANAEROBIC DECOMPOSITION OF SWINE EXCREMENT. Trans. ASAE, 13(3): 320-325.

Hart, S. 1963. DIGESTION OF LIVESTOCK WASTES. Journal WPCF. 35: 748-757.

Hobson, S.A. 1973. DIGESTION OF LIVESTOCK MANURES. Jour. WPCF. 35: 748-757.

Jewell, W.J. 1974. ENERGY FROM AGRICULTURAL WASTE. METHANE GENERATION. Agric. Engin. Bull. 397, New York State College of Agric., Ithaca, N. Y. 13 pp. (C) Popular overview.

Loehr, R.C. 1974. AGRICULTURAL WASTE MANAGEMENT. Academic Press, N. Y.

MANAGEMENT OF FARM ANIMAL WASTES. 1967. Proc. Nat. Symp. on Animal Waste Management, ASAE, $5.00. 1966, $14.00.

Meenaghan, G. et al. 1970. GAS PRODUCTION FROM CATTLE WASTES. Paper no. 70-907. ASAE.

Parker, R. et al. 1974. METHANE PRODUCTION FROM SWINE WASTE WITH A SOLAR REACTOR. Presented at Southeast Region Meeting of the ASAE, Memphis, Tenn., Feb. 5, 1974.

Savery, C.W. and D. Cruzan. 1972. METHANE RECOVERY FROM CHICKEN MANURE DIGESTION. Jour. WPCF. 44(12): 2349-2354.

Taiganides, E.P. et al. 1963. ANAEROBIC DIGESTION OF HOG WASTES. Journal of Agric. Engin. Res., 8: 327-333.

Taiganides, E. and T.E. Hazen. 1966. PROPERTIES OF FARM ANIMAL EXCRETA. Trans. ASAE, 9: 374-376.

Taiganides, E.P. 1963. ANAEROBIC DIGESTION OF POULTRY MANURE. World's Poultry Science Journal, 19: 252-261.

POPULAR OVERVIEWS AND SCALED DOWN DESIGNS

Acharya, C.N. 1958. PREPARATION OF FUEL GAS AND MANURE BY ANAEROBIC FERMENTATION OF ORGANIC MATERIALS. I.C.A.R. Research Series, no. 15, India. 58 pp.

Boshoff, W.H. 1963. METHANE GAS PRODUCTION BY BATCH AND CONTINUOUS FERMENTATION METHODS. Tropical Science, 5(3): 155-165. (Britain). Using plant wastes in tropical (East Africa) conditions.

Diaz, L.F. et al. 1974. METHANE GAS PRODUCTION AS PART OF A REFUSE RECYCLING SYSTEM. Fourth Annual Composting and Waste Recycling Conference, Proceedings, El Paso, Texas. In: Compost Science, 15(3): 7-13. Popular description of recent research.

Fairbank, W.C. 1974. FUEL FROM FECES? The Dairyman, May, 1974. Popular putdown of digestion. "Direct combustion is the simplest way of converting feces to fuel . . . digesters are dangerous . . . on-farm digesters are not practical . . . only municipal or corporate industry can muster money . . ." etc., etc.

Lapp, H.M. et al. 1974. METHANE GAS PRODUCTION FROM ANIMAL WASTES. Information Division, Canada Dept. of Agriculture, Ottawa, Canada K1A OC7. 12 pp. (C)

Mother Earth News. 1972. PLOWBOY INTERVIEW WITH RAM BUX SINGH. Mother Earth News, 18. Hendersonville, N.C.

Pfeffer, J.T. 1973. RECLAMATION OF ENERGY FROM ORGANIC REFUSE. EPA - R - 800776.

Po, Chung. 1973. PRODUCTION OF METHANE GAS FROM MANURE. In: "Proceedings of Biomass Energy Conference," Winnipeg. See Reviews. 80 cubic feet, and 230 cubic feet square block digesters connected in series, built from bricks and concrete, flowing into algae pond. For 20-head pig sty and family of 12 in tropics.

PROCEEDINGS: BIOCONVERSION ENERGY RESEARCH CONFERENCE. Institute for Man and His Environment. Univ. Mass., Amherst, Mass., June 25-26, 1973. Conference about conversion of waste and feedlot materials to methane.

Singh, Ram Bux. 1972. BUILDING A BIO-GAS PLANT. Compost Science, March-April, 1972.

Singh, R.B. 1971. GOBAR GAS EXPERIMENTS IN INDIA. Mother Earth News, 12: 28-31, Hendersonville, N.C.

Taiganides, P.E. et al. 1963. SLUDGE DIGESTION OF FARM ANIMAL WASTES. Compost Science 4:26.

Water Pollution Control Federation. 1968. ANAEROBIC SLUDGE DIGESTION. WPCF, 3900 Wisconsin Ave., Washington D.C. 20016 $2.50.

Whitehurst, Sharon and James. 1974. OUR FOUR-COW BIO-GAS PLANT. In: Producing Your Own Power, Rodale Press, Emmaus, Pa. See Reviews. Integrated Systems. Experiences with building and operating a 225 cubic foot continuous feed digester (old boiler tank) that utilizes manure from 4 cows on a Vermont dairy farm. Built with the help of Ram Bux Singh.

BIOLOGY/CHEMISTRY

Barker, H.A. 1956, BACTERIAL FERMENTATION. John Wiley & Sons, N.Y. 95 pp. (B)

Buswell, A.M. and N.D. Hatfield. 1936. ANAEROBIC FERMENTATION. Illinois State Water Survey Bulletin, no. 32.

Chamberlin, N.S. 1930. ACTION OF ENZYMES ON SEWAGE SOLIDS. N. Jers. Agric. Exper. Sta., Bulletin 500.

Fair, G.M. and E.W. Moore. 1934. TIME AND RATE OF SLUDGE DIGESTION AND THEIR VARIATION WITH TEMPERATURE. Sewage Works Journal 6:3-13.

Fair, G.M. and E.W. Moore. 1932. HEAT AND ENERGY RELATIONS IN THE DIGESTION OF SEWAGE SOLIDS Sewage Works Jour. 4: 242.

Golueke, C.G. 1958. TEMPERATURE EFFECTS ON ANAEROBIC DIGESTION OF RAW SEWAGE SLUDGE. Sewage Works Jour. 30: 1225-1232.

Gotaas, H.B. et al. 1954. ALGAL-BACTERIAL SYMBIOSIS IN SEWAGE OXIDA-TION PONDS. 5th Progress Rept., SERL.

Gould, R.F. (ed.). 1971. ANAEROBIC BIOLOGICAL TREATMENT PROCESS. ACS No. 15, Amer. Chem. Soc., 1155 16th St., Washington D.C. 20036. 196 pp. $9.00. (A)

Heukelekian, H. and M. Berger. 1953. VALUE OF CULTURE AND ENZYME ADDI-TIONS IN PROMOTING DIGESTION. Sewage and Indust. Wastes, 25(11): 1259.

Isaac, P.C. 1952. THE EFFECTS OF SYNTHETIC DETERGENTS ON SEWAGE TREATMENT: A REVIEW OF THE LITERATURE. New England Sewage and Industrial Wastes Assn.

Jeris, J.S. and P.L. McCarty. 1965. THE BIOCHEMISTRY OF METHANE FERMEN-TATION USING C^{14} TRACERS. Jour. WPCF., 37(2): 178-192. 70% of methane produced in anaerobic digestion comes from acetic acids.

Kinugasa, Y. et al. 1968. ANAEROBIC DIGESTION OF FECES WASTE BY ADDI-TION OF ENZYME PREPARATIONS. Suido Kenkyusho Hokoku, 5(1): 68-72, Japan.

Kotz, J.P. et al. 1969. ANAEROBIC DIGESTION. Water Research, 3: 459-493.

Lawrence, A.W. and P.L. McCarty. 1969. KINETICS OF METHANE FERMENTATION IN ANAEROBIC TREATMENT. Journal of the WPCF, 41 (2): R1-R17.

McCarty, P.L. 1964. ANAEROBIC WASTE TREATMENT FUNDAMENTALS: I. "Chemistry and Microbiology." II. "Environmental Requirements and Control." III. "Toxic Materials and Their Control." IV. "Process Design." Public Works 95: (9): 107-112; (10): 123-126; (11): 91-94; (12): 95-99. Great semi-technical introduction.

McKinney, R.E. 1962. MICROBIOLOGY FOR SANITARY ENGINEERS. McGraw-Hill, New York.

Nelson, G. et al. 1939. EFFECT OF TEMPERATURE OF DIGESTION, CHEMICAL COMPOSITION AND SIZE OF PARTICLES ON PRODUCTION OF FUEL GAS FROM FARM WASTES. Jour. of Agric. Research (USDA). 58(4): 273-287.

Sawyer, C.N. and P.L. McCarty. 1967. CHEMISTRY FOR SANITARY ENGINEERS. 2nd ed., McGraw-Hill, N. Y.

Stanwick, J.D. and M. Foulkes. 1971. INHIBITION OF ANAEROBIC DIGESTION OF SEWAGE SLUDGE BY CHLORINATED HYDROCARBONS. Water Pollution Control 70(1).

SLUDGE: ANALYSIS

Anderson, Myron S. 1956. COMPARATIVE ANALYSES OF SEWAGE SLUDGES. Sewage and Ind. Wastes 28: 132-135.

Bender, D.F. et al. (ed.). 1973. PHYSICAL, CHEMICAL AND MICROBIOLOGICAL METHODS OF SOLID WASTE TESTING. EPA, NTIS. $6.75. Analysis of com-post and sludge.

Coker, E.G. 1966. THE VALUE OF LIQUID DIGESTED SEWAGE SLUDGE. J. Agri. Sci., Camb. 67:91-97.

Moore, E.W. et al. 1950. SIMPLIFIED METHOD FOR ANALYSIS OF B.O.D. DATA. Sewage and Industrial Wastes, 22(10).

Vieiti, D. 1971. LABORATORY PROCEDURES: ANALYSIS FOR WASTEWATER TREATMENT PLANT OPERATORS. EPA/NTIS, $4.85.

Vlamis, J. and D. Williams. 1961. TEST OF SEWAGE SLUDGE FOR FERTILITY AND TOXICITY IN SOILS. Compost Science 2(1): 26-30.

SLUDGE: GARDENING AND FARMING

AGRICULTURAL BENEFITS AND ENVIRONMENTAL CHANGES RESULTING FROM THE USE OF DIGESTED SEWAGE SLUDGE ON FIELD CROPS. 1971. EPA, GPO. 62 pp. Results of experiments with Metropolitan Sanitary District, Chicago.

Allen, J. 1973. SEWAGE FARMING. Environment, 15(3): 36-41. (C) Popular overview.

Anderson, M.S. 1955. SEWAGE SLUDGE FOR SOIL IMPROVEMENT. USDA, Circular 972. GPO.

Glathe, H., and A. Makawi. 1963. THE EFFECT OF SEWAGE SLUDGE ON SOILS AND MICRO-ORGANISMS. Soils and Fert. 26: 273

Hinesly, T. et al. 1971. AGRICULTURAL BENEFITS AND ENVIRONMENTAL CHANGES FROM THE USE OF DIGESTED SEWAGE SLUDGE ON FIELD CROPS. EPA, GPO. $0.65.

INCORPORATION OF SEWAGE SLUDGE IN SOIL TO MAXIMIZE BENEFITS AND MINIMIZE HAZARDS TO THE ENVIRONMENT. USDA. 1970. Agricul-tural Research Station, Beltsville, Md. Most extensive and current USDA research on sludge farming.

Laura, R.D. and M.A. Idnani. 1972. MINERALIZATION OF NITROGEN IN MANURES MADE FROM SPENT-SLURRY. Soil Biol. Biochem. 4:239-243. Liquid slurry superior to sun-dried slurry and farm compost.

Law, J. 1968. AGRICULTURAL UTILIZATION OF SEWAGE EFFLUENT AND SLUDGE. An Annotated Bibliography. WPCF, GPO. 89 pp.

Shreir, Franz. 1950. PROBLEMS IN SEWAGE FARMING. Abstracts, Sewage & In-dust. Wastes, 25: 241. Spraying onto grazing areas is hygienically and biologi-cally the best means of sewage utilization.

Van Kleeck, W. Leroy. 1958. DO'S AND DON'TS OF USING SLUDGE FOR SOIL CONDITIONING AND FERTILIZING. Wastes Engr. 29: 256-257.

Wylie, J.C. 1955. FERTILITY FROM TOWN WASTES. Faber & Faber, London. 244 pp. (B) (OOP) Methods of sewage sludge disposal in agricultural country in Scotland.

SLUDGE: ALGAE SYSTEMS; GROWTH, HARVESTING, DIGESTION

Foree, E.G., and P.L. McCarty. 1970. ANAEROBIC DECOMPOSITION OF ALGAE. Environmental Science and Tech., 4: 842-849.

Golueke, C. et al. 1957. ANAEROBIC DIGESTION OF ALGAE. Appl. Microbiol. 5: 47-55.

Golueke, C.G. and W.J. Oswald. 1964. HARVESTING AND PROCESSING SEWAGE-GROWN PLANKTONIC ALGAE. SERL, Rept. 64-8. Also Journal, WPCF, April 1965. Handy description of process.

Oswald, W. 1960. LIGHT CONVERSION EFFICIENCY OF ALGAE GROWN IN SEWAGE. J. Sanit. Engin. Div., ASCE. 86: 71-94.

Lawlor, R. 1974. ALGAE RESEARCH IN AUROVILLE. Alternative Sources of Energy, 16:2-9. Research in India on simple algae systems.

Oswald, W.J. and H.B. Gotaas. 1957. PHOTOSYNTHESIS IN SEWAGE TREAT-MENT. Trans. ASCE, 122: 73-105. The paper that started people rethinking the potentials of algae production.

Po, C. 1973. PRODUCTION AND USE OF METHANE FROM ANIMAL WASTES IN TAIWAN. In: Proc. Internat. Biomass Energy Conf., Winnipeg. See Reviews. Simple description of a small sludge-algae operation.

TRANSACTIONS OF THE SEMINAR ON ALGAE AND METROPOLITAN WASTES. April 27-29, 1960. U.S. Public Health Service, Robert A. Taft Sanitary Engineering Center, Cincinnati, Ohio.

Water Pollution Control Federation. 1969. SLUDGE DEWATERING. Manual of Practice, 20. WPCF.

SLUDGE: ALGAE SYSTEMS; FOR METHANE POWER

Golueke, C. and W. Oswald. 1963. POWER FROM SOLAR ENERGY VIA ALGAE-POWERED METHANE. Solar Energy, 7(3): 86-92.

Golueke, C.G. and W.J. Oswald. 1959. BIOLOGICAL CONVERSION OF LIGHT ENERGY TO THE CHEMICAL ENERGY OF METHANE. Appl. Microbiol., 7: 219-227.

Oswald, W.J. and C.G. Golueke. 1964. SOLAR POWER VIA A BOTANICAL PRO—CESS. Mech. Engin., Feb. pp. 40-43.

Oswald, W.J. and C.G. Golueke. 1960. BIOLOGICAL TRANSFORMATION OF SOLAR ENERGY. Adv. Appl. Microbiol. 2: 223-262.

SLUDGE: ALGAE SYSTEMS; ALGAE AS LIVESTOCK FEED

Cook, B. et al. 1963. THE PROTEIN QUALITY OF WASTE-GROWN GREEN ALGAE. Jour. Nutrition, 81: 23.

Dugan, G. et al. 1970. PHOTOSYNTHETIC RECLAMATION OF AGRICULTURAL WASTES. SERL Rept., 70-1. (A) Classic study of chicken, digester, algae, feed systems.

Dugan, G. et al. 1972. RECYCLING SYSTEM FOR POULTRY WASTES. JWPFC, 44(3): 432-440. Popular account of 1970 study above.

Gran, C.R. and N. Klein. 1957. SEWAGE-GROWN ALGAE AS A FEEDSTUFF FOR CHICKS. SERL.

SLUDGE: HYDROPONICS

Bridwell, R. 1972. HYDROPONIC GARDENING. Woodbridge Press Publishing Co., Santa Barbara, Calif. 224 pp. (C)

Douglas, J.S. 1973. BEGINNER'S GUIDE TO HYDROPONICS. Drake Publishers, Inc., N.Y. 156 pp. (C)

Douglas, J.S. 1959. HYDROPONICS: THE BENGAL SYSTEM. Oxford Univ. Press. (C) A simple method making use of low cost materials.

Iby, H. 1966. EVALUATING ADAPTABILITY OF PASTURE GRASSES TO HYDRO-PONIC CULTURE AND THEIR ABILITY TO ACT AS CHEMICAL FILTERS. In: Farm Animal Wastes. Symposium, 1966. Beltsville, Md.

Law, J.P. 1969. NUTRIENT REMOVAL FROM ENRICHED WASTE EFFLUENT BY THE HYDROPONIC CULTURE OF COOL SEASON GRASSES. Federal Water Quality Admin., GPO.

Saunby, T. 1970. SOILLESS CULTURE. Transatlantic Arts, Inc., Levittown, N.Y. 104 pp. (C)

DIGESTER PRIVIES

Foster, D.H. and R.A. Engelbrecht. 1972. MICROBIAL HAZARDS IN DISPOSING OF WASTEWATER ON SOIL. In: Recycling Treated Municipal Wastewater and Sludge Through Forest and Cropland. See Reviews. Most complete recent review.

Gainey, P.L. and T.H. Lord. 1952. MICROBIOLOGY OF WATER AND SEWAGE. Prentice-Hall, N.Y. Good section on Coliform bacteria.

Gotaas, Harold. 1956. MANURE AND NIGHT SOIL DIGESTERS FOR METHANE RECOVERY ON FARMS AND IN VILLAGES. In: Composting (H. Gotaas) World Health Organization, Geneva.

Gram, E.B. 1943. EFFECTS OF VARIOUS TREATMENT PROCESSES ON PATH-OGEN SURVIVAL. Sew. Wrks. Jour. 15:

Nishihara, S. 1935. DIGESTION OF HUMAN FECAL MATTER WITH pH ADJUST-MENT OF AIR CONTROL. Sewage Wrks. Journal, 7(5): 798-809.

Wagner, E.G. and J.N. Lanoix. 1958. EXCRETA DISPOSAL FOR RURAL AREAS AND SMALL COMMUNITIES. World Health Organization, Geneva. 187 pp. $5.00. Many designs for privies . . . models for privy digesters.

Wiley, B. and S.C. Westerberg. 1969. SURVIVAL OF HUMAN PATHOGENS IN COMPOSTED SEWAGE. Appl. Microbiol. 18(6): 994-1001. Aerobic composting of sewage sludge destroys most pathogens.

ALCOHOL

ALCOHOL AS A BIOFUEL: COMING AROUND AGAIN??
by Richard Merrill and Tom Aston

PERSPECTIVE

For most people alcohol means liquor. But in its pure form alcohol is also a source of energy. It can be used for heating, cooking, lighting and as a motor fuel. We are not totally convinced that the production of alcohol is really practical for individuals or small groups seeking energy self-sufficiency. For one thing, the biggest drawback to alcohol as a fuel is that you can also drink it,* and the legal red tape controlling its production is almost insurmountable for small operations. For another thing it is becoming more and more difficult to justify using plants for anything except food and fodder. You can produce alcohol from organic wastes, but this requires a technology that is generally impractical for families, groups, or even cottage industries. As a final blow, sugar and materials for building stills (especially copper) are becoming harder to get . . . even the moonshiners are shutting down. In any event we only want to sum up briefly some information concerning alcohol as a biofuel. And in spite of the legal and material difficulties, alcohol is a beautiful, high energy, clean burning and totally renewable liquid fuel. Ideally it makes real sense.

Year	Molasses	Fermentation			Synthetic		Total
		Sulfite Liquors	Grain	Other	Ethyl Sulfate	Direct Hydration	
1934	72.5	--	5.5	2.6	6.4	--	86.9
1944	113.1	--	313.6	33.6	59.9	--	519.9
1954	36.8	2.7	4.8	1.2	126.3	27.4	199.2
1964	0.7	4.1	43.9	16.3	232.7	51.7	341.1

TABLE I ETHYL ALCOHOL PRODUCTION IN THE U.S., MILLION GALLONS (190 PROOF). FROM MONICK, 1969 (REF. 1).

There are two kinds of common alcohols: ethyl alcohol (ethanol or "grain alcohol" . . . the stuff you drink), and methyl alcohol (methanol or "wood alcohol"), a toxic alcohol familiar as a heating fuel for *sterno*. At the turn of the century, before cheap crude oil became plentiful, both ethanol and methanol were seriously considered as motor fuels in the U.S. and Europe. Today almost all non-beverage alcohol is produced synthetically from natural gas or ethylene and used as industrial chemicals rather than as a fuel source. Beverage ethanol is distilled commercially from grains and fruits and its production is strictly controlled at all levels by Federal

---

* *A general rule of thumb:* IF YOU PRODUCE ETHANOL FOR POWER, DON'T DRINK IT!! *Unless you are really experienced or on top of it, some of the byproducts of distillation, especially methanol, can kill you. Also alcohol is an organic solvent and will pick up most toxic organic substances that happen to be* in *the still or condenser.*

regulations. For industry, ethanol is denatured (laced with toxic materials) and, like methanol, it is used in plastics, solvents, drugs and food processing, etc.

In short, both ethanol and methanol can be produced in a variety of ways: from the organic compounds of fossil fuels or the sugars of natural plant products (Fig. 1). Only certain processes, though, qualify alcohol as a biofuel: ethanol, from the distillation of plant sugars; and methanol, from the destructive distillation of wood and heat conversion[1,2] of refuse, or from methane gas obtained by anaerobic digestion.

Generally speaking, methanol production, by whatever means, is a high-tech process and usually impractical for small operations. This leaves us with the traditional method of making ethanol . . . fermenting and distilling certain plants. As an example, consider the making of ethanol from a starch crop. This will give us a handle on the terminology and basic processes involved.

First the plants are finely ground and heated in water to form a gelatine or *mash*. The starch in the mash is then converted to sugar by malt (sprouted grain) which contains an enzyme *diatase* designed especially for this task.** Yeast is then added to the mash. The yeast contains another enzyme that *ferments* the sugar produced by the malt into ethyl alcohol.

The next step is to separate or *distill* the alcohol from the mash (mostly water). Fortunately alcohol boils into vapors at a lower temperature (77°C; 171°F) than water (100°C; 212°F). So by heating the mash to slightly over 77°C, alcohol vapors can escape and *condense* elsewhere on a cool surface as a more or less pure liquid alcohol. The purity of the alcohol produced depends on how efficiently the fermentation, distillation and condensation processes have converted sugar to alcohol, and separated alcohol from water. In fact the history of alcohol technology can be described in terms of fancier and fancier devices designed to make alcohol as pure as possible . . . without water or other byproducts. Many of these early devices can serve as experimental or even production models today.

ALCOHOL HISTORY

The earliest forms of alcohol were simple fermented beverages. As early as 4000-6000 B.C. the art of making crude beers and wines was flourishing in the Middle-East. By 2000 B.C., production breweries were well established in Egypt.

The Chinese were probably the first to distill alcohol directly from a fermented (rice) liquor around 800 B.C. About the earliest known apparatus used for distillation was the *Tibetan Still* (Fig. 2a), a clay pot in which various ferments were heated to drive off alcohol vapors. The vapors rose and condensed on a saucer-cover filled with cool water. Another pot (*receiver*) suspended inside the still collected the dripping alcohol which was then used for liquors. A major advance was made by the Peruvians who

---

** *Enzymes do not enter into a chemical reaction directly. They merely speed up the reaction by virtue of their chemical structure.*

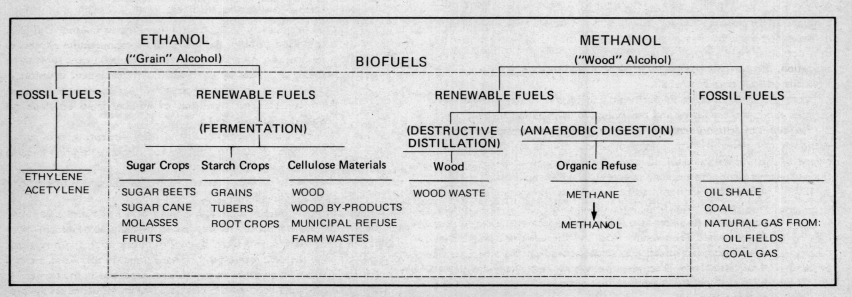

FIG. 1 PROCESSES FOR PRODUCING ALCOHOL

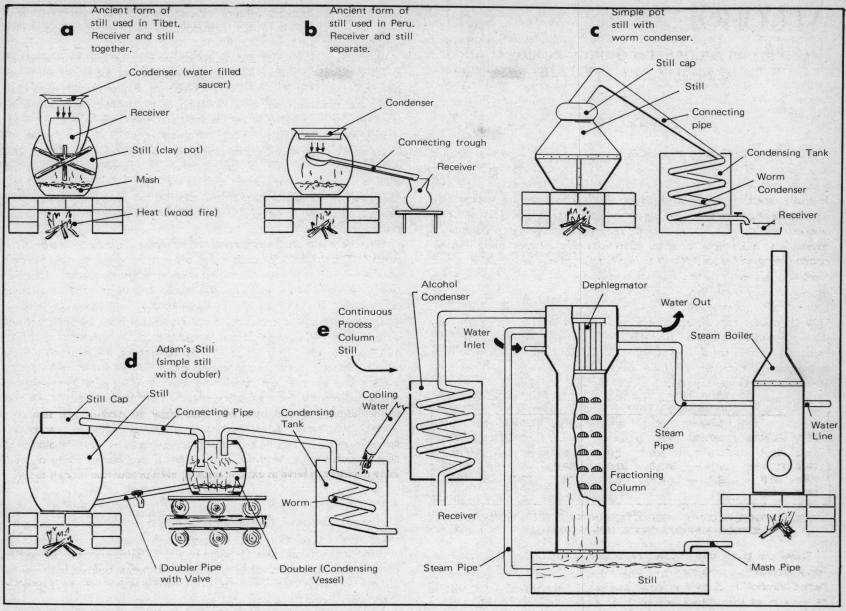

a Ancient form of still used in Tibet. Receiver and still together.
- Condenser (water filled saucer)
- Receiver
- Still (clay pot)
- Mash
- Heat (wood fire)

b Ancient form of still used in Peru. Receiver and still separate.
- Condenser
- Connecting trough
- Receiver

c Simple pot still with worm condenser.
- Still cap
- Still
- Connecting pipe
- Condensing Tank
- Worm Condenser
- Receiver

d Adam's Still (simple still with doubler)
- Still Cap
- Still
- Connecting Pipe
- Condensing Tank
- Worm
- Doubler Pipe with Valve
- Doubler (Condensing Vessel)

e Continuous Process Column Still
- Alcohol Condenser
- Cooling Water
- Receiver
- Steam Pipe
- Water Inlet
- Dephlegmator
- Water Out
- Fractioning Column
- Still
- Steam Pipe
- Steam Boiler
- Water Line
- Mash Pipe

separated the receiver from the still by a connecting trough (Fig. 2b). They were thus able to reclaim more alcohol by increasing the space of the still. The *Tahitian Still*, probably also of B.C. vintage, was similar to the Peruvian still except that a pipe, rather than an open trough, was used to run alcohol from the condenser to the receiver. This prevented evaporation and increased yields.

By 500 A.D. distillation technology had advanced to the point where relatively pure forms of alcohol were being used in cosmetics, perfumes and medicines. During the "Dark" Ages, knowledge of alcohol production spread through Europe, and by 1300, Italian monasteries were distilling alcohol from wine as "aqua-vitae." *Simple Pot Stills* (Fig. 2c) were used throughout Renaissance Europe. Many of them used a new kind of condenser called a *worm*. This was a coiled metal tube that led from the still to a container holding cool water. The worm increased the area of condensation, the purity and quantity of alcohol, and separated the condenser from the receiver once and for all.

From the 18th century to the beginning of this century, major discoveries about the chemistry and technology of distillation made it possible to produce ethanol cheaply from a variety of organic materials. Although our main interest is ethanol production as the most popular means of making fuel alcohol, it is worth noting some of the important finds in general alcohol technology over the last 175 years.[2-6]

a. 1801 *Adam Still:* First still to be used on an industrial scale. Used a condensing vessel (Fig. 2d). Vessel was kept at 78°C to condense as much water as possible. Extra ferment was also kept in the vessel. Thus vapors from the still were not only better dehydrated, but mixed with fresh vapors from the vessel.

b. 1819 *Acid Hydrolysis:* Discovery that wood wastes heated with sulfuric acid yielded a product that contained sugars suitable for fermentation.

c. 1820's *Continuous Still:* Allowed mash to be loaded and alcohol received without shutting still down. The savings in time and energy was revolutionary. With the simple still the weight of fuel consumed was nearly 3 times that of the alcohol produced. The continuous still reduced this to one quarter.

d. 1823 *Methyl Alcohol:* Discovery of a new alcohol produced by condensing gases from burning wood *(Destructive Distillation)*.

e. 1826 *Column Still:* Alcohol distilled by blowing steam through mash spread in layers over perforated plates in a column (rectifier). The column still was the first to produce nearly pure alcohol (94-96%) on a commercial basis.

The development of the *Continuous Process Column Still* (Fig. 2e) made possible for the first time the manufacture of ethanol in large enough quantities and at low enough prices for it to be available as a fuel by the 1830's. All subsequent advances in distillation technology were essentially variations on this theme.

f. 1828 *Synthetic Ethanol:* Synthesis of ethanol from ethylene gas dissolved in sulfuric acid.

g. 1830's *Alcohol Lamps:* Ethanol mixed with turpentine, coal tar or naptha and used as a light source. Ethanol begins replacing whale oil as a popular fuel.

h. 1900 *Commercial Wood Alcohol:* Industrial manufacturing of ethanol using acid hydrolysis.

In recent history, public interest in alcohol as a fuel has changed with the pattern of our war-prosperity-depression cycles: the development of distillation technology during wars, absence of public interest during times of prosperity and renewed interest during hard times. In this sense, alcohol is not much different than other energy sources described in the *Primer*.

Other things besides economic cycles have had an influence on the production of ethanol as an alternative fuel source. For one thing ethanol is not only a fuel but also a beverage. Since 1861 there have been a series of taxes and laws regulating its production. In general these laws have been so complex and arbitrary that they have all but prohibited the individual or small group from legally producing ethanol fuel in any practical sense. For another thing, since the 1900's alcohol has had to take a back seat to oil as a liquid fuel source. Until recently oil has been cheap, predictable and easily available, while the raw materials for ethanol production (grains, molasses, etc.) have been subject to the vagaries of weather, pest outbreaks and foreign policies. Except during wars and depressions, there has never been any real incentive to produce and use ethanol (or any alcohol) as a fuel. These trends are reflected in other historical events:

i. 1861   First *Federal Tax* on alcohol production (mostly beverage tax). Taxes plus rising prices from Civil War made alcohol too expensive to compete with kerosene.

j. 1890's   Rising taxes on ethanol limited its use as a fuel. Methyl alcohol (from destructive distillation) became a substitute for most manufacturers. Early *Heating Devices* used a Bunsen burner supplied with carborated alcohol from a pressurized reservoir. Alcohol stoves appeared.

k. 1907   *Denatured Alcohol:* U.S. tax laws changed, excluding denatured alcohol (95% ethanol, 5% toxic additives).

l. 1900-1910   Determined effort to expand use of denatured alcohol as all-purpose fuel. First major study[7] concluded that alcohol gave greater horsepower, higher compression, same mileage but lower thermal efficiency than gasoline. However, competition from petroleum continued to make alcohol non-competitive.

m. 1923   War-surplus alcohol mixed with gasoline (20/80 blend) and sold in some cities. Small corn crop of 1924 discontinued supplies.

n. 1920's-1930   European countries cut off from petroleum supplies during the war began post-war use of ethanol as a fuel. Sweden began production of ethanol from *Sulfite Liquors*, used 25/75 blend as motor fuel. Germany began alcohol economy from agricultural crops: 2/3 potatoes, 1/3 molasses, grains and sulfite liquors. Improved foreign balance of payments and reduced need for energy imports.

o. 1920's-1930's   United States industrial alcohol made mostly from molasses. Used in synthetic rubber, anti-freeze, munitions, cosmetics, etc. During 30's farm production of alcohol was slowly replaced by synthetic ethanol.

p. 1930's   Midwest research advocated use of alcohol in gasoline. Nebraska legislature passed a law that would refund $0.02/gallon to motorists who bought the blend. Petroleum industry campaign knocked out the plan.

q. 1940's   WWII put demands on alcohol industry, increased grains output of alcohol to 41% of total production by 1944. Many whiskey distilleries commandeered into war production and molasses-using plants converted to grains. Food shortages caused raw materials to change from corn to wheat. After the war, grain shortages caused potatoes to be used on a large scale for the first time.

r. 1950-present   Early 50's marked the end of farm products as a large source for alcohol. Since then, synthetic alcohol from fossil fuels has dominated the alcohol markets.

Today the specter of an "energy crisis" and fuel shortages have once again prompted interest in alcohol as a possible energy source. Special attention is being given to alcohol as an additive to gasoline in place of lead, since it would reduce pollutants and improve octane and mileage. Proponents have suggested that alcohol be produced from domestic grains,[8-11] natural gas from oil fields and coal gasification plants,[12] organic refuse[13] and other "waste" materials such as garbage, sawdust, scraps from logging, lignin discarded by paper mills, coal tailings, mine washings, etc.

Properties of Alcohol

Property	Ethanol	Methanol
Boiling point	172°F	148°F
Freezing point	-205°F	-176°F
Btu/Lb.	11,500-12,800	8200-9000
Btu/Gal.	90-100,000	65-70,000
Lb/Gal.	6.58	6.59
Specific gravity (at 20°C, water = 1.0)	.7905	.7924
Octane	99	106

TABLE II   BASIC PROPERTIES OF METHYL AND ETHYL ALCOHOL

ETHANOL PRODUCTION FROM FARM PRODUCTS

Basics

Ethanol can either be produced from gases such as ethylene, acetylene and carbon monoxide found in various fossil fuels or from carbohydrates (sugars, starches, cellulose)** found in various farm products. In the case of carbohydrates, the traditional methods of fermenting sugar to alcohol are the only ways to produce ethanol from renewable sources. Either the raw material contains sugars that can be fermented directly, or it contains the more complex carbohydrates (starches and cellulose) that must be broken down first to simple sugars before the yeast can do its work (Fig. 3).

** *Carbohydrates are compounds of carbon, hydrogen and oxygen. The hydrogen and oxygen are present in the same proportion as they are in water (H_2O), hence the name carbo-hydrate.*

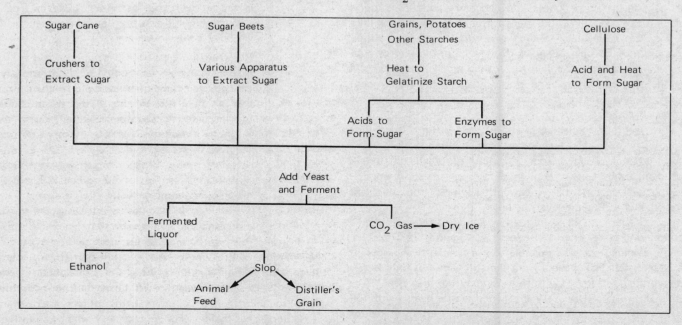

FIG. 3   BASIC STEPS IN ETHANOL PRODUCTION FROM FARM PRODUCTS.

The simplest sugars contain only one molecule (monosaccharides); these include dextrose (glucose or grape sugar) and fructose (fruit sugar). Still other sugars such as sucrose (table, beet or cane sugar), maltose (malt sugar) and lactose (milk sugar) contain two simple sugar molecules (disaccharides). The starches are even more complex carbohydrates made up of many simple sugar molecules held together by splitting out water molecules. When starch is treated with certain chemicals (acids and enzymes) the molecule takes on water and breaks apart into the original sugar molecules . . . a reaction called *hydrolysis*. Even more complex carbohydrates are the fibrous compounds called *cellulose*. Examples of cellulose are cotton, wood, plant stalks, paper and most organic refuse.

All of these carbohydrates can be converted to ethanol, but the more complex the compound, the more difficult and therefore the more costly and impractical the process becomes for small operations.

Ethanol From Sugar Crops

The simplest method of producing ethanol is fermentation and distillation of sugar beets, sugar cane, molasses and fruits. These crops contain high amounts of sugar which can be converted directly to alcohol by various yeast enzymes:

$$C_{12}H_{22}O_{11} + H_2O \xrightarrow[\text{Enzyme}]{\text{Maltase}} 2C_6H_{12}O_6$$

maltose + water   dextrose

or

$$C_{12}H_{22}O_{11} + H_2O \xrightarrow[\text{Enzyme}]{\text{Invertase}} 2C_6H_{12}O_6$$

sucrose + water   dextrose

then

$$C_6H_{12}O_6 \xrightarrow[\text{Enzyme}]{\text{Zymase}} 2C_2H_2OH + 2CO_2$$

dextrose   ethanol + carbon dioxide

There are, of course, many more considerations here than just the simple addition of yeast to a slurry of mashed fruits or sugar beets. Alcohol fermentation, like anaerobic digestion, is a biological process and requires special attention through a series of living reactions. For example:

1) Pure yeast will not produce alcohol from pure sugar, because a pure sugar solution does not contain the substances required to nourish the yeast. There are usually enough extra nutrients in the raw materials besides sugars to properly feed the yeast and set them on their way, but this may not always be the case. Special malts or other supplements may have to be added.

2) Like most biological processes, fermentation is actually a series of chemical steps . . . each one providing the basic materials for the others to follow in a *succession* of reactions. During the first period, the yeast grows in the mash at a temperature of about 82°F. The growth of the yeast becomes apparent by the gradual bubbling of carbon dioxide up through the mash. When alcohol is produced to an extent of 5%, the growth of the yeast stops. During the second period, carbon dioxide bubbles freely, and the sugar is converted to alcohol rapidly. The temperature at this point should not exceed 81°F. Water is often added here to dilute the mixture and permit further growth of the yeast. Finally there is a lessening of carbon dioxide formation and a lowering of temperature (77°-80°F).

There are really dozens of tricks to successful fermentation. Useful "how-to" descriptions of preparing mashes from molasses and sugar beets are found in books by Simmond[2] and Wright[6]. As far as fermenting fruits are concerned, probably the best sources of information are the many popular wine-making books now available on the market (e.g.[14-18]).

Ethanol From Starch Crops

Producing alcohol from potatoes, grains, etc., requires that the starch first be converted to sugar before it can be fermented. Depending on the crop, the conversion of starch to sugar is accomplished in three steps:

(1) Corn, rice and potatoes are steamed under pressure in a *converter* to gelatinize the starch and form the mash. (2) The enzyme diastase then converts the mash into a sugar solution. Diastase is found abundantly in all sprouted grains (malt), especially barley. This is why grains are often sprouted before they are fermented. (3) Yeast enzymes then convert the sugars into alcohol as described above.

An important step in the starch/ethanol processes is the preparation of the malt extract. An excellent description of do-it-yourself malting techniques is given by Wright[6]. The preparation of malts from commercial products is described in various popular books on home brewing (e.g.[19]). Good descriptions of preparing grain mashes are given by Carr[3], Simmonds[2] and Wright[6]. Wright, Simmonds and Wente[20] deal well with methods of preparing potato mashes.

One starch crop that deserves real attention as a raw material for ethanol production is the Jerusalem artichoke or wild sunflower (*Helianthus tuberosus*). Inulin, its major carbohydrate, is easily broken down into fermentable sugars. The plant is also easy to grow (a "weed" in many places), hardy and productive; its stalk can be burned for fuel and its flower serves as a food and habitat for many natural insect enemies of crop pests.

Ethanol From Cellulose Materials

It has been known since 1819 that when wood wastes are heated with a strong acid, a solution of fermentable sugars is obtained (Acid Hydrolysis). The idea was first put into commercial use in 1900. At about the same time it was discovered that sulfuric acid converted wood cellulose into dextrose when the mixture was heated to about 130°C, under pressure. The solution was then neutralized to allow the growth of microbes, inoculated with yeast and fermented in the usual manner.

Various processes since then have yielded from 16-40 gallons of '100% ethanol per ton of dry wood.[21, 22, 23] Other materials used in acid hydrolysis have been sulfite liquors (by-product of the wood pulp industry), sawdust, straw, cornstalks, nutshells and urban refuse.[13] However, acid hydrolysis doesn't seem to be a practical way to make fuel ethanol at home or on any small scale. The need for a system of recycling strong acids (to keep expenses and pollution down) and high pressure containers seems to make the process quite impractical. Perhaps a small acid hydrolysis plant could be operated in connection with a cottage industry mill or wood craft center . . . but it doesn't seem likely. There just are no simple ways to get alcohol from wood.

Ethanol Yields From Farm Products

It is impossible to obtain a complete conversion of starch into sugar and alcohol. Even under ideal conditions the yield of alcohol is, for various reasons, appreciably lower than the quantity theoretically possible if all starch or sugar could be converted into ethanol and carbon dioxide. The theoretical quantities are:

From simple sugars (dextrose etc.)	51.1%
From complex sugars (maltose, sucrose etc.)	53.8%
From starch	56.8%

Taking starch as the starting point, about 12-20% is generally lost in one way or another by the time the fermentation is finished. From 6-10% of the starch remains unfermented. During fermentation 2-3% glycerol is formed; a part of the sugar is used up in providing food for the yeast, and a little alcohol is lost by evaporation. In a badly conducted operation the alcohol produced may represent not more than 72% of the theoretical yield. A good yield is 6 gallons of absolute alcohol per 100 lbs. of starch, as compared with a theoretical yield of 7.2 gallons. Anything less than 5½ gallons per 100 lbs. of starch indicates something is wrong.

Table III gives some general information about the yield of ethanol from various farm products. The numbers are general and should not be taken too seriously. For one thing the crop yields are from 1970 USDA and California crop statistics. They are thus averages for large commercial farming operations. For another thing the estimates of ethanol yield per ton of raw material are in terms of the theoretical yield described above.

Raw Material (Lbs/Bushel)	Average U.S. Crop Yield (1970) (Tons/Acre)	Fermentable Content	Yield of 99.5 Ethanol Per Bushel Gallon	Per Ton Gallon	Per Acre Gallon	Residual Solids (Lbs/Ton)
MAIN CROPS						
Sugar Cane	41.1	11.0%	--	15	623	--
Molasses	237 gallons	51.0%	--	70	97	--
Sugar Beet	19.1	16.0%	--	22	420	100
FRUIT CROPS						
Apples (48)	14.4	11.0%	0.4	14	207	40
Apricots	5.2	10.4%	--	14	71	46
Grapes	7.9	11.5%	--	15	119	76
Peaches (48)	11.3	8.7%	0.3	12	130	34
Pears (50)	6.8	8.9%	0.3	11	78	58
Prunes, dry	2.3	55.0%	--	72	166	152
Raisins, dry	2.4	62.0%	--	81	195	166
STARCH CROPS						
GRAINS						
Barley (48)	0.9	54.3%	1.9	79	71	646
Corn (56)	2.0	57.8%	2.4	84	168	446
Sorghum (56)	1.4	54.5%	2.2	80	111	488
Oats (32)	0.8	43.6%	1.0	64	51	846
Rice (45)	2.3	54.6%	1.8	80	183	520
Rye (56)	0.7	54.0%	2.2	79	55	542
Wheat (60)	0.9	58.6%	2.6	85	77	538
TUBERS AND ROOTS						
Carrots (55)	11.8	7.5%	0.3	10	116	76
Jerusalem Artichokes (60)	9.0	15.2%	0.6	20	180	104
Potatoes (60)	11.5	15.6	0.7	23	263	76
Sweetpotatoes (55)	5.2	23.3%	0.9	34	178	92

TABLE III ETHANOL YIELDS FROM VARIOUS FARM PRODUCTS. CROP YIELDS (EXCEPT FRUIT) ARE FROM 1970 USDA AGRICULTURAL STATISTICS. FRUIT YIELDS ARE FOR 1970, CALIFORNIA AGRICULTURAL EXTENSION SERVICE.

Methanol From Wood Wastes

Wood, sawdust, farm wastes and urban refuse can be treated with destructive distillation to produce methanol. Like acid hydrolysis, the process has little practical value for small operations since it requires such high-tech equipment. For information, it is described here only briefly.

First the raw material is dried thoroughly and placed in ovens that are connected to condensers. The dried material is then heated to about 400-500°F.

Gases from the organic matter are then condensed and run into tanks. Charcoal is left in the ovens after heating. This can be used as a fuel also. While in the tanks, the distillate separates into a tar (which settles to the bottom) and pyroligneous acid (which forms an upper layer). Pyroligneous acid consists of acetic acid, 4% methanol, acetone and allyl alcohol. Pyroligneous acid is distilled to remove all tar. Water from the settled tar is then combined with the distilled acid. Pyroligneous acid is then neutralized with lime leaving acetic acid and alcohol. Acetic acid and alcohol are separated by further distillation leaving acetic liquors and crude alcohol liquors. The latter are distilled again in column stills to produce crude methyl alcohol.

Methanol From Bio-Gas

Last year over 1 billion gallons of methanol were produced, mostly from natural gas (methane). However methane gas can also be made from wastes and other renewable resources in anaerobic digesters. Since methane is so inconvenient to compress and carry in vehicles, it has been suggested that the conversion of organic wastes to methanol instead of methane would make this fuel more practical.[12] The conversion process involves the synthesis of carbon monoxide (CO) and hydrogen (H_2) by partial oxidation of the methane with water. In the original high pressure process, pressures of 300 atmospheres at 200°C were used in the presence of a zinc-chromium oxide catalyst. In 1968 a low pressure process was developed that used 50 atmospheres at 250°C. A number of other processes have also been described,[24] but again, they are not what you would call backyard or farmstead type technology.

LEGAL PROBLEMS

There is no Federal law that prohibits the manufacture of ethanol. Yet no one can make, sell or store ethanol without a permit from the Bureau of Alcohol, Tobacco and Firearms (ATF). The ATF used to be a division of the IRS, but since July 1972 it has been a separate bureau of the Federal Government. The ATF now monitors and regulates all production of ethanol in this country. If you write the ATF office in Washington (see reviews) you can get various pamphlets that outline the mind-boggling regulations concerning ethanol production.

As far as we can tell there are no explicit regulations covering the production of ethanol *as an energy source*; it would probably be a matter of interpretation, in or out of the courts. However, at this point in time, you will almost surely be subject to the same taxes and laws regardless of whether you are using your ethanol as a beverage or a fuel. This is an area where the right pressures might force legal changes. If you want to deal with the legal hassles, the thing to do is write the ATF office in Washington and ask for the address of your nearest ATF Regional office. Then start making contacts inside. Use words like "experimental," "small-scale" and "research." If you are still forced to oblige the laws, here are a few of the things you will have to do: (a) Register with the Regional Commissioner of the ATF and apply for a permit to erect a still. Failure to do so . . . $1000 fine or 1 year in jail. (b) Buy a bond making the Government the beneficiary. This is supposed to protect the Government against tax losses. (c) Build a special accommodation for your still, which may not be located in a private dwelling, shed, backyard or boat. (d) Provide an office for the exclusive use of the government inspector including a toilet and office furniture subject to the approval of regional commissioner. (e) Keep accurate records of all production and dispensation of your ethanol. (f) Pay an alcohol tax of $10-20 per 100-proof gallon, $55 per still and $22 per condenser every year. The list of regulations goes on. At this stage it would seem technically and economically absurd to produce ethanol for energy unless the laws are either changed . . . or bent . . . or ignored.

APPLICATIONS

Ethanol Plants on the Farm

Suggestions have been made that the United States follow the example of some European countries during WWII in developing an alcohol industry on the farm, consisting of very small plants, privately owned and operated, and adapted for using local raw materials. Indeed, the industrial-alcohol law of 1906 provided specifically for such a program and the production of ethanol from farm products has been part of several programs to boost rural economies in the U.S.[8-11,25] Clearly the present method of making ethanol from ethylene will be short-lived because of impending oil shortages. Instead we might return to the old industrial process of fermenting grains. One suggestion[26] describes a rural industry of 40 acre farms . . . 1.5 million of them . . . that combines the fermentation of ethanol from corn with the raising of pigs and cattle. The corn acreage would be fertilized with urban sewage effluent, the stills fueled with corn stalks, the labor provided by dispossessed urban dwellers and the byproduct slop would be fed back to the livestock.

It is hard to imagine how such a scheme would work given *today's* conditions. For one thing, the U.S. is going to come under increasing pressure to use its domestic grain supplies for foreign barter (oil and balance of trade), and diplomacy (starving Third World Countries). In light of this, the widespread use of food crops to produce an additive for gasoline seems absurd. For another thing, the availability of 1.5 million, forty-acre farms makes little sense in a society where land values and land monopolies are increasing.

Finally, any scheme that promotes the increased production of livestock has to contend with the gross inefficiency of our already over-meated diets. Perhaps the creation of small rural fermentation plants using farm *wastes* and within hauling distance to a central refinery might work, especially if the ethanol were used to supplement fuels used in rural areas. But speaking realistically, if alcohol is to become part of our fuel economy, it will probably be through the manufacture of alcohol from organic refuse in large still-factories near urban centers, or some other such operation.[12,13]

Alcohol Motor Fuel

The idea of using alcohol as a motor fuel has been around since the early 1900's[27-32] and has been suggested recently as an offshoot to the current "energy crisis."[8-10,33] Ethyl alcohol from farm products and blended with gasoline has been used as a motor fuel for years in several foreign countries (10-30% alcohol in gasoline). In the U.S. absolute limits to a gasoline economy are now obvious and anything that stretches the supplies will probably be used. Besides, alcohol is a good anti-knock additive for gasoline. High compression engines are more efficient than low-compression engines (more power and better mileage), but they have the tendency to "knock." Tetra-ethyl lead is now the most popular anti-knock compound, but the dangers of excessive lead in the environment are now well known.

There are real difficulties to overcome before alcohols can be used as undiluted or unblended motor fuels. They have high latent heats and thus don't vaporize easily in an ordinary carburetor. Also their low vapor pressure makes alcohol engines hard to start in the cold.

A comparison of gasoline and alcohol fuels at the same compression ratio and overall efficiency shows that the relative fuel consumption for a given power output is considerably higher for alcohol than gasoline:

Gasoline (grade 1)	100
Ethanol	161
Methanol	222

Alcohol for Lighting and Heating

Alcohol appliances (lamps, stoves and heaters) were in widespread use during the late 19th and early 20th century.[2,5,34] It is hard to find information about them these days. We located alcohol lamps in marine supply houses . . . but that was about it.

References Cited

[1] Monick, John. 1969. ALCOHOLS: THEIR CHEMISTRY, PROPERTIES, AND MANUFACTURE. Reinhold, N.Y.

[2] Simmonds, Charles. 1919. ALCOHOL, ITS PRODUCTION, PROPERTIES, CHEMISTRY AND INDUSTRIAL APPLICATIONS. Macmillan and Co., Ltd., London. 574 pp. OOP.

[3] Carr, Jess. 1972. THE SECOND OLDEST PROFESSION: AN INFORMAL HISTORY OF MOONSHINING IN AMERICA. Prentice-Hall, N.J. See reviews.

[4] Brachvogel, John. 1907. INDUSTRIAL ALCOHOL. Munn and Co., New York. OOP.

[5] Herrick, Rufus. 1907. DENATURED INDUSTRIAL ALCOHOL. John Wiley and Sons, London. OOP.

[6] Wright, F. B. 1906. DISTILLATION OF ALCOHOL. Spon and Chamberlain, New York. 194 pp. OOP. Describes processes of malting, mashing, fermenting and distilling alcohol from grain, beets, potatoes, molasses. Also alcoholometry and the de-naturing of alcohol for use in farm engines, autos, heating and lighting, etc. One of the best nitty-gritty, how-to books. Look real hard in libraries.

[7] U.S. Geological Service. 1909. COMMERCIAL DEDUCTIONS FROM COMPARISONS OF GASOLINE AND ALCOHOL ON INTERNAL COMBUSTION ENGINES. U.S. Geological Survey Bulletin, No. 392.

[8] Miller, D. L. 1970. INDUSTRIAL ALCOHOL FROM WHEAT. In: Report of 6th National Conference on Wheat Utilization Research, Oakland, California. November 1969. Agricultural Research Service, ARS 74-54.

[9] Miller, D. L. 1972. FUEL ALCOHOL FROM WHEAT. In: Proceedings of the 7th National Conference on Wheat Utilization Research, Manhattan, Kansas. November 1971. U.S. Agricultural Research Service, ARS-NC-1. Especially good bibliography on alcohol as a source of motor fuels.

[10] Scheller, W. A. 1974. AGRICULTURAL ALCOHOL IN AUTOMOTIVE FUEL . . . GASOHOL. In: Proceedings of the 8th National Conference on Wheat Utilization Research, Denver, Colorado. October 1973. U.S. Agricultural Research Service, ARS W-19.

[11] Acres Magazine. 1972. FARMER'S ALCOHOL. Acres, USA, June 1972. Box 1456, Kansas City, MO 64141.

[12] Reed, T. B. and R. M. Lerner. 1973. METHANOL: A VERSATILE FUEL FOR IMMEDIATE USE. Science, 182 (4119). Good description of methanol production schemes and overview of methanol as part of basic fuel economy. Good bibliography especially on performance of methanol in engines.

[13] Converse, A. O. et al. 1973. ACID HYDROLYSIS OF CELLULOSE IN REFUSE TO SUGAR AND ITS FERMENTATION TO ALCOHOL. EPA/NTIS PB 221-239.

[14] Mitchell, J. R. 1969. SCIENTIFIC WINEMAKING MADE EASY. British Book Center, New York. 246 pp.

[15] Mahan, Paul E. 1973. SMOKEY MOUNTAIN WINES AND HOW TO MAKE THEM. Arco Publishing Co., New York. 114 pp.

[16] Hardwick, Homer. 1954. WINEMAKING AT HOME. Simon & Schuster, Inc., New York. 218 pp.

[17] Carey, Mary. 1973. STEP BY STEP WINEMAKING. Golden Press, Racine, WI. 64 pp.

[18] Bravery, H. E. 1961. SUCCESSFUL WINE MAKING AT HOME. Arc Books, New York. 151 pp.

[19] Bravery, H. E. 1965. HOME BREWING WITHOUT FAILURE. Arc Books, New York. 159 pp.

[20] Wente, A. O. and L. Tolman. 1910. POTATO CULLS AS A SOURCE OF INDUSTRIAL ALCOHOL. U.S. Department of Agriculture Farmers' Bulletin 410, 44 pp.

[21] Kressman, F. W. 1922. THE MANUFACTURE OF ETHYL ALCOHOL FROM WOOD WASTES. U.S. Department of Agriculture Bulletin 983.

[22] Wise, L. 1949. WOOD CHEMISTRY. Reinhold, New York.

[23] Hawley, Lee F. 1923. WOOD DISTILLATION. Chemical Catalogue Department, Book Department, New York.

[24] Stanford Research Institute. 1973. CHEMICAL ECONOMICS HANDBOOK. SRI, Menlo Park, California.

[25] POWER ALCOHOL AND FARM RELIEF. 1936. "The Deserted Village," No. 3, Department of Chemistry, Iowa State College, 1936.

[26] Editorial. 1974. FEEDBACK: THE ULTIMATE PANACEA. New Scientist. May 16, 1974.

[27] Shepard, G. 1940. POWER ALCOHOL FROM FARM PRODUCTS: ITS CHEMISTRY, ENGINEERING AND ECONOMICS. Iowa Corn Research Institute, Iowa Agricultural Experimental Station, 1(3), June 1938.

[28] Jacobs, P. B. 1938. MOTOR FUEL FROM FARM PRODUCTS. USDA, Miscellaneous Publication, No. 327. Annotates early studies of alcohol as a motor fuel. Two and four cycle stationary engines, pure alcohol, mixtures and performance tests. Good overview of production techniques up to the times. Excellent bibliography.

[29] Ogston, A. R. 1937. ALCOHOL MOTOR FUELS. Journal Institute Petroleum Technology 23:506-523.

[30] Monier-Williams, G. W. 1921. POWER ALCOHOL: ITS PRODUCTION AND UTILIZATION. Henry Frowde, Hodder and Stoughton, London. OOP. Workings of internal combustion engines and applications for alcohol.

[31] Lucke, C. E. and S. M. Woodward. 1907. USE OF ALCOHOL AND GASOLINE IN FARM ENGINES. USDA, Farmers' Bulletin, 227.

[32] Davidson, J. B. and M. L. King. 1907. COMPARATIVE VALUES OF ALCOHOL AND GASOLINE FOR LIGHT AND POWER. Iowa Agriculture Experimental Station Bulletin 93.

[33] METHYL FUEL COULD PROVIDE MOTOR FUEL. 1973. Chemical and Engineering News. September 17, 1973.

[34] M'Intosh. J. 1923. INDUSTRIAL ALCOHOL. Scott, Greenwood & Son. OOP. Valuable for its discussion of the inner workings of early alcohol appliances.

AN INFORMAL HISTORY OF MOONSHINING IN AMERICA

We looked high and low for an in-print book on small scale alcohol production. This is as close as we got. The book is real dynamite for three basic reasons: (1) it outlines the technology of alcohol distillation in terms of the history of the practice from ancient to modern times, (2) it explains in step-by-step terms how stills have been built from simple materials (radiators, barrels, boilers, etc.) and how different kinds of mash are turned into alcohol, (3) it provides numerous photos and drawings of homemade stills that sing along with the text. Stills from the past. . . Tahiti, Tibet, Peru, etc., and the present. . . pot stills, submarine stills, groundhog stills, Alabama Box stills, Georgia type stills, barrel stills, mushroom stills, column stills, etc. etc. There is also insight into the complex and ever changing legal hassles that helped to form the various moonshining cultures in America.
—R.M.

Before the still is fired and put into action, it will be helpful to pause and review the preparation of the mash (ingredients to be distilled). For the demonstration, ten mash barrels, or boxes of 120 gallons capacity each, have been placed to the side of the still. Into each barrel is poured one bushel of corn, previously ground into meal. The still has been filled with water and a fire built underneath to heat water. (The still is uncapped, being used only to heat scalding water.) When the water is scalding hot, a sufficient quantity is poured into the mash boxes over the corn meal to "scald it down." This is stirred into a thick mush. Hot water has now started to gelatinize the starch, which is the first action of the mash. This mixture cooks for one hour, and then one gallon of ground rye and three-fourths gallon of malt is added to the top of the mush. After one hour, malt and rye are stirred down into the mush approximately six inches in depth and one gallon of warm water added. Slow mixing of rye and malt with the mush prevents overcooking the malt, which would kill it (destory its full effectiveness). The malt is the substance which will break down the starch and convert it to sugar, from which the alcohol distillate will be derived.

The Second Oldest Profession: An Informal History of Moonshining in America
Jess Carr
1972; 250 pp

$7.95

from:
Prentice-Hall, Inc.
Englewood Cliffs, New Jersey 07632
or WHOLE EARTH TRUCK STORE

ALCOHOL

Encyclopedic coverage of alcohol; composition, sources, production, chemistry, alcholometry and distillation technology are just a few of the areas discussed. For anyone who wants to know everything there was to know about small-scale alcohol production up to 1919 (not much has changed), this is where you'll find it.

Now in libraries, but definitely another one to bring back.
—Tom Aston

Alcohol
Charles Simmonds
1919; 550 pp

OUT OF PRINT

WOOD

HOME HEATING WITH WOOD
A Guide to Efficient Use of Fireplaces & Stoves

Dennis Dahlin
Environmental
Planner and Designer

After serving as the main home heating fuel for centuries, wood was largely abandoned when coal, oil, and gas became available. Fireplaces have continued to be a decorative feature in homes, but their role in heating has largely been neglected. However, as a supplement to conventional heating methods, properly-managed wood fires can cut use of scarce oil and natural gas. It is true that wood-fueled units probably can't equal the "convenience" of oil and gas heaters. But in the face of the increasing shortages and rising costs of fossil fuel, wood is becoming a welcome alternative.

WOODLOT MANAGEMENT

The ideal source of firewood on rural land is a managed woodlot. The obvious useful values of a woodlot are for timber and fuel production, but even a small growth of trees can have considerable ecological benefits as well. For example, some tough conifers can be planted on land that has been ruined by erosion and compaction following the clearing of a hardwood forest. Eventually, the soil can be restored by these pioneer trees to the point where hardwoods again can thrive.

Besides controlling erosion and rejuvenating soil, trees can have an important influence on the micro-climate of land by helping to moderate temperatures and humidity. When used as a windbreak, trees can also help to reduce heating needs for a home by as much as 30%, according to U.S. government research. Animals sheltered by a windbreak will tend to gain more weight during winter months. In addition, a woodlot provides food and shelter for wildlife. With all of these benefits in addition to firewood, it is well worth the patience to manage a woodlot.

If you don't have existing timber, the long period from planting to harvest is an undeniable problem. Some species such as catalpa and eucalyptus will begin to produce usable firewood in five or six years, but hardwoods such as oak will take much longer. But unlike timber production, you don't have to grow a full-sized tree to use the wood. Just pruning and picking up broken limbs can yield a cord of wood per acre every year. Diseased or deformed trees can be cut from existing woodland. Also, trees need to be thinned as they grow—just like many vegetables—and this can provide more fuel.

ECOLOGICAL IMPLICATIONS OF
USING WOOD AS A FUEL

On a widespread basis, indiscriminate use of firewood can be disastrous.

In *Home Fires Burning: The History of Domestic Cooking and Heating*, Lawrence Wright describes the "energy crisis" that hit England in the 1600's. England was still almost entirely dependent upon wood for fuel, and much of the country's forests had been cut down before there was a switch to coal. Likewise, many forested slopes of the Mediterranean countries were stripped of their trees to provide firewood and lumber, causing erosion and general ecological havoc.

Only a small fraction of America's fuel needs are now provided by wood, and it would be impractical and environmentally harmful for wood to be depended upon as a major fuel source. Harvesting trees for firewood, as well as for timber, requires careful management on a "sustained-yield" basis, allowing nature each year to grow back the amount of wood that has been removed. Since at least several acres of sustained-yield forest land are needed to supply firewood for a typical home, complete reliance on firewood heating is obviously not a realistic long-term answer to energy needs.

The potential pollution caused by smoke from wood fires also needs to be considered. The U.S. Forest Service notes, however, that wood is much lower in irritating pollutants than most other fuels. For example, wood smoke contains almost no sulfur dioxide, in contrast with heating oil or coal which can give off large quantities of this dangerous gas. Some of our concerns about pollution are based on psychological reasons rather than actual hazards, and most people consider smoke from wood burning fireplaces with nostalgia rather than disgust. It's still true, though, that adding even wood smoke to a dangerously-polluted metropolitan atmosphere can multiply the problems.

When the total picture is taken into consideration, the ecological advantages of carefully used wood fuel far outweigh any drawbacks. In a society becoming buried by its waste, it is refreshing to have a fuel that burns cleanly, leaving only a minimum amount of ash—which in turn can be recycled into fertilizers and soap. Using waste wood, such as broken tree branches and construction scraps, can also help to reduce the enormous volume of solid waste headed for the dump. According to the U.S. Forest Service, as much as 30 percent of the debris discarded by a city is reusable wood material. In contrast to fossil fuels such as coal and oil, wood is a renewable energy resource that can be continually replaced. With a little care, wood can be obtained without much damage to the environment, unlike the gouging, drilling, and processing needed to obtain fossil fuels.

SOURCES FOR WOOD

To consider using wood for fuel, it should be available at low cost in the immediate area, and should be obtained by methods that don't ruin the environment. Unless you have plenty of time for hand-sawing and splitting, you will need a power saw and this cost (plus fuel) should be figured into the overall balance sheet. Buying wood from commercial dealers is an extravagance, and may be supporting some damaging forestry practices. A limited amount of firewood, especially kindling, can be picked up at scrap piles on construction sites. People may also be glad to have you cut down a dead tree on their property and haul away the firewood.

If you live near a National Forest, this may be a good source of firewood. There are over 150 National Forests across 44 states, and some of these are near metropolitan areas. The U.S. Forest Service now allows people to cut unwanted timber or chop up felled trees, as long as the firewood is for personal use. A permit is usually required, and people who want to cut their own firewood should contact the supervisor's office or one of the ranger district offices within the nearest National Forest. Sending a postcard ahead of time is recommended. To get an address, check in the phone book under "U.S. Government—Agriculture, Department of—Forest Service." Most other local agencies of the U.S. Department of Agriculture also can provide an address.

HEATING VALUES OF WOOD

Firewood is measured by the cord, which equals a stack of wood 4 x 4 x 8 feet, or 128 cubic feet. (A cord or rope eight feet long can be used to measure the stack, hence the name.) Only about 80 cubic feet of this volume is solid wood, the remainder being air space. It is also sold by the face cord. A face cord is a 4 by 8 foot stack of wood cut into any desired lengths. Firewood can also be sold by the rick, which is a 4 x 8 foot stack of 16 inch logs.

Measuring wood by volume isn't a very good method, though, since the fuel value varies widely for different types of wood. Hardwoods (oak, maple, eucalyptus, madrone) have more heating value than softwoods (pine, poplar, fir). Heating value per cord of wood ranges from 24,600,000 BTU's for hickory to 12,500,000 BTU's for aspen.

For comparison, two pounds of dry hardwood have about as much heating value as a pound of good coal. One cord of a heavy wood such as hickory or oak is equivalent to one ton of coal or 200 gallons of fuel oil, although it takes 1½ to 2 cords of more lightweight woods to equal a ton of coal. Weight isn't the only heating factor in wood, though. Since resin provides twice as much heat as wood, per unit of weight, resinous woods such as pines and firs have more heating value per ton than some non-resinous woods. Heating values for some common species of wood, in BTU's per cord, are listed in Table I.

TABLE I. APPROXIMATE WEIGHT AND AVAILABLE HEAT OF DIFFERENT WOODS, GREEN AND AIR-DRY*

	Weight		Available Heat per Cord**		
	Green Weight (Lbs)	Air-Dry Weight (Lbs)	Green (Million BTU)	Air-Dry	Percent more Heat From Air-Dry %
Ash	3840	3440	16.5	20.0	21
Aspen	3440	2160	10.3	12.5	25
Beech, American	4320	3760	17.3	21.8	26
Birch, yellow	4560	3680	17.3	21.3	23
Douglas-fir, heartwood	3200	2400	13.0	18.0	38
Elm, American	4320	2900	14.3	17.2	20
Hickory, shagbark	5040	4240	20.7	24.6	19
Maple, red	4000	3200	15.0	18.6	24
Maple, sugar	4480	3680	18.4	21.3	16
Oak, red	5120	3680	17.9	21.3	19
Oak, white	5040	3920	19.2	22.7	18
Pine, eastern white	2880	2080	12.1	13.3	10
Pine, southern yellow	4000	2600	14.2	20.5	44

*Data from U.S. Forest Products Laboratory, except for Douglas-fir southern pine.
**Standard cord-to-stack 4 ft x 4 ft x 8 ft containing 80 cubic feet solid wood
SOURCE: U.S. Forest Service

It would be a mistake, though, to consider only the heating value of various types of wood. Other qualities such as easy ignition, rapid burning, freedom from smoke, and uniform heat are also important. Generally, soft woods burn more easily than hardwoods. However, a soft wood such as pine will give a quicker, hotter fire which is consumed in a shorter time than a hardwood blaze.

Another very important feature, if you're chopping your own firewood, is its "splitability." Naturally, the least line of resistance on a piece of wood is found along the grain, perpendicular to the rings. Woods which have straight grain, free of knots, are much easier to split than wood with twisted grain. The easiest woods to split are usually conifers, including pine, cedar, redwood, fir, and western larch. The most exasperating woods to split are elm, sycamore, dogwood, red gum, and black gum.

Most softwoods put out a lot of sparks, which can be entertaining but also can be a real hazard. Trapped gases and water vapor build up pressure in moisture pockets within the wood, causing these miniature explosions. Although thorough drying of the wood can reduce sparking, some resinous woods such as spruce, juniper, hemlock, and larch should be used with caution in an open fireplace.

Some woods burn more cleanly than others. High moisture content as well as resin in wood can lead to a smoky fire. Excessive smoke can cause a fire hazard by leaving soot and creosote deposits in a flue. These deposits can ignite suddenly, causing a dangerous chimney fire. Most softwoods are noted for putting out a lot of smoke, and any green, unseasoned wood can cause a real smoke problem unless used sparingly in a hot fire.

Some woods have special features which add to the pure enjoyment of sitting by a fire on a cold winter night. Wood from fruit trees, especially applewood, is particularly prized because of its superior flame and delightful fragrance, and, of course, any kind of properly dried driftwood makes an especially good flame. The following Table II, summarizes some of these overall qualities of firewood.

TABLE II. RATINGS FOR FIREWOOD

Name of trees	Relative amount of heat	Easy to burn	Easy to split	Does it have heavy smoke?	Does it pop or throw sparks?	General rating & remarks
HARDWOODS						
Ash, red oak, white oak, beech, birch, hickory, hard maple, pecan, dogwood	high	yes	yes	no	no	excellent
Soft maple, cherry, walnut	medium	yes	yes	no	no	good
Elm, sycamore, gum	medium	medium	no	medium	no	fair—contains too much water when green
Aspen, basswood, cottonwood	low	yes	yes	medium	no	fair—but good for kindling
Chestnut, yellow-poplar	low	yes	yes	medium	yes	poor
SOFTWOODS						
Southern yellow pine, Douglas-fir	high	yes	yes	yes	no	good but smoky
Cypress, redwood	medium	medium	yes	medium	no	fair
White-cedar, western red cedar, eastern red cedar	medium	yes	yes	medium	yes	good—excellent for kindling
Eastern white pine, western white pine, sugar pine, ponderosa pine, true firs	low	medium	yes	medium	no	fair—good kindling
Tamarack, larch	medium	yes	yes	medium	yes	fair
Spruce	low	yes	yes	medium	yes	poor

SOURCE: U.S. Forest Products Laboratory

HEATING REQUIREMENTS

If you want to heat your home with wood, how large does your wood-lot need to be? This will depend on the heating needs of your house as well as the growing characteristics of your timber. First, if you don't already know the heating requirements of your house, you can get a rough estimate by multiplying the floor area of your house by 30 BTU's, an average figure for the heat needed for each square foot per hour. This number should be increased somewhat if you live in a cold climate or if your house is not well insulated; an uninsulated house might require 45 BTU's per hour per square foot. This points out the logical first step in heating your home—make sure it's well insulated.

Next, multiply this heating value for your house by the number of "degree-days" per season in your area. A degree-day is a unit of heat measurement, used to reflect differences in climate, which shows how much the outdoor temperature deviates from a standard indoor temperature. To find the number of degree-days per season for your area, you can get in touch with a utility company, or the U.S. Weather Bureau.

The colder the climate, the higher the number of degree-days; southern California has less than 2000 degree-days per year, while northern Minnesota has 10,000. The heating needs of your house for one year thus can be shown by this formula:

$$\text{Heating} = \text{square feet of floor space} \times \frac{\text{BTU}}{\text{sq. ft.}} \times \text{degree days per season}$$

To find the number of cords of wood required to heat your home, just divide this figure by the BTU's available in the type of wood you're using. From this information the land needed to produce the desired number of cords can usually be determined. For average-growth hardwood, one acre should yield one cord of wood every year. This value can vary, though, from as little as one-fourth cord per acre from hardwood on dry slopes, to seven cords per acre from a good stand of eucalyptus.

In an article in *Organic Gardening and Farming* (March 1973) Jeff Cox calculated that a 1200-square-foot house in Pennsylvania would need about nine acres to produce enough wood for one winter's heating. Since not too many people have nine acres to use for growing fuel, this should emphasize that wood heating is best used in combination with another heating system.

Seasoning Firewood

For convenience as well as safety, it is important to use wood that has been dried properly. It is best to store freshly-cut wood for six months or more before use. For thorough seasoning, the wood should be stacked so that air can circulate around each log. An open-sided shed can provide a good place to shelter the wood from rain and snow, while allowing good ventilation.

Some of the best types of firewood can be a problem while drying. Hickory, beech, and hard maple are susceptible to rot and fungi. In contrast, cedar, redwood, live oak, black locust, and black walnut are considered very durable.

Other Wood-Based Fuels

Artificial logs, made of pressed sawdust and wax, are being used increasingly in fireplaces. Their heating value per pound is considerably higher than firewood. Although the use of sawdust in these logs recycles waste, the wax in the logs makes them unfit for use in cooking. Their cost, and the environmental effects of wax combustion, make artificial logs a questionable product for use, particularly in large quantities.

For recyclers, there has been a flurry of interest in making old newspapers into fireplace "logs." The papers are soaked in water or various solutions, then rolled into a cylinder, bound, and left to dry. Unless the papers are bound very tightly, there is a tendency for pages to curl off and leave messy ashes when burned.

WOOD HEATERS

There are two basic varieties of wood-burning space heaters: (1) the open heaters—masonry, adobe, and metal fireplaces plus charcoal braziers and (2) enclosed heaters—"complete combustion" burners such as Ashley heaters (see page 162) and closed metal stoves. Other enclosed heaters, which have a primary use other than space heating, include wood cookstoves, laundry stoves, and woodburning water heaters.

The difference between open and closed units is important. Enclosed heaters use fuel with greater efficiency than an open fireplace, because combustion can be controlled more carefully, with better radiation of heat. By gaining efficiency, however, the view of an open flame is sacrificed.

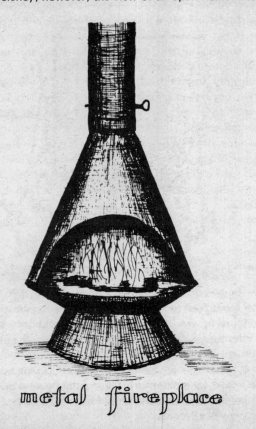

metal fireplace

Masonry Fireplace

Unlike all the other forms of wood heaters, a stone fireplace is made mostly of locally found materials. The traditional values of the open hearth, and the sense of permanency provided by the solid masonry, have a significance which isn't measured in BTU's. However, the masonry fireplace is not an efficient heater. A functional stove may provide more than three times as much "useable" heat to a room, with the same amount of wood. In cold climates, poorly-designed and operated fireplaces may even cause a net energy loss by sucking heat up the chimney. This "theft" of warm air most often occurs when the fire has died down but the damper is not yet closed.

With proper fireplace design and use, respectable heating efficiencies can be achieved. The most important technique is to use a metal heat-circulating unit (see page 158, last section of this article). Masonry fireplaces may cost several thousand dollars, but if you do the work yourself, and use local stone or used brick, it can cost a fraction of that amount.

Although there is great variation in the appearance of masonry fireplaces, their operation is essentially the same. Depending on local availability, brick, stone, or adobe may be used. A stone fireplace is considered the most difficult to build, with its need for thick wall sections and expert stone placement.

Metal Fireplace

These consist of a large metal hood supported over a base that holds the fire. Metal fireplaces have several distinct advantages over masonry fireplaces. First, they offer relatively high efficiencies for heating, since the metal hood and flue radiate heat into the room instead of letting most of it escape. Also, these units can be placed in the center of a room, providing more uniform heat distribution.

Prefabricated metal fireplaces are easy to install, and their cost usually is much less than a masonry fireplace. On the other hand, metal fireplaces cool quickly once a fire is out, in contrast to the heat-storage capacity of masonry.

Prefabricated metal wall unit fireplaces are also available. Due to compact chimney sections and efficient insulation these models can be placed directly on a wood floor and built against wood framing. From a heating standpoint, however, these units are at a disadvantage, since the metal construction is typically covered up with masonry veneer, preventing the kind of heat radiation of an exposed metal unit.

Charcoal Braziers

Although home heating with charcoal is a rarity in the United States, charcoal is commonly used for heating as well as cooking in many parts of the world. The traditional Japanese home, in a cool maritime climate, depended entirely on heating with charcoal braziers. In contrast to typical American central heating, no attempt was made to heat the entire house in winter. Instead, the occupants would wear thickly-padded clothes indoors as well as outside while three basic methods of selective heating were used. The *hibachi*, with a few pieces of charcoal buried in ashes, would be used for warming the hands and heating water for tea. On cold nights, a small oblong charcoal container called a *kotatsu* was placed in the bed. The *kotatsu* was also used in the daytime as a foot-warmer, being placed in a wooden cage under a table.

While use of charcoal in an airy Japanese house apparently wasn't too hazardous, except for the danger of fire, the use of charcoal in a well-sealed house or camper without proper venting can be very dangerous. Charcoal removes oxygen and adds carbon monoxide to the air without the warning smoke of a wood fire. With proper venting, however, charcoal braziers can be useful for heating rooms located away from the main stove or fireplace.

Franklin Stoves

There are several types of metal stoves used for space heating. Unlike metal hooded fireplaces, heating stoves have doors which can be closed to control combustion. The familiar "Franklin stove" is a metal unit with a design which hasn't been modified much since the early 1800's. There is some variation from Benjamin Franklin's original design, which actually was intended to fit into existing masonry fireplaces. The special advantage of the Franklin stove is its flexibility in serving as an open or semi-closed

yukon stove

franklin stove

heater. With the doors open, the blaze in the stove can be enjoyed. Closing the doors on the stove minimizes the loss of room heat up the chimney, by controlling the draft, while the metal surfaces can still radiate heat into the room. Franklin stoves (also called Franklin fireplaces) are available from Sears and other sources, at very reasonable prices (considerably less than most metal hooded fireplaces (see page 163).

potbellied stove

Closed Stove

For heating efficiency, closed stoves have an edge on the open-front stoves. The rounded shape of the potbelly stove makes it an efficient and widely-used model in the past. Coke and coal can also be used in potbelly stoves, although only small logs would fit in the rounded firebox. In contrast, good-sized logs could be used in box stoves, and their flat tops could be used for cooking. Short-legged parlor stoves, with fuel fed in from the side, are a smaller version of the closed stove.

Yukon Stove

This home-made brand of closed stove deserves special mention. A Yukon stove, made from a discarded 55-gallon oil drum or old buoy, etc., combines the benefits of recycling with a low cost. The barrel can be set horizontally or vertically, with a door cut into the end or the side, and a stovepipe fitted onto the top. An open fireplace can be made by placing the barrel horizontally with the lower portion of one end removed, but it's best to add a door. Since the abrupt angle of the added stovepipe isn't ideal for carrying smoke away, smoke is apt to collect inside the barrel and spill out into the room through an open front.

There are many variations of the basic Yukon stove. The door can be a simple piece of sheet metal, or a manufactured cast iron part with an automatic fire control mounted on it. The drum can be lined with firebrick, stove liner, or furnace clay to extend the life of the stove and provide extra heat storage. Grates can be made of reinforcing rod, or cast iron

grates can be used. Another drum, connected to the stove pipe above the first barrel, can be used to radiate additional heat into the room. And, recycling systems can be built to increase efficiency by forcing gases down through the fire again.

COMPLETE COMBUSTION BURNER

An automatic airtight stove, or complete combustion burner, is the most efficient wood heater available. Ashley and Riteway are the best known brands. The best models feature an air intake damper controlled by an automatic thermostat; the damper closes automatically if the stove overheats, and more air is allowed if the fire gets too low. A "secondary intake system," which circulates unburned gases back through the fire a second time, helps to increase efficiency. Automatic stoves can maintain a fire from twelve to more than twenty-four hours, easing the usual problem of facing a freezing-cold house in the morning. Coils for hot-water heating can be incorporated into some models. Most units will burn wood or coal. From the same quantity of wood, the better airtight stoves can produce twice as much heat as the older wood stoves. For a homeowner hesitant to rely only on wood heat, one Riteway model features a backup oil or gas burner. If the wood or coal fire burns out in the combustion chamber, the oil or gas burner takes over.

With these specialized heating features, complete combustion burners would be expected to cost more than simpler fireplaces and stoves. Surprisingly, prices on basic models are no more than medium-priced metal hooded fireplaces. Initial cost of the complete combustion wood/coal burners is usually more expensive than comparable gas furnaces though. This difference in price is made up quickly by reducing or eliminating fuel costs for gas.

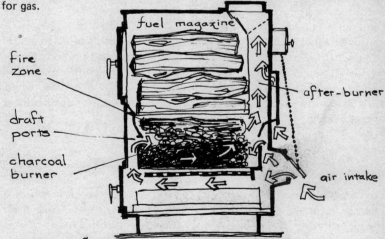

complete combustion burner

For a more limited budget, a variety of manual airtight stoves are on the market. Designed for use in small cabins, these models are less durable than the automatic heaters, but are lightweight and easy to move. The manual heaters also need to be tended more carefully than the automatic models.

The main disadvantage of the complete combustion burners is their appearance. Designed for maximum efficiency, the flames are hidden from view. For dependable and efficient heat, however, no other wood heater can approach their effectiveness.

CHOOSING A HEATER

If you're thinking about heating your home or cabin with wood, which method is best? Is wood heating worthwhile in your situation, or should you stay with conventional fuels? There are several factors, summarized in Table III, which enter into this decision:

TABLE III. COMPARISON OF WOOD HEATERS						
	Masonry Fireplace	Masonry Fireplace with Heat-Circulating Unit	Metal Fireplace	Franklin Stove	Closed Stove	Complete Combustion Burner
Relative cost						
—labor ($ or time)	very high	very high	low	low	low	low
—materials	variable	medium to high	low to medium	low	low to medium	medium to high
Comfort & Convenience	fair	fair	fair	fair	fair	good to excellent
Heating Efficiency	poor to fair	fair to good	good	good	very good	excellent

As mentioned earlier, wood fuel needs to be convenient and available under conditions that don't harm the environment. If some wood is available, but you can't depend on it for your total heating needs, a combination burner also using coal or oil should be considered. A backup solar heating system may also help.

Wood heating is excellent for a vacation cabin. You don't need year-around dependability. Since heating efficiency isn't of prime importance in an occasionally-used cabin, a masonry fireplace should serve well—if you have the time, the materials, and the money to build it. Lacking one or more of these commodities, a metal hooded fireplace or Franklin stove would be fine. For a quick, convenient, inexpensive heater, a manual airtight stove might be sufficient.

For your home, however, dependability and convenience are much more important. If you're depending entirely on wood for heat in a cold climate, only a complete combustion burner would be able to provide efficiency and comfort. The main heater could be supplemented with smaller stoves, fireplaces, or vented charcoal braziers. A wood heater with backup oil or gas heat provides the most convenience and reliability, if you have the money.

The initial cost of a wood heater can be deceptive. Most woodburners cost more than comparable conventional heaters, but pay off within a few years in fuel savings. Cheap wood burners can wear out quickly, and it may be best to invest in the higher-priced model from the start.

Nothing can match a fireplace of local stone or used brick, fueled with wind-pruned limbs and discarded wood. Even the most efficient metal woodburners have to be made from mined and processed iron ore. Where wood fuel is scarce, though, the efficiency of a complete combustion burner can help to prevent robbing Nature for fuel. Finally, any wood burner used with care is undoubtedly an improvement over conventional fossil-fuel heating.

EFFICIENT USE OF WOOD HEATERS

To obtain the maximum heat from your wood stove or fireplace, a number of techniques to increase efficiency are available. Three basic points for achieving maximum efficiency should be kept in mind:

1. Maintain proper conditions for the fire. The goal of a wood heater should be to achieve complete combustion. This increases efficiency and reduces smoke problems. Since combustion requires plenty of oxygen, an adequate air supply is needed. Fuel should also be selected for best operation.

2. Get the most heating value out of the fire. A maximum amount of heat should be reflected into the room, absorbed and circulated through ducts, or radiated from heated surfaces. Since metal has a much higher conductive value than masonry, use a maximum amount of exposed metal surface.

3. Prevent heat from escaping up the flue. The fireplace opening, throat, and flue should be kept as small as possible. Proper proportions should be used, and the flue should be closed when not in use.

More detailed methods of improving efficiency are listed on the following pages, based on these general rules.

For maximum efficiency, any heating unit should be located near the center of the space to be heated. This gives an advantage to metal fireplaces, which can be located in the middle of a room.

The fireplace size should be kept proportional to the size of fire desired for the room. There is much greater heating efficiency in a small masonry fireplace, with the flame close to the side and back walls, than in a larger fireplace with a similar flame. Much of the heat radiated from a fireplace comes from the heated firebrick behind and beside the flames. The closer the brick to the flame, the more it is heated. Also, a larger fireplace opening would require a larger throat and flue, which would allow more heat to escape up the chimney.

To achieve maximum heat radiation into a room, the walls of a masonry fireplace should be slanted (see Fig. 1). A splay of 5:12 is generally used for the side walls. The back wall should be sloped forward to reflect more heat into the room. While walls are usually of firebrick, iron reflectors have been used to radiate additional heat into the room. In a heat-circulating fireplace, the sides as well as the back are metal.

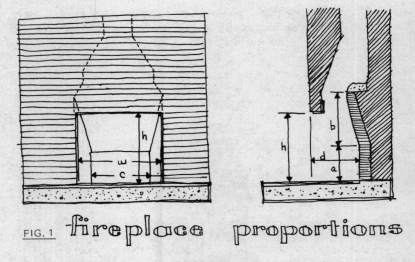

FIG. 1 fireplace proportions

1. Height of fireplace (h) = 2/3 to 3/4 of the width.
2. Depth of fireplace (d) = 1/2 to 2/3 of the height.
3. Effective area of the flue (f), the cross-section area of the pipe carrying away smoke, measured to interior dimensions:

   (f) = 1/8 x width x height of front opening (unlined flue)
   (f) = 1/10 x width x height of opening (rectangular lining)
   (f) = 1/12 x width x height of opening (round lining)

4. Throat area = 1.25 to 1.5 x flue area.
   Throat width = 3″ minimum to 4—1/2″ maximum
   (The throat of a fireplace is a slot-like opening above the firebox where fumes from the fire pass into the smoke chamber.)

TABLE IV	RECOMMENDED DIMENSIONS FOR FIREPLACES AND SIZE OF FLUE LINING REQUIRED (Letters at heads of columns refer to Fig. 1)						
Size of fireplace opening			Minimum width of back wall	Height of vertical back wall	Height of inclined back wall	Size of flue lining req'd.	
						Standard rectangular (outside dimensions)	Standard round (inside diameter)
Width w	Height h	Depth d	c	a	b		
inches	inches	inches	inches	inches	inches	inches	inches
24	24	16-18	14	14	16	8½x13	10
28	24	16-18	14	14	16	8½x13	10
30	28-30	16-18	16	14	18	8½x13	10
36	28-30	16-18	22	14	18	8½x13	12
42	28-32	16-18	28	14	18	13x13	12
48	32	18-20	32	14	24	13x13	15
54	36	18-20	36	14	28	13x18	15
60	36	18-20	44	14	28	13x18	18
54	40	20-22	36	17	29	13x18	15
60	40	20-22	42	17	30	18x18	18
66	40	20-22	44	17	30	18x18	18
72	40	22-28	51	17	30	18x18	18

SOURCE: U.S. Department of Agriculture

Over centuries of fireplace construction, general proportions have evolved for the fireplace opening and flue size. The chimney flue, serving to provide a draft as well as to eliminate combustion gases, should be designed to provide just enough air for complete combustion. The throat, or opening into the flue above the flame, should be kept as small as possible to increase the velocity of the rising gases in the flue. More detailed information is in Table IV.

A. The flue, or the hollow center of the chimney, carries combustion gases out of the house.
B. The smoke chamber is the transition area which connects the fire chamber with the flue.
C. The smokeshelf is a horizontal surface which deflects any downdrafts coming down the chimney.
D. The damper, located in the throat of the chimney, is a movable metal plate which is used to close the flue when the fireplace is not in use.
E. The fire chamber is the space in which the fire burns.
F. Firebrick is used for lining surfaces near intense heat.
G. The fire is built on the back hearth.
H. The front hearth protects the floor from sparks and embers.

parts of a traditional fireplace

Damper and Smokeshelf

A damper always should be used in a masonry or metal fireplace so that warm room air won't escape up the chimney when the fireplace isn't in use. The damper is a metal door that opens or closes the throat opening to regulate the amount of heating. It should be set open just enough to prevent smoking into the room—a wide-open damper promotes heat loss. The smokeshelf is needed in a masonry fireplace. It acts to deflect downdrafts back up the chimney so they don't cause smoking.

Air Intake

One of the most frequent mistakes in designing fireplaces is the failure to provide a good draft or fresh air to serve the fireplace. The hot air rising up the chimney must be replaced, and chimney downdrafts adjacent to the hot air column may be the result if there isn't enough fresh air at the fireplace level. In early American houses, there was plenty of air constantly moving in through cracks in the walls and doors. The opposite problem is often found in modern homes, with their tightly fitted windows and doors. The best solution is to plan the room layout so that incoming drafts cross a little-used area, or to install ducts to bring in air from the basement or outside. For very cold areas, bringing in air from another room is better, since directly-introduced cold air may not become sufficiently heated by the fire. For the average fireplace, the required air-volume flow toward the fire is about 3000 cubic feet per hour. Since this amount is almost double the established room ventilation requirement for a family of four, this shows how a fireplace can set up unpleasant drafts in a room. For this reason, the fireplace preferably should draw half of its required air from outside the room.

Use of Fuel

Heating efficiency can be drastically affected by the way a fire is built and maintained. Only seasoned wood should be used, since the moisture in green wood reduces the heating value. There are many different fire-building techniques for different fireplaces and stoves, but some general rules apply. Logs should be placed close together, since the narrow air spaces between them promote better drafts; also, combustion temperatures are raised and maintained by the heat reflected between adjacent surfaces. Ashes should be left to accumulate until they are just under the bottom of the grate, forming a bed for the glowing coals that drop through the grate. The ashes concentrate heat and direct drafts of air up to the base of the fire. A fire, banked by covering the burning logs with ashes, will retain glowing coals overnight, making it easier to rekindle the flames. Excess ashes can be used in the garden for fertilizer and pest control.

Use of Exposed Flues

The hot metal flue above a stove or fireplace can radiate a great deal of heat to a room, while the enclosed flue of a masonry fireplace lets most of this heat escape. Any method for increasing the radiating area of the metal can be a heating benefit.

With a closed stove, or even a Franklin stove, the metal flue can be run horizontally through the room before bending it upward again to go through the roof. For open fireplaces and stoves, though, a horizontal flue is apt to interfere with the draft.

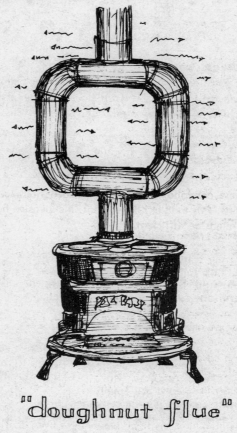

"doughnut flue"

The "doughnut flue" is another technique for increasing metal surface area. A sheet-metal tee is fastened onto the stove pipe above the heater, forming a double flue which is recombined into a single flue before reaching the roof. This arrangement has particular value in heating saunas.

Heat Storage

One problem skipped over by many books on fireplace design is the quick loss of heat when the fire is banked or put out for the night. Once the source of heat is gone, a metal fireplace cools off very quickly. In this respect, a masonry fireplace has an advantage, since the bricks store a great deal of heat and release it to the room over a longer period. Still, even with a well-banked fire, a room will be cold by the next morning unless there is a supplementary heat source. (A complete combustion burner does not have this problem, since a fire can be maintained for twelve hours or more.)

Where constant fireplace heat is needed, a heat-storage medium could be used. Solar houses have successfully used water and eutectic salts to store heat received during the daytime, which is then released gradually during the night. As a possibility, large water barrels could be built into a masonry fireplace, with air ducts conducting warm air (heated by radiation from the barrels) to the room. The barrels could be filled with a solution of Glauber's salt (sodium sulfate), an excellent heat absorbent. The warm air ducts could be built in conjunction with a regular heat-circulating device within the fireplace. The heat stored in this way would have only limited and short-term value, since storage space would usually be small. It could be of great value in certain situations, though, such as preventing water pipes from freezing while a house is vacant for a few days.

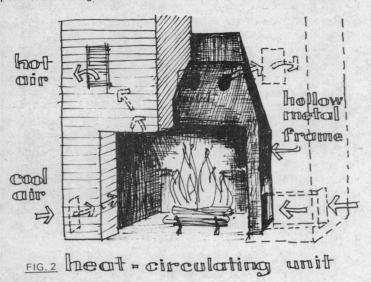

FIG. 2 heat-circulating unit

Heat-Circulating Units

This is the most important way to improve heating efficiency of a masonry fireplace (see Fig. 2). Heatilator and other companies sell metal frames which form a hollow box around the fire. Masonry is built around the outside of the frame. Air is taken in through intakes near the bottom, then is heated as it passes over the interior of the hot metal frame, and is returned to the room as hot air through outlets at the top of the unit. The outlets can be positioned in the mantle, the front or sides of the fireplace, or they can be extended to adjacent or overhead rooms. These units have been shown to distribute warm air to corners of a room which were cold when a non-circulating fireplace was in use. To improve circulation, a ventilating fan can be positioned in the outlet or intake.

Finally, hot-water coils can be used in a fireplace for supplementary space heating. While this technique requires some knowledge of plumbing, it offers the greatest potential for increasing the efficiency of a wood heater. A metal coil, usually copper, is mounted in the fireplace, either placed on the back wall or used as the grate. This coil is then connected to hot-water piping which can carry the heated water to baseboard heaters or concrete-slab heating coils in other rooms. Special solder is needed for connections in intense-heat areas. It is very important that relief valves are used in this system, since pressure can build up in the pipes and cause an explosion. A pump generally is needed to circulate the water. However, a careful piping arrangement, with the heating units located higher than the coils, could operate by gravity flow.

One of the best features of this system is its potential for combination with solar heating. In winter, when solar radiation is at a minimum, the fireplace could be used for hot-water space heating of the house. In spring and fall, solar collectors tapped into the system could be the heat source, without the need for separate interior heating units. In many climates a solar-plus-wood heating system would be the ideal way to have a comfortably-heated house in harmony with its environment.

REVIEWS/WOOD

WHAT WOOD IS THAT?

I had seen this book six months before I sat down to read and review it. I had found it to be hokey with its forty specimens of actual wood taped to the first few pages. Well, I take back my earlier scepticism. Here is a fantastic overview of how to distinguish woods from one another in the forest or in their man-transformed state of furniture, building materials and the like.

Basically wood identification is discussed in general and the forty woods whose specimens are included are discussed in particular. They are primary woods found or used in this country. Hardness, durability, density, color and grain is each covered thoroughly. This should be of more value to the carpenter/cabinetmaker than the wood burner. It creates reverence for wood.

—T.G.

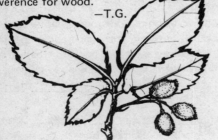

LEAVES AND WINGED SEEDS
OF AMERICAN ELM

What Wood Is That?
Herbert L. Edlin
1969; 160 pp

$7.95

from:
Viking Press
625 Madison Avenue
New York, NY 10022

or WHOLE EARTH
TRUCK STORE

FOREST PRODUCTS LABORATORY /USDA

The Forest Products Laboratory in Madison, Wisconsin studies wood. They review and research the properties and problems associated with timber used for industry and building as well as wood used for fuel. They provide most if not all of their information free. A few of their useful pamphlets are listed below.
—T.G.

Wood Fuel Combustion Practice
Fuel Value of Wood; Technical Note Number 98
Wood Fuel Preparation
Wood as Fuel for Heating

The following table is an approximation of the number of cords of seasoned wood of various kinds needed to give the same amount of heat as a ton of coal, on the basis of 80 cubic feet of wood, with a moisture content of 15-20 percent, to the cord:

1 cord	hickory oak beech birch hard maple	ash elm locust longleaf cherry	= 1 ton coal
1½ cords	shortleaf pine western hemlock red gum	Douglas-fir sycamore soft maple	= 1 ton coal
2 cords	cedar redwood poplar catalpa	cypress basswood spruce white pine	= 1 ton coal

From FUEL VALUE OF WOOD; Technical Note Number 98

Wood Information free

from:
U.S. Department of Agriculture
Forest Service
Forest Products Laboratory
P.O. Box 5130
Madison, Wisconsin 53705

WOOD: WORLD TRENDS AND PROSPECTS

By far the most discouraging aspect of reading through this study is to know that it is out of date. (The study projects analysis up to 1975 but the main input figures come from the 1960's.) Completed in 1967 it is an amazingly complete look at wood in the world. Consumption of fuel wood and industrial wood material are studied. Insightful economic analysis is given and the questions of what wood is being used for, by whom, and where it is growing are answered in tables, maps, and text.

—T.G.

	1960-62	1975	Change 1961-75
	.. Million cubic meters ..		1961 = 100
Europe	108.00	74.00	69
U.S.S.R.	101.00	80.00	79
North America . .	46.00	34.00	74
Latin America . .	192.00	220.00	114
Africa	183.00	246.00	135
Asia-Pacific . . .	458.00	545.00	119
WORLD TOTAL .	1 088.00	1 199.00	110

ESTIMATED CHANGE IN TOTAL CONSUMPTION OF FUELWOOD, 1960-62 TO 1975

Wood: World Trends and Prospects
Food & Agriculture Organization of the United Nations
1967; 130 pp

$2.50

from:
Unipub Inc.
P.O. Box 433
New York, NY 10016

or WHOLE EARTH
TRUCK STORE

ONE MAN'S FOREST

Short on technical information but long on personal experience, this book explores, rather thoroughly, the joys, dangers, and considerations involved in "developing" timber on an elderly couple's land in Vermont. It is a down-home look at wood lot management.
—T.G.

The Soil Conservation Service of the Department of Agriculture will prepare a land use capability map on an aerial photograph. Soil types and topography are identified to indicate appropriate land use such as cropland, hay, woodland, or tree plantations. Regional staffs are usually headquartered in each county seat. Vermont was the first state to establish a professional forester in every county to advise any woodland owner and make available the specialists in the state department of forestry for consultation on many critical aspects of forestry practice. Through state and federal funding all these services are supplied at no cost to the landowner.

One Man's Forest
Rockwell R. Stephens
1974; 128 pp
$3.95

from:
The Stephen Greene Press
Box 1000
Brattleboro, VT 05301

or WHOLE EARTH
TRUCK STORE

TREES OF NORTH AMERICA

Trees of North America is an attractive, tasteful, lively, sporty little book that lets you identify trees with a minimum of drudgery—and even some enjoyment. This book is a Golden Field Guide, created by people who started out making children's books. In comparison every other guide on the market looks stuffy.

Trees of North America covers all native trees, most larger shrubs, and just about every foreign exotic that has carved out its niche in our environment. The written descriptions are precise and helpful, but the strength of this book lies in its graphics—color drawings that are botanically accurate and at the same time pleasant to look at. A tree might be illustrated by drawings of its leaves, buds, twigs, bark, its general shape, perhaps a stunted form, the fruit, or the flowers—in short, by whatever features are most distinctive for that tree. There are also

distribution maps to give the tree's range. Finally the cover and all the pages are glossy and water repellent—a feature that should be a statutory requirement for all field guides.
—Malcolm Margolin

Trees of North America
C. Frank Brockman
1968; 280 pp

$3.95

from:
Western Publishing
Company, Inc.
1220 Mound Ave
Racine, Wisconsin
53404
or
WHOLE EARTH
TRUCK STORE

Furrowed Black Oak · Scaly White Pine · Plated Ponderosa Pine · Warty Common Hackberry

Shaggy Shagbark Hickory · Papery Paper Birch · Smooth Amer. Beech · Fibrous Coast Redwood

---

FARM AND GARDEN RULE-BOOK

These tables were taken from the *Farm and Garden Rule-Book*. The author, L. H. Bailey, has put together innumerable tables, recipes, and formulas for gardening, farming, forestry, and livestock raising. This book, originally published in 1915 by MacMillan and well worth its weight in gold, is long out of print.
—T.G.

HARDNESS OF COMMON COMMERCIAL WOODS

Shellbark hickory	100
Pignut hickory	96
White oak	84
White ash	77
Scrub oak	73
Red oak	69
White beech	65
Black walnut	65
Black birch	62
Yellow oak	60
White elm	58

FOREST YIELDS
APPROXIMATE TIME REQUIRED TO PRODUCE DIFFERENT WOOD CROPS (U.S. FOREST SERVICE)

Species	Location	Av. Diam. 6 In. (Posts)	Av. Diam. 8 In. (Handle, Pulp, Spool, or Fuel Wood, Props)	Av. Diam. 11 In. (Ties)	Av. Diam. 14 In. (Poles and Piles)
		(years)	(years)	(years)	(years)
Northern forests					
Aspen	Maine	30	40	60	--
Beech[1]	Michigan	--	80	100	200
Birch, paper	Maine	--	50	--	--
Hemlock[1]	Michigan	--	100	130	--
Maple, sugar[1]	Michigan	--	90	--	200
Pine, red	Wisconsin	32	40	55	75 100
Pine, white	New York	32	40	55	90
Central hardwood forests					
Chestnut[2]	Maryland	20	25	40	55 85
Oak, red	Kentucky	25	30	45	100
Oak, white	Kentucky	35	45	80	160
Poplar, yellow	Tennessee	--	45	--	110
Farm timber plantations					
Catalpa[2]	Illinois	20	--	--	--
Larch, European[2]	Illinois	23	--	--	--
Maple, silver[2]	Illinois	--	25	--	--
Walnut, black[2]	Illinois	25	35	--	--
Cottonwood[2]	Nebraska	--	18	--	--
Southern forests					
Ash, white	Arkansas	--	30	45	85
Cottonwood	Mississippi	--	15	--	30
Cypress	Maryland	40	--	65	75 90
Gum, red	South Carolina	--	--	30	55
Pine, loblolly	South Carolina	20	25	40	55 70
Pine, longleaf	South Carolina	--	--	75	100 130
Pacific coast forests					
Fir, Douglas	Washington	25	35	45	50 75
Hemlock, western	Washington	--	50	70	125
Pine, sugar	California	40	50	65	100
Pine, western yellow	California	25	35	45	55 80
Redwood	California	20	25	35	50 70

[1]Species tolerant of shade which should show better results in second growth.
[1]Species growing under favorable conditions when measured.

PLANT NOTES
NURSERY PLANTING-TABLE FOR FOREST TREES (FARMER'S BULLETIN)

Species	When to Collect Seeds	How to Store Seeds	% Which Should Germinate	When to Plant Seeds	Depth to Plant Seeds (inches)	Spacing of Seeds in Rows	Height of 1-Year Old Seedling (inches)
Ash, green	October	Bury in sand	35-50	Spring	1/2	Scatter thickly	6-9
Ash, white	October	Bury in sand	35-50	Spring	1/2	Scatter thickly	6-10
Basswood	September or October	Sow at once	5-50	Fall	1/2	Scatter thickly	6-12
Beech	Fall	Bury in sand	70-80	Early spring	3/4	2 inches apart	3-6
Butternut[1]	September or October	Bury in sand	75-80	Early spring	1	3 to 6 inches apart	10-14
Box elder	September or October	Bury in sand	40-60	Spring	1/2	Touching in rows	10-14
Catalpa, hardy	October or November	Cool, dry place	40-75	Spring	1	1/2 inch apart	14-30
Cherry, black	August or September	Bury in sand	75-80	Spring	1	2 to 3 inches apart	4-6
Coffee tree, Kentucky	September or October	Cool, dry place, or bury in sand	70-75	Spring	1	2 to 3 inches apart	3-6
Cottonwood[2]	June or July	Sow at once	75-95	Summer	1/2	1 inch apart	20-30
Elm, slippery	May or June	Sow at once	50-75	Late spring	1/8	Scatter thickly	15-16
Elm, white	May or June	Sow at once	50-75	Late spring	1/8	Scatter thickly	5-10
Hackberry	October	Bury in sand	70-80	Spring	1/2	1 to 2 inches apart	6-12
Hickory, pignut[1]	September or October	Bury in sand	50-75	Spring	1-2	3 to 6 inches apart	2-6
Hickory, shagbark[1]	September or October	Bury in sand	50-75	Spring	1-2	3 to 6 inches apart	2-6
Hickory, shellbark	September or October	Bury in sand	50-75	Spring	1-2	3 to 6 inches apart	2-6
Locust, black	October	Cool, dry place or bury in sand	50-57	Spring	1	Scatter thickly	6-12
Locust, honey	October	Cool, dry place or bury in sand	50-75	Fall or spring	1/2	2 to 3 inches apart	6-14
Maple, red	May or June	Sow at once	25-60	Late spring	1	1/2 inch apart	6-10
Maple, silver	May or June	Sow at once	25-50	Late spring	1	1/2 inch apart	12-20
Maple, sugar	October	Cool, dry place	30-50	Fall or spring	1	1/2 inch apart	6-12
Mulberry, Russian	July or August	Cool, dry place	75-95	Spring	1/2	Scatter thickly	8-10
Oak, bur[1]	September or October	Sow at once or bury in sand	75-95	Fall or spring	1-1/2	3 to 6 inches apart	5-9
Oak, red[1]	September or October	Sow at once, or bury in sand	75-95	Fall or spring	1-1/2	3 to 6 inches apart	6-20
Oak, white[1]	September or October	Sow at once, or bury in sand	75-95	Fall or spring	1-1/2	3 to 6 inches apart	5-9
Osage, orange	September or October	Cool, dry place	60-95	Spring	1/2	1 inch apart	10-15
Poplar, yellow	September or October	Sow at once	5-10	Fall	1/4	Scatter thickly	4-6
Walnut, black[1]	September or October	Bury in sand	75-80	Spring	1-1/2	3 to 6 inches apart	10-18

[1]Difficult to transplant on account of tap root. Advisable to sow seeds in permanent sites in field whenever possible.
[2]Easily grown from cuttings. Not necessary or advisable to attempt growing from seed.

WOODBURNERS HANDBOOK

Efficiency and care with a limited but renewable source of energy. This book gives a general overview of burning wood for heating and cooking. It has some practical tips on repairing old stoves, building stoves from 55 gallon drums, putting in chimneys and stove pipes and keeping them clean and safe from fire. Has some history of wood stoves, and information on the hardness, splitability, and moisture content of different woods.
—T.G.

EASY	INTERMEDIATE	HARD
Chestnut	Birch	Elm
All Pines	Maple	Beech
Redwood	Hickory	Black Gum
Cedar	Red Oak	Sycamore
Fir	Ash	Dogwood
Western Larch	Cottonwood	Red Gum

SPLITABILITY

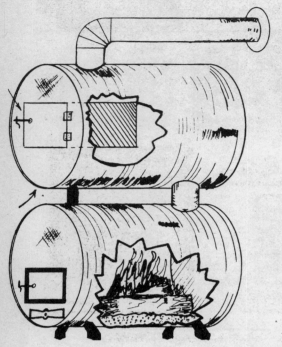

55 GALLON DRUM SMOKE EXCHANGER WITH BUILT-IN OVEN.

For green freshly cut from the forest, from six months to a year is usually required for thorough seasoning. The rate of evaporation of the moisture will depend on such factors as temperatures, relative humidity in the air, exposure to rain or snow, and movement of the air about the individual sticks. Splitting the pieces helps and is almost indispensable with some species such as birch and alder, which should be placed in fairly dry locations. Moreover, cottonwood is, for example, easier to split when green.

* *

A brick stove can be constructed by using cement for the foundation and the legs. A wooden form for the legs and foundation is made on the spot where the stove will rest, as it is a permanent structure. Reinforcement rods are used inside the concrete and should extend into the legs to insure that they are well secured to the structure. The forms are not removed until the concrete is "cured" or fully dried and settled. When the foundation and the legs are ready, the sides of the stove are built and the interior is lined with fire brick. Fire clay is used to secure the fire brick.

* *

The best equipment is a small Christmas tree and a long rope. Tie the rope to the tree so that two lengths dangle from top and bottom. Feed the length of rope attached to the top of the tree into the chimney from the roof. The person below in the house starts pulling gently on the tree and once the tree has reached the opening in the fireplace, the person on the roof pulls it back up. Repeat this process until soot ceases to fall down the chimney. It is best to acquire the help of a close friend for this task, as the one at the bottom will be rather dirty once the job is accomplished. The same process can be undertaken using a burlap bag filled with newspaper and a few bricks to weight it down.

Woodburners' Hand-Book
David Havens
1973; 107 pp

$2.50

from:
Media House
Box 1770
Portland.
Maine
or WHOLE EARTH
TRUCK STORE

BOOK OF SUCCESSFUL FIREPLACES

Though fireplaces and wood-burning devices may be used for cooking, most people will use them for space heating. We Americans have a tendency to over-heat just about as much as we have a tendency to over-eat. Probably we will find fireplace heating to be insufficient even in temperate climates. If we take the time, however, to realize that it is us (people)— not the floor, ceiling, walls, furniture, not the whole building—we are trying to keep warm, we may be able to lower our heating requirements. Certainly constructing smaller buildings, especially with lower ceilings, thus lower volume, will help lower our heating "needs." Constructing buildings to maximize the heat from winter sun will also help.

The *Book of Successful Fireplaces* is a complete volume. It presents tables and diagrams, information on construction do's and don'ts, and explores the various different types of fireplace designs. A fascinating section on the history of the fireplace discusses the two great fireplace engineers—Ben Franklin and Count Rumford—as well as others. Certainly the most discouraging part of this book is the posh fireplaces in posh homes which are rendered in glossy color photos and boost the price of this good book up to $9.00.

—T. G.

The Book of Successful Fireplaces
R.J. Lytle & M.J. Lytle
1971; 104 pp

$9.00

from:
Structures Publishing Co.
P.O. Box 423
Farmington, MI 48024
or WHOLE EARTH
TRUCK STORE

THE OWNER-BUILT HOMESTEAD

This is Ken Kern's sequel to *The Owner-Built Home* (see page 173). Originally in two volumes it stands by itself as a useful introduction and reference book for "how-to" information about homesteading. Kern is a pragmatist with some decentralist theorizing thrown in who puts homesteading in the perspective of being the real hard work it is. The book discusses water, soil and plant management, site selection, roads, shop and tools, animals, sanitation, human nutrition and has a good chapter on woodland management.

—T.G.

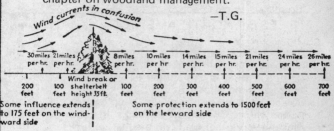

	Wind currents in confusion								
30 miles per hr.	21 miles per hr.		8 miles per hr.	10 miles per hr	14 miles per hr.	15 miles per hr.	21 miles per hr.	24 miles per hr.	26 miles per hr.
200 feet	100 feet	Wind break or shelterbelt height 35 ft.	100 feet	200 feet	300 feet	400 feet	500 feet	600 feet	700 feet

Some influence extends to 175 feet on the windward side
Some protection extends to 1500 feet on the leeward side

Correct pruning, thinning and cutting practices constitute the final factor for maintaining optimum woodland conditions. Woodland thinning is done to reduce the density . . . maintaining a fast-growing diameter and slow-growing height. It is better to make moderate thinnings at frequent intervals than heavy thinnings infrequently. And pruning and thinning should be done in early spring, just before the growing season begins.

TOLERANCE OF COMMON WOODLAND TREES

TOLERANT	INTERMEDIATE	INTOLERANT
CEDAR	DOUGLAS FIR	PINE
HEMLOCK	ASH	LARCH
REDWOOD	BIRCH	ASPEN
SPRUCE	CHESTNUT	BLACK WALNUT
BEECH	ELM	HICKORIES
MAPLE	OAK	WILLOW

DIAMETER GROWTH

RAPID	MODERATE	SLOW
EUROPEAN LARCH	DOUGLAS FIR	CEDAR
LOBLOLLY PINE	PONDEROSA PINE	HEMLOCK
ASPEN	REDWOOD	LONGLEAF PINE
BLACK LOCUST	SPRUCE	BEECH
COTTONWOOD	BLACK WALNUT	OAK - BLACK & WHITE
WILLOW	ELM	SUGAR MAPLE

The Owner-Built Homestead
Ken Kern
1974; 207 pp

$5.00

from:
Owner-Builder Publications
P.O. Box 550
Oakhurst, California 93644
or WHOLE EARTH TRUCK STORE

GARDEN WAY

Garden Way Publishing has three useful pamphlets on using wood for heating.

How to Sharpen and Use an Axe and Get the Most Use of Fuel Wood, 6 pp, is a good cheap introduction to sharpening and caring for an axe. $0.75

Curing Smokey Fireplaces, 24 pp, 1974, discusses 20 or more problems and solutions to smokey fireplaces. $0.90

Wood Stove Know How, 1974; 31 pp, was written by Peter Coleman the Director of Garden Way Research. It is a basic introduction to wood stove use and maintenance with information on heating values of various woods, different types of flues and more.

. . $1.50

from:
Garden Way Publishing
Charlotte, Vermont 05445

MASONS AND BUILDERS LIBRARY

As with most Audel books these two are good complete basic sources. With the information here and a little common sense anyone ought to be able to handle the immediate technical aspects of whatever masonry he/she might want to undertake. There is little here concerning design, but tools, composition of materials, and techniques for laying and repairing are clearly presented. Volume II—Bricklaying · Plastering · Rock Masonry · Clay Tile has a useful section on fireplace sizing and construction.

—Bill Duncan

Clay Flute
Smoke Dome
Down Draft Shelf
Insulation
Insulation
Damper Control
Metal Fireplace Unit
Ash Dump
Raised Brick Hearth

FIREPLACE BUILT ON A CONCRETE SLAB

Masons and Builders Library
Vol. I Concrete·Block·Tile·Terrazo
Vol. II Bricklaying·Plastering·Rock Masonry· Clay Tile
Louis M. Dezettel
1972; 356 pp and 375 pp
$5.65 each
$11.25 set
from:
Theodore Audel & Company
4300 West 62nd Street
Indianapolis, Indiana 46268

or WHOLE EARTH TRUCK STORE

FIREPLACES AND CHIMNEYS

The basics: construction, design and modification. Good advice, well illustrated.
—T.G.

MORTAR

Brickwork around chimney flues and fireplaces should be laid with cement mortar; it is more resistant to the action of heat and flue gases than lime mortar.

A good mortar to use in setting flue linings and all chimney masonry, except firebrick, consists of 1 part Portland Cement, 1 part hydrated lime (or slaked-lime putty), and 6 parts clean sand, measured by volume.

Fireplaces and Chimneys
USDA
1963; 23 pp
$0.40

from:
Superintendent of Documents
U.S. Government Printing Office
Washington, D.C. 20402

HOW TO PLAN AND BUILD FIREPLACES

The variations in types of fireplaces and how to build them could easily fill a book. Instead this book spends two-thirds of its pages illustrating and discussing where to put a fireplace in the home—in which room, where in the room and against which wall. A good deal of the discussion refers to the different styles of fireplaces and their "designy" aspects. The assumption is made that a fireplace will be used for "supplementary heating."

The remaining third discusses how to build a masonry fireplace in an existing house, how to install a prefabricated fireplace, and gives a number of useful tables and tips on flue-sizing, fireplace sizing, dampers, etc. In all, certainly worth the money but I can't help but thinking that more could have easily been said.
—T.G.

The heating action of a fireplace is principally that of radiation from the back wall, the sides, the hearth, and the fire itself. Because radiant heat travels in straight lines, its range is limited. The exception to this general rule is the heat-circulating fireplace, which heats by means of convection. Heat is distributed by air currents resulting from unequal temperatures and consequent unequal densities. A heat-circulating unit can maintain an even temperature throughout the room, whereas the conventional fireplace warms only that part of the room which is near the fire and in a direct line with the fireplace opening.

THE COMPLETE BOOK OF HEATING WITH WOOD

I am having trouble putting this book in perspective. It has not been published at the time of this writing so I read through a xerox copy of the manuscript with no illustrations. It is full of small tidbits of information not found in other books but on the whole lacks a certain cohesiveness and I wonder what is trying to be said.

Larry Gay has taken an optimistic view of heating with wood. He suggests that wood, even on a large scale, could be used to fill much of America's heating needs. He discusses wood lot management, what species of wood give the most heat, and what tools to use to cut down trees. Perhaps the best part of this book is a good look at how the three most efficient wood burning heaters operate; the Ashley, Riteway and Jøtul.
—T.G.

With a well stocked average woodlot you can count on about 1 cord per year from each acre. In the colder parts of the country about 6 cords per winter may be needed, a figure that comes down as insulation and burning efficiencies go up. This implies a woodlot of at least 6 acres, but with only 6 acres you would have to burn some trees suitable for lumber, spend time inefficiently cutting up some very small wood, and also rob the woodpeckers. It would be preferable, therefore, to have 12 acres or more to supply 6 cords of fuelwood annually. These figures can easily be adjusted according to forest productivity and heating requirements in your area.

The Complete Book of Heating with Wood
Larry Gay
1974; 128 pp
$3.00

from:
Garden Way Publishers
Charlotte, VT 05445
or WHOLE EARTH TRUCK STORE

RAISED BRICK HEARTH AND NATURAL CORNER SETTING HAVE PRACTICAL USES.

How to Plan and Build Fireplaces
Sunset Books
1973; 96 pp
$1.95
from:
Lane Book & Magazine Co.,
Menlo Park, CA 94025
or WHOLE EARTH TRUCK STORE

THE BEN MEADOWS COMPANY

A catalog-mail order house for forestry and engineering supplies. Everything from drafting supplies, t-squares and levels to pruning saws, axes, and timber carriers. All good quality.
—T.G.

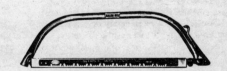

Timber-Jack, 9" hook opening, 4¼' handle
11 lbs. $19.95

Ben Meadows General Catalog
453 pp
$3.00 (credited to first order of $25 or more)

from:
The Ben Meadows Company
P.O. Box 8377
Station F
Atlanta, Georgia 30306

ASHLEY THERMOSTATIC
WOOD BURNING CIRCULATOR

The Ashley still seems to be the best heater on the market for the money. It is a combustion burner with a thermostat. The main body of the heater is made of sheet steel and needs to be replaced every few years; the door, top and legs are heavy cast iron.

—T.G.

from:
Ashley Automatic Heater Company
1604 17th Avenue
P.O. Box 730
Sheffield, Alabama 35660

or WHOLE EARTH TRUCK STORE
Limited availability through 1976.

Ashley heaters are cheaper the closer you are to the factory in Alabama. The above quoted prices are applicable to the West Coast.

ASHLEY CAROLINIAN
Model 23-EF
($143.95 plus shipping)

ASHLEY COLUMBIAN
Model 25-EF Regular
($159.95 plus shipping)

GREEN MOUNTAIN POWER

GREEN MOUNTAIN POWER MULLS USING WOOD AS FUEL

BURLINGTON, VT.—An electric utility here thinks it may have discovered a "renewable" source of fuel. It's called wood.

Green Mountain Power Corp. said it's studying the feasibility of burning wood chips in a generating plant boiler. The first step would be a pilot-plant test in an old 4,000-kilowatt power station. Favorable results could lead to using wood for up to 100,000 kilowatts in a new plant. The utility's peak power load now is 300,000 kilowatts.

Wood has about half the heat content of coal and would cost less than coal and far less than residual oil, Peter McTague, president, said. Burning wood also produces little pollution and yields an ash with "high nutrient value as a fertilizer," he said.

Use of wood for 100,000 kilowatts of generation would more than triple Vermont's timber industry, Mr. McTague said. But first, the utility must test the logistics and economics of collecting wood, grinding it into chips the size of 50-cents pieces and delivering it.

—Wall Street Journal 4/4/74

PORTLAND FRANKLIN
STOVE FOUNDRY

Manufacturers of the fine Franklin Fireplace and the finest wood cook stove, the Queen Atlantic.

—T.G.

Limited availability through 1976.

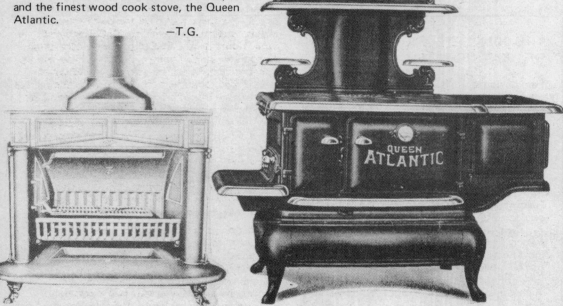

No. 3 Franklin Fireplace
(approximately $230 plus shipping)

No. 408 Queen Atlantic
(approximately $600 plus shipping)

from: Portland Franklin Stove Foundry, Inc., 57 Kennebee Street, Portland, Maine 04104

RITEWAY

The Riteway is said to be the most efficient wood burning heater on the market. Made of heavy gauge sheet steel, it has an automatic thermostat and a four cubic foot firebox. It is ruggedly constructed with over-all dimensions of 28" long, 17" wide, and 33" high. This heater is efficient and large enough to be most useful for heating a large space or a few rooms rather than one small room.

—T.G.

Riteway Radiant 2000

$295.00 plus Shipping

from:
Riteway Mfg Co.
P.O. Box 6
Harrisonburg, Va. 22801

or WHOLE EARTH TRUCK STORE

JØTUL

This is by far the most solidly constructed wood burning heater I have yet to see. These solid cast iron heaters are the standard wood heating units in Norway where they are manufactured. The Jøtul operates similarly to the combustion burner Ashley and Riteway and is said to be almost as efficient. These heaters should be looked at as a lifetime investment in quality and durability.

—T.G.

Manufactured by:

Aksjesekapet
Jøtul
Postbox 6206
Et, Oslo 6
Norway

Distributed by;

David Lyle
So. Ackworth
New Hampshire, 03607

L. L. Bean
Freeport, Maine 04302

Whole Earth Truck Store
558 Santa Cruz Avenue
Menlo Park, California 94025

No. 602 . . . . $200 plus shipping
25" high; 13" wide; 19" long;
5" stove pipe; green enamel finish

No. 118 . . . . $315 plus shipping
30" high; 14" wide; 29" long;
5" stove pipe; green or black enamel finish

WOOD BURNING FIREPLACE, HEATER AND STOVE MANUFACTURERS

Autocrat Corporation
New Athens, Illinois 62264
Automatic wood heater with modern style cabinet; wood cook ranges.

Enamel and Heating Products Ltd.
Suite 1002
1107 Broadway
New York, New York 10010
Corvette Solid Fuel Range (starting at $300) an imported stove with optional water reservoir and enamel finish.

The Firebox Company
P.O. Box 1
Richmond, Massachusetts 02154
Heavy gauge sheet steel heater with interchangeable wire mesh or solid steel door ($139 f.o.b. Richmond, Massachusetts).

Washington Stove Works
P.O. Box 687
Everett, Washington 98201
Olympic Franklin (starting at $200); Parlor Stove (starting at $250); and others.

Malm Fireplaces
368 Yolanda Avenue
Santa Rosa, California 95404
Freestanding metal fireplaces (starting at $150).

Atlanta Stove Works Inc.
Atlanta, Georgia 30307
Automatic wood heaters; pot-bellied stoves; laundry heaters; wood ranges; cook stoves.

The Majestic Company
Huntington, Indiana 46750
Freestanding fireplaces (starting at $150); built in heat circulating fireplaces (starting at $225).

Vega Industries Inc.
Mt. Pleasant, Iowa 52641
Manufacturers of the HEATILATOR heat circulating fireplace and also freestanding metal fireplaces.

King Stove and Range Co.
P.O. Box 730
Sheffield, Alabama 35660
Pot bellied stoves; laundry heaters; coal heaters; box heaters; automatic wood heaters; Franklin fireplaces.

United States Stove Co.
South Pittsburg, Tennessee 37380
Box heaters; coal heaters; Franklin fireplaces.

West Coast Fire-View Distributors
P.O. Box 370
Rogue River, Oregon 97537
A cylindrical sheet-steel heater with a glass door—rugged construction.

SOME OF THE BEST WOOD BOOKS

The Coming Age of Wood
Egon Glesinger
1947; 279 pp
Simon & Schuster (out of print)
Somewhat outdated information on wood: how it grows, what it is used for—plastics, alcohol, sugar, food, wood alloys, lumber, chemicals, wood gas, insulation, fiber and fuel, where it grows, and where it is consumed or used. A complete book about wood from a time (1940's) when wood was more of a universally used material than it is today.

Tree Crops
J. Russell Smith
1953; 408 pp
The Devin-Adair Co.
One Park Ave.
Old Greenwich, Connecticut 06870
$7.95
A call for the planting of trees to prevent soil erosion and depletion, specifically trees which produce food—tree crops—nut trees, fruit trees and acorn bearing trees. Tree crops around the world are discussed and so is tree crop management.

MORE HEAT

We came across three companies in our research on wood heaters which manufacture "attachments" to increase heating efficiency of a fireplace or wood heater. Of the three, Thermograte appears the most likely to be useful. It operates by drawing cool air into the hollow tubes at the bottom of the grate and then as the air heats in the grate it circulates out the top part of the tube. Both the Loeffler Heating Unit (for fireplaces) and the Heat Saver (for wood heaters) use electric fans to circulate the heat.

—T.G.

THERMOGRATE $69.50 plus shipping

HEAT SAVER $78.00 plus shipping

Information free

from:
Thermograte Enterprises
51 Iona Lane
St. Paul, Minnesota 55117

Heat Saver
The Hubbard Creek Trading Co.
Box 9
Umpqua, Oregon 97486

Loeffler Heating Unit Mfg. Co.
R.D. 1 Box 503
Branchville, New Jersey 07826
(Not shown — $75.00 postpaid)

Seeding and Planting in the Practice of Forestry
James W. Toumey
1916; 455 pp
John Wiley & Sons (out of print)
Somewhat outdated but still useful information on forestry. Aspects of gathering, drying, storing, and choosing seeds as well as planting, reforestation, aforestation, planting sites, plant spacing, nurseries and more are thoroughly reviewed.

Farm Wood Crops
J. F. Preston
1949; 455 pp
John Wiley & Sons (out of print)
A well illustrated look at wood on the farm. The economics of wood land production are discussed as well as establishment of new woodlands, trees commonly planted, information on nurseries (1949) and tools and equipment.

SHEET-STEEL VS. CAST-IRON

Most wood burning heaters are built using either sheet-steel or cast-iron or a combination of the two. Sheet-steel used for heaters generally comes in widths between 1/64" and 1/4". Sheet-steel has the advantages of: low initial cost, light weight and thin walls which heat up quickly when near fire. Sheet-steel has the disadvantages of: burning out (bending and breaking as a result of the expansion and contraction of the steel from heating and cooling). The thinner the steel the faster the burning out usually occurs.

Cast-iron has the advantages of: sturdy construction, generally long life and the ability to retain heat after the fire has subsided. Cast-iron has the disadvantages of: heavy weight and not being easily repairable if cracked or chipped.

CHAIN SAWS

Seven friends and I purchased a Homelite EZ Automatic with 16" bar a year ago. It works well and despite having eight different people using it we have only had to have it serviced by the dealer once. It cost us $200 and we put the saw into our tool coop. Since each of us realized that we wouldn't be using the saw a sufficient amount to own one ourselves sharing the cost and use of the saw made sense. The cooperation feels good.

With a year of experience under my belt I'll make a few comments—take 'em for what they're worth. There are a great number of chain saw manufacturers in this country and around the world. The three that have the best reputation in this country are Homelite, McCulloch and Stihl. Homelite and McCulloch are pretty much comparable saws. Their prices differ little and they both have a full range of sizes and styles. Stihl is said to be the best chainsaw on the market. Folks I have talked with have had little trouble with theirs and think quite highly of them. Stihl chain saws generally cost more than Homelite or McCulloch. In general I would suggest that one purchase a chain saw from a friendly dealer nearby. A local dealer will be able to sharpen the saw and then teach you how to sharpen it yourself. Further, a local dealer will be able to repair the saw which breaks down invariably when you need it the most.

On choosing the chain saw for you: 16" or 20" bars ought to be sufficient for most trees—you can usually rent a larger saw if you need it—automatic chain oilers are easier to use than the manual type; a compression release makes starting the saw much easier but is certainly optional equipment; light weight is worth searching for; and taking the time before you buy is good sense.

—T.G.

Information free and the name of a local dealer.

Homelite
A Textron Division
Port Chester, NY 10593

Stihl American, Inc.
107 Bauer Drive
Oakland, NJ 07436

McCulloch
6101 West Century Blvd.
Los Angeles, CA 90045

SWEDISH WOOD GAS

Gentlemen,

In reply to your inquiry I am pleased to send you some information about Swedish gas generators.

During World War II many different types of generators were manufactured but only very few types were sold in large series. The most well known of these manufacturers was Mr. Swedlund, who now is 81 years old. One of his old generators has recently been mounted on a new Saab (as a curiosity).

At the present time there is no manufacturer of gas generators in Sweden but the two automobile manufacturers Saab and Volvo are testing prototypes for automobiles, trucks, and tractors. No major changes in either car construction or in the motor are supposed to be undertaken when these types of gas generators are applied. If a real severe crisis in the gasoline supply should occur in Sweden, the generators could be in production half a year after a decision is made but the emphasis would probably be on generators for trucks, buses and tractors.

For your information, I enclose a short description in Swedish of how today's gas generators are working. Wood chips instead of coal are used as fuel. One m³ (cube meter) is approximately equivalent to 53 gallons of gasoline or 32 gallons of diesel oil. The gas generator is filled with wood chips and before starting the engine, the draught is kept up with an electric starting fan. The wood chips are then ignited with a special type of matches. Then the generated gas is filtered through a glassfiber filter. As the gas has a high temperature, 500-575 degrees F, the soot particles but not the tar are collected in the filter. The tar is not stiffened until it reaches the cooler. After passing through the cooler, the gas is mixed with air in proportions that can be regulated with the gas pedal which is connected to another damper in the gas mixer. The cost of the generator is supposed to be at least 1,000 dollars.

If you would like to have pictures of today's prototypes, I suggest that you write directly to Volvo and Saab. From Saab you will perhaps also be able to get the address of the pioneer, Mr. Swedlund, and some historical documents on the gas generators of the olden days.

Previously I have been in contact with the Engine Design Department at Volvo to try to obtain further information but they are not willing to give any technical descriptions unless there is a real interest in the US to buy large series of generators.

The addresses are:

AB Volvo
Fack
S-40508 Goteborg
SWEDEN

SAAB
S-58188 Linköping
SWEDEN

I hope that this information will be of some interest to you.

Yours sincerely,

Yngve Vesterlund
Asst. Scientific Attaché

Swedish Embassy
600 New Hampshire Ave., N.W.
Washington, D.C. 20037

SNOW & NEALLEY

According to our tool expert, Phil Bekeart, there are a whole bunch of small companies which manufacture axes and logging tools. Most of them sell direct to logging companies and other buyer/users.

Snow & Nealley Co., 155 Perry Road, Bangor Maine 04401, is one such company. They make beautiful looking axes, piveys, draw shaves, cant hooks and the like. Snow & Nealley doesn't sell direct to the public, but L. L. Bean, Inc., Freeport, Maine 04032, carries two of their axes. They sell postpaid a 28' hickory handle axe with either a 2½ lb or 3½ lb head for $11.75 and $12.00 respectively.

—T. G.

WOOD GAS BIBLIOGRAPHY

A Wood-Burning Conversion Unit for Household Furnaces
H. Hicock, A. R. Olson and L. E. Seeley
1912; 21 pp
Connecticut Agricultural Experiment Station,
New Haven
Bulletin No. 463
Discusses the experimental design and construction of a wood-burning household furnace in response to the energy crisis created by W.W. I.

Thermodynamics of Producer Gas Combustion
A. P. Oleson and Richard Wiebe
July 1945; 9 pp
Industrial and Engineering Chemistry Vol. 37, No. 7
The composition and heats of combustion of producer gas from various raw materials including wood. The application of this gas to internal combustion engines—carburetor modification, pressures, compression and efficiency are all discussed. Article is reasonably technical with numerous graphs and charts.

Engine Tests with Producer Gas
A. Middleton and C. S. Bruce
February 1946; 14 pp
Journal of Research of the National Bureau of Standards; Vol. 36; Research Paper RP 1698.
Bench tests with a four-cylinder stationary engine were made with gasoline and producer gas from charcoal as the fuels. A comparison of their performance revealed that maximum power from producer gas from charcoal is 55% of gasoline power, and that about 11.4 pounds of charcoal is equivalent to one gallon of gasoline.

Gasogens
Forest Products Laboratory
1944; revised 1962; 6 pp
Forest Products Lab.
Madison, Wisconsin
Report No. 1463
General overview of fuels used, principles, design and equipment for mobile and stationary engines using gasogens.

Gas Producers for Motor Vehicles
E. A. Allcut and R. H. Patten
1943; 162 pp
National Research Council of Canada
A committee report on possibility of replacing gasoline by gas made from charcoal or wood, as a wartime emergency measure. Road and stationary tests were made on a number of engines, and tables and graphs of results are plentiful.

Charcoal and Water are Converted into Gas That Runs Trucks
Popular Science
September 1944, page 141

Charcoal Gas for Motors: American Made Unit Available for Motor Vehicles
Scientific American
October 1944, page 174

Gas Producers for Motor Vehicles and Their Operation with Forest Fuels
I. Kissin; 1942
Technical Communication No. 1
Imperial Forestry Bureau, England

Experiments on a High-Speed Producer Gas Engine
A. F. Burstall and M. W. Woods
1939, 2 pp
London Engineer No. 167

Producer Gas for Motor Vehicles
Cash and Cash; 1942
Angus and Robertson Ltd.
Sydney, Australia

The Modern Portable Gas-Producer: Theory, Design, Fuels, Performance Utilization and Economics
B. Goldman and N. Clarke Jones
1939; Journal of the Institute of Fuels No. 12

Producer Gas for Motor Transport
E. A. Allcut; Part I 4 pp; August 1, 1943
Part II 5 pp August 15, 1943
Automotive and Aviation Industries.
Issues of the same journal published May 1 and May 15, 1941 and August 1, 1941 have articles on producer gas.
General overview of fuels, design of plant, amount of power, cooling the gas and comments as to efficiency, problems and widespread application.

Can We Use Wood to Beat the Gasoline Shortage
Popular Science, January 1944; reprinted The Mother Earth News No. 27
Brief general article explaining basic theory and practice of a particular truck converted to use wood gas.

Ersatz Motor Fuels
Gustav Egloff
Scientific American, July 1939
A largely economic look at Europe's use of producer gas for vehicle fuel. Illustrating that producer gas at that time (1939) was not economical on a large scale.

How to Run Your Car on Wood
Travis Brock; 5 pp; The Mother Earth News No. 27
A good overview of the various different types of producer gas generators as well as general information on the subject.

CHARCOAL PRODUCTION, MARKETING, AND USE.

This technical booklet provides useful information for people interested in going into the charcoal business. While some of the report covers large-scale charcoal production, most of the material is geared to the small operator with limited capital who wants to have a supplementary income. The booklet includes useful construction diagrams for various types and sizes of charcoal kilns. Regrettably, only brief mention is made of very small backyard kilns that can supply enough charcoal for home use. Also, little mention is made of the ecological implications of charcoal production, although the report does stress the value in using waste wood for making charcoal.

—Dennis Dahlin

Charcoal Production, Marketing and Use
U.S. Forest Service Report No. 2213
1961; 137 pp

Free

from:
U.S.F.S. Forest Products Laboratory
P.O. Box 5130
Madison, Wisconsin 5705

ARCHITECTURE

CONSERVE ENERGY

The buildings in which we live and work are huge consumers of energy. Building services (largely climate control devices) account for a third of the nation's energy consumption. Eighty percent of this energy is used in heating and air conditioning. The energy consumed in constructing a building has not even been calculated adequately. The energy input of various materials (i.e. cement, brick, steel, aluminum, etc.) must be determined if we are to lower the energy consumption of buildings.

In calculating the overall energy use of a building the short term energy input of construction must be weighed as well as the long term requirements for climate control. The National Bureau of Standards has estimated that 40% of the energy consumed in building services could be conserved with improved thermal design and construction practices. Present building practices based on low-first-cost objectives have accounted for significant energy waste.

In what ways can renewable sources of energy such as solar, water, wind and biofuels affect energy consumption in buildings? For the most part the cure-all to energy consumption does not originate at the source. It matters little what energy source we are using if we waste it through poor building practices, poor insulation techniques, over-building and general disregard for the consumption of resources. It will do us very little good to put a wind generator and solar collector on a poorly designed energy consuming house. To apply new sources of energy to old habits and faults approaches the problem of energy consumption from entirely the wrong direction.

So what can be done to conserve energy in buildings? On the owner-builder scale, compared with present practices, the possibilities are almost limitless. Conservative and judicious use of building materials is certainly a first step. For example, learning that the manufacture of aluminum requires a great amount of electrical energy and that aluminum window frames, one of the predominant uses of aluminum in buildings, allow much greater thermal conductivity than their wooden counterpart, ought to make aluminum a rarely used building material.

Building small will both decrease the amount of materials used and decrease the amount of energy required to "climate control" the structure. Well chosen and plentiful use of insulating materials on floors, walls and roofs will also lessen a building's need for climate control devices. Conservative use and placement of climate control devices within a structure will insure less energy consumption. Specific lighting rather than general lighting, window placement for light, ventilation and heat, selective heating rather than general heating and limited use of airconditioning will all lower the energy consumption of a building. Exposure to the sun and wind will also have an effect upon the needs for climate controls. Orientating the building so as to maximize winter sun exposure and minimize summer sun, and building windbreaks where needed will result in less energy being consumed to make the "climate" indoors comfortable. Finally, so-called passive design which utilizes the natural energy of the environment such as the sun and wind should be the rule not the exception.

What are the stumbling blocks to utilizing energy conserving techniques? Perhaps the first stumbling block is with architects and designers. Architects provide what the customer wants. For energy conservation techniques to be used on a widespread basis it will be necessary for both architects and their customers to demand environmentally sound architecture. It will often be necessary to spend more money initially in order to gain a well constructed building which saves energy and money on fuel bills in the future. The second stumbling block will undoubtedly be building codes. Les Scher's article *Building Codes* on the following pages outlines the situation in greater depth. The problem with building codes is either their being too restrictive or too lenient. Codes rarely require insulation in buildings and yet often restrict solar water heaters and windmills. For real energy conservation to work and new energy sources used to power buildings, building codes must change.

On the small scale, the owner-builder scale, energy conservation is up to you and me. How we build our houses and what we demand from architects in the way of energy conserving techniques will determine the energy consumption of future buildings. Before we can proceed to use renewable sources of energy in a meaningful way, we'd better get good at conserving the energy in the buildings in which we live and work now.

—T.G.

DESIGN WITH CLIMATE

Olgyay's explanations of the human comfort zone, climatic need timetables, sun path diagrams, shading effectiveness, and windbreaks are the best work on the subject I've seen. This book, since it came out, has been the basis for a lot of thinking and planning in architecture and it would be worth your time to read it.

— C.M.

The desirable procedure would be to work with, not against, the forces of nature and to make use of their potentialities to create better living conditions. The structure which in a given environmental setting reduces undesirable stresses, and at the same time utilizes all natural resources favorable to human comfort, may be called "climate balanced." Perfect balance can scarcely be achieved except under exceptional environmental circumstances. But it is possible to achieve a house of great comfort at lowered cost through reduction of mechanical conditioning. We will do well to study the broad climate layout, then apply the findings, through a specific region, to a specific structure. And one must be ever alert to regional variations.

Gains
1. heat produced by:
a. basal processes
b. activity
c. digestive, etc. processes
d. muscle tensing and shivering in response to cold
2. absorption of radiant energy
a. from sun directly or reflected
b. from glowing radiators
c. from non-glowing hot objects
3. heat conduction toward the body:
a. from air above skin temperature
b. by contact with hotter objects
4. condensation of atmospheric moisture

Losses
5. outward radiation:
a. to "sky"
b. to colder surroundings
6. heat conduction away from the body
a. to air below skin temperature (hastened by air movement-convection)
b. by contact with colder objects
7. evaporation:
a. from respiratory tract
b. from skin

Heat exchange between man and surroundings.

Design With Climate
Victor Olgyay
1963; 190 pp

$25.00

from:
Princeton University Press
Princeton, New Jersey 08540

or WHOLE EARTH TRUCK STORE

THE ARCHITECTURE OF THE WELL-TEMPERED ENVIRONMENT

A brilliant and lucid historical treatise on the past hundred years of architecture. Human beings altering and creating their own environment. Banham's hypothesis is that mechanical innovations such as air-conditioning and lighting have had a profound effect upon architecture. Many amazing architectural schemes are reviewed and illustrated including solar walls and natural ventilation. This book should be required reading for both the owner-builder and the architect.

—T.G.

The Architecture of the Well-Tempered Environment
Reyner Banham
1969; 295 pp

$5.95

from:
The University of Chicago Press
11030 South Langley Avenue
Chicago, Illinois 60628

or WHOLE EARTH TRUCK STORE

BUILDING CODES
by Les Scher and Carol Wilcox

Les is an attorney and consumer advocate. He authored Finding and Buying Your Place in the Country (see page 71), the best book there is on buying land. Carol Wilcox did a considerable amount of the research for this article.

For centuries legal controls in the form of building and health codes have regulated the manner in which homes and other buildings are constructed. This article presents two conflicting aspects of codes. On the one hand, they are written to protect the public's health and safety as well as to conserve energy resources through the use of new energy insulation standards. But, paradoxically, the way in which many of these codes are written inhibits the incorporation of new, often useful and inexpensive designs, techniques, and products. They also prevent many individuals from building their own low-cost houses, particularly in rural areas. The first part of the chapter presents the history of codes, what they regulate, and how they are enforced. The new energy conservation codes being adopted in many jurisdictions are discussed in detail. The last part of the chapter is concerned with the problems codes present to owner-builders and how one community is dealing with these problems.

Codes Defined

Each state government is permitted under the Constitution to exercise its "police power" and enact laws to protect the public health, safety, and general welfare. This legislative right has led to the enactment of such laws as zoning ordinances, health codes and building codes, all of which regulate the construction and use of buildings and the use of the land on which they are constructed.

Zoning power is generally delegated to city and county governments by the state legislature, since it is an accepted principle under the "home rule" doctrine that the local government can best determine the type of development suitable for its jurisdiction. Zoning ordinances provide a method of controlling land use by permitting a city and county to be divided into several districts, or zones, with each zone containing only specified kinds of development. For example, common zoning categories include industrial, business, residential, agricultural, forestry, or recreational uses. Within each zone, local regulations not only limit the type of activity permitted in the zone, but also dictate such things as the minimum size of a parcel or lot, the maximum permissible number of dwellings allowed on a parcel, and the minimum distance a building must be set back from the property boundaries.

Health codes regulate the construction of water and sewage facilities. For example many health codes prohibit outhouses and require the installation of septic tanks in rural areas. They also require that a permit be obtained before a septic tank or well can be installed on the property. Before an owner can obtain a building permit, he must first be in compliance with the local zoning and health regulations.

Housing codes are commonly confused with building codes. The former regulate the living conditions in existing buildings, whereas the latter regulate the construction of new buildings and substantial alterations of old buildings. Housing regulations protect the occupants, usually tenants, by requiring the maintenance of adequate heating, toilets, ventilation, lighting, exits, water supply, and garbage disposal. These housing laws are supposed to prevent urban blight by forcing owners, usually landlords, to maintain their buildings under the threat of criminal penalties and building condemnation and demolition. In some cases, housing and building laws may overlap.

Building codes set standards for new construction of residential, commercial, and industrial structures by regulating all aspects of building design and construction, including structural design (size and location of rooms, minimum ceiling heights, structural loads and stresses, foundations, floor systems, exterior walls), light and air (windows, ventilation, lighting), stairways, means of exits and fire-escapes, fire protection (fireproofing of materials, chimneys and flues, fire walls), and mechanical and electrical systems (heating equipment, sanitary equipment, plumbing, electrical wiring). In addition, building codes also control the issuance of building permits, which will be discussed later.

The History of Building Codes

Contemporary building codes were initially a product of the insurance industry, which set certain minimum standards for a building before it could be insured against fire. It was also discovered that the implementation of building standards is the best way to decrease property losses, loss of life, and personal injury resulting from fires and accidents in substandard dwellings. Codes were initiated in highly populated urban areas where fire was the greatest danger to public welfare. After each major disaster, codes became increasingly restrictive. There was an additional reason for the promulgation of building codes. The average purchaser of a real estate does not have the ability or knowledge to inspect a home or other structure before purchasing it. Ideally building codes ensure safe construction practices and thus become a form of consumer protection.

The first recorded building code in the U.S. was passed in New York (then called New Amsterdam) in 1625. The overcrowded conditions and the danger to life from fire in that city prompted the need for construction controls. This first code specified permissible types of roof coverings and locations of dwellings to prevent roof fires. In 1648, New York prohibited wooden or plastered chimneys, and inspections by "firemasters" were initiated. By 1656, straw and reed roofs were prohibited and ordered removed from all houses. Philadelphia went a step further in 1701 by passing

a law providing that any person whose chimney caught on fire would be prosecuted and fined.

Then as cities proliferated across the country, so did building codes, until by 1968, it was estimated that 5,000 different building codes were being used in the U.S. with some municipal areas, such as the greater Chicago area, having as many as 85 different codes. Generally, authority to impose and enforce building codes, like zoning ordinances, is granted to the local jurisdictions within a state by the state charter or legislature. Only a handful of states have mandatory state building codes that are imposed on the local cities and counties. Among these are California, Indiana, New Mexico, North Carolina, Ohio, and Wisconsin. However, all of these states, except California and New Mexico, exclude one and two family dwellings from the mandatory codes. Connecticut, Minnesota, New Jersey, and New York have general building codes that are optionally available for adoption by local jurisdictions. All other states permit local governments to draw up their own codes entirely or to adopt part or all of one of four national model codes.

The National Model Building Codes

Today there are four national model building codes in use throughout the U.S. They were prepared by private groups as models for enactment by local municipalities. When a municipality decides to adopt some form of building regulations, it can either draw up its own codes or adopt a pre-existing code in whole or in combination with its own independently developed standards.

The four model codes are being increasingly accepted because the groups that sponsor them have the facilities, money, and experts to experiment with new building techniques and materials, and this enables them to update the codes on a regular basis. These groups present their findings and code amendments annually to each jurisdiction that has adopted their codes. The jurisdictions generally accept the changes as a matter of course. Because less populated areas do not have the money to hire experts to draw up their own codes, a majority of the cities in the U.S. with less than 100,000 inhabitants have adopted one of the four major codes. However, many of these cities continue to independently amend the codes even after they adopt them.

The oldest model code is the National Building Code, which was originally drafted in 1905 by the National Board of Fire Underwriters, now called the American Insurance Association. It was drawn up by the insurance industry to minimize its risks by demanding certain minimum standards in the buildings it insured. This code has been adopted primarily by eastern jurisdictions. It is the exclusive code of the insurance industry.

The other three model codes are sponsored by associations of building officials made up of experts from the fields of labor, materials suppliers and manufacturers, and other building professionals. The second model code, the Uniform Building Code, was drafted in 1927 by the International Conference of Building Officials (ICBO), a California based organization (formerly called Pacific Coast Building Officials Conference). This code has been adopted primarily in the western half of the U.S., but some eastern jurisdictions have accepted it.

Many jurisdictions in the central states have adopted a third code, the Basic Building Code, which was drafted in 1950 by the Building Officials Conference of America (BOCA) based in Chicago, Illinois. Although no official studies have been made of code adoptions, BOCA claims that their code is the most commonly used code in the country.

The fourth code, the Southern Standard Building Code, was drafted by the Southern Building Code Congress (SBC) in Alabama to meet the unique needs of the South. It demands special construction techniques so that buildings can withstand hurricanes and strong winds. Its use is scattered among 20 southern states. (See "Useful Resources" at the end of this article for the addresses of all the model code organizations.)

Most of the building codes, including the model codes, incorporate practices established by the Uniform and National Plumbing Codes, the Uniform and National Electrical Code, and the Uniform Mechanical and Heating Code. The codes also utilize national standards promulgated by such organizations as the National Bureau of Standards, the American Society for Testing Materials, and the American Concrete Institute.

Problems of Code Diversity

Despite the wide use of the four model codes, there has not yet been a successful effort at formulating a single national uniform building code. Regional differences in labor practices, construction techniques, and climate conditions have prevented such an adoption. In addition, the large metropolitan areas that have drawn up their own codes have developed large bureaucracies which jealously guard their independence. Nevertheless, some attempts toward uniformity have been undertaken.

In 1971, all of the model code groups except the Southern Building Code Congress, jointly published the One and Two-Family Dwelling Code, but it has not gained acceptance yet. A group called the National Conference of States on Building Codes and Standards (NCSBCS) has prepared congressional legislation calling for uniform state building codes, but this legislation is still in the preliminary stages and no major efforts have yet been made to put it into law. Attempts to establish a National Institute of Building Sciences, a federal organization that would certify new building techniques, died somewhere in a Congressional committee.

The Federal Housing Administration (FHA) promulgated the Minimum Property Standards for Single and Multi-Family Housing that specifies the minimum standards a building must meet in order for the purchaser to get federal financial assistance in the form of an FHA loan to purchase the home. The standards also apply to developers and builders who want to participate in the FHA federally financed housing program. These are not actually building codes but rather definitions of eligibility for financial assistance. The federal government does not have Constitutional police powers over the states and local governments and cannot establish a mandatory federal building code.

The diversity of building codes has hindered the widespread acceptance and use of new products, designs, and methods in the construction industry. A producer of a new product or building method is faced with the overwhelming task of gaining approval from every jurisdiction that has its own code. In addition, each different code jurisdiction charges the manufacturer a fee for evaluating new products. For example, if a pre-fabricated dome design is found acceptable by the ICBO, it will generally be accepted only in jurisdictions that have adopted the ICBO Uniform Building Code. If the designer wants to sell on the national market, he will still have to seek approval in each code jurisdiction that has its own code standards.

The lack of uniform codes has also been the major impediment to the growth of industrialized, pre-assembled housing production, which the federal government is promoting as the best means of rapidly providing a large volume of low cost housing on a national scale. The costs are low because the houses are constructed on factory assembly lines and the traditionally huge expense of on-site construction of an entire home is greatly decreased. This type of housing is unique to the construction industry, traditionally a locally organized business, because the structures are assembled at a central location and shipped to the building site. This makes it difficult for the local building code jurisdiction to approve the construction, since their inspectors cannot be present when the structure is built. In addition, there is strong opposition from local building trades unions, materials suppliers, architects, and other people dependent on local construction for their incomes. Many code jurisdictions, being controlled by the local building industry, have refused to grant permits for factory built housing.

Because of these problems, the Federal Department of Housing and Urban Development (HUD) established in 1969 a federal program called "Operation Breakthrough." The program's purpose is to encourage the growth of industrialized housing production by attempting to "break through" such constraints as diversified local building codes. By 1972, the federal government had convinced twenty seven state legislatures to enact mandatory statewide "Factory-Built Housing Laws" permitting the use of factory-built housing in any jurisdiction in the state regardless of the requirements of the local building regulations. First the state evaluates and approves each industrialized housing system, and once approved, the local building codes no longer apply to that system. Many states are granting automatic approval to any housing system that has been authorized by HUD.

Specification and Performance Code Standards

All of the building codes utilize one of the two principles of building standards. The type most frequently adopted is the "specification standard," which spells out exactly the types, amounts, grades, and sizes of the acceptable materials and methods of construction that can be used to achieve an end result. In contrast to this is the "performance standard," also called the "functional" approach, that determines the acceptability of a type of building material or method on its functional performance requiring only that the desired effect is achieved rather than specifying how it is to be achieved. For example, a specification code would require that floor joists must be made of grade B, or better, lumber and be no less than 1–5/8 inches thick and 7–5/8 inches deep. A performance code would simply state that the floor joists must be capable of maintaining a floor load of 3,200 pounds per square inch.

The basic problem with specification codes is that many architects, engineers, and owner-builders believe that such codes inhibit modern building technology, product innovation, and freedom to build by imposing overly restrictive standards in construction. An example of this inflexibility recently occurred in San Francisco, where the city code prohibited the use of both plastic pipe in plumbing and plastic-coated electrical cable in electrical wiring. The U.S. Department of Housing and Urban Development (HUD), finding plastic pipe perfectly acceptable, threatened to hold back federal funds for urban renewal unless the city permitted the use of plastic in home construction.

The code makers, who are influenced by the construction trade unions, are reluctant to change these standards because in some cases changes mean less work and income for construction workers. For example, plastic piping is considerably easier to install than steel piping, which means less working time and therefore less money for the plumbers. In addition, new developments in construction often place the burden on segments of the construction industry to develop new building procedures, purchase new tools or materials, and train workers in new techniques.

Building Permits, Fees, and Inspections

Jurisdictions that enforce building codes require that a building permit be obtained before constructing or renovating a building. The courts have always upheld the right of a municipality, as part of the constitutional police power, to prohibit construction until a permit is issued.

Before a permit can be obtained, the owner must submit building plans to the local building inspector who determines whether they are in compliance with code standards. If approved, the owner must pay permit fees based on the value of the construction, which is often a set amount per square foot of structure. If the building is a conventionally framed dwelling of stud walls or masonry construction, the owner is usually permitted to draw up and submit his own plans. In cases of unusual design, the official may require plans to be prepared by a licensed engineer or architect. Other permits must also be obtained and fees paid for such items as a sewage disposal system and installation of plumbing and electricity. Once the plans are approved and a permit is issued, anyone can legally build the house.

During construction, most building departments make four inspections to insure that you are complying with your approved plans. The first is to look at the foundation before it is laid. The second is a frame inspection after the roof framing and bracing are in place and pipes, chimneys and vents are complete. The third is the wall inspection before plastering or siding is commenced. The fourth, and final, inspection comes after the building is completed and ready for occupancy. Many rural inspectors only make a single inspection after the house is completed.

Before a home can be lived in and after the final inspection, the building department will often be required to issue a Certificate of Occupancy, if all the standards have been satisfied.

Energy Conservation and Building Codes

According to data taken in 1971 by the Stanford Research Institute, Menlo Park, California, 33.6% of this country's total energy resources, which are comprised almost entirely of fossil fuels, are consumed in supplying commercial and residential buildings with various services such as heating and cooling, hot water heating, and electricity for lights and appliances. Heating and cooling alone account for almost 2/3 of this amount, or 20.4% of the total national energy consumption. At least 50% of this energy is wasted simply because buildings are poorly insulated and sealed. Nevertheless, until very recently few building codes required insulation, which is perhaps the most basic energy conservation item.

The federal government led the way in enacting energy standards in building design, when in 1965, the Federal Housing Administration (FHA) amended its Minimum Property Standards for Single and Multi-Family Housing to restrict heat losses to no more than 2000 BTU per thousand cubic feet-degree day. In 1972, these standards were revised to restrict heat losses to no more than 1000 BTU per thousand cubic feet-degree day. These heat loss reductions are to be achieved largely through the use of insulation and the control of air infiltration. Studies have shown that houses built with FHA loans between 1965 and 1972, and therefore subject to the earlier FHA standards, consume 40% more fuel for heating and air conditioning than they would if they were insulated and sealed according to the 1972 standards. Houses built before the 1965 FHA energy standards consume at least twice as much fuel as they would under current insulation standards. A group of engineers estimates that it is technologically and economically feasible to construct buildings that would have a heat loss of only 700 BTU per thousand cubic feet-degree day, which would cut fuel consumption still further. The FHA code is not a mandatory guideline for any construction other than FHA-approved housing. However, the federal government's influence in the construction industry is extensive since 37% of the construction done in the U.S. is either built for or financially assisted by the federal government.

Of the four model codes, only the Southern Standard Building Code includes insulation requirements. The energy standards of this code, drawn up by the National Mineral Wool Insulation Association (NMWIA), are performance-oriented standards, and specify the maximum allowable heat loss for a given building surface. Being performance standards, there are no specific types of insulating materials required. The NMWIA estimates that if every residential building used optimum insulation, a 15.9% energy savings could be realized over the next ten years.

On January 1, 1975 California will become the first state to require that energy conservation standards be incorporated into its building codes. They must be equal to or stronger than those found in the FHA Minimum Property Standards for Single and Multi-Family Housing and will apply to all new hotels, motels, apartment houses, homes, and other residential dwellings, including mobile homes. The building departments of every city and county will enforce the adopted provisions by refusing to issue a building permit unless the planned structures meet all building code requirements, including the new minimum energy insulation standards.

The new California Energy Insulation Standards begin with the general principle that "a building which is both heated and cooled shall be insulated against the most severe climatic condition for the location and type of structure involved." Then specific areas of construction are regulated, including ceilings and walls; glazing; floorsections, foundation walls, and slabs-on-grade; weatherstripping, loose fill, design temperatures, and duct and other insulation. The requirements are performance-oriented standards in line with the Uniform Building Code that California has adopted. Although these requirements have been passed and will become part of the California Building Code in 1975, attempts are already being made to amend them in hearings being conducted by the Commission of Housing and Community Development.

A second California energy bill, Senate Bill 753, was passed in September, 1973. It is now Section 14962 of the California Government Code and requires the State Architect to develop and apply rigorous energy conservation standards in designing new state buildings. Included in this bill is the rule that when computing the total costs to a building which the new energy regulations will require, both the extra initial costs and the amounts that will be saved in operating costs during the anticipated life of the building must be figured in to get a true cost analysis.

The third California energy insulation bill, Senate Bill 144, was passed on March 20, 1974, and calls for insulation standards for new non-residential buildings to be developed and adopted by July 1, 1975. The bill requires that the standards shall require the most efficient use of energy consistent with economic and technological feasibility, and shall take into consideration the indirect costs of energy production as well as the direct costs of energy use."

California Senate Bill 1575 has created a State Energy Resources Conservation and Development Commission to oversee the development of the above new code standards and to develop and coordinate a program of research and development of state energy supplies, including nuclear, solar, wind, and geothermal. The Commission will begin functioning on January 7, 1975.

Many other states are following in California's footsteps. In New York, a bill has been introduced that calls for minimum performance standards for insulation in new residential construction. North Carolina has adopted statewide the Southern Standard Building Code insulation requirements. Other states currently preparing energy insulation codes are Maryland, Nevada, Ohio, Oregon, Virginia, Tennessee, Texas, Washington and Wisconsin.

There is even a city that is preparing to pass its own energy savings building code. This is Davis, California, a city of 30,000 inhabitants situated in an area where winters are wet and cold and summers are hot and dry. The city expects to achieve a 50% home energy savings in space heating and cooling at little, if any, extra cost. The code will require, in addition to the more common insulation requirements, such things as the following: it will prohibit building construction that would block sunlight to adjoining structures in order to preserve solar heating possibilities in the winter (all windows would have to be shaded in the summer) and will require window placement geared to southern exposures, lighter colored roofs to reflect more summer heat, and ventilation openings on opposite sides of every room. Davis is making progress in these directions because of political pressure from a branch of the University of California that is located there.

All of the above energy standards have been adopted on a state or local level. The most far reaching national energy guidelines to date are now being evaluated for use in a set of federal guidelines, to be adopted by the National Bureau of Standards (NBS). This extensive and complex project began in July of 1973 when an emergency energy crisis workshop convened in Washington, D.C. This gathering of state building code officials and federal experts was co-sponsored by the National Conference of States on Building Codes and Standards (NCSBCS) and the National Bureau of Standards.

The government's ultimate objective is to facilitate nationwide adoption of energy standards by local jurisdictions that don't have the expertise to develop such standards on their own. This would be comparable to the present practice whereby jurisdictions adopt one of the four model codes. The NBS code can be considered a Uniform Energy Conservation Code.

Will Energy Standards Increase Building Costs?

One of the major and most frequent arguments against requiring energy saving improvements in buildings, particularly houses, is that the resulting increase in the initial cost of construction will make it even more difficult for the low and middle income wage earner to purchase a home. To determine the validity of this argument, the California State Commission of Housing and Community Development conducted a series of tests in 1973, prior to the adoption of the state energy standards, to determine the effect of the new requirements on the cost of owning a home. First, they determined the extra costs to a home built according to the new standards. They spread these costs over a 30 year period, the normal life span of a home mortgage, with amortization at an interest rate of 8–1/2%, the going rate in 1973. Then they determined the amount of fuel savings for heating the home that would be realized by the homeowner over the same period of time due to the increased insulation. They excluded the cost of air conditioning because it is not required under the building codes, whereas heating is. They compiled figures according to fuel costs in the various major cities in California, excluding Los Angeles and San Diego because the climate in those two cities is so warm that heating costs are negligible compared to the other major California cities. The conclusion reached by the commission was that the extra cost the energy conservation standards would add to the price of a home balances out with the fuel savings over a 30 year period, thereby showing that the costs of purchasing and maintaining a home will not be increased by the standards. Furthermore, there will be an increase in the quality of the dwelling which raises its resale value as well as its level of comfort. As fuel prices continue to rise, those factors will become even more important.

Energy Sources and Code Problems

At the present time codes do not deal with alternative energy sources, such as the sun, wind, water, or methane, which can be used in systems to heat water and generate electricity. Performance oriented codes, as they are now written may permit the use of certain systems if they are designed by licensed civil or structural engineers who can demonstrate that they are adequate for the dwellings and safe to use. For example, building and housing codes require that a dwelling be supplied with hot water. To meet this requirement, builders generally install a standard gas or electric powered hot water heater that is familiar to the inspector. But few inspectors have the expertise to determine if a solar water heater is adequate, and thus they may have a tendency to deny its use. They might claim that there are not enough sunny days to provide adequate hot water, or they might require a back-up gas or electric heater. Until systems are accepted by federal agencies such as the National Bureau of Standards, industrial groups such as the ASHRAE, or model code groups, gaining approval for these alternative energy systems, particularly in urban areas, will probably be difficult.

On the other hand, if fuel prices keep rising sharply, the codes of the future might begin to regulate the amount of energy consumed by appliances and demand that certain energy hogs such as frost-free refrigerators either be prohibited in the home or redesigned to use less energy. Codes might also permit only fluorescent lights since they provide three times more light per watt than the standard incandescent bulbs.

Zoning regulations, especially in urban areas, present another roadblock to alternative energy devices such as black solar collectors on roofs and large windmills. Communities are already showing a reluctance to accept these systems because the inhabitants don't find them aesthetically pleasing. This problem has occurred for, at least, one group of home builders. Interactive Resources, Inc., a professional group in Northern California that plans, engineers, and constructs homes, has designed a house that uses a built-in windmill electrical generator. Unfortunately, the Planning Commission refused to issue them a zoning permit because the local zoning ordinance prohibits any structures from being over 35 feet high. Most cities have a standard height limit of 30-40 feet. Although TV antennas, smokestacks, and towers are often exempt, windmills are not, yet. As of this writing, Interactive Resources, Inc. has failed to get a zoning permit to build this house with a wind electric generator. (See Useful Resources at the end of the chapter for the company's address.)

Interactive Resources, Inc. has also run up against another roadblock. They want to include a standard electrical hookup as a back up system for use when the wind doesn't blow. This electricity would be supplied by the local power company, the Pacific Gas and Electric Company (PG&E). However, PG&E has stated that they are not in the business of supplying "back-up systems," only "primary systems," and they refused to provide electrical installation to Interactive Resources, Inc. This reactionary attitude will undoubtedly be tested in lawsuits initiated to try to force utility companies to service dwellings that want to use the wind, sun, or methane as their primary power source.

Owner-Built Homes and Building Codes

An owner-builder is defined as a person who either acts as his own general contractor or provides all of his own labor for the construction of his own dwelling. Official Bureau of Census figures show that 20% of all the single-family homes built in the U.S. each year are owner-built and 40% of these owner-built homes are in rural areas. These statistics are actually underestimated since thousands of new rural residents have been building their homes without government recognition.

There are several reasons why there are not more owner-builders today, including a lack of access to land; discriminatory lending policies, especially by the federal government; the growth of mass produced housing packages, such as the mobile home; and last and foremost, restrictive building codes and standards.

Building codes are particularly restrictive to owner-builders in the rural areas. The codes were initially written for the welfare of highly populated urban areas where the needs and lifestyles of the people are very different from those of rural dwellers. Since urban dwellers generally buy their houses rather than build them, minimum code standards have been adopted to protect the ignorant urban house buyer from unscrupulous developers. Because the urban dweller's houses are generally built on small lots within view of other homes, the aesthetics of the buildings must conform to the tastes of the neighbors who want to protect their property values, thus a major reason for the similarity of building styles in urban and suburban areas. Urban homes also have easy access to all utilities such as water, sewage, gas, and electricity. Codes requiring such things as hot and cold running water under 40 pounds of pressure, electric wiring, inside plumbing, septic tanks if sewers are not available, a kitchen area separated from the rest of the house and minimum room sizes reflect cultural norms more than safe construction practices.

Rural dwellers, on the other hand, who usually live on more than an acre of land isolated from the view of neighbors, who must develop their own water supply and sewage disposal systems, and who sometimes are miles from the nearest electric lines cannot hope to build houses which meet many of these codes without incurring tremendous expenses, often for things they do not want or need.

One of the major obstacles faced by many of these rural dwellers is the lack of water supplies on their land ample enough to provide their homes with running water under pressure or to permit the use of 5 gallons of water every time they want to flush the toilet. Most counties will not issue a building permit unless a health permit is obtained first, and most rural jurisdictions will issue a health permit only if a septic tank, which uses tremendous quantities of water, is installed for sewage disposal. There are other types of systems that require little or no water that have been proven safe and effective but have not been approved by the codes. I will discuss one of these systems later in the chapter.

These rural owner-builders realize that the building and health codes were promulgated by an urban society for urban living and have not yet been adapted for the rural lifestyle, so they have ignored the regulations and built homes that, in many cases, do not meet codes. Nevertheless, many of these houses are structurally sound. I doubt if any building inspector or code writer would insist that the only safe house is a code house.

But what happens to the person who builds a house without following the codes and paying for the permits? Is there any means of fighting the building inspector? Because California is the staging ground for a significant social, political, and legal battle over owner-builders' non-compliance with the codes, I will summarize the California building regulations and their enforcement.

In 1961, the California State Legislature enacted the State Housing Law as part of the State Health and Safety Code, and directed the California Department of Industrial Relations, through its Division of Housing, to "adopt, amend, repeal, and in certain instances enforce rules and regulations governing most phases of construction of hotels, apartment houses, and dwellings" throughout the state. These rules and regulations mandated the local jurisdictions to impose building requirements equal to or more restrictive than those contained in the Uniform Building Codes of the ICBO, the Uniform Plumbing Code of the Western Plumbing Officials Association, and the National Electric Code of the National Fire Protection Association. Future amendments to these codes are to be "adopted by reference" into the local codes.

However, this legislation also provides ways for the state and local jurisdictions to work outside the accepted uniform codes. The State Commission of Housing and Development has the discretion to substitute alternative methods of construction and materials for those called for in the codes in three circumstances: when there is a shortage of approved materials; when the substitution will not create a hazard to health or safety of the public or of the occupants of the building; and in unincorporated areas where the population density is less than 300 persons per square mile.

Local jurisdictions within the state also have a major area of discretion, or "home rule," that they have been, and still are, ignoring. Regardless of the requirements of the building codes, any local appeals board that hears appeals from individuals or corporations regarding the building requirements may exempt an entire geographical area or an individual building from following the codes if it determines, after a hearing, that because of local conditions or factors it is not reasonable for the regulation to be applied. The California Attorney General has ruled, for instance, that if it can be shown that water or electricity is not, and will not be, available to a certain area in the immediate future, structural compliance with the uniform plumbing or electric codes becomes impractical and unreasonable. But, an area cannot be excluded from the requirements simply because it is rural. Some other reason must be given for a ruling of exclusion. The state cannot override a decision of the local jurisdiction to exempt an area from the codes. In practice, unfortunately, this home rule exception has rarely been put into action.

If an owner disregards the codes and his building is found to be in violation of the building codes in California, a local building inspector "tags" the dwelling by posting a sign on it putting the public on notice that the structure is "unfit for human occupancy." Any building that does not meet code standards is automatically unfit for human occupancy. "Tagging" is the first step in a process known as "abatement." If the county orders the abatement of a building, that structure must be brought up to code or be destroyed by the owner within a certain time period, usually 30 days. If the owner does not comply with the order of abatement, the county will destroy the building and bill the owner for the costs of doing so. In most jurisdictions, failure to comply with the order of abatement can also lead to a misdemeanor conviction with a possible penalty of a jail sentence, a fine, or both.

After a building has been tagged, the owner has certain appeal rights. Although the procedure varies among different jurisdictions, generally the owner is given 30 days to appeal the decision of the building inspector. A Board of Appeals, which is often the Board of Supervisors or other local governing body, hears the owner's case. At the appeal hearing, the owner can be represented by an attorney, present witnesses, and introduce evidence as to why his building should not be condemned. For most non-code homes, the owner's only case is to show that although his house does not meet code standards, it is still a safe dwelling and not a danger to the health, safety, and welfare of the general public. He can attempt to show that the codes are too restrictive to be applied in his particular case, and he can offer to pay the necessary permit fees in an attempt to destroy that part of the building inspector's case. Unfortunately, most Boards are very conservative and not easily persuaded, particularly where there are other factors involved that can sway their opinions, such as the lifestyle and physical appearance of the violators.

After the hearing, if the owner fails to convince the hearing officers that the law has been misapplied in his or her case, the Board declares that the building must either be brought up to code or be demolished. The owner can appeal the Board's decision by filing an action in the Superior Court to contest the validity and findings of the proceedings. Such appeals, however, require a lawyer, are very costly, and are rarely successful.

In actual practice, the decision to approve building plans is subject to the individual building inspector's discretion. He can be liberal or strict in interpreting and enforcing codes. Many inspectors will permit a certain degree of digression from the codes if a builder pays the required fees and either discusses his plans with the inspector or hires a licensed civil engineer to draw up plans for him.

The United Stand Story

A major battle between owner-builders and code administrators is now occurring in Mendocino County, California. Beginning in the late 1960's, Mendocino County attracted thousands of young people fleeing city life who wanted to create a new type of lifestyle in the country. Many of these people chose to ignore the local building codes because the codes were unreasonable for their needs. The rural dwellers that built their homes in defiance of the building codes in Mendocino County were not bothered by the building and health authorities until recently. In February 1974, the Mendocino Grand Jury passed a resolution to form a "Task Force" which would search out and tag dwellings built in violation of the building and health codes so the county could begin abatement proceedings against the offenders.

This Task Force has tagged over 100 homes. After the homes were tagged, each property owner received a letter stating that his or her home was in violation of the building and health codes and had to be demolished within 30 days. The young residents of Mendocino, aware of the futility of pursuing the normal appeals route on an individual basis, chose to pursue a more political course of action. They called a meeting of all the persons whose homes were condemned or who were in sympathy with those homeowners. Several hundred people showed up, and they decided to organize themselves into a single unit, called "United Stand," to combat the rigidity of the building codes and the action being taken against their homes.

United Stand adopted a strategy of communication and cooperation, rather than confrontation, with the county citizens and the local government officials. They found that even conservative old-timers resented the government telling them how to build their own homes on their own land. They asked the building inspector, the director of environmental health, the district attorney, and other county officials and members of the public to attend a meeting at a local church to hear what United Stand was all about. The invitations were accepted, and United Stand presented a well documented slide show of their lifestyle and a discussion of their position and proposals. The meeting was a success and resulted in a temporary delay in the abatement actions and the creation by the county of a special committee (the Building and Land Use Review Committee) to study building, health, and zoning regulations and violations and to formulate recommendations, to be presented to the Board of Supervisors, for new ordinances covering owner-built rural housing.

United Stand drew up and presented to the Committee the following proposed Owner/Builder Code:

1. The home must be built by the property owner with the aid of his or her family and friends with no renumeration. Anyone employed under contract must do code work with code materials.

2. The home may not be rented or made available for other contracted payment.

3. All non-code structures will be recorded on the property deed as such when a permit is issued for such a building. This will become part of any title report in order to put a future purchaser on notice that the building is not a standard code structure.

4. There will be no use of heavy equipment for grading or otherwise improving homesites unless approved.

5. Land used for owner-building must be compatible with zoning and must be in unincorporated areas.

6. The owner/builder has complete discretion in choosing his materials and architectural style as long as reasonable safety standards are maintained.

7. Permits will be issued for owner-built homes and fees charged. Permit fees will be based on the actual cost of the structure, not its size.

This Owner/Builder Code appears to be a just compromise. The owner will have to pay a permit fee and build a safe dwelling. In rural areas, the threat of fire is just as great as in the cities, and fire-safe homes should be required under the law. Perhaps an Owner/Builder Code should also require that a house be built to last and be built according to the insulation standards, thereby preserving the resources of the planet which benefit society as a whole. If a compromise is made in the United Stand case, the new code will probably include regulations that make a home durable, as well as safe, while excluding all requirements dealing with the actual type of lifestyle required in the home, such as mandatory hot and cold running water, indoor plumbing and septic tanks, electrical wiring, and minimum room sizes. However, it can be anticipated that professional builders and developers will either fight the enactment of such a code, demand to also be entitled to build under its standards as long as they put the buyer of such a home on notice of this fact, or insist that such an owner-built home cannot be resold at all unless it is brought up to normal code standards.

United Stand is also attempting to gain approval for a "new" sewage disposal system, called the compost privy. Compost privy systems are self-contained units that decompose excrement without the use of water or plumbing. They take the place of the flush toilet and septic tank and don't require heavy equipment to install. For a complete description of compost privies, write for United Stand's Presentation to the Board of Supervisors and Technical Bulletin No. 1—Composting Privy. (See Useful Resources for addresses.) These safe and sanitary systems have been approved by Sweden, Norway, and the World Health Organization. Since the compost privy only receives sewage, other waste water from washing must be diverted outside the home in some other fashion, but this can be done safely and cheaply. The Mendocino Health Department has started to give permits for the system, but the building

CLIVUS MULSTRUM WATERLESS TOILET

department refuses to issue a building permit unless the code-required indoor plumbing and septic tank system are included in the house plans, thus negating the effect of the compost privy health permit.

As of the writing of this paper (August 1974), the Committee in Mendocino County has not made its final recommendations to the Board of Supervisors. Under the law the Board can recommend the adoption of the new standards desired by United Stand, by arguing that they are "reasonable" for the local geographical, social and economic conditions are not a danger to the general health, welfare and safety of the community. However, the Board has let it be known that it will not adopt any new standards without first seeking approval from the State Commission on Housing and Community Development. It appears they will "pass the buck" to avoid local responsibility and political repercussions. Ultimately the owner-builders and their sympathizers will probably have to move full force into the political arena and elect their own supervisors who will be willing to adopt radical changes without bending to pressure from the state, the building industry, or local building inspectors. They might also have to institute a class-action law suit that will be expensive, time-consuming, and difficult to win. On the other hand, if each owner-builder is forced to pursue his or her case individually, the Appeals Board and the courts would be tied up for many years, an eventuality the government wants to avoid. Thus, the organizing tactics learned in the 1960's will have to be employed by those who thought they were going to the country to "get away from it all." You can keep informed of the progress made by United Stand and get ideas for organizing your own community by subscribing to the Mendocino Grapevine and United Stand News. (See Useful Resources.)

USEFUL RESOURCES

Information on the National Building Code can be obtained from:
American Insurance Association
85 John Street
New York, New York 10038

Information on the Uniform Building Code (ICBO) can be obtained from:
International Conference of Building Officials
5360 South Workman Mill Road
Whittier, California 90601

Information on the Southern Standard Building Code can be obtained from:
Southern Building Code Conference
3617 8th Avenue South
Birmingham, Alabama 35222

Information on the Basic Building Code can be obtained from:
Building Officials Conference of America (BOCA)
1313 E. 60th Street
Chicago, Illinois 60637

You can obtain the pamphlets listed below from:
National Technical Information Service
U.S. Department of Commerce
Operations Division
5828 Port Royal Road
Springfield, Virginia 22151

Self-Help Housing in the U.S.A.
NTIS No. PB-185 981

Self-Help in Housing
NTIS No. PB-196 376

Owner-Built Housing in the United States
NTIS No. PB-196 377

A Self-Help Housing Process for American Indians & Alaskan Natives
NTIS No. PB-196 401

Residential Energy Consumption
NTIS No. PB-212 306

You can obtain Patterns of Energy Consumption in the U.S. from:
Stanford Research Institute
Energy Technology Department
333 Ravenswood Avenue
Menlo Park, California 94025

You can obtain the Insulation Manual from:
National Association of Home Builders' Research Foundation
Rockville, Maryland 20850

You can obtain The Value of Thermal Insulation in Residential Construction: Economics and Conservation of Energy (Report ORNL-NSF-EP-9) and an Inventory of Energy Research from:
Environmental Information System Office
Oak Ridge National Laboratory

Post Office Box X
Oak Ridge, Tennessee 37830

You can obtain the pamphlets listed below free from:
Office of Policy Development and Research
U.S. Department of Housing and Urban Development
451 Seventh Street, S.W.
Washington, D.C. 20410

Economic Evaluation of Total Energy—Guidelines

HUD Research Newsletter (Monthly)

MIUS Program Information

Total Energy Feasibility Study Information

Residential Energy Conservation Measures and Information

Prototype Solar House Evaluation and Information

Organization for Social & Technical Innovation, Owner-Built Housing in the United States, Report No. 8 (1970)

You can obtain the Model Interim Building Code, the National Consensus Standards, The Performance Concept: A Study of its Application to Housing: (1968), National Bureau of Standards Report No. 9850, and a catalogue of pamphlets on housing and energy use, which has information on every state's research on energy and codes, from:
National Bureau of Standards
Office of Building Standards and Code Services
Center for Building Technology
Building 226, Room B226
Washington, D.C. 20234
Attn: Gene A. Rowland, Chief

You can obtain for $5.00 Draft Design and Evaluation Criteria for Energy Conservation in New Buildings, the proposed federal standards for efficient energy use in buildings (an interim document, guidelines only and open to improvement from readers) from:
American Society of Heating, Refrigerating and
Air-Conditioning Engineers, Inc.
345 E. 47th Street
New York, NY 10017
Attn: Nicholas A. La Courte

You can obtain the California energy insulation regulations for homes, non-residential and government buildings from:
Department of Housing and Community Development
1500 5th Street
Room 200
Sacramento, California 95814

For $2.00 you can obtain Energy Conservation Design Guidelines for Office Buildings, prepared by the American Institute of Architects, from any General Services Administration Business Service Center Branch or the national headquarters:
Public Buildings Service
General Services Administration
GSA Headquarters
Washington, D.C. 20405

A copy of United Stand's Presentation to the Board of Supervisors ($0.50) and other information about United Stand can be obtained from:
United Stand Office
Box 191
Potter Valley, California 95469
(707) 462-0102

A one year subscription to The Mendocino Grapevine, which includes United Stand News, costs $3.00 and can be obtained from:
The Mendocino Grapevine
1484 So. Main Street
Willits, California 95490
(707) 459-4755

You can obtain Technical Bulletin No. 1—Composting Privy (discusses health codes and how to get the compost privy accepted) for $2.00 from:
The Farallones Institute
P.O. Box 700
Point Reyes Station, CA 94956

The most inclusive legal discussion of building codes is the article: Courting Change: Using Litigation to Reform Local Building Codes by Steven R. Rivken, Rutgers Law Review, Vol. 26, No. 4, Summer 1973, pp. 774-802.

YOUR ENGINEERED HOUSE

Every home owner should read this book, not just prospective home builders. Roberts logically examines most of the functions that take place in a home. He relates them to traditional building solutions, and then the logical, simple "gee whiz, why didn't I think of that" solutions that offer a livable, inexpensive shelter. He makes engineering logic palatable with simple hand drawn sketches and light, readable text.

He neglects long-range environmental considerations in places, and I get the feel of sex role stereotyping once in a while. His logic and his refusal to take any building component at face value, though, makes this a worthwhile book to read even if you're only thinking of doing a little bit of redecorating or remodeling.
—C.M.

Your Engineered House
Rex Roberts
1964; 237 pp

$4.95

from:
M. Evans and Company, Inc.
216 East 49th Street
New York, NY 10017

or WHOLE EARTH TRUCK STORE

FREEDOM TO BUILD

The basic premise of *Freedom to Build* is "that as dwellers lose control over their living environments, shelter becomes a commodity of decreasing value to the individual and often an inordinate expense to society." The book is a collection of ten papers covering different aspects of owner-controlled housing construction and how building codes and other local standards "fail to distinguish between what things *are*, materially speaking, and what they *do* in people's lives." The impulse of planners and officials is to define housing values by the material quality of the house based on the minimum standards of construction. But, as editor John Turner continuously emphasizes, these standards cannot be used as measures of human value.

Where people want handmade houses, products of the woodbutcher's art, they should be permitted and encouraged to build them themselves, and governments and private sectors, such as banks and financial institutions, should aid this process. If they would do so, Turner estimates that 5-9 million families could own housing presently unavailable to them.

Freedom to Build is the first scholarly approach to recognize that the need to build one's own home implies a fundamentally different set of values and energies than those found in a society dominated by housing manufacturers, professional builders, and regulations that mitigate against the primal desire to exercise control over one's own environment. Every building official, legislator, and owner-builder should read this book.

—Les Scher

If housing is treated as a verbal entity, as a means to human ends, as an activity rather than as a manufactured and packaged product, decision-making power must, of necessity, remain in the hands of the users themselves . . . The ideal we should strive for is a model which concerns housing as an activity in which the users—as a matter of economic, social, and psychological common sense—are the principal actors.

One statistic seems particularly significant, since it reflects the role the federal government plays in guiding national energies. While the Federal Housing Administration (FHA) and the Veterans Administration (VA) assist the purchase of one out of every three developer-built homes by offering mortgage insurance, they perform this service for only one out of seventeen owner-built homes.

Freedom to Build
J.F.C. Turner & R. Fichter, Eds.
1972; 301 pp

$2.95

from:
The Macmillan Company
866 Third Avenue
New York, NY 10022

or WHOLE EARTH TRUCK STORE

THE OWNER BUILT HOME

This book is the bible of low cost building and design principles for the owner-builder. As an introduction to design principles for the beginner, as well as a source of new ideas for the experienced builder, it is probably the best. It is certainly unique, covering many innovative and not so well known discoveries in the field of house design and construction. The book is divided into four volumes: "Site and Climate," "Materials and Skills," "Form and Function," and "Design and Structure." All of the volumes are concerned with methods applicable to the home that is built and designed by the owner, i.e., cheap and simple. The ideas that Kern presents deal with how to make your house as efficient as possible, in terms of construction methods, use, and energy consumption. The volume on "Site and Climate" especially, discusses how to heat, cool, and ventilate your house naturally, without the use of gadgets. This idea of using the house itself to produce the desired climate is as important and revolutionary as developing new, improved windmills and solar collectors. This is not a construction manual; the detail needed for such a book is lacking. It is a book on design principles, and much of the information is not available anywhere else. Kern is an entertaining writer. The book is well researched and every chapter has a bibliography for further research.
—Larry Strain

The number one rule in plumbing fixture arrangement is: keep fixtures compact. Where possible, locate the toilet between the tub and the sink. For ease of installation as well as material savings, bathroom fixtures should line up on one wall. The opposite side of this so-called 'wet wall' could include perhaps food preparation and laundry functions. A complete mechanical core might well be planned to include water heating, furnace, fireplace, and main electrical panel, as well as bathroom, laundry, and kitchen. Some progressive plumbing designers have arranged plumbing fixtures so that all supply and drainage pipes are above the floor. This is possible now that the much-improved wall-hung toilet is available.

The Owner Built Home
Ken Kern
1961, reprinted 1972; 275 pp

$7.50

from:
Ken Kern Drafting
P.O. Box 550
Oakhurst, CA 93644

or WHOLE EARTH TRUCK STORE

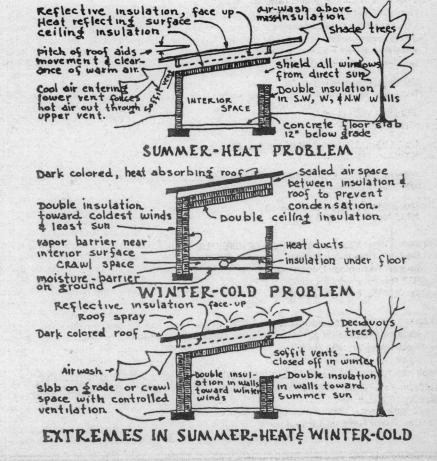

INSULATION AND HEAT FLOW

Larry Strain
Carpenter and Architecture Student

In dealing with energy conservation, one of the principal study areas is the heating and cooling of buildings. To understand the role this plays in U.S. energy consumption, it helps to look at some figures. According to the Scientific American book Energy and Power (see page 187), space heating and air conditioning consumed roughly 2/3's of all the energy used by the household and commercial sectors of the U.S. economy in 1970. That's about 16% of all the energy consumed in the U.S. that year.

Definitions

In order to understand heating and cooling in buildings, it helps to have some understanding of heat—what it is, how it moves, and how to control its movement. Here are some definitions.

Heat is defined as the result of the vibration of molecules. The more rapidly the molecules vibrate, the higher the resulting temperature.

Heat flow is defined as moving from hot to cold. An object loses heat to its surroundings if they are colder and gains heat from its surroundings if they are warmer.

Conduction, a method of heat transfer, takes place within solids, and is the result of energy being transferred from one vibrating molecule to the one immediately adjacent to it without any relative displacement of the molecules. Example: One end of a metal rod is placed in a fire, heat is conducted through the rod, and soon the other end of the rod heats up.

Convection, another method of heat transfer, takes place in fluids and is the result of a mixing of warm and cool portions of the fluid. Convection can either be natural or forced. Natural convection occurs when a portion of the fluid comes in contact with a heat source, absorbs heat, and becomes less dense. The warmer fluid rises, allowing a cooler portion of the fluid to come in contact with the heat source, which in turn rises causing a natural circulation. Example: Air comes in contact with the heating fins of a baseboard heater, heats rises, and starts the air circulating.

Radiation, a completely different method of heat transfer, accounts for 10% of the heat flow in a typical house. It does not rely on molecular vibration and is the only form of heat that can travel through a vacuum. Radiant heat can not be sensed as heat, it is simply a method of heat transfer. It becomes sensible as heat only when it strikes an object or a fluid and is converted to molecular heat. Example: Heat reaching us through the vacuum of space; also, most of the heat reaching us from a fire.

Space Heating and Radiant Heating

There are two methods of heating a house artificially. The first is convection heating (called space heating because what it does is heat up the space, or air, within the structure), and the second is radiant heating, which heats up the objects within the structure. In space heating a lot of energy is spent in heating the air in the house, which then transmits heat to the people and the objects in the house. Space heating involves convection, a form of molecular heat transfer. As there are relatively few molecules in air, it takes a lot of air to heat up the people and objects in the house. Radiant heat does not rely on molecules to transmit heat so the air can remain relatively cool while the objects needing heat receive it more or less directly. For this reason radiant heat is more efficient and is cheaper to operate. It uses less energy than space heating.

Insulation

Which ever type of heating system you have, or plan to have, it is possible to cut down the artificial heating requirements by making the house a more efficient heat retainer. This can be done by using insulation. The purpose of insulation is to slow down the flow of heat by obstructing one or more methods of heat transfer. In order to effectively resist all forms of heat transfer, insulation must incorporate reflective properties and fibrous or cellular properties. Reflective properties are effective against radiant heat transfer. They work by reflecting heat back the way it came. The brighter and shinier the surface the more heat will be reflected and the less heat will be absorbed. The fibrous or cellular properties work by utilizing a great number of tiny air cells. Because of their size, the individual air cells do not allow the movement of air, and heat by convection is thus slowed down. Heat by conduction is also slowed down because the continuity of the material is broken up by the tiny air cells.

There are four major types of materials used in manufacturing insulation. These are (1) fibrous or cellular mineral matter such as glass, silics, rock or slag, (2) fibrous or cellular organic matter such as cane fiber, wood or wood bark, (3) cellular organic plastics such as polystyrene and polyurethane, and (4) heat reflecting materials such as aluminum foil.

Insulation is marketed in four different forms. These are (1) blankets and batts, e.g. rolls of fiberglass, batts of rock wool, (2) board and slabs, e.g. mineral biberboard, polystyrene slabs, (3) loose fill, e.g. cellulose, vermiculite, and (4) rolls and sheets, e.g. rolls of aluminum.

The following is a list of the major types of insulation on the market.

Reflective insulation, the most common type of which is aluminum foil. Aluminum foil is generally produced in rolls or sheets mounted on a paper backing, or used as a reflective surface on various insulation products. In order for reflective insulation to be effective it must have an air space in front of it. Reflective insulation will work best in walls, as the vertical surface does not allow dust to collect. It also provides a good vapor seal.

Another form of reflective insulation useful in keeping heat out of the house is a light colored or shiny surface on the roof. This will reflect a lot of the sunlight away from the house before it can penetrate into the house. White rolled roofing or white gravel roofs are cheap and work well for this purpose.

Mineral wool is made by blasting molten glass, rock, or slag into long threads which form into a wool-like mass that traps many air pockets. Fiberglass accounts for about 85% of all mineral wool. Mineral wool is manufactured into rolls and batts anywhere from two to six inches think and it is often faced with foil or paper. In this form it is used between floor joists, wall studs, and roof rafters. It is also available in loose fill form and can be poured between ceiling rafters and inside hollow walls.

Foamed glass is made by expanding glass pellets under pressure and creating a cellular mass which is then fused into block form and cut into boards. It is used in roofs where it is placed between layers of hot asphalt, between layers of concrete, and in walls.

Perlite is a glassy volcanic rock which, when heated, pops like popcorn and expands four to twenty times its original size. The bubbles formed by this expansion serve as insulation. It is generally made into insulation board. It is also made into loose fill, as well as being used to make lightweight insulating concrete.

Plastics used for building insulation are generally cellular polystyrene and polyurethane. Thermoplastic and thermosetting resins are expanded by a blowing agent, such as a gas, which transforms the resin into a cellular structure. The result is lightweight and rigid and can be cut into boards or granulated and used as loose fill. Polystyrene and polyurethane are two of the best insulating materials available. To my knowledge, however, they are non-biodegradable, and they are made from oil, a limited resource. While they usually are fire resistant, they can release poisonous cyanide gas when they catch on fire.

Foamed rubber is made by incorporating chemical agents which decompose under heat, into rubber. When the rubber is heated nitrogen gas is liberated, which forms tiny air bubbles filled with nitrogen. Foamed rubber is used in rigid sheets to insulate walls, and as roof deck insulation.

Vermiculite is a group of mica-like minerals which expands under heat to a cork-like consistency. It is used primarily as loose fill insulation.

Insulation board is made by reducing wood, cane or other lignucellistic fibers to pulp and manufacturing them into boards. The air spaces between the fibers and the air spaces in the cells themselves create the insulating property. The lower the density the higher the insulating value. Densities generally range from 16 to 27 lbs. per square foot.

Cellulose is made from pulverized paper or wood impregnated with fire retardant chemicals. Cellulose is available as either loose fill insulation, or when mixed with binders, as a spray on insulation. This is a good way to recycle newspapers.

Non-commercial insulations include crumpled newspaper, corn cobs, sawdust, cardboard, earth banked up against the outside of a house, and many others depending on what materials are locally available. Any thing which incorporates small dead air spaces can serve as insulation. The danger with using non-commercial insulation is that many of them are flammable. There are, however, fire retardant chemicals that can be applied to reduce this danger. The benefits of using non-commercial insulation are obvious in terms of cost and self sufficiency. However, there are no figures available as to their various insulation values.

Building Heat Loss

In order to figure heat loss in a building some terms need to be defined. Some formulas and tables for figuring heat flow are necessary also, which can be found in the ASHRAE Handbook of Fundamentals. (See page 24.) The reference section of your library probably has a copy.

Btu	The British Thermal Unit is a measure of heat. It is the amount of heat it takes to raise one pound of water one degree Fahrenheit.
U, or U factor	The amount of heat in Btu's that will pass through a combination of materials and air spaces such as a wall or a floor in a given time. U is usually computed on the basis of each degree of temperature difference, per square foot, per hour.
k	Unit of thermal conductivity. The amount of heat in Btu's that will pass through one square foot of a material that is one inch thick, for each degree of temperature difference of opposing sides.
c	Unit of thermal conductance. The same as k but for the thickness specified.
r	Unit of thermal resistance. Equal to the reciprocal of k, or c, that is, dividing one by k or c. r is useful when you are dealing with a composite wall or ceiling section, in that you can simply add all the various r values of the various materials to obtain the total thermal resistance (R). Then by finding the reciprocal of R you have the U value for that particular wall or ceiling section. You cannot add up the various k or c values in the same way.
T	This refers to the difference in temperature between two surfaces. For example, if your house is 70 degrees inside and the outside temperature is 50 degrees, then T is 20 degrees.
L	Thickness in inches.
A	Area in square feet.
q	Thermal conductivity of the inside air surface. The thermal conductivity of the air right next to the surface is different than the thermal conductivity of the rest of the air. For this reason it must be taken into account.
q_1	Thermal conductivity of the outside air surface.

R_q and R_{q1} Thermal resistances of q and q_1.

The formula given here is for heat loss through conduction, since that is the way most of the heat is lost in a building. (If you are interested in heat losses through convection and radiation I again refer you to the ASHRAE Handbook of Fundamentals.) The formula for heat conduction through one material of the same substance (such as glass) is:

$$Btu/hour = \frac{kAT}{L}$$

However, most of the outside components of a house, such as walls, floors, and roofs, are made up of more than one material. Since it does not work to add up all the various k and c values separately, you have to add up all their values. These are often available from ASHRAE books. (See page 24.) If they are not, you simply have to take the reciprocal of the k or c value to get the r value.

Therefore, the way to figure heat loss in a composite wall is simply to add up all the r values to get the total thermal resistance, R. The reciprocal of R gives the U value.

$$U = \frac{1}{R} \text{ which} = \frac{1}{\text{the sum of all the r's}}$$

SAMPLE:

R_q = 0.68, inside air surface value
r_1 = 0.45, sheetrock value (½")
r_2 = 11.10, mineral wool insulation value (3")
r_3 = 2.06, insulating sheathing value (25/32")
r_4 = 0.79, drop siding value (1" x 8")
R_{q1} = 0.17, outside air surface value (15 mph wind)
R = $R_q + r_1 + r_2 + r_3 + r_4 + R_{q1}$
R = 0.68 + 0.45 + 11.10 + 2.06 + 0.79 + 0.17
R = 15.25
U = $\frac{1}{R} = \frac{1}{15.25}$ = 0.06

This means that 0.06 Btu are lost for every square foot of area and for every degree in temperature difference, T, per hour.

SHELTER

When the single family ticky-tacky houses all around you start to weird you out, *Shelter* is a welcome relief. Hundreds of pictures and lots of text to convince you that there are still some people left who know how to build liveable, beautiful, and individualistic structures. The density of information is high, there is no index, the annotated bibliography is complete, and the whole package is fun reading. This is an idea book, not a how-to-do-it book.
—C.M.

In times to come, we will have to find a responsive and sensitive balance between the still-usable skills and wisdom of the past and the sustainable products and inventions of the 20th century.

This book is about simple homes, natural materials, and human resourcefulness. It is about discovery, hard work, the joys of self-sufficiency, and freedom. It is about shelter, which is more than a roof overhead.

Shelter
Ed. by Lloyd Kahn
1973; 176 pp
$6.00

from:
Random House, Inc.
Westminster, Maryland
21157
or
WHOLE EARTH
TRUCK STORE

CLIMATE AND HOUSE DESIGN

Here's a condensed guidebook to intelligent shelter design, particularly in arid or humid tropical regions. Climatic factors are involved in all three steps of the design process, i.e., the sketch design stage, the plan development stage, and the element design stage. It's a very direct monograph on how to use solar, wind, and humidity information wisely. It has some short cut graphs to determine the sun path diagram, and a shadow angle protractor has been included. Olgyay's *Design With Climate* was the source of much of the material presented.
—C.M.

This neglect of the traditional designs and building methods, according to this group of experts, is partially due to the fact that virtually all professional training is oriented along the lines of the western countries, even in non-western societies. Not many architects from the developing countries would advocate their own countries' traditional designs and construction methods, national pride notwithstanding. On the contrary, it was mentioned that design solutions and building codes emanating from a by-gone colonial era and representing an entirely different cultural and climatic background are prevalent, and even promoted, in developing countries today. The minimum standards specified in many developing countries are hardly relevant to the situation of the masses of their populations who cannot afford even these minimum, which are not only of foreign inspiration but also urban in conception, whereas the populations concerned are mostly rural in character. It is far more practical, it was stressed, to start from what is found and what is feasible and improve upon the shanties and hovels that exist.

Climate and House Design
1971; 93 pp
Sales No. E.69.IV.11
$3.00

from:
United Nations
Sales Section
New York, NY 10017

or WHOLE EARTH TRUCK STORE

HOW TO INSULATE HOMES FOR ELECTRIC HEATING AND AIR CONDITIONING

A small booklet that shows how to install insulation for the greatest effectiveness. It is similar to the illustrated how-to- pages in the NAHB Research Foundation's *Insulation Manual*.
—C.M.

How to Insulate Homes for Electric Heating and Air Conditioning
1973; 32 pp
Free

from:
National Mineral Wool Insulation Association, Inc.
211 East 51st Street
New York, NY 10022

MINIMUM DESIGN STANDARDS FOR HEAT LOSS CALCULATIONS

A concise and practical guide. Resistance values for common building materials are given, as are instructions for calculating heat transmission through a building section. Appendix 4, "Overall Heat Transmission Coefficients of Typical Wall, Ceiling and Floor Sections," eliminates the need to calculate the coefficient if the building section is identical to one of the many sketched. It also gives instructions for calculating the heat loss from an entire building.
—Gail Morrison

Minimum Design Standards for Heat Loss Calculations
1973; 66 pp
Free

from:
U.S. Dept. of Housing and Urban Development
451 Seventh Street SW
Washington, D.C. 20410

or your regional HUD office

U.S. DEPARTMENT OF HOUSING AND URBAN DEVELOPMENT

HUD has printed a good many pamphlets on housing. Four that pertain directly to energy use and conservation in architecture are available FREE from:

U.S. Department of Housing and Urban Development
Washington, D.C. 20410

Insulation: Where and How Much;
1950; 9 pp
    Basic information on insulation, cost, fuel saving, etc. Also information on degree days for many major cities across the U.S. and Canada.

The Thermal Value of Airspaces
1954; 32 pp
    Formulas and data for calculating heat loss and heat retention.

An Egyptian Evaporative Cooler
1963; 2 pp
    Natural air conditioning using evaporative coolers.

Physiological Objectives in Hot Weather Housing
1963; 79 pp
    Tables, charts, graphs and informative text on solar heat effect upon humans and buildings. Mostly but not entirely relevant to countries with warmer climates than found in the U.S. Good, solid factual material.

INSULATION MANUAL: HOMES AND APARTMENTS

Here's an excellent book on the whys and hows of insulation. Locations, amounts, and methods for installation are illustrated and explained, and the reference section includes enough information for you to figure out your home's heating and cooling needs.

Insulation Manual: Homes and Apartments
1971; 44 pp
$4.00

from:
NAHB Research Foundation, Inc.
P.O. Box 1627
Rockville, Maryland 20850

INSULATION

Further information on insulation may be obtained from the following sources.

Thermal Insulation BC15.13-WP-1/1 (1971; 16 pp), free from the Canadian Wood Council, 77 Metcalfe Street, Ottawa, Canada KIP 5L6.

Insulation for Heating (1969; 12 pp), Small Homes Council, University of Illinois Bulletin, Technical Note No. 3.

"Thermal Insulation in Building Construction," *Construction Review*, U.S. Department of Commerce, November, 1973.

Heat Losses from House Basements (1969; 4 pp), Housing Note No. 31, and *Space Heating and Energy Conservation* CBD142 (1971; 4 pp), from the National Research Council of Canada, Division of Building Research, Ottawa, Canada KIA OR6.

CUNNING USES OF SOURCES AND SINKS IN THE PURSUIT OF NATURAL AIR CONDITIONING
Phil Niles

Our immediate thermal environment is loosely suspended between the sun at 10,000°F and outer space at -460°F. We like it best when it is in a narrow band around 75°F. The temperatures of most environments are either too low (arctic) or too high (equatorial). Even in the mid-latitudes the daily and monthly rise and fall in temperature may be through too wide a range for optimum comfort.

The mid-latitudes, which are usually too cold in the winter and too hot in the summer, are most amenable to natural air conditioning methods. These methods involve judiciously tapping the available natural heat sources and sinks, so that a comfortable balance can be maintained between them as much of the time as possible. The difficulty is that desirable sources and sinks are usually 12 hours, and frequently 6 months, out of phase with our needs. Indeed, that is why we are uncomfortable in the first place.

A systematic examination of natural air conditioning methods, particularly those involving the heat capacity and thermal resistance of materials, leads naturally to one of the most elegant and effective solutions to the problem of low energy heating and cooling of buildings. We have been studying this system for over a year in a house at Atascadero, California.

All natural air conditioning methods, including the system at Atascadero, have to work with the fundamental elements of natural heat sources and heat sinks. For comfort purposes, a source can be loosely defined as something hotter than about 75°F—a source can be used to heat our houses. A sink would be lower than 75°F—a sink can be used to cool. Of course, a source is no good if we already are too hot, and a sink is no good is we are too cold. We must find ways to minimize undesirable sources and sinks and augment the desirable ones.

Excluding conventional heating and air conditioning systems (which are artificial sources and sinks using energy imported to the site), the principal sources and sinks are:

Air: source or sink, depending on its temperature.

Sun: always a source when shining.

Evaporation: usually provides a sink and can drop surfaces 20 or so degrees below air temperature, depending on humidity.

Sky and Outer Space: usually provides a sink and can drop surface temperatures 20 or so degrees below air temperature.

Terrestrial surfaces radiate a net amount of energy to colder bodies. The upward radiation from a 75°F building will travel until it hits a non-transparent barrier that absorbs the radiation. For thermal (infrared) radiation, this barrier is the water vapor in the sky. It takes a few thousand feet of atmosphere to contain enough water to be opaque to radiation, the average temperature of this water is the same as the atmosphere, and is usually 10° to 50°F below ground air temperature. This is why on clear nights objects facing the sky can become 20° or so colder than the air.

Suppose one lives in a climate of hot days and cold nights. One of the thermally worst buildings to live in would be a tin building with no insulation. The inside of the building would follow the temperature of its walls, and they would follow the balance between the temperatures of the sources and sinks they are exposed to. The air temperature is the predominate influence on the wall temperature, and without the sun or radiation to the sky, the walls would follow the air temperature. When the sun is shining the walls will be hotter than the air temperature because of the direct sun radiation to them. When the sun is down and it is dry enough, the walls may radiate to the sky, which drops their temperature below that of the air. The roof temperature would drop lower than the walls because of its better exposure to the sky. Thus, the interior temperature cycles from colder-than-air during the night to warmer-than-air during the afternoon.

In order to deal with fewer influences, pretend that the effect of the sun, sky and air are combined into one factor—a fictitious air temperature that accounts for all sources and sinks. It would be higher than the actual air temperature while the sun shines, and lower at night. This is the temperature that the interior of the tin building would follow. This fictitious temperature is a standard but little used concept called sol-air temperature.

Sol-air temperature is defined as that temperature the air would have if it alone were to have the same influence on a particular opaque surface as the normal environment does. Sol-air temperature depends on the surfaces considered, because their ability to absorb depends on such factors as color and material. The difference between sol-air and air temperature also depends on the solar radiation on the surface of the material, the dew point of the air, and the ability of the surface to radiate heat (emissivity), particularly to the night sky. On a clear day and night in the mid latitudes, a typical sol-air cycle might go from 30°F at night to 120°F in the day at the same time as the actual air temperature cycled between 40° and 90°, depending on local conditions.

In contrast to the tin building, consider what happens when a building made of heavy material, like adobe or concrete, is subjected to an environment with the same sol-air temperature cycle. In this case, the indoor temperature will still oscillate about the daily sol-air mean, but the oscillation is damped—it doesn't have as big a peak or as low a minimum. If the mean sol-air temperature during the day (the 24 hour average) happens to be near 75°F, then all one needs for a comfortable building is thick enough walls to damp out the extremes. This, of course, is why heavy weight buildings (made from adobe, sod, brick, stone, etc.) have always been built in climates where the mean sol-air temperature is near the comfort temperature.

What materials are best at damping the temperature swing? Both insulating ability (Btu/hr, leakage per degree temperature difference) and heat capacity (Btu's stored per °F rise in temperature) are important factors in material selection. These factors help damp out the temperature swing because the insulation retards the flow of heat into or out of the wall, while the heat that gets through is soaked up in heating the heavy wall material. Thus, the wall never manages to heat or cool as much as does the sol-air cycle. The most effective combination of wall materials is insulation on the outside and heavy material on the inside of the wall. This is a much more efficient damper than if the wall elements are reversed. (A noteworthy improvement in damping is possible in ordinary insulated frame construction by adding multiple layers of sheetrock on the interior wall.)

The trouble with this type of wall is that even though the outdoor oscillations are damped out, the resulting average isn't necessarily comfortable. The problem may have been solved during one part of the year, but the other half of the year the average is too hot or too cold. How do you boost or depress the sol-air mean? Many mid-latitude natural air conditioning methods specifically address themselves to this problem.

The method we have been testing at Atascadero is essentially the next step up from the concrete wall discussed above. In this test house the roof is the main damping element, and its mass is composed of water in eight inch deep water bags (with twice the heat capacity of the same thickness of concrete). It is insulated on the outside with 2'' of rigid polyurethane foam. The key feature of the roof is the ability to remove the insulation for part of the day to get a controlled blend of daily appearing sources and sinks. To emphasize the sun and de-emphasize the night sky radiation loss in winter, the insulation is removed during the day. After heating the water, the insulation is replaced to protect it from the cold air and sky. In this way it is possible to boost the average temperature above the sol-air mean. Since the water mass can spread the heat out over 24 hours or longer, it boosts the room temperature evenly in time.

During the coldest part of the winter, the intermittently insulated roof has been able to keep the average temperature of the test house near 68°F with an average outdoor temperature of 45° and with a mean sol-air temperature of about 52°. This was done without the use of any heat except as collected from the sun and normal occupancy loads.

To increase the heating ability of the system, the vinyl water bags are made with a double top skin which is blown up slightly to give a transparent insulating layer of air over the water. The bags can thus collect heat on rather cold days if the sun is shining. One winter morning while it was still overcast, the roof opened to collect sunlight when it was only 47°F outside.

Does the house stay warm? Since early February, 1974 when the solar collectors were finished, the family living there has never used the auxiliary electric heaters. There were times, especially following breakdowns, when the indoor temperature dropped to the low 60's and a less active family probably would have used the heaters.

The house is a more complex system than it first appears—any new system is. It works well thermally, but needs frequent attendence to its breakdowns. Although the controls and mechanical system are fairly unsophisticated, they aren't off-the-shelf items and they require a lot of planning, design, and tune-up. The system need not be automated, but it is convenient and important to the effectiveness of heat collection, especially on scattered cloudy days when the automated panels can open to snatch heat between passing clouds.

To make a house like this successful, it is extremely important to understand its energy flow under different environmental conditions. It doesn't do much good to plop a collector on a house that is full of thermal hemorrhages. The closer the house is to being comfortable without a mechanical collector system, the better it will operate with one. This means attention should be given to the traditional natural air conditioning methods of tree placement, heavy construction materials, minimum window area, double glazing, window and overhang solar collection techniques, ventilation, insulation and the like.

A few natural air-conditioning references:

1. How to Cool Your House, Sunset, Lane Books, Menlo Park, CA, 1961
2. Primitive Architecture and Climate, Fitch and Branch, Scientific American, December, 1960
3. Architecture and the Sun, an International Survey of Sun Protection Methods, Ernst Danz, Thames & Hudson Publishers, 1967.
4. Climate and Architecture, J. Aronin, Reinhold Publishing Co., 1953
5. Housing and Building in Hot-Humid and Hot-Dry Climates, Building Research Advisory Board, National Academy of Science, BRAB Report No. 5, 1952
6. Thermal Performance of Buildings, Van Straaten, American Elsevier Publishing Co., New York, 1967
7. Building Physics: Heat, N.S. Billington, Pergamon Press, 1967

ENVIRONMENTAL TECHNOLOGIES IN ARCHITECTURE

Planning before building is a must. This is certainly true for structural considerations—for load, materials, stress etc., but it is equally true for environmental considerations—for heating and cooling, lighting, sanitation and noise control. This book discusses the environmental considerations in a rigorous technical manner with numerous tables and graphs mostly taken from the ASHRAE Guide and Data Book 1961. It is aimed at the architect and engineer rather than the owner/builder though the latter may, with some study get something out of this text. Considerable time is spent with examples and the tables and graphs enable one to calculate heating requirements and heat loss, acoustic requirements, sanitation needs, lighting needs and designs, and electric power use, distribution and wiring. Only passing mention is made of "future" energy sources.

—T.G.

Environmental Technologies in Architecture
B. Y. Kinsey Jr., H. M. Sharp
1951, 1963; 788 pp
$17.95

from:
Prentice-Hall, Inc.
Box 500
Englewood Cliffs, N.J. 07632

or WHOLE EARTH TRUCK STORE

SHELTER AND SOCIETY

All too often for too many people, architecture suggests the monumental building, styled by an egotistic architect and financed by an owner too heavy of purse and too light of mind. *Shelter and Society* introduces us to a broad cross section of vernacular architecture—that which has grown up through generations of watchful and involved "non-professionals" trying to make their daily life more comfortable and rewarding. In pictures and in sociological and historical essays, the perspective is presented that leads us away from our own narrow, angular and technologically dependent building designs to ones which flow, use native materials and reflect the wisdom of generations of ancestors.

I particularly enjoyed the article on the Norwegian Laftehus, with its chronicle of the development of these beautiful, functional farm buildings.

—C.M.

Shelter and Society
Ed. by Paul Oliver
1969; 164 pp
$12.50

from:
Praeger Publishers, Inc.
P.O. Box 1323
Springfield, Massachusetts 01101

or WHOLE EARTH TRUCK STORE

A BUCKET OF OIL

If this book were selling for five dollars I would recommend it without hesitation. It's written by architects for architects about how to save a bucket of oil (how to save energy) in building. Most of the information given is general and there is easily as much preaching as there is hard data. It's an introduction to building big buildings with the natural environment in mind and low energy consumption high on the priorities list. It has information on the use of glass, shading, cooling, wind reflection and how codes often prohibit energy conserving architecture. It's worth a read through because it illustrates many of the design combinations which can save energy and points to codes as one of the main reasons we don't have more energy conserving buildings being built.

—T.G.

A Bucket of Oil
Caudill, Lawyer, Bullock
1974; 87 pp
$10.95

from:
Cahners Books
89 Franklin Street
Boston, Mass. 02110

or WHOLE EARTH TRUCK STORE

ARCHITECTURE WITHOUT ARCHITECTS

Originally published by the Museum of Modern Art, this book is subtitled "A Short Introduction to Non-Pedigreed Architecture." Rudofsky spent some 40 years traveling and collecting pictures of architectural styles in many lands. Here he gives us a hint of the variety of communal architecture he found in his studies. Towns carved from rock, towns below ground, fortified places, arcades, woven structures—these examples, and many others, are presented, expanding our concept of housing and living away from just rectilinear grids and production line components. A beautiful book of black and white photos to help your mind roll on.

—C.M.

Architecture Without Architects
Bernard Rudofsky
1964; 143 pp
$4.95

from:
Doubleday & Company, Inc.
501 Franklin Avenue
Garden City, NY 11530

or WHOLE EARTH TRUCK STORE

THE GENTLE ARCHITECT

Malcom Wells works in an underground office in New Jersey. He designed it himself to take advantage of the earth's nearly constant temperature and the reduced operating costs/maintenance problems associated with underground structures. He was one of the first "design professionals" to advocate sensible, low impact architecture.

Wells has developed a rating system to evaluate building designs in fifteen categories. Scores range from +1500 for a total ecologically sound structure to -1500 for an energy absorbing, pollution causing, noisy, wasteful building. Here's a sample rating form. Draw vertical bars on it to see how well the structure you call home rates.

Malcolm Wells   —C.M.
Box 183
Cherry Hill, New Jersey 08034

The Architect

	1 Creates purer air	2 Creates purer water	3 Uses rain water	4 Produces its own food	5 Creates richer soil	6 Uses solar energy	7 Stores solar energy	8 Creates silence	9 Consumes its own wastes	10 Maintains itself	11 Matches nature's pace	12 Provides wildlife habitat	13 Provides human habitat	14 Moderates climate & weather	15 Beautiful
+100 Completely															
+75 Mostly															
+50 Partly															
+25 Slightly															
0 Neither nor															
-25 Slightly															
-50 Partly															
-75 Mostly															
-100 Completely															
	Destroys pure air	Destroys pure water	Wastes rain water	Produces no food	Destroys rich soil	Wastes solar energy	Consumes fossil fuels	Destroys silence	Dumps its wastes unused	Needs repair & cleaning	Disregards nature's pace	Destroys wildlife habitat	Destroys human habitat	Intensifies climate & weather	Destroys beauty

Malcolm B. Wells 1969

INTEGRATED SYSTEMS

So far in the *Energy Primer* we have been talking about separate energy systems . . . solar, wind, water and biofuels. Unfortunately, no *single* source of energy is likely to supply all, or even most, of the power needs of a home, group or community. The supply of each of these natural energy sources is intermittent and at any one time energy demand is likely to exceed energy supply. Furthermore, each energy source comes in a different form which makes it suitable for different uses. Solar energy comes as heat. Wind and water energy provide mechanical power. Biofuels are forms of chemical energy that are generally more portable and versatile. But integration of these sources, combining and sharing their energy loads and waste products, creates the real possibility of providing reliable and economic power supplies under a variety of conditions.

Integrated energy systems can be defined as diverse energy sources combined with one another to provide continuous energy. Picture them as inter-dependent. They are integrated during the process of production: a methane plant may receive waste heat from a solar collector and the gas produced may be compressed with the energy from a wind generator.

The trouble is that very little is known about integrated systems which combine *renewable* energy sources. The classic papers of Golding outlined some of the problems of arid regions[1] and remote communities in Third World countries.[2] A few recent papers have described integrated systems as alternatives in developed countries[3-7], and a few groups and research institutes in the U.S. and elsewhere have begun experimenting with a variety of combined energy resources.[8-16] But there is really little information about the economics, reliability, mechanics, or practicality of integrated solar, water, wind and biofuel operations.

PRACTICAL SMALL-SCALE RENEWABLE ENERGY SYSTEMS

What kind of renewable energy systems are really practical enough to deal with here and now? Table I lists what we believe to be technologies and processes that are available today and not totally out of economic reach, bogged down by laws, grossly inefficient or still on the drawing boards. Admittedly, clever minds or money can create more options. But for our purposes here we will limit our discussion to the "practical" sources listed in Table I and their relative conversion efficiencies in Table II. Table I cannot stand by itself as the final word. The discussions in the previous sections of the *Energy Primer* about these sources and their applications must be analyzed for this table to be meaningful in terms of specific situations.

BASIC ENERGY CONVERSIONS

The first thing to consider is how the five basic forms of energy interact with one another with respect to the "practical" systems outlined in Table I (see Fig. 1). When one form of energy is converted into another there is a loss (in the form of heat) of useable work that accompanies the conversion. For example, as explained in the *Biomass* section, the conversion of solar energy into chemical (plant) energy is only about 1-2% efficient, whereas the conversion of solar energy into useable heat energy is about 40-60% efficient. The important point here is that the more conversions there are between the forms of energy, the less efficient and (usually) the more costly the process will be.

There are exceptions to this rule. For example: in most cases it is more efficient to pump water with a wind generator than a windmill. A wind generator pumping water without batteries will go through two conversions: mechanical to electrical and electrical to mechanical (pump). The entire process will be about .40 x .90 = .36% efficient (Table II). On the other hand a windmill pumping water, which goes through one less conversion than a wind generator, is only about 30% efficient.

The reverse is also true; in some cases, depending on local conditions it is more practical to use less efficient systems to generate needed energy. For example, imagine a site with lots of wind and very little sun (like many

coastal climates). Probably the best way to get hot water under these conditions would be to go through the extra conversion and heat water with a wind generator (40% efficient), rather than rely on a slightly more efficient but less practical solar collector.

SOURCE	DEVICE	PRACTICAL USE	IMPRACTICAL USE
SOLAR	Collector	Space heat Water heater	Heat pump
	Greenhouse	Food production	
	Dryer	Food drying	
	Concentrator	Cooking	
	Photovoltaic cell		Electricity
	Steam boiler		Electricity
WATER (where available)	Water turbine	Electricity	Air compression Electrolytic (H$_2$) Fuel cell
	Water wheel	Mechanical power Air compression D.C. electricity Heat pump	Flywheels A.C. electricity
	Hydraulic ram	Pumped water	
WIND	Generator	Electricity	Air compression Electrolytic cell (H$_2$) Fuel cells
	Windmill	Water pump Mechanical power Air compressor Heat pump	Flywheels
BIOFUELS	Photosynthesis	Food	
	Food and feed	Sustenance	
	Organic waste (methane)	Combustible fuel	Mobile engine
	Wood	Heat	Wood gas Methanol
	Biomass		Ethanol Electricity
	Compost	Heat Fertilizer	

TABLE I   PRACTICAL AND IMPRACTICAL CONVERSION AND STORAGE USES. (AS OF LATE 1974)

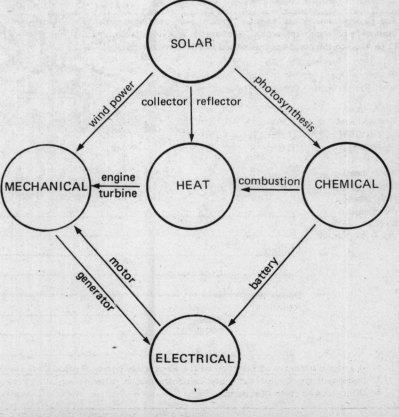

FIG. 1 DIRECT ENERGY CONVERSIONS

MECHANICAL	Wind Generator 40% Water Turbine 68-93% Steam Power Plant 40% Electric Motor 90%	ELECTRICAL
MECHANICAL	Flat Collector 40-60% Waterwheel 70-85%	MECHANICAL
SOLAR	Flat Collector 40-60% Concentrator 80-90%	THERMAL (Heat)
SOLAR	Photosynthesis 1-2%	CHEMICAL
CHEMICAL	Wood Combustion Burner 85% maximum Oil Furnace 65%	THERMAL (Heat)
CHEMICAL	Battery 80% (Storage)	ELECTRICAL
HEAT	Engine 25-36% Turbine 35-45%	MECHANICAL
CHEMICAL	Methane Digester 40-60%	CHEMICAL
ELECTRICAL	Resistance heating 99%	THERMAL

TABLE II ENERGY CONVERSION OF PRACTICAL SYSTEMS - Maximum Efficiency.

ASSESSING ENERGY NEEDS

If we are to build workable integrated energy systems we must carefully and accurately assess our energy needs (see page 83). As we pointed out in the introduction to this book it makes little sense to gear renewable energy systems to meet current high energy demands. The first step in assessing your needs is *energy conservation.* Make the distinction between your necessities and your luxuries. This does not mean that we must live in a primitive or totally austere way. It means that in measuring our needs we must first conserve what we have and then gear our needs to our resources . . . not the other way around. We cannot apply renewable energy systems to fill present high energy demands and think that we are doing anything about the environment in which we live.

Table III illustrates the energy source which may be applied to each major type of energy need. It should be obvious from looking at the table that the use of any one energy source will not produce sufficient power to meet all energy demands, but that an integrated system has the potential to do so.

MEASURING LOCAL ENERGY SOURCES

We can get a better idea of the availability of energy supplied by actually measuring our endemic resources. Gathering this information by calculating the available solar incidence, wind velocity, water head and flow, and organic fuels makes it easy to see the possibilities for integration of these sources. The following list gives the page numbers on which measurement data and methods may be found for each energy source discussed in previous sections.

Wind
velocity 75, 76, 77-79, 88, 90
generator 75, 76, 77, 80, 81, 85,
. 93-94
Biofuels
methane 144-147
wood 156, 159, 160, 162

Solar
insulation 17-23, 25-26, 29, 31
collector 22-23
Water
head 52-57
flow 52, 57, 67, 70
power 52, 55, 60, 61, 62, 65

STORAGE SYSTEMS

Inherent in any energy system with intermittent power sources is the

	STORAGE MEDIUM	STORAGE EFFICIENCY (%)	MAJOR LOSS CHARAC-TERISTICS	*RELATIVE COST	*DEGREE OF MECHANICAL COMPLEXITY
SOLAR (heat)	Water	75-90	Leaks (thermal & physical)	2	1
	Air	0	Leaks (thermal)	1	1
	Earth	-	Leaks (thermal)	1	1
	Rock	60-80	Leaks (thermal)	2	2
	Salt hydrates	75-95	Material breakdown	3	3
WIND/WATER (Mechanical)	Pumped water	50-70	Evaporation Friction	1	2
	Compressed air (Compressor)	40-50	Leaks Friction	2	2
WIND/WATER (electric)	Battery	70-85	Internal discharge	3	3
WOOD	Open air or shed		Loss — weathering; pests Gain — drying; seasoning	1	1
METHANE	Tank			1	2
	Tank (compressed)	50-60		3	3
ALCOHOL	Tank		Leaks Evaporation	1	1

* 1. Negligible
2. Intermediate
3. Considerable

TABLE IV RENEWABLE ENERGY STORAGE

Energy requirements are listed by "time of day" use. Renewable energy sources are used to fulfill each requirement. The sources are ranked according to desirability (1 to 4) given the conditions described in the "assumptions."

ASSUMPTIONS:
SOLAR (high solar incidence)
WIND (substantial and continuous)
WATER (sufficient for mechanical power, not electrical)
METHANE (small amount of organic waste sufficient for minimal gas production)
WOOD (poorly managed two acre woodlot)

RANDOM (DAY OR NIGHT)	DAY (NO PRECISE TIME)	DAY (PRECISE TIME)	NIGHT (PRECISE TIME)	SOLAR	WIND MECH.	WIND ELECT.	WATER MECH.	WATER ELECT.	METHANE	WOOD
Water heating				1		2			3	4*
Space heating				1	2■	3	2■			2
Refrigeration				1						
Appliances				1						
Media				1						
Water distillation				1		2				
	Lighting			1		2				
			Lighting			1				
		Cooking		1		4			2	3
			Cooking	2		4			1	3
	Domestic Industries +					1	2			
		Water pumping		1		2	1			

KEY:
* If water is heated in conjunction with a wood space heater or wood cook stove this becomes more desirable.
+ Stationary agricultural machinery; carpentry shop or other. Small or large scale.
■ When hooked up to heat pump.

TABLE III   MATCHING RENEWABLE ENERGY SOURCES TO ENERGY REQUIREMENTS

need for various storage devices to hold the energy received until it can be used whenever needed. Again the question of practicality comes up. Table IV attempts to put in perspective the practical and proven storage devices.

ECONOMIES OF SCALE

Renewable energy systems cost money. . . to build or buy. In some cases (e.g., water turbines and wind generators) the cost of technology is beyond the means of the average person. In most cases it is cheaper to develop renewable energy systems when the cost is spread over a large number of people. Economists refer to this as an economy of scale.

For example, imagine a wind system supplying 1 kw/per person. A 2 kw Quirk's with inverter costs about $9,000 installed or $4,500 per person for two people (1974). A 70kw NOAH rotar wind generator costs about $45,000 (1974) or about $642 per person, for 70 people. Another example: the solar space heating costs (60% of the heat) of a 1000 ft² house (for 2 people) is about $2500. A small community of 45 houses buying similar equipment to solar-heat their individual houses would receive a standard price break of about 25% or a savings of $625 per house. These are economies of scale. Notice that the solar collectors are used in terms of the individual living units whereas the wind generator (and presumably digesters, turbines, greenhouses etc.) are more efficiently used on a cooperative basis.

However there need to be some qualifications. Most economies of scale are based on the availability of cheap fossil fuels. To use fossil fuels economically, large generation and distribution facilities are necessary. As these operations become larger, this leads to a dis-economy of scale in which sheer size and complexity begin to create hidden costs. Although there is very little information about it, the same can be said for renewable energy systems. The difference is that fossil fuels require centralized economies and centralized politics and both seem undesirable. As our graph below suggests, small-scale renewable sources have small-scale economies. Fossil fuels can't be "used" on a small scale. Renewable energy resources can.

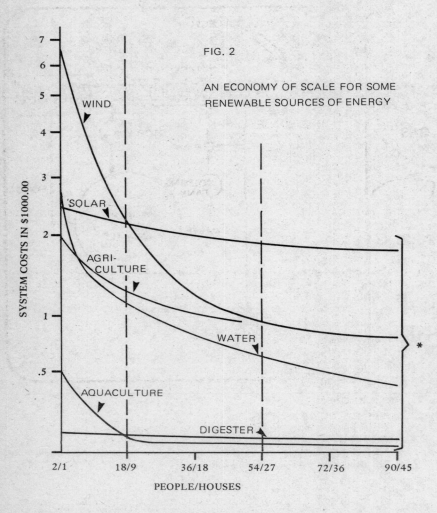

FIG. 2

AN ECONOMY OF SCALE FOR SOME RENEWABLE SOURCES OF ENERGY

ASSUMPTIONS:

1. Wind or water (electricity): 2KW/2 people; 10 mph wind or equivalent head and flow of water; system has 20 year life. Source: T.W.
2. Solar heat: 2 people/1000 ft² house; 60% space heating; below 40° latitude; 20 year life. Sources: Löf and Tybout in **Solar Energy**, (vol. 14:253), Zomeworks, and Ecology Action/ Palo Alto.
3. Digester (gas): 15 ft³/person/day; available organic matter; cooking only; 5 year life. Sources: Ram Bux Singh, Spirogester Co., Lakeside Engineering Corporation, 222 W. Adams St., Chicago 6, Illinois 90606, and Maximum Potential Building Systems.
4. Aquaculture (food): 70 grams of animal protein per day/person; 10 year life; see page 133. Sources: Solar Aquafarms and New Alchemy Institute.
5. Agriculture (food): .5 acre of land; standard U.S. diet; sufficient tools, water, seeds, etc.; vegetarian diet (vegetables, grains, herbs, fruits); intensive garden farming. Sources: Ecology Action/ Palo Alto and New Alchemy West.

Within the ranges we looked at, there was an economy of scale, i.e., the more people that were involved in an integrated renewable energy community, the cheaper it was per person. Obviously this has limitations, and it should not be inferred that "the more people the better." Quite the contrary. At some point the pressures of population and the inefficiencies of large energy devices begin to reverse the trend. The major point suggested by the figure is that somewhere between 20 and 60 people the price per person of the separate systems begins to level off suggesting that perhaps after all a tribe or a small community is the most efficient group level. THIS FIGURE IS A FIRST APPROXIMATION ONLY.

References cited:

[1]Golding, E.W. and M.S. Thacker. 1956. THE UTILIZATION OF WIND, SOLAR RADIATION AND OTHER LOCAL ENERGY RESOURCES FOR THE DEVELOPMENT OF A COMMUNITY IN AN ARID OR SEMI-DESERT AREA. Proceedings of the New Delhi Symposium on Wind and Solar Energy, New Delhi.

[2]Golding, E.W. 1958. THE COMBINATION OF LOCAL SOURCES OF ENERGY FOR ISOLATED COMMUNITIES. Solar Energy Journal, 11(1): 7-12.

[3]Clarke, R. 1973. TECHNOLOGY FOR AN ALTERNATIVE SOCIETY. New Scientist, 11 Jan., 1973.

[4]Merriam, M. 1972. DECENTRALIZED POWER SOURCES FOR DEVELOPING COUNTRIES. International Development Society, International Development Review, 14(4): 13-18.

[5]Thring, J.B. and G.E. Smith. 1974. INTEGRATED POWER, WATER, WASTE AND NUTRIENT SYSTEM. Working Paper, Technical Research Division, Dept. of Architecture, Univ. Cambridge, England.

[6]Weintraub, R. and D. Marier. 1974. LOCAL ENERGY PRODUCTION FOR RURAL HOMESTEADS AND COMMUNITIES. In: "Radical Agriculture." R. Merrill (ed.). Harper and Row. (In Press).

[7]Marier, D., R. Weintraub and S. Eccli. 1974. COMBINING ALTERNATIVE ENERGY SYSTEMS. In: "Producing Your Own Power." Rodale Press, Emmaus, Pa. Revised and abridged from reference 6 above.

[8]NEW ALCHEMY INSTITUTE. 1974. Journal of the New Alchemists. No. 2. Box 432, Woods Hole, Mass. 02543. See also pages 133-135 and 181 of PRIMER.

[9]Blazej, R. et al. 1973. PLANS FOR GRASSY BROOK VILLAGE . . .A PROSPECTUS. RFD 1, Newfane, Vt. 05345.

[10]INTEGRATED LIVING SYSTEMS. See pages 181 and 189 in PRIMER.

[11]CENTER FOR MAXIMUM POTENTIAL BUILDING SYSTEMS. Austin, Texas. See pages 100, 144, 181, 192 in PRIMER.

[12]Hughes, F.P. 1973. THE ECO-HOUSE. Mother Earth News, Vol. 20, March 1973. Description of the autonomous house being built in England by Graham Caine.

[13]Vale, R.J. 1974. SERVICES FOR AN AUTONOMOUS RESEARCH COMMUNITY IN WALES. Working Paper, 5, Technical Research Division, Cambridge University, (Dept. Architecture).

[14]Golueke, C.G. and W.J. Oswald. 1973. AN ALGAL REGENERATIVE SYSTEM FOR SINGLE-FAMILY FARMS AND VILLAGES. Compost Science 14(3).

[15]THE ECOL PROJECT, Minimum Cost Housing Project, McGill University, Montreal, Canada.

[16]Davis, A.J. and R.P. Shubert. 1974. ALTERNATIVE NATURAL ENERGY SOURCES IN BUILDING DESIGN. College of Architecture, Virginia Polytechnic Institute, Blacksburg, Va. Last section of the book describes several working or proposed autonomous housing units using integrated energy systems.

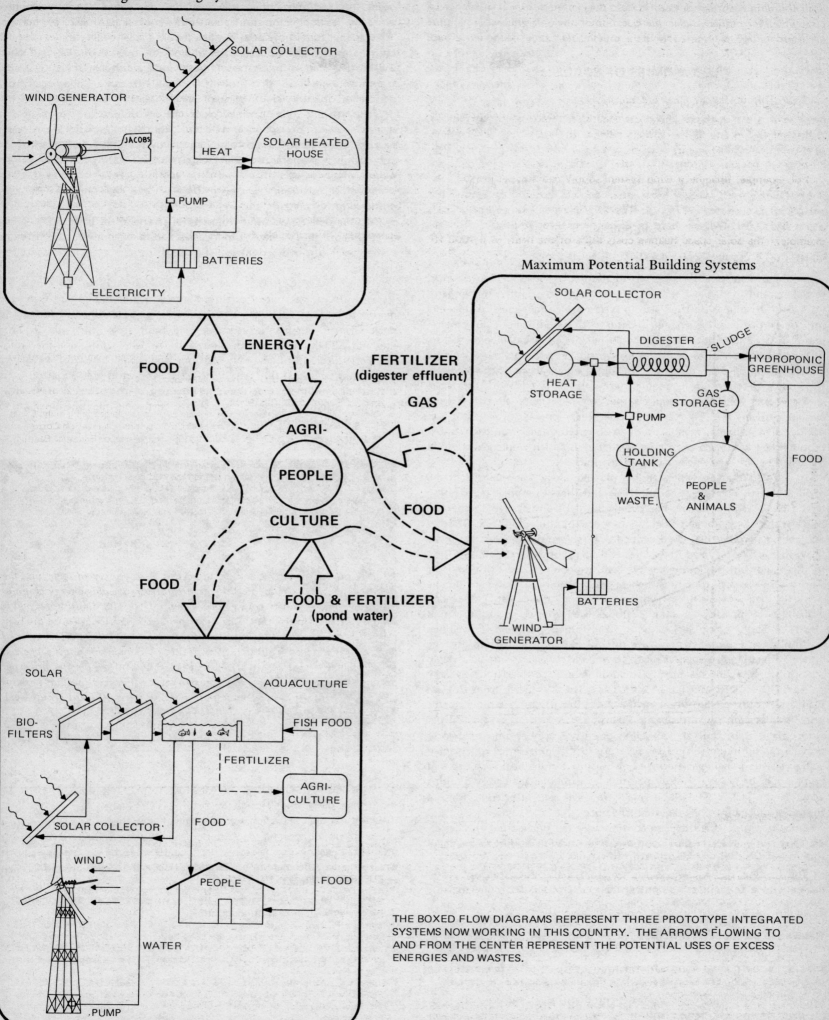

Integrated Living Systems

WIND GENERATOR

JACOBS

SOLAR COLLECTOR

HEAT

SOLAR HEATED HOUSE

PUMP

BATTERIES

ELECTRICITY

Maximum Potential Building Systems

SOLAR COLLECTOR

DIGESTER

SLUDGE

HYDROPONIC GREENHOUSE

HEAT STORAGE

GAS STORAGE

PUMP

FOOD

HOLDING TANK

PEOPLE & ANIMALS

WASTE

BATTERIES

WIND GENERATOR

ENERGY

FOOD

FERTILIZER (digester effluent)

GAS

AGRI-

PEOPLE

CULTURE

FOOD

FOOD

FOOD & FERTILIZER (pond water)

SOLAR

AQUACULTURE

BIO-FILTERS

FISH FOOD

FERTILIZER

AGRI-CULTURE

SOLAR COLLECTOR

FOOD

WIND

PEOPLE

FOOD

WATER

PUMP

New Alchemy Institute

THE BOXED FLOW DIAGRAMS REPRESENT THREE PROTOTYPE INTEGRATED SYSTEMS NOW WORKING IN THIS COUNTRY. THE ARROWS FLOWING TO AND FROM THE CENTER REPRESENT THE POTENTIAL USES OF EXCESS ENERGIES AND WASTES.

The following article by Ken Smith (now with Ecotope in Washington) describes the evolution of a methane system and its gradual integration with other forms of renewable energy. Max's Pot is one of the few groups we know of that has been struggling with an integrated system from the beginning. At each step along the way something was learned about the practicality and demands of methane, solar and wind energy supplies, and some of the experiences are shared here.

Max's Pot has plans available for their integrated bio-gas plant which is described in the Reviews of the methane section. Also see page 192 of Integrated Systems.

MAX'S METHANE: DESIGN AND INTEGRATION

by

Ken Smith

Our approach to methane digesters was an attempt to synthesize many of the things that were being said about alternative energy, self-sufficiency, recycling, and humanized forms of technology. In addition to the hardware considerations, we tried also to synthesize certain social parameters into our prototype. We wanted a design that would benefit not an elite group of dropouts, but one that could be applied in low-income sectors of our society as well as in the "Third World". It was a basic feeling from the beginning of the project that it should benefit those who would feel the greatest effects in economic terms from a crisis of shortages.

The basic philosophy required that we seek materials which were available to anyone. To carry this philosophy one step further, it was decided that a list of available products and performance standards should be published with each prototype so that each design would be carefully evaluated before receiving widespread distribution.

It was felt that an understanding of technology was essential in the application of low-impact technologies and that widespread application would only result from the combined use of readily available materials, "off-the-shelf" equipment and simple construction methods. Readily available materials could be described as simple nuts-and-bolts hardware as well as easily recycled items like used 55-gallon steel drums. "Off-the-shelf" equipment are more complicated items such as hand pumps or marine (low water) toilets, and these items would be evaluated on the basis of their environmental impact as well as their cost and general availability. Simple construction methods were considered as those that could be easily assembled without special machine work or welding.

With these criteria in mind, we set out to build our first prototype system, integrating a methane gas generating sewage treatment system and a water recycling system into an autonomously serviced house system.

VERTICAL DRUM BIO-GAS PLANT: The "Vertical Drum Bio-Gas Plant" was our first prototype methane digester. Its three basic elements were a 55-gallon steel drum, a 20-gallon steel drum, and a 32- gal. Rubbermaid trash can. The 55-gallon drum was used as a heat jacket to provide the optimum (95° F) temperature to the inner drum which acted as the digestion chamber. Recycled oil was used in the heat jacket so that there would be no worry of evaporation, as would be the case with using water in the jacket. The Rubbermaid trash can was inverted to capture the gas produced from the digestion chamber.

Since it was designed to be a continuously fed (loaded daily) digester, we used two-inch water pipe to transport the new manure into the digestion chamber and to remove the effluent fertilizer.

The heating element was a burner from a discarded gas hot water heater with a thermostat to control the temperature. We found that the thermostat was unnecessary since the pilot flame provided enough heat. Our intention was to use the methane to sustain the temperature. Propane was used to get the first batch going.

A mixture of chicken manure, kitchen vegetable material and water was used in proportions of one part water to one part solid materials. The first gas was observed five days after initial loading (mostly CO_2).

From the initial load, the prototype produced approximately 30 ft^3 of gas over a four-week period, and this gas was burned in a Bunsen burner for demonstration.

We decided that the vertical drum design was inadequate and that a larger digester was necessary to provide even the simplest of cooking needs. We had approached the design of the size of plant in a rather assuming fashion without first collecting enough technical information. The gas that could have been produced from the vertical drum would have been barely enough to sustain its own heat requirements. We had made the mistake that so many people have made about the energy available from manure. We had first thought it possible to run a Volkswagen from a 55-gallon drum digester in place of the rear seat!

Talk of cars running on chicken manure or drawings of basement digesters which provide not only fuel for the automobile but space heating for the home have perpetuated the myth that we can get something for nothing, or more out than we put in. *We cannot, as many people believe, easily replace fossil fuel with alternative energy sources without some rather significant changes in life-style and consumption.* This was the lesson from our first prototype.

The one defense we offer to justify this experiment is its aid in giving us confidence that we could produce gas, and the incentive to improve our system so that it could meet realistic needs for an autonomously serviced dwelling.

WATER RECYCLING — AN INTEGRATED APPROACH: While the Vertical Drum was under construction we acquired two low-water-use marine toilets and began the installation of a garbage disposal which could recycle water. Our first toilet was a hand pump style which was acquired used for $30.00. The second toilet, with its electric flush and macerator (grinder), disposed of material with one and a half quarts of water in a single, two-second, 1,000-watt WHOOSH! Known as the Supertoilet, its cost is eleven times what the hand pumped machine had cost us. The feeling in offering this option was that some people might be unwilling to use a hand-pumped version.

HORIZONTAL DRUM BIO-GAS PLANT: In the summer of 1973, we set forth to design the "Horizontal Drum Bio-Gas Plant".

Using national statistics, we determined that the daily per capita gas consumption for cooking was 7.5 cu. ft. Next we determined that a digester of three 55-gallon drums would produce 15 to 18 cu. ft. of gas daily. It was to be fed the manure of 35 chickens and the excretion and kitchen wastes of two humans.

The following calculations for the 15-18 ft^3 of gas are derived directly from the New Alchemist publication.

(2) human:	.6 lb. V.S. x 5 ft³ =	3.0 ft³ daily
(35) chicken:	2.1 lb. V.S. x 5 ft³ =	10.5 ft³ daily
(2) kitchen:	2.0 lb. V.S. x 3 ft³ =	6.0 ft³ daily
	Total gas available	19.5 ft³ daily

With these numbers we developed the preliminary design for the "Horizontal Drum Bio-Gas Plant."

The Digester Unit: The basic plan was to connect three 55-gallon drums together lying on their sides so as to form a long tube. This arrangement constitutes a displacement style digester as opposed to the vertical style digester we had built previously. The main advantage to the displacement style digester is that the greater surface area is less susceptible to clogging from scum formation, which retards or stops the production of gas.

To connect the 55-gallon drums together, we decided to use recycled automobile inner tubes rather than welding. This was accomplished by first slitting the tubes down the middle of the outside circumference. The slit tubes then acted as short pieces of rubber hose that were clamped between drums by using the bolt down, locking rings used to secure the removable tops on some 55-gallon drums.

In order to conserve heat, we decided to bury the entire unit. To have the earth act as insulation rather than a heat sink, we placed sticks of polyurethane foam around the digester barrels. The one drawback to burying a digester in this fashion is that it is very difficult, if not impossible, to clean out; we advise against it.

The digester unit was buried and covered with approximately six inches of soil. The existing two-inch bungs in the drum were used to input the organic matter and release the effluent (fertilizer). A marine, hand operated bilge pump was connected in line to pump the material.

INTEGRATING A SOLAR COLLECTOR: Since small digesters hardly produce enough gas to provide their own heat requirements, we decided to use a solar water heating unit to provide the desired temperature for the new digester.

To best use the hot water from the solar water heater, we used 50 feet of coiled copper tubing. The heat coil is a much more efficient heating system than the heat jacket used in our previous digester. In a heating coil system all of the heat is absorbed by the slurry. In a heat jacket system only one surface gives heat to the digester while the other is exposed to losses, requiring insulation.

The 50 feet of coil is approximately twice as much as is necessary. We found that 1 ft^2 of coil surface was enough for each 100 ft^3 of digester capacity. Using 50 feet of 5/8 inch diameter coil gave a surface area of 0.68 ft^2. Three 55-gallon drums equal 29 cu. ft. of digester area; therefore, we used twice the needed length of copper coil — another case of intuitive rather than calculated consideration.

Hot water was circulated from the solar flat plate collector unit into a storage tank and then to the coil in the digester unit. The storage tank, a recycled 30-gallon gas water heater, was also used as an auxiliary heating unit during overcast periods.

Water was circulated around in the system by an 18 watt (12VDC @ 1.5 amps) Teel pump available in the marine industry for less than $20.00. The electrical power to run the pump was provided by a 200 watt "antique" Zenith "Wincharger" wind generator.

The Solar Heating Unit: Our design calls for two solar heating units (60 ft^2). The collectors are insulated 4'x8' boxes covered with five-year greenhouse vinyl. The internal collection plates consist of 3/4 inch galvanized water pipes sandwiched between two sheets of corrugated aluminum roofing material. The roofing material is pop-riveted together to form a tight contact with the pipe. The piping is a parallel system. The major drawback was the expense of the unions (1/3 the cost). The total cost of the 180 ft^2 was about $300.00 (1972) or approximately $1.70/ft^2.

Unions were made from radiator hoses and stainless steel hose clamps. We used a double glazing to cover the insulated box: a layer of five-year greenhouse vinyl topped with 1/16 inch (single strength) window glass. We learned that this glass and plastic would result in good insulation with better heat retention within the collector than with a double layer of glass.

We have been pleased with the performance of the single collector (30 ft^2) which has been observed to give about 3,000 BTUH during the sunniest part of a spring day. The circulating temperature is rather low with an exit temperature from the collector of about 106° F. This is, however, sufficient to raise the digester temperature from 75° F to 90° to 95° F.

GAS STORAGE: The gas storage system consists of a H_2S and CO_2 scrubbing device, a bicycle-powered refrigeration compressor, and a 100-gallon, 100 psi pressure vessel which is capable of storing about 96 ft^3 at a pressure of 100 psi. Regular air compressors are not well designed and have a tendency to leak compression into the crankcase area of the compressor, whereas refrigeration equipment is designed to run with closed cycle refrigerants and cannot afford such leakage. For high pressure storage there are surplus, multi-stage compressors used in aircraft applications. These are available from surplus outlets such as Airborne Sales, Palley and Master Mechanics. The name of the compressor is Cornelius, and it costs under $100.00. These compressors are capable of 2,000 psi and operate on 12 or 24 VDC.

FUTURE PLANS, INTEGRATED DIGESTER SYSTEM: At the present, Max's Pot is making plans for a complete digester system using holding tanks for different kinds of wastes, a 2-drum digester, solar collector, wind generator and a hydroponic vegetable garden for receiving sludge. See page 144 of the *Primer* for more discussion.

ENERGY AND SOCIETY

This work traces man's use of energy, from readily available but low-yield sources . . . to more complicated but high-yield forms . . . The thesis is that the amounts and types of energy employed condition man's way of life materially, and set somewhat predictable limits on what he can do and on how society will be organized.

With that, Cottrell set out on an elegant description of history as moved by the energy sources people have used. His chapter "The Industrialization of Agriculture" was one of the first convincing analyses showing modern agriculture to be an energy sink rather than an energy producer. By using energy as the common denominator for history, Cottrell succeeded in predicting 20 years ago most of today's dilemmas.

—R.M.

Energy and Society
William F. Cottrell
1955; 330 pp

$13.00

from:
Greenwood Press Publishers
51 Riverside Avenue
Westport. Connecticut 06880
or WHOLE EARTH TRUCK STORE

ENERGY FOR SURVIVAL

Wilson Clark has done a superb job of assembling up-to-date energy information and using it to tell a comprehensive story on a largely non-technical level. Many readers will feel the main value of the book lies in its conservationist-ecologist views of energy use and development. It is also an extensive information source, as well as a guide to sources. About one thousand references are given. The book covers the history, sociology, politics, and corporate structure of energy and its use, as well as technical and environmental aspects.

This book is a major contribution to what ought to be a raging national debate over prevailing attitudes and responses to the coming energy and materials shortages and the fall-out of pollution from our high-consumption life style. One of the really outstanding sections of this book is "Electricity from Nuclear Fission." After reading Clark's massively documented account, I don't see how anyone could feel present government-industry safeguards protect us from a radio-active future.

Wilson Clark is not strong on quantitative analysis. Numerical data is frequently presented, but seldom used to derive quantitative conclusions, though such conclusions by others are quoted. The real value of Clark's evaluations lies as often in the questions he raises in his conclusions.

This book is a veritable who's-who and what's-what of "new" energy technology. Fossil-fuel and energy conversion processes are extremely well covered, and a better guide to developments in solar and wind energy probably doesn't exist.

The book is well worth its price for this alone.
—Roger Douglass

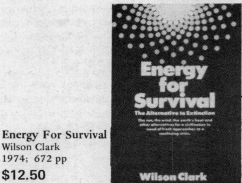

Energy For Survival
Wilson Clark
1974; 672 pp

$12.50

from:
Doubleday & Co., Inc.
501 Franklin Avenue
Garden City, NY 11530
(Paperback version due August 1975)

or WHOLE EARTH TRUCK STORE

ENERGY

Steve Baer turned us on to this book. His comments were "beautifully clear, concise, with a broad view—gives you the intellectual tools to forage through the energy wilderness."

With all the talk about "energy crisis" these days, few of us have a good theoretical understanding of what it's all about. Most of us equate an "energy crisis" with long lines at the gas station, but do we know the finer points of the subject? What's the difference between potential and kinetic energy? What relation does heat, radiation and electricity have to the concept of energy? What are the basic mathematical formulas and units we use when discussing energy? The author, a Harvard professor when this book was written, takes us through the complexities of this broad subject as only a master of the subject can—simply, clearly and directly.

If you were sorry you never took an introductory physics/chemistry/mechanics course, or you bombed the one you did take, read this book. I think you will find its clearly stated perspective enjoyable and rewarding.
—C.M.

Energy
Bruce Chalmers
1963; 289 pp

$9.25

from:
Academic Press
111 Fifth Avenue
New York, NY 10003

or WHOLE EARTH TRUCK STORE

SMALL IS BEAUTIFUL

As a Quasi-economist, and a rather troubled one, I have searched a dozen years for a "leading" economist willing to discuss some plain, present questions that arise under the label of "people's economics."

In this search, I characteristically ask the candidate mentors I meet "What is it you can

say or do to be helpful to that sub-culture of reformers who are willing, working and positive—and who are interested in some specifics, starting if possible next Thursday morning."

Needless to say, the answer I usually receive has something to do with the year 2000, or after a new political system is achieved, or when the population is converted to a condition rather resembling sainthood.

E. F. Schumacher appears to be an exception. He knows how to rise above 20 year projections, statistics and theories (which he doesn't avoid, however) to deal with "intermediate technology," "Buddhist economics," and village development, for examples.

His analytical style displays his training as a Rhodes Scholar and his experience as advisor to the British Control Commission in postwar Germany, and his twenty years of service as the top economist at the British Coal Board. But his snappy conclusions and recommendations connect plainly to his career as president of Britain's oldest organic farming organization, and as sponsor of the Fourth World Movement (for political decentralization), and as director of the renowned worker-controlled Scott Baler Company.

In his book he pops a number of dust-covered balloons. For example, he pricks the illusion that the poor will someday share the bounties of the rich, and quotes Gandhi: "Earth provides enough to satisfy every man's need, but not for every man's greed."

His discussion of labor as a "noble pursuit" is as poetic as it is radical and worth considerable mulling, especially in terms of "right livelihood," which is a Buddhist term that Schumacher incorporated comfortably into his economic analysis. He sees deep and personal value in work, not just "characterless cost to be reduced to a minimum."

In this age when old-time economists have nothing to say to straighten up the world's mess, Schumacher sounds serene and sane to us who live in the cracks of this weird dinosaur establishment.

—Richard Raymond

We shrink back from the truth if we believe that the destructive forces of the modern world can be "brought under control" simply by mobilizing more resources—of wealth, education, and research—to fight pollution, to preserve wildlife, to discover new sources of energy, and to arrive at more effective agreements on peaceful coexistence. Needless to say, wealth, education, research, and many other things are needed for any civilization, but what is most needed today is a revision of the ends which these means are meant to serve. And this implies, above all else, the development of a life-style which accords to material things their proper, legitimate place, which is secondary and not primary.

Small is Beautiful
Economics as if People Mattered
E. F. Schumacher,
1973; 290 pp

$3.75

from:
Harper & Row
10 East 53rd Street
New York, NY 10022

or WHOLE EARTH TRUCK STORE

ENVIRONMENT, POWER, AND SOCIETY

In recent years studies of the energetics of ecological systems have suggested general means for applying basic laws of energy and matter to the complex systems of nature and man. In this book, energy language is used to consider the pressing problem of survival in our time...the partnership of man in nature nature. An effort is made to show that energy analysis can help answer many of the questions of economics, law and religion, already stated in other languages.

This book bent my mind the first time I read it. It is difficult to sum up swiftly, but you might think of it as an energy I Ching. The book is packed with unique energy flow diagrams, tables of energy data and flashes of inspirational prose. With further readings, however, you get the idea that Odum tends to stretch the analogy between physical and biological systems a bit too much, and we are left with life forces being managed like machines and reduced to little more than kilocalories:

Read Cottrel first and then read this...carefully.

P.S. Odum has also written two papers that are perhaps the most concise examination of the global energy situation to date. 1) *Energy, Ecology and Economics* (written for the Royal Swedish Academy of Sciences), and 2) *More Perspectives on World Energy Relationships.* Both are reprinted in *The Mother Earth News* No. 27 and the *Whole Earth Epilog.*

— R.M.

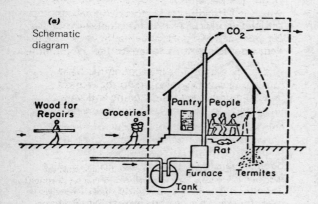

(a) Schematic diagram

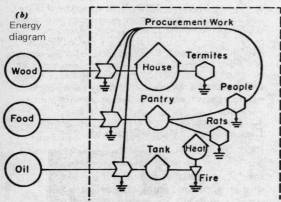

(b) Energy diagram

Power circuit diagram for a human habitation showing three outside energy sources, work by people, and steady-state maintenance of population and the structures of furnace and house.

Environment, Power, and Society
Howard T. Odum
1971; 331 pp

$6.95

from:
John Wiley and Sons, Inc.
One Wiley Drive
Somerset, New Jersey 08873

or WHOLE EARTH TRUCK STORE

SCIENCE AND TECHNOLOGY IN A DECENTRALIZED SOCIETY

Ever since Goldwin's *Political Justice* the idea of a decentralized society has rubbed like grit against the traditional centralist thinking of Socialists, Marxists and Capitalists. The political dichotomy is not, as we are led to believe, between the left and the right, but rather between government and no government... or at least between centralized bureaucracies/industries and self-sufficient local economies. As central governments decay under their own weight, there becomes a growing imperative need for regional control of resources and institutions. Indeed, belief in a society where power rises upward from the common base rather than downward from a concentrated power runs thinly but persistently through modern history. Yet, such notions are typically suppressed as being outcries of chaos, violence and utopia.

Part of the problem is that political alternatives are usually analyzed in a political context. Few people have sought to describe the science and technology that could make a decentralized society work... or at least get off the ground. Two recent books attempt to deal with the problem. *Post Scarcity Anarchism* by Murray Bookchin is an anthology of essays written originally for the now defunct "Anarchos" magazine. Bookchin is better known in Europe than this country, but three of his essays;"Ecology and Revolutionary Thought";"Listen Marxist" and "Toward a Libertarian Technology" have changed as many heads as any written pieces I know of. Bookchin argues that a truly alternative society must integrate an ecologically based science with a libertarian theory of human activity. Some of his ideas on the technologies involved in the new society need to be updated a bit, but the message is clear. The concept of "dominating" nature emerges from the domination of man by man; the quality of technology is as important as the quantities which it provides; scale down and diversify the energy resources of technologies, integrate them more to natural laws...make them the tools of people and not the other way around.

Dickson in *Alternative Technology...Change* seems more concerned with putting down the myth that technology is politically neutral. Unlike Bookchin he talks about the place of intermediate technologies in the Third World... a valuable contribution.

Both books are well worth reading several times over. My only major criticism is that they seem to be written from the point of view of reporters rather than participants... but then participants wouldn't write about this anyway.

—R.M.

Alternative Technology and the Politics of Technical Change
David Dickson
1974: 224pp.   **$1.25 plus postage**

from:
Collins Publishing
14 St. James Place
London SW1, England

Post Scarcity Anarchism
Murray Bookchin
1971; 288 pp

$2.95

from:
Ramparts Press, Inc.
P.O. Box 10128
Palo Alto, CA 94303

or WHOLE EARTH TRUCK STORE

ENERGETICS, KINETICS, AND LIFE: AN ECOLOGICAL APPROACH

A good book to read before *Perspectives in Ecological Theory.* Both books are superb sources of information regarding society's relationship to the environment and the place of energy in that relationship. Miller's text is *not* complicated and covers the subjects lucidly. He has also compiled an excellent bibliography for further study.

—T.W.

Water is the real key to life and to growing food. One half of the water used in the U.S. is for agriculture. Our spaceship has a large fixed load of water, but most of it is not *usable* water. Over 97% of our water is in the salty oceans. Robert and Leona Rienow have provided a striking example of just how much water on this planet is really usable. Imagine a 12-gallon jug as representing the total water supply on the planet. The entire supply of fresh water would then be about 5 cups. However, all but two-thirds of a cup of this are tied up in glaciers. When you remove the additional fresh water sources deep below the earth's crust, along with that contained in the top soil and in the atmosphere, and the amount we have polluted, then the useful water that we have amounts to only about *six drops* in the bottom of the 12-gallon jug.

In the past 50 years the per capita use of water in this country has increased twenty-five fold, and our water demands are expected to double by 1980. We expect, or think, we shall be using 650 billion gallons of water per day by that time. The Senate Water Resources committee indicates that by 1980 we shall have allocated every last drop of our water from natural resources. You can see why a *usable* water famine is predicted in the U.S. by 1980.

Energetics, Kinetics, and Life
G. Tyler Miller, Jr.
1971; 360pp

$6.95

from:
Wadsworth Publishing Co., Inc.
10 Davis Drive
Belmont, CA 94002

or WHOLE EARTH TRUCK STORE

PERSPECTIVES IN ECOLOGICAL THEORY

Four lectures delivered in 1966 at the University of Chicago. Probably the most lucid account of recent ideas in ecological theory. In a simple manner (once the terms are understood) Margalef explores and attempts to integrate the dynamics of ecological feedback systems, biological diversity and stability, energy flows, information theory, evolution, the organization of ecosystems, the effect humans have on these systems, plus the changes of natural communities as they move through time in the short run (succession) and the long run (evolution). Margalef gains insight and draws examples from his own work with ocean plankton, an ecosystem subject to rapid changes. This book just doesn't provide another intellectual branch to cling to . . . it projects one into a totally different frame of biological reference and ecological consciousness.

—R.M.

Perspectives in Ecological Theory
Ramon Margalef
1968; 111 pp

$5.50

from:
University of Chicago Press
11030 S. Langley Avenue
Chicago, Illinois 60628

or WHOLE EARTH TRUCK STORE

INTEGRATED SYSTEMS ANTHOLOGIES

ALTERNATIVE SOURCES OF ENERGY: THE NEWSLETTER AND THE BOOK

ASE Newsletter is a four-times a year information exchange, dependent upon volunteers for input and readers for financial support. Started in 1971, this Newsletter has grown in size and quality with almost every succeeding issue. It is the best available source for continuing information on all aspects of renewable energy sources.

ASE Book One is a compilation of the first ten issues of ASE Newsletter. Articles and letters have been grouped by subject: combined systems, solar, wind, and water power, fuels from renewable resources, transportation and other systems, agriculture, architecture and the arts, networks—groups—schools—conferences—people getting together, the philosophy and politics of energy, sunrise, and a long classified bibliography.

—C.M.

ASE Newsletter
$6.00/year

ASE Book One
Edited by Sandy Eccli & Others
1974: 277pp
$6.95

from:
Alternative Sources of Energy
Route 2, Box 90A
Milaca, Minnesota 56353

or Book One is available from the
WHOLE EARTH TRUCK STORE

PRODUCING YOUR OWN POWER

Producing Your Own Power is an anthology of articles about renewable energy systems (solar, water, wind and methane digesters). One third of these articles are reprints from other publications: the water section is reprinted information from VITA on small water power sites and the hydraulic ram; half of the methane section is a partial reprint of the New Alchemy West Newsletter on methane systems; one of the wind section articles is largely a reprint of Henry Clews own pamphlet *Electric Power From The Wind*; Eugene Eccli's *Conservation of Energy in Existing Structures* appeared previously in an issue of "Alternative Sources of Energy" Newsletter.

By far the best original article presented is "Heating and Cooking With Wood" written by Ken Kern. The article lacks significant information on woodlot management and forestation but has some of the best tips and data available on wood stoves, heaters and fireplaces. Also included are useful architectural design ideas for wood heater placement.

Both of the solar articles are originals. They cover space heating and water heating and are elementary enough to be easily understood by the novice and meaty enough to provide some design information for the serious experimenter. The second methane

article discusses a four-cow Bio-gas plant built on a Vermont dairy farm. The second wind article by Jim DeKorne discusses using an air brake governor (Wincharger) and a surplus aircraft generator to build a wind generator modeled after a "Jacob's Model No. 15."

The Appendix includes numerous source and bibliographical listings and a fine article on combining alternative energy sources.

—T.G.

Producing Your Own Power
C.H. Stoner, Editor
1974; 322pp
$8.95

from:
Rodale Press, Inc.
Book Division
Emmanus, PA 18049

or WHOLE EARTH TRUCK STORE

THE MOTHER EARTH NEWS HANDBOOK FOR HOMEMADE POWER

"Mother," as she fondly refers to herself, has been encouraging "back-to-the-land" folks for about five years now. She is good at it, providing a continuing array of new articles and tips for the homesteader in the form of *The Mother Earth News*. As with most mothers, you appreciate her for the things she does well and wish she wouldn't try so hard to do the things she's not so good at. Information gathered and presented on gardening, farming, animal raising, food preparation and homesteading are generally all top notch very informative pieces. Mother loses her footing when she enters the more technical areas, specifically energy. The articles presented are often hopeful rather than realistic or sufficiently researched.

The . . . *Handbook of Homemade Power* is mostly a compilation of articles from back issues of *The Mother Earth News*. It lacks technical information but the basics are there. The most complete water power article written to date concerning small scale systems, a 1947 Popular Science piece, is reprinted entirely. This book is worth reading. As a resource for continuing information on energy, other sources are certainly more useful, though Mother will probably get better at giving energy-related advice rather than give up trying.

—T.G.

The Mother Earth News
Bi-Monthly
$10.00 (one year 6 issues)

from:
The Mother Earth News
P.O. Box 70
Hendersonville, North Carolina 28739

The Mother Earth News
Handbook of Homemade Power
374; 1974
$1.95

from:
Bantam Books, Inc.
666 Fifth Ave.
N.Y. N.Y. 10019

or WHOLE EARTH TRUCK STORE

NATURAL ENERGY WORKBOOK

The title page calls it the "new and revised *Natural Energy Workbook*." I haven't seen the earlier version. This one is a pleasant booklet giving some background, some technical details, and lots of sketches of ideas and plans for doing-it-yourself with wind and waterpower, solar collectors, and methane generators. I think a lot of it is sound - some parts more sound than others - but there are few faults bad enough to call for yet another new and revised edition. If technical details are given then they ought to be accurate. Who knows, someone might actually use them. If you are actually going to build anything, you should go to more reliable sources of data.

The book does have lots of sound ideas and discussion. There's a good discussion of choosing a wind power site, instructions on making a Savonius rotor, a good exposition on types of water wheels, step by step instructions on making a parabolic mirror and a methane producing sewage digester, and hints and an offer of help to get approval of the county health officer.

Roger Douglass

Natural Energy Workbook
Peter Clark
1974; 100 pp
$3.95

from:
Visual Purple
Box 979
Berkeley, CA 94701

or WHOLE EARTH TRUCK STORE

ENERGY AND POWER

This is a classic primer for what shall be referred to as "the energy crisis." It consists of eleven essays which first appeared in the September 1971 *Scientific American* and which are now reprinted in a fully illustrated paperback. These essays have been editorially composed into a gallery of energy portraits illustrating the key concepts and phenomena in the energy cosmos. The book's intention is to be comprehensive. It succeeds well. Freeman J. Dyson's "Energy in the Universe" *could* give an overly susceptible person religion, whereas William B. Kemp's "The Flow of Energy in a Hunting Society" makes one long for the good old prehistoric days when the world was young and easy (and other illusions).

Ultimately, as it must, the scientific overview becomes awesome in its unmanageable enormity and disquieting in its subtle assault upon our precious standards of humanity, fairness and individuality. *Energy and Power* takes the holistic view of our resources and our manner of using those resources. The inevitable outcome of that use is a look into an appaling future with delicate language. Inevitably, the view turns back upon the viewer, as an individual. We are forced to ask the untiring, unanswerable questions, "Who are we? Why are we here? What are we supposed to do?"

—Pennfield Jensen

Energy and Power
A Scientific American Book
1971; 144 pages.

$3.50

from:
W.H. Freeman and Company
660 Market Street
San Francisco, Calif. 94104
or WHOLE EARTH TRUCK STORE

THE LAST WHOLE EARTH CATALOG WHOLE EARTH EPILOG

These are probably two of the finest source books in print. Generally well known, not much need be said other than they list and review books and hardware on topics such as crafts, building, education, cybernetics, gardening, community, land use, communications and more.

The Soft-Technology sections of each book includes reviews of energy-related books and hardware. Information on windmills, water turbines, solar power, composting and methane is presented. The information in the Soft-Technology section of the *Epilog* is more plentiful and current than *Catalog* listings.

The *Epilog* is considerably more professionally researched and presented than the *Catalog*. The *Epilog*, however, lacks the humor and prose (funk) of the *Catalog*.

Certainly the main criticism of these publications is that they are "wish-fostering." Because cause they present so much information and lack depth in the areas they do cover, there's almost an information overload. Many people, upon leafing through these books, find themselves saying, "Wish I had, "or" Wish I knew." We need fewer wishers in this world, and more doers.

—T.G.

The CoEvolution Quarterly is a continuing magazine supplement to the Whole Earth Catalog/ Epilog. Like the Catalog and the Epilog it reviews books and hardware. It also includes in depth articles on food storage, ecology, land trusts and more. Published quarterly, it is available for $2.00 per issue or $6.00 per year (four issues) from CQ, 558 Santa Cruz Avenue, Menlo Park CA 94025 or your local newsstand.

The Last Whole Earth Catalog
448pp
$5.00

from:
Random House
457 Hahn Road
Westminster, MD 21157

or WHOLE EARTH TRUCK STORE

Whole Earth Epilog
319pp
$4.00

from:
Penguin Books, Inc.
7110 Ambassador Rd.
Baltimore, MD 21207

or WHOLE EARTH TRUCK STORE

SURVIVAL SCRAPBOOKS

Energy is the latest in the series of Survival Scrapbooks. Loose and easy, lots of illustrations.
—C.M.

Survival Scrapbook: Energy
Stefan A. Szczlkun
1973; 112 pp
$3.95

from:
Schocken Books
200 Madison Avenue
New York, NY 10016

or WHOLE EARTH TRUCK STORE

PERIODICALS

ENERGY

The National Technical Information Service publishes several "Weekly Government Abstracts." The one I find most useful is titled *Energy*. As most federally funded, unclassified energy research is completed, reports on it are sent to NTIS for cataloguing and dissemination. *Energy* gives access information and abstracts on topics such as Energy Sources, Power and Heat Generation, Energy Conversion and Storage, and the like. This weekly summary is the best way to keep up with the published results of all aspects of federally funded energy research, including solar.

—C.M.

Weekly Government Abstracts—Energy
$35 per year

from:
National Technical Information Service
P.O. Box 1553
Springfield, Virginia 22161

POPULAR SCIENCE

Popular Science, by Times Mirror Magazines, is probably the most valuable publication they own. The price is right—$0.60/issue. It covers the subjects, materials, and products that we use today more inclusively than any other source I've found. Possibly the Last Bargain in this country.
—T.W.

Popular Science
Monthly
$0.60/issue
$6.00/year, subscription

from:
Popular Science
Subscription Department
P.O. Box 2871
Boulder, Colorado 80302

ENERGY DIGEST

The grass-roots, low-tech movement has big brothers. NASA, Institute of Gas Technology, Oil Companies and other centralists, high-techers and energy conglomerates are exploring and dealing in the wings, soon to rush in, snap their meters on the sun and wind and lay their spread of Madison Avenue ASE devices on a befuddled public. Be aware of what the power base is up to. . . at least on the surface. Expensive scroll this. . . but it really lays out legislation, grants, contracts, etc. of energy happenings. . . fossil fuel, nuclear and renewable. Muckraking and factual, but poor on motives and priorities.

—R.M.

Energy Digest
semi-monthly
$125.00/yr

from:
Scope Publications Inc.
1120 National Press Bldg.
Washington, DC 20004

ENERGY ABSTRACTS FOR POLICY ANALYSIS

Energy Abstracts for Policy Analysis (EAPA), formerly *NSF-RANN Energy Abstracts*, is sponsored by the National Science Foundation and the Atomic Energy Commission. Published monthly, *EAPA*...

provides abstracting and indexing coverage of selected publicly available nontechnical literature contributing to energy-related analysis and evaluation in the following areas: policy; conservation; research and development studies; economics; supply and demand; forecasting; systems studies; and environmental effects. Specific fields of energy that will be covered are: energy sources...; unconventional energy sources, including solar, wind, geothermal, tidal, and waste products; electric power; energy conversion and storage; and energy consumption, including residential, commercial, industrial, agricultural, and transportation sectors and intersectorial studies; and efficient energy utilization in these sectors.

EAPA covers pertinent material from Congressional Committee prints; USAEC, NSF, FEA and other Federal agency and department reports; regional and state government documents; news reports; books; and conference proceedings and papers. In general, only documents considered to have significant reference value and published within the past two years are included.

Information on publications within the scope of EAPA is appreciated. Please send copies of publications to Miriam P. Guthrie, EAPA, Oak Ridge National Laboratory, P.O. Box X, Oak Ridge, TN 37830.

Energy Abstracts for Policy Analysis
Monthly

Inquire About Cost

from:
Energy Abstracts for Policy Analysis
Oak Ridge National Laboratory
P.O. Box X
Oak Ridge, TN 37830

LIVING IN THE OZARKS

Joel Davidson is the *ASE* Newsletter contact in the Ozarks, founder of the Upper Friley Organization School, and editor/publisher of *Living in the Ozarks*, a low-budget monthly newspaper for Ozarks' folks. Joel has built several methane and solar devices and he's willing to help neighbors do likewise. His fine newspaper covers most aspects of rural, low-tech living. We need more alternative regional newssheets like this one.
—C.M.

The cold frame pictured below is the cheapest and easiest one we have ever built. Our thanks to the folks at the Garden of Joy Blues commune for the idea. They call it "The Ozark Organic Coldframe." With a few windows, some 8" wide lumber and bales of hay you can have fresh greens all winter. It is a great way to get a headstart on spring planting by starting your seeds in it. On cold nights you can cover the windows with a blanket or tarp to keep the heat in. If you don't have access to bales of hay, bundles of newspapers will work just as well. The cost of this project is almost nothing and the windows can be re-used.

Living in the Ozarks
Monthly periodical
$5.00 per year

from:
Joel Davidson
Upper Friley Organization School
Pettigrew, Arkansas 72752

UNDERCURRENTS: THE MAGAZINE OF RADICAL SCIENCE AND PEOPLES' TECHNOLOGY

There are several excellent British publications that we should see more of in the U.S. *Undercurrents* is certainly one of the best. Originally published as a collection of odds and ends mailed in a clear plastic envelope, it now is a nicely printed and bound bundle of alternative news and views. Articles on Velikovsky, "Technology for De-Centralisation," alternative technology guides for Europe, and much, much more. The latest issue, No. 7, is "dedicated to the liberation of communications." Unfortunately, issues 1, 2 and 3 are out of print.

"Transfiguration Among the Windmills," by Peter Harper in issue No. 5 is dynamite. It started a storm of reaction; we quote from it here:

—C.M.

I think we have to recognize that the old, "unified" conception of AT (alternative technology) is dead. What is biotechnic is not necessarily non-exploitive or cheap; what conserves resources is not necessarily fulfilling or interesting to work with; cooperative production is not necessarily efficient enough to avoid hassles over distribution; what is simple to manufacture may require great expertise to maintain and be deadly to use, or vice versa.

Our dreams of a magic technology—the distillation of all our hopes, without any compromises—must be over. We rejoin the human race, and with it the unavoidable conflicts and tradeoffs of economics and technology.

We have to decide what we want, then decide what we are prepared to sacrifice for it in terms of things we want less. It's my guess that, faced with the real choices and the real costs, nearly everybody would opt to stay in the straight society as things are at the moment. Apparent successes of cheap AT have on the whole been achieved through hidden subsidies of time or resources which could not be generalized throughout society.

* *

I expect biotechnic research to continue, if only because there's bound to be at least a Sunday Colour-supp market for it in the coming decades. I expect "autonomous housing" research to continue, partly for the same reasons, partly to meet genuine needs in remote areas, and partly as a hedge against rising fossil fuel costs. Many people will attempt to build "eco-houses" to demonstrate a principle of independence or to avoid exploiting anyone else, but I doubt if these aims will be realized without hidden subsidies.

I pray that someone can prove me wrong.

Undercurrents
Six approximately bi-monthly issues

$5.00 Surface mail (2+ months delivery)

$10.60 Air mail to U.S. & Canada

$0.90 Each back issue, surface mail

from:
Undercurrents
275 Finchley Road
London NW3
England

WALL STREET JOURNAL

When you walk by the newsstand, check out the headlines of columns 1, 4 and 6, particularly column 4 on Monday, where they write on various economic subjects. If a headline grabs you, buy the paper. The reporting is usually very thorough and readable. They've reported on subjects like food and energy shortages long before anything appeared in the popular press.

—C.M.

SOME SCIENCE PERIODICALS

It is easy (but not cheap) to stay on top of current events in hard science and environmental issues by reading from the genre of science periodicals. Often these also include ideas, research and fantasies about renewable energy systems. Perhaps the best of the lot is *New Scientist* from Great Britian. I like it for two reasons: First, it is very well written. . .poetic when describing new theories of cosmology, wry when discussing nuclear power, oil in the North Sea etc. Second, it gives a good view of environmental problems in Europe and the Third World, plus an "outsider's" objective view of what's coming down in the U.S. scientific establishment. *New Scientist* is easy to read from cover to cover. *The Ecologist* is also from Great Britian, sharing the same address as the Low Impact Technology Group. It is more political and more meaty in areas of agriculture and solar energy than *New Scientist*. *Nature* is Britian's prestigious weekly anthology of current scientific research. Informative, but often esoteric.

Science is the U.S. equivalent of *Nature*. Published by the American Association for the Advancement of Science (AAAS), the editorial policy is cool and objective (read conservative). 19 April 1974 has a very good issue on Energy. *Scientific American* comes out monthly as a series of review articles about areas of scientific research, both specific and holistic. Written in a popular style, it has the Madison Ave. touch with the best graphics in the business. Each September issue is devoted to an entire discipline: 1969, "The Ocean"; 1970 "The Biosphere"; 1971, "Energy and Power" are current classics of information. *Bio-Science* is a popular style journal of the American Institute of Biological Sciences. Avid readers claim that by reading the editorials over the past decade, one could have predicted what's happening today. The articles are good too.

—R.M.

New Scientist
128 Long Acre
London, England WC2E 9QH
Weekly
$34.00/yr

The Ecologist
73 Molesworth St.
Wadebridge, Cornwall, England PL27 7DS
Bimonthly (10 issues per year)
$12.00/yr

Nature
Macmillan Journals, Ltd.
Little Essex St.
London WC 2R 3LF, England
3 weekly editions
$108.00/yr

Science
American Association for the Advancement
of Science
1515 Massachusetts Ave., N.W.
Washington, D.C. 20005
Weekly through membership in AAAS
$30.00/yr

Scientific American
415 Madison Ave.
New York, N.Y. 10017
Monthly
$10.00/yr

Bioscience
American Institute of Biological Sciences
3900 Wisconsin Ave.
Washington, D.C. 20016
Bimonthly through membership to AIBS
$18.00/yr

ENVIRONMENT

There are only a few magazines that I regularly read—*Environment* is one of them. Published ten times a year by the Scientists' Institute for Public Information, it combines good feature articles on various aspects of the degradation of our environment with timely and succinct news briefs in the centerspread "Spectrum" section.

Recent issues have featured the "Oil Glut" ("genuine concern about long-term energy supplies has been manipulated to justify artificial immediate shortages"), "Energy: Some Aspects of the Crisis You Haven't Heard Much About," and "Urban Transportation."

—C.M.

"I could pick three to five ex-Underwater Demolition, Marine Reconnaissance or Green Beret men at random and sabotage virtually any nuclear reactor in the country. . . There is no way to stop such activity other than to maintain a system of civil surveillance more strict than that maintained during the last world war. . ." Testimony of Bruce L. Welch, former Navy demolition officer and present associate professor of environmental health, Johns Hopkins School of Medicine, before the Joint Congressional Committee on Atomic Energy, March 15.

Environment
Ten issues per year

$10.00 per year

from:
Environment
438 N. Skinker Boulevard
St. Louis, Missouri 63130

SYNERGY

"A directory of energy alternatives. The 1200 U.S. and foreign sources include publications, major articles, conferences, research associations, manufacturers, and facilities through July 1974." Lots of source info, but access info isn't always accurate.

—C.M.

$3.50/copy, individuals

$6.00/copy, institutions

Synergy
P.O. Box 4790
Grand Central Station
New York, NY 10017

DESIGN AND ENERGY, NATURALLY

"A resource list to facilitate the use of natural energy in the design of buildings." Almost exclusively devoted to solar energy. Gary Farber and Carl Steinberg welcome inquiries regarding their research and design services.

$3.00/copy

—C.M.

Gary Farber
1131 S. Rexford Drive No. 2
Los Angeles, CA 90035

SYNERGY ACCESS

"A global newsletter on futuristic communications, media and networking." Topics include soft technology, video, and an events calendar. Jam-packed with names, addresses, dates and annotated book reviews.

—C.M.

Synergy Access
Bimonthly

$8/year

Synergy Access
21st Century Media, Inc.
606 5th Avenue
East Northport, New York 11731

INTEGRATED SYSTEMS COMMUNITY GROUPS

LOW IMPACT TECHNOLOGY

LIP is an active consultancy and design group working with ambient energy systems. In addition to thinking services, they offer a broad range of hardware for sale. Unusual items they carry are steam engines, Stirling engines, heat pumps and "Tabitha's Fireless Cooker," in addition to the usual run of solar collectors and aerogenerators. Andrew MacKillop, Managing Director, has edited a *Water Power Manual* ($4.00), and another do-it-yourself book, *Methane Gas Plants* ($4.00). They also offer plans and specifications for a light steam engine ($12.00).

—C.M.

Low Impact Technology
73 Molesworth Street
Wadebridge, Cornwall
United Kingdom

INTERMEDIATE TECHNOLOGY DEVELOPMENT GROUP LTD.

Intermediate Technology was founded by E.F. Schumacher, soft-technologist and author of *Small is Beautiful* (page 184). He claims to have started it with £ 100. Now it is a group of four companies: a consulting firm, a training and education firm, a retail shop in London selling Third World goods and a publications company.

In many ways it is similar to VITA. They both aid predominantly developing nations, usually with soft-technology answers to problems. Both use consultants, training programs, and publications as their vehicle. Intermediate Technology seems the more advanced and professional of the two.

Intermediate Technology, in addition to its extensive publications list (a few samples of which are listed below), has just begun publishing a new journal. Entitled *Appropriate Technology* it is published quarterly and sells for £ 2.00 surface mail or £ 3.50 air mail for four issues. It is a fine source for continuing information on soft-technology.

—T.G.

	BY AIR	SUR-FACE
GUIDE TO HAND-OPERATED AND ANIMAL-DRAWN EQUIPMENT 82pp	$5.80	$4.10
MANUAL ON BUILDING CONSTRUCTION 360 pp	$5.20	$2.90
COOPERATIVE ACCOUNTING	$1.20	$0.50
THE STIRLING ENGINE 32 pp	$3.00	$2.70
SIMPLE DESIGNS FOR HOSPITAL EQUIPMENT	$0.75	$0.60
OIL DRUM FORGE DESIGNED FOR LOCAL CONSTRUCTION	$2.90	$2.30
WATER TREATMENT AND SANITATION	$3.80	$2.65

Intermediate Technology Development
Group Ltd.
9 King Street
London WC2 8HN, England

THE NEW ALCHEMY INSTITUTE

The New Alchemy Institute arose out of a dissatisfaction with conventional science . . . the answers it was giving and, indeed, the questions it was asking. Today the New Alchemists have a small research community in Massachusetts and loose centers in California and Costa Rica. NAI is a prime mover in the area of aquaculture, and one of the only groups we know of that is researching ways to integrate aqua/agricultures with solar energy systems. Their latest publication (Journal No. 2) describes, among other things, designs for a sail-wing water pump (see page 101 of *Primer*). and over 4 years experiences with various self-contained aquaculture systems maintained by solar/wind power (see page 133 of *Primer*). Membership is $25.00/year. Write and ask for their "blurb." It describes their goals and lists available publications.

—R.M.

The New Alchemy Institute is a small, international organization for research and education on behalf of man and the planet. We seek solutions that can be used by individuals or small groups who are trying to create a greener, kinder world. It is our belief that ecological and social transformations must take place at the lowest functional levels of society if mankind is to direct his course towards a saner tomorrow.

Among our major tasks is the creation of ecologically derived forms of energy, agriculture, aquaculture, housing and landscapes, that will permit a revitalization and repopulation of the countryside. The Institute has centers existing, or planned, for a wide range of climates in several countries, in order that our research and experience can be used by large numbers of people in diverse regions of the world.

New Alchemy Institute
Box 432
Woods Hole, Massachusetts 02543

PROJECT ASSOCIATES

Project Associates is a Portland-based team of engineers, architects, planners and energy systems specialists now involved in
- the UN—Canadian Urban Demonstration Project for Kingston, Ontario involving solar heating, wind-electric systems, and low-energy architecture.

- the Soap Lake (Wash.) Solar Community Project involving the transition of a 1200 population town to solar energy.

- the Squaxin Island Indian Home Project involving pole-construction and wind-electric systems.

- the AIA Solar Energy & Housing Competition involving the design of prototypical solar homes and evaluation of National Bureau of Standards interim performance criteria for solar heating & cooling.

Enclose a stamped, self-addressed envelope for response - - we are interested in working on specific consulting projects.

Project Associates
3111 SE Chestnut St.
Oak Grove, OR 97222

INTEGRATED LIVING SYSTEMS

The work that ILS and Bob Reines have been doing for the last few years has been touted highly in *Shelter* and the *Whole Earth Epilog* as well as numerous newspaper articles. Certainly this small but ambitious experiment is worth watching to see the nature of its failures and successes.

ILS is a research laboratory integrating solar collectors and wind generators and autonomous living units. The hope is to develop a unit model or prototype for implementation on a larger scale.

—T.G.

ILS Labs is a laboratory. It in itself is an experiment. We are not a business but a team of ten people who design, construct, and live in systems which can ultimately be brought into society by other impact groups. Our goal is to build a larger laboratory with some two hundred scientists, engineers, designers, lawyers, doctors, artists, anthropologists, communications people and the like, working together in a new way with a sense of urgency to provide new tools, models and methodologies to grapple with the broad problems of energy, people and habitat. We have the hardware to build a very inexpensive physical plant for the laboratory in a very short period of time. The ILS system hardware allows for the first time energy autonomous communities to be built.

Integrated Living Systems
Star Route 103
Tijeras, NM 87059

COMMUNITY TECHNOLOGY

From a distance, applications of renewable energy source systems in urban areas seem to be difficult to find.

The amount of land available is usually small, health and sewage codes are strict, wind currents are often blocked by buildings, and solar insolation is often not available to everyone, especially people living in apartment houses. So we readily make the assumption that renewable energy systems are better suited for rural settings. Across the board this assumption is probably true. But if we take a city situated in a mild climate with high insolation rate and a high average wind speed and compare that with a rural setting in a northern lattitude with a low solar insolation rate and low average wind speed the former location may provide significantly more possibilities than the latter.

Community Technology in the Adams-Morgan section of Washington D.C. is exploring the possibilities of urban renewable energy systems. In conjunction with the Institute for Local Self-Reliance and other community groups they have proceeded with a number of research experiments. Fern Wood Mitchell has successfully been raising trout in recirculating tanks in basements for over a year. C.J. Swet and others have been building and experimenting with a new design in solar cookers. Wind patterns are being studied to see if wind power is feasible and hydroponic gardening is underway.

Information from Community Technology is available for $1.00 and a stamped self-addressed envelope. Further information will be available in a new magazine they will soon issue entitled *Self-Reliance*.

—T.G.

from:
Community Technology
1520 New Hampshire Ave. N.W.
Washington, D.C. 20036

CERRO GORDO

I think the most exciting new community/renewable energy project in the country is now coming together near Cottage Grove, Oregon. A rapidly growing group of families (100+) from all over the country has banded together to purchase 1200 acres of beautiful forested hillside land, fund a detailed land use study, and start planning for a new town that will eventually be home for hundreds of families. The automobile is being planned *out* of the community, and personal sharing, renewable energy sources and energy conservation are being planned in. We are looking for more people to help us plan this dream, fund its future and build its reality. Send for more free information or subscribe to the future resident's newsletter.

—C.M.

Above all we are seeking a mode of life which promotes a deeper appreciation of our shared humanity and recognizes our interdependence. . . a mode of life which respects our ultimate dependence on natural cycles of energy and physical resources. . .an ethic of self-determination, freedom, cooperation, and personal growth. . .a decision-making process that encourages expression of individual values and reflects diverse points of view. . .a teaching-learning community with educational opportunities learner-centered and open to all. . .

The Cerro Gordo Experiment:
A Land Planning Package

$3.00

The Community Association Newsletter
Monthly

$15/year

from:
Cerro Gordo Community Association
704 Whiteaker Street
Cottage Grove, Oregon 97424

GRASSY BROOK VILLAGE

Dear Chuck:

Thanks for the invitation to send material for the upcoming book, the ENERGY PRIMER.

Here is basically how I got into this alternative energy "business:"

My long-time vague curiosity about solar heating and windpowered electricity was brought to life by—are you ready?—the Whole Earth Catalog. But this remained a sort of kinetic interest until I began viewing the environmental movement, of which I was a tiny part, as too much protesting and not enough practical answering. This led me to the logical realization that, I, as a building contractor, was not part of the solution but part of the problem! In the spring of 1972 I began actively seeking moral and financial support for some sort of experimental building project that would involve solar heating and windpower, as well as other environmental considerations. Grassy Brook Village was "born" as a corporation several months later, and the project as described in our printed sheets evolved over the next year or so.

My thinking has been brought into focus by the extended planning process for this project along with the influence of hundreds of people with whom I've come into contact subsequently. After starting out with some very vague environmental goals, I've now developed a fairly clear (to me) picture of what I'd like to see the future bring, insofar as human habitation is concerned, and I'd articulate it as follows:

1. Housing will be on a human scale.
2. People will control their housing and the life support systems involved with their housing.
3. People will have a personal responsiblity for the consequences and effects of their housing lifestyle: (1) and (2) will provide a clear understanding of the interrelationship.
4. Housing will be clustered, with obvious environmental benefits.
5. Solar heating and other alternative life support systems will be enhanced through application to group housing.
6. A number of positive personal, social, environmental, architectural, and synergetic benefits will flow from such arrangements.
7. Grassy Brook Village will prove to be a successful first step towards achieving these results in a form that is replicable and falls within a viable economic framework.

Can a hippie-capitalist backwoods Vermont contractor make it all come true? Tune in next week, same time, same station . . .

Richard D. Blazej
R.F.D. No. 1
Newfane, Vermont 05345

ECOTOPE: ECO = HABITAT + TOPOS = PLACE "A SPECIALIZED HABITAT WITHIN A LARGER REGION"

Ecotope Group is a coalition of designers, builders, engineers and scientists working on energy and shelter systems. We consult, design, build, conduct research, provide information and education on options available for creative survival. Ecotope Group works with Housing Assistance Service in Seattle, Project Associates in Portland, and OPEN Northwest Information Network. We are presently involved in a bio-conversion project (methane digester) at the Monroe Washington State Reformatory Dairy Farm—funded by the Washington State Department of Ecology. Other areas of interest are: energy conservation in housing; wind power applications; and solar home heating.

We are interested in communicating and sharing information. To communicate, send a self-addressed stamped envelope to:

Ecotope Group
Box 5599 U. Station
Seattle, Washington 98105

OPEN

Information network that publishes an Index to builders and designers of alternative sources of energy in the Pacific Northwest. Send $.50 and a large self-addresses stamped envelope to OPEN for a copy of the Index.

—C.M.

OPEN Northwest Information Network
P.O. Box 692
Port Townsend, Washington 93638

WITH SYNERGY . . . COOLING'S THE THING

After living without electricity for 3 years let me say that the greatest need for external energy (whether gas or electricity) is not for light, heat or entertainment but for cooling/refrigeration/freezing. Alternative energy methods for cooling *are vital to even approximate a satisfying standard of living*, and regardless of what you have heard, the old methods just don't work well enough to keep large amounts of food from spoiling. (How do you store gallons of milk or cheese or a whole beef until it is used?) Would some of you gifted energy thinkers get to work on a refrigeration system that runs continuously, efficiently with only moderate capital cost on dual solar/wood heat (or other). Here in Montana either the wood stove is going during the cold or it's so hot that the sun could handle the job easily. All other energy/electrical needs can be handled by 12/120 V D.C. wind power and wood. Methane is the obvious answer but too few of us produce enough on a continuous basis to satisfy needs of a refrigerator and a 15-20 ft³ freezer.

George Oberst
Box 609
Noxon, Montana 59853

OMSI ENERGY CENTER

The Oregon Museum of Science and Industry's Energy Center sponsors classes, workshops, conferences and displays on various energy topics. Lee Johnson is the resident wind energy resource, and Marcia Lynch is the compiler of information files and distributor of alternative energy information sheets and abstracts.

OMSI Energy Center
4015 S.W. Canyon Road
Portland, Oregon 97221

AERO

AERO is a publicity, promotion and organizing offshoot of the Northern Plains Resource Council. If you think of Montana as nothing but big sky country, guess again. Beset by stripmining coal companies on one hand and nuclear interests on the other, Montana has a real need for a group that supports renewable sources of energy. They are particularly against mineral depletion allowances.

—C.M.

Alternate Energy Resource Organization
418 Stapleton Building
Billings, Montana 59101

ROARING FORKS RESOURCE CENTER

"RFRC is a non-profit corporation set up to promote, direct and develop the exploration of alternative energy sources, to provide public information and learning experiences, and to explore the architectural opportunities of alternative energy."

RFRC has a growing newsletter, and they are now in the reprint business. Send a stamped, self addressed envelope for a listing of the articles they have for sale.

—C.M.

Roaring Fork Resource Center
P.O. Box 9950
Aspen, Colorado 81611

INTEGRATED SYSTEMS
UNIVERSITY-RELATED

FARALLONES INSTITUTE

Farallones Institute is a non-profit research and educational institution that designs, constructs and evaluates:
1. innovative, inexpensive ways of building
2. components for self-renewing energy supply and resource recycling
3. improved means of food and fiber production, field crop, aquatic and wildlife management.

We offer an apprentice program in these study areas and are beginning a number of projects in Northern California including the conversion of a standard urban house to self-sufficiency, an adobe and earth building project (with Peter Van Dresser), improved composting privy design and testing, biological control of urban pests (Bill and Helga Olkowski), eco-system management and aquaculture (Sterling Bunnell), and instruction in small-scale building design.

The group includes:
Sim Van der Ryn—architect
Art Boericke—builder
Sterling Bunnell—psychiatrist and naturalist
Bill and Helga Olkowski—biologists
Chuck Raymond—physicist
Paul Duffy—master machinist
David Katz, Michael Stusser—agriculturalists
Barry Shapiro—photographer

Over the winter and spring of 1974, a group of U.C. Architecture students in a class on Natural Energy Design taught by Sim Van der Ryn, Jim Campe and Carl Anthony, designed and built a structure to illustrate and test the integrated design and use of low tech natural energy devices suitable for household application. The pavilion, costing $2500 in materials, included:

—a complete water heating and recycling system: two types of flat plate collectors, a parabolic focusing collector, sand filter and solar still to purify water. Dirty water was pumped from a holding tank to the still using a 12 volt pump powered by a 200 watt Dynaflow wind generator.

—a nutrient recycling system: including a methane digester privy designed around the John Fry inner tube digester, and a Van der Ryn design composting privy. Spent sludge from the digester was funneled to the privy. The digester was housed in a closed compartment with temperature maintained by a solar heated water bed. A redwood lath-polyethylene skinned greenhouse with portable planting boxes completed the system.

Bureaucratic hassles made it impossible for someone to live in the structure and use all the systems continuously. However, a monitoring program was carried out for several months. The 4 x 8 foot solar collectors produced 30 gallons of 130° water in several hours of sun; solar still output was a maximum of 12 gallons per day (still area: 60 feet). The privy digester produced small amounts of gas and is not recommended for household use. Because of the short use period, the composting system was not begun.

Basically, the Pavilion was an attempt to reproduce and connect up "first generation" natural energy hardware and learn something about the operation and use of an integrated system for household use. The experiment clarified for us that hardware by itself can do very little towards reducing reliance on fossil fuels, although given vastly reduced demands and the willingness to fit one's life to the parameters of natural energy design, we can live lightly and well.

A technical bulletin describing the project and including the detailed how-to-do-it designs and costs of its energy systems, will be available for $2.00 from:

Farallones Institute
P.O. Box 700
Point Reyes Station, CA 94956

ECOL OPERATION: MINIMUM COST HOUSING GROUP (McGILL UNIVERSITY)

Table of Contents
1. 12 ways of building ecologically
2. Sulphur technology
3. How to make sulphur interlocking block
4. Building the house
5. Water and power
6. Living in an eco house

The Ecol Operation describes the experience of developing, building and living in an ecological house. It deals with the use of industrial waste as building material, the use of solar and wind energy for cooking, water purification and production of electricity, and the development of a self-sufficient water and waste system. The methods use intermediate technology and self-help as a basis for ecologically non-destructive building.

—T.W.

The Ecol Operation
Ortega, Rybczynski, Ayad, Ali and Acheson
1972; 100 pp

$5.00

from:
Minimum Cost Housing Group
School of Architecture
McGill University
Montreal, Canada

ENVIRONMENTAL ACTION OF COLORADO

There are only a few energy groups in the US that impress me as being really together—at the top of my list is EA of C. Like most groups of its kind, it formed around Earth Day activities four years ago; unlike most groups since then, it's gotten better and better.

EA has a reprint service it calls EARS. Send them $.25 for a copy of their latest EARS catalog. Their articles are pro solar, wind and conservation, against nuclear. Bumper stickers, posters and a "Solar Energy" button are also listed. One article they offer, Egan O'Conner's *Solar Energy—How Soon?* is must reading. We had hoped to reprint the whole thing in this book, then we ran out of room.

The "Grand Slam" package includes all their solar, applied solar and wind energy reprints, plus bumper stickers, a button and an EARS catalog. This would make a nice gift for the solar Freak in your Family.

And finally, Carolyn Pesko is compiling a Solar Energy Directory. Now able to complete it with a little outside financial help, she should have this available in September, 1974. I think it will be the best guide yet on who's making what, who's helping others and where to find information.

—C.M.

EARS Catalogue
1974; 16 pp
$0.25

"Solar Energy" Button
$0.50

Solar Energy—How Soon?
1973; 6 pp
$0.30

"Grand Slam" Package
$4.95

Solar Energy Directory
Carolyn Pesko
1974; approx. 900 entries
$15.00

from:
Environmental Action of Colorado
University of Colorado—Denver
1100 14th Street
Denver, Colorado 80202

MAX'S POT

As for our work here at the Center for Maximum Potential Building Systems, the enclosed booklet will give you a rough idea of some of the things we've been up to. The Lab's only been in existence since the fall of 1972, when we came down here, but even so, most of the projects in the booklet are from '72-'73. We've got a bunch of others going on now—including organic gardening, algae ponds, solar walls for space heating, integrating a low water using bathroom/kitchen complex with the bio-gas plant and this in turn with the garden and algae pond—gradually getting around to making things work together in a whole system where all outputs are inputs, which gives as no-waste, or low-waste, a system as possible.

Another of the main things we've been up to here in the lab (which is a branch of the School of Architecture) is to develop a whole series of modes through which people can begin to deal with alternative sources of energy and of methods and materials of building. The modes are on the one hand purely informational, while on the other hand they are physical examples, from full-scale working prototypes built by students and community members to one inch scale models of energy systems. These allow students and others to explore the design potentials of integrating alternative concepts with whole house designs, rather than just tacking them on as usual.

Max's Pot is doing some of the best, if not the best, university related work on integrating energy systems in the United States. The ideas generated there are novel, they pursue them 'til the ideas work, and they share information at reasonable costs. Plans are now available for (1) a horizontal 55 gallon drum bio-gas plant sized for a small homestead, and (2) a woodburning 55 gallon drum stove that works with an afterburner that ignites excess wood gas. The latter has been used for two years without any problems.

By mid-1975 they will have plans available for a sonic nozzle aerobic toilet that uses sound vibrations to entrain water with micron-sized bubbles, making aerobic waste treatment far more efficient. By late-1975, plans and systems should be available for electrostatically spraying sulfur, a building material found in great quantities in Texas.

By mid-1975 they also will have plans and kits available for their Kit O'Parts Windgenerator, alias the Wind Cycle Wonder. It's an 1800 watt, 12 volt system designed around the use of mobile home—recreational vehicle appliances. For about $500, including batteries, you can get 2-3 days of storage capacity (4100 watt-hours). Only three simple tools will be needed to build the system, and no welding, threading or fiberglassing will be necessary.

If you stop by to see the little organic Max's Pot spread in Texas, ask Pliny and Daria Fisk, Lab Directors, about the 70 foot recycled Dutch canal boat (vintage 1897) that they are converting to a floating alternative life support vessel.
—C.M.

Horizontal Drum Bio-Gas Plant Plans
$5.00

Woodburning Stove Plans
$3.00

from:
Center for Maximum Potential Building Systems
6438 Bee Caves Road
Austin, Texas 78746

CAMBRIDGE UNIVERSITY

The Department of Architecture at Cambridge publishes an amazing set of pamphlets dealing with autonomous housing, renewable energy sources and argiculture. Occasionally the information presented lacks depth and sometimes the geographical area discussed only applies to Britain. These papers, however, present one of the best places to start reading and understanding about houses which are energy self-sufficient (autonomous).

—T.G.

Although there are voluntary movements away from consumption growth there has so far been little analysis of the consequences; saving in one resource may lead to increased consumption of others, as seems the case with substituting autonomous plant and ambient resources for the central and non-renewable varieties. Using the household as a model of the world it seems clear that the most energetic and fortunate members have a duty to help the remainder, not only through technological and financial aid but by lowering the goals of attainment and redistributing the means to attain them.

Publications List Available Free from:

University of Cambridge
Department of Architecture
Technical Research Division
1 Scroope Terrace
Cambridge CB2 1PX England

RATIONAL TECHNOLOGY

The Rational Technology Unit of one of England's best architectural schools has been doing lots of work lately on many alternative building system components. A sample of their work is included in *Rational Technology Unit 73-4* (84 pp, $2.00). Some chapter headings are "Sulphur—A Potential Building Material," "Rammed Earth and Soil Cement Construction," and "The Energy Cost of a House."

—C.M.

There is a new vernacular of building to be learned in which we come to terms with the existing fabric of our built environment: the days of rip it down and replace it are gone. There is a new attitude required, a gentler one, in which we conceive man in relation to his environment not as a dominant force but as a related part of the totality. There is a place for the sun, and growing things and a re-use for what used to be called waste. We have to learn how to live without surplus of energy; people did so in the past and we will have to do so in the future.

Rational Technology Unit
Architectural Association
34-36 Bedford Square
London WC1, England

SWOPSI

The Stanford Workshop on Political and Social issues in in the process of publishing a book entitled *Design for Alternative Lifestyles: Better Homes and Garbage*. The book, which discusses renewable energy sources and applications, is one of the best university hatched publications we have seen. Write SWOPSI, Stanford University, Stanford, CA 94305, for price and date of availability.

—T.G.

ACCESS

ACCESS is an option at the School of Architecture, University of Wisconsin, Milwaukee. Under this option,

. . . students and others can do full scale built experiments that may serve to conserve human and natural resources. The experiments are in the area of low-cost, low impact, environmentally responsive shelter and life support subsystems.

Concept: is to utilize the university context to develop and disperse responsive environmental technology, both soft and hard, for people who choose to be responsive to environmental problems, but don't yet know how they have the technical ability to implement that choice. Learning takes the form of directed experiments based on our knowledge of the current state of the art in the specific area of user built intermediate technology.

Operation: is based on the concept that the university ought to do more than serve as an adolescent holding tank; and that architectural education ought to involve active implementation to improve—directly—the global environment, rather than decorate it or help speed its unguided capital growth.

With little but basic support from the School, this program depends on the scrounging ability and generosity of students and friends. So far, they've built reflective insulating shutters, light weight roof-mounted solar heaters, solar heated greenhouses, and many other projects. They have a 70 year old house on the east side of Milwaukee to use as a full-size, real time laboratory. A Work Manual describing many of their projects is available for $2.00.

ACCESS   —C.M.
c/o John Schade
School of Architecture
University of Wisconsin
Milwaukee, Wisconsin 53201

OUROBOROS

Applying solar thermal collection technology to residential architecture is a joint project of the Mechanical Engineering and Architecture Departments at the University of Minnesota, Minneapolis. The project, code-named Ouroboros (a mythical dragon that survived by consuming its own tail, symbolizing recycling and energy conservation), is a study of architecture's role in energy conservation through research, design, and construction of two full-scale residences.

The first residential project, called Ouroboros/South, is a 2000 square foot, two-level house which incorporates energy-conserving design features such as increased wall and window insulation, Thomason-type solar water and space heating, a 5-kilowatt Aero Generator, and sewage and water recycling.

The dwelling, as shown, is trapezoidal in shape with the largest wall facing south. The earth remaining after excavation of the basement was later pushed up against the north, west and east walls to provide added insulation against the winter cold. The long north roof is covered with sod.

The second residential project, called Ouroboros/East, is the redesigning and retrofitting of an existing, older house into a solar house. The completed project will demonstrate via a public educational program possible methods of reducing fossil fuel energy consumption of an existing house, including the application of solar collectors on the south roof and walls, reinsulation of windows and walls, alterations of minimum space volume standards, etc. The first floor of the experimental house will contain a video/seminar space for community energy conservation education, and the basement will provide a community toolshop to be used by people who want to retrofit their houses.

THE HOUSE IS DESIGNED TO CAPTURE SNOW LIKE A SNOWDRIFT. SNOW IS AN EXCELLENT INSULATOR. THE RIDGE VENT ACTS AS A SHADING DEVICE FOR SNOW IN WINTER.

A book, *Ouroboros/East*, describing plans for that project was published in early 1974. The proceeds from the book's sale will help finance the remodeling. It has loads of ideas, drawings, sources, and references and is highly recommended for natural and low-energy architecture freaks. In addition, it includes information on how to grow plants and keep bees—there's something for everyone.

—C.M.

Ouroboros/East
1974; 209 pp

$5.50

from:
University of Minnesota
School of Architecture
110 Architecture Building
Minneapolis, Minnesota 55455

CONVERSION FACTORS

Because different conventions historically have been used to measure various quantities, the following tables have been compiled to sort out the different units. The first table identifies the units typically used for describing a particular quantity. For example, speed might be measured in "miles/hour".

Most quantities can also be described in terms of the following three basic dimensions:

length	L
mass	M
time	T

For example, speed is given in terms of length divided by time, which can be written as "L/T". This description, called "dimensional analysis", is useful in determining whether an equation is correct. The product of the dimensions on each side of the equal sign must match. For example:

$$\text{Distance} = \text{Speed} \times \text{Time}$$
$$L = L/T \times T$$

The dimension on the left side of the equal sign is length, L. On the right side of the equal sign, the product of L/T times T is L, which matches the left side of the equation.

The second table is a Conversion Table, showing how to convert from one set of units to another. It might be necessary to take the reciprocal of the conversion factor or to make more than one conversion to get the desired results. The following handbooks might be referred to for futher information:

CRC HANDBOOK OF CHEMISTRY AND PHYSICS, 55TH ED. R.C. Weast, ed. CRC Press. Cleveland. 1974.

PHYSICS: PARTS I AND II. D. Halliday and R. Resnick. John Wiley and Sons. New York. 1966.

IES LIGHTING HANDBOOK, 4TH ED. J.E. Kaufman, ed. Illuminating Engineering Society. New York. 1966.

STANDARD HANDBOOK FOR MECHANICAL ENGINEERS, 7TH ED. Baumeister and Marks. McGraw-Hill. New York. 1967.

MEASURED QUANTITIES AND THEIR COMMON UNITS

Length(L)	Area(L^2)	Volume(L^3)
mile(mi.)	sq. mile(mi^2)	gallon(gal.)
yard(yd.)	sq. yard	quart(qt.)
foot(ft.)	sq. foot	pint(pt.)
inch(in.)	sq. inch	ounce(oz.)
fathom(fath.)	acre	cu. foot(ft^3)
kilometer(km.)	sq. kilometer	cu. yard
meter(m.)	sq. meter	cu. inch
centimeter(cm.)	sq. centimeter	liter
micron(u).		cu. centimeter
angstrom(Å.)		acre-foot
		cord
		cord-foot
		barrel(bbl.)

Mass(M)	Speed(L/T)	Flow Rate(L^3/T)
pound(lb.)	feet/minute(ft./min.)	cu. feet/min.
ton(short)	feet/sec.	cu. meter/min.
ton(long)	mile/hour	liters/sec.
ton(metric)	mile/min.	gallons/min.
gram(g.)	kilometer/hr	gallons/sec.
kilogram(kg.)	kilometer/min.	
	kilometer/sec.	

Pressure($M/L/T^2$)	Energy(ML^2/T^2)	Power(ML^2/T^3)
atmosphere(atm.)	British thermal unit(Btu.)	Btu./min.
pounds/sq. inch	calories(cal.)	Btu./hour
inches of mercury	foot-pound	watt
cm. of mercury	joule	joule/sec.
feet of water	kilowatt-hour(kw.-hr.)	cal./min.
	horsepower-hour (hp.-hr.)	horsepower(hp.)

Time(T)	Energy Density(M/T^2)	Power Density(M/T^3)
year	calories/sq. cm.	cal./sq. cm./min.
month	Btu./sq. foot	Btu./sq. foot/hr
day	langley	langley/min.
hour(hr.)	watthr./sq. foot	watt/sq. cm.
minute(min.)		
second(sec.)		

TABLE OF CONVERSION FACTORS

MULTIPLY	BY	TO OBTAIN:
Acres	43560	Sq. feet
"	0.004047	Sq. kilometers
"	4047	Sq. meters
"	0.0015625	Sq. miles
"	4840	Sq. yards
Acre-feet	43560	Cu. feet
"	1233.5	Cu. meters
"	1613.3	Cu. yards
Angstroms (Å)	1×10^{-8}	Centimeters
"	3.937×10^{-9}	Inches
"	0.0001	Microns
Atmospheres(atm.)	76	Cm. of Hg(0^0C)
"	1033.3	Cm. of H_2O (4°C)
"	33.8995	Ft. of H_2O (39.2°F)
"	29.92	In. of Hg(32^0F)
"	14.696	Pounds/sq. inch
Barrels(petroleum, U.S.) (bbl.)	5.6146	Cu. feet
"	35	Gallons(Imperial)
"	42	Gallons(U.S.)
"	158.98	Liters
British Thermal Unit(Btu)	251.99	Calories
"	777.649	Foot-pounds
"	0.00039275	Horsepower-hours
"	1054.35	Joules

MULTIPLY	BY	TO OBTAIN:
"	0.000292875	Kilowatt-hours
"	1054.35	Watt-seconds
Btu/hr.	4.2	Calories/min.
"	777.65	Foot-pounds/hr.
"	0.0003927	Horsepower
"	0.000292875	Kilowatts
"	0.292875	Watts (or joule/sec.)
Btu/lb.	7.25×10^{-4}	Cal/go
Btu/sq. ft	0.271246	Calories/sq. cm. (or langleys)
"	0.292875	Watt-hour/sq. foot
Btu/sq. ft./hour	3.15×10^{-7}	Kilowatts/sq. meter
"	4.51×10^{-3}	Cal./sq. cm./min(or langleys/min)
"	3.15×10^{-8}	Watts/sq. cm.
Calories(cal.)	0.003968	Btu.
"	3.08596	Foot-pounds
"	1.55857×10^{-6}	Horsepower-hours
"	4.184	Joules(or watt-seconds)
"	1.1622×10^{-6}	Kilowatt-hours
Calories, food unit (Cal.)	1000	Calories
Calories/min.	0.003968	Btu/min.
"	0.06973	Watts
Calories/sq. cm.	3.68669	Btu/sq. ft. Watt-hr./sq. foot
Cal./sq. cm./min.	796320.	Btu/sq. foot/hr.
"	251.04	Watts/sq. cm.
Candle power (spherical)	12.566	Lumens
Centimeters(cm.)	0.032808	Feet
"	0.3937	Inches
"	0.01	Meters
"	10,000	Microns
Cm. of Hg(0^0C)	0.0131579	Atmospheres
"	0.44605	Ft. of $H_2O(4^{\circ}C)$
"	0.19337	Pounds/sq. inch
Cm. of $H_2O(4^0C)$	0.0009678	Atmospheres
"	0.01422	Pounds/sq. inch
Cm./sec.	0.032808	Feet/sec.
"	0.022369	Miles/hr.
Cords	8	Cord-feet
"	128(or 4x4x8)	Cu. feet
Cu. centimeters	3.5314667	Cu. feet
"	0.06102	Cu. inches
"	1×10^{-6}	Cu. meters
"	0.001	Liters
"	0.0338	Ounces(U.S., fluid)
Cu. feet($ft.^3$)	0.02831685	Cu. meters
"	7.4805	Gallons(U.S., liq.)
"	28.31685	Liters
"	29.922	Quarts(U.S., liq.)
Cu. ft of H_2O (60^0F)	62.366	Pounds of H_2O
Cu. feet/min.	471.947	Cu. cm./sec.
Cu. inches($in.^3$)	16.387	Cu. cm.
"	0.0005787	Cu. feet
"	0.004329	Gallons(U.S., liq.)
"	0.5541	Ounces(U.S., fluid)
Cu. meters	1×10^6	Cu. centimeters
"	35.314667	Cu. feet
"	264.172	Gallons(U.S., liq.)
"	1000	Liters
Cu. yard	0.76455	Cu. meters
"	201.97	Gallons(U.S., liq.)
"	27	Cu. feet
Cubits	18	Inches
Fathoms	6	Feet
"	1.8288	Meters
Feet(ft.)	30.48	Centimeters
"	12	Inches
"	0.00018939	Miles(statute)
Feet of $H_2O(4^0C)$	0.029499	Atmospheres
"	2.2419	Cm. of Hg(0^0C)
"	0.433515	Pounds/sq. inch

MULTIPLY	BY	TO OBTAIN:
Feet/min.	0.508	Centimeters/second
"	0.018288	Kilometers/hr.
"	0.0113636	Miles/hr.
Foot-candles	1	Lumens/sq. foot
Foot-pounds	0.001285	Btu.
"	0.324048	Calories
"	5.0505×10^{-7}	Horsepower-hours
"	3.76616×10^{-7}	Kilowatt-hours
Furlong	220	Yards
Gallons(U.S., dry)	1.163647	Gallons(U.S., liq.)
Gallons(U.S., liq.)	3785.4	Cu. centimeters
"	0.13368	Cu. feet
"	231	Cu. inches
"	0.0037854	Cu. meters
"	3.7854	Liters
"	8	Pints(U.S., liq.)
"	4	Quarts(U.S., liq.)
Gallons/min.	2.228×10^{-3}	Cu. feet/sec.
"	0.06308	Liters/sec.
Grams	0.035274	Ounces(avdp.)
"	0.002205	Pounds(avdp.)
Grams-cm.	9.3011×10^{-8}	Btu.
Grams/meter^2	3.98	Short ton/acre
Grams/meter^2	8.92	lbs./acre
Horsepower	42.4356	Btu./min.
"	550	Foot-pounds/sec.
"	745.7	Watts
Horsepower-hrs.	2546.14	Btu.
"	641616	Calories
"	1.98×10^6	Foot-pounds
"	0.7457	Kilowatt-hours
Inches	2.54	Centimeters
"	0.83333	Feet
In. of Hg (321F)	0.03342	Atmospheres
"	1.133	Feet of H_2O
"	0.4912	Pounds/sq. inch
In. of Water (4°C)	0.002458	Atmospheres
"	0.07355	In. of Mercury (32°F)
"	0.03613	Pounds/sq. inch
Joules	0.0009485	Btu.
"	0.73756	Foot-pounds
"	0.0002778	Watt-hours
"	1	Watt-sec.
Kilo calories/gram	1378.54	Btu/lb
Kilograms	2.2046	Pounds(avdp.)
Kilometers	1000	Meters
"	0.62137	Miles(statute)
Kilometer/hr.	54.68	Feet/min.
Kilograms/hectare	.89	lbs/acre
Kilograms/hectare	.0004	Short ton/acre
Kilowatts	3414.43	Btu./hr.
"	737.56	Foot-pounds/sec.
"	1.34102	Horsepower
Kilowatt-hours	3414.43	Btu.
"	1.34102	Horsepower-hours
Knots	51.44	Centimeter/sec.
"	1	Mile(nautical)/hr.
Langleys	1	Calories/sq. cm.
"	1.15078	Miles(Statute)/hr.
Langleys	1	Calories/sq. cm.
Liters	1000	Cu. centimeters
"	0.0353	Cu. feet
"	0.2642	Gallons(U.S., liq.)
"	1.0567	Quarts(U.S., liq.)
Lbs./acre	.0005	Short ton/acre
Liters/min.	0.0353	Cu. feet/min.
"	0.2642	Gallons(U.S., liq.)/min.
Lumens	0.079577	Candle power(spherical)
Lumens(at 5550 Å)	0.0014706	Watts
Meters	3.2808	Feet
"	39.37	Inches
"	1.0936	Yards
Metric ton/hectare	.445	Short ton/per acre

MULTIPLY	BY	TO OBTAIN:	MULTIPLY	BY	TO OBTAIN:	MULTIPLY	BY	TO OBTAIN:
Micron	10000	Angstroms	Pounds/sq. inch	0.06805	Atmospheres	Sq. yards	9(or 3x3)	Sq. feet
"	0.0001	Centimeters	"	5.1715	Cm. of mercury(0^0C)	"	0.83613	Sq. meters
Miles(statute)	5280	Feet	"	27.6807	In. of water(39.2^0F)	Mile/hour	.447	Meters/second
"	1.6093	Kilometers	Quarts(U.S., liq.)	0.25	Gallons(U.S., liq.)	Meters/sec.	2.24	Mile/hour
"	1760	Yards	"	0.9463	Liters	Tons/long	1016	Kilograms
Miles/hour	44.704	Centimeter/sec.	"	32	Ounces(U.S., liq.)	"	2240	Pounds(avdp.)
"	88	Feet/min.	"	2	Pints(U.S., liq.)	Tons(metric)	1000	Kilograms
"	1.6093	Kilometer/hr	Radians	57.30	Degrees	"	2204.6	Pounds(avdp.)
Mililiter	1	Cu. centimeter	Sq. centimeters	0.0010764	Sq. feet	Tons(short)	907.2	Kilograms
Millimeter	0.1	Centimeter	"	0.1550	Sq. inches	"	2000	Pounds(avdp.)
Ounces(avdp.)	0.0625	Pounds(avdp.)	Sq. feet	2.2957×10^{-5}	Acres	Watts	3.4144	Btu./hr.
Ounces(U.S., liq.)	29.57	Cu. centimeters	"	0.09290	Sq. meters	"	0.05691	Btu./min.
"	1.8047	Cu. inches	Sq. inches	6.4516	Sq. centimeters	"	14.34	Calories/min.
"	0.0625(or 1/16)	Pint(U.S., liq.)	"	0.006944	Sq. feet	"	0.001341	Horsepower
Pints(U.S., liq.)	473.18	Cu. centimeters	Sq. kilometers	247.1	Acres	"	1	Joule/sec.
"	28.875	Cu. inches	"	1.0764×10^7	Sq. feet	Watts/sq. cm.	3172	Btu./sq. foot/hr.
"	0.5	Quarts(U.S., liq.)	"	0.3861	Sq. miles	Watt-hours	3.4144	Btu.
Pounds(avdp.)	0.45359	Kilograms	Sq. meters	10.7639	Sq. feet	"	860.4	Calories
"	16	Ounces(avdp.)	"	1.196	Sq. yards	"	0.001341	Horsepower-hours
Pounds of water	0.01602	Cu. feet of water	Sq. miles	640	Acres	Yards	3	Feet
"	0.1198	Gallons(U.S., liq.)	"	2.787×10^7	Sq. feet	"	0.9144	Meters
			"	2.590	Sq. kilometers			

INDEX, THE

IN THE INDEX

This type face refers to a subject listing,
this type face refers to a book or periodical, and
this type face refers to an individual or group.

PORTOLA INSTITUTE

Portola Institute is a non-profit tax exempt corporation established to encourage "learning in the world." For almost eight years Portola has been a facilitator for educational risk-taking. The groups who have been aided in setting up their projects here include:

Whole Earth Truck Store Big Rock Candy Mountain Ortega Park Teachers Laboratory
Music Resources Program DeSchooling/DeConditioning Scripps Off-Campus Project Center
Kids Teaching Kids Project Whole Earth Catalog Word Wheel Books

Currently, Portola is helping research and launch a holistic health center, a food cooperative, a coop auto shop, and the *Energy Primer*. Efforts are also going on to facilitate networking of "Briarpatch" enterprises, especially in Northern California. We define "Briarpatch economics" as caring-based economics focused around simple living, right livelihood, and sharing of resources: materials, money, knowledge, etc. Portola hopes to continue its work in publishing and disseminating useful educational information for the people actually involved in alternative economics via *Briarpatch Review*, business clinics, workshops, networking, and conferences. Portola is a working foundation, not a fund granting foundation; as such it has no money to give away. Portola welcomes substantial contributions to aid its work in Briarpatch economics.

Portola Institute
540 Santa Cruz Avenue
Menlo Park, California 94025

THE WHOLE EARTH TRUCK STORE

The Whole Earth Truck Store exists as a supplier and source of books, tools, and information which allow people to become better acquainted with the world around them. We supply goods for urban and rural survival which promote cooperation, independence, self-sufficiency and the ability to expand control over one's own life and environment. To the extent that it is possible, we carry goods that people need rather than items which they simply want; we do not carry *stuff* we consider to be frivolous.

We have a small local store in Menlo Park, California and a world-wide mail order business. Through the mail we sell books and hardware listed in the *Energy Primer*, *The Last Whole Earth Catalog*, the *Whole Earth Epilog*, and the *CoEvolution Quarterly*. In our Menlo Park store we carry all the mail order items as well as gardening tools, functional clothing, children's toys, culinary equipment, knives, and many additional books.

Whole Earth Truck Store
558 Santa Cruz Avenue
Menlo Park, California 94025
415-323-0313

NEW ALCHEMY WEST

New Alchemy West is a small California-based group working with, and writing about, renewable food and energy systems. Publications include: *Designing Experiments for the Organic Garden*, *Modern Agriculture and the Quality of Life*, and *Methane Digesters for Fuel Gas and Fertilizer* (New Alchemy Institute Newsletter No. 3). Future plans include putting together workbooks about small scale aquaculture and wind systems.

ECOLOGY ACTION/PALO ALTO

In 1970, several volunteers started a recycling project - this was the beginning of EA/PA. By 1972 the City of Palo Alto had taken over the recycling program and EA's focus changed to organic gardening research. It now supports a large biodynamic/French intensive garden where John Jeavons is documenting the exceptional harvest yields this method is capable of producing. (See page 119 for a review of *How to Grow More Vegetables . . .*)

In addition to its research activities, EA provides free community garden plots for area residents and, through Common Ground, sells related supplies. Once a week sessions in urban homesteading skills are offered regularly, as are classes on the philosophy and methodology of the biodynamic/French intensive gardening technique. As they have for five years, EA's activities still depend on the energy and resources of its volunteers.

ALTERNATIVE SOURCES OF ENERGY NEWSLETTER

ASE Newsletter (see page 186) started in 1971 when Don Marier put an ad in the *Mother Earth News* wanting to get in touch with others interested in solar, wind, and water power. He found much interest but little experience, and he began a network-newsletter as a forum where people could exchange ideas, tell what they were doing or wanted to do, ask questions and get feedback. The Newsletter's circulation has grown rapidly and each issue is bigger than the last. It's a volunteer-run, non-profit operation, all contributions donated, not edited for content, viewpoint, or style.

In addition to the Newsletter, *ASE* maintains a lending library with special emphasis on practical and hard-to-find information. Readers are encouraged to file an Interest Questionnaire as a help to contacting others with similar interests.

If you have questions, comments, or additions to the Energy Primer, send them to ASE. Your input will be directed to a Newsletter contact near you.

Energy Primer
c/o ASE
Route 2, Box 90A
Milaca, Minnesota 56353

COPIES OF THE ENERGY PRIMER MAY BE ORDERED FROM THE WHOLE EARTH TRUCK STORE. ORDERS SHOULD BE PREPAID AT THE PRICE ON THE BACK COVER OF THIS BOOK. CALIFORNIA RESIDENTS SHOULD ADD 6% FOR SALES TAX.

HOW TO ORDER

A considerable amount of access information is provided in the Energy Primer - access to the information, tools, and hardware with which to build renewable energy systems.
—The reader will find addresses of publishers and suppliers under book and hardware reviews.
—If "or Whole Earth Truck Store" appears under the address of the supplier, the item may be ordered from:
 Whole Earth Truck Store
 558 Santa Cruz Avenue
 Menlo Park, California 94025
—Usually, the price of the item is listed. **All items are postpaid by the supplier at the listed price unless otherwise noted.** *Shipping on items not postpaid, especially large items, can cost a good deal of money. Consult the supplier or your local post office for postage rates.*
—State sales tax must be added to the listed price or cost if the supplier and the customer are within the same state. Periodicals are exempt from sales tax. (California sales tax is 6%).
—Send a check or money order for the items you wish to purchase. Cash has been known to get lost in the mail. The Post Office charges extra for C.O.D.
—Many names and addresses are given for further information. The group may or may not have any product to sell. If you are requesting information, send a stamped, self-addressed envelope and perhaps a quarter or more to help defray the cost to the group. Small groups have gone broke trying to answer hundreds of inquiries. Besides, your quarter is likely to get your letter answered.

CREDITS:

EDITORS
Richard Merrill (R.M.) Thomas Gage (T.G.)
Chuck Missar (C.M.) James Bukey (T.W.)
LAYOUT
Jeanne Campbell Richard Gordon
TYPESETTING
Trudy Smith Emily Smith
Mary Lamprech Phyllis Grossman
Evelyn Eldridge
COPY EDITING
Yedida Merrill
PROOFREADING AND INDEXING
Dian Missar Yedida Merrill
ART
Beth Amine James Bukey
Dennis Dahlin Robin Saunders
Lynn Smith Cayla Werner
PHOTOGRAPHY
John Gaylord Lynn Houghton
RESEARCH ASSISTANCE
SOLAR
Harry Burris Fred Godfrey
Lee Johnson Dian Missar
Carolyn Pesko Judy Raak
Paul Shippee Gary Smith
Dave Weiman E.N. Whitney
WATER
Nancy Bellows Bruce Franklin
Byrd Helligas Vic Marks
Yedida Merrill
WIND
Catherine Brown Jim DeKorne
Dr. Richard Dickey Karen George
Don Kozak Alvin Miller
Albert Nunez Carolyn Pesko
Carolyn Sheehan Ken Smith
Alan Sondak Ben Wolfe
BIOFUELS
Evan Brown Bill Campbell
Len Dawson Henry Esbenshade
Dr. Isao Fujimoto John Jeavons
Kurt Kline Dr. Perry McCarty
Bill McLarney Darryl McLeod
Yedida Merrill Annette Mowinckle
Steve Nelson George Oberst
Mike Perelman Ann Poole
Steve Serfling Carolyn Sheehan
Dr. William Shupe Sim Van der Ryn
CONVERSION FACTORS
Kim Mitchell
GENERAL
Multi Fassett Bob Gaylord
Becky Jennison Elisabeth McAllister
Jacqueline Meyer Anna Meyer
Ray Oszewski Bob Parks
Richard Raymond Wally Thompson
The Truck Store Staff ASE Newsletter Staff